**The Untold Story of Sabina Spielrein:
Healed & Haunted by Love**

Unpublished Russian
Diary and Letters

The Untold Story of Sabina Spielrein: Healed & Haunted by Love

Unpublished Russian Diary and Letters

Translated by Henry Zvi Lothane
With the collaboration of Vladimir Shpilrain

New York:
The Unconscious in Translation

General Director: Jonathan House
1050th Fifth Avenue – New York, NY 10028
www.uitbooks.com

The Untold Story of Sabina Spielrein:
Healed & Untold by Love
Unpublished Russian Diary and Letters

First paperback edition May 2023
Editor: Stephan Trano
Cover art by David Polonsky
Cover and Central Portfolio design by Christian Bowden
Book design by Jodi McPhee

ISBN 978-1-942254-20-1 (paperback)
Library of Congress Control Number: 2023932916

In memory of my wife, Malca Lothane.
To my daughter, Shara Lothane.

H.Z. Lothane

"And when put it in the grave let young life play and uncaring nature shine in eternal magnificence."

Sabina Spielrein

Editor's Note

As General Editor and Publisher of The Unconscious in Translation I am proud to publish new and important work by a major scholar like Professor Doctor Henry Lothane. I believe this work is not only important for psychoanalysis and the history of psychoanalysis, but has an importance that reaches far beyond psychoanalysis.

It is an honor for The UIT that Dr. Lothane has chosen to have us publish this work.

Personally, I am proud and honored that Dr. Lothane chose me to be involved in other aspects of his work such as choosing me to be on the committee on Free Association which he led for the International Psychoanalytic Association.

All that pride and honor pales beside my pleasure in being able to call Henry my friend.

Jonathan House

Table of Contents

Abbreviations

CITATIONS

C	Carotenuto 1982
Car	Carotenuto 1986

LETTERS

S S	Sabina Spielrein[1]
AO	Abraham Ott
C J	Carl Jung
CM	Cavendish Moxon
CO	Charles Odier
C S	C. Sheitler
E B	Eugen Bleuler
EC	Edouard Christin
EO	Emil Oberholzer
E S	Eva Spielrein
ESo	Eugenia Sokolnicka
EmS	Emil Shpilrain
F S	Fania Shpirlrain
I S	Isaak Shpielrein
GS	Gaston Rosenstein
MS	Menikha Spielrein
NL	Nachmannsohn-Leibowitz
NS	Nikolai Spielrein
OP	Oskar Pfister
P S	Pavei Sheftel
RK	R. Kleiner
S F	Sigmund Freud
Ter-O	Revekka Ter-Oganesian
WS	Wilhelm Stekel
UC	Unknown correspondent
Y S	Yan Spielrein

1 Spelling and pronunciation of the name Spielrein Footnote #33

Foreword

Russian-Jewish Sabina Nikolayevna Spielrein (1885–1942) from Rostov-on-Don received her medical degree in Zurich, Switzerland. While in medical school, she was trained as a psychiatrist and psychoanalyst by Professor Eugen Bleuler and Dr. Carl Jung who were also supervisors of her doctoral dissertation. She was later accepted by Sigmund Freud as a member of the Vienna Psychoanalytic Association and went on to publish many psychoanalytic papers. In this book Spielrein's development as a person and a professional is revealed in her Russian diary and letters all of which are presented for the first time in English translation and simultaneously are being published in Russian in Moscow by Vladimir Shpilrain. Additionally, included are her German diary entries and letters not previously published in English.

The relationship between Sabina Spielrein and Carl Jung was noted publicly in the *Freud Jung Letters* published by William McGuire in 1974 but did not at first arouse attention. This changed drastically after the publication of Spielrein's German diary and correspondence by Aldo Carotenuto first in Italian in 1980 as *Diario di una segreta simmetria—Sabina Spielerein tra Jung e Freud* and thereafter in English in 1982 and 1884 as *A Secret Symmetry, Sabina Spielrein Between Jung and Freud.* It was reviewed by Bruno Bettelheim in 1983 as "Scandal in the Family" in the *New York Review of Books* and reprinted as "Commentary by Bruno Bettelheim" in Carotenuto 1984. The scandal was an alleged sexual relationship between Spielrein and Jung an allegation rebutted in the *Afterword* in the present book. Carotenuto (1982) contained Spielrein's German diary (1909–1912), letters from Spielrein to Freud (1909–1914), from Freud to Spielrein (1909–1923), and letters from Spielrein to Jung (1911–1918)—but no letters from Jung to her which were subsequently released by the Jung heirs. The aforementioned German diary and letters, including the letters of Jung to Spielrein, were first published in Germany in 1986.

Although from 1987 to 1997 I had discussed Spielrein in four publications, I was not aware of the Russian diary and correspondence until my colleague Dr.

Fernando Vidal, author of papers on Spielrein and Jean Piaget, told me about a 1993 German dissertation of Wackenhut & Willke the manuscript of which was later sent to me by its supervisor Professor Wolfgang Eckart. The dissertation contained the German translation of the Russian diary and correspondence of Spielrein and it was an eye-opener! In 1998 I traveled to Geneva to visit Mme de Morsier, owner of the Spielrein archive, who graciously allowed me to examine the materials and compare the German translation with the originals. In the process I discovered key letters, not included in the dissertation. These letters were exchanged between Sabina and her mother. They offered new insight into the Spielrein-Jung relationship so I published them in 1999. My article made the German dissertation known to subsequent scholars studying Spielrein.

Some of the German material previously translated by Jeanne Moll (1983) and Brinkman & Bose (1986) has been retranslated for this book. A part of the 1993 German dissertation was included in a paperback by Traute Hensch in 2006 titled *Sabina Spielrein nimm meine seele tagebücher und schriften* (S. S. take my soul diaries and works), published by Edition Freitag. The words 'take my soul,' seem to copy *Prendimi l'anima*, the 2002 feature film by Roberto Faenza, titled *The Soul Keeper* in USA. In her well-researched 2005 book (republished as a paperback in 2008) Sabine Richebächer quoted sentences and passages from the Wackenhut & Willcke dissertation, my 1999 article, and from some Russian letters published in full in this book.

In 2003 in Moscow I met with Sabina's nephew professor Evald Emilievich Shpilrain to discuss the publication of the entire Russian diary and correspondence. He suggested I contact his son Vladimir Shpilrain, mathematics professor at City University of New York (CUNY), who lived just a few blocks from me in New York City, now heir to the Spielrein archive. We later decided to collaborate on this project. In 2018 copies of the entire Russian archive were sent to me by Mme de Morsier and Vladimir Shpilrain found a professional manuscript expert, Svetlana Subbotina, who deciphered and transcribed the letters for us.

This diary, written in Russian until 1905 and continued in German till 1906, covering the period from age 11 to 21. Its pages depict the evolution of a precocious and perceptive teenager into a sophisticated medical student and an innovative psychiatrically trained psychoanalyst. For the first time English readers can see Sabina and her sophisticated family emerge as real-life people: with their characters, conflicts and conquests; their dreams, deeds, desires, and defenses; their destinies and dramas as shaped by the Bolshevik Revolution and the first and second World Wars.

Henry Zvi Lothane, New York, 2023.

Acknowledgments

We are grateful to Mrs. Hélène de Morsier for sharing with us Sabina's archive that was in her possession, and to Sabine Richebächer for giving us permission to include Sabina Spielrein's unique letter to Max Eitingon. We are also indebted to Anna Komarova and Svetlana Subbotina for their invaluable help at various stages of our work on this manuscript. Our special thanks to Dr. Fonya Lord Helm for copy editing the Russian diary and correspondence, and to our editor in New York, Stephan Trano.

Chronology of Life and Work of Sabina Spielrein

Father Nikolai Arkadievich Spielrein ("Warsaw resident Naftel' Moshkovich Shpilrain"), wholesale merchant of agricultural products 1861–1938

Mother Eva Markovna Lublinskakaya-Shpilrain 1863–1922, dentist

Sabina Nikolayevna Spielrein born October 25, 1885 in Rostov on/Don

1885–1890 With parents in Rostov

1887 Brother Yan (Yasha) born

1890–1895 Attended Fröbel Kindergarten in Warsaw, Poland, learns German and French

1891 Brother Isaak (Sania) born 1895 Sister Emilia (Milochka) is born

1896–1904 Attended Catherine female gymnasium in Rostov, graduating with a gold medal

1899 Brother Emil (Milchik) born

1901 Death of sister Emilia Naftelevna of typhus

August 17, 1904 After a month-long stay at Dr. Heller's private psychiatric sanatorium admitted as patient of Eugen Bleuler and Carl Jung at the Cantonal Burghölzli Hospital

April 1905 Matriculated and attended lectures at the Medical School of Zurich University

June 1, 1905 Discharged and moved to apartment in town

1905–1911 Student of medicine, after premedical courses mainly taught psychiatry, psychotherapy, and psychoanalysis by Eugen Bleuler and Carl Jung

1908 Spent summer vacation in Rostov, corresponded with Jung, in the fall she and Jung had a few dates

1908 Fall wrote the German "Essay on transformation"

1909 Jung reported anonymously to Freud about a "scandal," i.e., row, while Spielrein wrote to Freud revealing Jung's name

1911 January Finished dissertation supervised by Bleuler and Jung graduating as medical doctor

1911 In Munich studied music (composition, counterpoint, harmony), art, the Nibelung myth and psychoanalysis

1911 Published dissertation "On the psychological content of a case of schizophrenia (dementia praecox" in *Jahrbuch für psychoanalytische und psychopathologische Forschungen* edited by Jung

1911 Enrolled by Freud as member of the Vienna Psychoanalytic Society in October, she lectured in November at Society's meeting 152 "On transformation" (antedating Jung's 1912 paper on "Transformation and symbols of the libido" published in the *Jahrbuch*) and also briefly mentioned "destruction as the cause of coming into being"

1911 Third International Congress of International Psychoanalytic Association in Weimar, Germany, with Jung presiding, Spielrein did not attend

1912 Lectured on psychoanalysis in Rostov and met Jewish doctor Pavel (Faivel) Sheftel whom she then married in synagogue 1912 Published "Destruction as a cause of becoming" in the *Jahrbuch* 1912–1914 Lived in Berlin with husband

1913 Birth of daughter Irma renamed Renata

1913 Published "Contributions to knowing the infantile mind" in *Zentralblatt für Psychoanalyse und Psychotherapie*, renamed after Stekel's breakup with Freud as *Internationale Zeitschrift für ärztliche Psychoanalyse* (*IZP*, international journal of medical psychoanalysis, IJMP), the other new journal, *Imago,* launched in 1912; in both were published Spielreins shorter clinical observations and long methodological papers from 1913 to 1931

1913–1916 Published short papers in *Internationale Zeitschrift für ärztliche Psychoanalyse, IZP, Imago*

1914 Moved with Pavel Sheftel and daughter from Germany at war with Russia to neutral Zurich

1915 Sheftel left Sabina and Renata to be drafted for military service in Russia

1915–1920 Lived with Renata in Lausanne 1917–1918 Renewed correspondence with Jung

1920 At the 6th International Congress of International Psychoanalytic Association in Hague, with Ferenczi presiding, presented "On the question of the origins and development of speech" Thereafter moved with Renata to Geneva

1920 In *Beyond the Pleasure Principle* Freud noted: "A considerable portion of these speculations have been anticipated by Sabina Spielrein (1912) in an instructive paper"

1920–1923 In Geneva, active in Institut Jean-Jacques Rousseau founded by Claparède, member of the Swiss Psychoanalytic Society Published seminal papers in German and French

1921 Published "Russian literature" in Beihefte der *IZP*, Nr. III *Bericht* über *die Fortschritte der Psychoanalyse 1914–1919* (report on advances of psychoanalysis); analyzed Jean Piaget

1920–1923 Published short papers in *IZP*, *Imago*; and "L'automobile-symbole de la puissance mâle" (the car as symbol of male potency) and "Rêve et vision des étoiles filantes" (dream and vision of shooting stars) in *The International Journal of Psychoanalysis*, 4:128–132, 1923

1922 Presented at the 7th International Psychoanalytic Congress in Berlin "Time in subthreshold mental life"

1922 Published "The origin of the infantile words papa and mama" in *Imago*

1922 Death of mother Eva Spielrein

1923 Published "Time in subthreshold mental life" in *Imago*

1923 Published "Some analogies between the thinking of children, aphasics, and unconscious thinking" in *Archives de Psychologie* founded by Claparède

1923 Returned to Moscow with Renata, husband did not rejoin them

1923 Member of the Russian Psychoanalytic Association (with Ivan D. Ermakov as president and members Wulf & Kannabich (of the International Psychoanalytical

Association); member of the Children's Home (founded by Ermakov and Vera & Otto Schmidt), later reorganized as the State Psychoanalytic Institute (GPAI) linked with Children's Home Laboratory "International Solidarity"; co-directed a psychoanalytic clinic founded by Ermakov and Wulf; taught a special course "on psychoanalysis of subconscious thinking" and a "seminar on child psychoanalysis"

1924 First quarter taught a course the "psychoanalysis of children" at the National Institute of Psychoanalysis

1924 First half: Worked as "child psychology researcher" in the psychology section of the Institute of Philosophy, presented at meetings: on March 3rd lectured on "Unconscious thinking and the laws of infantile behavior on the 16th "Processes of subconscious awareness and infantile behavior," and director of psychology section of the First Moscow National University

1924 Left Moscow for Rostov, rejoined Pavel Sheftel, worked as doctor and pedologist, had a couch, unknown if practiced psychoanalysis

1924 Nina Snitkova born out of wedlock, daughter of Pavel Sheftel and Dr. Olga Snitkova, half-sister of Sabina and Pavel daughters Renata and Eva

1925 National Psychoanalytic Institute (GPAI) Psychoanalysis abolished by decree of the Soviet of National Commissars

1926 June 18, second daughter Eva born to Spielrein and Sheftel

1930 27th July Official decision to outlaw of the Russian Psychoanalytical Association

1931 Published last paper "Children's drawings with eyes open and closed" in *Imago*

1932 Liquidation of the journal *Pedology*, the profession of pedology attacked as "pedological distortions of in the National Education system"

1935 The NKVD (People's Commissariat for Internal Affairs) arrested Isaak Spielrein

1936 Abolition of pedology 1937 Death of Pavel Sheftel

1937 Isaak Spielrein executed in Moscow by firing squad 1938 Yan and Emil Spielrein executed

1938 Death of father Nikolai Spielrein

1941 June 22 German invasion of the Soviet Union

1941 Summer, Renata leaves music studies to vacation in Rostov and stays there

1941 November 21 to 29, first repelled German occupation of Rostov during which many civilians were killed; thereafter continuous aerial bombings of Rostov, the worst in July, until the summer of 1942

1942 24th July Second occupation of Rostov, with mass murders of civilians, Jews, and military prisoners led by former doctor of law Walter Bierkamp and now chief of Einsatzgruppe (firing squad) D and doctor of law Kurt Christmann, chief of Einsatzkommando 10a

1942 August Sabina and her daughters were last seen in a column of about 27,000 Jews marched by the Nazis to be murdered in Zmiyevskaia ravine, Rostov's Babi Yar

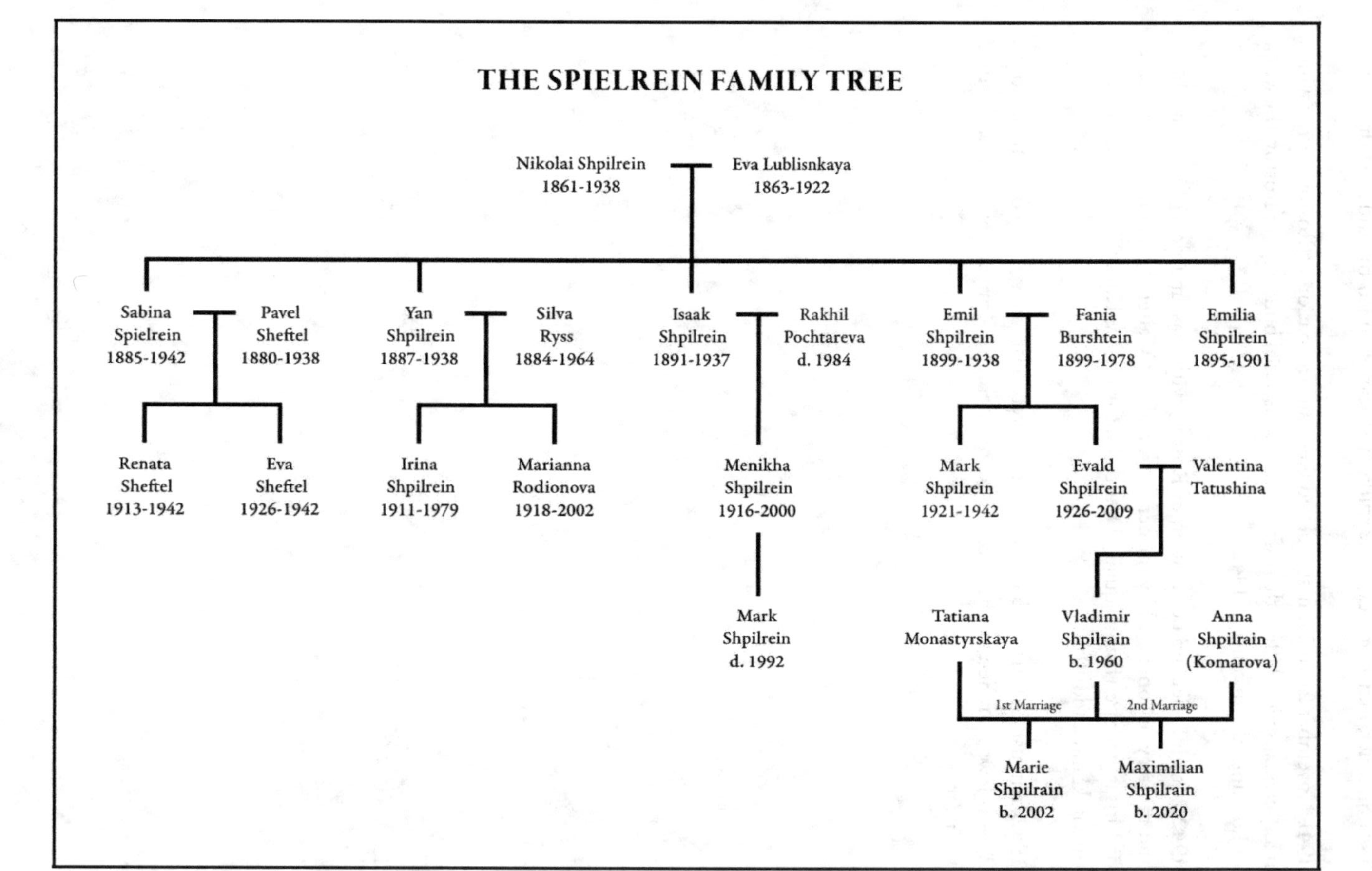
THE SPIELREIN FAMILY TREE
Nikolai Shpilrein 1861-1938
Eva Lublisnkaya 1863-1922
Sabina Spielrein 1885-1942
Pavel Sheftel 1880-1938
Yan Shpilrein 1887-1938
Silva Ryss 1884-1964
Isaak Shpilrein 1891-1937
Rakhil Pochtareva d. 1984
Emil Shpilrein 1899-1938
Fania Burshtein 1899-1978
Emilia Shpilrein 1895-1901
Renata Sheftel 1913-1942
Eva Sheftel 1926-1942
Irina Shpilrein 1911-1979
Marianna Rodionova 1918-2002
Menikha Shpilrein 1916-2000
Mark Shpilrein 1921-1942
Evald Shpilrein 1926-2009
Valentina Tatushina
Mark Shpilrein d. 1992
Tatiana Monastyrskaya
Vladimir Shpilrain b. 1960
Anna Shpilrain (Komarova)
1st Marriage
2nd Marriage
Marie Shpilrain b. 2002
Maximilian Shpilrain b. 2020

Introduction[1]

Henry Zvi Lothane

Diaries and letters are afforded a special place among historical documents. The diarist's need to record her own suffering, self-doubt, and imaginary or real character flaws, sustains the diary's veracity. As remarked by Tchaikovsky (2000): "To whom shall I pretend in the diary?" (p. 41). Similarly, letters provide a safe vehicle for confession, emotional discharge, and self-expression. Furthermore, diaries and letters provide a window into the life story of the dramatis personae, their characters, conflicts, and evolution.

In the hospital records and secondary literature Sabina Spielrein and her parents were stereotyped with various labels: she as a seductive hysteric, her mother a vain hysteric with a shopping addiction, her father as autocratic. In the diaries and letters they all emerge as real life persons interacting in dramatic events, scenes, and situations.

Real life dramas are actions in the here-and-now in, spoken in monologue or *dialogue*, with tone of voice, feelings and emotions, with facial expressions and body gestures and postures, and pertain to *dramatology*.[2] *Dramaturgy*, on the other hand, refers to invented dramas, as an art form on stage and in films. *Narratology* deals with *description* of past dramas, stories of events that occurred there-and-then. The past, once established or recorded, becomes an unchangeable historical fact. Subsequent narratives about such facts vary continually for they are shaped by the narrator's interests, ideologies, goals, or any other motives; they may be true or false, conscious lies or unconscious, i.e. repressed errors of memory. This calls for distinguishing established facts from imagined or invented fictions. One can either narrate facts or interpret facts, the difference between knowledge and opinion and the difference it makes. Authors of psychiatric and

1 Numbers with dot, e.g. 47., refer to diary entries. Numbers in parentheses with abbreviations refer to letters. The words in square brackets [ ] are clarifications added by transcriber or translator.
2 See Lothane, Z. 2009 http://www.archivespp.pl/uploads/images/2011_13_4/Lothane29_APP_4_2011.pdf and Lothane, H.Z. 2014.

psychoanalytic case histories and biographies have tended to conflate fact and fiction (Lothane, 2016), resulting in a proclivity to represent interpretations as biographical facts, e.g., as Freud in his 1911 interpreting Schreber's procreation fantasies as actual homosexual desires (Lothane, 1992). The crucial fiction here is the alleged sexual relationship between Spielrein and Jung as patient and doctor.

Moreover, some fictions become ingrained as societal myths, involving labeling or stereotyping a person or a people in characterological, racial, national, political or sexual terms, and such myths acquire a tenacity difficult to challenge or cancel. Such personal myths, nay archetypes, played a role in the lives of Jung and Spielrein. An example of a collective stereotype is Jews who have been labeled—and libeled and persecuted—as Christ murderers (Poliakov, 1974); or as vermin by Hitler, therefore disenfranchised and exterminated during WWII. Concrete examples are the murder of Sabina Spielrein and her daughters (Lothane, 2019, 2020) by the Nazis; or Stalin's purges and show trials that led to executions of people, even party members, labeled as enemies and traitors, as happened to all three of Spielrein's brothers.

Here I offer a tour d'horizon and commentary on key life events of Sabina Spielrein and her family as revealed in the diary and letters.

Spielrein's childhood and school years 1896–1904

Sabina was an amazingly intelligent child. Between five and ten (1890–1895) she was sent to a Fröbel kindergarten in Warsaw and at age six spoke German and French. At age ten she started attending a girls school in Rostov and writing a diary which was lost. She also learned to play the piano (Minder, 1994). At age eleven Sabina started writing the present diary, eager to describe events at school and at home. Depending on her mood, gaps of varying length occurred now and then. Her penmanship was calligraphic but at times sloppy due to haste or fatigue, or when writing in bed. Her command of the Russian language, its grammar, syntax and idioms, her keen observations and precise descriptions in a sophisticated style are beyond her years. She produced fascinating accounts of travels to Taganrog (47) and Warsaw (62, 65) in the Russian empire. She was enchanted by Germany and Austria (65–68) and the Germans (70–73). She also displayed an early interest in language and linguistics (73,74) which she would develop in her psychoanalytic writings. Sabina also expressed her feelings and emotions in dreams (29) and in verse (39, 82, 83, 84, 86).

On the first day Sabina couldn't wait to get to school (1) because studying is a "joy," especially when she was praised as a good student (2). She was eager to study Russian and other languages, many other subjects, e.g., chemistry (80), and drawing. She "trembled" at school when she made mistakes because father demanded that all her grades should be above excellent, i.e. 5+, and she feared his criticism (5, 8). She would remain vulnerable to criticism as a wound to her pride, or *ambitsia* as it is called in Russian, in her relations with father and later with Jung.

At home first-born Sabina was surrounded by parents and siblings: brothers Yasha two years, Sania six, and sister Emilia ten years younger. The staff included a maid, a cook, and a governess; the latter used to beat the children frequently since corporal punishment was then an accepted method of child-rearing, and by parents as well. In a 1905 letter to Freud Jung would state incorrectly that father beat her on her bare buttocks between the ages of "4–7" when she was actually in Warsaw part of that time; Jung also referred to beatings by father and mother between the ages of 11 to 13 but there is no mention of those in the diary. However, beatings per se do not explain Sabina's entire emotional crisis in 1904 that led to her hospitalization as Jung's patient.

The governess was ineffectual in managing the fights among the boys, she even fostered antagonism, but neither mother nor father intervened. The house was often in an uproar. When the maid carelessly broke a glass she blamed Sabina for it, was rude and spit but mother did not rebuke her; but savvy Sabina noticed that the maid "disappears for hours, probably with some men"(4). And Sabina reflected: "sometimes I see myself as a little girl, sometimes as a big girl, and I don't know how to write, as a little girl or as a big girl" (7). This contrasts with the unruly behavior of her brothers who one day started a fire in the apartment (7).

Sabina was also concerned with truth-telling and outspokenness, a theme that would recur in her relations with Jung (see "Afterword") and others later in life. She noted that father told her to lie about the reason for missing a day in school (14). A classmate prevaricated when caught misbehaving (5) and the teachers got angry with the girls. She was also upset by father's anger: "papa is different from mama, because at times he becomes utterly furious...when our things were lying around the table he wanted to burn them all down" (18). Father also instigated fights between the brothers (46). Sabina would use the word "furious" quite frequently but did not mention her own angry emotions during this period or later. There was only one instance of father being angry at his son Yasha, whom he also pressured to be a high achiever (29). Thus, his irascible temper aside, father did inculcate a desire to strive for excellence in school and in life, as Sabina would acknowledge in 1909: "fundamentally I feel that I have an unusually good, wholly unselfish father, to whom I owe much gratitude" (C, p. 37).

At times, the tensions and tumult at home made Sabina feel anxious, lost and helpless, e.g., when she almost froze on the way to school (3). Besides, being a student was demanding both at school and due to a heavy load of home work and there were days when she had no time to write in her diary. She was friendly with some girls had but had no close friends to share confidences with. And she lamented: "I cannot express my emotions,... I am having too many agitated emotions to be able to write in a diary" (20). Despite these continuous tensions Sabina was an excellent student: "I try very hard to study and to be on my good behavior at home" (11), she has "got 5's all around and was promoted without an examination" (21), and she "passed with first prize" (25).

A sad episode was mother's plan to attend a doctors' convention in Moscow and her wish to take Sabina along so that Sabina, suffering from stomach complaints, could be examined by one of the professors. Father canceled the trip and Sabina was disappointed, and "of course [she] cried." Her desire to go to Moscow can be seen as an important identification with mother, a university graduate and a dentist, thus a seed of her early interest in medicine, her future great passion (28, 29). Her other reaction to the cancellation was that she dreamt that "papa arrived and said that Yasha does not want to travel at all. We were about to resume our travel when I remembered that I had forgotten my books... I see a dog spinning in the air...I guessed it was a rabid dog and I knew it would attack me" (29), perhaps an expression of her anger at father. The dream shows an early psychological ability foreshadowing her future interest in working with dreams as a psychoanalyst.

Sabina described various daydreams: "I keep imagining how I will grow up and be an adult and let my children read my diary" (13); "when...I become grown up I will not get married and will not have my own children...I will adopt a few tiny orphans" (42); "I have a little son Adiuk. He was born on Tuesday 27th October 1898 [around the time of her 13th birthday]...was given the name Abram (in Russian Adolf)" (51); "I want to write how...I will be a housewife... but there is no place for it in a diary" (61). These were an adolescent girl's nascent maternal and womanly feelings which would play a significant role in her relationship with Jung and in her meditations (*Essay on Transformation* below) and published works (Spielrein, 1912a).

Some of her daydreams and fantasies were enacted, e.g., as in 16th July 1898 mock wedding scene in which the siblings "exchanged rings...then San'ka blessed us...we kissed each other...and made a feast...Mama also took part in the feast.

I very much wished that in a year I should have a child, a girl, and a year later a boy" (45). This scene suggests an awareness and a curiosity about procreation and sexuality in a girl who has reached puberty. This scene is remarkable as a contrast to the lack of any sexual education by mother at home and none at school, not until her medical studies in Zurich. Six months later a harbinger of a nascent maturity was seen when a "contract" was agreed upon between Sabina and father whereby as of "25th January 1999 "papa…will no longer reprimand me and he confirmed this with his own word of honor coupled with me giving my word of honor that I will observe all the rules that will be presented to me." (50). In July of 1900 she reminisced about that mock wedding: "I simply cannot believe… I was capable of writing such nonsense…that I would have children as a result of this comedy? No, I just expressed a wish knowing it cannot be realized…Despite all this the memory is very dear to me…Now I am fantasizing quite differently: I expect that when I get married my husband will be crazy about me and I about him…God only knows what my fate will be"(56).

A major event in 1900 was the death of her maternal grandmother "who stuck up for me when…mama was angry with me for no good reason [and] San'ka vicious and not sick…I would unburden to grandma all my grief that piled up in me…for a number of days." And now "there is nobody who will intercede for me in the daily scenes with San'ka [father's favorite]. San'ka is the good child and I am an idiot, the mean one, the beast, the witch" (57), an important family dynamic and more important than beatings. Sabina suffered from her father's preferring her brothers while criticizing her, a wound to her self-esteem and an injustice. She found an outlet in identifying with the fictional American Georgie (18). Similarly, when feeling criticized during her hospitalization and in medical school she would repeatedly enact various pranks (94).

The next great loss of her life happened in 1901: the death of her sister Emilia, unmentioned in the diary but noted by Jung: "the sister was six years old when she died. She loved her sister "more than the whole world. The patient was 16 when her sister died of typhus. Her death made a terrible impression on her" (Minder, 1994).

Becoming more mature created a new burden: taking care of "a nervous mama about whom I felt utterly responsible," a woman disorganized in handling the demands of traveling and distraught by a number of travel accidents, to which Sabina reacted with "severe pains in [her] feet which became so swollen that mama was forced to make a stopover in Kharkov" (63–65). Otherwise these travels in Austria and Germany were rich and rewarding and she could not find enough superlatives to express her admiration for German architecture, orderliness, neatness, and manners, a stark contrast to the scene in Russia. This enthusiasm was a prelude to Spielrein's enthusiasm for Germans during her years in Berlin prior to WWI and later her reluctance to listen to the warnings of her niece Menikha Isaakovna (daughter of brother Sania) about Nazi atrocities prior to WWII. Instead Sabina would dismiss those claims as Soviet propaganda (see Menikha's letter to me of 20.12.1994 p.XXX). That letter also explains how Sabina was lulled into a false sense of security during the first Nazi occupation of Rostov in 1941 versus the lightning-speed second occupation in 1942 which made it too late for her to flee. Furthermore, Sabina could not have known about Jung's speeches on Radio Berlin, and his publications in 1934, in support of Hitler's regime (Lothane, 2007).

In contrast to the aforementioned negative portrayal of a nervous mother, in the essay composed in 1901 in honor of her mother's birthday, Sabina expressed positive feelings towards both her parents. It is a complex story about an old man reminiscing about his past life. In "childhood he showed a great passion for chemistry...at the university [he studied] chemistry... sacrificing family tranquility for the sake of science." After many trials and tribulations the old man is deeply depressed and hears "the tender voice of his...daughter" who soothes him: "have you forgotten what you had repeated...when I was a child...to give oneself wholly to an idea without regard for one's feelings?...He became ashamed of his faintheartedness...The face of the old man shone with a noble and proud benevolence" (80). This imaginary tale suggests that Sabina attributed her own love of science to both her parents: the mother who studied medicine at the university and father who studied chemistry, while she herself was dreaming of attending a university.

But she was also inspired by her maternal grandfather: he wanted to marry "the daughter of a physician...a representative of the Christian community" but his father forced him to marry a Jewish girl. But "my grandfather must have unconsciously retained the image of his first love, for he considered Christian sciences more important than anything else. His daughter [Sabina's mother] was supposed to study, only study, he sent his daughter to the Christian Progymnasium and also saw that she was educated at the university" (C, 22–23). It shows grandfather to have been influenced by 19th century Jewish enlightenment, the Haskala. She also sees herself as the daughter healing her mother's anxiety but her father's depression as well.

Of particular interest is Sabina's 1902 "essay" that follows, which is actually a short story in the style of Anton Chekhov (1860–1904), whose many stories were subtitled "little scenes" (*stsenki*). Sabina displays a literary flair in crafting the scene of an encounter in a railway car between a Russian couple and a young female student "traveling all by [herself] to a distant country to study" (81). The Russian lady instantly "felt a liking to toward [her]...you remind me of my youth...so passionate to study, to be useful, to help the oppressed." Mixing benevolence with sanctimoniousness, the lady proceeded to rebuke the young woman for throwing away her money on a mendacious mendicant; but the young woman held on to her convictions. Finally the lady asked the girl's name and address and was dumbfounded to hear her say: "my name is Revekka Samuilovna Bornshtain...a Jewish name...I am a Jewess...The girl stood up proud and erect...[T]he lady's...little sweet smile turned into a contemptuous grimace... she is really a Jewess" (81). Bornshtain rings somewhat similar to Shpilrain: Sabina identified with the young woman's pride in her Jewishness.

The last story, without title or date, is about herself and a small group of boys and girls on a walk in the forest (85), with only two named characters, girl Ninotchka and a boy called "I." It is the only scene of Sabina in the company of both sexes but without any suggestion of dating. The proper custom in those times was for young people to meet as arranged by a matchmaker. Here Sabina again combined external pictorial descriptions of scenic nature with portrayals of internal scenes of moods and emotions in the style of pathetic fallacy and daydream fables: she imagined seeing a forest king, a fairy named Meri, "someone of my people...[her] gaze pierces me through and through, as if the entire sorrow of mankind, the deep hidden suffering, and an unspoken reproach, are all combined in it."

Sabina graduated from the gymnasium with a gold medal in 1904. And in the summer of that year her life seemed to come apart.

Spielrein's hospitalization at the Burghölzli 17 August 1904 to 1 June 1905

There were two reasons why Sabina was brought to Zurich in 1904: (1) *to study medicine*, as recalled by Sabina: "No one could have been happier than my grandfather when he learned I had decided to study medicine" (C p. 23); and as recorded by Jung: "In the gymnasium she particularly liked scientific subjects. Wanted to study medicine" (Minder 1994); (2) *to be treated* for an emotional crisis. There was no mention anywhere whether the parents also supported Sabina's desire to study medicine.

As recorded by Jung, after a month's stay in Dr. Heller's hospital she was "agitated due to disappointment by a young doctor whom she admired." The last straw was a violent scene at the Baur en Ville hotel whereupon she was taken to the Burghölzli "accompanied by her uncle and a policeman. Laughing and crying, a curiously impulse-driven behavior. A mass of tics; rotates her head in a jerky manner, sticks out her tongue, her legs jerking." On the day of admission she "complained of a terrible headache. She was not crazy, she just became agitated at the hotel, could stand neither people nor noises. *History*: *Always somewhat hysterical. About three years ago* [*1901*] *a serious illness*." Skipping procedure Jung did not perform a physical status examination on Spielrein. The next day she displayed "a constant play of laughing, crying, her head jerking, with flirtatious (*cokettierenden*) glances." On another occasion Jung observed: "Last night during the visit the patient was sitting on the couch half-lying in her habitual oriental-enticing attractiveness with a dreamy-sensuous expression on her face" (Minder, p. 110). Sensuousness or voluptuousness may be a seductive allure but this impression may also indicate Jung's projected emotions. Moreover, 'oriental' is a euphemism for 'Jewish,' and this could be a reason for Jung's attraction to her as the "*other* woman" (Feldman, 1964). This phenomenon where one belonging to a different ethnic community holds a particular allure can also be seen in Sabina's mother's attraction to Christians(C p. 23). Spielrein wrote to Freud that "Dr. Jung...admitted to me that he had excused his passion for me by speaking to you in terms of love for your daughter" (C p. 104). Jung's attraction to Freud's daughter Mathilde (born in 1887 and whom Jung met during his visit in Freud's home in 1907), "actually did not originate with her but with Frl. S.W." (C p. 106), i.e., Jung's cousin Helen Preiswerk[3]): "a dark-haired hysterical girl called S.W. who always described herself as Jewish (but in reality was not)" (C p. 105). And Jung confirmed: "As I have indicated before, my first visit to Vienna had a very long unconscious aftermath, first the compulsive infatuation in Abbazia, then the Jewess popped up in another form, in the shape of my patient" (*FJL*, p. 228).

The striking fact is that Jung did not document more details about Sabina's *present* illness: he did not explain what happened during the violent scene at the hotel; he was more interested in tracing her childhood traumas. Jung did mention a number of past "big scenes" with her father but did not consider the role of aggression and anger in her current state (see "Afterword"). Instead of respecting Sabina's paramount wish to study medicine the father, I submit, may have planned to marry her off with a sizable dowry which Sabina did not

3 S.W. figured prominently in Jung's 1902 doctoral dissertation "*On The Psychology and Pathology of So-Called Occult Phenomena*," published in Leipzig by Oswald Mutze in 1902, read by Sabina. In 1903 Mutze published Schreber's *Denkwürdigkeiten*, Jung acquired the book and passed it to Freud in 1910.

want (88) and she furiously fought back. Furthermore, Spielrein was not the only one who wanted to study medicine in Switzerland. As recalled by Chaim Weizmann (1949), the first president of Israel, about Vera Chatzman of Rostov, his future wife: Vera studied medicine in Geneva because

> the schools of her own country were closed to her...But the small group of young women to which [she] belonged differed in a marked way from the general run of Jewish girl-students...of that time. Their looks, their deportment, their outlook on life set them apart. They were far more attractive than their contemporaries from the Pale of Settlement...they were less absorbed in Russian revolutionary politics;...they paid more attention to their studies, and less to the public meetings and endless discussions that took up so much time of the average student abroad... who for the most part seemed underfed, stunted, nervous, and sometimes bitter—and easy prey to revolutionary propagandists (p. 70–71).

Spielrein named two other young Rostov women who studied with her in Zurich and with whom she corresponded later: Esther Aptekman and Revekka Ter-Oganesian (see their letters to Sabina).

Spielrein was a patient not only of Jung but also of hospital director Dr. Eugen Bleuler and Jung's boss, both concurrently and when Jung was away, and both corresponded with Spielrein's parents. With Bleuler's approval Sabina took part in the association experiments of Jung, in Franz Riklin's studies of myth and fable, attended lectures, studied in the anatomy laboratory, had meals with the medical staff, took care of a patient named Rähmi (90), and finally matriculated as a medical student while still an inpatient. Bleuler was her first dissertation supervisor followed by Jung. There are no reports of Bleuler's sessions with her but he applied one essential treatment approach: isolating Spielrein from any contacts with her father except for some visits with her mother, to provide relief from antecedent sources of trauma. In October 1904 Bleuler informed the father that Sabina "decided to begin her medical studies...and a return to Russia for a longer period is not recommended...Your daughter needs a completely autonomous and independent development, namely, she must be free from all compassionate cares for the family and its restrictive factors...Your daughter is of the opinion that these are the preconditions for her healing." Seconded by Jung. Bleuler wrote again in May 1905: "Miss Spielrein was very upset because she was expected to take care of her brother...She must be absolutely free of any obligation toward the family." In April Bleuler gave Spielrein this certificate:

"Miss Sabina Spielrein who resides in this Institution and plans to matriculate at the medical Faculty is not psychotic (*geisteskrank*).[4] She came here for treatment of nervousness with hysterical symptoms. We are duty-bound to recommend matriculation." Bleuler's diagnosis is most compelling: nervousness is not necessarily a disease and, furthermore, as colloquialisms, the words hysteria and hysterical commonly denote behavior marked by a high degree of emotionalism and a proclivity to exaggerating. Sabina was vindicated: she was never crazy, she had been highly agitated, angry and stressed-out because she could not have her way and thus dramatized her emotions in various enactments, like Dora before her (Lothane, 2009). It is also remarkable that Jung did not make any diagnosis in her chart either. My colleague Dr. Axel Hoffer (2001) suggested a diagnosis of "adolescent turmoil" (p. 123).

Jung's method of treating Sabina was twofold: (1) complete dedication in spite of her trying his patience with numerous pranks; (2) following Freud's theory that sexual trauma caused hysteria, excavating Sabina's childhood sexual traumas as stuff for an abreaction. In an undelivered report to Freud dated 25.9.1905 Jung concluded: "I have analyzed the clinical condition almost completely with the help of your method and with a favorable result from early on. In the course of her treatment the patient had the *bad luck to fall in love with me*. She continues to rave blatantly to her mother about this love and her secret spiteful glee in scaring her mother is not the least of her motives. Therefore the mother would like, if needed, to have her referred to another doctor, with which I naturally concur" (italics added, Lothane, 1996, p. 205). This report remained in Spielrein's possession (C p. 101) and would give her an excuse to complain to Freud about mistreatment by Jung during their crisis in 1909. As in the chart, there was no mention of aggression or anger in this report.

Remarkably, adolescence and adolescent appear 20 times in Freud's *Standard Edition* (Guttman, 1984), showing that Freud privileged the developmental role of childhood over that of adolescence. However, the latter is quite important here. Sabina's adolescence and puberty can fairly be dated as starting at the age of eleven and lasting at least till the age of nineteen, when she was admitted to Burghölzli, with events and consequences that would play a determining role in her later life.

4 Geisteskrank is often erroneously translated as "mentally ill", the latter term referring to neuroses as well.

Spielrein in Zurich medical school 1905–1911

During this period Bleuler and Jung were no longer her psychiatrists but her teachers. There were two periods in her relationship with Jung: (1) 1904–1908, first three years of medical studies until the summer vacation, marked by non-erotized friendship and altruistic love; (2) fall of 1908 to1911, erotized friendship with conflicts and clashes, until her graduation, dissertation, and departure for Vienna.

During the first days at the university Sabina was gripped by conflicting emotions: admiration for Jung and elation alternating with self-doubt and depression (87–90). This was her paramount need: "I want a good friend to whom I could bare every little trait of my soul; I want the love of an older man so that I can be loved the way parents love and understand their child (soul affinity)[5]... If only I were as wise as my Junga!"[6]. But she is still easily hurt by "even the smallest... criticism... Only from Junga can I endure everything."(88). "This unavoidable, unbearable pain caused by him (and sometimes by the Professor [Bleuler] as well) is at the same time often felt by me as pleasurable and I am glad when he gets angry and I gloat over my humiliation" (90), because she must inhibit her wish to protest vocally. However, "The truth be told that I am not as vicious as I appear to people. I often say what I do not think and it seems that I am terribly heartless, while actually I am so glad when I succeed in helping someone" (88). In her German diary Sabina refers to her old prideful *ambitsia* which drives her once again to "engage in creating scandals, i.e. I invented thought scandals and was completely dominated by the wildest anti-social pranks," like threatening people with a syringe filled with fake KCN (94). Above all this, she had one all-encompassing necessity: "The only thing that I now possess in this world is freedom and I guard this blessing with all my might" (90). Later that year she wrote to her mother that she was "madly happy as almost never before in my life...the cause of all this is Junga. I visited him today...because Junga told me that I should not be wearing a hat with holes in it and that I should also have my shoes mended...he forced me to accept 10 francs from him for the hat and the repair of the shoes" (SS 1). She sent mother a witty letter about passing the anatomy examination (SS 2).

5 Probably a reference to Goethe's 1809 novel Elective Affinities (Wahlverwandschaften) in which he viewed interpersonal relations between man and woman as analogous to chemical reactions.
6 An affectionate Russian form for the name Jung.

In 1908 Sabina was planning to spend the summer vacation with her family in Rostov. Prior to her departure Jung arranged dates with Sabina both at the hospital and downtown. On 30.VI.08 he wrote: "my dear friend, I want to tell you how very, very happy it makes me to be able to hope that there are people who are like me, people in whom living and thinking are one; good people who do not misuse the power of their mind to dream up fetters but rather to create freedoms...How great would be my happiness to find that person in you, that *esprit fort* [= strong and independent spirit] who never descends into sentimentality, but whose essential and innermost prerequisite for life is her own freedom and independence" (Car p. 189–190; all my translations).

On 12.8.08 Jung wrote: "My dear friend!... I admire the truly wonderful disposition of your parents. Tell your mother that I admire her for that. Your father will have an easier time of it because an idea man can more easily espouse new viewpoints and new life values than a woman who is conservative by nature... In me everything rises and falls like a volcano, now all golden now all gray. Your letter was like a sun ray amidst clouds...I notice that still much more of me is attached to you than I ever imagined. But I am always awfully suspicious and always believe that other people just want to exploit and tyrannize me...But you are not like this!... All last week I was a bit hysterical...and your letter had also a good effect on my mood and my energy level has risen since. How do you like being back in you homeland? Do you go on walks in the steppe? What did your old Bombuchna [nanny] say to you? Was she glad to see how beautiful you have now become? We read here in the newspapers that there is a cholera epidemic in Rostov. Do not drink any unboiled water and do not eat any raw lettuce and be careful with uncooked fruit because of bacteria...A warm kiss from your friend" (Car pp. 191–192). Two weeks later Jung sent her a postcard dated 27.VIII.1908: "My Dear! You deserve a great bonus of friendship along with the heartfelt wish that your life should be successful and with a minimum of inexpedient goals and the pain connected with them. Never lose hope that work done with love will lead to a good end" (Lothane, 1999, p. 1195). Love was mentioned here for the first time and, curiously, on a postcard[7] others could read; but it was love writ large.

Back in Zurich Sabina got a heart-rending letter from Jung on December 4, 1908: "I regret a great deal and regret my weakness and curse fate that is menacing me...You will laugh when I tell you that lately I am *constantly flooded with early childhood memories* [Jung's emphasis]...Will you forgive me that I

7 The postcard and the 1909 letters of Sabina and mother were first published in Lothane, 1999.

am who I am? That I am thereby offending you and forgetting my duty as a physician toward you?... My misfortune is that I cannot live without the joy of stormy, ever changing love in my life...Since the last scene I have completely lost my sense of security toward you...I need definite agreements so that I do not need to worry about your intentions. Otherwise my work will suffer, and that seems to me more important than the momentary problems and suffering in the present. Give me at this moment something back for the love and patience and unselfishness that I was able to give you during the time of your illness. Now I am the sick one" (Car, pp. 195–196, Lothane, 1999, p. 1197).

The last letter, of the second period, marks a milestone: Jung's supportive love for Sabina turns seductive and sensual: "four and a half years ago Dr. Jung was my doctor, then he became my friend and finally my "poet," i.e., my beloved[8]. Eventually, he came to me and things went as they usually do with "poetry." He preached polygamy, his wife was supposed to have no objection, etc., etc." (C p. 93). Sabina responded in kind but for her it meant something different: "It was my first love. Not to live with him, or at least for him, for the child I wanted to give him, seemed impossible" (C, p. 12), combining the sensual longing awakened in her by Jung and the instinctual maternal longing for a child with him, thus an essential difference between a man's and a woman's attitude toward sexuality. While playing passionate Faust to Spielrein's chaste Margaret Jung is also shrewd and self-serving in pressing the aforecited "definite agreements," in effect making it clear to his student that he will neither divorce his wife nor marry her, nor forfeit his wife's riches. Moreover, knowing the intensity of her passion, and the danger of making her pregnant, would restrain Jung from intercourse. Sabina is also aware of the reality of her situation: "His wife is protected by the law, respected by all, and I, who wanted to give him everything I possessed without the slightest regard for myself, I am called immoral in the language of society—lover, maybe maîtresse!...and I have to skulk in dark corners... we must conceal our feelings...to be kept secret from her" (C p. 12), echo of trauma as a child (57).

Back in Zurich Sabina also receives a letter from her mother with excuses for having opened and read Jung's letter to her, perhaps the aforecited letter of 12.VIII.08, with this wise caveat: "Had you wished to cause him to divorce his wife, then it would be a different matter...you can get him but it is not worth it... continue meeting him as a friend" (ES 1). In response Sabina reassures mother:

8 This word in Carotenuto is "lover" but Geliebter also means beloved, i.e., dearly loved, which is who Jung was for Sabina (Lothane, 1999).

"We are both either equally guilty or not guilty…The question whether we should separate was also considered…It ended with having things out…We stood motionless in the most tender poetry…So far we have remained at the level of poetry that is not dangerous and we shall remain at that level for a long time, perhaps until the time I will become a doctor, unless circumstances will change" (SS 3, her emphasis). In 1909 Spielrein's expressed her "yearning for love, fear of emotional atrophy" in her diary (C, p. 5). As to "friendship…Mother says it is impossible for my friend and me to remain friends once we have given each other our love. A man cannot sustain pure friendship in the long run…I will pray here: dear Fate, allow us, my friend and me, to be exceptions…to form one soul…allow me to be his guardian angel, his spirit of inspiration, always spiriting him to new and greater things…at least till I find a husband…please, allow there to be a pure, noble friendship between us…allow this feeling to satisfy me completely and to become a ray of light in my solitude" (C p. 6). See also her undated German letter to Freud about her feelings toward both (p. 443).

Sabina graduated with these grades (highest being 6): pathology 4; internal medicine 5, surgery 5, gynecology 4, psychiatry 6, ophthalmology 4, pharmacology 4, hygiene 5. She passed the preliminary examination on 11/5/1908; written examination December 1910; oral examination on 20/1/1911; dissertation 2/9/1911 (Swales, 1992). After defending her dissertation Sabina moved first to Munich and then to Vienna where she joined Freud's circle. In 1913 Jung got a new patient, Antonia Wolff, who would become his sexual partner and Emma Jung's friend and be recognized as member of the family (Bair, 2003, p. 248, 265).

In this period Sabina wrote her dissertation, a pioneering analytic investigation of the meaning of a schizophrenic woman's productions with "the advantage of surveying the spontaneous course of associations" (Spielrein, 1911, p. 330, my translation), a method Freud would name free association (Lothane, 2018). In 1910 Jung started reading the manuscript and was delighted by some parts of it and critical of some others (Car p.197). In November of 1910 Spielrein wrote that

> much more important to me is my second study, "On the death instinct," and there I must admit I greatly fear that my friend, who planned to mention my idea in his article in July, saying that I have the rights of priority, may simply borrow the whole development of the idea…to refer to it as early as January. Is this another case of unfounded distrust on my part? I wish…that my second study be dedicated to my most esteemed teacher, etc. How could I esteem a person who lied, who stole

> my ideas, who was not my friend but a petty, scheming rival. And love him? I do love him, after all. My work ought to be permeated by love! I love him and I hate him because he is not mine. On the other hand it is good that my father has come to stay with me until I take my exams. Father wants to take me back to Russia…I don't want to go to Russia! The German language, which I have adopted for writing my journal, clearly shows that I want to stay as far away from Russia as possible. Yes, I want to be free! Where shall I go? " (C p. 35).

Working on this text was not easy as reflected in Sabina's hitherto unpublished fragment in German about meeting Jung:

> …and my great exhaustion, to boot. I wanted to visit him today in Küsnacht at 9 o'clock in the morning. I looked so dumb and tired that I thought it unbearable to appear in this state but on the other hand to suffer greatly if I didn't. But I went there mainly because of my paper so that he wouldn't get terribly angry and just simply send me the paper back. When I arrived in Küsnacht I could not find his house. First I went toward Herrliberg, then back all the way to Zollikon, but to no avail! Just around half past ten I called him from Zollikon that I rather come some other day. His voice sounded so cold. I wanted to leave but was overcome by such a wild despair that I could not bear it any longer and…

In July of 1911 Jung was curious to see her new paper on destruction (Car p. 193). In next letter in August, having partially read it, he considered her thought to be daring, wide-ranging and philosophical but not suitable for the *Jahrbuch*, of which he was the editor. Rather, he found it to be a good fit for a journal dealing with applied psychology (Car, p. 193–194). However in December Jung notified Spielrein that her paper would be published in volume IV of the *Jahrbuch* "should Prof. Freud wish it as well. **I congratulate you on your success**" (Car, p. 205). But then, surprisingly, on March 18, 1912 Jung confessed that when he finally "leafed through [her] paper [he] found uncanny parallels to [his] own new paper [on transformations of the libido] of which he had no idea because until now he always misread [her] title as 'distinction' instead of 'destruction' and was astonished" (Car p. 201), a bizarre slip suggesting his ambivalence toward and rivalry with Spielrein. Eventually on March 25 1912 Jung sounded reassuring: "You are getting upset in vain. When I said there are "uncanny" similarities, you again took it too literally. I wanted to give you a compliment. The paper is exceptionally intelligent and contains excellent ideas the priority of which I readily acknowledge...Nobody can presume you borrowed from me... Perhaps I have borrowed from you" (Car, p. 208).

Jung's last stratagem was to insert a long passage into Spielrein's published paper (1912a, pp 465–466) to make it look as if she had borrowed the idea of destruction from him.[9] In her footnote on page 466 Spielrein stated she found that passage in Jung's "*Wandlungen und Symbole der Libido* (transformations and symbols of the libido). *Jahrbuch*, III." I searched in vain for that passage in Volume III, published in 1911. Reviewing this paper Paul Federn[10] (1913) both agreed and disagreed with Spielrein's theses. He acknowledged "the ambivalent components, the destruction drive and the emergent drive of sexuality" (p. 90), but "since a solution to these problems is so far unavailable one would forego polemics against her hypotheses and be grateful for her highly interesting and comprehensive work" (p. 91). Federn also noted her discussing the "splitting of complexes" in schizophrenia, an idea anticipating Melanie Klein on splitting; "the struggle between two antagonistic currents, the species ego and the individual ego"; and ideas about "words, art, sadomasochism" (p. 91). He underscored, however, that "whereas one would not object to trying to determine representations of destructive processes, one would all the more question the completely unfounded assumption that processes of destruction and transformation have their own underlying drive...rather than result from individual strivings" (p. 93), with which I agree. In 1932 Wilhelm Reich vigorously repudiated Freud's theorizing that "masochism [is a] *primary biological* tendency to self-destruction" (Reich's emphasis), thus a denial of its source in conflict psychology (p. 307) and sociology (p. 308).

By January 19, 1911, having passed all her examinations, Sabina noted: "He [Jung] is gone, and 'tis good thus. Good at least that my parents are now happy" (C p. 38) and by January 7 1912 she went "away from Zurich and to Montreux on vacation ...from there to Munich for art history [where] she finished [her] paper on 'destruction' " (C p. 40); and from there to Vienna to "become a member of the Vienna Psychoanalytic Society on the strength of

9 There Jung writes: "libido has two aspects...it beautifies all...and destroys all...A woman...that succumbs to passion rapidly experiences the destruction...Anxiety about the erotic fate...explains death fantasies and renonciation of the erotic wish."

10 Paul Federn (1871–1950), was a Viennese physician who joined Freud's circle in 1904 and 1913 became a most loyal follower. He pioneered applying psychoanalysis to treating psychoses; settled in New York in 1938 and committed suicide in 1950 fearing his cancer was incurable.

my dissertation. Prof. Freud, of whom I have become very fond, thinks highly of me and tells everyone about my magnificent article he is also very sweet to me personally" (C. p. 41).

The third international psychoanalytic congress took place from the 25th to the 26th of September 1911 in Weimar which Sabina neither mentioned in her diary nor attended. Jung's letter to Sabina in 21/22.IX.1911 is an ardent homily filled with character analysis, advice and encouragement, assuring her that he had "removed all bitterness from [his] heart" (Car, p. 201), and stating emphatically: "**under no circumstances should you have missed to attend the Congress, this was a big mistake**" (Jung's boldface, Car, p. 201). Apparently while in Munich Sabina was referred by Freud to see Dr. Seif.[11] Now Jung writes: "I see your situation clearly. I can hardly consider that there is something organic with your foot for the psychological situation is most significantly traumatic. You needed to find a reason not to go to Weimar. Namely, you wanted to arrive here with a certain wish fantasy which you then had to repress. But you should have come anyway, because life demands sacrifices..." (Car p. 201).[12] There was foot trouble before (63) and a "hyperesthesia in the feet with abasia" observed by Jung in December 1904.

On November 29 1911 Spielrein was the "speaker" at the 152nd scientific meeting of the Vienna Psychoanalytic Society. The title was "On transformation" but her actual goal was to lecture on destruction. Her aim was not a death instinct in the sense of Freud's instinctual death drive. She invoked "a normal death instinct (Mechnikov)" (Nunberg & Federn, *Minutes*, 1974, p. 329), without citing Metchnikoff's book she may have read. According to Metchnikoff (1903) the long-lived biblical patriarchs had "the instinct of natural death," i.e., an *intuitive* knowledge of death, and "it may seem altogether surprising and improbable that an instinct for death should arise in man, since we are imbued with an instinct of an opposite nature...the desire of life and the fear of death are manifestations of an instinct deeply rooted in the constitution of man" (p. 281). In 1908 Metchnikoff wrote: "The instinct of natural death is far from harmful...[it] would contribute to the maintenance of the life of the individual and of the species" (p. 129). Metchnikoff also noted that "in the animal world...an instinct is blind and generally very precise, in man we find

11 Leonhard Seif (1866–1949), German neurologist turned expert in education in Munich and a follower of Alfred Adler (German Wikipedia)

12 The other woman who did come to Weimar, greatly admired by Freud, was the attractive and seductive Lou Andreas-Salome, mistress of Nietzsche, Rilke, and Tausk, who would eclipse Spielrein as a prolific letter-writer and member of the Vienna Psychoanalytic Society.

nothing of the kind. The social instinct appears in him in endless variety" (p. 306), for example, in the "maternal instinct that furnishes [the woman] with certain rules of conduct but…is not enough…to rear the child until the age when it can live independently" (p. 319). Metchnikoff's real scientific interest was senescence. There are only self-conservative and reproductive drives, there is no death drive.

As summarized by Rank, Spielrein's idea was that the component of death is contained in the sexual instinct itself…these relationships are then pursued to the Siegfried myth and the legend of the Flying Dutchman; in this connection…it is in the manner of Freud's savior type that Wagner's heroes love, in that they sacrifice themselves and die…These relationships prove to be analogous throughout in the worlds of man, animals, plants. For the instinct of propagation requires the destruction of the sexual instinct. Man has a need to come into existence and to perish (*Minutes*, 329–330).

Another possible juxtaposition was the Wagnerian *Liebestod* versus the then high mortality of women in pregnancy and childbirth.

> The last to speak was blunt Spielrein
>
> Express[ing] regret that as a result of her failure to take into consideration the fundamental chapter of her work: "Destruction a the cause of coming into being," a conceptual confusion has impaired the discussion. In her view, the sexual instinct is a particular case of the drive for transformation. In speaking of conflict, she referred to the personal ego, and to the cosmic ego. Whether death wishes are directed against oneself or against another person depends on the preponderance of either the masochistic or the sadistic component. The desire to be consumed is a normal tendency; among women, it is often expressed as a fantasy of destruction (*Minutes*, p. 335).

Clearly, with her ideas about masochism and sadism she was years ahead of Freud, Theodor Reik, and Helene Deutsch. This brings me to her German *Essay on Transformation*, composed in 1908 (Chapter 8).

As nontechnical words, transform and transformation suggest a *change* in character, nature or function, e.g., water is transformed into ice or steam. Spielrein would have read these words in Freud's works on hysteria, dreams and sexuality. She first mentions "transformation" and "transformation drive" in 1906 (95). She also quotes from Mach's (1959) important work on the analysis of sensations[13] in which ideas akin to transformation are expressed in related terms such as adaptation, change, modification, transition, transfer, and continuity.

Sensation is defined in The Oxford English Dictionary (1933) as "1. The operation of the senses; 2. A mental feeling, an emotion. Now chiefly, the characteristic feeling arising in some particular circumstances"; 3.An excited or violent feeling" (Volume IX, p. 456). Bertrand Russell (1984) defined as follows: "Sensations resulting from a stimulus *within the body* will naturally not be felt by other people; If I have a stomach ache I am in no degree surprised to that others are not similarly affected" (p. 45; italics added), thus distinct from external events perceived by many. Such painful somatizations of feelings and emotions occur in states of anxiety and depression while pleasurable sensations accompany feelings of satisfaction and happiness.

With considerable complexity and subtlety Spielrein continues to argue that psychologically woman is different from man. Mach's book inspires her to claim that "one can simply explain the abreaction drive: it is a procreation drive...the transformation drive. The entire sexual complex, in the broadest sense, is the sum total of the sensations experienced toward the beloved including all that has been felt along with him." She also formulates an ego psychology: "The ego seeks to assimilate and transform itself... as soon as the complex is out...the more one believes oneself to be understood, the more the ego is assimilated...The sexual drive, a drive for the renewal of the whole personality, is a partial case of the transformation drive." Next comes "transformation in the form of works of art...a sexual complex can, in the extended sense, become a powerful motivating drive for everything in art, but it does not have to be." In her conclusions she states: "The expression "libido" (i.e., "sexual emotion" in its narrower sense), when applied to art and science, is strictly speaking, false, for there is no specific sexual feeling that is the foundation of all feeling...but a transformation drive; it perhaps can tend toward a sexual aspect and then it can be called "libido." With this 1906 text Spielrein has established her priority with the concept of transformation of instinctual drives, emotions, and impulses, without denying Freud's sexual libido. Jung used the word *Wandlung* (= change, transformation, metamorphosis) in the title of his 1911–1912 revisionist landmark essay, "Transformations and symbols of the libido," thus a heresy from Freud's libido, foreshadowing their final break in 1914, as documented in the *Freud Jung Letters*.

13 A further discussion of sensations as conceived by Mach and by Spielrein in her Essay on Transformation.

Sabina's essay ends mysteriously: "In my case the family has now arranged that I am snatched from my studies and remain stuck in the complex. The misery is once again immeasurable. Will I be able to get out of it unscathed once more?" At this point the family is not interfering with her studies as they did during the violent scenes in Zurich, when Sabina refused to get married off and insisted on studying medicine. On the other hand, the complex she is stuck in now is her relationship with Jung: he healed her as his patient in 1904–1905 but complicated her life falling in love with her by 1908. After their separation in 1911 Sabina would be haunted by memories of their romantic love, complicating her relationship with Paul Sheftel.

In the 1911 volume III of the *Jahrbuch* both Freud and Spielrein published their pioneering psychoanalytic contributions to psychiatry about meaning in psychosis: he was interpreting the content of a book, Schreber's 1903 *Memoirs of My Nervous Illness*[14] (Lothane, 1992), she was decoding the fantasies and emotions of patient Mrs. M. with whom she interacted by following her free associations, viewing the woman's utterances as "symbols of her sexual personality." As Spielrein notes: "Freud and Jung have shown that delusional systems are not nonsensical but meaningful, thus a reworking of complexes based on the lawfulness of dreams" (p. 396). Schreber's fantasies about "little Flechsig" led Spielrein to the "transformation-thoughts of our patient" (p. 397) and her feelings in mentioning "little Forel" (p. 350), the former director of the hospital, thus hinting at Bleuler and Jung. Spielrein also noted that instead of expressing "something definite and concrete in the complex," she spoke in symbols, "expressing it via another person; instead of 'I experience [she] says 'she experiences,'...a dissolution of...the complex [thus] stripped of its personal character" (p. 399).

Spielrein connected Mrs. M.'s "present conflicts" (p. 398) to a "representation of her sexual activities by means of death symbolism" (p. 400), foreshadowing her future 1912 paper on destruction as a cause of becoming, widely accepted as a precursor of Freud's death instinct. But in 1920 Freud propounded a "*dualistic* ...opposition... between life instincts and death instincts" (p. 53, his italics), misconceiving death due to aging, i.e., biological senescence as a process of gradual deterioration. In 1923 Freud noted: "love impulses transform themselves into aggression...[via] the murderous id" (p. 53). He also linked "the dangerous death instinct" to "aggressiveness" and "suppression of aggressive-

14 In the 1912 "Postscript" to his 1911 paper Freud cited: "See Jung (1911, 164 and 207); and Spielrein (1911, 350) (p. 80, footnote 2, which went unnoticed so that only the 1920 mention of Spielrein was cited.

ness" (p.54), a dynamic he had himself suppressed for decades in deference to his sexual libido theory.

However, in 1920 Freud also added this footnote: "A considerable portion of these speculations have been anticipated by Sabina Spielrein (1912) in an instructive and interesting paper which, however, is unfortunately not entirely clear to me. She there describes the sadistic components of the sexual instinct as 'destructive'" (p.55, emphasis added). Freud was right, because his ideas about the death instinct in 1920 and Spielrein's ideas about destruction in 1912 were two different theories. In fact, continuing the concepts of the dissertation, Spielrein focused on the feminine fusion of "the procreation drive and the destruction drive" (p. 489) as "transformations" of antagonistic (p. 503) images of pleasure and pain, love and hate (p. 488), sadism and masochism (484), "transformation" of love and aggression (p 484). These ideas are based on "biological facts" (p. 466, 503); clinical observations (her Mrs. M.); mythology (water symbolism); and in literature (the *Liebestod* in Shakespeare's Romeo and Juliette and Wagner's Brünnhilde and Siegfried ("let love reign paramount in sorrow and in joy," p. 494). Spielrein cited two sources of inspiration: (1) Friedrich Nietzsche (who "became man and woman" (p. 481), and (2) Wilhelm Stekel's[15] "Eros and Tanathos" (Stekel, 1909, p. 489), on page 478, there making an curious slip copying "Tantalos" instead of Thanatos.

Differentiating a collective "species psyche" from an individual "ego-psyche" (p. 474), what takes place in psychosis and in art is a dissolution, a "transformation" of the image of personal self into a "typical ancient species image" (474), a transformation of the personal "ego" into a collective "us" (das *Wir*). This idea can be seen as a precursor to Jung's collective unconscious and archetypes. Remarkably, Freud never used Thanatos as a synonym for death instinct.

In the winter of 1911/1912 Sabina traveled to Rostov and lectured on psychoanalysis to the Rostov medical society where she met the Jewish doctor Pavel (Faivel) Sheftel. They were married in June 1912 in Rostov in a traditional Jewish wedding ceremony in a synagogue. I submit that for Sabina it was a marriage on the rebound, after a brief courtship and without first having mourned the separation from Jung. The newlyweds moved to Berlin and in December 1913 her daughter Irma was born. Later Irma's surviving an illness meant to Sabina

15 Wilhelm Stekel (1868–1940), physician and "specialist for psychotherapy and nervous disorders in Vienna," a most gifted founding member of the Wednesday Society that became the Vienna Psychoanalytic Association in 1906, banished by Freud in 1912. In 1911 published Die Sprache des Traumes (language of dreams): "the philosophers have repeatedly illuminated the connection between Eros and Thanatos" (p. 96).

that she was reborn, renata in Latin, and she changed her name to Renata and the pet names Renatchen and Renatochka. She reminisced about Renata in 1922: "we often had fun with our little daughter singing all kinds of folk songs one after the other, the way it occurred to us. It occurred to me that I was associating the next song with the word content of the preceding one whereas the child, then two-and-a-half to three years old, associated according to similarity of the melodic lines. This was not due to the child's ignorance for she knew those texts and some of them word for word" (p. 241, HZL translations).

In 1912 Spielrein published "Contributions to knowing the infantile mind" which included her self-analysis based on a "diary she kept as a ten year old and corroborated by her uncle and brother" (p. 166). Here are some examples Sabina narrated:

> my parents, actually my mother, were proud of the 'purity' and 'naiveté' of their daughter. In the gymnasium, for the sake of a respectable education, animal reproduction was eliminated from the biology curriculum. I ended liking myself for my "innocence" and felt a certain horror of a knowledge that would render me feeling impure. So that the first time I became acquainted with sexual matters was during my zoology lectures at the university (p. 144; her italics)...

> at age five I was aware that a mother has a baby in her body to which she then gives "birth"... Where children come from was to me a terra incognita and I queried about it, and who created mother and father... and god" (p. 147).

> One day I asked an old mother if I could also have a child, like mother. "No," she said, "you are too small to have a child, now you could perhaps give birth to a kitten. I ruminated a lot about the kitten... and here you have the sexual etiology of anxiety: the kitten...was the longed-for child...The child was thus perceived as a dangerous or fatal illness. I often see in women this depiction of pregnancy and labor as a form of serious illness...consciously or unconsciously a woman imagines the child as growing to the detriment of its mother. Interestingly, we react to these destruction fantasies now with pleasure and now with anxiety, or at least with unpleasure. The fear of an infectious disease was for me also connected with the fear of the child, and, moreover, the fear of the seducer or the kidnapper (148). As a child...I had no "idea" of the

> sexual meaning of the father...he was there only to earn money and yet I looked for the kidnapper, i.e., the man" (p. 149). In my clinical years, as any beginner, I had the well-known anxiety concerning infectious diseases...going back to my childhood (p. 145).

Sabina had a rich fantasy life:

> Until the age of 6–7 I feared "*no devil*"...I mocked my younger brother and scared him by jumping out of a dark hiding place or telling scary stories. I had grandiose fantasies of a goddess that ruled a vast realm; I possessed a power I called '*partun power*' that gave her the power to know everything and achieve everything I wanted...I was sure of being chosen by God...Inside me there was a critic who knew the difference between reality and fantasy (p. 145; her italics.)

But she was also aware that these fantasies "were pleasurable and from my earliest childhood on served unconsciously as a need for a substitute for parental love"(p. 150). This need was especially acute in relation to father who rebuked her for scaring her brother:

> "*Just wait, fate will punish you, you will also be afraid one day and then realize how scared your brother was.* I did not take this threat seriously and yet it had obvious consequences; then one day I was greatly terrified when...I saw two black kittens sitting on the dresser. It was an illusion and yet so clear, I thought, "*this is death*," or "*the plague*." With this shock I was plunged into an anxiety period: in the dark, I clearly saw many horrible animals, I felt I wanted to wrench myself away from the power of my parents...With great fear and interest I wanted to hear descriptions of various diseases which I discovered within myself that in the shape of persons wanted to "*attack*" me or "*snatch*" me. For a non-psychoanalyst it was clear: the child was intimidated by father, his threats, acted suggestively and the child was terrified. But only now can a psychoanalyst ask: did these fantasies have any connection with sexuality which is missing in this description? I must answer this in the affirmative (p. 146; her italics).

However, both evaluations have their validity and would play an important role in her later years.

Sabina was also thrilled by watching the "transformation of a little zinc rod dropped into a solution of lead salt into a '*real*' tree. In this way I can artificially create '*life*'! And thus began my passion and enthusiasm for chemistry...At the university I was passionately fascinated by organic chemistry lectures; each time it happened, it occurred to me that I had known all this long ago" (p. 150; her italics).

Berlin 1913 to 1915

Sabina, Pavel and daughter Irma have now been living in Berlin. In 1913 Freud wrote to Sabina: " I am sorry to hear that you are still consumed with longing for J.[ung]...I imagine that you love Dr. J. so deeply still because you have not brought to light the hatred he merits...I can hardly bear to listen when you continue to enthuse about your old love" (C pp. 119–120). But she was not making money as an analyst. She asked Freud for referrals and got this response from him in 1914: "Now you are going crazy [*meshugge*] yourself...and your argument that I have not yet sent you any patients!... I have not seen a patient from Berlin for the last six months, or anyone else I could have sent on to you...I do not know whether Abraham is able to hand over many patients, but I am sure he will take your wishes into account unless you distance yourself from the work of the Association" (C p. 121–122). Sabina accepted Freud's explanation but did not contact Abraham. She would later hold a temporary job at the famed Charité Hospital run by psychiatrist Karl Bonhoeffer, salary unknown. Similar concerns were expressed by Eva in 1914: "Sabina, I would advise you to avoid seeing J[Jung]" (ES 17); in 1915 Eva asks: "Are you seeing Jung" (ES 27). Her answer is unknown. She would not tell mother about having renewed her correspondence with Jung in 1917. Similarly, her Burghölzli friend Ter-Oganesian wrote: "It appears, that [Jung] is still... quite deeply lodged [in your mind], what a disappointment that you have not yet abreacted this" (Letter #5).

After her husband's return to Russia in 1915 Sabina went back to Switzerland. After a brief trial in Zurich she settled down in Lausanne.

Lausanne 1915–1920

During the time in Lausanne Spielrein corresponded with Jung from 1917 to 1918 (C pp. 50–90). She composed an unpublished fragment of a novel, *Les Vents* (the winds), and two papers in 1915: "An unconscious juridical ruling" and "The manifestations of the Oedipus complex in childhood" (Spielrein,

1987.) Thereafter she attended the 1920 international psychoanalytic congress at The Hague an read her paper on the origin of the words papa and mama. The congress was also attended by current and future luminaries: Anna Freud, Karl Abraham, Sandor Ferenczi, Max Eitingon, and Melanie Klein. After the congress she moved to Geneva.

Geneva 1920–1923

These were her most productive years of her life in the West with 20 papers published in various journals (Spielrein, 1987). The Hague paper, a major contribution, appeared as "The origin of the child's words papa and mama" in *Imago* in 1922. In 1923 she published a pioneering paper on the similarities between the thinking of children, of patients with aphasia, and unconscious thinking, also in *Imago*,[16] that was quoted in an important treatise on the psychoanalytic method by Roland Dalbiez (1941). Discussing the method of free association, Dalbiez focused on the "regression of thought towards the image, oneiric or hypnagogic dramatization," and cited in detail two of Spielrein's cases, "two simple examples of the 'visualization' of thought borrowed from Frau Dr. Spielrein (p. 93)... Thus the subconscious thought expresses by image what the conscious thought would have expressed in words" (p. 94). Spielrein utilized Freud's method of free association in studying unconscious processes as did Bleuler (1912), Silberer (1912), Varendonck (1921), Reik (1948) and others.[17]

In Geneva Spielrein became acquainted with Édouard Claparède (1873–1940), an early supporter of Freud since 1901, founder of the *Archives de Psychologie*, who cited Freud on associations in 1903. In 1912 he founded the Institut Jean-Jacques Rousseau and Spielrein became his assistant in 1920. Claparède, who married Jewish-Russian woman Hélène Spir (Lothane, 1999), was not a psychoanalyst but he enabled the spread of psychoanalysis in Switzerland and France. Spielrein was the analyst of Jean Piaget and Charles Odier, the future founder of the French Psychoanalytic Association. She was also befriended by Swiss Pierre Bovet and Emil Oberholzer (1883–1958), born in Germany, trained by Bleuler, analyzed by Freud, and married to Polish Jewess Mira Gincburg whom he met at the Burghölzli[18]. In 1919 Gincburg, Oskar

16 All Spielrein's articles from 1911 to 1931 were published by Traute Hensch in 1987, a volume 389 pages long.

17 This method was later continued by my teacher Otto Isakower (Wyman & Rittenberg, 1992, Lothane, 2018).

18 See Jung's letters 153J and 154J (*FJL*, pp. 243–245).

Pfister and Oberholzer founded the Swiss Society for Psychoanalysis of which Oberholzer was president until 1928. In 1938, fearing Nazi persecution, the couple fled to New York and practiced psychoanalysis there. Spielrein was a member of the Swiss Psychoanalytic Association and reported on its activity in *Internationale Zeitschrift für ärztliche Psychoanalyse* founded by Freud in 1913. In 1921 Spielrein published a detailed survey of psychoanalytic literature in Russia and translations of Freud's work into Russian from 1909 on.

1923 turned out to be a decisive year. In January Freud wrote about Dr. Spielrein to an "esteemed colleague" in Geneva, most likely Oberholzer, that if the possibilities of staying in Geneva were dwindling, and since the likelihood of having a psychoanalytic practice in Vienna nil, on Spielrein's only option, as Freud had already told her, was to settle in Berlin. In the meantime, pressure was mounting from parents, husband, and brothers for her to return to Russia. After years of indecision, Sabina finally yielded. By August, brother Yan sent her the schedule of trains to Moscow.

The years in Russia 1923–1942

The first surge of interest in psychoanalysis in Russia took off with the translation of Freud's works from 1909 to 1913 and articles by 18 authors including Nikolai Ossipov, Nikolai Vyrubov, Tatiana Rosental, Moisei Wulf and Yuri Kannabikh (Spielrein, 1921) the last two appearing on the masthead of *I.Z.P.* Remarkably, Freud was first published in Russian before any other European language (Litvinov, 1994). In 1912 Freud had told Jung: "In Russia (Odessa) there seems to be a local epidemic of psychoanalysis," and in the footnote: "Two members of the Vienna Society were in Odessa Leonid Droznes, who attempted to analyze the Wolf Man...and in Jan. 1910 brought him to Vienna... and Moshe Wulf (1878–1971)" (*FJL*, p. 495). Wulf left the U.S.S.R. in 1927, resumed his work in Berlin, settled in Palestine in 1933 (the year Hitler seized power); he became a co-founder of the Palestine Psychoanalytic Society. The other co-founder was Max Eitingon (1881–1943), formerly a member of Freud's "Secret Committee" and the architect of the Freudian system of psychoanalytic training, also settled in Palestine.

After a fallow period during the war, the second surge of psychoanalysis started in the 1920's. In 1921 the Children's Home-Laboratory and The Psychological and Psychoanalytic Library were founded by Ivan D. Ermakov, aided by Moisei Wulf, and Vera and Otto Shmidt. In 1922 the Russian Psychoanalytic Association was founded by Ermakov and Wulf. In 1923, with the

Children's Home as springboard, those aforementioned members and Spielrein organized the State Psychoanalytic Institute (GPAI) and the Children's Home Laboratory "International Solidarity." In 1924 psychoanalytic research was also supported in St. Petersburg by the All-Union congress on experimental pedagogics and pedology, the latter a synthesis of psychology, pedagogy, and pediatrics.

During the year Sabina stayed in Moscow she was the only staff employee in the aforementioned institutions. She saw children in the outpatient clinic, acted as consultant, taught a course on unconscious thinking and led a seminar on child analysis. She also lectured at the meetings of the Psychanalytic Association and taught a course on "psychoanalysis of children." In 1945 Wilhelm Reich recalled that "many pedagogues...with psychoanalytic orientation such as Vera Shmidt, Spielrein and others attempted to institute a positive sexual education... all in all, the *sexual education of children in the S.[oviet] U.[nion] remained sex-negative*" (p. 238; his italics). In 1925 the commissars outlawed the State Psychoanalytic Institute and by 1930 the Psychoanalytic Association ceased to exist as well. Remarkably, Spielrein succeeded in publishing her last article, on children's drawings with open and closed eyes, in 1931 in *Imago*. In 1932 the journal *Pedology* was closed down and by 1936 pedology was outlawed too.

During those years new stars were rising in Moscow, psychologist Lev Vygotsky (1896–1934) and neuropsychologist Aleksandr Luria (1902–1977). Both were at first interested in psychoanalysis but eventually, whether due to personal disillusionment or official pressure, denied its importance for psychology. Arguably, in Moscow Spielrein was head and shoulders above her colleagues which could create envy and frictions. And since all politics is local politics, wearing the mantle of Freud was no guarantee of continual success either. In spite of her superior qualifications she may have been cold-shouldered by the Moscow elite, hardly the glorious recognition foretold by Freud. Furthermore, Pavel did not travel to meet her in Moscow: it seemed inevitable that she had to return to Rostov. There she found out, we are not told how, that her husband had been living in a common law marriage with Dr. Olga Snitkova who bore him a daughter Nina in 1924 (Etkind, 1997, Launer, 2015). In 1926 Eva, the second daughter of Sabina and Pavel was born. Sabina continued her daily work as school pedologist, and after 1936 as doctor, with occasional trips to Moscow.

In 1990 Etkind interviewed Nina Pavlovna Snitkova, her daughter's half-sister, gleaning the following story. The Sheftels and the two daughters lived in a former stable, in the courtyard of the old family house. In one empty room there was a "huge sofa" but it is unclear whether she practiced psychoanalysis since it was illegal under Stalin. Nina Pavlovna recalled that

> people remembered her as terribly impractical, she only wore clothes given to her. She looked like a little old woman although she was not that old. She stooped, wore an old black skirt reaching the ground and boots with buckles nowadays called "goodbye, youth," probably brought from Berlin. That is how grandmother dressed. Clearly, she had been broken by life (p. 176).

Pavel Sheftel died of a heart attack in 1937. Later Sabina and Nina's mother became friends and agreed to take care of each other's daughters should something happen to them.

In the 1930's, cut off from the West, Sabina could not have known what Jung said on Radio Berlin in 1934: "the Aryan unconscious...has a higher potential than the Jewish...Freud did not understand the German psyche... Has the formidable phenomenon of National Socialism, on which the whole world gazes in astonishment, taught them any better?" (Lothane, 2007, p. 85); nor that concentration camps Dachau, Sachsenhausen and Buchenwald were opened in 1933 and 1937 respectively; or that during the "Night of Broken Glass" in November 1938 Jewish homes, businesses, and synagogues went up in flames.

The Nazi invasion of Russia began on June 22 1941 with a blitzkrieg and taking about 1.5 million of prisoners. In its wake the Wehrmacht, the Armed SS, and the paramilitary Einsatzgruppen (death squads) tortured and murdered communists and partisans, Gypsies and Jews, culminating in September with the massacre of 33,700 Jews in the Kiev ravine Babii Yar. In the summer of 1941 Renata joined her mother and sister in Rostov and from November 19th through the 21st the city was briefly seized by the Germans. Niece Menikha recalled that the two sisters played music for the invaders (MS 1) which could explain how Sabina was lulled into a false sense of security even though Jews had already known about German atrocities elsewhere. In July 1942 the Red Army still held Rostov while German aerial bombardments continued nonstop until Rostov's second occupation on July 24. Emil's widow Fania and her second son Evald were miraculously able to escape to Central Asia but Sabina stayed on.

The mass killings of Russian prisoners of war, civilians, and Jews were organized by former jurists: Walther Bierkamp, chief of Einsatzgruppe D, supervised by Kurt Christmann, chief of Eisatzkommando (firing squad) 10a, and Obersturmführer Dr. Heinrich Herz. Both were Nazi party members who had held positions in the Nazi security system already before WWII. Bierkamp committed suicide at war's end. Christmann was tried and convicted as war criminal and imprisoned. Sabina and her daughters were last seen in a column of thousands of Jews driven to be shot and buried outside Rostov in the Zmieyovskaia ravine. I am sometimes haunted by the image of an exhausted Sabina clutching her daughters and tormented by the realization of the fateful mistake she had made.

COMMENTS ON THE RUSSIAN CORRESPONDENCE

These letters from her parents, siblings, and others were written to Sabina during the 19 years she lived in Western Europe from 1904 to 1923 in Zurich, Vienna, Munich, Berlin, Lausanne, and Geneva. Only a few letters from Sabina to her mother survived. These letters offer a window into the physical and mental states of Sabina during this period.

LETTERS FROM FATHER

Sabina's father, Naftul (Naftali, Naftel) Moshkovich Szpilrajn, was born around 1861 in Warsaw where his whole family lived. Since the former Polish Kingdom was annexed by the Russian Empire, Naftul was able to settle in Rostov on Don in 1883 and change his given name to Nikolai Arkadievich and last name to Shpilrain in Russian and Spielrein in German. Sabina's maternal grandfather Mordechai Lublinskii, with a name pointing to origins in the eastern Polish city of Lublin, may have moved to the Russian city of Ekaterinoslav. Nikolai rose from poverty and was educated as agronomist in Germany at his own expense (Ljunggren, 2001). In Rostov he founded a successful import business of fertilizers[19] and amassed a considerable fortune. As a first guild merchant Nikolai earned the right to own land and build a house whereas the poor Jews were constrained to live in a region called the Pale of Settlement. At birth Sabina's Yiddish name was Sheive, Yasha's name Yankev, and Oskar's, also called Sania, Isaak.

With such renamings, assimilated and secularized Jews like the Spielreins maintained their cultural and social distance from poor and traditionally religious Jews and victims of official anti-Semitism and violence. Furthermore, they did not discuss anti-Semitism in their letters. Thus Nikolai expresses reservations about his son's in-laws as "an old stagnant world not ennobled by anything" and money-hungry (NS 2). In addition to Polish, Yiddish and Hebrew, Nikolai knew

19 N. A. Spielrein also owned Fabryka chemiczna (chemical factory) in Schweinfurt on Main, was "representative in Russia and the Kingdom of Poland and an agricultural office in Warsaw."

German and French. As a nouveau riche he tended to be stingy with money to his young children, as described and hinted by Sabina (86), at a "rich man who lived like a miser"); but he was generous when they grew up, and especially with Sabina, while apparently controlling with his wife, who used to have her own income.

To be sure, Nikolai had his emotional problems: "he objected to touching people and refused to take anyone by the hand" (Ljunggren, p. 79–80), he suffered from depression, and saw Freud in Vienna for treatment (NS 8). But he became a different parent and person when Sabina started medical school: he was friendly, his advice still authoritative but not patronizing (NS 1). Four years later father empathized with Sabina's loneliness, allaying her self-doubt by expressing his belief in her (NS 3) and promising her a big dowry. During Sabina's and Pavel's years in Berlin (1913–1914), in an effort to dispel her doubts about the husband, he defended him with words of appreciation and empathy for his circumstances (NS 5, 6, 7). In an undated letter Nikolai bared his soul to Sabina because Freud could not help him and that she "had observed this even before he did" (NS 21). Nikolai respected Freud's ideas (NS 23) and the great Jewish-Polish educator and author Janusz Korczak (NS 4).

By 1915, with WWI underway, Pavel was drafted and was back in Russia, Sabina decided to return to Switzerland and her serious money problems began (NS 12–14). This was further complicated by difficulties with money transfers abroad and wartime inflation (NS 17, 18). In 1916, Nikolai congratulated her on her 31st birthday and admiringly mentioned Sabina's newborn niece Menikhochka, Isaak's daughter. In 1917, with the "storm" of the great Russian revolution, father's advised her to keep out of politics (NS 14), perhaps worried by Isaak's membership in the "Socialist Revolutionary Party and Socialist Revolutionaries' terrorist organization" (Ljunggren, p. 83). By 1918, with the storm over, Nikolai sent Sabina a long soul-searching letter, including a long dream, in which he declared his plan to collaborate with the new regime under Lenin: "to give back to society what I have acquired as an excess payment for my work" and to bequeath his fortune toward establishing a university in his name (NS 15). Nikolai did not grumble that the state had requisitioned his Rostov townhouse, even though the parents and Emil's family were cramped in two of the many rooms they once owned (NS 19). As recompense, Nikolai as entomologist was commissioned by the government to develop methods of protecting crops from parasites (NS 20) and was sent on many official business trips representing the new Soviet state. Jung's aforementioned prediction in his letter of 12.8.08 came true: "Your father will have an easier time of it because an idea man can more easily espouse new viewpoints and new life values than a woman who is conservative by nature."

Nikolai ended his 1916 letter (NS 26) with the words "money" and "person"—spelled in Russian and English letters—a topic rarely discussed in psychiatric or psychoanalytic literature. Money was a central issue in the lives of Jung and Freud. The theme of having money, making money, and spending money is a crimson thread that ran throughout the entire correspondence of the Spielrein family.

LETTERS FROM MOTHER

Sabina's mother, born Khave Mordekhayevna Lublinskaya (1863–1922), had her name russified to Eva Markovna. Her rabbi father Mark Lublinskii considered "studying Christian sciences more important than anything...and saw that she was educated in the university...Mother was also afraid of falling in love with a Christian" (C p. 23). "In her youth my mother loved someone else...they became engaged...[then] the break came about...She met my father who soon won her over by...his intelligence, his firm and noble character, his tender concern for her. In spite of all this she did not love him...They became a couple. One could hardly imagine two more different people" (C p. 7). Arguably, her mother's past history affected Sabina's relations with Jung and her marriage. Eva practiced dentistry until 1903 and thereafter only sporadically while devoting herself to home, children, and philanthropy. These letters from mother show her in a new light: a person of dignity and dedication to her children, her distress of missing them year after year, worrying about their diseases and deprivations, all of which caused a progressive deterioration of her health and untimely death at age 59.

In these letters Eva was constantly worried about all her children and grandchildren, but especially about Sabina and her child, and how all this affected her physical and emotional health. Eva urged Pavel and Sabina to take some medical tests. Alluding to the mood in the marriage and sensing some malaise, she advised them to take it easy and have fun (ES 2). She worried about Milia's schooling and in spite of her poor health is happy to make a few extra rubles practicing sporadically as "papa spends a lot of time reading...I hope business will improve and then everything will be fine" (ES 3). Sensing Sabina's loneliness in Berlin and her contemplating a move she advised her not to go to Geneva but to Zurich, where she knew some people (ES 4). Since Sabina held a job, mother advised her to have a nanny rather than a nurse to care for her daughter (ES 4,

5). Father's business was slow. So as not to upset father, mother lied asking him for money to buy herself a dress while planning to buy a dress for Sabina. (ES 5); she was relieved to see that "papa's attitude to money has changed... Papa will send you money but it cost me a lot of effort to achieve this" (ES 6). It was war time, Eva worried "that all of you are suffering hunger and this torments me," so she got busy sending them food parcels and clothes (ES 7). But she also continued to worry about depressed Nikolai: "It is painful to look at him, he turned into some kind of a machine or a dead person, nothing more" (ES 8–9). She was also busy trying to get patients for Pavel and sent his visiting cards around (ES 10). As she continued to worry about Sabina's marital relationship, Eva found solace in charitable work, sewing clothes for needy children (ES 13). Complaining about Yasha's meddlesome mother-in-law, Eva painted herself as one who never "reproached" Sabina's husband (ES 13). In 1913 Sabina would publish a psychoanalytic paper, "The mother-in-law" in *Imago* (1987), analyzing both the positive and negative types." But Pavel did go back, leaving wife and sick daughter, to be drafted. But did he have to or did he choose to?

Early in 1915 Eva complained of Pavel's standoffish behavior, careless about protecting the privacy of their correspondence, especially if the subject of a possible divorce were to be mentioned and his family would catch wind of it. In the postscript Eva changed her tune after reading a recent letter from Pavel in which he mentioned renting two rooms from her family and waiting for patients. Eva also reported that she helped Pavel to get registered for the draft as a doctor (ES 20). Sabina missed hearing from Pavel and the mother wrote: "I would not like to even remember anything about "him"... but anyway for your sake I will try to find out" (ES 21). The husband was now in Rostov but remained incommunicado. However, as the war dragged on, the post office services broke down and letters got lost or portions of them were missing due to negligence of censors (ES 23). Eva was pleased that Milia continued to meet with Pavel, a contact mentioned before (ES 22), an opportunity to mend fences with Pavel.

And then came Eva's most poignant remark: "It is strange for me that you still have not written to me about why you broke up with your husband under such strained conditions" (ES 25), echoing father's indignation over Pavel's abrupt abandonment of his family (NS 13). The reasons for this fatefully tragic breakup are still an enigma: it cast a dark shadow on Sabina's entire life.

As previously, Sabina was not earning an income as an analyst and got a job in a hospital for "blind patients" whereas in Rostov, "your dear husband rented a room in which he is receiving patients...from 3–5...he is working and living in a hospital" (ES 28). Meanwhile the subject of divorce surfaced again. Eva was pleased she had "told Sheftel that that you have enough money...as I gathered that they brainwashed him that the child was poorly cared for, that there is no money...to argue in court that the mother is impecunious... So my purpose was...to make him regret that he mentioned divorce...[but] he avowed to me... that the divorce had already happened" (ES 29). Three months later there was a glimmer of hope: "I see that in spite of everything you are still interested in him and that he is very dear to you...There were some moments when he was ready to be a little bit softer but I did not yield... [but] lately he has been calling you Sabina...wrote to me...whether it was possible that the two of you could get back together" (ES 31). After Sabina informed her mother that her husband "sent [her] a letter ten pages long" Eva admitted that "a mother with a daughter and son-in-law makes her nervous when [she] sees that everything is not alright with them" but was pleased that now Pavel "is talking about you with great satisfaction," he showed her Sabina's letters and "called [her] Sabina," instead of the formal Sabina Nikolayevna (ES 34, 37). Eva made a rare comment about the situation in Russia: "One scene is more horrible than the other: hundreds of refugees are wandering around the cities, homeless and hungry, exhausted both morally and physically...victims of the barbaric Germans, victims of the war" (ES 35). But, in their way, so were her children

A new development was Sabina's request to find out how easy it would be to get a medical diploma in Russia: was she thinking of returning? (ES 38). Congratulating Sabina on her birthday Eva declared: " I am now a partial fatalist, I believe what will happen will happen" (ES 39). In addition to her physical ills she was also "feeling nervous and I requested a visit from a doctor of nervous diseases" (ES 40). She opined that Renatochka "inherited her constipation from Sabina: "I had a lot of trouble with you" (ES 41). Is this connected with Jung's analysis of Sabina's bowel habits? Eva also noted that "papa, being a man, does not understand many things" (ES 41). But Sabina was ill herself "with the ear, then the teeth, and now a new story with her surgery" (ES 42), not further specified. But surgery as a profession was another matter and Eva held that Sabina's "surgery was completely unnecessary" while father opined that "the only important field is psychiatry and it is very much needed in Russia" (ES 43). Did Sabina consider becoming a surgeon, seeing that months later Eva congratulates her on "passing the surgery examination" (ES 49). Eva also promised "to find out everything about the university"—another indication that Sabina might have been thinking of returning to Russia (ES 44). Throughout1916 Eva continued to worry about her children, her problems with Yasha's wife and mother-in-law, her own son-in-law and her poor health. About coming to Russia Eva wrote: "To have you travel back to Russia would need a great deal of time and papa is afraid in that if you do, you will neglect the university...therefore you should not come back at this time" (ES 49).

1917 was the year of the October Revolution: the collapse of the monarchy and of the republic of Kerensky and the civil war; the return of Lenin and victorious Bolsheviks founding the Soviet Union. It remains unknown what Sabina thought about it except for the appearance of Kerensky in her dream (C, p. 81). On May Day Eva exulted over "a free democratic Russia!" and the breath-taking "solemn procession" in Rostov, with "flags and banners" and slogans. "It's a pity that all of you are not in Russia now where every person is needed...for the renewal of Russia" (ES 56). Reading these lines Sabina may have thought it corroborated her thesis that the destruction wrought by the revolution was necessary for this renewal to come into being. And Eva added: "I had already thought that you were coming to us and imagined what to arrange" (ES 58) and this was also vital for her since "now that Milia will also leave us, it will become completely empty" (ES 59). It also hurt her that Sabina's "letters are filled with so much sadness" (ES 60). There, was, however, a change in Pavel: "he turned up... you could feel that he had softened...he spoke about Renatochka and you too with great enthusiasm...about all with such love... and told a great deal about himself...he spoke in a completely different tone compared to past times...he got emotional." Given the current "world problems," Eva wondered how past "paltry events [could] poison a human life" (ES 62). Eva advised Sabina to ask people she knows for a loan: "and what about Jung? He would not refuse you" (ES 63). Sabina did turn to Jung and asked for referrals and, as before with Freud, she got a harsh refusal in 1917: "Dear Frau Doctor! It is hardly possible for me to pick a suitable case for you as I am so busy" (C, p. 212).

In 1918 Eva repeated her "wish you could come here, it would be a big relief for us all," given Sabina's "mental state and worries." This year Eva got a report from her physician Dr. Tsaitlin, a "certificate" about her medical condition (ES 64). Eva kept pleading: "Please ask for a loan from Jung, Bleuler...don't they trust you", adding that, realistically, Sabina could "only make [her] own money by doing translations at home," with father chiming in: "all mama's advice is good but it would be better if you could think about earning something with your own work" (ES 66).

In 1919 Eva informed Sabina that that she had no news from Sania for nine months and that Yasha was toiling like a simple laborer (ES 68). No word from Sabina in eleven months either but "we are making plans to get you out of Switzerland" and "Pavlusha can't wait for you to return" (ES 71). But the revolution hit the family hard: their house "was requisitioned, eight strangers live in our home and we huddle in the dining room and bedroom, that's all we have." Sania has not yet come back; "Yasha has been promoted to professor in Ekaterinodar"; "Pavel wanted to travel and fetch you but this cannot be done." And Pavel added comforting words of compassion greeting her on her 34th birthday (ES 72). Eva wrote about indelible signs of aging for the last five years (ES 73) and that she "is reduced to complete penury" (ES 73).

In 1920 Eva wrote that times were she till hard and she wavered: "it is now better that you are living abroad but morally it is quandary" (ES 74). The old problems with sending money to Sabina continued (ES 75, 77), and Eva still "[wanted] only one thing…that we shall meet again" (ES 78), but she was "very happy with [her] scientific accomplishments" (ES 79). Moreover, Eva found some solace in the markedly improved relations with Pavel and his family: "Yesterday was [Pavlusha's] birthday. I bought pastries and we went to his sisters to have tea. We spent close to an hour together" (ES 79).

Money matters also cropped up in 1921, but again, Pavlusha came through: "he writes to us very frequently and all his letters are filled with suffering for you and the child. He is longing and he is sad. On the whole, he got very emotional" (ES 80). Mother's entreaties grew more urging: if Sabina just came "temporarily, for a month or two…with appropriate documents… to go back…in Rostov or Moscow give a few lectures in [her] specialty. Yasha is getting ready to write to you about it" (ES 81).

The Spielreins were now in Moscow and were suffering too: "we are now living in terrible conditions. We are all in one room with Sania: papa, me, Yasha and Pavlusha. Some sleep on the floor others in beds "(ES 82). Missing Sabina's letters, Eva apologized for "repeating [herself] frequently and it gets boring and annoying, and now for the hundredth time…" (ES 83). Eva congratulated Sabina on her 35th birthday and advised her to "turn to the professor [Bleuler], explain to him your financial situation and ask him for a job" (ES 84). It seems that Sabina had some lung disease which reminded Eva of her past chronic bronchitis (ES 85). Surprisingly, Sabina's looking for work in Berlin was mentioned (ES 84). By year's end Eva was back in Rostov "living in one room with Milia and Fania because all the other rooms are occupied by strangers" and being visited by "Pavlusha almost every day, and every time my heart aches for him seeing how he suffers" (ES 87). But these are not social visits from Pavel, he is now acting as her doctor, alongside other physicians treating her steadily deteriorating health. Death robbed her of seeing Sabina and Renata.

LETTERS FROM YAN SPIELREIN TO SABINA

In the first five letters Yan, Yasha, or Jean Spielrein writes about his Jewish religious wedding with Silva Ryss, highlighting the contrast between a secular and assimilated Jew as compared with guests invited by his in-laws: "mangy and non-mangy Yids," Zhids in Russian, the pejorative version of the polite Russian name Yevreys (YS 1). Yan also declares: "I am not a Zionist" (YS 3). Yan is energetic, jolly and witty, who can turn sarcastic toward his younger brother Emil, then fourteen years old. Financially he seems to be more successful than Sabina or brother Oskar. Yan's marriage has issues echoing problems in Sabina's marriage with Pavel Sheftel, who "in all his life he has not learned how to speak Russian without a Jewish accent" (YS 8).

After a seven years hiatus Yan questions Sabina: "why are you working for Claparède for free?...We have considered...your coming to Soviet Russia. Undoubtedly, you would be successful... but you cannot live in Russia and could only come here under the absolute condition that you would be able to return abroad" (YS 8). The problem is Sabina, not Claparède, whom Yan respects and is willing to promote his book in Russia (YS 10).

Yan Nikolayevich Spielrein studied music at the Conservatoire de Paris, later mathematics and physics, graduating from the Sorbonne and Karlsruhe University. As a physicist he specialized in electrotechnology, was member of the Academy of Sciences of the Soviet Union, editor of the *Journal of Electricity* and the section on electrotechnology of the *Technical Encyclopedia*, and author of the standard *Textbook of Vectorial Analysis* applied to electricity also published abroad in German. He was not a member of the Communist Party. As scientist and teacher he became dean of the faculty of the Moscow Energy Institute. However scientist Yan was also quite familiar with the psychoanalytic scene in Moscow. In a long letter in 1923 Yan is no longer in doubt: "you should, according to personal and familial considerations, return to Russia" and sends his sister a detailed road map how to achieve success as a psychoanalyst in soviet Russia (YS 14). In his last letter Yan informs Sabina about the best train connections to Moscow (YS 15).

LETTERS FROM ISAAK (OSKAR) SPIELREIN TO SABINA

Sabina's younger brother Isaak distinguished himself in psychology and became a leading authority on the application of psychology to the new science of psychotechnics, a method of raising industrial productivity (Shpilrein,

1924); he is cited in Misiak & Sexton (1966). Isaak married Rakhil Pochtareva and their daughter Menikha, aforementioned in the letters as Menikhochka, was born in 1916 and died in 2000. She was discovered in Moscow by Slavic Studies professor Magnus Ljunggren and thus became known in the West and was invited to speak at conferences. In her letters to me she provided important information about her aunt.

A major contrast between Yan and Isaak was Isaak's identification with being a Jew: he reverted from Oskar to his Jewish names Isaak Naftulovich, Itshe Maier and Izak, and addressed Sabina by her Jewish name Sheive (IS 1, 2). Isaak spoke and published in Yiddish (Shpilrein, 1926), in part enabled by Lenin's condemnation of anti-Semitism and liberal politics toward minorities. According to Ljunggren (2001), during the 1905 Russian revolution, when virulent state sponsored anti-Semitism and pogroms spread to Rostov, the 15–16 years old Isaak took part in self-defense patrols and became a member of the terrorist Socialist Revolutionary Party. The Spielrein home was searched by the police, revolutionary leaflets were found, and in desperation Isaak shot himself in the mouth, but the wounds were not life threatening. He abandoned pro-revolutionary activity and left to study in Germany.

Between 1906–1909 Isaak studied philosophy with Wilhelm Windelband (1848–1915) in Heidelberg, psychology with Wilhelm Wundt (1832–1920) in Leipzig, and learned psychotechnics from William Stern (1871–1938) in Breslau, publishing with him as co-author (Erdelyi, 1933). In Berlin he was also befriended by the neo-Kantian Hermann Cohen (1842–1918) since 1912 professor at the Institute for Judaism in Berlin. In 1929 Isaak was a member of the delegation of the Soviet Union to the International Psychology Congress in New Haven, along with A. Luria and the great Ivan Pavlov (1849–1936) and in 1931 he was host to the International Congress of Psychotechnics in Moscow and similar congresses in Paris, Prague, and Utrecht. From 1919 on he was lecturer at Tiflis University. In 1920 he became a member of the Bolshevik Communist Party. In 1922, as director of the psychotechnics laboratory, he was invited to join the National Labor Commissariat of the Russian Soviet Federative Socialist Republic. From 1932 he was director of the section of labor organization at the Institute of War Industry in Moscow. In 1935 Isaak was arrested and accused of counterrevolutionary propaganda in a book "The language of a Red Army soldier" and in manuscript on "mass political literature and its readers," denounced as "anti-Soviet nonsense having nothing to do with scientific research" (Ovcharenko, Vekhi). Convicted of counter-revolutionary activity, he was sent for five years to a "correctional" forced labor camp in

Karaganda, moved from there to the Butyr prison in Moscow in 1937: there accused of being a spy for the German secret service, which he denied, Isaak was convicted and executed by shooting the same day. Isaak was rehabilitated twice, in 1956 and 1957.

LETTERS FROM BROTHER EMIL SHPILRAIN

In none of her letters did Eva mention care or concern about Emil, nor did Yan or Isaak. It was with Emil, the youngest son who stayed in Russia, that Eva shared a profound love and devotion. Tracing his life from birth in 1899 (57) and recorded in letters by Emil, Nikolai, Eva, and Yan, we see a steadfast, uncomplicated character, musically gifted, brimming with generous and noble emotions. Emil was also very attached to his father and adored him as a great man (EmS 6, 12). Emil's marriage with Fania Burshtein seemed harmonious, happily raising their precocious son Mark, born in 1921, also called Marka and Marochka, mentioned by Eva (ES 80–86). Emil cared heroically to keep his sick mother alive and left a moving description of her last days and death (EmS 5, 8). He also encouraged Sabina to return to Russia (EmS14).

Emil graduated from the Rostov male science gymnasium in 1916 and from the Don State University as biologist and zoologist in 1924. By 1936 he rose from lecturer to chair of the department of biology, then to dean of the biology department of Rostov University. He taught general and evolutionary biology, did experimental work, and made two inventions. In 1937 he was dismissed from the university, excluded from Communist Party, arrested in November 1937 in Rostov and accused by a Rostov military court as a member of a "rightist-trotskiist terrorist organization" aimed at assaulting party leaders and sabotaging industry sites in Rostov. In a closed court trial Emil Shpilrain denied all charges, was convicted and executed by a firing squad the same day. He was posthumously rehabilitated.

Emil Nikolayevich Shpilrain had two sons. Mark was a Red Army soldier killed in 1942. The second son, Evald Emilievich Shpilrain (1926–2009), survived the war in Barnaul in Central Asia. In Moscow he became a leader in thermophysics and energetics engineer. Nominated professor in 1965 he became a corresponding member of the Russian Academy of Sciences and director of the department of high temperatures of the Russian Academy of Sciences. He was on the board of many Russian and international journals of thermophysics and energetics and published more than 300 papers and 12 monographs and textbooks on thermodynamics and the theory of solutions (Ovcharenko). I met with him and Ovcharenko in Moscow in 2003 and later in New York I met his son Vladimir Shpilrain (born in 1960).

LETTERS FROM PAVEL SHEFTEL TO SABINA

Sabina's husband has been an obscure dramatis persona until recently. For Launer (2015) "Pavel was not as intelligent as Spielrein" (p. 157), but this is not what Pavel's letters show. Launer also quoted a "poignant phrase [in Pavel's letter] that Richebächer used for the title of her German biography [2005]: that he reproached [Sabina] with being impractical and having an 'almost cruel love for science' (*eine fast grausame Liebe zur Wissenschaft*)" (p. 208). But the word 'cruel' and 'inhuman, was added by Richebächer because Pavel only mentioned "a deficient fitness for practical life and *a passionate penchant* for science (и страстному влечению к науке)" (PS 10; my italics). Moreover, Pavel recalled "realizing the plan we had formulated about our travel abroad in 1912...[for] science can give moral satisfaction and consolation in this vale of suffering " (PS 5); "the goal you had set yourself while you were still in Russia and about which we were day-dreaming during our long heart-to-heart talks lasting until early morning when we were betrothed: the goal of a scientific career" (PS 11). In fact Pavel Sheftel was very intelligent and his prose style was that of an educated doctor with an interest in psychiatry, psychoneuroses, and psychoanalysis, and he encouraged Sabina's choice of profession. However, he admitted to having a character weakness: "I confess I do not possess the hard, steely tenacity persisting for many years that sometimes helps a person to achieve a difficult goal" (PS 11).

In the first three letters written during the early days of the "revolutionary frenzy" Pavel was emotionally distant from his wife, unsure whether to address her politely as "You" or intimately as "thou" and seemed more interested in his daughter than in his wife. Pavel also complains of Sabina's suspiciousness: "you have repeatedly slipped in reproaches about various Rivkas or Khayas, or perhaps you perceived something intuitively" (PS 3). And later: "I have nothing against your reproaching me, but I recall [around their wedding in 1912] you were saying that my words were like something you read in a book;...It was a sad and painful picture...these were vain, unnecessary, superfluous torments caused by morbid suspiciousness" (PS 12). Was Sabina having second thoughts about her marriage? Was she longing for Jung? Pavel also confessed : "when I left both of you...the eighth year already already...it may well be that all that happened, my separation, should not be blamed on the war, for it is we who are directly to blame, for we were the makers of our happiness, not only victims of various accidental events and *fatalité*" (PS 11). But Pavel is silent about his reasons for leaving and the riddle remains unsolved. But despite having "lived through a lot of grief, doubts, hesitations, conflicts together and separately" he ends on a hopeful note (PS 12).

In 1921 Pavel reports that in Russia, in Sabina's "specialty there are ardent pupils of Freud" and "various pedagogico-psychological institutes where both academic and practical psychologists are working (your brother Sania is an example thereof)" (PS 8). Pavel writes a moving letter to widowed Nikolai, how Eva showed him kindness and compassion when he faced his "pathological self-love and excessive suspiciousness", despite his having "offended her mercilessly"; and in a long postscript to Sabina he wishes to be with both of them again (PS 13). In addition to being an internist, Pavel informs Sabina that he has also started working as a pediatrician, lectured on "pedagogy" which has now "changed into a new science, pedology...ripe to establish a new scientific pedological society" (PS 14). Pedology was based on applying the unified methods of medicine, biology, and psychology to developmental psychology. Upon her return to Russia Sabina will work as a pedologist. Pavel now offers concrete plans for Sabina's return (PS 16).

By 1923 there is crescendo of voices from Pavel, the three brothers, and father clamoring for Sabina's return. Sabina is also encouraged by Freud: "Dear Frau Doktor, Your plan to go to Russia seems to me much better than my advice to try out Berlin. In Moscow you will be able to accomplish important work at the side of Wulff and Ermakov"(C p. 127). The die was cast.

LETTERS FROM SPIELREIN'S VARIOUS FRIENDS

These letters provide interesting comparisons between these women's characters, careers and marriage choices versus fleeting infatuations with other men from Eugenia Sokolnicka (ESo 1), Revekka Ter-Oganesian hinting at Sabina's possible lingering nostalgia for Jung (Ter–0 5), and Esther Aptekman who longs for Zurich and offers an opinion about Jung's state of mind (EA 1). While we do not know what statements of Spielrein's these women were reacting to, at the very least, they suggest that she might still be reminiscing about Jung. This raises the question whether Sabina continued to be haunted by her love for Jung, or the unfulfilled wish to have married him, thus connected to Sabina's long separation from her husband, or with her mother's wondering "why you still have not written to me why you broke up with your husband under such strained conditions" (ES 25).

Other interesting echoes to Sabina's issues are found in correspondents cited in "Various Letters." A unique find is the unpublished 1923 letter from Freud. The messages in the "Miscellaneous Letters" from patients and colleagues who admired Sabina speak for themselves.

1
The Russian Diary of Sabina Spielrein

1. 12th September Thursday 1896

The first visit to the gymnasium[20] taking an examination.

I woke up quite early in the morning and I could not wait for the moment when for the first time I had to go to the gymnasium not for taking an examination. I was even unable to perform well in my music lesson. Finally the moment arrived. I was a little bit afraid to go there by myself, I asked papa to accompany me there but papa did not want to. Our house is across the street from the gymnasium. Papa showed me the door through which I had to enter and he himself went out into the street to see how I would enter. I entered through one door and wanted to go in but the doorman told me to go in through the gate. I wanted to approach one of the girl students but I did not know whom to approach. Until then I did not meet Vera Sabsovich. A few minutes later the students were called to enter the classrooms. I came with a notebook and a pencil but the headmistress told me that I did not need that. I became very curious what we would be doing without a notebook and a pencil. Then the classes were led into the hall. It was so beautiful and so pleasant that I could not wait for our class to be led in. One girl from the preparatory class came to where [text break] The headmistress asked the girl which class she belonged to and when the girl told her, she showed her to her place. Then the girl started crying and the headmistress asked her elder sister if she was also crying. This seemed to me so comical that I smiled. I was very hungry and very happy when the class was let out and I could go home.

2. 20th November 1896,

Wednesday Joy

Today I was very glad. Today the headmistress herself said that I excelled in diligence. I was particularly happy because I was able to provide great joy to

20 Hers was an all-girl school. The very first grades were called the Progymnasium.

papa and mama. This happened during the drawing lesson, my favorite lesson; it made me so happy but I could not wait for the lesson to end. The teacher told me that I draw better than everybody. This is how it happened...I am tired and cannot write any more.

3. 1st February Saturday 1897

How I almost froze

Sania got sick with scarlet fever. We, Yasha, myself and Milochka, were sent to our grandmother; (this happened a long time ago). Today we were walking to the gymnasium. It was far away, since grandma lived on Nikolskaia Street, just before reaching the Sobachyev alley from the railway station, in the Mukhin building, and the gymnasium was on the right side of the city park on Pushkinskaia street, which was faraway; moreover, this was happening in winter, and we could be late, so grandma sent her servant Osip to accompany us on the horsecar. I also forgot to mention that the boys' gymnasium was farther away on Taganrogskaia street, closer to the steppe. We were waiting for the horsecar and finally I decided that if we continue to wait for the horsecar we would surely be late; but Yasha did not agree with me and decided to wait. However, on the whole, I do not like riding in a horsecar and therefore I decided to continue on foot. I was in a great hurry. Yasha called out to me; I turned back to look and fell down. We were to have a geography lesson and therefore I was also carrying a big atlas. I began to feel I was gasping for breath and squatted down, even though at this moment Mademoiselle was running ahead with the other girls. But it was time to go. I got up, was walking and walking and gasping for breath, so I squatted down again and then walked again. But at that moment I was not even able to get to a bench, I leaned against a wall and I was thinking, "I am going to die any minute now." I was almost starting to cry and was gasping for breath. Some girls were passing me by, but none of them looked at me. Only one of them asked me why I was standing there. I told her why, and she walked away, and I was thinking, "I'm going to suffocate now"...But presently two other girls approached me and asked: "You must be freezing?" I said, "Yes." Then they said: "Oh! You poor thing, if we hadn't come you would have been stuck here." They grabbed me and one picked up the backpack and the other the atlas, and then gave me a glove (because I did not wear any gloves), and they quickly ran with me to the gymnasium.

What should I write about today? Today we did not have a Russian lesson but we were writing conjugations of strong German verbs and a German dictation. I get very fearful when I write a dictation because when I make mistakes I get the grade 5-[21] and then papa says it is a shame and a disgrace. Today I made a drawing from papa's photograph and got from him a 3+. Papa says that when I get only one 5+, then it is the same as another girl getting a 3; but he would consider me excellent if I had 5+ in everything. Usually I tremble every time I am called out [to the blackboard]. The arithmetic teacher Maria Sikerdonovna did not give us any homework today because today or tomorrow will be a big holiday, but perhaps this is enough for today.

4. 2nd February 1897 Sunday

Today is Sunday and I did not go to the gymnasium. I have just finished the homework in geography. We were cooking orange marmalade and I gave the larger part of it to nanny because I had promised it to her. The three of us made very tasty marmalade. Milochka kept asking for "more". We have a nursery governess. As young children we could not pronounce the word *mademoiselle* so we called her Madmas'ka[22] and we got so used to calling her Madmas'ka that we kept addressing her by that name. She was not particularly pretty, she had a long nose, but the main thing is that she was very vicious. She always defended Sania and beat us irrespective of whether we had been guilty or not. She was very skinny, tall and very dirty. She hated us and always quarreled with us and beat us. She was born in Warsaw. She was Polish. When I treated everybody to the marmalade but gave none to Madmas'ka Milochka said: "Mia (this is how she calls me) gave bomba (she calls Mad-mas'ka bomba) 'malmade'" [marmalade]. Then Madmas'ka said: "Oh, what a golden child! She remembered her bomben'ka! [diminutive of bomba]." Truly, Madmas'ka was a very ridiculous woman. How many times did we laugh at her! She very rarely called me by name Sabina; most of the time she called me Sabinka, Sabukhna, Sabul'ka. Quite often she didn't understand what the problem was and complained to mama, and mama believed her and then attacked us for nothing. How often mama believed Madmas'ka's tales and attacked us and beat us; however, about Sania, who himself beat us and hurt our feelings, she would say in our presence that he was skinny and pale, that we were nasty, rotten children, and that he should neither study nor play with us. This made us very angry and therefore we were unable to love him. Therefore, he acted like a spoiled brat, but mama said that he learnt all his dirty tricks from us.

21 Student grades were from 1 to 5, where 1 was the worst and 5 the best.

22 The s' indicates a soft-spoken s

Yasha was playing an instrument, and nanny said to Milochka: "Here is music, music is heard," and Milochka asked: "But where are the players?" This, however, was not as funny as in other such incidents which I do not remember. On the 3rd of March Milochka would have been two years old. Yesterday I played the piano a lot but papa said that I did not play at all. Mama said that Sania had fever. I did not want him to get sick.

There was a big commotion in our home today: Milochka was crying, mama was screaming, and so was Madmas'ka. Yasha was playing music and at that moment our housemaid Nad'ka ran in yelling. (She was very vicious, with a long face and dirty hands; when she cleaned knives and forks, she spat on them; and when mama asked her whether she spat, Nad'ka answered: "What are you saying, my lady! You have got to be kidding!"). She also lied a great deal. She often beat us, she scolded us or spat at us, and when we told mama, she would say, "Why are you lying, Sabinka?" or "Why are you lying, Yashka?" When she was sent some place she disappeared for hours, probably with some men. Now she was standing there with her fingers stuck in her mouth. Should Sania get sick, the situation would get much worse. Today mama went to the theatre with papa, Moisei and, I believe, with uncle Noi as well. Moisei is mama's first cousin, he is married.

An evening scene.

Here is what happened to us yesterday. We were sitting at the table (this happened in the evening) having supper. Suddenly Nad'ka came in running and yelling: "Sabinka, why did you break the wine glass? Now I'll be punished for it!" I asked: "What is it? What happened to you? I broke no wine glass." Nad'ka kept cursing and cursing and finally spat and left the room. While she was cursing I kept silent and thought, "Let the little dog bark," but when she spat, I shouted: "How dare you spit?" and slammed the door. I do not want to tell more because I got tired. Sania also started writing a diary. I made a paper notebook for him for this purpose.

5. 3rd February Monday 1897

A gymnasium story

During the Russian lesson Maria Alekseievna was explaining pronouns to us. At first we were reading. Maria Alekseievna (this is the Russian language teacher) made six students read the same story because they read it poorly. During the German language lesson something unpleasant happened: I received a 4 for dictation, a 4 for copying and a 5- for declension. In the declension I wrote *Ploral* instead of *Plural*. In copying (we copied syllable by syllable) it seemed to me that Anna Genrikhovna had told us to write like this: *vie-lleicht* [perhaps].

To me it seemed odd and, therefore, I made a note of it in the book. It turned out that Anna Genrikhovna (this is the German language teacher) had told us to write this way: *viel-leicht.* I even left out other German words. I also missed [German word in gothic script]. In dictation I wrote *Ggimnasium* and the teacher had even written that word on the blackboard... Then I even got wild: at first I wrote the word *wir* [we] correctly, but then I heard the teacher pronounce it as a long vowel, so everything got mixed up in my head, and I forgot the folly I was committing, and wrote *wier.* I also forgot to mention that during the Russian lesson while copying, I wrote *Mosk-va,* but the teacher corrected it as *Mo-skva.* Now papa has come, and I am so sad; I am sure he will start putting me to shame. Why is it that when other girls get a 3, they are allowed to be happy but if I get a 4, I have to suffer? Anna Genrikhovna will not enter our grades in the class logbook because almost everybody got either a 1 or a 2. And another thought occurs to me: if another girl gets a 1, she will not feel as hurt as I when I get a 4; she will not be teased at home as I am teased. Because of papa, I cannot wish that other girls should get a 5 or a 5+ because papa says that if a [Christian] girl should get a 5+, then I get a 5-. Anyway, papa will surely find out. Oh, I am so sad, my heart is so heavy. So what, I can do nothing about it. It is time to do my homework. I will be playing the piano now and later I will do my homework. I sat down to play but was unable to make a go of it, I could not get rid of this awful thought, "Let me do the homework, perhaps it will be more successful than music?"

Madmas'ka bought Sania a little fish. He first called the fish Mashka and then Lidka. We liked that little fish so much that we asked that such a fish be bought for us as well. At first, Madmas'ka was cross with us but afterwards she promised that when she goes to the market tomorrow she will also buy one for us. The fish Madmas'ka bought for Sania was amazing. The cook carried the fish wrapped in paper and it did not die without water. But the cook said the fish will die in a few days because here, that is the water in our jar, is not the same as the water in the Don. Now it is time to go to bed; otherwise I will not be able to get up tomorrow to go to the gymnasium.

6. 4th February Tuesday 1897 A few words

At least I will write a few words. Today I was not called out to the blackboard. Tomorrow we will be making written answers about grammar. It will be interesting to see how we will write. I now know I can get a 5 for this task but I do not know how well I will write in the classroom. Soon it will be Rozalia Yakovlevna's birthday. Rozalia Yakovlevna was our former teacher who prepared me for the first class and Yasha for the preparatory class. She is a [relative] of ours but I don't know in what way. Her birthday is on February 14th. I would have written even more, but it is time to go to bed. It is now 8:45. I will now collect my books and sharpen my pencil (because tomorrow we'll have a drawing lesson), I will tie the pencil-case with a little ribbon because the key is broken, and go to bed. It is not worth it to write all this down, but I am doing it in order to write something. I will get ready everything that I mentioned and in addition, I will write down for Sania a list of what he has to do until my return from the gymnasium because I had promised him.

7. 14th February Friday 1897

I always forget to write down something that is very interesting. For example, on Saturday 8th of February 1897 a small fire started in our home. This is how it happened: Yasha and Sania were playing with a little oil lamp (the small wick was burning in the oil and the iron cup caught fire); then they went into the living room and put out the fire. Then Yasha played, and Sania and I had time to play together. Suddenly Yasha yells: "Fire! It is burning! Fire! Help..." I shall finish this story next time, now it is already late and, moreover, I have to consume some buckthorn berries because I have a sick stomach. Before I forget I need to mention that I gave Rozalia Yakovlevna as a gift a little basket of buckthorn berries with sugar and I wrote a little poem for her: "I greet you cordially and send you buckthorn berries with sugar." The time now is 9:55, time to go to bed!

I'm doing my best not to forget to have time to write more in my diary tomorrow and I imagine how I will be reading it when I grow up; sometimes I see myself as a little girl, sometimes as a big girl, and I don't know how to write —as a little girl or as a big girl. But it is time! My thoughts, "Do not get into my head anymore, I'm not going to write you down anyway..."

8. 26th February Wednesday 1897

It is time

I have become so used to write the year as 96 that I forget and write in my notebooks 96 instead of 97. It is time to go to bed, or else papa will see... Trouble... With every knock I imagine that papa is coming, and I tremble. Goodbye today. The time now is 9:55. And papa is coming. It is time...

9. 28th February Friday 1897

In order to give us a bigger room papa and mama decided to renovate and change the distribution of the rooms and therefore yesterday and today there was a dreadful disorder. I forgot to mention that on the day we had the fire papa bought a plot for 20,000 [rubles] and in ten months from now we will have our own house. For now the living room was transformed into a children's room, mama's consulting room into papa's office, the bedroom into uncle Mosia's office, a part of the living room also became a hallway, papa's office was turned into mama's consulting room, the children's room into uncle Mosia's bedroom and office. In the living room only the dining room, kitchen, terrace and hallways remained unchanged. Next time I will describe everything in greater detail. I wish that tomorrow they should call me out at the gymnasium. However, it should be noted what time it is and it's time to go to bed, anyway; for quite a while now I have had a headache and I am sleepy... It is now 9:33. Sania is still awake.

10. 8th March Saturday 1897

It always happens like this: as soon as there is anything to be explained I stop writing, as it happened on the 20th of November 1896. I wrote, "It happened this way," and then I stopped writing, or on the 14th of February 1897, I wrote, "Yasha is yelling 'it's burning! fire! help!'" and again I stopped writing. I always read my diary, and I regret very much that on the 12th of September I did not write what we were doing at the gymnasium on a day we had neither notebook nor pencil handy. Now I have become so accustomed to going to the gymnasium that I find it strange that previously I had been so afraid of it.

Yesterday Yasha brought home a two-days-old white puppy. Were it not for my mother, the puppy would have stayed with us, but mama could not stand its squealing and we had to give it away to the cook downstairs to be trained. But I think she will either throw it out or take it home. Today Ter-Grigoriants (this is the tenant on the floor below) gave us as a gift a two-months-old pug puppy. We named him Mos'ka[23] to tease uncle Mosia, because we are involved in a quarrel with him. I think that the white puppy is a bulldog but Yasha thinks it is a pug.

At a time when I still did not know what a diary is I wanted to write down all my thoughts and actions and keep them secret from everybody. Now I am a long way from writing down everything in my diary. And everybody can guess why. (I don't want Yasha to read my diary). First, I do not write everything because later on I will give my diary to my children to read; second, I will not say but it is anybody's guess.

---

23 Possibly an allusion to Krylov's fable *The Elephant and the Pug* in which the puny pug barks at the giant to feel important. Pug in Russian is mos'ka and thus a pun on the uncle's name 'Mosia.'

11. 15th March, Saturday 1897

Today ended the third quarter [of the school year] and we were promised to get the grades for this quarter. I try very hard to study and to be on my good behavior at home and at the gymnasium. Oh, how mama is fond of music, she is most happy when we play well. It pains me so much that drawing is such an unimportant subject in the gymnasium. I wish it would be the most important subject. In the gymnasium they promise us everything but they do not fulfil anything...It is now 9:45.

12. 17th March Tuesday 1897

I will not describe a certain interesting event and for the same reason.

13. 21st March, Friday 1897

Oh, how little I have written on Tuesday March 17! At first I do not know what to write but afterwards so many thoughts come to mind that I am unable to write everything down. Anyway, I have already written more than on the 17th of March. I keep imagining how I will grow up and be an adult and let my children read my diary, how they all will gather around me, for them it would be a punishment, should I deny them reading it. Or perhaps, it will be of no interest to them. [It is also?] possible that I will have no children.

14. 25th March, Tuesday 1897

I am back writing in my diary. During the music lesson papa made Yasha wear eyeglasses N[umber]-24. He is near-sighted. I was away from the gymnasium for a whole week. And I do not like when people tell lies. Papa wrote a note in which he said: (with me and Yasha he speaks French, with Sania he speaks German, Yasha and I speak to each other in German) [in French with Russian letters]: "Kant on te demandra koman ete tu malad alor di ke le z'ye te feze mal [when they ask what was your illness, then say that your eyes were hurting you]". But the doctor said that I had perfect vision. And what if they ask me what kind of doctor I saw and will find out what eyesight I have? I had better tell them that this was a nervous episode. It is high time to go to bed. I will now check the time and go to bed. It is now 9:33. Tomorrow I will tell something unless I forget it.

15. 26th March Wednesday 1897

I have not forgotten! Now it seems of no interest at all. Papa opened the front door with the key and wanted to come in but I locked it again. We are a terrible class. Today during the arithmetic class somebody made a clicking noise.

Maria Sikerdonovna said: "The person who made the clicking noise should stand up." Nobody stood up. Then Maria Sikerdonovna thought of Chikalova because she is always naughty. Chikalova was making excuses. Then Maria Sikerdonovna earnestly pleaded with the class to tell the truth, she said that the girl who confessed she had done it would not be punished. Then she told the girls they should be ashamed, but this did not work either. Then she got terribly angry and told everything to the supervisor. Therefore we were on lockdown at the school. The girls became noisy and screamed that Chikalova was guilty of everything so that the headmistress came to the class. But earlier Olga Aleksandrovna (this is our supervisor) had put in a note in Khenkina's notebook that she (i.e. Khenkina) laughs and chatters a lot during lessons and Khenkina started crying. At first the headmistress started screaming that we did not know how to behave and asked us what happened during the arithmetic lesson. She was told what happened. She approached Chikalova and pleaded with her for a long time to confess. Chikalova kept denying and denying her guilt and finally started crying. The headmistress let go of her and approached Khenkina. She thought that Khenkina had confessed and she was very glad. Finally she told the headmistress why she was crying. The headmistress asked her why she was laughing. Khenkina told why and her story (pity I did not hear the story) made Olga Aleksandrovna, Mihailova, Malinovskaya, and even the headmistress laugh. It turned out that during the lesson Khenkina was remembering stories told by Mihailova. The headmistress said: "You see, you remembered this during the lesson." And she left the class laughing herself. When Khenkina was telling the headmistress that a critical comment was entered in her notebook, I saw that Olga Aleksandrovna turn red.

16. 27th March Friday1897

Today an extremely unhappy event happened. I forgot (during a lesson on German declensions) the plural of the word *Schaf* [sheep] and wrote *Schäfer* [instead of *Schafe*]. Therefore I thought I would get a 2. And today a happy event occurred: I did not get a 2 but a 3. Soon after the Jewish Easter will be mama's birthday. I am completely unable to come up with an idea what to give her as present. I will now do my homework, there is a whole lot of it. There is also a whole lot to write about in my diary. I will first change into other clothes.

17. 29th March Saturday 1897

Mama is badgering me to play the piano and won't give me a quarter of an hour to write in my diary. On Monday I did not go to the gymnasium therefore I did not what homework they gave us in geography for Saturday (we have geography lessons on Mondays and Saturdays). On the blackboard they wrote: "Determine in which countries are these volcanoes located." And that is what I prepared. It turned out that we were told to do additional homework. Now for Monday I wrote down sea currents (as homework, now a repeat); but it is impossible that we had been given two pages of homework.

Ter-Grigoriants gave away to somebody else the puppy he had given us as a gift. Mama and papa said that this was very mean of him. Yasha and I are of the same opinion. We named the white puppy "eggwhite," the puppy is now very funny. We took it with us to bed and it licked our faces and tickled us! We laughed a lot. And it is eating so much! The puppy cannot aim at its saucer (I won this saucer in a lottery in Slaviansk). We called it the great Chinese ashtray but actually it was just a small saucer. I do not know what metal it was made of but on its rim is written *Mirror and fancy goods trade company P. Braz & Ya. Gordon, Odessa.* Sometimes the puppy turns the saucer upside down or hits it with its paws and sniffs and grimaces vigorously. And Nad'ka grabbed it by its paws and hurled it with its head down.

18. 30th March Saturday 1897

Tomorrow they will issue us the quarter (this is how I call the grades for the quarter). Mama wants me to finish only seven classes in the gymnasium. Now I will not let daddy dear[24] read my diary anymore because he told me that if I had to be pushed hard to study music, he would burn it (that is, my diary). I do not even have a quarter of an hour to get busy with my diary. Either there is homework, or one has to go to the gymnasium, or to do drawings, and on top of it this disgusting music. How many times, whenever they force me to play the piano, the thought occurs to me, and I even tell mama, that I do not want to study music. And yet it is a pity, I can abandon it at any time, and I may not be able to study it later, and even if I could, daddy would not let me. I feel very sad should I have to write my diary only for myself and not even allow mama and papa to read it. But daddy dear is different from mama because at times he becomes utterly furious and then I myself [many times?] do not want him to read my diary. When our things were lying around on the table he wanted to burn them all down, he grabbed our common book (it contains many lamp[?] patterns), Yasha's diary, and many little papers (thankfully my little one, as I call my diary, was not on the table), some kind of small box used for parquetry, and

24 Daddy dear is this time different from the usual papa: the Russian word is papishka, a diminutive of papa, contains the suffix -ishka, here with the connotation of something derisive or sarcastic.

some kind of a paper notebook belonging to Sania. For a long time we begged him (papa) to give us back the common book and Yasha's diary, and especially Sania's guidebook (it seemed to us that papa also took that guidebook; previously he had given Sania as a present a no longer needed guidebook [it is now old?] and tattered, and even missing many pages, and I don't know why Sania likes it so much. There is nothing better than this old guidebook). Daddy said he did not take Sania's guidebook or Yasha's diary. And finally, after many Yasha's tears [Sabina's striking], I cried a little, I felt sorry for Yasha's diary more than he did himself. I do not understand how one could be so uncaring. He says: "I will consider that I have not started writing one at all yet." Earlier papa had even teased Yasha and told him how happy he would be now had he possessed a diary of his childhood and could read it. Then Yasha started to weep violently. He called for papa. And papa came, and Yasha pleaded with him in earnest to forgive him this time. Finally papa agreed. Yasha threw himself upon him to kiss him and cry with tears: "Mersi [merci], papa, mersi!" What was he thankful for? This is very similar to Zhorzhi[25] [Georgie], (which I read in the diary of the little prankster), who almost killed a young boy, but who, as people got angry with him, thought to himself, "They should thank me that he didn't die." No, [after all?], let daddy dear read my diary. For if I don't give it to him now he will never want to do it again.

19. 5th April, but it is not the 5th but the14th April 1897

On the 12th of April, Saturday, I gave mama as a present a bunch of paper roses which I made from a paper book that had been given to me by papa and I wrote a poem for her. I was taught how to make such roses by the landlord's daughter when I was five years old and that is why I gave mother these flowers as present. I first told Yasha and the maid (we now have a new maid whose name is Katia, she is very good-natured). I approached mama and handed her the poem. Mama started getting dressed when Katia or Yasha rang the doorbell. One of them opened the front door, Katia and Yasha said: "My lady, somebody brought you flowers! Mama, they brought you flowers." Grandma (she lived with us during Passover) approached mama and whispered something to her, it seemed to me that grandma told her everything. Mama got dressed quickly and entered her consulting room. She had also said earlier, "These probably came from Patt." When she entered she said, "Oh, what wonderful flowers, but Patt

25 Russian for Georgie, the hero of the 1880 book *A Bad Boy's Diary* by American novelist Metta Victoria Fuller Victor, translated into Russian and German in the 19th century.

would not have sent so few flowers." And nanny said: "Yes, please smell them, what fragrance!" Mama smelled them and said: "These are not live flowers, I am sure it was mademoiselle who gave them to me." Madmas'ka answered: "Pani [milady in Polish] these were made by tsatsul'ka!!"[26] Mother asked: "Sabina, was it you, is it really true?" I then said to her that it was Madmas'ka. I then asked mama to give me a word of honor that she did not know that it was I who made them and that when she entered the room she thought those were live flowers, and mother gave me her word. In addition to the roses I also made her a flower which I stuck into the rose bunch. I do not know the name of that flower; I saw it at milliner Sotnikova's place when I went there with my mother on April 11th. Now I am going to draw. I wish my first diary should end soon! There are four more sheets, one page, and three and a half lines. Now there are only three incomplete lines and now a little bit more than one. Now there are exactly four sheets and one page.

20. 7th May Wednesday 1897

It has been a long time since I have written something in my diary. I have passed up many, many interesting things. Now I will briefly describe one thing because I cannot write long. My thoughts run ahead of me, and they run so quickly that when I want to write down one thought I forget the other ones. I wish that my thoughts and actions, and everything that I would like to write in the diary, should write itself. I remember my diary every day and would like to write down everything. But either I have no time, or playing is too interesting, but the main thing is that I become at times so agitated that it seems to me I will not be able to write everything down. But even more than that: I am unable to express my emotions. I wish it would explain itself why I am so often unable to write in my diary. It's not that I cannot, how can I explain this? Well, I am having too many agitated emotions to be able to write in a diary. Right now I am also very agitated and I cannot explain it. Well, now we, that is, more correctly I, will begin to describe this matter. I will give it a title (yes, anyone would give this matter such a title): laying down the foundation stone.

Regarding our house (on the land, which we bought for 20,000 rubles on which we decided to build the house) it was decided that the foundation stone will be laid on Sunday the 4th of May 1897 at 4 o'clock in the afternoon. Yasha was impatiently waiting for that today but I not especially so. Papa did not want to invite anybody, he said: "Anyone who would like to come should decide him-

26 Sarcastic diminutive of the Polish word cacka, pronounced tsatska, meaning gem, treasure.

self." But mama wanted very much to invite Olga Yakovlevna Bershanskaya, I do not know why she didn't want papa to know about it (I will begin to write with a pencil because I don't have my inkwell because Yasha misplaced it somewhere). When papa came into his office I had a feeling I could not explain, and instead of staying there I left and will write with a pencil because papa does not allow taking his inkwell to another room. It means I will continue writing the story. Mama asked me if I could ask father if I could invite Maniechka, the daughter of Olga Yakovlevna, and should papa permit it, go and fetch Olga Yakovlevna and Mania (Yasha brought me papa's inkwell, and I am now writing with a pen). We went and met Olga Yakovlevna while Mania went to the Armenian garden so Yasha brought her sister Nadia, a somewhat silly seven year old girl.

Grandpa was supposed to lay down the first stone but he announced that he would not be able to come before 5:30 because he had to go to the slaughterhouse. But it was no longer possible to postpone the foundation ceremony because it had already been postponed from 10 in the morning to 4 in the afternoon in order to accommodate him. Moreover, the guests and the workers were already there, and the food was also ready. Mother and I were very upset by all this. I have forgotten to mention that since I cannot walk as fast as Yasha, he had to fetch Nadia. I was afraid that Yasha would be late. All of a sudden I heard the bell ring and I thought that Yasha had come. But oh joy, – it was grandpa who came. I was very glad but very worried about Yasha. What is this? Everything happened so unexpectedly on that day. I also met Yasha and Sania there, that is at the construction site. Among the guests who came were also Mr. Patt, and Mr. Tiurk, and Mr. Gerainimus, our contractor was there too, and grandma came as well. At first mother did not want to come, she said it was not proper for women. In the end mother came as well, only the architect (Zelinskii) did not come. Mother said that it was unbecoming of Zelinskii, or the architect (I don't recall how she put it, but it's not important) to make us wait for him. Uninvited guests also came, two peasant women with a girl and a student from the science school or just a gymnasium student, I did not take a good look. The workers brought with them musical instruments: an accordion and some kind of a rattle with little bells. Finally, the architect came as well. Grandpa laid the first four stones, then mother laid three stones on the left side of the opposite street, when you stand with your back to the gymnasium, then I laid one stone. Moreover, I forgot to mention that uncle Noi came even before the architect, laid one stone on the right side, and then Yasha one foundation stone, and Yasha did it so well that papa said to him: "Well done!" Then papa himself did it. We do not remember whether grandma, the architect and Olga

Yakovlevna laid any stones. I will ask mama and write it down. Of course, the workers received tips. The bricklayers received ten rubles and the navvies five. In addition, they were given presents: some workers were given shirts as presents, but I don't know which ones. I forgot to mention that money was put under the stones, and papa put his photographs. We left the site. Suddenly, I heard the cries of: "Hurray, hurray, hurray!" I looked, it is the workers tossing papa aloft and hollering. Earlier Yasha and I had an argument: Yasha said that grandpa would lay a stone anywhere and I said that architect would show him where to lay it. It turned out that I was right. You understand me, and now the foundation stone ceremony was over.

21. 8th May Thursday 1897

Today we were dismissed after three lessons. The supervisor told us we would have examinations on Monday, the 12th of May in Russian dictation and on Tuesday, the 13th of May, in arithmetic (earlier Maria Sikerdonovna told us during the last lesson Wednesday, the 7th of May, how to write this examination. She told us to buy two sheets of paper each one costing a kopeck and put a sheet of blotting paper in between, but I lost it all because I would not be taking this examination. (I did not pay special attention to Maria Sikerdonovna's explanations as I knew that I would not take this examination). On Tuesday, the 20th of May, I took the German examination. We waited for a long while for the headmistress to come. I prayed to dear God that I should be promoted to the next form without taking an examination. Finally the headmistress came with some sheets of paper and began reading. I do not recall word for word in what order she was calling the students and what she was saying. I was very agitated. But this is not important. She sat down and started: "Galkina you got only a 3 in arithmetic but the rest of your grades is good. You, Galkina, will be able to pass the examination in arithmetic if you learn how to calculate, and then you will get more than a 3 in arithmetic." Galkina said that she cannot expect to get more than a 3 and therefore will not take the examination. Then the headmistress continued: "Golub also improved her grades and is also promoted to the next form without taking an examination, and so is Niestatnaya – without an examination. Chikalova, although your behavior was bad, you are quite a clever girl, and besides your health is poor, you will also be promoted without an examination. Now Shpilrein, Shpilrein got 5's all around and is also promoted without an examination. This means I will be in the second grade. Tomorrow I will write more. Now it is too late, namely exactly 9:45.

22. 9th May Friday 1897

I cannot write a long and interesting story in this diary because my diary is ending. Today I will buy another diary and will start writing in it many interesting things. Papa is angry with Yasha for something. He has probably told mama about it. Probably papa will do nothing to Yasha. Hurray! My diary has ended. Goodbye!

23. 10th June Tuesday,
1897 Story of a life

I did not expect I would have to wait for so long to write in my diary. Papa went away on a trip and mama either had no money or it was too hot, or mama sent me to have a new uniform made—because the other uniform was dirty—which had to be done in one day. Papa returned yesterday at 5 o'clock in the morning. I either have a bad pen or bad ink. When papa was away Frida Leontievna came to see us. Formerly we were her students; she ran a Fröbel[27] type [pre]school. I remember we were told that a new school had been opened in which only the very best ten children were accepted so that we had to kiss each other or else we would not be admitted. It so happened that we were quarrelling with each other but then we kissed each other.

24. 10th June Wednesday 1897

Thereafter Frida Leontievna used to come to us and then she stopped coming because I was getting ready to start the preparatory class for the gymnasium and because now, as in the past, we were going to Frida Leontievna to take music lessons. At first we took music lessons with Ida Eduardovna Brodskaya, then we took an examination at the music school on the 6th of August 1896. After we took an examination on the 6th of August 1896, we started to study with Anna Samuilovna Filonova who had been recommended to us by Ida Eduardovna. We studied in the gymnasium and had no time to go to school and also do the homework for the music school and for the gymnasium; therefore, we started studying music at home with Filonova. I did not interrupt getting ready for the preparatory class (Fridman was the teacher preparing us). We moved to another apartment and started working again with F. L.; only then Yasha and I began to prepare ourselves: I for the first grade and Yasha for the preparatory class for the gymnasium, and again we stopped studying with F.L.

27 Based on the preschool educational method of pedagogue F.W.A. Fröbel (1782–1821)

25. 13th June Friday 1897

We were admitted to the gymnasium and passed with first prize. Earlier [illegible] F.L. came, she wanted that [illegible]. I will finish writing this later because I have no time to write now, and because I will make as a present for Yasha a small picture [in a frame with a little leg]. His birthday is tomorrow.

26. 22nd July Tuesday 1897

Previously Frida Leontievna wanted us to live with her and only go home to sleep but she asked too much money. So mother arranged that F.L. should come to us in the morning from 9:30 to 12 and from 6 to 9 in the evening. We, i.e., mama, Yasha and I were making a (I don't know what to call it [illegible]) for an etagere[28] and a very pretty little frame for papa's photograph, and afterward we'll make one for mama's as well.

How I did the laundry

Yesterday I laundered and ironed a chemise of a doll that had previously belonged to me and had been completely wrecked by Yasha, Milochka and a little bit by Sania; I washed it very thoroughly but ironing was not so successful. Later yesterday I washed the dress of Milochka's doll; then papa's, mama's, and my handkerchiefs (Sania's handkerchief was all the time with Milochka); a girdle of the dress of Milochka's doll, Miss Ida Germanovna Kurts, who is infatuated with her Avedik; and a pillow case. I have not yet ironed the latter, but perhaps I will iron it today, but I washed it very thoroughly; I rinsed in blue only the dress of Milochka's doll, but the little girdle came out very well. I also stained my fingers blue because instead of using washing blue I used a blue paper from a colored cigarette book that papa had given me as a present on Sania's collection day. Some other time I will explain what collection days are all about because it is a long story. Today my finger nails are still blue. Yesterday Ivanovna, the cook of Ter-Grigoriants (whom we call 'lower', because she lives below us, under [illegible]), and for some other reason I don't know). Yasha also calls her a snub-nosed pug. When we sit on the stairs, she likes to grab us by our shoes, pull the shoes off and give them back. She is a very good cook, and she takes excellent care of cats, healthy and sick, as well as dogs, ducks and geese; she cooks and she helps tidy up the rooms, she serves the food and clears the table, she washes all the dishes, and she always has free time to sit in the street and chatter. She gave us as present a small but very tasty melon

28 Also called a whatnot.

which we divided into five parts and shared with Yasha, Sania, Madmas'ka, Fräulein[29] and myself. A story about the time when mama first wanted to travel to Moscow and then decided otherwise.

27. 9th August Saturday 1897

An affair that was caused when mama first wanted to travel to Moscow and then decided otherwise. I forgot to write about an important event: a doctors' convention in Moscow to which doctors could travel first class free of charge to Moscow and back and get food and everything at half price. Mama also planned to travel there and wrote asking for the ticket to be delivered to her. She wanted to take me with her in order to get some advice from a professor about my stomach. At first papa wanted mama to take me with her, then he did not want to, and then wanted [again?]. Earlier mama wanted to travel on the 3rd of August with Dr. Dubrov but then she was very worried about Milochka...

28. 10th August Sunday 1897

Mama decided to travel on the 4th and requested Dr. Dubrov to book a hotel room for her and be met at the train station, then she decided to travel on the 5th, saying that she was having a bad premonition [illegible], her heart was breaking when she remembered about traveling, and, perhaps, she would not travel at all, even though she had ordered a very expensive ball dress from milliner Vengerova. On the evening of August 4th she went to Olga Yakovlevna, the sister of Rozalia Yakovlevna, to ask for advice and said she would do what Olga Yakovlevna would advise her and she took Yasha and me along. Olga Yakovlevna and grandma, who also came, advised mama to go, but when mama said that she was afraid something might happen to her in the railway car, Olga Yakovlevna said: "If you do not expect to get any pleasure there, then clearly it is not worth going there." Mama sent Yasha to find out if papa had come, because when he came back, he would be angry that mama was not there and he would want to drink tea. No sooner was Yasha out of the gate than papa arrived and took mama home. Mama took me by the hand and led me in the direction of home. Yasha came and started saying that I should come to play at Olga Yakovlevna's place. I had such a heavy feeling in my heart and did not feel like going. But I went with Yasha anyway.

29 Gouvernante in French, governess in English, woman employed to teach and train children in a private household.

There we played the game of opinions and Olga Yakovlevna said this about Nadia: "unattractive." About me they said: "a beautiful kvass lover" (because I like kvass very much) and "a humble kvass-lover." I immediately guessed that it was Nadia who said "beautiful" and Yasha who said "kvass-lover" but that the other two were not true, because it was Olga Yakovlevna who said that I was humble and Mania said that I liked kvass, but I had said it the other way around. About Nadia Mania said that "she is a doll lasher" and that Yasha is "fidgety," and I do not remember what I said. About Mania O.Y. said "lazy," Yasha said "a bit fat," I said "a bit plump," but I don't recall what Nadia said. Nadia was mentioned twice, the second time she guessed all the opinions correctly and we lifted her in the air to express our hurrah like the workers who had lifted papa. And O.Y. also guessed all the opinions but we didn't lift her. Regarding her Mania said "clever," Nadia said "kindhearted," Yasha said "mama liked her," and I said "she likes mama." Then in response to something O. Y. said to Mania: "I will break all your ribs" and Mania answered: "You will not get to touch my ribs."

Earlier we had also played a magician's game. I played the magician and the stairs were the house. Yasha was on the third stair and [illegible; to jump down?] and Nadia [illegible], and they both [came tumbling down?]. I wanted to catch them, caught hold of Yasha, and I also fell down. Yasha was crying but we were laughing; it was altogether so funny, and we were laughing so hard, that I was sure I was going to cry, because I knew why I might cry, because I had good reason to cry; therefore the whole time I tried to suppress my laughter so as to be able to travel to Moscow. I wanted to go home as soon as possible so as to stop laughing. O.Y. wanted to accompany us as mama had requested, but, as bad luck would have it, Semion arrived (I will write later who he is) and O.Y. got involved in a conversation with him. Then Yasha wanted to play chess but Mania did not want to and neither did O.Y., but finally she agreed to play. Also, earlier Mania lit a candle in order to look for the chess set but I blew the candle out. Mania lit the candle again; but no matter how she tried she could not find it. And I just quite simply found it on the second shelf of the whatnot. And here is something else in their apartment: the sublet part of their apartment and the terrace are separated by a wooden partition and between this partition in the wall there is an empty space, and Yasha suddenly shoved a stick into the tenants' part.

When mama and I came home, I really cried. Everybody was saying it looked that I would not be travelling, and papa said emphatically that I would not travel. Papa and mama went for a walk on the boulevard. When mama came home and heard that I had been crying, she said that should Motia, (the son of

Semion who works in our office), secure the tickets on the evening, when she spoke with him, then she would travel the morning after, but should he obtain them the next day, then she would travel that evening. The next day mama told me I should give my things ready to be packed. I did that and was, of course, very glad. But as bad luck would have it, it turned out that the basket was broken, and as it was being mended, mama changed her mind about travelling and told me I should put away my things and that we would travel later. Of course, I figured out this meant "No" and, besides, papa had told me...

29. 11th August Monday 1897

Of course, I cried. Mama explained to me that during the convention the professors did not see patients, that had they been seeing patients, she would have traveled but this way it was pointless to go. She asked me how I would feel if something happened to her in the railway car and she also asked me why I wanted so much to come along. And I myself did not know why. Today I had the following dream.

My dream

Mama hailed a cab and took Yasha, Sania and me along, and we were traveling to Moscow. Yasha was awfully naughty in the cab and mama sent Yasha and Sania back home to fetch something. Mama and I were traveling along Sobornaia street that runs parallel to gardens and past Sobornaia leads toward the steppe. I thought that Yasha and Sania would be very upset. All of a sudden papa arrived and said that Yasha did not want to travel at all. We were about to resume our travel when I remembered that I had forgotten my books. Mama said, "How is it that you remembered this only now," and told me to go rapidly (I cannot recall what was the name of the last street before leaving Rostov). I went but I was very afraid to walk alone. I walked so rapidly that just before reaching the corner of Skobelevskaia Street—(I also dreamt that around the little shops on Sobornaia street was also Skobelevskaia Street)—I saw a dog spinning in the air (it seemed there was nobody else on the street beside myself). I guessed it was a rabid dog and I knew it would attack me. I grabbed its snout but it still managed to bite my hand but without causing pain. I started to fight with it and woke up. I wanted to go on dreaming and began imagining that I was not running toward the steppe but that I fetched the books and was traveling with papa and mama to Moscow. But the moment I imagined I had boarded train I fell asleep again but do not remember what I dreamt about. Following the dream I had described, I woke up early in the morning and fell asleep a second time and woke up late.

A visit with Rozalia Yakovlevna

Yesterday, after being scared by a rat grandma fell down and broke her arm. Yesterday morning mama went to visit her, took us along and with her and also picked up Rozalia Yakovlevna. Rozalia Yakovlevna got married. When I asked her whether I should come to her wedding she said "No, you better stay home." I felt very offended by this. When mama and I arrived at her home mama told her about this. R. Y. asked me not to be angry and said that I would not have had a good time at her wedding. She showed me her wedding dress. In honor of her birthday, Yasha wanted to add: "that you should happily give birth on your wonderful birthday." But I did not add anything. A few days after celebrating her birthday she gave birth to the boy Volodia, on the 25th of February 1897. She was married in 1896 or 1895, but I do not recall which month, may be in January or February, March or April, May, or June, July, or August, September, or November, or December. No, it cannot be October, because that month is my birthday, so most probably in July. Mama wanted Milochka to see Volodia. Fräulein took Volodia in her arms and Milochka started crying, so I picked up Milochka and then Volodia, but I was afraid that the gentleman might dirty me with feces so I gave him back to R. Y. I have forgotten that Yasha had told me that R. Y. used to beat him all the time. And I remember a few things. Yasha said that in the month when there are grades he would know his geography real well and in all the other months he would be getting only grades 5. He further explained that papa said that one 5+ is not enough for him, that he should be getting a 20. Earlier he had said that for calligraphy he got a 3. Then he told a story about a peasant who was following a lady and felt she was reeking of an odor... and so forth. And also, because mama asked us to ask for a glass of milk for Milochka, Fräulein or Yasha asked for milk, but Yasha said: "If you do not want to give, mama will pay you."

What are collection days.

We organized collection days in order not to quarrel about which thing belongs to whom. Early on I collected from mama, Yasha from papa, Sania from uncle Noi. Rarely did we get things from mama and from uncle Noi; and, moreover, papa and mama gifted everything to Sania because he did not have anything, so nobody was satisfied. Therefore we organized collection days: one day for Sania, another for Yasha, and a third one for me. And now everyone gets from papa, mama, and uncle Noi. Many times, when there were no collection days, Yasha wanted to collect from papa, and so did Sania, and they quarreled and hit each other; so for the time being I did not want any collection days. Yasha was against me and Sania was on my side and papa did not approve that there should be collection days.

Some news

As long as there is no school I am absorbed in my diary. Later I may have no time to write in it. I have not yet completed my homework, there is still a lot to finish, and one more task: to learn by heart the fable *The Liar* (by Krylov), to mark all the punctuation signs, the subjects and predicates, and all the explanatory words. I also need to repeat geography. The day before yesterday papa gave me as present (and Sania, too) another slim book with samples of multicolored cigarette papers. In Warsaw I had a dream that God clad in a gray dressing gown and a cap came down and was saying to papa and mama that they should treat us more strictly, and either the second or the first time I dreamt of a fire, but I do not recall how. Thereafter we traveled to Rostov and uncle Mosia put on a gown like the one in which God appeared in my dream and said he will send us to Africa. I did not believe him at all and Yasha believed him and was afraid of him. And then uncle Mosia was saying that he was God, and because we did not believe he was God, he would dispatch us to Africa. I told Yasha not to be afraid. Uncle Mosia should have been arrested. He used to call us insufferable and in general spoke of us as nasty children. Then he grabbed Yasha. Yasha started screaming and I told him not to be afraid. I said to uncle Mosia that he should send me away. Uncle Mosia said he did not want to send me away. Finally I convinced Yasha not to be afraid. Uncle Mosia put him under the couch and said he was already in Africa. It seems this happened a few days after the story about the gown. After I persuaded Yasha we kept begging uncle Mosia to send us away but he kept making excuses and delaying, until he got caught out.[30]

12th August Tuesday 1897

Pigeons

A boy was selling pigeons in our courtyard. Mama had given me 2 rubles in coins for my tenth birthday. Papa took the coins from me and gave me back a half-imperial.[31] Later I drew orders as pictures and was paid a kopeck or more. I thus accumulated about ten rubles. Papa took them from me again and gave back the ten rubles. Then papa took them from me and said that he would give it to me if I needed anything. Yasha had 15 rubles and papa took them from him as well. At first the boy selling the pigeons wanted 40 kopecks for a pair and now he agreed to take 10 and then daddy did not want to give more

30 This episode illustrates uncle Mosia's exploits as "a school-boy 13–14 years old who likes to impress us with being important" (see Spielrein, 1912, p. 149).

31 A gold coin worth five rubles.

than 6 kopecks of our money for the pair. He did not want to give us any money as long as the construction of the house remained unfinished. I did not know I would be writing so much today. Earlier I thought I would not be able to write at all, and then I thought I would write no more than one line, because I am again so agitated...I did not expect I would be able to describe such an affair.

A letter

Today I have a great joy that deserves to be described. It appears that on 2nd July I received from the grandmother, not from these parts[32], a letter in a separate envelope, with a seven kopeck stamp, addressed personally to me. This seven-kopeck stamp which I used to hate as a matter of habit now became the most cherished stamp of all, even more than the American ones. Of course, this letter was a response to mine. I will not describe my joy today because it will take too long, and I have to go to the club, and I am too irritated. I have not been to the club for five days. Yesterday the brother of uncle Noi's bride arrived. He made a poor impression on papa and mama and me as well. The reason was that he said that when a woman of his acquaintance knits or darns socks he approaches her and snatches them. If the women knitting or darning socks or eating sunflower seeds are strangers, then, if he could, he would like to tear the socks to pieces. And it so happens that last night we were eating sunflower seeds. Mama picked up a few sunflower seeds and gave them to him and he handed them to uncle Noi. And he ought to be ashamed to speak while they are eating; for he well knows that mama would stop eating them because of him, since for us [illegible] eating sunflower seeds is a great pleasure.

30. 16th August, Saturday 1897
[Nr. 11a note]

Today I went to the gymnasium and we were told to come back on the 20th and look on the door when we should come.

31. 29th October Wednesday,
1897 My birthday

I will at least mention the day of my legal age, that is my twelfth birthday, which I reached on Saturday, the 25th of October 1897. I wanted to celebrate my birthday on Saturday and not on Sunday so that I would be able to go to the

32 The paternal grandmother in Warsaw.

gymnasium. But eventually papa and mama decided that Yasha and I should not go there. Moreover, I began to fear some troubles because should something happen on a birthday, it might be happening all year long.

32. 8th November Saturday 1897

I was up.

Yasha and papa could not wait for me to come into the living room and receive the presents. And I myself was as impatient as they were. I dressed, combed my hair, drank tea and went to the living room. I thought the presents were in the consulting room, I do not remember who told me that they were there. All of a sudden, through the open anteroom door, papa congratulated me and asked me to give him my word of honor that I would be well behaved, and [I saw] a colossal doll sitting next to the piano. This was a present from papa and mama, on the window there was porcelain furniture consisting of a little table, two armchairs, and a chair. The latter was a gift from Sania but of course, papa and mama bought it and gave it to him so that he could give it to me as his present. Yasha gave me as a present stamps from his album (I will later explain from which stamp-album, but I am sure I cannot remember which stamps), and, in addition, he gave me, the same way as did Sania, a chess set. Milochka gave me a little fan that cost 25 kopecks. The chess set cost three rubles. The furniture cost one ruble, and the doll, I think, 10 rubles, but papa got a discount. I thought the guests would arrive very late, after 2 o'clock, when I was due to come back from the gymnasium, at 2 PM, and usually guests arrive later. But the guests came at 1 o'clock, of course, not all of them. The first one to arrive was madam Tsaitlin with her children Sasha and Lelia (Lelia is older than Sasha), and she brought me no present, because... [I will write more later.]

34. 9th November Sunday 1897

My collection day Continuation

We had an agreement that mama would tell them not to bring any presents. Then, presently, the Kantoroviches. I just had the time to think... [text break]

35. 11th November Tuesday 1897

What a pity that the Kantoroviches will not be coming, but presently they did come. Each of them brought me as present a box of candy, and, in each of these boxes, there were pretty little bottles with rum.

36. 12th November Wednesday 1897

Lelia Tsaitlin wanted to hold my doll all the time and screamed, even though Lelia had thrown down her Lida or some other [doll], so she could have smashed [my doll]. Sashka and Lelia Ts. had a fight.

37. 5th April Sunday 1898

We moved into our house.

38. 13th April Monday1898

The day before yesterday we moved into our own house. Two days prior to that we lived in grandma's place and we were going to practice in our aunt's place because our own piano was taken away to be repaired. It is standing on the first floor.

As there is nothing to do: a fragment

Today was the first time we went to the gymnasium after the holidays. Those who did not participate in religion classes had only three lessons and they also missed the Russian lesson. A.F. (our supervisor) told us to bring a book to read and the grades but I do not know where those were. Today I had to attend the needlework class. The teacher told me to come to see her after the three classes. I went there but she was not at home. I got very tired and I am writing in the diary because I have nothing else to do. I will tell in detail what we have been doing in the gymnasium. Before the classes started we were laughing. I myself and all the Jewish girls did not know when the prayer would end and when one had to bow. Before the first class and after the prayer A.F. told us we should bring books to read and the grades and those who forgot should make a note of it in their report notebook. I don't want to write about this.

39. 14th April Tuesday 1898

My album

I am not in the mood to write and I wish everything should write itself. I myself do not know where to start. I am terribly bored. There are no interesting events. However, something did happen today but I do not want to write about it. And why I don't I want to write about this event I won't tell, because it is self-evident. Mama wrote to A.F.: "Dear A.F., forgive my girl if she does not bring a book to read and the grades tomorrow but only a few days later since we have moved and her things are packed with other stuff, and [we] do not know where they are. Respectfully yours, E. Shpilrein[33]." I wanted so much to sign with the word 'pretend' before 'respectfully' and send it. So it would have been: "pretend respectfully, yours E. Shpilrein." Mama hates A.F., she says that she's a dirty creature and that she regrets very much that A.F. is our supervisor, yet she writes to A. F. with such esteem.

In our gymnasium there are girls who have albums in which boys write love verses. I made this kind of album for myself from a book with color samples on the cover which is written "Gans [Hans] vunder [Wunder = miracle] in Berlin." The cover of this book is green. Since I had nothing else to do, on the first page I started writing the following little verse: It is getting dark,

The stars are rising,
The hut is quiet.
Only a curly-haired boy
Is crying at the window.

At first I wanted to give this verse the title "Vokra", as if it were the boy's name, but then I changed my mind. And when Yasha asked me "what does Vokra mean?" I told him this is not a title but the name of a color. I then left two pages empty to finish the verse and made lines on the fourth page, glued in a little picture, and thus created an album like the other girls. On the third page of the album, or on the sixth page of the booklet, classmate Kleiner wrote:

Written on the four corners was the following:
When you open it, remember; when you close it, do not forget.

Remembering Sabina 14th of April 1898.
I fulfil your wish
I write verses in your album
I wish you all the best and happiness
But I will not sign my name.
What for? You know it
Other people do not need to know
Who had the idea to write verses

33 Eva's signature is Russian, pronounced like 'rain' not 'brine'. Vladimir spells it Shpilrain. Brother Isaak, in Russia, signed Shpilrein, Yan, in Germany, signed Spielrein.

In this little album.
On the sixth page of the album, Yasha wrote me the following:
14.IV.1898
Obeying your wish,
I take a pen, sit down to write
Why deprive an innocent creature
Of an innocent joke.
Y. Shpilrein

Yasha took a book with samples (I cannot state which samples) of papers and said that this will be his album. On the first page I glued in a little picture for him as a present. I wrote for him a composition that was almost entirely done by myself. Well, let's assume it was not mine at all.

To Yasha, in the memory of 14th of April 1898.

I take a pen, sit down to write.
What should I write? I do not know.
What then, perhaps wish happiness?
All right, I wish it.
S. Shpilrein.

40. 9th May Saturday 1898
A present for Sania's birthday
The 13th of May is Sania's birthday. I thought of giving him a book but I was afraid I would not be able to write something in it on time. I have there three stories one of which was lost. I remember that in Warsaw uncle Mosia had written us a letter in block letters.

41. 10th May Sunday 1898
On Monday [illegible] there was a 2nd prize. If I do not get the 1st prize, I will not attend the commencement ceremony. Yesterday we traveled to see Frida Leontievna so that she would come to see us. She said she could not do this before 8 o'clock (and we had gone to her at 6 = 6+6 o'clock), because she was teaching a girl student. At parting F.L. gave us some nuts. Yasha wanted to pay her two kopecks, but she said all she had was nuts for half a kopeck. Then Yasha said: "I cannot give you half a kopeck, because I left it at home, so give me change of one kopeck." And he gave her two kopecks. She did not want to take them. So

Yasha gave them to F.L.'s husband. He did not want to give change. Then Yasha said that if he does not want to give change let him keep the two kopecks. But to prevent Yasha from paying, the husband of F.L. gave the money to Fräulein, but I saw it, and told Yasha about it. Then Yasha took the money back from Fräulein and ran back to F.L. I do not know how it all ended. However, I will ask Yasha. He forced Yasha to accept the money. Yesterday after breakfast we took a walk with papa and drank lemonade at Armaganov's. Before we left F.L., he said that it was printed in the newspaper that two boys and a girl were drinking lemonade with their father. We asked to see that paper but F.L. told us that the paper was torn up.

A walk in the steppe

After we left F.L we went for a walk in the steppe. We bought sunflower seeds for two kopecks and persimmon for one kopeck and for three kopecks Yasha and Sania took a ride on the merry-go-round. There was no kvass and I wanted to get a drink so we went to Fräulein and drank our fill. Then we went farther and bought a quarter of a pound of croissants for two kopecks so that everybody got one-and-a-half croissant. Then we continued walking and I became terribly thirsty. On our way we found kvass costing one kopeck per cup but it was so sour that Sania [and I] were unable to drink it. Fräulein also bought herself a cup of kvass and Yasha drank from our cup. Yasha paid for our cup and Fräulein had the impression that she had lost her money, that is one kopeck, and was unable to pay. I said that we have already paid for ourselves and that Fräulein had to pay for herself so Yasha set his cup of kvass aside. Fräulein found her money and paid but Yasha did not finish drinking his cup. We got terribly tired and wanted to sit down at the mill but Fräulein did not want to. I had no desire to go to the grove but Yasha wanted to, but we went the way I wanted to go between the crop fields, and we arrived at the railway tracks.

42. 11th May Monday 1898

Daydreams

When I become a grown up, I will not get married and will not have my own children. But I decided I will adopt a few tiny orphans and train them that I am their mother and raise them in the Jewish religion. We have two janitors (*dvorniks*) and both are named Vassilii or Vas'ka. To tell them apart we call one the white Vas'ka and the other the black Vas'ka.

43. 14th May Thursday 1898

About pigeons

Mr. Vainshtein made us a present of eleven pigeons. The black Vas'ka also has pigeons. Daddy fired him because the gate lock had been stolen. He departed and left us two pigeons. Presently Yasha came and told us that our pigeons hatched two chicks. That means we have fifteen pigeons.

44. 21st June Sunday 1898
    2nd note
    We, that is Milchik [i.e., Milochka] and I, were bathing in one big tub. I am now going to make a game for Milchik with little cups and dolls and therefore stop writing.

45. 16th July Thursday 1898
    Our wedding
    I now resume writing in my diary. Yesterday the marriage of Yasha and me took place. Before that we were marrying San'ka and Milochka but this failed because both before and after the marriage the bride wanted to be breast-fed and we all laughed during the wedding. We got married the same way they did, namely, at first we prayed that God grant us a happy marriage, then we exchanged rings, then San'ka blessed us in the following manner: Yasha shouted out to San'ka and Milchik: "Bedbug and bedbug powder give us your blessing." Milchik did not want to, so San'ka blessed us with these words: "Be happy, devils, never kick the bucket, devils," whereupon we kissed each other. Then we were married. We made a feast and spent our two kopecks and mama's ten. Mania and Nadia persuaded us to accept five kopecks more, but we lost one. We played a game of croquet. Nadia and Sania started first and had to pass forward and we, Yasha, Mania and I, started second and had to pass forward and backward. But first Nadia got tired of it and then Mania and we stopped playing. Then we danced the polka, Yasha with me and Sania with Nadia, and then Nadia and Mania went home. Mama also took part in the feast. I very much wished that in a year I should have a child, a girl, and a year later a boy.

46. 18th July Saturday 1898
    A fight
    Yesterday it rained all day and I was afraid that there might be a flood. Should the water inundate only the lower floor, and even our floor too, we would have to climb to the third floor and would not be in danger anymore, we would just have to go hungry. Yesterday we got up at 5:45 in the morning and when I started getting dressed it was 5:55 o'clock. Today I was not yet fully dressed at 7:35. Then mama hid the sugar and even though I was already fully dressed I had

to wait half an hour for [tea?]. During tea Yasha found a picture of an orangutan taken out of San'ka's book. San'ka said that Yasha tore it out of his book. Yasha was saying all the time: "No." But finally he said: "Alright yes, let it be yes." Then San'ka started hitting him with his fists. Yasha pushed his hand away. Then dear papa ordered both of them to fight each other for a whole hour. San'ka burst out crying twice. Papa gave Sania a fork to pull Yasha's eyes out but Yasha would not let Sania do it. Mama heard the noise, came in and took Sania with her, and papa said should they start fighting like this again, he will lock them up somewhere and force them to fight each other for three hours, but should only one be hitting the other, then he will...

47. 22nd July Tuesday, 1898

Sania's name

Not very long ago, Mr. Ganemann came to have dinner with us and said that he was also called Oskar. A conversation ensued about Sania's name, that when he grows up he will be called Oskar, so we finally agreed that as grownup Sania should be called Osia. I liked this very much. Previously, we used to call Sania Niusia, then we called him Sania, and now we can also call him Osia. Oh, papa will probably not like it.

The journey to Taganrog

Papa told Yasha and Sania: "He who finds mama's [card game?] will receive an award." Yasha found the card game and said: "I would like to be rewarded with a trip to Taganrog by steamer, but you will not do this, so choose what you like." However, papa agreed. Yesterday Yasha got up at 6 o'clock in the morning. Suddenly it started to rain and papa changed his mind about traveling. We knew nothing about it. The maid and mama were very eager to travel with us. After breakfast we started getting dressed. I had no special desire to travel: I was afraid that I would see nothing but water and sky. Papa phoned that he would not be leaving without mama. Mama told us to get dressed and go to cry in papa's office. Yasha was sure that papa would travel and I myself was not particularly worried and only Sania was screaming. I was very afraid to travel. For the journey mama gave us six bread-and-butter sandwiches with meatballs, three cucumbers, and 16 candies. We said goodbye to mama and Milochka and left. Papa wanted to go on foot, but, thankfully, Yasha's shoes turned out to be too tight so we begged father to take a cab. We had to wait a long time for the steamer to cast off. We started watching as it was being loaded. I regretted very much that we had rushed papa to leave home. Yasha and Sania started to fish with hook and bait. Earlier I was frightened by the first horn whistle. The sun was burning terribly and the air in the stateroom was stifling. Papa bought a bottle of beer, gave me a glass, and drank the rest. The beer was very bitter. Suddenly I was frightened again by the second whistle. Yasha said the steamer was about to cast off in ten minutes. I could not wait for this moment to arrive. These ten minutes felt like an eternity, especially since papa fell asleep, but I consoled myself with a thought that nothing was forever. Eventually, the boat has to cast off. And I waited ten minutes more. Finally the third whistle was heard, papa woke up and called me to watch how the steamer started to cast off. I was hungry but did not want to go to the stateroom by myself. More than the sight of Rostov I liked the view of the opposite bank of the river. Then we sailed through the railway bridge. After we passed it papa showed us how the bridge was raised. Then Yasha brought us some food. I started getting seasick. I ate two candies. Father lay down to sleep and charged me with watching Sania. I did not like this at all. I myself could hardly move. Yasha and Sania went into the stateroom. I sat down on an anchor cable and behind me was sitting a gentleman. It seemed to me that he was either a bandit or a madman and that he wanted to kill me. I could not look at him and turned around. He must have noticed my gaze because he turned away. I also felt uneasy but I could not help looking at him. Finally Yasha came. He slandered me to the gentleman that I was afraid of the sea, of the boat rolling, etc. All of us together, Yasha, Sania, and I, went to join papa in the stateroom. Yasha and Sania climbed to papa's top birth and I lay down below. The air in the stateroom was too stifling again so I went back to sit on my anchor cable and Yasha with Sania joined me there. Sania was playing with a little boy named Kolia. We started throwing little pieces of paper into papa's beard. I combed my hair and sat down with Yasha on my spot. The gentleman said that we would soon reach the open sea. I will never forget the impression the sea has made on me. I was not afraid at all. I was enchanted by this magnificent sight: a wonderful, as if silvery surface with light waves, as if chasing and swallowing each other. The banks were no longer visible. The sky seemed to be merging with the sea to form one blue expanse. Even the sky never looked to me as beautiful as it did now: little clouds floated one after the other extolling its splendor to me. An enormous mother-cloud got hold of the little ones as if fearing they might make a graceless movement. The pale-blue part of the sky was so bright that I could not look at it. In the sea the young waves rolled quickly and the old waves flowed slowly behind them. These waves were mocking us, showing us how insignificant we were compared to them. All they need is to rise more and the steam-boat would be damaged and scores of people would become prey of these proud waves. I would have continued to contemplate this wonderful sight had I not become hungry. Papa bought tea for 30 kopecks, four pieces of lemon for 20, half a portion of butter for 25, and pastry for 10[34]. Presently we arrived. I took leave of the sea and have now noticed a similarity between the sky and the sea. Sky waves are clouds, sea clouds are waves. During a storm both clouds and waves turn dark. I got terribly tired and therefore suggested that we walk up the hill and take a rest on the grass. Papa agreed. Papa, Yasha, and I got very tired. But Sania not at all. Then we went to the train station. On the way papa bought one pound of plums and two pounds of pears, then a bottle of lemonade and a glass of seltzer. We arrived at the train station; I was not hung...[text break].

48. 23rd July Wednesday 1898

I was not hungry and afraid the train would leave without us. Papa led us into the railway car and went to buy the tickets. I asked papa to buy us eggs or sandwiches, for even though we were not hungry now we could become hungry later. But papa said that it was not worth it because we would have supper at home. Papa came back quickly. We got bored again waiting for the train to start moving but it was not too long. The train started moving, then suddenly stopped at a station and stayed there for a terribly long time. Presently the train started moving again. To me...

49. 28th December 1898 Monday [empty]

50. 1st January Friday, 1899

Contract and events of 1899

In the new year I am starting to write in my diary again and will try to write down everything that has happened that day. Except for one contract and one event I will not describe anything concerning 1898. I will only say that 1898 was the unhappiest year of my life and that the happiest year I remember was 1896, that is when I started writing my diary, and half of 1897, that is the year I attended the first grade. I made the following contract on the 2[5?]th of December 1898. Papa made an agreement with me that until the 25th of January 1899 he will no longer reprimand me and he confirmed this with his own word of honor coupled with me giving him my word of honor that I will observe all the rules that will be presented to me on the 25th of January. I will then be presented with rules of good behavior. I will omit describing those rules for I am sure I won't forget

34 The Russian word is franzolka, which could mean both pastries and rolls.

them. I wanted to describe some of my own rules but the inkwell overturned which means I intended to do something bad.

Now I will describe the event itself. Yesterday at 8 o'clock in the evening we went to the Asmolov theatre to see the play "At the Maneuvers". This play is a very funny four-act comedy. At the theatre we met Osip Il'yich, Yasha's supervisor. Yasha and I were walking around in the theatre and if madam Sanieieva were on duty today, she would have approached me and asked: "Who is that boy with you?" She had posed this question to the girl Nakhmanovich when she was seen walking around with her elder brother, a gymnasium student. However, instead of Sanieieva we were confronted by the comparable dragon on duty who told me I could no longer stay in the theatre since the masked ball scene was about to begin and the headmistress had strictly forbidden the students to watch it. This was the ending of the comedy. I told this to papa and mama. Papa immediately came over to the woman and told her that live scenes would be shown now. Then she agreed that I could stay. But at this moment the fat mug of a man entered our box, Fiodor Nikonovich, supervisor of the upper classes of the boys' gymnasium, who told Osip Ilyich, and later papa, that there was a regulation and there was no way Yasha could stay. Then papa took us home. This was about 11 o'clock. At 11:50 papa, mama, and bald Mr. Patt came back from the theatre; he said that he wanted to celebrate the New Year together with us. I opened a bottle of tokaj wine and served everybody a glass. For the first time in my life papa celebrated New Year in Rostov. Usually, around Christmas he traveled to Warsaw. Papa made a speech usually made with the passing of the old year; we clinked our glasses and drank the wine. Papa turned on the light in all the rooms. My heart was very heavy, but I did not want to spoil anybody's mood. However, to tell the truth, the mood was not a happy one and the conversations were sad. Then Yasha and I sat down to play piano four hands, then we had desert, and when we finished, Yasha went to bed, and I, after drinking tea and listening to Mr. Patt's story till the end, went to bed as well.

Today, first Yasha then I, wore paper costumes which I had made and which we tore in short order. Mika [Emilia] wore a sky blue angel's dress with a light pink bow and little wings and a picture of a rose on her chest. I was wearing a light pink bra and red pleated skirt with a green girdle. I do not want to describe the costumes of Yasha and Sania, I'm going to bed.

51. 2nd January Saturday, 1899
    My little son
    I did not write that I have a little son Adiuk. He was born on Tuesday 27th

October 1898. Exactly one week later he was given the name Abram (in Russian Adolf). On the 3rd of November I left after the second lesson in order to attend the ceremony. The bald Mr. Patt was the godfather.

The last memory of 1898 was losing a black pencil on 31st December 1898. I was drawing a pattern with this pencil when suddenly it fell down and no matter how hard I looked for it I could not find it. I lost a little knife the same way and I put an eraser in a pocket and could not find it the next day.

A secret

What I won't let anyone read, I shall write in a secret language, for example my rules.

52. 3rd January Sunday 1899

Third note

Today I visited Madam Bortsmaier and was gilding little terracotta plates which I had bought for papa's birthday at Ivashchenko's. I do not want to do gymnasium homework. I myself do not know when I will do it. On the 7th of January we will have a public prayer and lessons will resume on the 8th. Lately I feel very weak and I'm sure it will be difficult for me to sit through five lessons at the gymnasium. It is even difficult for me to get dressed. Already for two days, today and yesterday, I did not drink my morning tea.

At the theatre

Yesterday we went to the Asmolov theatre to see the play "The Conquest of Izmail[35]." We sat in the orchestra in the fifth armchair row. We came in the middle of the second act. Papa phoned us at the end of the first act and told us

35 The 1790 siege and assault on the Turkish fortress Izmail by general-in-chief Suvorov.

to get dressed immediately and go to the theatre. We went. We sat for some time in the hall on the second floor. Then an employee came and asked: "Where is the boy?" and led us to our seats. I liked this play very much.

53. 4th January Monday 1899 Madmas'ka's illness

I forgot to mention that Madmas'ka left us already at the beginning of October 1897 and returned in December 1898. Now she is sick and lying in bed. Dr. Tsaitlin has already made two visits.

At Bortsmaier's

Today I visited Bortsmaier and brought her three little brushes; at her place I painted four little leaves, four little stems, and a piece of blue background. Bortsmaier has two little dogs, Kotik [little cat] and Tsyganochka [little gypsy]. They dislike terribly when one of the servants enters the room and bark dreadfully. Especially Tsyganochka is afraid of the former servant Grania. All Mrs. Bortsmaier has to do is to utter the name "Grania" and Tsyganochka starts barking furiously followed by Kotik. While I was painting I accidentally looked at Kotik's eyes and saw that they sparkled like two flames. I'm finishing this page. I have written enough.

54. 17th Saturday April 1899 The illness

I was ill. I fell ill already on evening of that Thursday the 8th of April. This is how it happened: on Wednesday at the gymnasium I got a pain in my hand. I had already thought earlier to skip gymnastics and then I decided that if I had to do exercises with my right hand I would decline. But the gymnastics lesson turned out to be easy and even though we played ball I did not need to refuse. Toward evening my right hand was hurting even more and I told mama about it but mama paid no attention because that evening papa was leaving for another city and this created a big turmoil. The next day I was getting dressed to go to the gymnasium, and the little back buttons were fastened up by Madmas'ka. She [a few words in code language] was also combing my hair because my hand was hurting badly and the pain in the hand was making it difficult even to lift a glass of tea. I felt that in the gymnasium I would not be able either to draw or write. Mama told me to stay home. Then mama smelled out that I had fever and undressed me. I had fever of 38.6° and the back of the hand started getting swollen. Then I got a headache and mama daubed the painful part with iodine. Toward evening mama asked Dr. Margulis to come. He prescribed a medicine that made me feel better and said that if I start coughing he should be called to come again for it would mean either pleuritis or, if not, rheumatic fever. On

Friday I stayed in bed all day. In the morning papa came back. On Saturday morning my hand stopped hurting but my chest started hurting and coughing began. Mama was not aware of this while papa gave me permission to go out into the courtyard. In the evening papa got angry with Yasha and it became a big mess. I went out into the courtyard wearing a summer dress and of course my cold became more severe. Toward evening I had a temperature of 38° and toward night it became even higher. Next day, that is on Sunday, I became much sicker. I had two big hemorrhages from my nose and Dr. Dubrov came to see me three times. I did not sleep all night and was coughing a great deal. The doctor said that I had pleuritis. Up until Tuesday he was visiting us twice a day. On Tuesday he only came once and yesterday he gave me permission to get out of bed and go out into the courtyard. He will come to see me again today. I forgot to mention that Mika also got sick on Tuesday and recovered completely yesterday. Yesterday Sania took ill. He had 37.9° fever but today he is running around in the courtyard. Mama also had 38° fever. Briefly, our home was hit by an epidemic.

55. 9th May Sunday 1899

We were dismissed on Wednesday the 5th of May. I was promoted without an examination. The headmistress told many students, "Promoted without examination for good behavior, diligence, due to illness, etc." And to Kleiner, Polidorova, and me she said, "Promoted for excellent grades." Consequently, I am now in the fourth grade, I am especially glad that my friend Naumova was promoted without an examination. She did not get very high grades but was promoted for her diligence. She was terribly afraid of examinations. On Friday the 7th of May we took the first examination, written French. Today we went to take part in the rehearsal for the Pushkin anniversary jubilee. During the jubilee the first class will sing "Through waves of mist." The second—"God's bird never has a worry." Our class—"The feast of Peter the Great." Some other classes will sing "The storm," "A roaring wave is running in the river," a little fragment from "The Mermaid": "Gone is that time, the golden time." Then "The Maidens." I wished mama could attend the jubilee. On the 15th of May papa is traveling to the Caucasus and would like to take Osia, Yasha, and me along.

56. 25th February 1900

I have not written for quite a long time. How my views and plans have changed since then. I simply cannot believe, how only two years ago, I was capable of writing such rubbish. For example, regarding the description of the journey to Taganrog, I am still haunted by this stupid, aping expression ("as if it was extolling me..." etc.) and I would like to tear out that page from it. Or when I described our wedding with Yasha, is it really true that I was able to think that I could get children as a result of this comedy? No, I actually just expressed a wish, knowing that it cannot be fulfilled. Altogether, the entire style of those times, all the expressions seem to be terribly silly for my age. But enough of that. Nevertheless, this memory is precious to and it is still interesting to know how I was as a child. Now I fantasize quite differently. I reckon that when I become an adult (by the way, I am not little anymore), I will get married, my husband will be crazy about me and I about him. We will have a very clean, very simple and cozy small apartment; when papa and mama will come to visit I shall serve them coffee with cream and whatever else they like [a word in code]. In the evening, illuminated by a bright light of a lamp, we will sit down at the table covered with dishes that papa and mama like. I will be sitting next to a squeaky-clean samovar serving tea and my husband will be treating my papa and mama and buttering their sandwiches. We will all be so happy! Then I will buy special armchairs for papa and mama and I will not let anybody touch them. Each one of my children will have its own glass and each child will wash its glass and put it in its place. These are really sweet dreams. Oh, if only they would come true. Mama once had similar dreams and would now pay a high price to be a young maiden again. All happiness is in the hands of fate. God only knows what my fate will be and whether what I often think about will be fulfilled even approximately. I would like to become an adult sooner in order to get to know and experience my happiness should it really happen this way. Since January 31st of this year mama has started to save for my dowry. However, for the most part my head is filled not with happy but with sad thoughts, about which I will not write now so as not to ruin my mood.

(Note. 11th November 1899 I got sick with measles, this happened on Thursday, and from Tuesday until the 26th I was sick with scarlet fever).

57. 26th February 1900

I forgot to describe a whole series of very important events: 1) we traveled to Tiflis and then to Borzhom; 2) at that time grandmother, whom I loved more than anybody else, died; 3) on the 1st of July 1899, my brother Milchik [Emil] was born; 4) grandfather took another wife, a very good-natured woman but a very silly one. It is very difficult for me to live in this world without my grandmother. How often when I am overcome with some dark fear, it seems to me that only grandma would be able to protect me. I cannot write anymore...

And when I remember how many times she stuck up for me, how she pleaded with mama when she was angry with me for no good reason! How grandma consoled me when I was in some distress! How often she agreed with me that San'ka was vicious and not sick and taught me how to deal with him. How I had a habit of climbing on the bed with mama and grandma and start dreaming about my future. How lovingly grandma played with my hair and how pleasant were these minutes for me. Now I have to endure all this misery by myself. There is nobody to tell it to, nobody to talk with about what so interests me. I would convey to grandma all the sorrow that piled up over a number of days, how happy I was when she came, and how much I liked to drink tea at her place. I have never had a chance to treat grandma to tea served in my little cups. Or maybe I did succeed in achieving this, but I just do not remember it. Yes, what is the use of remembering all this, anyway it will not bring grandma back from the dead. There is nobody who will now defend me during the daily scenes with San'ka. San'ka is the goody-good child, and I am the idiot, the scoundrel, the beast, the witch. This was not happening when grandma was alive.

58. 29 February 1900

The diary fell into my hands, so this means I should write something. But what should I write? It's already one and half week since I stopped going to the gymnasium even though I am now completely healthy. By now I should be getting busy with geography. I do not want to think about what I wrote on the 26th but it comes to mind involuntarily. Poor grandma! Just yesterday we were remembering her. Pinia Mints came to visit. He is leaving for America and came by to say goodbye. He, mama, and Aunt Tania talked a lot about her, but I just sat and listened. Yes, I will not forget this for a long time although I appeared completely indifferent. Milchin'ka is crying. I have to see what happened to him.

Reviewing now all that I had written previously, I find it not as stupid as it appeared to me at first sight. True, there are some parts there which I dislike terribly but on the whole I can reconcile myself to the writing of those times, all the more so since I write particularly for myself. It is not to my liking that papa forbade us to go into the main rooms without asking permission. It is very inconvenient that I have neither a pen nor ink. It is simply horrible how crooked my handwriting is. Let us also assume that it is impossible to write any better while lying in bed. Since I have nothing to do, I am talking to myself. In spite of having been writing my diary for all these years, until now I have only filled one and a half books or notebooks (I do not know how to call them).

Milochka and Milchin'ka are sick with whooping cough. Yasha, Sania and I the sa[me?].

59. 5th March 1900

Today I received a new pencil. Papa brought a little box with pencils and let each of the four of us pick one that we liked. I picked a light brown one. On the 3rd Milochka had her birthday. Mama bought her a doll; I made for her 6 little [people?] movable [illegible] by blowing air. Sania gave her two soldiers, [a canon], and a [cardboard] soldier. Papa gave her little fireworks as present. It is [painful?] for me to write.

60. 17th April Monday, 1900

On Saturday mama had her birthday. I gave her a pillow covered with designs under the supervision of Bortsmaier (Anna Timofeievna). Yesterday Yasha started writing the chronicles of their army, that is a description of their fights since the time when our former tenants, the Kraselshschiks, were joined by their eleven-year old elder son Sania.

61. May 1900

I want to write how I would like to live when I myself will be a housewife but there is no place for it in a diary. I will prepare a separate notebook where I will write all that is pertinent to this subject, and, as time goes on, and as my convictions will change, I will write them down. Well, in a [word], all this will become evident. I would also like Yasha to be writing a diary. I do not feel like writing. Uncle Abram came to visit. He is in love with mama and I am with him. Yesterday this uncle gave Milochka a doll as a gift and me a box of candies. On the 28th of May Sania took an examination in arithmetic for the first grade. He had to take the Russian examination on the 30th, but he will probably take it on the 31st, it is not clear why. The first one he took was not on the 28th but on the 29th, and he got a 5. On the 5th of May I was promoted to the fifth grade. The lady administrator authorized various games for the school garden. I have quite often played those games since the head-mistress gave us permission to use the little school garden for that purpose. The games were the following: two of croquet, cerceau, air bilboquet[36], jump rope, balls, and hoops.

62. 17th August 1900

I am now sitting in the train. On the 1st of August mama and I left Rostov and on the 4th we arrived in Warsaw, i.e., the destination of our journey. I like Warsaw very much; it is a pity that we did not have enough time to see it because we spent all the time visiting milliners and stores. When we arrived in Warsaw we were met at the train station by the son of Chmokalka[37], i.e., the long-nosed Adolf, who adores Yashen'ka, and babtsia [babcia in Polish, the paternal grandmother]. Papa sent a telegram to Chmokalka that Yashen'ka was on his way, but since Chmokalka was not at home it was his son who came. At first babtsia seemed repulsive to me but once I got to know her more intimately I became receptive to her. At first we stayed at Aunt Bronia's who had left for her cottage. At the entrance to Warsaw I liked very much the Visla [Vistula river] and the iron bridge above it, stretching for quite a distance in the form of a pavilion-like structure covered with shingles; the massive, four to five story high very beautiful buildings; and the roadway built by Germans upon which one rides without jolts or hearing noise; the gardens in the part of Warsaw called "Novyi Svet" [in Polish Nowy Świat = new world] where I saw (as I recall it) a monument to Copernicus and one or two to Mickiewicz[38]; the 1st and the 6th gymnasiums for boys; and the castle of the governor. Then, accompanied by my cousin Mitia, we visited the Fotoplastikon[39] where we saw sights of Switzerland. Bronia's apartment is located on a square called Zhelazna Brama [the Iron Gate Square] on the 3rd floor. On the same square there is a market. I have never seen such big crowds as on this Warsaw market. When I was looking at the people from Aunt B.'s balcony they seemed like ants. In Warsaw there are several gymnasiums for boys, four or five gymnasiums for girls, five science schools, a university and plenty of educational establishments. On the way to the Fotoplastikon, or perhaps on the way back, I do not remember, Mitia took us to a candy and pastry shop that was constructed in the form of a cave which consisted of an anteroom and an actual cave on the ceiling of which were hanging cruciform branches decorated

36 Cerceau is a game of rolling a hoop by beating it with a stick; air bilboquet is tossing a small ring on a string attached on the other end to a hand-held stick and catching it.

37 Chmokalka, a word derived from Чмокать chmokat,' make a smacking sound with one's lips or give smacking kisses. Thus Adolf's nickname.

38 Adam Mickiewicz (1798–1855), Polish poet laureate

39 The Warsaw Fotoplastikon was a theatre of rotating stereoscopic images, the oldest in Europe.

with multicolored electrical light bulbs that created a somewhat dimly-lit and fantastic appearance. Naturally, the entire cave consisted of rocks, as if covered with grass, out of which at intervals were peeping out all kinds of animals. Two times we visited Aunt Sabina living in Svider [Świder], a picturesque hamlet in a pine forest which gets its name from the river Svider that flows in the shape of a French letter S hence the name Svider.

63. 11th June 1901

On the 17th of May of this year we, i.e., my mother, Milochka, and I for the first time left our native land and went abroad to seek medical treatment. Our journey was filled with most varied impressions. As we were leaving Rostov, an enormous crowd saw us off: three of my friends with whom I do readings (Kleiner, Sokolova, and Feldman), Feldman's brother and his friend Pet'ka Lublinskii, who had just arrived in Rostov from Tiflis, grandfather, the bald uncle from Taganrog, and our three boys with papa and the nursemaid. Despite this crowd I was nevertheless very sad: leaving my native land, leaving behind all my relatives and girlfriends and traveling to foreign lands which in my imagination appeared grandiose and austere, and on top of it with a nervous mama for whom I felt utterly responsible. Overcome to such a degree by an inexplicable fear and a hopeless melancholy, that when papa was saying goodbye to us on Gnilovskaia street and suggested that I should stay home, I was unable immediately to decline his suggestion. As the train started moving, and papa with Yasha, Sania, and Pet'ka were waving their handkerchiefs and hats for the last time, I overcame within me, although just for the sake of appearances, my intense sadness and settled myself at the window to look at all and describe all I was seeing so that at the very least our journey would not be in vain. But my intentions were not meant to be realized: toward evening I developed severe pains in my feet which became so swollen that mama was forced to make a stopover in Kharkov. One little lady loaned me her shoes in which I was barely able to arrive at the hotel. This mishap upset me so much that mama, in order to calm me down, said that should there be an opportunity, she would take those ill-fated old shoes to Warsaw, where that little lady lived, to give them back to her. But this was not destined to happen, it was impossible to give the shoes back to her, because in Warsaw we did not meet the little lady again and because mama had forgotten to ask her last name and address. We spent three days in Kharkov, which caused mama to make enormous expenses, and if mama had not taken with her 65 rubles as a reserve we would have had to cable papa. The journey to Warsaw was terrible: for until the last train change, we were seated in the only second-class car.

64. 15th June 1901

The car was so terribly crowded that our things were piled up on the floor of the car and we were sitting on them; an unbearable heat, a screaming infant, angry grumbling of women (we were traveling in a car for women), who certainly did not offer us a friendly welcome—all this enhanced the charm of our journey. With my sick feet I was unable to move and step out on the car's outdoors platform for a breath of fresh air. But I was not sad and laughed wholeheartedly at those angry little ladies, at the fat station master who found that there was enough room for everybody in the car, and at the comforts of our trip. At first, our fellow female travelers were sulking; finally they started laughing and it turned into a conversation. Then the women fell asleep and mama went out on the platform with Milochka and I remained completely alone. It was very, very trying to wait for the train change. However, this time we were lucky to get a whole compartment to ourselves and I, still affected by what we had just lived through, diligently guarded it against undesirable fellow travelers.

65. 25th June 1901

All night long we were the only ones sleeping in the compartment and mama was even a little bit afraid. In the morning, a young man whose nationality we were unable to guess, entered our compartment: it turned out that he was a Lett. As we were approaching Warsaw the weather got colder and finally it started to rain. I will not describe my impressions of Warsaw because I have too much to write about yet; I will only say that it was very hard on me due to family circumstances. After having spent there about five days we continued to Berlin. I wanted to see Berlin but it gave me the creeps to find myself among Germans who, as I heard, were not very friendly toward Russians. I was in an unusually excited state and anticipated something unusual. This state was becoming more pronounced the closer we were getting to Aleksandrov, that is to the frontier. And here a little trouble happened: unaware that passports are required at the frontier, mama had put hers away in one of the luggage baskets. When we arrived in Aleksandrov all the cars were locked down and we were visited by imposing persons wearing helmets and demanding passports. The car fell immediately silent, mama got agitated about the passport and Milochka, ready to start crying, was fearfully clinging to me and eyeing the visitors with great curiosity; and I myself could not figure out what was happening to me: I was either very gay or miserable; I felt unusually daring, I wished something terrible should happen, I laughed and was getting ready to face it. Mama soon found the passport but then another trouble occurred: after changing trains it turned out that traveling abroad required Milochka to have half a ticket. While mama went to buy the ticket the chief conductor announced that he would hold the train, but as mama had already bought the ticket and was coming back, he blew his whistle. Mama thought that the train was already moving, became terrified and started running toward us. I started screaming, because I was afraid that something might happen to mama due to fright, and Milochka started crying. Naturally, our screams attracted a crowd of curious people; however, this is not interesting. But there was no end in sight to our "unhappy adventures": when mama was running toward us she lost the luggage receipt, and since we had to undergo a luggage inspection in Thorn [now Polish Toruń], we were faced with a big inconvenience and the fear of losing our basket. Luckily, we were approached by a very polite gentleman who went to the luggage room and arranged that mama should be issued the basket, of course, provided mama would tell beforehand what was in it. Without this man's intervention mama would have had to wait till they inspected everyone's luggage. This way we were the first to be inspected. The inspection turned out to be so thorough that they did not even touch the things we had with us in the wagon and were content with our answer that we did not carry anything that was prohibited. When all the excitement was over I started looking around our car, reading all that was written, looking out of the window, and singing songs. Nobody except Milochka could sleep because there was not enough room.

In the morning we arrived in Berlin at the Friedrichstrasse station which is where we were supposed to arrive. I have not seen anything like this before. A magnificent two story train station, and the main thing is that above the train is running on the roofs and below is the luggage, etc. The walls of the upper train station are made up of small, fine, multicolored glass windows; everywhere there was extraordinary cleanliness and wonderful architecture. Berlin is a big, clean and [sumptuous?] city with asphalt roads, broad streets and most luxurious buildings. But most of all I liked the little Germans themselves. Lovely people: agile, helpful, gay and, by no means stupid. Had we been in Rostov in a similar situation, that is without knowing any street or any restaurant, we would have certainly been exhausted from hunger and fatigue before we found anything. But here when you address a little German he will take you under his wing, will ask detailed questions about everything, will show and explain everything. When one is in trouble, they all will share it with so much warm sympathy and all will be ready to help. We stayed at the Berlin hotel Wiesbadener Hof that was recommended to us by a gentleman who, in his own words, knows Berlin like "his own pocket."

66. 1st July 1901

This is really a very sumptuous hotel: firstly, such cleanliness, so that I did not succeed when I tried to dirty the soles of my new shoes and rubbed them on the floor in order to pass them without paying duty. On the third floor we got a room for five marks with laundry service and clean linens every day and with plush furniture. Moreover, the chamber maid we got was a very nice girl whom mama even wanted to take back with her to Rostov; she herself manages the entire hallway and keeps all the rooms remarkably clean; moreover, she is an educated girl, like all the Germans. In the evenings we had conversations with her and learned many interesting things.

67. 2nd June [should be July] Monday 1901

We stayed on the Neustädtische Kirchenstrasse, not far from the train station, but far from city center and God only knows where their city center is. A few times we needed to use Berlin cabs which are very expensive and very original. Each cab is equipped with a taximeter that is a tablet which, as it travels and wheels are turning, pops up to show the amount that has to be paid. The one thing I do not like is that the coachmen are dressed up in top hats and gloves which gives them the appearance of a truly trained little monkey.

68. 6th June [July] 1901

In general, in places in Germany and Austria we visited, dogs often carry out the work of horses: dogs transport heavy loads and sometimes people ride dogs. I should also add that in Berlin we didn't go anywhere either because of rain or lack of time or because we were going from store to store to buy what was necessary. Everywhere in Berlin prices are astonishingly low. The stores are enormous and luxurious; for example, there are those like "Wertheim" and "Herzog" where you can get anything a person might need[40]. They occupy entire enormous buildings and always have many customers. I cannot say anything more about Berlin because we only spent two days there. From Berlin we took the express train to Karlsbad [today Karlovy Vary].

The way to Karlsbad was quite interesting apart from the picturesqueness of nature: houses of German design, tall with pointed tiled roofs, are located below so that railroad tracks run above allowing trains to pass. Many little houses, as if toys, are buried in verdure and all around leading up to them are very clean

40 Sabina describes department stores established at that time also in other major modern cities like London, Paris, and New York.

stairs or pathways. In open spaces adjacent to the houses there are little gardens and flower beds, even with little fountains and multicolored spheres. I wanted to find out what kind of crops grow in their fields but the train was traveling too rapidly. Here the peasants are dressed up like all men, clearly without frock coats but seemingly wearing sashes, but in this respect peasant women resemble our peasant women. I was particularly struck by the fact that women do the same work as men do, they dig in mountains, carry heavy loads, work in the fields, etc.

At the frontier, probably in Bodenbach, they were supposed to search the luggage traveling with us in the car, but the inspection of the basket was postponed until we reached Karlsbad. Here I found out that an inspection would probably be done, as we say in Russia, in a slipshod manner, but as an added precaution we put on all the new clothes we had bought in Berlin, and the books I had bought I held in my hands, because Mrs. Feldman had told me that they do not check hand luggage; and Milochka loaded herself with her toys. Then men came in and told mama to untie our things (they would not do it themselves). Then they asked us if we were carrying tea. Then I answered that we did not bring any from Russia and we would not drink German tea even if it were free; that what we have is only sausage and candies and we could treat them to some. That was all they wanted and left. In Karlsbad they did not search our basket at all because mama was laughing.

Karlsbad was not how I had imagined it: I thought it was a little settlement of villas like Borzhom but with nature not as beautiful as in Borzhom; it turned out that it was a whole city with four and five story tall houses, stores, big hotels, restaurants and even with such luxurious medical institutions as Kaiserbad, where there are bathtubs, treatments with electricity, massage, and Swedish gymnastics, the drawing of which and the purpose I have on my little poster. In Karlsbad we first stayed at the hotel "Rossiya" and then we found

69. 7th July 1901

an apartment in the "Kaiser Wilgelm" [Wilhelm] on the fourth floor with an elevator for 24 gulden per week. The first few days were difficult for me, but then I got used to it. We also made some acquaintances, but more about it later. With its constant dreary weather, Karlsbad makes a painful impression on a person not used to it, all the more so since we had to stay indoors till we got used to this raw weather. In front of our building there was a big mountain with paths and signs at the crossroads so that even a very small child that could read would be able unaided reach a trip's destination. On the way there are many restaurants so that one can eat something if the trip is very long. In any case, such paths are everywhere in Germany and Austria and it is forbidden to walk on grass. Well, generally speaking, what rules do we have in our gardens, it's only here that there is a lush wild nature, wonderful air, and cleanliness. We were climbing up "our mountain" in the direction of the "Drei Kreuzberg [Dreikreuzberg] der Kronprinzessin Stephanie Warte" [three-cross-mountain of crown princess S. W.], and on the way we stopped now and then and gazed at the town that seemed to be buried in verdure and looked very lovely among the mountains. And also here we came across a glade with a castle and a gravestone workshop. Not far from our hotel "Kaiser Wilhelm" there are the two restaurants where we had our meals: "Hotel Post" and "Goldener Löwe" [golden lion]. As far as the first hotel is concerned, I liked it very much and in particular its garden; I had nothing against it and enjoyed my meals there; the second one was not always remarkable for the tidiness of its food. There I was terribly irritated by the canary twittering the same disgusting song everyday, as well as by a fat pug and an old head waiter with bulging blood-shot eyes. I do not know whether in Rostov it is the practice for both waiters and boys to serve at their own expense [i.e., only for tips].

70. 9th July 1901

At Hotel Post, in closed rooms, there are women servants i.e. girls whom men are not shy to pat on the cheek in the presence of others; in general, the Germans are a free people: married people sit close next to each other and express to each other signs of mutual and most tender love; the feeling of shame is much less developed in them than in us Russians; in a dress store women stand before men in their underskirts; in the presence of women men take off their frock coats if they are too tight; husband and wife bathe in the same bathtub, men massage women, etc. To some degree I even like such lack of embarrassment. At the same time the feeling of spousal fidelity is very rarely violated among Germans; a person guilty in this respect is liable to a three month prison term.

71. 10th July 1901

In general, Germans are very conscientious in fulfilling social duties toward individuals and society. They are all very honest, take each other's word for it, and treat each person with equal respect, courtesy, and instant readiness to do a good turn; a person has the right to think and say what he or she wants; in general, this is what is called personal freedom. The following fact is of interest: when mama, a complete stranger, went to see a dentist named Schild to place an order for teeth and wanted to give him a down payment, the doctor felt offended and said that in such a case one would have to consider all people cheats if one could not take their word for it. I am especially pleased that here everyone has to go to school from the age of 6 to 14; and he who is not particularly interested in studying can attend a so-called "Bürger Schule" [Bürgerschule school for practical professions] that offers a reduced program but still for the duration of eight years. How pleasant it is when there is no dividing mankind into simple folks and lords and everybody is treated equally. When we were leaving Karlsbad the elevator man held his hand out to mama; cabbies and servants were quite at ease asking us where we were from, what was the purpose of coming here, they wanted to know how we were, etc.; Gogol[41] is, indeed, right when he says a German will never understand all the subtleties of how Russians treat each other.

72. 13th July 1901

I cannot write because I have no ink. They [illegible]

73. Austria 15th July1901

Germans are taught courtesy from childhood on: all day long you hear nothing but *Guten Tag* [good day] and *küsse die Hand* [kiss your hand]. Recently I have read an article in the paper that Russians grasp foreign languages more easily than all other nations; but in my opinion this is still a big question. Germans, Frenchmen and Englishmen can speak perfectly all the mentioned languages and with the best accent; but as far as the Russian language is concerned, it shows a complete contrast to all three in pronunciation. I have noticed that here tiny children at first swallow the sounds of consonants and pronounce only the vowels greatly prolonging them, especially before the letter *r*, which grown-ups also pronounce softly; on the other hand, our small children prolong the accented vowels and pronounce the rest unclearly, for the most part incorrectly, and even combining them with superfluous consonant sounds. I have noticed that in words ending with a consonant the Germans pronounce more or less clearly only the last one but do not finish the preceding sound, similar to the French silent *e*; and that the German *i*, not *ie* and not in the beginning of the word, sounds harsh and abrupt; and the letter *n* before a *g* has a somewhat nasal sound; and word endings are predominantly soft whereas we pronounce them the other way around, it is impossible to enumerate everything.

41 Gogol, Nikolai Vasilievich, 1809–1852, writer, the father of realism in Russian literature, author of *Dead Souls* and the play *Inspector General.*

74. 16th July 1901

As far as these features are concerned, the Russian and German languages show a complete contrast. 1) At the very least, I have never met a Russian speaking German who could fake being a German, let alone the fact that based on pronunciation I can always tell a Russian from a German. However, Russians do not notice how abominably they pronounce German words, similar to Germans expressing themselves in Russian who do not understand how they distort our words even when their grammar is correct. 2) On the other hand, the Russian language is notable for countless, most diverse endings, which, moreover, are not pronounced the way they are written. 3) In no other language have I found so many irregular accents as in Russian. I will cite as an example a number of disyllabic nouns ending with the accented letter *a,* for example, [water]: i[ndicative] *vodà,* g[enitive] *vodý,* d[ative] *vodé,* a[ccusative] *vódu*...[sister] indicative *sestrá,* genitive *sestrý*, dative *sestré*, vocative *sestrū*...[hand] indicative *ruká*, vocative *rūku*... [leg] *nogá*, vocative *nógu*... indicative [bag] *sumá*, vocative *sumū* etc. The trisyllabic irregular words are even more difficult for a foreigner. Finally, do you want to see more? Even Poles, who easily grasp foreign languages, are unable to adjust to Russian, even though the latter is a language related to theirs. Even children of Germans can perfectly speak French, English, and in rare cases even Polish, but not Russian. Considering all this, one can only show that speaking Russian is significantly more difficult than the four aforementioned languages. But in any case, it does not follow that Russians grasp foreign dialects more quickly than other nations. Well, all right, this is too long a subject for a diary! I will omit mentioning French because I know too little about it.

75. 18th July 1901

I am now continuing. Karlsbad is a city with asphalt roadways and electrical lighting. All city employees, like mail carriers or messengers, ride around on bicycles; automobiles are also widely used (apparently you can hire those for about two gulden an hour); using dogs for transporting heavy loads is also very much in vogue here; in addition to taximeters local cab drivers fasten poles to carriages, similar to those fastened to our horsecars, to be used for instant stopping because narrow streets are hung with signs saying "*schrittfahren*" [drive slowly] and violators have to pay heavy fines. Instead of horsecars, which are not seen here, people ride buses and streetcars (small cars on oversize wheels). These omnibuses make stops and are always jam-packed; some omnibuses have an upper level used only for luggage, and are sometimes accessible by climbing small stairs.

76. 19th July 1901

On the second day of our arrival in Karlsbad mama invited Dr. Rosenzweig. This doctor, a friend of uncle Adolf, has lived in Warsaw for 12 years and speaks Russian perfectly; he is a big "dandy in a top hat." He is very jovial and likes to joke. It is remarkable that all Germans generally excel in their joviality and vivaciousness; they overflow with good spirits and good health; here it is amazing that everyone knows how to settle even on the most meager means and enjoy every minute of life; pleasures that are positively free compared to ours. For example, for 60 crowns per person, we went to the "*Stadtpark*" [city park] to see the "*Deutsches Sommerfest*" [German summer festival], how much pleasure we got for these 60 crowns i.e., 48 kopecks! The entire park was illuminated and the whole river glittered with the bright light of lampions; wonderful concerts of really original and typical music; various solos, duets, and quartets, etc. I particularly liked the harp sextet and playing the xylophone. I thought that the xylophone was a kind of trumpet but it turned out to be a keyboard instrument which had to be struck with little hammers. But with what dexterity and flawlessness did the artist perform the most difficult variations on this instrument and at an unusually fast tempo! I have never heard such tender, wonderful music. Then the park was illuminated with Bengal lights that were blazing up between the branches in many different colors which gave the park a completely magical appearance, enhanced by the sounds of music. And how wonderful the countryside is! No charming corner of nature is left unused, paths lead to each of them, and each has a shelter.

77. 21st July 1901

Of all the out-of-town places I like most is the one called "Hans Hailing"[42] where a rapid stream flows between steep rocky mountains in the midst of verdure. Actually, the rocks called Hans Hailing signify a petrified wedding. About the latter there is the following myth: a young man fell in love with a mermaid and was expected to marry her; but soon the empty-headed man became unfaithful to her and wished to marry another girl; the very same moment the wedding party and musicians were passing by the river where the mermaid lived, she emerged from the water and changed the bride and the musicians into rocks.

42 Hans Heiling rocks (Svatoš rocks), in the Loket national park, Czech Republic.

78. 25th July 1901

Such a little locality deserves to be described in detail but there is no time for it. So I continue. Dr. Roz[enzveig] prescribed for mama treatments in Kaiserbrunn and Mühlbrunn. I have a drawing of the Mühlbrunn colonnade, so that I do not need to linger to describe it. Like everybody else mama bought for herself a little cup on a small strap and a tube for drinking the mineral waters, as these are too hot to drink straight. On some cups there are portraits of Karlsbad doctors but mama did not buy any because she did not know about such. Obviously, countless people come here to drink the Karlsbad waters. People come here from all corners of the world; however, as I was told, I did not meet here any "eccentric" persons with enameled or golden teeth. But I have seen a lot of eccentricity even in the smart clothes of children, completely dressed up to look like little lapdogs, but that does not interest me at all. It is very difficult to write after such a long time: you cannot know what happened earlier, what later, and that is why I will try to get done as quickly as possible with Karlsbad.

Before long, Milochka and I started going to Kaiserbad to do Swedish gymnastics: Milochka simply to develop her muscles and I to get treatments for my stomach and hand and standing straight. I can recommend this establishment to everyone without reservation, as I became convinced of the real benefits of this treatment. There was an enormous well-lit exercise hall with masses of machines, where, in addition to specially trained female attendants, the exercises were also observed by a number of doctors. I was able to appreciate this wonderful arrangement after I had visited a similar establishment here in Aussee that belongs to Dr. Schreiber: a little hovel with strings and sticks. In addition, the difference in price was unbelievable: in Karlsbad a week costs 10 gulden (8 rubles), 20 days—25 gulden, and in Aussee each day costs 3.5 gulden. And the best part of Karlsbad is in the vicinity of Hotel Pupp, which we always used to pass on our way to gymnastics. I think the only people who live here are either the richest dandies or unsophisticated people, who accidentally end up here because the rooms here are positively worth their weight in gold, and year-round stores attract lots of ladies buying clothes of "the newest fashion," because those are so expensive. Passing by Pupp is the omnibus route to Kaiserpark, and from there to Pirkenhammer, where we exited the park in order to visit the porcelain factory. But due to the Russian habit of not paying attention to time, we came there on Sunday and found the factory was closed, so we had to make do with bestowing our presence on the local restaurant. Even though nature here is gorgeous, it pales in comparison with "Hans Hailing". People come here mainly to look at the factory.

All right, I am done with Karlsbad. We are going to Vienna. I will make note of two little habits of all Germans and their Austrian "friends": to say "*danke bestens*" [thank you very much] and "*bitte schön*" [you're welcome]. The expressions "*gnädige Frau*" [milady], "*küsse die Hand*" [kiss your hand] and "*habe die Ehre*"[have the honor] are only used in Austria. We were very glad to leave Karlsbad.

I liked the way to Vienna very much, especially beautiful was the Danube at night, the sight of which overwhelmed me with a feeling of something native, something close to me. After passing through an endless number of Viennese train stations we finally reached the "*Franz Josef Bahn,*"[43] which is where we needed to arrive. Numerous lit up restaurants were glittering close to the Danube amidst the night darkness; the noise and thumping [illegible] immediately startled me. However, as a result, I again forgot an accident with our ill-fated basket, which seriously ruined our mood as we were entering Vienna. The thing is that after the "Karlsbader Cur" [the Karlsbad treatment], mama felt so poorly that until the last moment she did not know whether to travel directly to Aussee or via a detour in Vienna in order to visit the professor[44]. Finally, when we arrived at the train station with all our luggage, mama decided to do the latter; it is clear that in such a state of mind, mama was unable to handle the basket, and I was busy with Milochka, and that is why the basket was left behind at the Karlsbad train station. It is self-evident that losing such a basket, which contained all our traveling belongings and even mama's diamonds, could not but take a toll on our peace of mind, and all the more so since she could not remember the number of the porter and thus make a claim that the basket had been left at the train station. Everybody was trying to reassure us that the basket could not get lost, that a porter caught even in the smallest theft is liable to a three year jail term; they finally tried to prove that even wallets with money that had been left behind in a railway car were always returned to their owners. Of course, a cable was sent from the train requesting the delivery of the forgotten basket to Vienna. Finally, the basket arrived in Vienna, but the two days of searching and worrying had left their mark. Had such a loss really happened, it would have disappeared forever...

Vienna is indeed beautiful in the center where there is a lot to see, but since we hope to visit Vienna again, I will now only describe "Wenedig [Venice]." Wenedig is a park on the Praterstrasse [Prater road] where a little money can buy

43 Actually Franz-Josefs-Bahnhof or station.

44 Presumably Professor Freud.

lots of various pleasures. There is a mill illuminated with red lights, an operetta, various concerts, dances of Little Russia and Spain, donkey and camel rides, but the best of all is the "*Rutschbahn*," a colossal Ferris wheel hung with many cars. This wheel is set in motion by one man sitting and pressing on wooden boards with his feet; all this is based on the power of water. Suffice it to say, when a car was very high up above the city the sight was exhilarating. Vienna seemed to be awash in a sea of light which harmonized especially at night with the Danube and with numerous jutting out tiny buildings. I will not touch upon the "*Kunsthistorisches Hof Museum*" [Vienna Imperial Art Museum], as I am leaving for Aussee. On the way there we saw so many combinations of nature's beauty that the sights which had delighted me previously did not captivate me anymore. Here there were the highest mountains, rapid rivers and raging rivulets, forests, glades, old castles, statues, picturesque hamlets, villas; briefly, whatever was your heart's desire. Most of all, I remember the Traunsee [See = lake] with its calm, mirror-like and pensively green water: it is located high up in the mountains and surrounded by the most charming little houses; then we saw a mountain that looked like the sleeping Greek princess, and numerous tunnels through which reached Aussee, completely blackened by soot. Aussee is a small town or rather a little hamlet in Styria (*Salzkammergut*). Many people say that this is the most picturesque place in Europe, a little Switzerland. Aussee is divided into Markt-Aussee and Alt-Aussee, the latter bordered by a lake carrying the same name; on the other side of Markt-Aussee is the Grundelsee, and behind it the Töplitzsee and, finally, Kammersee (*Salzkammergut*). This whole place is surrounded by chains of the highest mountains and is bathed in verdure, mainly pinewoods; it is carved by raging streams; briefly, a continuation of what I had described above. The climate here, as in any other mountainous places, is very changeable; it is always so foggy in the morning that you cannot see any trace of the mountains. Sunny weather can suddenly change into a storm and the other way around. At least during our stay here it rained just every day and once it even rained nonstop for two days and two nights. In general, the climate here is very healthy and rainy weather does not discourage Germans, hardened from childhood on to practice their daily "*Ausflucht* " [an excuse, a play on the word *Ausflug* , an excursion]. The population of Aussee is extremely mixed but clearly Austrians and Germans are the vast majority. In Aussee we stayed at the hotel Kauders Villa in the midst of a pine forest; next to our villa to this day is located the "*Ausseer Radfahrer Klub*" [cycling club] (in the Praunfalk Park). During the very short stay there we made a great acquaintance of many men-servants and cabbies who showed great pleasure in conversing with us.

But to tell the truth, during the first one and a half to two weeks we were terribly bored, in spite of such pleasant company, but as time passed we made the acquaintance of our German neighbors named Schwarz who were very kind to us. Mr. Schwarz, having found out that mama wanted to make a "*Rundreise*" [circle boat ride], spent many hours to procure her a ticket, displaying the most amazing knowledge of the smallest sights of his country. Not only this gentleman but all Germans know their homeland inside out. Later a Russian dokhtur [mocking spelling] from Perm, whom we met accidentally in Dr. Schreiber's waiting room, latched on to us; later on, accompanied by the Russian doctor, I attended a charitable festivity held at the "*Alpenheim*" (Kuranstalt = sanatorium); this happened because mama had bought two tickets and because of Milochka mama could not attend, and the extra ticked was given to the doctor. The festivity was wonderful, but what amazed me most was *Schnellmalerei*, speed painting, executed by Dr. Schreiber's daughter as follows: during an eight bar song plus a short refrain, which was very brief, she was able to depict with great accuracy various characters and scenes; I was amazed how she was instantly able to make a picture of her elderly father with his hair, his tired appearance, wearing his usual broad-rimmed hat and overcoat. Moreover, it was pleasant to see the genuinely hearty laughter of the audience which finally became so unusually enthusiastic that the laughter and the applause drowned out everything else.

Perhaps I will add something else later but now there is something more interesting. We are now back in Berlin, staying at the same hotel on the second floor instead of the third. Berlin felt like something native in spite of the previous rumors that Germans are hostile to Russians. True, a Berliner is serious, meticulous, he does not like unnecessary loquaciousness and cannot stand Russian disorderliness. But it doesn't follow that a Berliner cannot be helpful and cheerful toward Russians. Their consciousness of national pride and attachment to their homeland, is, I believe, much more developed than even in Austria, which one can detect instantly by the speaking and bearing of each one of them...

79. 19th November 1901

I am now a student in the famous 6a class that became notorious in the entire gymnasium for its bad behavior and, at same time, which is quite strange, for its very good accomplishments (not to speak ill of madam Sukhanova and company). Let me examine this strange phenomenon in an orderly fashion. Let me begin with the day when we, the girls, settled down in the 6a class and were faced with a very unpleasant surprise: instead of the former good supervisor E.P. Rashevskaia, whom we had in the 5th and 4th grade, we were met by Lida A. Kolunova, according to hearsay an outright loathsome person. We felt desperate and having decided to get rid of her without fail, we went to E.P. to ask her advice how to do it most skillfully. E.P. got red in the face as if she were the guilty one, and strongly urged us not to go to the headmistress with this request, and not to rebel because anyway nothing good would come of it. We yielded: as a matter of fact, the headmistress would have gotten angry and perhaps Lida was not as loathsome as people were saying. Who knows? Perhaps all this was nonsense?...

80. 28.3.1901

Essay of 28th March 1901 dedicated to mama on her birthday

The day was raw and rainy. The city became empty and gloomy; the wind was raging angrily, mercilessly jerking the risk-takers who dared to be outdoors during such a tempestuous state of nature. Everybody stayed locked up in their homes or hid wherever possible. In a small, dilapidated dugout a sad old man was sitting at a table laden with books, sadly absorbed in deep thoughts; in the corner, behind the oven, his little grandson was telling his little sister scary tales about beech trees and witches. The old man was reminiscing about his entire life: he was the son of poor parents but from childhood on he showed a great passion for chemistry. The parents, aware of their resources, tried to dissuade the boy from such a "folly" so that he would be able to earn his own daily bread. But all their arguments only produced the opposite effect, inflaming his passion more intensely. In high school the boy devoted himself completely to reading books and making experiments in his beloved profession, dreaming how much good he will bring people with his knowledge. After graduating from high school, in spite of mother's entreaties and father's threats, the young man decided to apply to a university department of chemistry, saying that he was sacrificing family peace for the sake of science. However, before long, the father made peace with his son and the youth, thanks to moneys sent him by his parents, and supplemented by income he earned by giving lessons, was able to continue his education. The professor could not praise him enough and foretold him a glorious future. But good fortune cannot last forever; the youth was visited by a blow that had an effect on his entire life: he received news about the death of his father and the illness of his mother who demanded his presence. One can imagine how this affected the son! He took care of his mother for three years and when they ended, she died in his arms. The young man became almost insane, unable to fathom what was happening to him, he ruined his health so much that his friends had to force him to take the water cure. Having stayed in the spa for almost a year in a semi-conscious state the patient improved thanks to his neighbor, a young girl who took pity on the unhappy man and ministered to him with maternal tenderness. He fell in love passionately with his woman savior and from then on improved rapidly. A little later, due to the usual emotions between people in love, they were married. Having become a husband, it was necessary to take the trouble of satisfying life's needs; the idea of graduating from the university became unfeasible, so that he got a job as an official in a government department. The good wife, knowing the passion of her husband and realizing that he sacrificed his dream for her sake, undertook to work sparing no effort to earn money and buy for her husband books and necessary accessory items to study chemistry. Two years later a daughter was born to the happy parents. The father doted on the child and devoted all his free time to her. As the girl grew up, the father developed in her emotions of altruism: he taught her to see herself as part of the mechanism of life that must act for the common good, disregarding one's own feelings, because one's personal feelings perish with a person's death, whereas traces left for the benefit of the common organism will not be erased. Father's words were not spoken in vain. True, at first the child understood them poorly, but the closer she reached the age of a young girl, she pondered them more often, understood their deep meaning, that made possible turning thoughts into deeds. The daughter grew up, then married; and before her father knew it, he was a grandfather of three grandchildren. And suddenly a new terrible disaster visited the father from which the poor man has not been able to recover until now. For quite some time he had in mind to submit to the judgment of his adored professor his essay on chemistry, which he wanted to dedicate to people thirsting for knowledge; but he had not been able to make up his mind to travel to see him. When he visited the professor, he was in seventh heaven: the essay exceeded all his expectations and the professor noted that he had not placed his hopes on such a talented student in vain. Our hero took [no] money for his work, true to his goal and obligation to serve science for free. And at the same moment as this noble man was speeding to get home in this happy mood, terrible news stopped him in his tracks: an outbreak of cholera killed his wife, daughter, husband, and granddaughter. This news hit the old man like a bolt from the blue: he was hit by a severe and prolonged illness during which his grandchildren were cared for by friends. No sooner than he recovered that he had to take care of feeding the orphans and paying off debts incurred by his treatment.

For the last year the old man has been living in the dugout where we met him and working as a teacher in the village school: white-haired, hunch-backed, sick, and having to care for two grandchildren. The old man thought about this subject for a long time. All of a sudden he heard a tender voice saying "papa." "Papa, what are you sad about?" asked the voice again, in which he recognized his daughter. The poor man burst out sobbing, moved by a feeling of self-pity and he bared his whole soul to his daughter, how all alone he had become, old and sickly despite all the good he had created all around. "Papa," said the daughter again, "have you forgotten what you had told me when, sat on your lap as a child? Have you forgotten that one has to give oneself wholly to an idea, without regard to personal feelings?" "My child, I am weak, I am old, my death is near," exclaimed the father, "how terrifying this is!" "No, my dear, this is not terrifying, you are weak but your spirit is not weak; you are old but your spirit is young; you will die but the good seed sown by you will never die and will surely leave a trace in the collective idea. Act as much as your strength allows and disseminate the luminous thought you have implanted in me, in your grandchildren, and in the young people surrounding you. Offer all of yourself, as you did in bygone days!" Having said this the daughter disappeared. For a long time the old man followed her with his eyes; he became ashamed of his faintheartedness; he thought hard over his daughter's words as she had thought in the old days. His face shone more and more. "Grandpa, what are you crying about? The sun is so bright, look how good it is! Why are you sad?" The old man started. The granddaughter threw her chubby little arm around his neck. Indeed, the sun was bright, the sky was radiantly blue with little white clouds; on the grass and the trees sparkled the still wet little tears of rain; everything sparkled and rejoiced. It also felt alright and bright in grandfather's soul. For the first time in the aftermath of his disaster he covered his grandchildren with kisses, and resolutely standing up straight he murmured: "No, grandpa will not be sad anymore, grandpa is still capable of taking care of himself for the sake of society; gone is the spook that confounded me; the old grandpa is back!" And the face of the old man shone with a noble and proud benevolence.

81. 9th August 1902

A composition (a little scene of life)

It was about 4 o'clock. The car was dusty and stuffy; the train was barely moving; the passengers exhausted by the long journey were either sleeping or dozing off sitting, swaying from side to side as if drunk; only at one window a rather lively conversation was going on between a young girl and an elderly lady; the young girl appeared to have a fresh complexion, her attractive little face strongly marked by childlike naiveté was flushed, the black eyes were shining as if she was getting ready to take a fateful step. "Please, tell me," her companion, a brown haired woman about 45 years old, kept exclaiming admiringly: "You're such a young girl and traveling all by yourself to a distant country to study. And you know, as strange as it may seem, there are sometimes people who are instantly attractive to one; as soon as I saw you, I immediately felt a liking toward you, dear girl, don't you believe me? I give you my word of honor. It is true. I told the same to my husband: What a lovely girl is standing at the window, isn't she, Pol?" – "You are right," answered a deep low baritone voice. – "But how can you pay me such compliments if you don't know me at all?" – "Oh, my dear, you are still so inexperienced; in a good person goodness is inscribed in the face. You remind me of all my youth: I myself, as I recall now, was then so trusting, affectionate, so eager to learn, to be useful, to help all the oppressed; sometimes, like you, when in the street, I would see a woman wiping her eyes with a handkerchief, so help me God, I would not be able to go by without offering her something. And how they took advantage of me because of that! While a student I would arrive at the university with a full trunk and come back home like a pauper. I would give everything away to various starving people who would use my money to drink and have a good time and I would be sitting at home freezing without dinner with my teeth chattering. That is how it was, young lady! Yes, life will teach you everything; you cannot be too good if you yourself want to live; and you will perish, mark my words, you will perish if you do not change. For example, this morning you gave three rubles to that old woman and I can guarantee you anything that the whole story she told you about herself was nothing but a fat lie from beginning to end." – "Oh, why do you think this way; you can't get into a person's mind. Is it not possible that she really had no money to travel to see her dying mother? This is terrible! No, I rather throw away three rubles than that it should turn out that I refused to help such an unfortunate woman. If I want to serve all mankind, I cannot refuse help to an individual irrespective whether I succeed there or not while here a live human was already dying. No, no, I was obliged to give her!" – "Yes, don't get excited, my dear. I do not want to dissuade you; you will live and you will see that I am not a cruel person, I give a fair amount to committees and various charitable purposes, and if you believe somewhat in the importance of culture and progress, you'll understand that it is sometimes necessary that individuals should suffer for the common good: that by giving alms to every female beggar you develop in the people a carelessness and a loathing toward work and..." – "Masha, we will soon be changing trains, you forgot you need to arrange the things and that it is time to wake up Seriozha," bellowed the basso profundus [deep bass] of Pol, the lady's husband. – "Yes, indeed, I really got carried away chatting with you, my dear girl, but do not forget, visit me in St. Petersburg without fail, make sure you do not lose my address. And what is your name and patronymic, miss?" Pol interrupted again. – "Oh, how absentminded of me! Until this moment I did not realize I forgot to ask with whom I had spent such a pleasant time!" said the amazed wife. –"My name is Revekka Samuilovna Bornshtein." – "This is impossible, you must be joking," smiled the lady and a sudden light pallor appeared on her face. – "Why do you think that I am joking?" – "Yes, but this is not a Russian name. What kind of name is it?" – "This is a Jewish name. Yes, it is a Jewish name and I am a Jewess" the girl stood up erect and proud. – "I don't believe it! You are Greek, Italian, Armenian, just not a Jewess!" – "It is pointless for you to think that: I give you my word of honor that I really am a Jewess" asserted Revekka Samuilovna once more. Thereupon the expression on the lady's face changed instantly, the little sweet smile turned into a contemptuous grimace, she turned to her husband and whispered with disgust: "Pol, she really is a Jewess!"

POEMS

82. 10.06.1897–07.1901
    For her little tiny chicks
    Mother craved to give her life.
    Misfortune hit! Perfidious fate
    Denied her having any chicks.
    Now she roams the world entire,
    But cannot find her chicks.

83. X 1904
    Empty, gloomy, and cold,
    Empty and gloomy all around.
    You are alone in the world,
    You are completely alone.
    There is no father,
    There is no mother,
    There is no shelter of one's own.
    There is nobody to tell one's thoughts to.
    My head,
    My little tired head,
    Nobody to bow to.
    My poor heart,

My broken heart,
Why do you pound so anxiously
And so plaintively, so painfully?
Gloomy expectations
And disturbing frights.
Oh, my youth is gone,
Oh, my life has perished.
[below under the drawings]
Spielrein

84. 25 X 04
People do not like
When one whines endlessly.
One should be friendly.
And make them happy.
My soul is so cold,
Black and dark.
My throat is choking with tears.
Never mind.
One has to be goody-goody,
Not to be reputed as wrathful.
Stupid life,
My bitter life.

85. Undated

This happened on a wonderful moonlit winter night. We were climbing a mountain through fresh snowdrifts. Our black long shadows stood out against the bluish snow. On the right down below we saw a lake covered with a hazy fog through which the lights of the houses twinkled faintly. The lake was amidst mountains that looked either silvery, or bluish, or dark blue depending on location and height. The sky's edges were covered with dark clouds that, especially in one place, formed dense narrow rows remarkably reminiscent of wrinkles. Ahead of us there was a dense forest all covered with brightly glistening snow. There was a light frost; the air was fresh and biting. Not a soul to be seen. Dead silence all around. The crunch of our treads sounded like something impertinent, defiant. But that was what we needed, we felt with our whole being that we were young, it was breathtaking, making our heart pound; we were eager to discharge the excess of energy, we pined for secret terrifying adventures, we wanted romp and daring, and we wanted to throw down the gauntlet to aloof and majestic mother nature. We enter the forest. Ah!

The snowdrifts are above the knees. "ee/ee/ee, ai" – squeaks one of the young ladies and stops short – "I lost my galosh!' The voice is ringing, unusually melodious: "aaaa" softly repeats the echo. But people, especially young people, are remarkably heartless: "uaaaa," we keep teasing our poor little friend, splitting our sides with laughter. One perfidious person imperceptibly comes behind Ninochka and with all his might kicks the trunk of the nearest fir tree. Suddenly a whole snow avalanche lands on the poor girl's head, knocks off her hat and cold pieces of snow get under her collar. Ninochka, forgetting to look for her galosh, picks up her hat, gathers a heap of snow and runs after the prankster. But to no avail, there is no trace of him! "You just wait!" was all she could shout in self-consolation. We are delighted to arrange all kinds of "surprises" for each other. Without noticing it, we got farther and farther into the depths of the forest. "Hey, guys, isn't it time to go home?" asks a certain I., the I. whom we address by his name and patronymic in view of the "stoutness" of his body build. "Forward, forward!" We go farther.

Nature looks fantastic. I walk a little distance behind the rest of the people: I have a wish to daydream. Between the trees becomes clearly visible the figure of the forest king wearing a sparkling crown. Near him there is a whole crowd of various fairies in shining costumes. One of them stands sad, leaning against a tree, her eyes are downcast; she is holding something resembling a guitar; presently, quiet gentle sounds are heard, as if some person is singing, the heart breaking with pity. I come closer, I peer closely into the pale attractive face and she seems unusually congenial to me, someone of my people. She slowly lifts her eyes, with a weary movement of her hand she throws back her black flowing loose curls. This gaze pierces me through and through, as if the entire sorrow of mankind, the deep hidden suffering, and an unspoken reproach are all combined in it. Her lips are moving as if to say something, when all of a sudden the trenchant voice of the forest king is heard; like a shadow, the girl turns around and walks toward him. The king is sitting in a golden armchair, dressed in a sparkling green mantle, pale, immobile, frowning. In the distance the clatter of horse hooves is heard; I look around: a crowd of young knights, surpassing each other in the richness and color diversity of the garments. "Ho, ho, ho" they laugh. I want to see what impression this crowd has made on my fairy. I look around for her, but in vain. What the hell? She and the forest king disappeared and the knights hid somewhere! Instead of them I now see our group.

We decided to spend the night in a hut. A "hut on chicken feet[45]" flashed through my mind. And indeed this little "hut on chicken feet" turned out to be a small coaching inn, inside grayish and faded. The owner, as if on purpose, was a small one-eyed bony old woman. "The witch Baba Yaga, the bony leg:" to me she seemed very vicious, especially due to the peculiar reddish hue of her seeing eye. I communicate my impression to my companions; they laugh and complete the scene. The rag in the corner is a roasted child; the stool broken in the middle is a mortar; in the adjacent room somebody desperate is breathing heavily and moaning – this is the poor Ivanushka being roasted in a cauldron; he is exhausted, he cannot scream anymore, that is why his voice is so quiet, etc. But we were the exhausted ones. Only now did we begin to feel it. We were terribly wet and hungry. The group decided to have a supper first but I was no longer able to stand on my feet and chose to go to bed immediately. Moreover—and perhaps this was the main reason—I could not stop thinking about the wonderful fairy.

The room that was assigned to us, the three young ladies, was not particularly comfortable. It was a shabby room; the beds were arranged like in a hospital; nothing could be done about it. I decided that the best thing was to imagine that I am in the open air lying on sweet-scented hay. But this turned out to be too difficult, so I brought a three-legged stool and sat down by the open window. Strange, how warm it was! A soft breeze tousles my hair. A completely summer-like night! Everything around is so fantastic. The moon is broken by narrow, long clouds, the sky takes on a milky-bluish coloration. Stars keep disappearing and reappearing, only one stubborn star refuses to disappear even for one second. The window has a view over a small garden; one can feel the hot breath of earth and plants. Dimly-lit shapes of trees transport me far into to a world of fairy-tale monsters; a soft breeze plays with my hair, like the little nanny in the remote days of childhood; I see the kind, wrinkled face of the old woman leaning over me; I hear her quiet monotonous voice: "In a certain kingdom, in a certain realm there once lived a good princess..." A "burble-burble" is heard from the garden; this is a stream of water playing in the fountain; especially beautiful are the separate silvery drops. And now a lake in the distance! A strange boom is coming from there. It is not a lake, it is a boundless blue, blue sea. It is so blue that it hurts to look at it. In the middle of the sea there is a high and steep rock, dark and gloomy with yawning chasms; from each chasm is peeping out a head of some terrifying monster with fiery red eyes, enormous wings, and horrible claws. Thousands of

45 An allusion to the fairy-tale house of the witch Baba Yaga in a fairy tale.

snakes with shining multicolored scales are crawling on the steep rocks, opening their black maws, ejecting a long spiral tongue; they must be hungry and looking for prey. Clear and melodious sounds are heard coming from the crest of the rock; shadows are moving there; they become more and more visible. It is a crowd of girls all dressed in white, with flowing hair, pale and transparent ghosts. One of them emerges out of this crowd and languidly throws back her thick black curls. What a familiar gesture! The face is stern, pensive, and pale. The thin lips are tightly pressed together; the brows are frowning. The gaze is heavy [intense?] and so powerful that it is felt from an infinite distance. In her whole person one feels a tension, an incomprehensible inner struggle. Who is this wonderful girl? I must have met her somewhere... yes...true... it is the same forest fairy! Her name is Meri. How do I know that? God only knows, but for me it is a fact that I know her name for sure. She is saying something to me! I am enchanted by her deep, magical chest-voice and am therefore completely unable to grasp the meaning of her words. What is it! A wind blows across the sea; the sea is restless; the waves are turning into white foam. The boom is getting louder and louder. The sea is roaring, rushing like a wild, furious animal; the waves furiously pound the rock and with a groaning and thundering noise break down into billions of minutest sprays. The sky is black. Thunder is booming. Lightning is flashing. The girls have disappeared. Only Meri, all "bespattered by the storm's foam,"[46] standing alone on the rock and holding a burning torch in one hand and a guitar in the other. The wind is tearing at her hair and dress but she is standing there motionless, defiant, every now and then illuminated by lightning. Her eyes are transformed and sparkle with a feverish and piercing brilliance. It seems that she is ruling and commanding the storm. Her slender fingers are gliding on the strings of the guitar. A gentle and tremulous sound is distinctly heard. Meri leans her head back and sings. The sounds, at first even and sad, are becoming more and more thrilling and powerful. The voice is getting louder and overflows into a trill evocative of desperate, heart rending sobbing. As if the sorrow of mankind entire is embodied in these sounds, weighing upon the soul and unable be expressed. I began to wonder that Meri is not singing with words but differently however I understand what she is singing about. This happened many years ago. Meri, the unapproachable, proud princess, lives on that rock.

---

46 Possibly influenced by the first line of an untitled poem by Stepan Petrov Skitalets (1869–1941) published in 1902: "My life—this stormy night on the waves."

86. Undated

1.

[a man is speaking; lines crossed out by Sabina]
Do you remember, we were in the forest?
And we were looking for lilies of the valley,
The paths were overgrown with moss.
But we ~~were not dejected, we almost fell down~~.
I held your hand,
We ran quickly downwards.
Where did the madness lead us!
The wonderful time passed
I was in terrible hell
And you...you...in a madhouse!
This happened in early spring
We loved each other
~~The young moon shone on us~~
And the nightingales echoed us
We were both young
And we were gay,
Everything laughed with and was blooming
Brooks babbled to us
The sun shone brightly for us.
And little birds sang freely.

2.

[a woman is speaking]
I saw a little birch
She was bent down
A little birdie was singing
But it stopped singing.
The heart knew joys
But it forgot.
Why singing birdie did you fall silent?
Heart, why did get to know
Black grief?
Oh, they killed the birdie
The furious snowstorms.
They killed a fellow
With evil rumors.

The birdie should have flown
To the blue sea.
The fine fellow
Should have run away
Into the dense forest.
Far in the sea the waves are roaring
But not snowstorms.
In the forest there are cruel animals
But no people.
3.
On a clean field
On velvety meadows,
A little river flows.
A storm will come, a storm will pass
But it is always bright.
The storm will disturb it somewhat,
But it won't know it was a wave.
Neither groves nor leafy forests
On its little banks grow
But shrubs with azure flowers
Bloom there admiringly.
The little river meanders
Gliding on the peebles.
It gets lost in a little hole
And then it shines again.
She knows no decrease
But forever in all her beauty
Is grateful for any increase
From the heaven's dew.
But how long will the little river
Flow along the flowers?
The ocean's abysses
Are awaiting it in the misty distance
4.
There was once a little man, a poor little man
With a house full of children
But nothing in his barn or coop.
The children are squeaking

The need is squeezing him.
Oh, trouble, trouble, trouble!
Bitter trouble!
There was once a rich man
Who lived like a miser
The miser has a house full of silver
The miser sleeps on his coffer
With the key in his hand.
He wakes up every minute Fearing for his coffer
Oh trouble, trouble, trouble!
Bitter trouble!

87. 24.4.1905

The devil! The devil's child

As a matter of fact, it is unpleasant to ponder a new era of my life in such a stupid situation. The courses at the university start tomorrow but I am anticipating this blessed moment with a somewhat murderous melancholy. My head is splitting, nausea, weakness. I have no faith in my powers; I have no faith in anything. Junga [Russian variation on Jung] is rushing down the hall. Now he will barge into me: I need to hide the notebook so as not to show him what I am doing. Although why not show? The devil take it!

88. 25.4.05

What the devil! I was at the university. I have a pile of impressions but no patience at all to describe it. I was particularly impressed with zoology professor "Lange."[47] I was passionately interested but presently a reaction kicked in and my heart is heavy again! I cannot become friends with the students; I am closed off from them; what they will see is the cheerful, superficial side of my soul but its very depth will remain hidden from all. It is somehow impossible for me to open up to these children, I feel that I am much more solid, serious, critically developed, independent... But unfortunately, I'm still far from knowing whether I will be able to work scientifically: first, will my health permit it? And most importantly: will I be sufficiently capable? Meanwhile for me life without science is completely unthinkable. What else is left for me without science? To get married? But this thought fills me with dread: sometimes my heart aches so much,

47 Arnold Lang (1855–1914), Swiss professor of zoology and comparative anatomy at Zurich University.

I have a desire for tenderness and love, but this is only a deceptive, temporary, superficial splendor hiding the most pitiful prose. This alone is tantamount to an enslavement of the personality! And then there is emptiness and boredom as soon as the first moment of passion is over. No! I do not want such love: I want a good friend to whom I could bare every little trait of my soul; I want the love of an older man so that I would be loved the way parents love and understand their child (spiritual affinity[48]). However, between me and my parents it is as if nonexistent...This story is known all too well so there is no need to go into details. Well, if only I were as wise as my Junga! The devil! I want to know right away whether I will ever amount to anything. Moreover, it is silly that I am not a man: men get what they want much more easily. Besides, it is such chutzpa that everything in life is arranged for them. And I do not want to be a slave!

89. 8.VI.05

Why such an oppression, such a heaviness in my soul? I am all alone in the whole world. There is nobody around me. Strange how all people are so shallow, for example, today one young lady affirmed that hard drinking and depravity are caused by either poverty or wealth. "Unfortunate paupers drink and are debauched due to distress while vulgar rich men drink due to satiety and prosperity," they do not know what to do with their time. Other causes do not exist for her. In general, opinions of this kind are as childish, as I was capable of thinking when I was in the 5th grade. Clearly, the girl has a kind heart but her critical thinking is not worth a dime. "Now I am waiting for a fellow, ykhm" (that is how she always says it). She is even a very narrow-minded person; what can I do about it? Even though I had invited her rather in order to excavate her complexes, to talk to her, to help her. I wish somebody would help me! I am really not as vicious as I appear to people. I often say what I am not thinking and it looks as if I am terribly heartless, while actually I am so glad when I succeed in helping someone or at least providing some small pleasure. To give to children a treat, to bring a tidbit to patients, I am enjoying all this so much! I myself economize as much as I can but often cannot stop myself from giving treats to little children.

90. 8.VI.05

Once again it is so hurting and hard! I am somehow afraid to get close to people. I fear losing my freedom. The only thing that I now possess in this world

48 Perhaps an allusion to Goethe's idea of elective or compatible affinities.

is freedom and I guard this blessing with all my might. I cannot endure even the smallest infringement on my person even in the form of simple guidance or reprimand. And the more rights a person has over me, the more apt he or she is to infuriate me even with a most friendly rebuke (why there is such a phenomenon is all too well known to me). Only from Junga can I endure everything. I am so unbearably hurt when he is displeased with me or criticizes me. Then I want to cry, I implore him to stop because I feel it as a humiliation, a repression of my person but at the same time I cannot oppose him altogether. This inescapable, unbearable pain caused by him (and sometimes by the Professor [Bleuler] as well) is at the same time often felt by me as pleasurable and I am glad when he gets angry and I gloat over my humiliation. If only somebody knew how it hurts me to write these lines! What an effort it costs me to write and to reflect on such humiliating words and phrases! I have got an awful headache!

This morning I again went to the hospital and took Miss Rähmi [a patient] to loaf about in the mountains. Our walk lasted from 8:30 until 11:30.

As far as I can recall, the only moment I experienced as pleasant was when on the way back we lay down in the hay. I am crazy about hay, the quiet all around and the peasants working. How hard it is! How murderously hard! And, as if mocking everything, nature is so gorgeous. I have such a fervent desire to study, I want to know as quickly and as much as possible but I do not know definitely what to take up first: science is so vast! In the library (I was there today) books are arranged alphabetically in catalogues; of course, it is impossible to read an entire catalogue in order to stumble on a book with an interesting title. What Junga recommended, (Roux, *Archiv der Entwicklungsmechanik*) and Lang (Hertwig and Hatischek),[49] could not be found. They do not loan nonfiction. Anyway, I am not interested to write about this in detail. Tomorrow I will go to the medical library (Kantonal 13) and perhaps take out Hartmann's "The Unconscious"[50] upon which I came across in the catalogue. Since I saw this book at Junga's, I believe it is worth reading. Then a man gave me the address of a certain Pestalozzi Society where I can take out fiction works. We shall see! It is with people that I am unable to deal.

---

49 Wilhelm Roux (1850–1924) German anatomist, pioneer of experimental embryology and founder of *Archiv für Entwicklungsmechanik der Organismen*. Oscar Wilhelm August Hertwig (1849–1922) German professor of anatomy, zoology, and developmental biology. Berthold Hatschek (1854–1941), Austrian zoologist and embryologist.

50 Karl Robert Eduard von Hartmann (1842–1906), German philosopher, author of *The Philosophy of the Unconscious,*1869.

The day before yesterday I had a quarrel with a former *Unterassistentin* (female intern) of our hospital named Trepa: I told her that the little medical student whom she greeted was a shallow and smug fellow. By the way, in her presence, I have often expressed opinions about the outward appearance of people, and I was always right. But she exploded that I always criticize and that one should not treat people in such a manner. Finally she found me guilty in relation to her as well: that I do not have the right to express an opinion about a person based on physiognomy and especially since that person is an acquaintance of hers (but only since a few days). The young lady demanded that I should be careful with [her]...but she forgot how she had offended me when I was still a patient at the hospital and so sick! When I told her that one should be careful with people, especially when they are sick, she answered that she could not hamper herself in this way and mind every word. She hit me in my most painful spot but I never touched upon her wounds. But what if she had just considered what the two of us could talk about? About her complex, about Jung, which simply means about criticizing people, which she had never renounced herself, all the more so since she did so for her personal reasons. So the day before yesterday I cut her short saying that I am who I am, and in response to further objections I said: "This means it is all over between us!" Later I was again in such pain, especially when I thought that mama would come to visit, that she is the only one!—only mama!—who knows how much suffering is attached to this word. I do not need kindness. Forget it! I only want peace. She should catch a fever! That would be just fine! On the other hand, I was even glad that we had broken up so that I would remain alone and would not have to go to her in order to speak with her. Last night we met in the street and naturally made peace with each other. I was glad we met and I also wished her she should return to Russia as soon as possible and that I should hear she was happy. Then I will be at peace with myself. People. When I feel that people are under my influence and that I am helping them, I am satisfied, but this way...only to feel constantly obligated to groan, and show compassion, and be eternally admonished... Come on! Perhaps I am expressing myself too sharply, but I cannot give an account of my feelings!...

Pet'ka should arrive in a few days. I will have to busy myself with him all day. He does not understand what this means to me! The main thing is his manner of eternally hugging me, eternally declaring his love, but instead of love, if love has to happen on demand (or else the other is offended), the result will be irritation and disgust. It will soon be a quarter past nine o'clock. It is time to go to bed. If only I could catch some fever but instead there is only this dull oppressive headache. I will re-read what I have written today. (I am writing by candlelight as I lost the habit of using a lamp when I was in the hospital). I could have said many more things but this is enough. I am going to bed.

2
Drawings, Undated Fragments and Words

Piglet! Calf! Blockhead! Devil's son! Unwashed mug!
Were it not for my maiden modesty,
That forbids me to say certain words,
I would have told you off more severely,
You impudent knave!
Mars Mars devil devil devil scandal devil it's stupid scandal go to hell!

The words that follow appear in this drawing dated 3/XII:

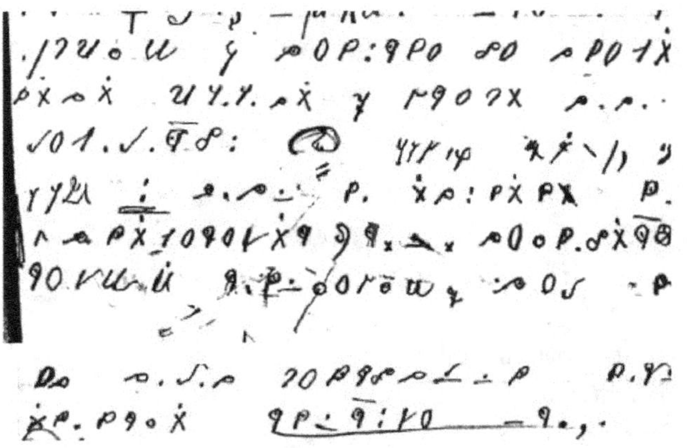

Damn you
It was supposed to depict, if it depicted
In the middle of the night you are gorgeous like the night
All wet with storm's foam.
With a proud smile (scandal!), with a loose black braid,
Your image shines in the glare of lightning
The torch is burning brightly, the wild wind

[on the left side] A LOW ANIMAL
fence says nothing to me

[follows a poem in rhymes]

Mad at the whole world,
[a piano] invented a secret
In order to an[ger?]
But it was nothing
It suddenly occurred to him
To write poems
To badger Junga.
Heartened by success
The good-for-nothing invented Excavating complexes
In order to banish Kirshbaum. Since then the poor wretch
Having cursed our pernicious world Dejectedly wanders the earth
And find a place to rest.
His victims are millions
Only Bleuler is spared
And why? He who steals the key
Will guess the answer
[a Pushkin (?) rhyme omitted]

[Word associations]

coal	stove
moderate	[illegible]
song	beautiful
assume	[knew that, illegible]
pain	laughter and I
lazy	not good
moon	is shining
to laugh	now don't recall effect of a beverage
coffee	excites
broad	[illegible]
child	I like O! how good
air	fresh
plate	guest
carry	heavy

tired	yes, I am
thread	will break
they intend	no don't know
key	door closed
I thought	to write
uncle	don't know
table cloth	broad (long?)
doctor	don't know (has nothing in common)

3
Sabina Spielrein's Interests, Readings, Remarks

3.1 MIXED RUSSIAN AND GERMAN[51]

ON FREUD'S PSYCHOANALYSIS

The theme of psychotherapy. Freud. I am a member. First two theor[ies] Then the [psychoanalytic] Association. Various co-workers. In February a new journal will be published. The source of the theory is the book. It is better that I become known to him as Freud's student. Freud wanted...by means of psychoanalysis. For the sake of convenience I will start with the well-known biological truth about the two instincts, the sexual instinct according to Freud. One can control the instinct of self-preservation but not the sexual instinct, but one should not eliminate it. In the subconscious. The subconscious. As it is known by the French. Splitting of the personality. Jung. A conversation between different personalities. Freud about the subconscious. What is contained in the subconscious. The laws operating in the subconscious, how to make the subconscious accessible. *Wünscherfüllung* [wish fulfilment]. Examples when one is thirsty. A resultant dream. The role of criticism. Pain, the representation of pain, etc.

A The sexual instinct. Byron's dream
N Formation of symbols (Freud)
X The censorship. The dream of the cutlet (the deeper meaning)
I The testimony of a pat[ient] with Dem[ementia] praec[ox]
E The subconscious, how do we get access to it, do we think like ancestors
T Siegfried and Brünhilde, Erdmännlein[52], "he," "she," "it"
Y Dem[entia] praec[ox] of a [female] patient's disgusting sex life with an unloved husband

51 From here on all underlining is by authors of the texts.
52 The "little man of the earth" or dwarf, legend of the famous cave Erdmannshöhle, Germany.

R. Have you ever had a fata morgana? [fata morgana in: "On a psych.[ological] cont[ent] of a c.[ase] of schizophr[enia][53]," the poetry of tropes and water symbolism

I Yes.

R. Have you ever seen eyes in the snow?

I I don't understand, how do you imagine this?

R. You know, water is the tears of heaven

I Yes, but how should we one understand this?

R. Water freezes so snow is created I And what are the eyes in this case?

R. In the eyes becomes manifest the soul, congealed like snow crust due to torments she had lived through and God saves us from these sorrows. Moreover the woman explains that God saves her by impregnating her with his rays. Indian mythology. A three-legged donkey.

Recapitulation

The sexual instinct enters unconsciously into our consciousness clothed in symbolic forms—censorship, fulfilled wishes, anxiety

Sexual instinct in children [illegible], disgusting.

Examples with Sisters of Mercy. The mother's breast. Non-localizable instincts.

Examples of it are symbols. *Verlegung nach oben* [displacement upwards]. Fairy tales about a childless czar's daughter. Made pregnant with fruit, fish. The king's son, like the frog in bed, is turned into the king's son or a bear. Also in dreams—in the first act, an animal, e.g., a cat, a cock; in the second—a human being. Athena out of the head of Zeus. The patient's dream. The scene of the patient with a cracked head. Smoke emerges from the crack, the smoke—the oven chimney

[to the left of the indented paragraph printed vertically, as above, the following words: sexual excitation, menstruation]

Jung's patient. Stomach disorder. Nausea after coffee with bread. Bread—body, coffee—blood. Aversion as with thoughts of carnal love. The patient with this diagnosis was cured.

Masturbation in a woman with epilepsy. Erogenous zones. Probably the very young children do not differentiate sexual excitations as adults do. But in the beginning, also in adults, and especially in women, love has a more erotic character but without so-called "dirty thoughts." But such dirty thoughts occur in every love, no matter what love it is. Byron's dream. Anxiety (the same cause of

53 Perhaps a reference to Spielrein's 1911 published doctoral dissertation.

anxiety is observed in analyses of children). Adults are aware of infantile love. The predominance of mother love in boys. Women differentiate less. Poets worship the mother, not the father. "Polygamy" is no substitute for the mother. Directly or symbolically as in S[iegfried] and Br[ünnhilde]. The author is Sieg[fried], the mother Br[ünnhilde]. Compare Graf. Perhaps my mother looked like this—Oedipus. We are oriented this way in our thinking but we ought not to know this. [Acad. T...illegible].

The need to suffer. Bodily punishments. Increased localization of manifestations. It seems that all children masturbate. Inhibition of the natural functions of the organism. Gratification. The recognition of the sick and the healthy. The struggle against bad habits. Adults know their children poorly. Anxiety regarding masturbation or sexual fantasies suppressed by consciousness. More [illegible] victory. Neurosis. Psychosis—children—anxiety-

3.2 LIST OF FREUD'S WORKS

On the psychical mechanism of hysterical phenomena [Freud, 1893]

Some points for a comparative study of organic and hysterical motor paralyses [Freud, 1893]

The neuro-psychoses of defense [Freud, 1894]. Retention hysteria. Defense hysteria Conversion hysteria.

On the grounds for detaching a particular syndrome from neurasthenia under the description 'anxiety neurosis' [Freud, 1895]

Studies on Hysteria by Dr. Josef Breuer and Dr. S. Freud in Vienna

Obsessions and phobias their psychical mechanism and their aetiology [Freud, 1895]

A reply to the criticism of my paper on anxiety neurosis 1895 [Freud, 1895]

Further remarks on the neuro-psychoses of defense *Neurolog. Zentralblatt* 1896, No. 10 simple neuroses (neurasthenia, anxiety neuro-sis—also harmful neuroses, see article on neuro-psychoses of defense (hysteria, obsessional neuroses) infantile-sexual source. Heredity and the aetiology of the neuroses) [Freud, 1896]

Heredity and the etiology of the neuroses. Revue neurologique IV, 1896

The aetiology of hysteria [Freud, 1896] *Wiener klin. Rundschau* 1896 No. 22 to 26

Sexuality in the aetiology of the neuroses [Freud, 1896] *Wiener klin. Rundschau* 1898 No. 2, 4, 5, and 7

The psychical mechanism of forgetfulness *Monatschrift f. Psychiatie u. Neurologie*, volume 4 pages 4–36 [Freud, 1898]

Screen memories *Monatschrift f. Psychiatie u. Neurologie* volume 6 page 215 ff. [Freud, 1899]

The Interpretation of Dreams Leipzig and Vienna, Franz Deuticke, 1900, 2nd edition 1909

On dreams. Wiesbaden, J.F. Bergmann, 1901 (*Grenzfragen des Nerven und Seelenlebens* edited by Loewenfeld and Kurella)

The Psychopathology of Everyday Life (Freud, 1901). Lindner. On thumb-sucking. [1879]

3.3 READING FRIEDRICH NIETZSCHE AND MAX NORDAU

Sabina copied from Nietzsche's *Thus Spake Zarathustra*:

"Now about the time that Zarathustra sojourned on the Happy Isles, it happened that a ship anchored at the isle on which standeth the smoking mountain, and the crew went ashore to shoot rabbits. About the noontide hour, however, when the captain and his men were together again, they saw suddenly a man coming toward them through the air, and a voice said distinctly: 'It is time! It is the highest time!' But when the figure was nearest to them (it flew past quickly, however, like a shadow, in the direction of the volcano), then did they recognise with the greatest surprise that it was Zarathustra; for they had all seen him before except the captain himself, and they loved him as the people love: in such wise that love and awe were combined in equal degree. 'Behold!' said the old helmsman, 'there goeth Zarathustra to hell!'"

Here is what Max Nordau (1898) wrote about normals and degenerates:

"In order, however, that the association of ideas may fulfil its functions in the operations of the brain, and prove itself a useful acquisition to the organism, one thing more must be added, namely, attention. This it is which brings order into the chaos of representations awakened by the association of ideas, and makes them subserve the purposes of cognition and judgment" (p. 45). "Every stimulus which reaches a place on the cerebral cortex results in a rush of blood to that spot, by means of which nutriment is conveyed to it" (p. 68). "Moreover, the thought of a healthy brain has a flow which is regulated by the laws of logic and the supervision of attention. It takes for its content a definite object, manipulates and exhausts it. The healthy man can tell what he thinks, and his telling has a beginning and an end. The mystic imbecile thinks merely according to the laws of association, and without the red thread of attention. He has fugitive ideation" (p. 118).

SPIELREIN'S COMMENTARY ON NORDAU AND FREE ASSOCIATIONS

Every perception is composed of a stimulus and a sensation [caused by] this stimulus. The sensation of the stimulus depends on attention. There are essentially three kinds of attention that are basically different from each other. The first is the momentary ability to take notice and in this sense, there is an attentive person, who at the same time is receiving more sensations (which does not mean that his sensations are becoming more thorough or deeper but only more numerous). The second attention, as Nordau understands this concept, is: that each stimulated brain cell propagates this stimulus farther and with every idea [illegible] a lot that is not suitable is aroused. Thus the function of attention is to suppress the unsuitable ideas and to make the needed ones clearer. And there, says Nordau, the cells that have the needed ideas are richly supplied with blood and that is why the ideas become clearer whereas in other cells the opposite takes place. For example, when we speak of heaven it occurs to us immediately to think of "blue," "red" and other colors and then of various colored objects and events, etc. The function of the 2nd attention is to suppress ideas that do not correspond with our main thought. The 1st and 2nd attention belong to fantasy and dream. When we employ only the 1st and 2nd attention we must always either fantasize or dream. A young woman has a dream (Forel's example): "I am looking for a young girl who lived in a certain house. This time

I undertake [followed by a devil's face "insane asylum", "mama"] dependence on will. The non-freed[om] of will. The concept "autosuggestion." Actually everything is "autosug[gestion]." In hypnot[ism] we have autos[uggestion] and the other way around. We always have autosug[gestion] and sug[gestion]. There is no precise difference. Dreams are autosug[gestion]. Habit and autosug[gestion]. Conscious auto-sug[gestion] in dreams. Pathological wish dreams [followed by nine lines of letters and numbers] The dream is autosuggestion. Illusions, hallucinations. Example, mixing up fantasy with reality (e.g., in children). The difference between sensation and perception is merely quantitative. Autosuggestion in hallucinations. Due to the stimul[ation] of the retina we see a picture and produce associations based on external similar[ity] (flight of ideas, no correct ability to judge). As with various cloud shapes, we imagine various figures and end up finding a similarity to certain persons etc. and the same in dreams. So we create pictures for ourselves and we suggest those to ourselves, and we believe in them because a broad overview of the situation is too tenuous. For example, I am dreaming that they are coming to us in the gymnasium and we are standing together with the history teacher and showing him something in the textbook. I am thinking, "this is impossible for he does not speak Russian." But I instantly find an excuse: "but we speak German." It does not occur to me that I have not explained anything about the matter and I believe what I myself have invented (sug[gestion]). However, since I seriously doubt that they could come to us I gaze at them more carefully and realize that the person in question is somebody else or something like that. We then have the hunch that it is just a dream and since we don't find an adequate excuse the suggestion is demolished and we realize it was just a dream and wake up or oftentimes pass into another dream in which we say with conviction: "but now this is already reality" and then we invent proofs. During a heavy dream we try to wake up: "it was just a dream," and we attempt in vain to open our eyes (because we are under sug[gestion] and are unable to add something to it). The successful suggestion strengthens our belief that the dream is reality; in case of the opposite we wake up. In the next dream we can readily obt[ain] a wish dream. Hunglig (sic) = [hungrig, I'm hungry?]. A mem[ory]. I am awakened to go to the gymnasium [illegible], dreams [illegible] etc. Dreams of Sch[illegible]. It is not true that we do not dream about strongly feeling-toned matters. In Interlak[en] [hospital] I mostly drea[mt] thoughts nachmit [nachmittag? = in the afternoon]. For example, we are touched on the throat. Exaggeration [wrote this word in Russian]. We suggest to ourselves that robbers want to stran[gle] us. "It is a dream." What is the evidence? "But I am feeling it so distinctly." Probably in general with eyes closed sensations become violent (blind people) because there is less control of and more freedom for the power of imagination. Forel is right. According to Jodl[54] in the dream there is a pure criticism-free correction of a series of perceptions through the content of the overall consciousness.[a page is missing]

In the dark, [I] I see something blurred and round that evokes the image of a ball. I close my eyes. To the ball I associate a child at play. Then I see the child. I notice the child has a little lock. (I have recently made a draw[ing] of a child's head with locks). This evokes the pictures of my little sister, who also had locks. Then I see that the girl resembles my little sister. Then I open my eyes. Here is an association connected with exterior likeness, flight of ideas. The little sister is for me a feeling-toned complex and therefore her image is in the associated ideas and a strong image at that. (The more is a matter important and feeling-toned for us the more often we think of it while awake and the more it enters into a great number of associations.) Here we have an example of attention—in the sense of Nordau—that is not directing the images at all. The image of the little sister is the deepest and most prevalent and therefore it steers attention to itself and thus becomes a leading image around which all the other relevant images group together. As soon as I close my eyes I see various reminiscence images that have something connected with the little sister. Gradually concentrating on the main image becomes stronger and stronger and the concern for the overall situation, the ability to control, becomes more labile. (As Jodl says, there is no criticism in the dream, no correction via a perception series, via the content of the total consciousness.) Like a child playing at being a soldier often suggests to himself that he really is a soldier, and he firmly believes his imagination and because all his attention is concentrated on the soldiers' image, he is hindered from correctly analyzing the overall situation. In children we always encounter such autosuggestions because in them the images are stronger and more one-sided, that is, they are more strongly illuminated by attention and therefore have not enough attention for the overview of the whole situation (the critique is too weak). It is the same one-sided attention that allows a sufferer from tertiary syphilis to jump from a high floor to get his cane. The image of getting hold of the cane is so intensely illuminated that the images of height, danger etc. pale in comparison. Similarly in my example. Eventually I take my imagining for reality

54 Jodl, Friedrich (1849–1914) was a German philosopher and psychologist, author of a textbook on psychology (1896). The quotation is: "In the dream there is no criticism; no correction of a perception series by the content of the overall consciousness" (p. 123).

and images become perceptions. Is this not autosuggestion? However, I believe in the reality of my imaginings not because I reached this conclusion using reason but just the opposite, because I concentrated my attention on one image and did not want to be bothered with any logical judgments. For as long as there is still a residue of an ability to judge such an event feels to me unnatural. How is it possible that I saw the little sister as real when in reality she had been dead for a long time? Clearly, can the dead be brought back to life? (It is the same if I ask this question with words or with feelings.) Sometime it seems a little bit (repetition, in Russian)like an incomplete judgment, so this arouses the general realistic judgment and thus the autosuggestion is wiped out. However, most of the time I don't bother about the real environment. (The wish to see the little sister still acts as a suggestion) and then I tell myself: "I do not know how this could happen, but it is happening; the child lives again."

It is not true that we don't dream about strongly felt things. In Interlaken I mostly dreamt about thoughts in the afternoon. Similarly, somebody touches our throat (repetition, in Russian). We suggest to ourselves that it was a robber who wanted to strangle us. "It was a dream." The proof is that I am feeling this so clearly. Perhaps when the eyes are shut the sensations are stronger (blind people) because there is less control and a freer imagination. According to Jodl (or Forel), there is no self-criticism in dreams, no correction of a series of perceptions by the content of the fully conscious mind.

4
Russsian Letters of Sabina Spielrein and Family

4.1 LETTERS FROM SABINA TO HER MOTHER

SS 1

Dear mamochka [mummy] [Zurich] 26.8.05[55]

I am now somewhat tired but I am completely at peace. I am madly happy as almost never before in my life. At the same time, for some reason, I am in pain and I want to cry from bliss. You have certainly figured out that the cause of all this is Junga. I visited him today. He reassured me about Rähmi [a woman patient treated by her at Burghölzli]: in his opinion, he tells me, her condition has markedly improved; thereafter he advised me not to take back the money I had spent on her. I should now get the money from a charitable society; on the other hand, the society could use that money to help another person and etc. in this vein. We had broached this subject because Junga told me that I should not be wearing a hat with holes in it and that I should also have my shoes mended. I replied that I had run out of money and that I had already received so much that I could not ask my parents for more. Thereupon he compelled me to tell him what I had spent the money on. Then he made a proposal to loan me 100 francs and write to both of you about it. But as I objected vigorously, he forced me to accept 10 francs from him for the hat and the repair of the shoes. How do you like this chicken feed? I was so ashamed I wished the earth should swallow me. I was ready to resist but you cannot win an argument with such a man. On the other hand, I was delighted that he had done a good deed and decided not to be a hindrance. Do not breathe a word to him about it. Strange how it is somehow pleasant to be an object of his "charitable attentions" and have him spend money on me. Naturally, I shall soon pay him this money back but he

---

55 Misdated as 26.8.1908 in Wackenhut & Willcke. Confirmed by 1905 Calendar: Jung's planned to visit Sabina on Friday September 1st. In August 1908 Sabina was in Rostov (see Jung's postcard).

does not know this as yet. So there, can you see what kind of a person he is, my Junga? When I left the Professor [Bleuler] today I felt like one condemned to death but he [Jung] restored my faith in my abilities and made me so happy! He is coming to visit me on Friday (1st of September) at 3 o'clock. If only I could learn to cook borscht before then! Today I dragged along Junga as he made rounds at out hospital. There are quite a lot of women there who adore me! But sleep is getting the better of me, I am going to bed. I was so excited that I forgot to convey to him your apology about the gift you had sent him; but I did not forget to tell him how I scared you when I had presented you Rähmi's letter to me as his letter. He read this letter and told me I should not have tortured you in this manner. Today the mathematics teacher... [On the margin] Tomorrow he will come again to prepare me for the examination and then organize the program of activities.

SS 2 (Russian and some German)

My dear ones! [parents] Undated

I wanted to send you the rough drafts of my written examination papers, but I decided it was not worth it. I believe that in all probability I have passed the examinations. Officially, the result is still unknown, therefore I am not telegraphing you yet. To tell you how it all happened? But I have already told it so many times! However, of particular interest was the anatomy part. I was the first to finish my work. As soon as I was coming through the door with the paper and other accessories, students flocked around me: "How was it," and more in that spirit. So, I told them, all together and separately. I felt rather important. Of course, every moment on the way home I met other people who kept asking me to tell them again or to congratulate me. And this was the general impression: that before an examination they all huddled together pale-faced and trembling while red-faced Shpilrein, as usual, was walking down the hallways and singing, etc. I sang, either "Ah, look how pale I am, oy, oy, oy, oy, oy, oy, oy! I fell in love with an unfaithful friend, oh you, my God!" Or then: "Poor, poor, poor me! My poor bitter fate!" [Then] "*Ich bin der Doctor Eisenbarth kurier die Leut nach meiner Art*"[56] etc. It was especially so prior to Taule's examination. " (physiology). "What is our exam? A toy! Ah, what a darling our Taula [russified] is! Ah, what a lovely hour when Taula is with us!" And prior to the test in anatomy: "Aunties!

56 "My name is doctor Eisenbarth I cure the people in my manner," a popular student drinking song mocking professors.

Oy, Oy! It's all over with us! God is my witness, I will get Kleinhirn![57]"—and more in that vein. And then everybody was astonished when it was my luck to get Kleinhirn as my examiner! I wrote down everything that could be written about the slide. But then a small misunderstanding occurred during the oral anatomy examination: I correctly read my slide (heart muscle); some time later professor Ruge came over to me again: "Well, what do you see there, Fräulein?" I told him again: "heart muscle" "But that is completely wrong." –"Yes, how so?—"What you are seeing there is not heart muscle at all!!!" – "Yes, naturally! So what is it?" I looked into the microscope once more and it was the "liver." It dawned on me: "Oh God, this *is* the liver! Really, Herr Professor, I have not noticed that you have given me another slide!" – "Well, I never!! It is the first time such a thing happened to me!" – "What have you been doing all this time, looking at the window instead of thinking about your slide?" – "But really, Herr Professor, I did not notice that another slide was given to me; I did look a little bit at the window and listened a little to what the others were answering." Well, it's gone, it went off alright. In the macroscopic part it did not come off without excitement. I described to him with the greatest detail the course of the vertebral artery; but I contrived to count the neck vertebrae not from above but from below and as a result Ruge asked me to repeat it a few times as I was demonstrating upon myself; then he realized: "Ah yes, you are counting from below? We all count from above." To which I, "Oh, yes! After all, the atlas is the first vertebra." Well, he also burst out laughing. As I finished he said to me: "Good, now go back to your work." The aunties were saying that the way I answered was one of the best. Well then, it means that everything was all right. Everybody finds that my exam was typical for me.

In physiology we had a family examination. I was as if answering all of the questions. We were answering in groups of three and I was in the middle; he only asked me once, and not much at all, but the others he asked twice and a lot (he passed me over two times). After we finished he told us: "You all passed, even though it was nothing special." Perhaps he was thinking only about those other two? Because I answered better than they; he showed that while he asked the others twice, he only asked me once. What the devil, what a caricature!

---

57 *Kleinhirn*, literally small brain, is the German name of the cerebellum, here the nickname of anatomy professor R , i.e. Ruge. Georg Hermann Ruge (1852–1919) was a German doctor, member of the Sauerbruch circle, director of the Anatomy Institute in Zurich.

SS 3

Dear mamochka, [1908]

I am unable to write because it does not matter, it is impossible to communicate important matters in a letter. One would have to say so much. Unfortunately, Rostov is too far from Zurich, and I cannot send you his letters because it is too risky, and to tell all is too long and too tiring. If I were able to make a firm decision, I would be living in a fairyland; as it is, I get exhausted thinking and it makes no sense, because *ducunt volentem dei nolentem trahunt*, which means "gods guide the one who desires and drag one who does not desire."[58] Just recently [1908] Junga finished his paper "Über die Rolle des Vaters im Schicksaale [sic] des Einzelnen"[the role of the father in the fate of the individual] in which he shows how the choice of a future love object is determined in the first years of the child's relations with its parents. That I love him is as firmly determined as that he loves me. He is a father for me and I am a mother for him, or, to be exact, the woman who for the first time acted as a substitute for the mother (seeing that his mother came down with hysteria when he was two years old) and he became so passionately attached to this woman that when she was absent he would see her in hallucinations, etc, etc. Why he fell in love with his wife I do not know, although this is certainly also determined and he even wanted to tell me about this, but the time passed and now I am afraid to ask. Evidently, let us say, his wife is "not completely" satisfactory and now he has fallen in love with me, an hysteric; and I fell in love with a psychopath, and is it necessary to explain why? I never saw my father as normal. His fanatical striving "to know himself" is best expressed in Junga for whom his scientific activity is above all else in the world, namely, scientific activity in a definite and appropriate direction. An uneven despotic character coupled with extraordinary sensitivity, a need to be suffering and compassionate 'ad magnum' [to the fullest]. With love and kindness you can do with him what you want and get what you want. Twice in a row he became so emotional in my presence that tears were just streaming! If you could only hide in the next room and hear how concerned he was for me and my fate, you would be touched to tears yourself. Then he starts reproaching himself endlessly for his sympathy, a kind of something sacred to him, that he is ready to beg for forgiveness...etc., I do not want to quote the phrases, and all this is a bit sentimental, but you can very well imagine it all. Remember how papa used to apologize to you. Word for word! It is unpleasant for me to quote the accusations he leveled at himself because we are both either equally guilty or not guilty. Look, how many female

58 Seneca the Younger, "ducunt volentem fata, nolentem trahunt, fates guide the willing drag the unwilling. *Epistles*, 107.

patients were seen by him and, without fail, each one of them would invariably fall in love with him, however, he could only act as a physician because he did not love in return! But you yourself know how desperately he struggled with his feelings! But what could be done? He suffered through many nights thinking about me. The question whether we should separate was also considered. But this solution was rejected as unfeasible if only because we are both living in Zurich. He felt responsible for my fate even though he howled as he pronounced these words, but he was ready to renounce everything in order not to stand in the way of my happiness, although it would have been necessary first to figure out where this happiness was [illegible words]; that so far he had grounds to fear for my immediate future (should we separate).

This conversation took place almost two weeks ago and we both were so overwhelmed that we became literally speechless etc. It ended with having things out *ducunt volentem dei, nolentem trahunt*. We stood motionless in the most tender poetry..."Let tomorrow bring darkness and cold! Today I shall offer my heart to [sun's?] rays! I shall be gay! I shall be young! I shall be happy! That is what I want! [gay, young and happy are here grammatically masculine, perhaps referring to Jung's mood as well as her own]. Then I get a postcard and a letter in one day saying that I should not be sad. Last Friday, that is the day before yesterday, he visited me again. Poetry again and then again more of the same: will I ever in my life forgive him for what he had concocted with me; he did not sleep the whole night, became exhausted and could not fight it any longer. But by the same right, I should also be saying: "Will he ever forgive me for what I have done to him!" The difference is that I know that for him scientific activity is above all else in life and that he will be able to bear everything for the sake of science. And again, almost two hours passed in speechless bliss. I said I would not go along with this whole business, as was discussed previously. I will always be capable of resisting. The question is only how will my intellect regard this whole business and the whole trouble is that the intellect does not know how to regard it. Anyway, I should not be writing to you about him and his family but about me and this raises the question, whether to surrender with all my being to this stormy vortex of life and be happy while the sun is shining, or, when the black days of parting come, to transfer my feelings to a child and to science, i.e., scientific activity that I love so much? Firstly, who knows how this whole business will end? "Inscrutable are the fates of God!"[59] Furthermore, today's youth looks at these matters differently and it is very possible that next

59 Sabina wrote "fates" but in the *Epistle to the Romans* it says: "How unsearchable are [God's] judgments and how inscrutable his ways," 11:33.

time I will fall in love with another man and will be successful, i.e., consummate legal matrimony.

Just don't you forget that this is still very far off in the future, and therefore do not worry. So far we have remained at the level of poetry that is not dangerous and we shall remain at that level for a long time, perhaps until the time I will become a doctor, unless circumstances will change. I am writing to you now only because I cannot feel happy without a mother's blessing, that is, without your approval of my ways of acting and that you should be happy that for now I am doing well. And afterwards? In the best of cases, we cannot say what will happen afterwards and where is happiness awaiting us. Consider a recent example. One of Jung's patients, in her attempt to get over her love for him, took to the mountains and became infatuated and sexually involved with a young man so that soon she will give birth to his child. The man who seduced her turned out to be a most small-minded person and abandoned her forthwith. Now she cannot stand him anymore, and in desperation wants to end her life, and would have done it, had Junga not saved her once again.

SS 4

Dear Mamochka, Undated

Truly miracles happen in this world! No more, no less, without intending I managed to hypnotize Junga. How did it happen? He arrived five minutes earlier than was agreed upon. He knocks. I answer, "Ja!" [yes]. He enters and I feel greatly embarrassed as I did not expect it was him and I stand there with my hair half-loose comb in hand. Well, to send him away was awkward and I did not have a suitable sitting room. Well, he sat down on the couch and promised he would not look, however, I knew beforehand that "not looking" to him means he covers his face with his hands and peeps through the spaces between the fingers. I had to make do with this situation. I hurried to finish getting dressed, tossed a red shade over the lamp, and walked over to him. We greet each other as if after a long separation. Then, as always, he launches into long speeches: he did not sleep all night and was thinking; he wants me to be happy forever etc. in this style. I tell him that that at the moment I find such speeches disturbing, that I love him anyway, and if one day circumstances will make us part then we shall part; but that this will happen later, and right now I am not thinking about anything, and I am fine. Then he kisses me and bawls, "Was ist?"[what's the matter], and he is immediately radiant with delight. I am a mother for him, he is a father for me, it is the best of all possible worlds! But the best of all, he had the idea to make me a new hairdo and he did this in this manner: he pulled the most showy comb out of my hairdo and loosened my hair, whereupon he became ecstatic that I looked like an Egyptian woman (!) On the whole, I had to play the role [text break]

4.2 LETTERS FROM SABINA TO DOCTORS

SS 5 (in German)
D[ear] P[rofessor] [Freud] Undated (possibly 1909)
Since a long time

At last I am sending you the letter I have promised, this will be the last one. Why this decision now? Because, for the first time, I saw you represented in my dream as good-looking. I wished to write to you a few months ago, but I had to abandon it, only because in my dream you appeared with female breasts, as old as professor Forel, and ugly-looking to boot. You also appeared there as extremely cunning. I came to you with the brother (Dr. Jung) and you paid attention to the brother but none to me. I have to confess that after I received your first two letters I immediately experienced a great joy in my dream which appeared to me quite appropriate. History is silent about your third letter.

Back to today's dream: I am in the hospital and you and Dr. Jung are having a conversation in the adjoining room. Should I leave, because soon you will enter the room where I am? No, I continue with my work and perhaps I will be able to poke some fun at both of you. You enter and I feel that you are thinking about me: "Is this the beauty I should compare with my daughter?" In the process I see myself in the mirror and feel embarrassed because I don't find myself beautiful at all. I feel that you are attributing a sexual meaning to every movement I make; I feel stupid and pull some mischievous pranks. I only know that Dr. Jung is quite friendly toward me but not you. Presently both of you go back to the adjoining room. At the same time I am looking at your face; it is youthful, beautiful, and remarkably likable. I feel awful, my heart and throat contracted painfully, and I put a compress to my head; why doesn't he want to listen to me? Why does he think so poorly of me? Should I go into the adjoining room or shouldn't I? At this moment a female friend of mine is calling to me through the window: "I want to tell you something interesting!" I answer angrily: "What can you possibly tell me?" She throws a little bag with candy at me. "This is nothing special!" say I, and the friend leaves. At this moment Dr. Jung notices my hesitation through the open door and calls out joyfully "Come on in!" I come nearer toward the room and think: "I am mainly interested in his opinion, not in Dr. Jung himself. Is it possible that this face hides a great genius? I just want to look at him!" Then you turn your chair around so I can only see your back. Finished. So you can see how a young person works through your letters in the depth of her personality! Firstly, the dream tells me about you that you now possess a better apparent personality (in this respect my unconscious never deceives me) and, secondly, it shows me that overall I am not indifferent to what you think about me, and that in the heat of the moment I forgot that in fact you don't know me at all, that instead of sending you some evidence, I simply wrote to you that it was so and so. Naturally, you think it is all my fantasy and whatever is connected with it! A perfidious manipulation! Now I am ready to give evidence for all that appeared insufficiently believable in my last letter. The conscious now thinks that I don't give a damn who professor Freud is and what opinion he has of me. I naturally don't want to hide this letter from Dr. Jung. Yes, I wanted to send Dr. Jung to you so that he himself could read it to you, but as the saying goes, "Opportunity makes the thief." Do not betray my little doubt to Dr. Jung: when he is sure that one believes in his honesty, then it becomes a big support for the better part of his personality, as happens to such a proud character with such labile affects. There is another reason here that you might point out to him: I am sending the letter directly to you so that he should not think that I want to "catch" him. Overall, I am not Dr. Jung's enemy, or else I would not have hung over the piano the painting (by Segantini[60]) he had sent me. He seems to me as my oldest little child to whom I have devoted so much of my energy so that he can now live independently; when I speak with you about him it is because you love him: when I first decided to write to you, I did not know yet that he told you something about me. You know that! I also need to explain my "prophecies" (in the letter). I do not consider that due to some happening, both Dr. Jung and I had been ordered, and that I had to execute this outright. The determination and the will I felt was due to the existence of Dr. Jung's love for me, for example, not only during the examination but also during the three preparatory courses about which I had received certain symbols intended for me which I interpreted as the effect of suggestion. I experienced a strong will that wanted this and that, and that somehow the Professor had sensed it too, which made him set up the needed slide; I myself had naturally selected the correct number. Could a gentleman, a complete stranger to me, correctly predict what I would get? Or think it was a coincidence? Wouldn't there be too many coincidences, as you will see from that letter? I am inclined to attribute to the complex a bigger influence

60 *Ave Maria Crossing the Lake* by Giovanni Segantini (1858–1899), a famous Italian landscape painter.

on the outside world than can be proved by science, for a complex is after all a necessity, I might say, "born" of all the possible components of the outside world. It is quite certainly true that the principle in the "role of the father in the fate of the individual"[61] is valid. However, I am surprised that relatively recently Dr. Jung tried to convince me that I could just as well have loved any other doctor like him; I then had to write him a long epistle (which is still in my procession) that there cannot be such a coincidence, that one loves the similarities in one's object and therefore first one loves one's own people and then one always discovers similarities in one's beloved. Doesn't it ring funny that my mother should rob me of my beloved for the third time? Before Dr. Jung I was infatuated with two [men]; (I was still too immature for love). Both of them even liked me very much but since I was still a child, both the first and then the second fell in love with my mother head over heels.

SS 6 (new letter to Freud)

Dear Professor Freud! Late 1913

The big one, or more properly, the little anonymous one, is here. She is a big, vigorous little animal, totally autoerotic and absolutely asocial. Her greatest love is her own little hand which she treats as a feeding organ, even while she is drinking; it cannot be ruled out that in this way she is obtaining some vivifying salts which she needs like so many other little young animals. Naturally, she possesses all the necessary wisdom appropriate to her age, she is very energetic, and when she wants to get something she screams with a real fury; but sometimes she is indeed tender and helpless like a little bird. Otherwise she is very interested in the world around her: the nanny gave her as present a little Christmas tree and lit a candle. The little animal looked at it for a moment and then tossed her little head back and yawned ever so sweetly. I am always disturbed when I am writing and I tire quickly. The periodicity theory of Fliess applies to the little girl, she seems to be a spitting image of myself including the little mouth and the little mouth resembles that of my mother's. I am now "one minute on top of the world, the next down in the dumps" [Goethe]. A pile of thoughts and feelings, [text break].

SS 7 (in German) Fragment of a letter to Jung

Dear Doctor! Undated

In the introduction to the second edition of your paper, "The conflicts in

61 Jung, C.G. (1909). Die Bedeutung des Vaters für das Schicksal des Einzelnen. *Jahrbuch*, 1:155–173.

a child's soul," you say that early infantile sexuality could just as little be called sexuality as calling brain the external neural plate of the fetal brain. This is incorrect because:

At any moment infantile sexuality can lead to a real sexual function "as long as the conflicts have not been resolved"; however, the external neural plate cannot at any development stage, or development inhibition, perform the functions of the normal brain.

We only know two drives (*Antriebe*), the drive to self-preservation and at higher stage the sexual drive. Out of these primal drives can later awaken in us something "higher," i.e., differentiated. Therefore in the child we can find representations of both these drives and perhaps also their sublimated derivatives.

It is not absolute that suppressed sexual wishes but that <u>every suppressed wish</u> can cause our energy (libido) to be transferred to another field. In children, as well as in primitive people, wishes are closer to the life of the drives, therefore one will observe the suppression of the animal drives mostly by the sublimation drive; on the other hand, in adults, we will observe the regression process...An artist, who momentarily doubts his task has immediately to devote himself to a different field; if he cannot find an equivalent field, then the libido regresses to infantile contents and even onto those out of which develops the future artistic course; or even to the complete infantile constellation, because it is impossible to set any limits to this. This is the neurosis of the adult.

I now have an everyday opportunity to observe many different children who masturbate and I must say that children masturbate extremely frequently or at least hold their little hand where it "does not belong." This happens at the earliest age, including neurotic children, whom one should count along with the aforementioned. In those early years, when the little ones can hardly babble, who can have any knowledge of this state; then it is surely not the suppression of the ability to comprehend that drives them in the direction of masturbation. The drive is simply there and not much is needed to arouse it, or, better yet, to observe its manifestations. It is mostly adults who unconsciously stimulate the child sexually. Therefore I had often to deal with this with my nannies and also observed it in others, that when they take the child in their arms, they always grasp with the [text break]

SS 8 (in French) [probably to Claparède]

Sir, Geneva, 15.V.1921

Despite all hesitations, I cannot act otherwise. Therefore, do not think badly of me: since I am your assistant, it would be impolite toward you if you should learn about my lecture at the Institut Rousseau—otherwise than from me directly. Not having made you aware of this earlier was solely due to modesty, fearing to impose myself in case you found it uninteresting or if you had something else to do. Mr. Bovet has perhaps already communicated to you the date and time of the conference. In spite of it, I owe you this letter and ask you to forgive for almost having failed to be polite.

Sincerely yours, S. Spielrein-Scheftel

SS 9 Letter to Doctor Eitingon

[Dear][62] Doctor, 24.8.27

If only you knew how sorry I am that I will not be able to see you all at the Congress on 1–3 September![63] The main obstacle is my second child, my sweet one-year-old little daughter whom I can neither leave here nor bring with me. Yet I owe our Association some account of our activities here in the North Caucasus region. – Interest in psychoanalysis is very widespread here, but superficial. One has 'no time' to devote oneself to the subject, because more essential 'practical' interests stand in the way. The official representative of the psychiatric clinic in Rostov-on-Don[64] is able to value the achievements of psychoanalysis – but warns against 'exaggerations' in the sphere of sexuality. The assistants at the clinic practise analysis on their own account – at the same time they are all actually against analysis.

It is the fate of analysis – understandably from the viewpoint of drive theory – always to arouse resistance where we display the greatest passion. So in Russia we face a completely unjustified resistance that is totally unknown abroad; it is the fear that psychoanalysis, 'product of the capitalist system', goes against the interests of the working classes. Psychoanalysis is accused of tracing everything back to sexuality and thereby denying the achievements of Marx, who, as is known, derives everything from socio-economic conditions. There is a great mistake here that cannot be clarified in a couple of lines: the teachings of Freud and Marx do not need to exclude each other and can co-exist perfectly well.

62 [Translator's note]: The transcript reads 'Sehr Herr Doctor': the gap implying that 'geehrter' ['Dear'] was to be inserted.

63 The 10th International Psychoanalytical Congress took place in Innsbruck from 1–3 September 1927.

64 The person in question could not be identified.

A number of our colleagues such as Prof. Reissner,[65] the young Prof. Luria,[66] the late Dr. Rosenthal[67] and others have already spoken and written about this. A second accusation is that psychoanalysis includes much that is subjective and mystical; hence it contradicts the demands of the biological trend in recent Russian psychology, known as 'reflexology' (Leningrad) or 'reactology' (Moscow). This viewpoint has even gained support among the great figures of Russian science, so that we also have to contend with such opponents as Prof. Bekhterev[68] in Leningrad, Prof. Hackebusch[69] in Kiev, amongst others. Prof. Wulff[70] and Prof. Luria had a fierce battle to fight. Finally I myself felt the necessity of giving a lecture in the local Society for Neurology and Psychiatry on reflexotherapy and psychoanalysis. In it I showed how little there is of the subjective or mystical in Freud's teaching and how a good part of Freud's teaching found confirmation in biological psychology or 'reflexology'.

This winter I was put in charge of two courses on 'The Significance of Psychoanalysis for Child Studies'. These courses were aimed at perfecting the scientific education of school and kindergarten doctors, one for doctors of the city of Rostov, the other for those of the North Caucasus region in general. Each of these courses had a six-hour theoretical part, followed by a practical one. In the practical part I demonstrated how I would carry out psychoanalytically based psychological tests of children in school day clinics, schools and kindergartens.

---

65 Mikhail Andreevich Reisner (1869–1929), as a lawyer and philosopher of law and government, concerned himself primarily with social psychology and the sociology of relition. He belonged to the Communist Party. In 1927 he became a member of the RPA.

66 Aleksandr Romanovich Luria (1902–1977), a psychologist from Kazan, moved in 1923 to Moscow where he became a member of the RPA. For several years he was committed to psychoanalysis, but then withdrew from it. Afterwards Luria studied medicine and pursued a second career as an internationally recognized neurologist and neuropsychologist.

67 Tatyana G. Rosenthal (1885–1921: death by suicide) studied medicine in Zurich. From 1911 to 1921 she was a member of the Vienna Psychoanalytic Society. After her return to her native city of St Petersburg she first worked as a psychoanalyst in private practice, then Bekhterev put her in charge of the polyclinic for the treatment of psychoneuroses.

68 Vladimir Mikhailovich Bekhterev (1857–1927), psychiatrist and neurologist, from 1918 to 1927 the Director of the Institute for the Study of the Brain and Mental Functions in St. Petersburg/Leningrad.

69 Prof. Hackebusch taught at the university psychiatric clinic in Kiev. For a time his attitude towards psychoanalysis was benevolent (see *IZ* 1924, p. 115; 1926, pp. 227–229). However, he soon distanced himself from it and openly criticized it (Kloocke, 2002, p. 83, n. 152).

70 Moshe Wulff (1878–1971) studied medicine in Berlin, where he encountered psychoanalysis. From 1911 to 1921 he was a member of the Vienna Psychoanalytic Society. In 1914 he returned to Russia and was among the founders of the RPA, of which he was voted President in 1924. In 1927 he travelled to the IPA Congress in Innsbruck and did not return to the Soviet Union. He went first to Berlin and in 1933 emigrated to Palestine (Kloocke, 2002).

As far as the time permitted, I also carried out Jung's association experiments on the doctors taking part in the course.

The lectures and demonstrations aroused great interest. In spite of that I did not escape the usual reproaches that one encounters when one does not wish to keep strictly to the Binet-Simon type of intelligence scale. It is not worth telling you more here about the test methods I use, since in a few days I shall submit a work which should be appearing shortly.

It is now over a year since I received the friendly invitation to engage in a literary collaboration with Dr Cronbach from America.[71] Until now I have left his letter unanswered, because for a long time I was suffering badly from malaria and could not trust myself to take anything on. But I have tacitly accepted his suggestion: I have collected the necessary material, worked on it and given a lecture on it at the pedagogical society of the North Caucasus University at Rostov. The lecture is entitled: 'The results of an investigation into the animistic ideas of children from 3 to 14 years old in Moscow and Rostov-on-Don'. I am not having the lecture printed here as I wish to rework the results of the investigation in a study for Dr. Cronbach.[72]

If you should see Dr Cronbach at the congress, dear Doctor, please be so good as to communicate this to him. I will write to him soon. But for the time being I send him my apologies and a promise to submit the work to him for publication as soon as possible (the honorarium to be credited to the psychoanalytical journal. Should it be too late, then it can go into one of our analytical journals.)

Unfortunately I still have nothing to report about my colleagues in Rostov. I am still the only trained analyst here and this is connected with my sickness that has prevented any undertaking. I have no material means of signing up to our journals or other literature, so that we are extremely poor on literature here. I got close to ordering the literature for the North Caucasus prophylactic out-patient clinic. But then I was too hopelessly depressed as a result of my illness and did not trust myself to take on the post offered to me at this clinic. The post was thereupon given to an assistant ('junior doctor') of the local psy-

71 Abraham Cronbach (1882–1965), son of an immigrant from Germany, was a rabbi in Ohio and Indiana and gained a reputation as a teacher, pacifist and author of numerous works, including *The Psychoanalytic Study of Judaism* (Cronbach, 1931–2). He corresponded with such analysts as Ernest Jones, Wilhelm Stekel and Fritz Wittels. No correspondence with Sabina Spielrein or her brother Isaak survives among his papers (Abraham Cronbach Papers) and none is mentioned anywhere (according to an inquiry of 7 February 2008 to the Marcus Center of the American Jewish Archives, Cincinnati).

72 This sentence was subsequently inserted at the foot of the page. The study mentioned has not yet been found.

chiatric clinic. He has no respect for psychoanalysis. In his lecture course he did speak of psychoanalysis too, but only in order to take contemporary events into account. He sees getting hold of the literature as totally pointless. – As we are so poor in literature, I would be very grateful to any colleague who might want to send me an off-print of their work.

Now I am healthy again and, despite all the difficulties, my mood is consequently no longer so pessimistic. I think I will manage to get work in the university at Rostov too, as in Moscow, and that if I want I will be granted a lecture course on psychoanalysis. The main obstacle to that is that our professor of psychiatry,[73] who knows me well, is travelling abroad the day after tomorrow and only returning in November. If I don't have success at the university soon, I don't even know whether it's a matter for regret: I will still have the opportunity of teaching psychoanalysis privately to a few capable people and also to offer them a practical introduction according to all the rules of the profession. Once we have more colleagues, then my recommendations on the literature will have more success.

My report on the state of psychoanalysis in Rostov deals with this winter semester. I sent the due formal report at the time on the previous working period to Dr, now Professor, Wulff.

As you also know Russian, Doctor, I recommend you to read a book entitled: 'V.N. Voloshinov: Freidizm. Kriticheskii ocherk. Moscow-Leningrad: Gosudarstvennoe izdatel'stvo 1927'.[74] You will see there how little we have been understood so far and with what stupid objections we still have to contend. My husband[75] brought me the book yesterday. With this I will close my brief account of psychoanalysis in the North Caucasus area. Would you communicate it in some suitable form together with the reports from the branch societies?[76]

---

73 Prof. A. Yustchenko (1869–1936) held the Chair for Nervous and Mental Diseases at the University of Rostov, later the Chair for Psychoneurology at the North Caucasus University. Apart from that he was Director of the psychoneurological clinic, and from 1927 to 1929 also the Chair of the North Caucasus Pedagogical Society (see Movshovich, 2006)

74 Voloshinov (1927) [*Freudism: A Critical Essay*. Moscow-Leningrad: State Publishing House, 1927].

75 Pavel Naumovich Sheftel (1881–1937) came from Kiev. He was a doctor and paediatrician in Rostov-on-Don, where he met Sabina Spielrein in the winter of 1911–2, during one of her visits home. On 1 June 1912 they were married by the rabbi in Rostov. The first child, Renata, was born on 17 December 1913. From January 1915 onwards the couple lived separately—she in Switzerland, he in Russia. In 1923 Spielrein returned to Russia. In 1924 she arrived back in Rostov and continued her marriage with Pavel Sheftel (see Richebächer, 2005).

76 In fact, in his chairman's report at the Innsbruck Congress, Eitingon made little mention of the situation of psychoanalysis in Russia, and none at all of that in the North Caucasus region (see *IZ*

Apart from that I have another request of our colleagues: I would very much like to have uncomplicated dreams with representations of a) car b) aeroplane c) sun or stars d) weather e) spiders f) shoes g) telephone, telegraph or radio h) hat i) thread or stitching –

It is important for me to collect as many dreams of this type as possible; preferably written down by the dreamers themselves before analysis. In addition a short analysis would of course be desirable. Together with the dream details I would like the age, sex, profession and a very short account of the dreamer's personal situation. Where that is not possible – just details of the age, sex and profession will suffice. I would also like to have the name and address of the person sending the dream.

Why this collection of dreams? – it is difficult to explain this in a few words: I am interested in how individual objects are represented by different dreamers. Many thanks in advance.

And now the personal part.

I am longing to get together with all of you – that may be why I am extremely inhibited about writing. It was curious: as soon as I found out that Prof. Freud was seriously ill – I could not say a word to him. I felt a desolation around me and was as if fettered. Now I know that Prof. Freud is well again[77] and yet feel a certain hesitation about finding out that he has, even so, perhaps deteriorated physically, perhaps is also mentally downcast. Nevertheless – how is Prof. Freud?

Neither could I react to the news of Dr. Abraham's death.[78] It is too terrible. What could I say, so many thousands of miles away from everything and yet sharing your feelings so intensely?

I conclude with my best wishes to all participants in the congress and with my heartfelt hopes that our association will flourish. May this congress be particularly successful!

Dr S. Spielrein-Scheftel.

at present: Rostov-on-D. Dimitrievskaya 33[79]

1927, p. 486).

77 I.e. after his operation for cancer in Oct–Nov 1923.

78 Abraham died on 25 December 1925 at the age of forty-nine.

79 The street is now called Shaumyana. This address was Sheftel's three-room apartment in which his mother had previously lived.

4.3 LETTERS FROM NIKOLAI SPIELREIN TO DAUGHTER

NS 1

On the stationery of N.A. Shpilrein Agronomist Agricultural Bureau

My dear little friend! Rostov/Don 17 September 06

You are suffering, my dear! This is evident, first of all, from your headaches against which you must arm yourself with all your might, so as to prevent their return. Be strong, my dear! Time is a great healer, it will also heal your emotional torments. It is only necessary that you should find within yourself the needed equilibrium and this you will achieve only through quiet, systematic acquisition of positive knowledge. As a matter of fact, you still do not possess any considerable knowledge: everything you have acquired is as if by accident, from the most varied fields, without consistency, just the way it happened "helter-skelter." Thus you were fascinated by mathematics, and chemistry and electricity, and even lately you have been ready to embark on philology. Of course, every field is by itself of enormous interest the deeper you penetrate into its secrets. But such an encyclopedic effort does not offer either true knowledge or a firm foundation upon which you will later be able to erect a new structure of your own. Anyway, you recognized this yourself, when you recently decided to choose psychiatry. I'm confident that the further you progress the more will psychiatry satisfy you, and when you will fathom all what modern science has contributed to this field, then following this path you will reach the heights, which... [break].

NS 2

My dear one! 20.4.10.

Finally, thanks to the holiday, I can have a conversation with you. The great family event [Yasha's wedding] has taken place, but I do not feel great joy. I did not dream of such a setting for my diamond. Such a marriage will not assuage the sweet torments of my quests, nor transport me to vertiginous heights. On the contrary, given his character, it is to be expected that the wife will drag him down. Their love is strange, one gets an impression of something quite puzzling. It would all be good if Yasha had realized that he had to liberate his wife from an off-putting environment, but he has neither the strength nor the ability to fathom this. It's a pity, there was nobody there to educate Silva; she was able to get a superficial sheen, but given her nature she is a representative of her surroundings. But her environment has all the characteristics of an old stagnant world not ennobled by anything, its sense of superiority based on financial well-being. All right, so forget about it, may they be happy. Even if I lose this battle I will not see it as a labor lost because my other children will get their own, it is pointless to think that all four children will rush to heaven the same way.

Are you interested to know how they arranged the celebration? Exactly as only ordinary, nonintellectual people can do – there was a disorderly "*yidishe khasene*" [Yiddish, a Jewish wedding], all the originality came from the people invited by our family. Isai and Iliusha delivered beautiful speeches, I also made a speech, which I enclose. With you, my dear little friend, it will be different. I'm sure of that but it is more difficult to achieve. The easily found ones are representative of the herd, not deserving of my Sabina. But I have no doubt that a rare man will appear, surely a man also incapable of having a relationship with an "ordinary" woman. Your little verse touched me deeply; I read it many times and each time I found in it a new charm. Simple, tender words and how picturesque they are. It would be good to set it to music in a suitable spirit. But you make some mistakes: you write "alein" instead of "allein" [alone]. What is the meaning of your signing your last letters with the word "soli"? Is this the plural of the word *solus* [alone]? I also remember an old error of yours: *Fortrag* instead of *Vortrag* [lecture]. I'm glad that you passed the examination in surgery, but I was not surprised at all; no, I have the outmost confidence in my Sabina. From Sania I received the enclosed sheets which are very witty. It seems that he, Sania, is becoming a very nice man. You should not worry about me; I am healthy, but pining for more spiritually satisfying work. Also, you need not worry about financial matters for now; as it is, we have not become impoverished and I will try to amass an even bigger fortune for you all. Don't forget that I have <u>ready</u> for you (and these are not empty words) 75,000 francs as your dowry. This shows that we are not poor. Good bye, my dear.

[abbreviated signature]

NS 3

My dearest daughter, my dear joy! 10/6.10

Of course, your letter dispelled my depression, reassured me, and filled me with delight. Oh, it is for nothing that you doubt your capabilities. I believe in you, I strongly believe in you, my dear child. It is hard to be lonely and it is of course very painful. But it cannot be helped: have patience. What you need, what will give you satisfaction is not easy to come by. But you will find it – I have no doubt. Your mother has already been introduced to a number of gentlemen, and when you finish and get a name, they will be trying to ingratiate themselves to you even more. Do not forget, Sabochka, that you have a sizeable dowry. Mother and I have set aside for you the sum of thirty thousand rubles. This is a considerable capital, equivalent to 80,000 francs with which a lot can be done. Have patience, child. Soon you will see mama. I would even suggest that you and mama spend a whole month in Karlsbad or Kolberg and get a rest. I think of coming to visit you in the fall and perhaps spend time with you during your examinations. Your mama definitely needs some good treatment. It seems to me that psychoanalysis would do wonders for her illness so that all the other treatments will prove unnecessary. I am now writing to grandpa, sending him a letter from mama. By the way, I'm informing him of your successes. I am writing to him in Yiddish. The old man will be happy. He is now living in Yekaterinoslav and doing very well amongst his relatives. His face is even beautiful, the cheeks are pink as always, sight and hearing are still good, but his legs are almost disabled. How happy he will be when his Sabinochka finishes, gets married and lives a happy life.

Goodbye my dear. [signature]

The day after tomorrow I will send you 300 francs for the month of July.

NS 4

My dear one! Warsaw 9 II.13

As you see, I'm turning to you without any preliminary invitations. There are areas about which you want to talk to a person whom you respect (and perhaps even love) – not because that person is physiologically close to you, but only because you can understand each other spiritually, and this one finds attractive. This is my present state of mind. Today I went specially to have a talk with doctor Goldszmit[80] (pseudonym Korchak) about whom I have recently written to you. Thanks to donations he was able to find a home for orphans and half-orphans, sheltering 50 children of both sexes. This is a charitable institution for the children and for society, but for him, for the doctor, it has been but a field for investigating various phases of child development. Of interests are the tables and the curves he studies, weighing the children every week, measuring their strength with a dynamometer, observing the duration and depth of sleep, noticing developments of sexuality (in each sex separately – of homosexuality and interrelations between both sexes), developing in them self-mastery and self-guidance by instituting procedures of surveillance and order (for which the children are paid), by having them elect judges of their own courts, etc. The growth and

80 Henryk (Hersz) Goldszmit (1878 or 1879–1942), known by his pen name Janusz Korczak, was a Jewish-Polish doctor and pedagogue in Warsaw who wrote children's books and pedagogical works (*How to Love a Child*). In 1942, refusing to save himself, he was deported with his children to the Treblinka gas chambers.

weight tables are correlated with this or that food (by its caloric content) given to a child, growth tables are correlated with states of fatigue, laziness, a desire to rest in bed, to be up late at nights and to stay long in bed during daytime. In a word, every child is a whole universe, and a very interesting universe, there is a great deal to admire. He showed the curve of a girl who was overfed which resulted in a troubling weight gain. It turned out that the weight gain of a whole kilogram a week, during a number of weeks, had been created artificially, but when this force-feeding was stopped the organism gradually returned to its previous normal. There was some transient dyspepsia that had given some cause for concern. In connection with this problem, I recalled our attitudes to our son Milia. We spoke at length about education in children's homes, about this form of social life which offers an alternative to the atrophied "family", about how every educator has to function as a doctor, a psychologist and a pedagogue. It's wonderful that this doctor is not a dry scientist, but a man of exceptional joie de vivre. We have very similar views on an "esthetics" not pressed into the service of artificial forms of communal life, but one that is confirmed by those inner emotional sensations that are our perceptions. He told me how his professor was one day showing the students with great delight a half rotten, stinking lung, and speaking with eyes glowing with happiness, "Just take a look at these gorgeous classical tubercles, etc." Is this not also a kind of esthetics? The only difference is that other people will not find here "a beautiful" landscape with regular lines or the fragrance of "milfler" [French mille-fleurs, a thousand flowers], nor "a harmony of spiritual sentiments." So isn't the rapturous delight which the professor's psyche received from those "classical" tubercles also filled with harmony?

Dr. G. knows Freud personally and prays for him, not because he agrees with all his conclusions in all relations, but only because Freud so courageously and daringly penetrates the heretofore dark field of psychology which still scares most people. He [Dr. G.] speaks of absolute "freedom," which is indispensable for his aspirations, including matrimonial and financial freedom. He has a private practice but doesn't see more than four patients a day so as not to devote too much time to other matters. He only works in order to reach an income of 200 rubles a month, to be able to live independently. A lucky man, I envy him so much! How happy am I that I was able to give my children financial independence, giving them the possibility to [break].

NS 5

My dear! 23/6.13

Yesterday I received a letter from Pavlusha, and answered him, and today your letter arrived. I probably won't go abroad now, but I'm going to Warsaw next week. There my address is as usual the French Hotel. Don't be sad about your future, and don't worry about your financial situation. As long as I live everything will be all right. And when I'm gone, your capital will be intact, not a kopeck is touched. Perhaps in a few days I will deposit your money at 9½ % annually for three years and this is a very good investment. In any case, there are already 2,850 rubles (about 7,500 francs), so something will come of it and both of you will be able to achieve something.

Do not blame your husband; you have in him a very good and decent fellow. Unfortunately, you have created for yourself the image of an ideal husband like your own father. However, this will not do: such husbands and fathers, so undemanding and so self-sacrificing people as myself, you will not readily find. Accept, my dear, what fate has given you. You lucked out. In general, where is there assurance that with another man, a "strong" one, you would be happy? Do not worry, years will pass, you will get closer to each other, everything will be smoothed out, you will have a goal in your life and will be happy. Just don't be impatient, do not demand from a man molly-coddled by his family and loving it that he should instantly forget everybody and belong all to you. But if you insist on this, then entice him so that he'll forget everything, but do it without arguing, without pushing. Keep asking yourself, "What have I done, what have I sacrificed for the husband, what have I arranged to make him forget all his relatives and lose himself in the paradise created by <u>me</u>?" And whatever answer you will get to this question from yourself expect to get the same from your husband. So, for example, consider it as a trivial matter that he has reserved a room for himself for some time. This did not ruin you both and the more so, if he really intends to renounce something else; it is the other way around: as a loving wife you must see to it, and especially in your absence, that he should enjoy life, that he should not feel the absence of a "family" principle. The more smoothly it runs and the happier he will be, the more he will willy-nilly transmit to you all that ease and happiness and share it with you. After all, you are a psychiatrist, a psychoanalyst, whose main foundation is the conviction that "shared joy is double joy" (*geteilte Freude ist doppelte Freude*). On the other hand, a suffering person, a dissatisfied one, unconsciously carries within herself this emotional state and transmits it to the people around her because she actually feels unconsciously that "shared sorrow is half the sorrow." But then this is hard on him, he must cast off the half of his burden. No, my dear, no; Pavlusha is a very nice man and you could be very happy with him. Make an effort, ignore trifles, give him sincere and warm love so that he will not notice any deprivation, and you will see that you are in paradise. Surely, before long, a witness or critic of your relations will make an appearance. For his sake and your own, prepare the soil for peaceful happiness, which, before all else, is based on an indulgent-patient attitude to what in the other is not the same as what is in one: as I understand it, as I got used to it. Believe me, my dear, my only little daughter; I speak sincerely. I respect Pavlusha a great deal and I love him no less than all of you, because he is a fully worthwhile person. Never mind certain shortcomings of his character due to methods of education different from ours. These are small matters – the main thing is that the foundation is unconditionally good and <u>noble</u>. You should be glad a thousand times, as am I, that in him you have found precisely a <u>noble</u> person with a good unspoiled heart. I have also got to know Ania [his sister] more closely and all his family as well. I'll repeat what I have written to your mother: these are people with good, kindhearted and noble inclinations. As far as getting settled is concerned, again, it is not surprising that he has not been successful as yet. It is easy for you abroad, you have spent there almost half of your life, but he spent all his life here. If you're exhausted by having to struggle, then forget abroad and get both of you settled in Russia. Here he will advance quickly, especially after the good job he had done in Berlin. If you do not want Rostov, then choose Odessa, Moscow, Saint Petersburg, Warsaw, Saratov – briefly, some university town. He is a hard-working man, he will fulfill his obligations quite well, and will be able to provide for the family. And since you feel that you have a calling to create something new, then go ahead and create it, and bring light to Russian darkness; there, in the West, besides yourself, there are many people with serious ideas which they are unable to disseminate in Russia, not knowing the country or its language. On the other hand, you are in a favorable situation; what you took from there transplant in your homeland; "Sow goodness and the Russian nation will say thank you." Is the political life difficult? True, [break].

NS 6

My dear! Warsaw, 30.8.13

As far as "education" is concerned, about which you write, I will explain to you that in this case it is a matter of "re-education", and this requires a very good and skilled outside pedagogue, since you will rarely find such people among those who are "<u>self-taught</u> pedagogues," or else why would Socrates have to proclaim his famous "*gnoth[i] seauton*"(know yourself)? As I have already told you before the wedding, the matter of re-education or, more precisely, interpersonal education, lies almost entirely in your hands, my dear. With love, kindness and logic, [one can] persuade even the most stubborn person. Clearly, you need a lot of patience, a lot of knowledge, in other words, at the same time one has to enhance one's own education. That Pavlusha, is, let us say, resisting, is not surprising, or else he would be a dishrag. Considering that this or that is very "unappealing" from our point of view, is indeed the reason why he needs to be re-educated; or else, why does one need to fence a garden [word-play, in Russian garden already means fenced]? I think you understand what I mean. One should not act according to a "categorical imperative," but, little by little, with a great supply of patience and love. What kind of sculptor would he be who would apply the same method to every matter: "he hits with an axe once and gets a nose, a second time and gets lips," etc. This is only possible when you are facing a Sobakevich,[81] but not a cultivated and educated person. However, you as a psychiatrist, find that he has a "complex" regarding financial matters. But if from the first moment after the wedding you would pummel this complex with your hand, then you are not psychologically savvy. Listen, my dear child. Wishing you well is equivalent to wishing well to myself. And I say to you sincerely, "You have worthy matter in your hands; mold it, and you will create, squeeze it and you will destroy". But don't worry, interacting with your relatives will improve once he is really able to love the hand that comforts him. However, a hand that is continually throwing salt on a man's psychological wound—and demanding, that while writing in burning pain, he should say, "Yes sir, I will do my very best, your highness"—cannot kindle heartwarming love. I will agree with all your reasons that prove that the task is a difficult one but I will never agree that it is an insoluble task. "If you want to hear the echo in the wonderfully sounding distance, then you must accordingly shout to the forest" ("*Willst Du das Echo in Klingender Weite vernehmen, dann must Du entsprechend in den Wald hineinrufen*")[82] With my best wishes, my dear one. Be happy, all three of you.

NS 7

My Dear! Hotel Kahlenberg Vienna, 21/6 Sunday 1914

I slept or just layed in bed and slept only for 12 hours and got up to be ready for a visit from Rakhil, expected within the next half hour. For many

81 Allusion to a character in Gogol's novel "Dead Souls" (1842): a man coarse, stingy, and bigoted.
82 This text could not be found but there is this German proverb: *wie man in den Wald hineinruft, so schallt es heraus* (as you shout into the woods, so it echoes back out), one is treated the same way as one treats other people.

hours I have been thinking about you, both of you. I have decided to write to you once more about the problems that are tormenting you. I repeat what I told you before: be calm, everything will be all right. It is only necessary that Pavel should become more steadfast. This will not be easy for him, first of all, because he is weak by nature, and mainly, because he feels guilty toward his relatives. It is certain that Pavlusha must have been told many times that when he got married, he would obtain 30 thousand rubles of dowry (this was a minimum) and take care of all of them. And if he has offered them concrete promises, then the claims of his relatives to his money are all the more justified by the situation of his mother and sister Ania. Consider the situation thoroughly, and you will understand that I am speaking sincerely and not just to calm you. After her husband's death, the mother was left (I made a slip using the masculine instead of the feminine verb, which, interpreted the Freudian way, means that the role of husband and breadwinner was transferred to her) with seven children of which two daughters and two sons had to be raised and given a decent education. The small pension she got was insufficient to feed such a family, and life was getting more and more expensive. Willy-nilly, the widow faced hard times that forced her to look for support, and first and foremost from her children. She probably got help from Ernestina, from Izrail and Pavel who was tutoring, etc. (all these are my suppositions). She mainly hoped to get help from her sons. S. A. [the mother] did not allow independence, everything was determined by her edicts. She married off her son Izrail, acquiring 4,000 rubles, and hefty skirmishes with her daughter-in-law, but with time everything was forgotten. The second son married without money; they hated his wife, and after the husband's death, this hatred was transferred to the daughter-in-law.

S.A. even ordered to stop the dinners, which the hospital was sending to the daughter-in-law and her son, a nice little boy. Ania was lucky in her marriage, as Senia turned out to be a very soft man; he became the financial sponsor to a considerable extent, contrary to, perhaps, Ania's own wishes; and perhaps Ania, who is by nature not such a good person, having seen all the troubles mother has had, wanted to save money to cover any future disaster, which of course is not itself blameworthy. However, the demands of the mother have been getting bigger and bigger: the young maidens are growing up, they need to be well dressed in order to show themselves to full advantage and cover up their poverty, they are also provided with education and the necessary glitter. And that costs a lot of money. The children are not taught how to deal with money, the mother takes care of everything herself and the children's only duty is to obey mother's orders. But mother is herself bad at dealing with money, she sets all her future hopes on Pavlusha who with his kind heart, is willing to take care of all of them. And now this Pavlusha, this commonly shared hope of future prosperity, has been coaxed by everybody, persuading themselves that all this was only a sign of true love. And now it is Ania's turn, or she herself takes a leading role. She has great faith in the magnificent match of Pavlusha (mainly regarding money), she has faith in his honesty and that he will give everything back, she has faith that he will conscientiously share with her the labor of dragging the sisters to get married. Moreover, she is flattered by having the role of the leader, which she inherited from her mother, especially since she has no children of her own (either consciously or unconsciously). Thus Ania, having assumed the role of mother, takes Pavel under her wing. And understandably, the brother obeys: he pushed and the amount of his dowry was fixed; the *shadkhens* [matchmakers] do their business, offer expense money, so what does he have to worry about? And so they hear about a bride with 30,000. She herself is a doctor, it means that there is *ikhes*[83], the only daughter of a father who is a wealthy man. Pavlusha is pushed, he is ready to go. And now, unfortunately, Ania has to leave town. She leaves calmly, and without worrying that the whole deal will be done soon and without her permission or blessing. And what is the horror: that for the first time Pavlusha has dared to act. And this is already a reason to get angry – but with whom? Of course, with his wife. Mother is also angry, so that she doesn't even want to see her other son (nobody of course is thinking about the daughter-in-law), about whose arrival in Kiev she had been fully informed. And even if she had to travel to Crimea to get treatments, how difficult would it have been to come for a day or two to Kiev, for her, who was used to travel to Rostov and back without getting tired? The son with the daughter-in-law... they are angry all the time, especially when Pavel continues to show disobedience. Ania demands that he come to visit her in Franzensbad[84] and he disobeys; she demands that he come to Berlin and, again, he refuses to go. Aha, that means that he feels guilty. He would have gone but "she" [i.e. Sabina] won't let him. Naturally, the result is a displacement (*Verlegung*) to "her": the guilty one, the one who dashes hopes, is "she." But her old man [i.e., Sabina's father], without demurring, is paying off all of Pavlusha's promissory notes. So it's not that bad. Hopes revive again and they begin to be reconciled. Pavel sends them 150 rubles... He is invited to attend a family celebration but he doesn't come. Again anger, again "she". Time passes, one wants to marry the

83 Yiddish/Hebrew yichus, pedigree, bragging based on a respected family history.
84 The famous Bohemian spa town now called Františkovy Lázně in the Czech Republic.

daughters off no matter what, and the cherished hopes regarding Pavel do not come through. The mother starts getting angry again, rather under the influence of Ania, not being able to find a way to cast off the burden. Sabina gives birth to a daughter; jealousy is added to the previous show of anger. Ania is beside herself. A son is born to Izrail, Ania doesn't have enough words to express her delight with this little boy; she can't stop talking how much she had suffered, having worried about the woman who had given birth, etc. However, she definitely said not one word about Irmochka [Sabina's daughter].

The mother is more intelligent; she is older and more experienced. And perhaps she recognizes that it is wrong to be angry with Sabina who is not guilty of anything. And yes, the latter is very attentive to her; why answer evil with evil, why not accept a fait accompli and not recognize her new dear daughter? Finally, she will travel to her son; she will try to persuade him to return to Russia, and with the right kind of oversight, in view of the changed circumstances, everything will go in the right direction. After all, she is a person, and a mother who undoubtedly loves her children. Managing all of them is her life's purpose, and in them is her future peaceful old age. It's not for nothing that she cannot forget her more peaceful, financially secure life with her husband to whom she still keeps referring as "my dear husband," and, to be precise, not "my late husband, " but "my dear one". This is how things are and I consider Pavel guilty to the extent that once he had accepted certain obligations toward his own family he had the duty to remember those obligations and make a show of it in the presence of all of them, especially given the important changes in his personal life. Here is an example: for many years doctor Adolf confessed a great love for Sabina at a time when she had no dowry. This would have gone on for a long time, but mother (your mother) put an end to it by telling him point blank. Then he answered that he could not get married; for only if his sister told him that he must give 2000 rubles to the parents, he would consider himself to be a free man. And since Sabina doesn't have the money, then he would like to accumulate this sum and then think whether he wants to get married. The relatives together gathered 2,000 rubles, which they handed to Adolf, the wedding took place without further ado[85], and from then on his relatives had no further complaints.

Immediately after your wedding, I vividly imagined all the aforementioned issues and was able to calmly accept the news, which reached me incorrectly, of Pavel's debts. I went even further: in consideration of all the facts presented and concerning the weakness of Pavel's character, I expressed my independent

85 It is unclear what wedding took place, but it could not have been wedding Sabina.

intention, through your mother, to offer full financial help to Pavlusha's mother or his sisters, which amounts to the same thing. Mother informed Pavel about this. But instead of understanding the tactfulness of our family, or in general evaluating the situation simply and sincerely, Pavel thought it necessary to demonstrate an honorable attitude, falsely understood by him (regarding all the relevant matters), and declared that I am prohibited from giving them help, because his mother is not a beggar. How shortsighted of him and what a weak character! Now mother and Ania are expected here. The latter, probably guided by her mother's advice, will start by saying that "she feels ten years younger" in your presence, she will say how delighted she is to see Irmochka, etc. For sure, she will bring Pavel another present like last time and will not forget about you. The mother is bringing you a golden ring with a diamond. Nothing you can do about it, of course, you will accept the present and try to repay with something; she, certainly, will treat you with a lot of feelings as long as the real problem is not mentioned. It is at this point that you should muster all your prudence. At no time should you forget the true picture, it seems to me, that I have painted for you; you have to take the side of his mother and recognize that from her point of view she is certainly right. To this you will probably answer, may be, "let's pay it off." So my dowry will become a little bit smaller." But you see, my dear, I have no intention of punishing Pavel for the imprudence he had committed at the time. I even want to forget that now it looks more like paying a "good producer". I simply do not know how strong your relationship is, i.e., whether it will survive the attacks on Pavel by his relatives. Therefore I repeat what I have already stated in my previous letter: do not worry, take it easy. Tell Pavel to solve by himself the problem of his weak character, as long as he does not make new promises that might infringe on your person, your freedom and your wishes. Embrace your husband's relatives with full dignity and respect as befits an intelligent and self-respecting person. But as soon as you notice any attempts to intervene in your personal and family life with your husband, please request, in a dignified manner and again without personal offence, to present this problem to you and your husband for a mutual evaluation, and this without any contact either with your relatives or your husband's relatives. That is all I wanted to tell you. I do not know if you will want to inform Pavel about the content of this letter. This is your business. I do not hide what I honestly and sincerely think. I have no intention of offending anybody. Should it be proven to me that I am mistaken and that with my mistake I caused someone unjustly some kind of distress, then I will gladly and publicly express my apology without feeling ashamed for my mistake, because "*errare humanum est*" [to err is human].

Just one more thing: ask Pavel seriously to consider serious problems. I sincerely respect him as a good person; therefore let him not look for hidden insinuations in between the lines. But he is doing just that is revealed by the signature of his last letter: "in many respects unattractive." But this criterion also reflects <u>my</u> point of view, the way I'm used to view life. Similarly, from his point of view I probably appear to <u>him</u> as unattractive in many respects. Why see premeditated evil in everything? When people of different viewpoints meet, frictions are unavoidable. But it is necessary to understand each other. It is beautifully stated in the Bible:

красиво сказано по …

על כן-יעזב איש את אביו ואת אמו ודבק באשתו.

In translation: therefore every (husband) leaves his father and mother and clings to his wife.[86] It is like "heads" and "tails" on a coin, like "cathode" and "anode;" without this the wholeness of life is unthinkable, in the same way we do not know light without shadow and vice a versa.

Good bye to you. [signature]

NS 8

Dear! Vienna 6/7 14

Tomorrow is the birthday of your Pavlusha. I have felt a flood of unknown to me warm feelings, which made me very happy; I view them as a result of my treatment. I wrote such a [warm?] letter to Pavlusha but did not send it, because I recalled his distrustful attitude, and especially now when his relatives are around here, and given his suspiciousness, he would've reacted to my letter with a certain bias. Therefore, I tore up my letter and sent him a more sober postcard. In addition, I ordered for him two volumes of the compositions of Wagner, which the editorial staff promised to send immediately, so that I assume that by tomorrow they will be in Berlin. I'm not sure whether he will get pleasure from this, but I do not regret what I've done because I acted from a sincere desire to make him happy and not for the sake of propriety. It seems to me that they took him "to task" despite the assurances of S.A. [Pavel's mother] that she and her son hold no secrets toward his wife. I always remember my stepmother, who made peace with her own son under mama's pressure, when asked by mama whether she was glad about it, answered: "What is there to be glad about, what do I get out of

86 "A man shall leave his father and his mother, and shall cleave to his wife," Genesis, 2:24.

him?" This is an old-fashioned way of thinking that parents should "get something" from their children, that they should be paid for their labors, care and expenditures. In this case, I am especially aware of the influence of and plotting by Ania, who feels obligated to help mother but of which, understandably, she would like to get rid of, at least partially, for she is an insincere person. She won't even hesitate to sic her own husband against someone even as she is enjoying that person's hospitality. I shall be glad to be proven wrong. I can only imagine what mama is going through there now. I must stop now. Osip, the brother about whom I've just been speaking, had just walked in. He happened to be in Vienna, attending a funeral of an heir on behalf of the editorial office, for which he works. We are going out to take a walk. I'll finish my letter later. [signature]

[postscript] I came back home from a walk. He promised to visit you on his way and try his best to help you. He likes to get carried away, like all "journalists". I received a letter from Pavlusha and I'm going to answer it. It seems that my suppositions are being confirmed. At the beginning of the letter he is nervous, he crosses words out, corrects words, makes long lines in the end of words, as if he is angry with somebody, as if he is "mit dich nicht' ["not with you" in German], etc. God help him, clearly he is suffering. Were he not so wildly suspicious, I would have shown him that in me he doesn't have "a father"—which I consider to be a [ridiculous?] propriety—but a real and devoted friend, upon whom he can lean with confidence. But at least you should be good and indulgent toward him, after all, he is your husband and the father of your daughter.

[postscript] I have just received your letter with yesterday's date. We shall talk about [text break]

NS 9

My dear! [Illegible] 3/6.15

I received your letter to mama of 21/5. Mama cannot write now, she is busy: she took upon herself the task of making various clothes for poor children. She bought all kinds of materials for 500 (five hundred) rubles and now day after day volunteers, girls and ladies are sewing here. It is strange how she has got the health and strength, seeing that ten times every day she has been definitely dying or at least saying, "This time I feel that I will die soon". True, she does get tired because it is lots of work, almost 200 complete sets of various shirts, pants, towels, etc. In general, so far everything is alright. Your "dream," about which you are writing, will come true if you will strive to fulfill it; nothing will happen by <u>itself</u>. You should join a suitable society and be aware that this implies that external appearances play an important role. True, Sania's wife Rozochka is far from perfect in this regard; however, she is more demonstrative than you and, besides, not everyone treats people the way Sania, you, me, etc. do – first of all looking for some inner content in a male or female friend. Anyway, you ought to, the sooner the better, to move to [Montreux?] and [pick a place to settle down?] and [then be dressed] well and in good taste. For this purpose, this year I am willing to make you a special gift of up to 2,000 francs in addition to the money you have already received.

It is a big sum of money, and you should spend it judiciously. Perhaps this will prove insufficient if you need to order outerwear for winter, and this is also necessary because you do not have anything decent to wear. If so, I will give you five hundred rubles more specially for the outerwear. Prepare an approximate estimate and let me know, in the meantime I will be sending you a few hundred francs every month until the full amount is reached (about 3000 francs). Are you satisfied, I hope? So look, don't order any rags, only something substantial. Are you receiving <u>all</u> my letters? Write [illegible words] you received my letters of March, April, and May.

Goodbye. [signature]

[a postscript from mother]

Sabinochka! I'm very busy doing something great thus I don't have a single minute to write letters. I am just letting you know that everything is alright here, you all should not worry. Let the children know about it. Sarra Pochtareva [Isaak's mother-in-law] has been staying with us for the last three days, tell Roza [his wife, whose Jewish name is Rakhil]. Everyone in her family is doing well. Write to me as frequently as possible, let everyone write to me often, or else I will have <u>a breakdown</u> if there are no letters.

Goodbye and write.

Your mama.

Dear Renatochka! My dearest child! Be always well, cheerful and gladden your mother and all of us. Your grandma.

[a postscript from father] Sabina, notice a complete absence of the [usual?] oh's and ah's – and just one word at the end "I will have a breakdown."

NS 10

My dear! 19/7.16

I am writing following a message I received today about a very important matter. As you know, I have already received a protective certificate No. 65211 for the production of sandals in Russia. Now I also want to obtain a patent abroad, and have therefore selected neutral Switzerland. There must be a patent office in

Lausanne that will give you all the necessary explanations. Based on these data, register immediately the patent in my name at the appropriate Swiss institution (the Swiss Ministry of Finances or some other office), if that is possible, and if not, submit it in your own name. Do not be to too trusting there, as anywhere, else they grab the idea and create a patent, and then go and sue them. You just find out what formalities need to be carried out and immediately submit a petition to the appropriate place with the required amount of money. As far as I remember, it should not be too expensive. You just have to translate it into German or French (if in Lausanne, then of course a French translation will be needed) and attached to it a detailed description as I had submitted to our Ministry of Commerce. In addition, I am attaching a drawing of the sandals. The most convenient way is to talk to the owner of the patent office there, who will undertake to arrange everything for a small fee of some 25 francs, I believe, and you should have very little trouble. But don't put it in the back drawer and get to it urgently. In any case, I expect an immediate response from you to this request.

Sania's silence is very troublesome for us. If it were not for your assurances, I would be entertaining very pessimistic assumptions. By the way, on the pages of a tear-of-calendar I found a few Jewish [Yiddish] poems. Send them to the proper address; apparently he [Sania] will be very pleased. Yesterday, the brother of our Susanna, with his wife, came here to receive some inheritance of a deceased female relative. Pity, you could not be here. The result was a brilliant psychological study. Yes, Sabina, money is an infinitely vulgarizing stuff. You know, when [Maksim] Gorky in an emotionally articulated speech pronounces the word "person", one is able to realize that in between the letters was insinuating itself the poisonous word "money" – it is a weed on a splendid field of a human life, having a stupefying effect and turning a person into a frenzy of Cain. Oh, my dear! Be well, write immediately.

ЧЕЛОВЕК	PERSON
д е н ь г и	m o n e y

NS 11

My dear ! 25.10.16

Today is your birthday; we cabled you, and we are now adding our best wishes. Today we received your undated postcard (stamped by the post office as 13/10) in which you are "begging fate" etc. Before long, you will start going to houses of prayer, make bows, and recite prayers to God. In a word, a complete picture of a superstitious fear becomes apparent. But seriously, I warn you, my dear; take hold of yourself or else you will end up in an unbearable state of mind and as a result cause irreparable damage to the child. Do not overdo it, do not exaggerate, do not beg any fate, be the fate yourself, and raise the child firmly and rationally, both physically and mentally, without fears and apprehensions that will only confuse the mind.

Today I received a letter from Marcel Poznanskii. He requests to inform his relatives that he is in a cheerful mood and is asking to be told how the family is doing. I am attaching press clippings about Beba's death. The article by Sevskii is so-so but the one by Tamarin is one big misunderstanding, one can see that it was all in vain. The whole pride of the family is in those letters: a millionaire, a Liebknecht[87], and a son [illegible]. By the way, he [Marcel] is a "real Jew" who does not know a word of Yiddish, who never had anything in common with Judaism, and who married a French gentile woman.

All the best to you, [signature]

NS 12

My Dear! Rostov-on-D 3/8.17

I received your letter of [?]. You do not write <u>from whom</u> you received 712 francs, i.e., whether as instructed by one of the local Petrograd banks or by a special office of the credit department of the ministry of foreign affairs. The thing is that until now it was possible to send you money via private banks, and when this became prohibited I turned once more to the special office. I assume that the 712 francs according to the current exchange rates are equivalent to 500 rubles. Today the exchange rate for a Swiss franc is 117 kopecks and since the maximum that can be transferred is 500 rubles it will be equivalent to no more than 428 francs. It's good that you have some savings. As far as Sevtsa [a relative] is concerned, your reasoning about her is in part incomprehensible. I have already written to you once that I believe it's our obligation to support her and there is no need to compute and compare that you are spending 50 francs a month on her. The only thing that seems strange to me is that she is in need. So where is the capital in cash of 20,000 rubles which she had; did she have to return this to her father? Moreover she had plans to marry a Frenchman; so what happened to that gentleman? At home we are all doing well. I am taking a holiday because there is no business. The renters are bothering me because

87 Karl Paul August Friedrich Liebknecht (1871–1919) was a socialist member of the original German Socialist Party (SPD) and later a co-founder with Rosa Luxemburg of the German Communist Party. He married Sophie Ryss a sister of Yasha's wife Silva (p. 184).

they are fighting about rents and repairs, etc. But this is now a common phenomenon: fights about money are everywhere. Mama is still sick, it's awful. If all of you came back it would certainly cheer her up. Our Fania has been seeing a fortune teller from Nakhichevan who reads beans which may be the origin of the word "bobkes."[88] Fania asked her to read your fortune and got the answer that you and the child are somewhere far away and that you feel very lonely and unhappy; that your husband loves you and that both of you long for each other but that "two women" are interfering with your ability to become good friends and live together. About Yasha, this Armenian said that he is on a long journey somewhere, that he is already sitting in a railway car on his way home, but that here (pointing to her forehead) there is something is wrong, but that all this will pass: he will come back and we will be happy and he will be happy all his life.

Mama and I have just come back from a wedding. The daughter of our dvorniks (janitor) was getting married, and they celebrated their wedding in our office. I and mama, were invited as sponsor parents of the wedding. We saw the young couple again when they came back from the church and blessed them with bread-and-salt and an icon. We stayed a little with the guests and left. Mama gave them a gift of a tea set and 100 rubles in cash, in one word the celebration was completed and the "satisfaction" infinite.

[signature]

NS 13

My Dear! Rostov on/Don 21/8.17

Today I was notified by Azovbank that the money for June (1,500 francs) was not transmitted to you because they did not have your address. I believe this is a misunderstanding because you are living on Avenue Solaire and you must have left your address in Villars. In any case, I instructed that the money should be left at the bank in Lausanne at your disposal, i.e., until you ask for it. This bank is called Société Banque Suisse Zurich à Lausanne. Even if you were to leave before receiving this letter, it will do no harm to leave the money there; it might be useful for Sania. Let us know when you will be leaving, but don't take all the money with you; it is necessary to leave it there so that in case he needs it, Sania will be able to use it, or else he'll have nothing to eat. By the way, I ask you once more to take from [other] banks [illegible] all the sums which you have received during all this time. I will have to do an accounting with the local banks and then it will be necessary [a line is missing]. I received a photo of the girl; I am

88 A pun on the Yiddish word for beans, also spelled bubkes, i.e., chickenfeed.

looking at this lovely face and thinking what happiness that you are [illegible] a mother, that you can't avoid experiencing conflicts that were undoubtedly once enacted between your parents during your early upbringing. Every cloud has a silver lining, and I consider it to be a supreme happiness that you alone in this case acted as you saw fit. I am confident that you will raise the child skillfully and properly; for these first inclinations are the whole guarantee of the future. On this photo Renatochka is a rare beauty; I just don't know how slender she is. I have one fervent wish: that your husband should prove worthy of your daughter and worthy to call her his daughter. It is perhaps in vain that he might love her, this Natochka, for he should earn the right and honor to this love. He left you and abandoned her while she was in a state near death, and, clearly, he may not consider himself worthy of her love. In general all our granddaughters are rare both in their outward and inward spiritual beauty. I assume that Menikhochka[89] will be a wonderful person if only the harmonious life between Sania and Rakhil will in the future remain the same, it seems to me, as it was from the very beginning of their life together. We received [Menikhochka's] photograph, a very intelligent face that promises a great deal. As far as Yasha's girls are concerned, I confess, I fear for them. Yasha lacks a backbone. True, they might turn out to be pearls in a dunghill, but something as free and creative as I would like to see in them can only be produced by a strong and energetic hand, which Yasha is yet to find in himself; but he cannot until he realizes that without him this matter leaves much to be desired. I would love to have my boys close to me. I need their help, their support. It is difficult to do everything alone. I am in Petrograd soliciting to obtain Yasha's freedom and our foreign office has already made contact with our consulates in Stuttgart and Copenhagen but so far no results. Meanwhile we are receiving desperate letters from Yasha which make mama terrified. It is especially necessary that you and Sania should help him to cheer up and not give in to his mood. Something bad is happening with your mother; she is suffering immeasurably for all of you, but she worries especially about Yasha since his last letter. By the way, here is an interesting observation: when she is suffering greatly, her hair turns gray; when she starts to calm down, her hair gets blacker as you are watching it happen. How strange to get such striking confirmation of the interrelationship between a person's mind and body. I have also made an observation of Sarra Pochtareva, a truly classical example of

89 Menikha Isaakovna Spielrein (1916–2000) would be discovered in Moscow by the Swedish Slavic Studies Professor Magnus Ljunggren (erroneously cited as "journalist" by Alexander Etkind (1997). Ljunggren published her reminiscences about the Spielrein family.

Freud's theories. But enough for now, I have to write to Sania, and soon dinner will be served. Goodbye, signature

[postscript] The news is that Milia transferred to study agronomy in Kharkov; he was [admitted] to the Novoaleksandriiskii Institute, the section of agriculture.

NS 14

Rostov on/Don 23/11.17

I held on to mama's letter because I wanted to send it in a special way, as a valuable parcel, to be sure that it will get to you. In the meantime I got ill with an attack of lumbago. I had to stay in bed for a few days and today we received your telegram without showing the date it was sent, that you finally received 354 francs and 1,500 francs, but I don't understand how the first sum was calculated. In addition, there are various sums underway. One of those sums is for June, also 1,500 francs. Make inquiries at the bank, insist strongly upon verification and I don't doubt that you will get it. What will happen next I don't know. I am transferring, more precisely, I am giving money for you to many people hoping that one of these sums will get to you but it's also possible that you will get nothing and you will have to get a job. It's a pity because of the child, but don't whimper and don't sit idly by. Anyway I think that Sevtsa should be able to help you with the little one. Although she lacks experience, she can learn, but she is a relative and she's still acting the part. When you first wrote to me about Sevtsa's situation I answered that it is necessary to give her lodging without worrying about the expense. Now since the situation has changed, we have no possibility to send you money to cover expenses. Sevtsa has to acknowledge her obligation to help you with Renata, but if she doesn't understand it (not due to her bad character but due to a faulty development), then there is no reason for you to feel ashamed. You have to explain this to her in a friendly manner and I am sure that she will perform her task willingly; otherwise I would see her as an unintelligent person. It is possible that due to current events you will soon be able to leave. The question is does it make sense for you to travel before the storm passes. From the selfish point of view I would say "come sooner, we'll all be together, etc.," but from the point of view of reason and sincere devotion to both of you, my children, I can resolutely say: "You have suffered so long, suffer a little bit more even if it becomes, as they say, unbearable." You are young, you have your life ahead of you, take care of it. You will be able to create a lot of things for the common good. And should I perish in this whirlwind, it would not be so terrible: I have already achieved a great deal by having raised four children the way I wanted to. It means that actually my life will not perish, you will continue it, willy-nilly, along the trail blazed by me provided that you do not consider this trail to be incorrect or unreasonable. Should you get involved <u>now</u> in the evolving cataclysm, you will not create anything, and under these conditions you will risk becoming useless victims which I consider to be devoid of all logic. Should I face death, I will feel sorry in the last moment that I was not able to be with you and personally take leave of you, but this will be a momentary weakness of self-love, and I will send you my benediction for your continuing life's journey with a deep satisfaction that what I have sown has created good results and one has to assume will yield correspondingly good fruit. But you, my children, don't worry; do not think that I am in imminent danger or that I have some premonition. Nothing of the kind; I am just soberly observing the events, and anyway I would like that you should accept the inevitable as calmly as I do. It's a pity that Yasha has been so unfortunate and my only wish is that he should not feel it. It could have been possible, had Silva been a wise woman but it didn't happen: she is very limited, very poorly brought up, and one should constantly fear the collapse of his insight. But he is such a rare, wonderfully rare person, that suffering caused by someone who completely misunderstands him and does not value anything in him for his own sake, can have a deleterious effect on his creativity and, as a result, his peace of mind. Oh, if only she could have insight and were able to appreciate what a great treasure fate had entrusted to her to preserve!

[postscript] Have you written down all the sums which you have received until now?

Postscript from Father: The photograph we received through Yasha is poorly made, the retouching is bad. How come?

NS 15

My Dear! Rostov on/Don 17/1 18

Today I am starting a letter to you which, as expected, will be quite long. Therefore it will have to be written in segments and finished in a few days. The difficult part is that I must express and bare my soul to the censors, who continue to fulfill their civic duty regarding the Germans, while the latter are better informed about our ministry of internal affairs than we are ourselves. But nothing can be done about it so I begin: in fact, I thought of writing about today's theme to Yasha and Sania, but I am addressing this letter to you, assuming that it will reach you more easily than them. It is a matter of all my experiences and decisions taken by me in connection with events taking place in Russia. I have already hinted to you that you may not find me alive when you return home. Now I wish to confirm this possibility even more, because the storm here is growing enormously almost by the hour. There are no data to determine whom this epidemic will spare because every reasonable person, especially if he is a man, has to be ready for what will happen when his turn comes. I say "man" because it is quite natural, because of our contemporary order of "the fight for survival," because it occupies a dominant role in the male gender, and in the present transvaluation of all values, it is a "he" (a man) who has first of all to be personally responsible for everything. By the way, this fact is most remarkable from the psychological point of view and more than ever before I would like now to converse with Professor Freud. The relations between the sexes have been completely destroyed in all the warring countries and it is particularly striking here in Russia where internecine wars have turned many men into victims. One cannot escape thinking that measures will be taken to restore an equilibrium either by way of legalizing polygamy or in some other way. What will then become of our concepts of morality, of the purity of morals, of paeans to love, of high ideals, of transvaluation of all values? That means QED [*quod erat demonstrandum* = that which was to be demonstrated].

I am getting back to the real purpose of my letter. I repeat, I am a man like everybody else, consider the possibility that I will become a victim of what is happening now. I have already mentioned in one of my previous letters that I view this possibility with complete serenity, that I consider my life cycle as fully completed, that until now I have been in all respects satisfied with the fruits of my creativity, in a word, that my life has not been in vain. Of course, I would like to live some more, and to have the opportunity personally to say goodbye to all of you, my children; would like to see the results of great and extraordinary efforts of the contemporary human spirit. Finally I would like to make with you, my dear, a little tour of this beautiful world: across America, Australia, India, Japan, for about two to three years. How much knowledge we would garner during that time, to die for! And then...and then...to fly high in a hot air balloon, and then hug you, all my children, to my heart, to hug and release so that I can gaze from afar how you will be marching ahead, each following his path until the moment when I will finally bid you farewell. Finally, indeed? I don't think so, because I believe in continuous life, in a self-renewing life, in eternal life. And what a beautiful dream I dreamt recently. I rarely remember my dreams so clearly as this one, so clearly do I recall this time the form, the contours, and the color of the objects seen, let alone their location, in a most detailed manner.

Here is the dream: I hear the whizzing (ein Zischen = a hissing) of a flying rocket and seem to be waking up, and I am surprised to have heard this sound, since "you hear no sounds in dreams"; but the dream with sound, that has apparently woken me up, does not stop, and I see a violet grey cone-shaped cloud rising from the earth upward; this cloud resembles a beautifully trimmed conifer, the kind used to adorn flower beds in gardens. This beautiful form with even, perfect borders astonished me; it is more correct to say, it did not astonish me but provided a certain pleasure. Little by little from above small tongues of fire began to appear, and all this was pleasant and beautiful. Presently, this thick internally burning cone disappears, as if bursting into an enormous flame on my right. The space is ablaze, but it is not a conflagration inspiring terror, but a fire that is both beautiful and transparent and pleasant; and now the fire goes out and against its background four hills appear, starting with a big one and gradually getting smaller and lower, so that they are symmetrical; these hills are not scattered around, but advance in a straight line getting lower on the right side. I ask myself, where has the fire gone, seeing that the hills are now violet grey, like the aforementioned cloud. The shape of these hills is also conical, but not with even borders, as I described above, but shaped like real hills. And at the same time as I am asking myself where the fire has gone, the [edges?] of these hills become illuminated by an extremely beautiful bright band of sunshine, as we often see on Swiss mountains at sunrise or sunset. As the hills are beginning to disappear on the left side, or more precisely on the left side of the burning cloud (it's amazing that this cloud, as I call it, had disappeared a long time ago, but I feel as if it is still here, and this process is still perceived by me as taking place either to the right or to the left of it). So, on the left side I see something like a monument (but it is not a monument as I tell myself in the dream), consisting of three circular, broad, and easily accessible steps, one on top of the other; the landings between the steps are wide and smooth; above the third step there is a big landing in the middle of which stands a column, not especially high, the height of a person, and about 30 centimeters in diameter. The top of the column is completely straight, horizontal. The color of this whole "non-monument" is a dark beige, and it is all smooth, sparkling (all of a sudden I remember both the color and the sparkle of that ceiling about which I had written to you when I told you about my dream of a bird, an electric technician, etc.; that ceiling was the same color and sparkled with exactly the same brilliance "as if somewhat dull", i.e., not glaring). As I was looking at this "monument," I was aware of a certain particularly present, even calm, sensation of something pleasant and even tranquil. It also seemed strange to me that I was not seeing this "non-monument" all around, but only the front of it facing me, not seeing the back of it. It is there, "in space," but I can see no contour of it. All of a sudden, on the steps I see a rug (it now reminds me of a Persian rug in our living room), but I have the sensation that this rug is incorrectly laid out. I cannot explain in what way is it irregularly laid out. Everything disappears, I see an empty space, like an open field, green, but after some time I see the monument again in its previous place. Now, on top of the column I see a black bird, an owl, I see its owl's eyes, but they are not scary (I think that an owl has scary looking eyes); its gaze is not malicious, and then in place of it there is another black bird but quite inoffensive, but I can't make out the species, and now I see below on the steps once again the Persian rug, and again now I see its bright fringed border; but I am again surprised that the rug is not laid out straight and even on these steps, but lying like a wedge, a corner, or a cone (!), as if everything is moving forward and upward. Then everything disappears, and I fall asleep. In the last part of the dream, starting with the appearance of the monument, at first on the left side; I see it not as if I am in a dream but just see it with closed eyes and not asleep, but now, as the vision disappears, I feel that I am pleasantly falling asleep and not because I am tired, but simply, naturally, "falling asleep." But the overall impression of this dream is somehow pleasant, satisfying and creating a feeling of tranquility. In part, this dream reminds me of another dream I had, of being in the living room and looking at the ceiling and seeing the bird flying etc. which you interpreted as related to Silva, remember? However, this time, there is no alarm, no troubling problems, only observing the pictures that give me a sensation of something beautiful and pleasurable. Maybe all this is connected with my thoughts about the children (four hills, three steps, plus a column equals four), all this is obvious.

Meanwhile, mama and I are having heated arguments about the events as a result of which she fears becoming a "beggar," no matter how I reassure her that she will never be deprived of anything as long as I live, and, well, it did not work. "I am not afraid for myself, but for my poor children", and "you will destroy them with your insensitive attitude;"; to try and prove to mother that our children are neither cripples nor imbeciles is useless. Her anxiety has increased since I started to treat our capital "lightly." Not long ago, on the anniversary of grandfathers death, we donated 10,000 rubles to an untouchable fund of both our grandfathers (mother's and mine) to establish two scholarships for a children's shelters best suited for raising most gifted boys and girls among inmates of these children's homes and to pay for their high school and even university education; mama's grant for studying medicine (5,000) and mine (also 5,000) for any designated department of learning as chosen by the honoree.

Therefore, this great revolutionary alarm bell has aroused me to analyze my almost 35 year-old system of accumulating wealth under the pretext of insuring my old age and my children. I understood that the accumulation of wealth is fruit of the highly inflated payments which we received from society as compensation for our work and for services we rendered to society. Therefore, I consider it just that this excess of payments received by me from society should be returned to society in full. Under the present social regime, this excess can be established only after my death. Since I lived all my life as I saw fit and supported my family financially, raised children, and left a so called inheritance, then obviously this inheritance is precisely that excess, and every honest and decent person is obligated to give it back to society. Therefore, I have decided that after my death, all my property, both movable and immovable, will be bequeathed on the city of Rostov that gave me the opportunity to earn all this capital. Nevertheless, I will neither touch mother's property, nor your dowry, only my own. Nonetheless, mother is in utter desperation over my "crazy" action; she cries and wails that I am "destroying" my family, but I did take into account the fact that you, my children, have not yet adjusted to independently earning your money because the war interfered with you. And here is what my testament says: immediately after my death, a balance sheet of my businesses should be executed, all my debts should be paid, and the net worth determined in whatever form it will take. That capital in its entirety is bequeathed as property to the Don University in Rostov-on-Don, on condition of founding at the university a department of social sciences (not only a chair but precisely an entire department). I will explain below how I imagine the organization of such a department; however, securing this capital for itself, the university will allow this capital to be used by all my children, along with their (the children's) reciprocal responsibility for each other, for a duration of ten years and without paying any interest. In the course of these ten years they are obligated to return to the university the entire inherited capital, as determined after my death, in the following order: at the end of the year, starting with the confirmation date of the university's right to the inheritance, my children will pay the university 10% (ten per-cent) of the inherited sum; at the end of the second year, they will transfer to the university the second 10%, and so on in this order; and at the end of ten years, the inherited sum will be paid to the university in full. Thus I am causing no harm to my children: in the course of ten years, after my death, they will get back for their use all the remaining capital without extraordinary toil. Although the university will fully receive 100% of the bequeathed capital, you, my children, will have to pay only some 60% of the entire capital because you will use the interest or other earnings created by this capital. And if my inheritance will also include real estate, then in ten years its value will also increase and my children will benefit from that as well. This will result in a situation as if I managed to live for another extra ten years. I consider this bequest quite ingenious because I am safeguarding the interests of my children and, as justice requires, I give back to society what I have acquired as an excess payment for my work.

And now a few words about how I imagine the organization of this new department of social sciences and, by the way, that it should be completely free from any kind of formality. Anyone can apply without checking his educational qualifications; there is no matriculation, the lectures are free and there are no obligatory examinations. Anyone, even without having attended a university, has a right to come to the office and demand that he be examined in the subject taught in a given department. A person desiring to be examined is obligated to present his curriculum vitae and also a written dissertation on a theme related to the subject in which he wants to be examined. Following this a council of professors will choose no less than five examiners who will determine the times of the examinations. The examinations may be attended by the public but without a right to vote. Upon completing the examinations the results would be published in the "University Bulletin" and local newspapers, approximately in this form: "On this day, so-and-so was examined on such-and-such subject. The examiners were so-and-so. Among the latter, three, namely so-and-so, gave positive testimonials about the examinee while two spoke against him. The three positive responses mean that the examinee passed the test, four positives of course mean something more favorable for the person, and five positives would be a unanimous decision, and a confirmation of the examinee's splendid knowledge. This publication dispenses with and abolishes the need for diplomas. The titles are also changed. Only persons who have received a unanimous recognition in all the subjects have the right to use the title of scientific specialist, without conferring on him any privileges or social status. The main subjects, about which lectures will be offered, are the following: political economy, psychology, jurisprudence, social hygiene, urban planning, style and eloquence. Topics like old age insurance, financial planning, education, etc. will be subsections of related chairs. Of course practice will show what further instructions and changes etc. are needed.

It is clear that my capital is too small for the realization of my thought, but I hope that I will be followed by other people, more so since at the end of the day, people will have to realize that one has to begin to see and underback the excess is reasonable; it should not frighten the capitalists, on the contrary it should attract them with its simplicity and practicality. For: after his death, the father continues both to have revenue and to take care of the material needs of his own family; contrary to the German proverb, easy won—easy gone (*leicht gewonnen—leicht zerronnen*), the children will not be able to squander the remaining capital because it actually does not belong to them, on the contrary, even a stimulus to work is created, the result of which has already been outlined; based on the commonality of interests and a mutual responsibility of the remaining members of the family, the result is a fusion, a common cooperation, a symbol of a social cell. My testament is drawn up; it is finished in a separate form as defined by law; it will always be kept in the middle drawer of my desk. I will only point out that the sum of 20,000 rubles, for which I insured my life, is not part of the total amount of the inheritance. According to the previous instruction known to you, this sum is earmarked separately for cultural-educational goals according, my children, to your personal [break]

NS 16

My Dear! Rostov on/Don1918

I am in a hurry because an Austrian troop train is now leaving for Austria and one soldier is taking this letter and promising to mail it to you. You probably know from the newspapers that Rostov is now occupied by Austro-German troops. There is a war with the Bolscheviks and shells are flying on the outskirts of the city, and here it is a little bit calmer. What we are living through is difficult to describe, and there is no time. The main thing is that we all, Yasha's family and the Pochtarev family, are healthy and unharmed at this time. We should be thinking about your travel here; I assume that I will travel to meet you in Kiev. As soon as the telegraph office starts working again we will agree how to go about it. I am ending here; Milia is hovering over my head and urging me to finish. Tomorrow a new troop train will leave and I will have time to think this over and write again. Let Sania and Rakhil know that the Pochtarevs are fine. Goodbye,

[signature]

PS. Get in touch immediately with Yasha and Sania although we [illegible] at the same time. However maybe one of these letters will reach its destination. I will transfer the money as soon as possible, for the time being no transfers can be made.

NS 17

Hello, my dear! Rostov-on-D 26.8.18

I take the opportunity that the Swiss consul Mr. Amsler is traveling to Switzerland. We received your letter of 3/8 which was 19 days underway. All is well with us, I am only worried about mother: she started complaining of heart pains and the smallest, the most negligible irritation, affects her heart. Now, after Yasha's tales about you and Renatochka she became ill , does not sleep nights. We sent you a whole pile of money, 4,000 crowns, through a certain Rotshtein who left for Vienna; 3,885 crowns through a captain (Walcker) addressed to Yasha; and 1,300 crowns through a lieutenant to Sania's address. Should you receive all this money you will be a rich woman. But since we have no news, we will have to keep sending. I am now soliciting to get some time off for a while; and if I succeed to travel to Germany, I will certainly try to visit you. In the meantime, mama is inconsolably sick at heart. Yasha has arrived but he is constantly restless. True, he traveled safely for 21 days to reach Rostov guarded by a German sergeant-major. He is running around upset; obviously, he has to endure a lot from the Ryss family; he wants to mend the relationship between Silva and mama and thinks he'll succeed to bring Silva closer to us. Actually, I don't know what the latter is for, unless temporarily to prevent a new breakdown. Thanks to Yasha's arrival, Milia has started to get gradually interested in music. For how long remains to be seen. By the way, he is very nervous. The family is more or less well all around, except for the death of uncle Pinia about two months ago. Uncle Noi is having some problems: Adia, his elder son, got involved with a young lady, who does not take him seriously while exploiting the opportunity to suck him dry financially. As a violin player he is paid 500 rubles for playing with a club orchestra and all this is spent on love. Uncle Mosia is still busy cheating this one and that one but still living in poverty. His [daughter] Emka has finished high school, got a job in a private library and is getting a salary of 150 rubles. All is calm in town, there was a hike in the price of securities, and, as usual, the Jews are afraid because they are used to carrying the more or less important historical events on their backs. The prices are rising not just daily but by leaps and bounds. We are already paying two rubles for a simple glass to drink water, 700 for a pair of women's shoes, 3,000 for a man's suit (we just made one for Yasha), 80 rubles for a student cap, 50 rubles for a plain women's blouse, 15 rubles for one arshin [= 0.71 square meter] of calico, six rubles for a watch glass, 150 rubles for the simplest kind of watch, ten rubles for shoe laces for a pair of boots. Briefly, everything is fine. Goodbye.

[signature]

[postscript from mother] Everything is alright, everybody is healthy, and it would be great if all the children were together.

[postscript from mother] We just received six letters from you, of which two are for Pavel, which I immediately forwarded to him.

NS 18

My dear Sabinochka Rostov on/Don 25

October, 1919

Today is your birthday again, and we are again celebrating it separated from each other and in circumstances worse than before because it has become more difficult to make contact with you, and the most awful thing is that we can't send you any money. We have to buy foreign currency here but speculation with it has gotten crazy: the French franc (not the Swiss franc) goes for 24–26 Don rubles; this is a nightmare, isn't it? We hope all the time that perhaps it will get better, but on the contrary, it is getting worse and worse and our ruble is tumbling lower and lower. The cost of living is turning into something out of a fairy tale: a pair of ladies shoes costs 11,000 rubles, a simple man's suit costs 5,000–6,000, a better quality suit costs up to 12,000, 10 eggs cost 45 rubles, a pound of butter costs 120 rubles, potatoes 3 rubles, one cucumber 3 rubles, a pound of cabbage 3 rubles a pound of coal for heating which cost one ruble 25 kopecks is now 50 rubles. Only bread costs 5 rubles and 50 kopecks a pound and flour 6 rubles. We, the deep pockets, groan and bear it, but what about of people, how do they fare? It's incomprehensible. No wonder that one expects all kinds of riots and this is why on the one hand, it is good that you are staying where you are, but perhaps for us it was not difficult to bear. On the other hand, due to your finances, you have to owe money and even suffer hunger and this is no joy either. And why wouldn't you take the Swiss state examination that would give you the possibility to earn money in private practice? After all these years of living in Switzerland you would be able to get the Swiss citizenship easily and, one should assume, would be able to earn a modest living or even hire a good person to take care of Renatochka, so that you won't be tired by taking care of her. If not, you would have to start working in some hospital; I think you will be able to get a position that will allow you to keep the child with you. If you weren't so lonely, which you must endure, I still would consider it better for you to live far away from the horrors we are living through. On the other hand, we want to live together, so as to know constantly what is happening with each one of us and not to have to be waiting in constant pining for some bit of gratifying news from afar. We would want to live together so that you wouldn't have to think constantly about money and could live like us and not have to forgo food, clothing, or heat. This is why we all insist that at the first convenient opportunity you should come back home. I think you might find an opportunity to do that. From time to time various delegations arrive here from Switzerland. Not long ago a certain Jules Kushcher [?] of the Société pour le Commerce avec l'Orient à Genève [society for trade with the east] arrived here accompanied by two Swiss gentlemen. If you make the effort, you might be able to join such Swiss people and they would readily accept you as a translator, and perhaps pay for your comfortable journey here, especially since now they are all traveling not only to Russia's south but especially to Rostov as a center of the politico-economic life of the country. Moreover, you would be able to get in touch with Mr. Gorgos Algardi of the Banque Impériale Ottomane, Galata-Constantinople. Not too long ago, this gentleman married a relative of ours (family name Aptekman, the relationship approximately similar to that of Nadia Bershadskaya), visited us at home and promised to give you every help possible, i.e. to tell you how to travel to Constantinople and there put you on one of the best steam boats that would bring you to Novorossiisk. It is possible that he will be in Paris and make contact with you from there. However, other than this gentleman there are many other opportunities from time to time; you could also reach out to the Swiss consul here, Mr. Amsler, and ask him to let you know when somebody from Switzerland will be coming here. Furthermore, in Lausanne lives a Mr. Panpe [?]; he is a son of a rich man from Peterburg now living in Rostov and renting an apartment in our house (where the Koyre's once lived). Finally you could travel to Warsaw where all my relatives live even though I don't think they are all doing well, and, therefore, it is probably more difficult to feel lonely amongst your own than amongst complete strangers. In one word, figure out yourself what is best for you and organize everything based on what your reason is telling you given the current situation.

We at home are all doing well: Milia is serving in a student unit from where, after a recent suspicion of typhus, he came home three weeks ago with scarlet fever, luckily a light case thereof. His bride, Miss Fanni Burshtein, was taking care of him. She's a student who lived with us throughout his illness. They will probably get married soon. Yasha has been unanimously appointed as professor of electricity and general physics at the Ekaterinograd Polytechnical Institute, the youngest and the only Jew. For now everybody there loves him and it is only his wife that is not happy that he gives so little to the family, 6,000 a month. In December he will be getting 8,000 and in January 10,000 a month. Sania is in Tiflis, we have not seen him yet, there he is a lecturer at the National University. He is living with Moisei Lublinskii (on Velikokniazheskaia Street No. 34), he misses life abroad and would like to escape to Switzerland, but who knows if he will succeed. Today, on the occasion of your birthday, we got a visit from Pavel and he brought mama flowers. In expectation of your birthday not long ago he sent us a letter for you (from his place of service) which we sent to you a few days ago. And so I am ending. Be healthy and happy together with your little daughter.

[signature]

NS 19

Dear Sabinochka! Rostov-on-D 15.II.20

Recently our acquaintances have received letters from Germany via Reval. Therefore we haste to take advantage of this route again, because evidently other letters have not been reaching their destination. It is almost a year since we had no news from you, and we will be extremely happy to know how you and Renatochka are doing. Or perhaps Pavel was able to migrate to you? You are asking how are we? Here is what is happening. We are living in our former apartment and mama and I are occupying our bedroom, which also serves as dining room, kitchen, and living room. We get heat from the stove because central heating is not working. Milia and his wife (he got married a year ago – 25/II.19) are living in a room with the balcony facing the street, also sleeping there at night is the maid with her child. Fanni (Milia's wife) will soon give birth. Mother is reacting to everything in a morbid manner, I am working in the Don Agriculture Department as a specialist in entomological technology. Milia works for the abolition of illiteracy. Yasha works in his specialty, right now he is not lecturing, and he is on leave till January. All the relatives are alive and well, and living as best as they can. Some time ago we sent you some clothes via Olga Pavlovna. I hope you received those together with mama's letter. We have the most incomplete idea regarding your financial situation; are you really the only one who failed to pass [lost!] an examination, and failed to get [lost!] a private practice? If I if get a business trip abroad, I would certainly be able to meet with you, but it will take some doing. You are probably receiving letters from Sania in Tiflis. He serves there in the legation and doing pretty well financially. I am attaching two letters, use them and put your return mailing address on each. I yield my turn to mama who will tell you everything in greater detail and with full expression of emotions. Dear children, be healthy and happy.

[signature]

NS 20

Greetings my dear! Moscow 24/5.21

As you can see, I happen to be in Moscow. This was the result of a business trip. I am busy here with carrying out my cherished idea of opening the Institute of "Plantakuria" [healing of plants], a report about which is attached. It is not difficult to realize that in an agrarian country like Russia, the highest attention should be paid to the most important industry, i.e., farming. Every other industry, the metallurgical, textile, chemical etc., will develop by itself, will revive and grow at a fast pace once the storm has passed. But this revival, and in general, the entire economic and social welfare of our country, should be based on the agricultural industry exclusively. In agriculture, the world of plants is of foremost importance. Our first concern should be the protection of plants from losses. Such losses amount each year to a destruction of one third of the seedings due to zoological parasites alone. And if the social relationships of the population are primarily determined by the quantity and quality of its economic welfare, then it is not difficult to understand how less painful it would be to achieve all kinds of social reconstructions, if it were possible to salvage a considerable part of one third of the food supply for humanity and animals that is destroyed each year. Animals also suffer due to being fed by grasses infected by all kinds of diseases (for example certain parasites on clover cause a pathological condition called bovine tympanitis). It's self-evident, that making feeding grasses healthy, we will get healthier cattle, which is so important for work in agriculture and as a source of food for humanity. All this makes clear the necessity for creating a plant institute for the study of plant medicine in its entirety and not fragmented and uncoordinated as it has been until now, as embodied in the representatives of entomology and mycology, etc. People graduating from higher agricultural academies certainly have an idea about diseases affecting plants but these are general ideas. This does not amount to a totality of plant medicine, of plant hygiene, and its representatives in practical applications. Just as there is a need for agronomists with a general knowledge of plant pathology, while there is no need for specialists, and lecturers with general ideas about agriculture. These plant hygienists should be distributed over the entire country and they should teach the people (the peasants) how to safeguard their greatest possession, plant riches. I have already had negotiations about this with the National Commissariat of Agronomy (section of plant protection), but here in Rostov and in Moscow it proceeds with difficulty, it's hard to get things done. They tell you that establishing such an institute is premature, that we do not have cadres to serve as faculty, that there is no way to build laboratories, etc. But this is incorrect: one can start with establishing cells attached to existing universities, to give lectures at first (the first two years let us say), with eight lecturers in natural history and general medicine and then specialize in plants. By that time there will be available specialists for heading additional courses in special plantakuria and laboratories exist already at any established old university. Oh, I would like to live long enough to see my dream realized and should I see that I can get nothing from the agriculture section, then I will turn to Lunachrskii[90] with the proposal to include the institute of plantakuria in the general network as one of the higher specialty institutes. Sania came here with me, I think he will probably get a job at the Commissariat of Foreign Affairs. Of course, he will stay here, his wife and child are still in Rostov. There Rakhil has to pass half of her doctoral examination and then she will come here. Yasha and his family will arrive here any day now. He will be working in his specialty, electrification. It is a grandiose beginning of an idea and its realization. For now, staying in Rostov with us is Milia and the family. To tell the truth, I would like all of us to move to Moscow. Now it is too difficult to live in the provinces. In the capital, life is more interesting and incomparably calmer and more balanced. The food conditions are quite difficult here, but it is not getting any less difficult, either, in Rostov. And how is it with you, my dear? Your last letters sound more encouraging; you are living a full life. But materially, you could make it easier for yourself if you were not too fussy. You should not be giving free consultations to patients, you are needy yourself and you are unable to take care of the child. As you reported, your debts are growing and there will come a time when you will have to repay them. You cannot fully rely on us because we can hardly make ends meet by selling what is left, and even that is coming to an end. You had better go to Berlin and dispose of the remaining things or else everything will get lost and the debt for storage keeps increasing considerably. Before my leaving, we received a letter from Pavel sent from Feodosia. He is still a serviceman and clearly his financial situation is not great. In addition, he is sad because he is completely alone. You can write to him there to this address: Voyennaya Street No 14. By the way, letters arrive either directly by mail, directly from abroad. Here in Moscow you can write to Yasha and Sania and "S.A. Kogan, Novinskii Boulevard No. 32 Apt 58. Alright, I am ending my dear, goodbye to you and Renatochka. Will I live long enough to get acquainted enough with my granddaughter?

Just now Kogan received your photograph dated "Summer of 1920" forwarded by Olga Pavlona. As usual, you are again photographed with a hat on, so that your whole face is hidden. One gets the impression as if you are ashamed of something. It is time, my dear, to act more courageously in life, to have more faith in yourself, and rely more upon yourself. Actually, the present circumstances of your life are as if organized to enable you achieve such self-confidence; but

---

90 Lunachrskii, Anatolii Vasilievich (1875–1933), a soviet government activist, President of the National Commissariat for Education (1917–1929)

you are still afraid of being obliterated by other peoples' envy or other motives. Get rid of it, don't pay attention to ill-wishers, do your own thing if you will, be able to stand up for yourself.

[signature]

NS 21

Dear Sabinochka! 5.22

Do you remember that some time ago I wrote you that a certain psychological change has developed in me? This is a positively interesting fact. You may recall that many years ago I had told you, and have kept maintaining since that time, that feelings of love, even toward my closest people, have completely vanished. When I was away, I would have no desire to write to my relatives; when I came back, I was not moved to kiss them, etc. At that time, I used to tell Freud about it, kept asking him to help me. He would just smile at me and explain (you had observed this even before he did) that this was proof of an excess of feelings. Of course, I was skeptical about this explanation. And all of a sudden, and especially since I took leave of mama in Moscow, I began to experience toward her, and all of you, exquisite and unusually tender feelings. Lately, I have even felt a need to write to you quite frequently, and to mama daily. I was myself stunned by this, informed you about it, and wrote to mama as if apologizing for writing too frequently, as if I were not a relative. In my letters I avoided mentioning unpleasant topics; on the contrary, I made an effort to provide as much pleasure as possible to recipients reading my letters. I connect this with a phenomenon I had mentioned to you a number of times, that I have been having "prophetic dreams," as if these were forebodings. And, just imagine, I receive a telegram from Pavlusha and Milchik that mama has fallen severely ill and wanted me to come back. I am therefore abandoning all my business affairs here and rushing back to Russia. We will see what awaits me there. I am ready for everything. You might be surprised, my dear, that I am reasoning so coolly. This is once again an interesting psychological phenomenon. Despite this, or perhaps because of this, I am an inveterate enemy of fanaticism and therefore always ready for any unavoidable outcome, and my only concern in relation to this boils down to this: that my end should occur far away from my beloved and dear ones, and that they should suffer from it as little as possible. This is definitely my attitude toward myself and that is why I am not surprised that this is also my attitude toward mama's illness. And the situation must be extremely serious, since I received a telegram; for despite of the current circumstances, difficulties with travel they sent a telegram anyway. Of course, I will travel with a heavy heart and as soon as I arrive I will send a cable to Yasha and he will forward it to you. But I beg you, my dear, do not get upset by any worries, any telegrams, any inquiries etc. Anyway, nothing can be found out before I get there, and as soon as I get there, you will be informed. So be armed with utmost patience so that it will not interfere with our acting in a calm and goal-directed manner. There is no need for me to add anything more but that you should make every effort to spare Renatochka and not make her anxious, for, my dear, she is so sensitive. And so, my darling daughter, be prudent and patient. My very dear ones, be healthy and happy. Confirm you received this letter. I am not sure it will reach you.

NS 22

My dearest Sabochka! Berlin 15/6.22

Yesterday I flew back from Moscow. I was in Rostov. Sania and Milia are doing tolerably well, at this time they do not intend to go abroad: the former does interesting work in Moscow on psychotechnics and the latter wants to graduate from the university and then specialize abroad. Milia has an exceptionally wonderful boy who is 16 months old. He pronounces everything clearly, his young mind is amazing, I will elaborate when you arrive here. Make up your mind sooner about you and Renatochka. Pavlusha is pining for you, wants to escape from here and travel to be with you, however, we will talk about it when you come. Only, when leaving Switzerland, do not forget to get a permit to "go there and back" or else they might not let you come back should you need it. On the 14th we celebrated the anniversary of your wedding. I sent a telegram from Moscow to Rostov. In Moscow was opened "The Children's Institute-Laboratory for Research of Child Psychology." There is an extraordinary interest in psychoanalysis, they are looking for specialists. Goodbye my dear.

[signature]

NS 23

My dear child! Moscow 31/12/22

Now I am here together with Sania, it is about half past 10 pm and in an hour and a half will be the new year 1923. Yasha went to Rostov; Rakhil and Menikhochka went to Malakhovka to celebrate the new year and are expected to return next year that is, tomorrow evening. I received your registered letter of the 20th of this month with an addition. Sania is telling you about all his new titles. He is working like an ox, it is impressive how he manages to be everywhere on time. Of course, this affects his health, but he persists in pursuing his goal. Moreover he is now living in the most dreary conditions; true, it is an oversize room but uncomfortable, with black wallpaper, there are neither cupboards and nor a chest for things, everything is piled up. But they are now eating better, they do not deny themselves anything. Sania is making a good salary, more than a billion a month. I am living with Sania, I am not trying to have a room for myself as I am expecting to get a business trip to Tiflis (via Rostov) and Tashkent. It is a very hard and tiring trip and it will be a lot of work but this is what attracts me because I cannot sit idly around and have nothing to do, it is boring. Anyway, actually work is my holiday, it is my rest, and the more intensive, the more gratifying it is, and the more I sense my rest, the more productive it is, the brighter my holiday. So don't worry about me in this regard: movement is life, and I still want to live more. It is so interesting to be alive now; I had a life, it was given to me, but now I create it myself and therein lies all its beauty for me. Activity, my dear, is not sitting next to each other and admiring each other. We all, my dear children, are all united in spirit, and that is all. It is the other way around, I think, the more we are separated from each other, the greater the space in which we create, the happier is our present life, not just physical existence.

I do not agree with Freud when he faint-heartedly maintains that (*Mann Wünschhätten wir* [sic]), "one could have omnipotent wishes," because (*Wünsche haben eben Allmacht. Die Allmacht äussert sich in Wünsch und das ist der Wille zur Macht*), "wishes do have omnipotence. Omnipotence expresses itself in a wish, and this is the will to power."...All our "cogito" as applied to life is split into newer and newer wishes, and therefore the result is "cogito – ergo sum."[91] Therefore it seems that Freud abandoned his dictum that "dreams are wish fulfillments" (*Träume sind Wunscherfüllungen*) to which I still strongly adhere. And that is why every wish ("*Wunsch*") (I am speaking of serious yearnings and wishes) at first appears in the form of a weak, powerless "dream" (a utopia, a soap bubble, an insane delusion, etc.); and then when the dream cashes in on the will to power ("*Wille zur Macht*"),[92] it gradually gets stronger and is transformed into reality. It is clear that Freud, having written that wishes possess omnipotence ("*Mann wünsche Allmacht hätten*"), merely expressed an ordinary and trivial "everyday thought" (*Alltagsgedanke*); however "*quod licet bovi...*"[93]; but such a dictum should not have issued from Freud's mouth. This is the tragedy of those to whom much has been given, because "noblesse oblige".

91 I think, therefore I am, the most emblematic statement of René Descartes (1596–1650), the father of modern philosophy.

92 Nikolai conflates Freud's omnipotence with Alfred Adler's will to power, inspired by Nietzsche.

93 The complete Latin saying is: *quod licet Iovi, non licet bovi*, what is permitted to Jove is not permitted to a bull.

I did not think of Renatochka's birthday, I forgot, so may she be happy without my greetings. Forget your financial worries, we will join forces and support you. You should calmly pursue reworking your published papers lest they get old and uninteresting. Life goes forward and if you put brakes on it, for this or that reason, it will do without you and others will leave you behind. I very much like Renatochka's song. I am sending her letter to Pavlusha. And so, the dear children wish you a happy year.

My Dear Renatochka, greetings for the new year, grandpa [French in original]

NS 24

My dear Sabinochka! Tashkent 21/3/23

It has been a long time since we have corresponded. I am traveling all the time on business trips so that there is no time for writing letters, especially here, in Asia, where I am for the first time in my life and find such an infinite number of interesting things. I have accumulated a great amount of interesting material and we will discuss it during the whole year ahead. Are you planning to come to Russia? This is my next worry. According to Narkompros [national ministry of education] there is a limitless mass of opportunities to work as a psychiatrist but you have to be prepared for many hardships, because Narkompros is particularly [illegible] with rooms or apartments. But, as Sania is in the habit of saying, "Got iz a tate" [Yiddish, God is a daddy].

We will all act together and it is very possible that I will get employment at the Narkompros so as to collaborate with all of you, my dear children. Please send if you can the latest photos of Renatochka, grandpa wants to be able to brag about his wonderful little grand-daughter. Good bye, my dear ones.

[Postscript 1] Ma très chère Renée! Est-il possible que nous nous voyions bientôt? J'attends le moment avec grande [illegible]. A bientôt, Gpand'pa [my very dear Renée! Is it possible that we could see each other soon? I am awaiting this moment with great...Till soon, grandpa]

[Postscript 2] Do you remember Sarra who often forwarded to you greetings from the your parents' home in the years 1915–1920? Now Nikolai Arkadievich is staying with us in Tashkent taking care of official business, his stay has provided my little family, consisting of a husband and little Ella (a four-year old chatter-box), with many happy hours. Warm greetings to you and Renatochka about whom grandpa is raving. Sarra Lublinskaya Bykova.

22.III.23 Postscript. I would have liked to send Renatochka money to buy some paper, which she is in need of, but it is impossible.

NS 25

Dear Sabinochka! Moscow 4/5/23

You reacted to my letter with too much anxiety, therefore I hasten to calm you. I am now living with Yasha (Moscow, Taganka, Lower Radishchevo No. 10, entrance 1). I bought myself a soft couch, sheets, and from Rostov Milia sent me a pillow and a blanket, so everything is alright. We worry about your journey; we did all that could be done from here. The rest has to be undertaken there. The journey, once you get a seat in the so-called soft car, will be neither horrible nor tiring (in Russia we do not have classes in trains anymore, only cars with either soft or hard seats and backs). In express trains, which are the only ones in which you should travel, there are also restaurants. The cars will not be extremely hot, because you will be traveling in the Northern latitude. In sum, nothing to be afraid of, and once you come here we will try to arrange everything so that you could rest for some time. Of course, you will not have the same cultural comforts as you had abroad and in this regard I am particularly sorry for the child, but there is no other solution, since you are financially strapped, and the family relations have to be mended as well. You don't have to bring anything for me personally, except the things stored in Zaidman's apartment, and only if you get permission to take these out of Germany and bring them to Russia, which are my costume, a rubber overcoat, a pair of shoes, some linens, which are all used items and therefore duty free; the rest will be subject to duty. Therefore, <u>if it isn't difficult for you</u>, buy a few items for women which were requested by our relative Sara Lublinskaya in Tashkent. These items are a pair of women's stockings, good summer stockings size 9, one blouse or jacket (or sweater I don't know what you call it), a light-weight light brown, size 44. This is worn like a man's jacket with belt and pockets, open and unbuttoned. In addition, one pair of slippers size 37 and finally two pairs of gloves 6½ which, as I requested, have already been bought by Silvochka. Should you be coming via Warsaw, which is best, you could rest there and see your relatives; it is nearer and quicker and cheaper. And if not, then come via Riga. Yasha will write to you separately.

As soon as we establish a connection with Petrograd there will be a possibility to send money either to all of us or one of us, I will immediately take full advantage of such an opportunity. In the meantime don't be sad, face life without fear even though it is hard at the present time. What is awaiting me will become clear; I am ready for everything and so, my dear daughter, be reasonable and patient. Be well and happy my dear ones.

[signature]

NS 26 (in German)

My dear! 10/9/18

I take advantage of the opportunity to write a few brief lines to you that we are all in good health, and only mama causes us to worry a great deal because she cannot bear the separation from both of you. So perhaps it will be possible that you will come back home again, after all, the way back is no longer so dangerous. Money matters are finally also becoming more promising. Via Sania, you will receive four thousand crowns, which Mr. Emil Rothstein in Vienna had transferred. Should you not receive this sum in due course then write immediately to the above named at this address: Vienna, Maria Torczico Street 11. I myself am looking for every possible means to come to you. However, I am unable to travel for many reasons including mama's condition. One fortunate remedy is that Jean [Yan] is now at home with us. He is of course first and foremost with his wife and children but this will only last a short time; he will leave his family there and will soon return.

So, my child, cheer up. A better time will come soon. You need no longer unduly restrict your spending. You have to get a full set of clothes for you and Renatchen, so that in case you return to the homeland, you won't have to think about tailors and shoemakers, but will be able to take a real good rest. Just now we received in the mail a very interesting book by Privat-Docent Zweng of Vienna "Therapy of gastrointestinal diseases." The book was printed by a Jewish publisher so the mailing was probably arranged by Sania for Paul.

All right, goodbye my child, warm greetings to all from your

Signature

NS 27 (in French)

Good day, my dear granddaughter! Rostov on Don, 3rd July 1921

Here is a letter you did not expect to receive, is it not? It comes from your grandfather Spielrein who is living in the south of Russia with his wife, your grandmother Eva. And in Russia you have another grandmother, it is grandmother Sophie Scheftel living in Kiev. In addition, you have three aunts named Scheftel and three aunts Spielrein as well as three uncles Spielrein and three [female]cousins Spielrein, and a tiny [male] cousin Spielrein, this one only five and a half months old. It is a big family, is it not? And you see, the Spielreins are the parents of your mama and the others, the Scheftels, are the parents on your father's side, also named Scheftel, Mr. Paul Scheftel. And we love you very much, because, dear, you are beautiful, kind, and good, and that you in turn love all of us. Do you truly love us? However, you do not know us at all. It was only when you were still a very little baby and could neither walk nor talk and were lying in a baby carriage, which also served as your crib, that your grandmother and I and your uncle Emile and uncle Jean saw you in Kissingen, Germany. This was in 1914, just seven years ago. How changed you are now since that time! You have little white teeth, you can talk and you can run, and read and write. Because your mama sent us one of your letters which you had sent her. I am sure, my dearest, that we will see each other again, when the world will become more reasonable and there will be no more obstacles to travel. We will then come to see you in Switzerland or you will come to us with your mama. In the meantime you can send us letters written by your little rosy hand. You will put your letter in the attached envelope and drop it into a mail box. We will receive your letter and read it with great pleasure and answer you immediately. A thousand big kisses, my beloved Renée, from your grandfather.

4.4 LETTERS FROM EVA SPIELREIN TO DAUGHTER

ES 1

Dear Sabinochka! Rostov on the Don, 21.9.1908

I cannot find peace after your departure, and I do not know where to write. I was unable to rest for one moment, got busy cleaning the rooms, so as not to have time to think about myself. I thought of you and him all night, and after having lost all hope of receiving any news, when my suffering for you reached a climax, I suddenly received a letter [from Jung] addressed to you. I was so upset, I could not read a word. I ask you a thousand times to forgive me for opening the letter, but I opened it because you would have let me read it anyway and I had to know what it held for you, because my entire mood depended on it. His letter calmed me down. It expresses deep friendship, lightly colored by something else, which is quite natural. He often thought of you, of the cholera, of your soul. He is probably in the throes of a conflict and his counsel to you and to himself is not to let the feeling of love grow but to suppress it, though not to kill it completely. Did I get it right? He who is able to do it will be victorious, or else will find himself in the reverse situation. I am sure he will be victorious. He writes that this is necessary for the sake of the loved ones, that is, his wife and children. And what about you? Perhaps I got it wrong? Anyway, I like the tone of his letter very much, especially the limits within which he places you and himself. It seems to me that it could not be any better. You have in him a person devoted to you, with a touch of love (more than that is <u>not permitted</u> and you have to remain content with that), a person for whom you have profound respect and appreciation, which you also have from him, so what more do you need? You should be happy because it is more than you should wish for. Had you wished to cause him to divorce his wife, then it would be a different matter, but if not, then you must not go any further. The important thing is that you can get him, but it is not worth it. You cannot have it better than the way it is. Do not torment yourself, suppress your feelings so that they do not make you suffer and continue meeting him as a friend. He also needs you, but he is not suffering, on the contrary, he is getting better. Please, please, do not tell him I opened the letter. As far as the jam is concerned, tell him that you brought along fruit for him but were unable to bring more. Rent a lavish apartment, invite him and write to me with all the details. You can talk to him about love but remain unyielding; you only stand to gain from it. For the time being, do not hide your feelings...

ES 2

[on stationery of] Sanatorium on Königgrätzerstrasse 105[94] near the Anhalt railway station

My dear children! Berlin, 26 March 1913[?]

Unfortunately, I have to forego the pleasure of seeing both of you until Saturday, most probably! I will let you know. It is a big deprivation for me, but what can I do? It has to be this way. Of you, Sabinochka, I have to ask a big favor, and you must do it: <u>have an analysis done</u>. I have noticed that you have lost weight and it pains me a great deal. After you left yesterday I was very nervous. I hope that this request will be fulfilled. I hope you will [illegible]; I will not ask you again, truly! Order [things] for yourself, i.e. buy yourself, a dress and a hat for now and tell me by telephone or by a letter how much it cost and I will immediately send you the money and then we will discuss everything else, alright! And regarding you, Pavlushen'ka, the matter may seem more difficult, but I as [illegible] person do not feel like losing heart. I saw with my own eyes that you looked pale, and it would be advisable for you to consult the professor. You seem to think that you are completely healthy and God help us that this should be true, but it can't hurt to get the assurance that this is so. What is the risk? 20 marks? I will gladly pay it to have peace of mind. Do this for me, my dear one, I beg you! I am not asking something impossible, am I? You know well how scrupulous and cautious I am when it comes to asking favors. I also

94 This was one of a number of sanatoria for "nervous" disorders in Berlin without naming the doctor who owned it and acted as therapist (Edward Shorter, personal communication).

wish you both to have a useful and enjoyable. Go once more to the theatre or to a concert, I will be glad to pay for it all. Live in friendship, harmony, peace and happiness, and I will be glad looking from afar at both of you.

Your mother.

PS. From Olga Pavlovna, I received an invitation to come to her Sunday evening with both of you. I don't know about you but I will tell her that I cannot give an answer now but will answer on Saturday.

ES 3

Dear Sabina! Rostov-on-Don, 17.I.14

No letters from you. This worries me a great deal. I think that your home is in disorder, that you are busy, and therefore do not write. How is your health? How is the little baby? Is she still ill? Poor little baby! The main thing is to have a good nanny, and an experienced one, because you yourself are inexperienced. I would like to know how much wiser she has become since I saw her last time. Is she already smiling? Is she saying hello? How is she reacting to the objects around her? I would sacrifice everything just to be able to see her for one hour! I have myself been very occupied with running the household, and therefore I didn't miss her that much, but now I am free from household chores, I have a very good staff, everything is in order and now I feel that I miss her. It's a pity I cannot see how she has been gradually growing up and how she is turning from a chrysalis [of infancy] into a self-aware person. Now that household work is like a well-functioning machine, there are of course still special tasks around the house that require an expenditure of effort; however, there is no longer any rush about it. The main task has been accomplished and the door curtains can be hung two weeks later, and thus I gave myself a complete rest. Yesterday resting the whole day in bed, I asked madam Tsaitlin to come and give me a massage and toward evening I got out of bed. As soon as I recover I will go out for daily walks.

Two days ago I called on Milia and went for walks with him after dinner. Milia has not yet passed any examination; he is terribly afraid because the teachers are very strict, some teachers are not normal and some even anti-Semitic. He keeps procrastinating, the study course is getting bigger and he has not been able to study everything, and it pains me to look at the poor boy and how nervous he is. Poor me, I tried to get busy and help him with physics and chemistry so that I could tell him this and that and ask him questions. Of course, I have myself forgotten a great deal, but if I don't know the answer and open a book, he gets angry.

I did not finish the letter, the doorbell rang, and then one patient walked in, one of the first ones I treated, a certain Isayeva, you know her. When I told her that I no longer accept new patients she became terrified and told me that she would not leave here tonight. "How can I go to another dentist? I will die, but I will not go to anybody else. The other doctors are this and that and they hurt, etc." I was trying to convince her that I'm not the only one, that there are other good doctors, and that she just got used to me; but nothing worked. I looked into her mouth and told her to come back at 3 o'clock. Now the instruments are being sterilized, and I sent for medications from the pharmacy, I got everything ready in the treatment room and recalled the past. I won't deny that I was very pleased to have been able to inspire such trust in my patient; she has been suffering with her teeth for the past three months, did not sleep nights, telephoned here and finding that I was not in she decided to wait. However, I have pains in my leg and it's difficult for me to work but, on the other hand, I have a great moral satisfaction and 10 rubles in my pocket and will put them in a special place, and if she orders new teeth I'll earn another 30 rubles, but this is doubtful. The laundress said and Milia confirmed, that a fair number of patients have come and that some of them said that no way would they go to other doctors but will wait for my return.

Enough about that, I am getting back to Milia. His face has turned yellow. He looks tired. He studies very intensively. In school there are six lessons daily, in stuffy rooms; after five or six hours of studying he eats his dinner, and a mathematics teacher comes for an hour and a half. Milia has difficulty completing the course, and thereafter there is an hour-long music lesson; after 8 o'clock, he starts doing homework on various current subjects, and there is a lot more work to be done. It is very difficult to memorize everything. The students have received a great number of 2 grades for their homework from the new teachers. Milia has to pass an examination for a course that lasted for two quarters, and it is very strict. And so it goes on and on. I was thinking to go to the director and ask him that he should be examined gradually, I am seriously worried about him. Papa is doing very well; he is living a quiet and peaceful life and eating well. Masia has joined our business, went on a trip, and everything was very successful. I am pleased that he has applied himself to this task with great energy. Mas'ka is a very capable and very intelligent man. It is only unpleasant for me that papa spends a lot of time reading but there is nothing I can do about it; on the other hand, he is completely at peace with himself. I hope business will improve and then everything will be fine. I am awaiting your letter with great impatience. I get very worried when I have no letters from you. As far as I'm concerned, I only want to be healthy,

I have fallen seriously ill lately, but I've got everything: I have books, newspapers, periodicals, a piano, good people around me who like me, and a peaceful family life. Papa in wonderfully touching way [text break]

ES 4

Dear Sabina! Undated

So as not to delay answering your letter I am now writing a few words to give you some news about me. I write many letters to you, but I either destroy them or leave them without mailing. I don't know what to do [with the last letter?]. Personally, I think that it will be hard on you to be alone in Geneva; it will be especially hard for you to be lonely. In Zurich you have people close to you. It is very difficult to send advice from afar when you do not know what the motives are. I think that you are now in Locarno; try to improve your and the child's condition. It is odd that you took along with you a nurse instead of a nanny, it must be [enormously expensive?], for hiring a nurse is more expensive than a nanny. Why is it that here everyone hires a nanny and where you are everyone hires a nurse and then the child will get used to the nurse, and it will be very difficult to switch to a nanny. I will write to you in a few days. Please, send me photographs of you and the child. For the time being I do not advise you to send your photograph to Sheftel, this is my advice [text break].

ES 5

Dear Sabinochka! Undated

The child needs a good nanny, an experienced person, my advice to you is that you should look for an experienced adult and not a young girl. You yourself are inexperienced and it is not good to leave the child with a young girl. A nanny should be no less than 30 to 50 years old. Pay more and hire a good person; I'll give you the rest of the money to make sure that the child is in good hands. I think that you can have an experienced person for 35 marks. Perhaps Silva's nanny knows an acquaintance. Write immediately about the child's health; I am very worried and awaiting your letter with great impatience. I feel so sorry for the child. Anyway, do not take the child outdoors until spring, remember! Who will you leave her with? Let in fresh air into the rooms as much as possible, and that should suffice for now; in the spring she will take more walks. I would like to know how you're doing, if you got a new nanny and a new maid. What a pity that Lisa is leaving; in Germany it is possible to find a woman who is a jack-of-all-trades. At Sania Lipknekht's home, a woman cleans all the rooms and cooks dinner for the whole family. At Anna Naumovna's [Pavel's sister], a woman cleans part of the rooms and cooks. One should be demanding of household servants and not cuddle them. The child, the child... I think about her all the time and can't wait to get a letter. Boris Ilyich visited me again and came to say goodbye, he says he would not take anything from me for you, as it is too much for him. How is your health? How is [food?]? Write to me immediately about your health. How is Pavlusha? How is his mood? How does he like the charm of family life? Would he prefer to live in an apartment or in boarding house?

Today I took 25 rubles from father for a dress and this way repaid a part of my debts. It's hurting me that I have to lie to him but I want to spare his health. I am giving him some rest from you and then I will ask him to send you money to live on and "to buy a hat". I hope that by spring he will be able to make some money, and then I'll talk to him. Papa is here; I am ending my letter. Be well, keep calm. Greetings to Pavlusha.

ES 6

Dear Sabinochka! Rostov-on-Don, 2.16.14

There is somewhere a letter with all kinds of accounts and I will finish that one separately. but now I am taking advantage of a few free minutes to talk to you. A seamstress will come to me the day after tomorrow, and I'll start sewing clothes for our little baby. I will start sewing dresses for the age of six months, because by the time she gets it all she will be already older. The seamstress is a specialist for children's clothing and I will work together with her, it will give me many happy moments. The dresses are all white and a summer coat is also white. Tomorrow, on Monday, I will buy a European magazine for children, beginning with newborns. I also took money from papa to buy a dress for myself and to order a winter house coat for you. I will sew it in the same fashion as mine with violet ribbons, but in a different color for you and I think it'll fit you well, it will have only one seam which can either be let out or left in place.

Papa will send you money, but it cost me a lot of effort to achieve this. I received your letter after he sent the money. As to my solicitations in Rostov, do not worry. I will do everything I can to help you with Pavel's practice; the only obstacle is not having enough calling cards. On Monday, I will order the cards, because only today did I get the telephone number. Pavlusha will soon receive a visit from a certain Pustovoitov sent by [Panin?]; he is waiting for the calling cards. On Tuesday I will distribute Pavlusha's calling cards to a number of doctors and also [to Panin?]; (he will certainly have patients to refer), and I swear, there will be work. At first there will be a little, then more. I will do everything I had promised you, but I cannot do it all at once. I have made a lot of debts, but God forbid you should let papa know about it, he will be very upset that I hid it from him, but I did it only so as not to upset him, being upset could affect him very badly. I must save 50 rubles a month and I barely saved 25. Papa's attitude to money has changed, thank God, he will send you everything and I will not have to bear this expense.

I've got ready a parcel for you and will mail it tomorrow. The price of caviar is now eight rubles a pound. If I send this to you, I would want this to be only for you and Pavlusha. It's too expensive as a hors d'oeuvres to be served to guests. A pound of caviar gets eaten very fast and one invitation could cost 20 rubles or even 40 [marks?]. That would be too much. My maternal advice is not to make such receptions. Germans do not usually serve a lot of food, they make everything look <u>beautiful</u> and do everything for the evening to be interesting. I am curious, did doctor [Abragim?] invite you to supper? He used to serve fruit and sponge cakes. And even this is in Berlin quite a hefty expense considering your budget. If you invite people to supper once, you become obligated to serve supper always. I recall when our odontology society met once at Anna Pavlovna's place, she only served tea, a sponge cake and fruit, but we all stayed until midnight. You cannot do otherwise, if you intend to see people frequently; otherwise you will have to run an expensive household, and you will have to spend no less than 15,000 marks a year. I would not economize with your <u>own food</u>; you have to eat well or else you will not be able to work well, and economizing on food could save no more than 30 marks a month and all the rest costs hundreds of marks. Personally, it is very important for me that you should eat well, sometimes go to the theatre, be <u>properly</u> dressed and healthy, and it is not necessary to entertain people at great expense. But food is not all. Put yourself in the place of your guests and ask yourself, what does one look for in people when one goes to visit them? My concern is the principle. Tomorrow I will send what you asked for, although it pains me that you shall have to pay duty on it, and I feel sorry for every penny you have to spend.

I would sacrifice anything to be able to see Natochka, even for an hour. My heart aches when I remember her. Now her mind will be developing every day; she will become more and more interesting as time goes by. Tell her, please, that her grandmother is taking care of her wardrobe. It would be nice if I could find someone to send it with. I hope that all this is not for nothing. I have to end this letter. I should be writing all the time; however, I do not write to Yasha and Sania at all.

It is now three days since I've been very ill, and I started receiving treatments in a clinic. I spent four days in bed or on a couch holding my foot on a pillow. In addition to gout, I got phlebitis, and I was in terrible pain not only because of the illness but because I was dependent on others for little things, I imagined I would become a cripple for life and being lonely for days increased this feeling. I was also worried about papa and Milia, I was unable to do a thing for them. An old chambermaid came to the house from the hospital and stayed with me, she had appendicitis but no surgery was performed. I had a lot of trouble with her, before it was with her child and now with her. I am recovering slowly and walk around the room; in the street, I only get around in a carriage, but being upset affects me greatly. Nothing I can do about it, I had to go to doctors, etc. As you requested, papa will place advertisements everywhere. In another letter I'll tell you about my talk with doctor Ryndziun;[95] very interesting, but I am too tired now. Doctor Strashunskii[96] has asked a great deal about you. I wish you all the best, don't worry, everything will be all right. Greetings to Pavlusha and Leibovich[97]! Why does not she write to me? All I got from her are two letters. Find out about her and let me know. Is she all right? Is she working? Where does she want to spend the summer? Once more, be well.

Your mother.

[postscript] Kisses to Irmochka. Send me a recommendation. I am writing everything in a half sitting position.

ES 7

Dear Sabinochka! Undated

I wrote a letter to Yasha in French and, of course, it was very difficult for me. I am completely alone, writing without a dictionary, just the way it occurs to me, and I feel that the turn of speech is incorrect and that there are many errors but what can I do? He is not getting our letters. Until now we had no letters from Yasha except one, I cannot understand this. Tell the children that I sent pastries to all of them, and I don't know if they got them. Then I bought 3 ½ pounds of sturgeon caviar and another 5 5/8 pounds of same, 3 pounds of olive oil, and I was busy with this package for a whole week but it was disallowed, and I didn't know, I cannot even send it to you. I will now ask about sending jam and sausages, and if possible, will send. In any case, papa asked you to send them

95 Ilya Galileievich Ryndziun, Russian physician (1848–?) founder of a hydrotherapy spa in Rostov.
96 Klimentii Solomonovich Strashunskii, a doctor in the Jewish hospital in Rostov; Eva was in contact with his wife concerning Sabina.
97 Rachel Leibowitz. Eva met her at the Sheftels' in Berlin. A graduate of Zurich medical school she married Zurich-trained Dr. Meir Shimon Nachmannsohn, originally from Yaffa, Palestine. See her letters to Sabina (see NL 1,2).

these necessary comestibles and present a bill every time, and he will pay you back later. Please write to us more frequently, I am very upset when there are no letters. Milia is now in a military camp and we miss him. Every day I send him his dinner which he eats cold and which he is allowed to do as a vegetarian. This takes up a lot of my time, I have to get up early to make sandwiches, boil water and milk (a small amount of albumen was found [in his urine]), therefore I get busy because of him, because he has to start studying Latin and pass the exam in August. He'll start preparing for it once he is done with his military service. He has to prepare documents for matriculation at the university and I am busy with that now. There is a lot to do. He has no time now and will not have it later. Milia got terribly sunburnt, beyond recognition. Yesterday he slept at home for the first time because today is Ascension day, and they allowed everything.

I beg you, Sabinochka, tell Yasha that I am giving a lot of presents to his children, very expensive presents. I wish he should have a pleasant time, that his family should not abandon his children. I give the children pleasure at every step. Tell him and he'll be very glad. Tell Roza that I recently paid a visit to her mother. Everybody's healthy in her family, but Aron got really sick, the poor mother was very worried, and I feel sorry for her. Sarra, her mother, is sending me desperate letters; I will visit her again. I think that all of you are suffering hunger and this torments me too; something like this is peeking through in the letters from Yasha and Sania. Oh, oh, oh, I could say so much, but you cannot commit it all to paper! I don't have a free moment, can't catch my breath, I work a lot; oh so many worries and I am not healthy. I am not complaining, my child, I am only saying that the times are hard, oppressive, and you will be surprised to see someone who is lighthearted. But we won't lose hope that better times are yet to come and we will be able to give joy to each other. In the meantime write to me more about the child for it works like a balm. What is she saying? I am glad that she is smart and kind-hearted. Irochka [Silva's daughter] is very selfish, beautiful, smart, cheerful, but can't make strong attachments. Her little sister is deeper. Renatochka on the other hand, would become more attached, if one gave her as much attention as to Irochka. Silva comes to visit us, but she is still a stranger; somehow she is not one of us. I give her lots of attention, I send her flowers. Strangely, she has never invited me to visit her, and Olga Pavlovna keeps silent. Strange. Goodbye, write more frequently. Greetings to Sevtsa and Leibovich. Tell Aunt Elena that I sent her son tea, sugar, cocoa, candy, nuts, biscuits, etc. We send money each month, separately for calling cards, I sent books. I kiss you and dear Renatochka

[from here to the end probably a fragment of another letter]

Let's assume that you have a son like Milia. You see that he has friends who may have a deleterious effect on him. You cannot l eave him without peers altogether, and in one class you might find two decent friends (there is one), but not very solid. There is only one who visits, someone dull, and others (I consider) dangerous for him, one has to be vigilant. Smallpox is raging in Rostov, also typhus, and another storm cloud is approaching, the plague, it is near Baku. Tell me honestly, would you risk leaving him alone without mother and father? He doesn't have an aunt or a grandmother. What would you have done? I am fearfully waiting for him to finish so as to take him away.

I said that he doesn't want to travel and this is the reason why I cannot travel. I had to act in this way. I did a favor to papa—one worry less for him. For the last two weeks I have been thinking of admitting myself to an infirmary. In the meantime I will pack all the rugs, will hide all the small things in the house, will try to sell some pieces of furniture, will cover the lamps, the statues, furniture, etc.; in the remaining week I'll rest and pack the things, I cannot leave before the 4th of June. Previously I did not think where I would like to travel, I thought to take some treatments, to rest, and wanted to decide in the last minute what to do. I repeat: I did not know that you <u>needed</u> me for the child, because I was sure that the child would be cared for by S. Ab., and was therefore surprised that you did call for me.

Now the problem is as follows. It will take a month before we can meet. During that month stay with the child either in the vicinity of Berlin in some good place or in Kolberg, at the seaside. If you stay in the vicinity of Berlin , then your underwear can be washed at home and the maid will do the laundry, because she won't have much to do. This is the way it is done everywhere. To cook for one person, to clean the rooms, and then there is nothing else to do. During that month I'll do my best to save 200 marks and send it to you specifically to cover the extra expenses, and we won't tell Papa about it. When I come, we'll decide how to organize things. If you want, I'll take you and the child to Switzerland, if you want you can stay in Kolberg. I am only afraid that a lack of experience getting organized will make you spend a lot of money. Look, get organized carefully, I will gladly throw money at all of you, but anyway don't forget that papa is only one person and has to work for all of you. So Sania has to pay 500 rubles for his doctoral exam marriage, and birthday. Within the year there will be a child there, too, and there is only one papa. True, says Sania, he won't take any money from papa but he'll have to take if he doesn't have any. I will not deny that we are wealthy but we may not deplete this wealth because papa will not be able to work forever and then we'll have to live on the savings of our capital. Of course, the child cannot be left in the city. So make up your mind and write to me immediately. What is most important to me is my need to discuss many things with you. I want to arrange that you will not have to spend anything on the child, i.e., her wardrobe, I will sew for her to last for a whole year. I'll buy her small stockings, short stockings, shoes, sandals, I'll make all the lingerie, warm dresses, woolens, night blouses or a warm jacket, a bonnet, and handkerchiefs, I'll buy her toys. This also means that she will need a nanny, milk, and a doctor, also laundering underwear. We'll talk about it. So, independently of what papa is giving, I will give you 200 marks for this month, but just don't talk about departure to him. It seems to me that there are beautiful spots in the vicinity of Berlin; I recall that the professor once said that there are also mountains covered with forests. So I advise you to go there for one month with the child until I arrive. What would it cost to feed two people?

I am now staying with Milia and two servants, and I spent 2 rubles at the market. Petia Shainov had supper at my place. The nanny can cook dinner for both of you in one hour on two kerosene burners; the soup on one, and meatballs or cutlets on the other, with one vegetable. In the morning eggs, cheese, milk; for supper scrambled eggs with tomatoes, something [salty?], and changing every time. It's not difficult at all; you can prepare a fruit salad for two–three days or just fruit, sometimes you can buy prepared foods and I assure you that you don't need to have a kitchen for two people; sometimes bring a prepared dinner home. Rent two rooms and make sure that you always have hot water for bathing the child. and a place for ice to keep the milk, and a place where you can wash the diapers, and pay an extra 5–10 marks a month. You should always have boiling water for making tea. Silva had the same arrangement but in a boarding house; but you should rent two rooms with the right to cook. Buy yourself a lot of fruit, fruit salads, cheese, butter, frankfurters, sausage, ham, eggs, milk, sour milk, potatoes, spinach, everything that can be prepared quickly for healthily breakfasts and suppers. You should rent space immediately in such a place where there is a doctor; otherwise it is a risk for the child. I am rushing to mail this letter, it's about 2 in the morning and I am writing another letter following this one or else the letter will not be mailed. I started the letter yesterday and am finishing it today. Goodbye,

your mama

ES 8–9

Dear Sabina! 29.II.14?

I have just read papa's letter to you and, obviously, I'm very upset that the letter will distress you greatly. I have suffered a lot because of his state of mind and I see no way out. Of course, I wrote nothing to you about it; I didn't want to worry you, but since papa had written to you too I can no longer remain silent. It is painful to look at him; he turned into some kind of a machine or a dead person, no more. I wrote about it to Yasha and asked for his help; but I hid it from you and Sania. I do not know what is better for him: to go to see Freud or just take some rest, as he works from dawn till night. He wrote to you to ask for your advice what to do with himself, to whom to turn so as to, so to speak, rise from the dead. True, I am neither a Freud nor a psychiatrist, but I could explain a lot about his state of mind. The most essential cause is a tremendous fatigue and a complete dissatisfaction with his spiritual strivings.

You will find the second cause in the long letter, which I wrote a long time ago but never sent to you, but I still may do it. If to what I have already said above you will add your guesses and your knowledge of psychiatry, then everything will become clear to you. Should your father say that it is all the same to him, then this would be a lie; it only seems to him that way, for it is only smothered, pressed down, and he is not aware of it. How pleased he was when Margulis praised you, and how much he himself added to it. And he praised you sky-high to Fabrikant, that there is nobody like you; he spoke with enthusiasm and pride and kept repeating "my daughter". He gets angry when somebody does not appreciate your true worth or is unable to understand you. It is also not this way as far as the child is concerned. He himself said to me: "Sew shirts for the child, write to her about this or that", but there is a certain "but" between him and the child, this is what I think, or even probably know for sure, and as I told, you would understand. All of this is not so terrible, such a feeling, which I <u>understand</u>, comes upon him for minutes due to known causes, but the child is dear and important to him and he is happy when you describe that the child as good, but sometimes he says he does not care, and this does not surprise me. He has suffered a lot, like no other father, he was exposed to utterly frivolous people and undeserved slaps on the face. Please, consider that all this is my own conclusion based on many conversations. I am unlike your father, I do not have such a psychosis, but I do have some distressing weak spots. Of course, I support father and he always answers: "I don't care". But he does care. He <u>arrived</u>, became reconciled to his situation, and stopped talking. I understand, though he did not tell me, that he does not want to go to Berlin, he is instinctively afraid to pick at his wounds, he wants to heal them, to be as uninvolved as possible, so as not to feel those well-known weak spots, but he is not aware [text break]

I have just had a visit from [Dr.] Margulis, and he spoke about you with such enthusiasm that my heart was filled with joy. We talked about you a great deal. "How unusually wise she is," he said, "she is a fine girl and she will go far", etc. I gave him 12 calling cards of Pavlusha and 3 of yours. He promised to do everything he can. Through acquaintances I also sent cards to doctors in Ekaterinoslav. Osip can also do something; I gave him cards. Fabrikant is at our place, he will send out Pavlusha's and your calling cards to relatives and doctors with a request to distribute the cards. He took many cards from me for Petersburg. Here I gave cards to five doctors and in a few days I will do the same for the pharmacies. We can expect patients only after Passover. A practice cannot be launched immediately so do not lose heart. Uncle Adolf referred a [patient?] either to you or Pavlusha, I do not know, probably uncle Osip knows if it is true.

[postscript on the margins] this really "long" letter will tell you a great deal.

[postscript] You mentioned once that you wanted to speak with me in person, I'm waiting for the address. Please, use the address of P.M. Lublinskii, Tkacheskii Lane, Kireyev's house, for E.Sh. [Eva Shpilrain].

ES 10

[Dear Sabina] March 27

Fabrikant left yesterday, I gave him cards for doctors and acquaintances, he promised to write to me from every city about the results. In his home in St. Petersburg assemble seven doctors and a big crowd of relatives. He promised me a great deal and now I am writing to Rozalia Solomonovna. He will place advertisement about both of you in the newspapers *The Russian Word* and *Word*. You will be famous in a week. I baked a lot of cakes at Aunt Esphir's [Esther's] because our [...] was out of order. I had been busy with it for two days and as a result I caught a cold, which can develop into pleuritis again, therefore I decided to hurry up and finish the letter. Baked goods included a cake specially baked by Aunt Esphir. This is a cake that requires a lot of materials and labor. The aunt was preoccupied all day baking two cakes, which I am sending out to the children. Thank her, send her a postcard with a few words. I am also sending a cake to Olga Pavlovna [Yasha's mother-in-law]; so don't send her anything. For now just eat the honey cake and the three-cornered cake and save money for a sponge cake. These three-cornered cakes are stuffed with almonds and are very tasty. I am afraid that you will give away the cakes to everybody and there will be little left for you to eat. So, for your information, I worked very hard so that my children should have pleasure and save money, and I am sending out cakes to everybody, and I spent more than 30 rubles for 6 families. Silva will probably know how to handle this cake wisely, and I sent her more because she and Yasha like them. Sort the various pastries and put them in jars and store the rest to serve with tea and treat your guests.

ES 11

Dear Sabinochka! 11.4.14

In a few days Shura will go to Berlin; he left a short while ago. I will go to see him tomorrow or in a few days, and if he has room I will give him a jar of sweets to take for you; he cannot take more than one pound, and I don't know if he can even do that; then I will send some candy for Irmunia. I want to buy boots or shoes, and for you I am sending a diamond ring, I am afraid it will be a small one, although a size bigger than your wedding ring. Eat [cured sturgeon?] and candy to your heart's content and remember us more often. I am now very busy and as usual not particularly healthy; the house is again full of disorder and I feel pinned down: the cook was suddenly called away to her village to arrange a marriage. I hired another cook and I'm teaching her how to prepare our meals; the chambermaid had her child brought back to her again; the boy has lost so much weight, it's a pity to look at him, and my nerves are in tatters because of that. Indeed, the mother wishes her child to be dead, what a drama! She asked our wet-nurse to abandon the child at somebody's doorstep. I took her under my wing, but I don't know what to do with her. Such a sweet, intelligent face, so lovely! Here is a new dilemma for me, but I don't have the strength to deal with that. I have to refer this to the "Society for the Protection of Women".

Today papa sent you money to cover your deficit of 25 marks, which I took three for the laundress and the remaining 22 marks to buy a little bed for the child. I'm afraid this will not be enough, so I will give a few more marks to Shura—the money I brought back from Berlin, 5–6 maybe—I don't know how many exactly; they are in my purse. If a bed costs less money, then buy something else for the child with the rest of the money. I think a white bed with a net costs around 30 marks. But look, without fail buy a deep enough bed with a net. Papa is thinking of taking a vacation soon. I am sure he will leave some money for the child. He says one thing, but he thinks something else. I received no telegram from Yasha on my birthday; I only got it on the10th. Papa was worried, sent them a telegram and asked how they were doing. Their telegram surprised me, then papa admitted that he had been worried [they had the following conversation] –"But you say it's all the same to you, that you feel nothing?" – "Then be happy that I do have some feelings and don't make a fuss about it" – "Alright, so what will you do then when you visit Sabina and see the child?" – "I will probably kiss the child and love her, take her in my arms, but it seems that sometimes I experience emptiness," etc. He will visit you and you can talk to him yourself. He came to me himself and offered to buy the bed; usually I'm the one who asks. And sometimes he says, "You will probably want to buy bagels for your granddaughter, go and buy as soon as possible." But he doesn't say what he wants, so as not to show his feelings. Oh, he is a strange, very strange man! You'll see him soon! In fact, he also lives for his children only and cannot live alone at all.

I have no definite plans for the summer, only a few approximate ones. Papa suggests that I should go with him to Switzerland and buy there a summer property, and you would be able to come and visit us there, but then I thought to find a dwelling in the vicinity of Dresden, or perhaps not to leave Rostov at all, I have become very tired of traveling. However, all this is in the future; we will write to each other about it. Are you happy with the nanny? Give her my greetings; we should think about her as well, I forgot about her. Write me about her.

Good bye, write to your mother. Greetings to Pavlusha. Kiss Irmochka.

ES 12

Dear Sabina! Rostov-on-Don 2.V.14

I am rushing to the post office. It is absolutely necessary for me to come and see you and I will come if you are not too busy, but do not rent a room for me yet, I will decide everything on the day I arrive. I would be leaving here in three days but in the meantime there was an accident with Milia's hand; I'm waiting for the wound to heal. I will not leave before the 10th, probably after the 13th. I am indeed quite ill, but where did you get the idea that I would come to "serve" you? How happy I would be to serve my own children if I were in good health. In two days Natochka will be six months old. Don't forget to take her photograph. Kisses and I wait impatiently to see her. I'm bringing with me a whole wardrobe for her. Be well see you and please write to me.

Your mother.

Greetings to Pavlusha.

Postscript. I bought a lot of books. It is the only pleasure I have. I am reading "The Great Initiates" by the French author Schuré[98] and also the book "Out of the caves and labyrinths of Indostan" by Blavatanskaya [should be Blavatskaya[99]],

---

98 Philippe Frédéric « Édouard » Schuré (1841–1929), French writer, philosopher, and musicologist, best known for his *The reat Initiates An essay on the secret history of Rama, Krishna, Hermes, Moses, Orpheus, Pythagoras, Jesus.*

99 Elena Petrovna Blavatskaya (Madame Blavatsky) (1831–1891), a famous Russian occultist and cofounder of the Theosophical Society in 1875 (see Webb, 1980).

a book told to me by many people, which might be of interest to you and papa. I'll bring them along. The book, which is recommended to you to read as suggested by aunt Sabina, save for me. Presently Ilya Grigorievich is coming to tea with me, we frequently share business these days.

ES 13

Dear Sabina! Rostov-on-Don VI.12.14

I always await letters from you and other children with trepidation, read them avidly, and do not find what interests me particularly, mainly about your health, mood and about <u>your</u> relationship with your husband. I do not know how to hold my ground with people, and what to answer them. All your letters and cards were sent to him through the office and the address was always printed on the envelope because we do not correspond with him; this means that the address is there on the envelope, but it doesn't tell us whether he got these letters or not; he probably gets them, because we send the letters by registered mail. Through you we got Yasha's letter about Olga Pavlovna, I feel sorry for poor Yasha, seeing that he spoke this way about his mother-in-law, which means that she had exasperated him. I wish your husband should see what kinds of mothers-in-law there are and how they talk about "money." I, on the contrary, always asked my son-in-law if I could take the liberty of doing this or that and never reproached him. Olga Pavlovna took the liberty to reprimand us repeatedly, that we spent a lot of money on our son-in-law and our daughter, that we do not think about her son and give him a little, etc. She rudely intervened in our lives.

But let us forget it, I'm telling you this only to say to you that I would never allow myself to tell Olga Pavlovna that I know of such an exchange of letters between her and my son, for the happiness of my child is too important for me. So you can be calm about this, because neither she nor any matchmaker has ever entered our house and never will. I know that they have already been here for a month and a half. I expected that she would make a gift of 10,000 rubles for [illegible], but she only gave 100 rubles, we gave more than 1000 rubles, 1350 rubles, precisely, but could we have done otherwise?

Very frequently I host at our home many ladies who are my acquaintances and others whom I do not know, who come to me to help me sew clothes for children, these are people who care a great deal about the needs of children. There was a terrible commotion in my home here, women were working on five sewing machines, others were sewing tabs and buttons, and two were taking turns in making cuts. Tell Roza that at the same time Sara learned to sew and she sewed even the children's aprons, she has lived with me for two weeks and helped me a great deal, even though I carried most of this burden. Now everything is done and tomorrow I will do the packing. It's pleasant to see how all these parcels contain 12 things apiece: pantaloons, shirts, aprons for boys and girls (100 for girls and 100 for boys), sheets (140), towels (125) and handkerchiefs. Children were asking whom I am seeing, tell them that in the daytime I see many people and at night I see nobody as I worked with Sara till late at night and rarely had time to go to the balcony.

June 17

This is how busy I am. On top of that I am busy looking for a position for Masia, his family cannot even afford bread, [illegible] refused to hire Masia on the spot, he will give him 500 rubles in cash (before that in [illegible] he lost 500 rubles), thus Alia will have money for food for a month. Now I'm going around visiting different offices and banks to find a job for him. I suffer so much for them that I nearly lost my mind. I'm in a hurry my dear. Kisses my dear wonderful baby, I wish her health. May God preserve her for us. All the best, tomorrow I will write to Yasha and Sania. I miss you all very much. Give the enclosed photograph to Roza, it is from her sister, Roza's sister is living with me.

ES 14

My dear child! Rostov-on-Don 3 September

Will I be able to see you and dear Renatochka soon? What are you doing there, my dear ones? What do you live on? Where do you get the money? Every time we eat, we remember you. Sabinochka, I wrote to you a long time ago that I had for you 80 fells for a fur coat, the best fur, first rate. I was offered 320,000 rubles for these fells; that is 4000 for one, but I didn't sell them, I wanted to save them for you as the money would've been spent very quickly in view of today's high prices. I did not send any money for it is not permitted to send money. Therefore, I sent you 10 fells with Olga Pavlovna, so that you could sell them and have at least a little bit of money to live on. If you can sell one piece for 100 francs, for ten you will get 1000 francs to live on. I would like to know whether you received the money sent to you by a London check, a total, I believe, of five pounds sterling. I sent this money to you a long time ago through Sania to whom it was supposed to have been delivered by Bebochka as she was leaving Rostov. Did he receive the 140,000 rubles from us? We sent them to him approximately 8–9 months ago, I think: 40,000 rubles you [owed] him for the money you borrowed from him and 100,000 for you to live on, which he was supposed to give you little by little at your request. There were many [opportunities?] to send [small amounts?] of money. I hope that now you will be able to inform me in detail about all of this and in general about your life and about dear Renatochka. My dear Sabinochka, now write to us via Sania's address, i.e. to Olga Pavlovna, and she will then forward the letters to us. Olga Pavlovna promised me to do for you everything she can, this reassured me a little bit. However, I cried a lot after Olga Pavlovna left because I was unable to support you financially. I wanted to see you and the child. Let me at least get some news from you soon. Kisses for you and the lovely little granddaughter.

Mother

[Postscript on top of the page] I have not heard from Pavlusha for a long time, according to the latest news, he was in Crimea. I hope that poor Pavlusha will have a chance to see you. [at the bottom] In our family everybody is in good health and they send their regards to you and to Renatochka.

ES 15

Dear Sabina! 29.IX

I am not in the mood to write; I am waiting for the Mintses and the Shereshevskiis to arrive in an hour, and I don't know if they will come [text break]

I started this letter, it got mislaid, and there is no other paper at hand. I'm so busy I can't breathe, I do not have a free minute for myself. Papa is angry that I am even busy evenings and he [thinks?] there should be no more work after seven in the evening and no business conversations. I don't think this will be possible. Until last night I was working alone and only yesterday Sarra came to help me keep the records. Now I am writing while waiting for the seamstress to come, we will be making cuts; when she comes I will have to stop. I'm very tired and this is causing me insomnia at night. As far as doctors are concerned [I learnt?] that as a formality they are obligated to pass some kind of examination in order to be licensed as "Russian doctors".

When I do not get any letters from you I am [losing my mind?]. I always imagine something happened to you when there are no letters from you. Work is my salvation from thinking, even though it is ruining my health, but free time for thinking is sheer torture. It always seems to me that you are suffering, that you are unhappy, and this is killing me. Are you and the child healthy? How did you get settled? I believe you should not get settled too firmly in one place. I have not had any letters from Yasha for a long time, I feel sorry for the poor boy, he is also alone. Why has Silva left him? Now they will not be able to see each other until the end of the war. Just imagine, he will not be able to see his children for such a long time. It is strange, very strange! I do not want to think about it any more. I do not understand what could have caused him to become separated from his family in such difficult times. I'm stopping, the milliner came, and I want to mail this letter. Kisses to you and Renatochka.

Mama

[postscript on top] I will repeat once more: borrow from Bleuler and others a little bit at a time so that it should be enough for the next 2–3 months and in the meantime the problem may be solved . Kisses to you and Renatochka.

ES 16

Dear Sabinochka! Undated

We have received many letters from you with one and the same content—all about money. I'm writing to you about this so that you won't worry whether any of your letters reached us. Do not think that we are not trying to send you money, papa has already tried everything but nothing can be done for now. Papa sent you 500 rubles for one month and then another 900 rubles, but the 900 rubles were returned to us and probably the 500 rubles will also be returned. All this just makes me desperate. Perhaps you will be able to get a loan from someone until we can send you money. It pains me terribly that it is your fate to suffer so bitterly. But no matter how much we are suffering and sighing we are now unable to help those who are in trouble. Today papa visited Strashunskii and learnt that there was a time when it was possible to transfer 10,000 francs to his wife; and recently he was in Petrograd and, as a military doctor, he was able to obtain, after much trouble with the ministry, a monthly payment of 1,000 francs for his wife for two months. I will write about it to your husband (we made an agreement with him), and as soon as it is possible he will travel to Petrograd. Believe me, it is getting done and we shall be doing everything possible, and how happy we would be if we could send you a thousand rubles a month. Try to borrow from everyone you know. Do not be ashamed, in time like these anyone can become impoverished. I am awfully sorry that for now all we can send you is hopes. I still hope to see you soon.

How is Renatochka? Does she go hungry? How is your health and the child's? For the last three months Silva and the children have been living luxuriously in a sanatorium in Kislovodsk: for two children and the nanny she pays more than 1,000 rubles and for herself 500 rubles. By the way, this is what they were paying in Essentuki; Kislovodsk may be even more expensive. Yasha is no longer on her mind. She spent a few days in Rostov, did not come to visit us, just made a casual inquiry about Yasha. Oh, poor, poor Yasha! Thankfully he knows nothing about this. Everything is fine with us. We mainly suffer for our children for whom we live and [breathe]. I want to believe that with your energy you will be able to find money and will not leave the baby alone.

[postscript] I repeat once more: ask for a loan from Bleuler and others, a little at a time, so that you will have enough for the next two to three months, and then perhaps you will find a solution to the problem. I kiss you and Renatochka.

ES 17

My dear ones! Rostov-on-Don, 28.XII.14

We finally received the long awaited letter from you, but no matter how many times I have read it, I still did not find in it what I was looking for. I have an infinite number of questions but I can't get an answer any time soon. Certain questions were also asked by father in his letter (I read his letter last night) and I would like an answer to the following: how does Pavlusha plan to travel to Russia? Such traveling is now totally impossible, perhaps only via [illegible names], but with his sick heart this would be very risky. If it were in my power, I would certainly restrain his impulse. On one hand, such a severe rheumatism, on the other, such a sick heart! He will not be able to bear it. And what does he need it for? For God's sake, Sabina, advise him to think seriously about his health, let him seek the advice of his doctors. And don't forget to provide him with a nutritious diet.

Further, did the Fräulein come along with you? Too bad if she didn't, because she is a very good and experienced nanny and you won't find anyone like her in Switzerland. How are you all doing? How did you get settled? In an apartment or in furnished rooms? What things did you take with you? Did you really leave a whole chest with things and silver behind? Moreover, what will Sania do with the furniture come April 1st? Do you have any plans? Did you really leave all of the dishes to Sania? He is inexperienced and you might lose all your possessions. It is a pity, really. I beg you to answer all my questions, because all this concerns you and is of great interest to me. Sania has really scared us: it has been five weeks since we last had a letter from him, and Roza [his wife] was in need of some money for herself. Through the ministry we received a telegram from her to send 200 rubles, of course we sent the money immediately, but it made us worried. Roza forgot that she had been getting money from her mother, she told me herself that she and Sania were living on the 400 marks we been sending her; and finally her sister told me that for a long time Roza had not been getting any money, she [illegible words] mother should send her (as Pavlusha wrote to me), etc. But, thank God, we recently got a letter from Sania and today we received a cable from you about Sania.

In Rostov everything is calm; but the mood is, of course, dreadful, life is dreary. We feel miserable. Since our return papa and I have not visited anybody, we always stay at home. Almost every evening some member of our club comes to visit us but the conversations are all about one thing… There is no special news, except perhaps that Elterman, Strashunskii and many other doctors have left town and madam Elterman [illegible] the practice here.

As to you, Sabina, I would advise you to avoid seeing J[Jung]. What do you need it for? Personally, I do not like even the idea that you decided to live in Zürich. I am writing to you not because I am doubting <u>you</u> in anyway, but because it simply distresses <u>me</u> that you should be seeing him. Anyway, this is your and your husband's business, do as you will.

I do not recall if I wrote you about Milia's progress with his grades, he got five 4's and five 5's. He studied very hard to achieve this as he did not yet have a chance to show himself to be a good student, and I hope that in the next quarter his grades will be even better. Today he had his third music lesson, he needs to make up for lost time. Yesterday he visited his friend Shura Mints and stayed there almost till 4 o'clock am, it was Shura's birthday. I am glad he was able to get away from his books for a little while. I bought lottery tickets for everybody and each ticket can win up to 20,000 rubles. I purposely bought tickets with different numbers to have a better chance. I bought tickets for you, Pavlusha and Renatochka, for Sania and Roza and Yasha, Silva, Irochka and future children, for myself and Milia. We will see who wins. Presently I gathered all the tickets together but had no time to check the numbers I have as there was a lot to do before the holidays; I will check them and send you your tickets, the drawing will take place in March. The lottery is supposed to benefit a charitable institution. I wish with all my heart that one of you should win.

I have learnt, Pavlusha, that your sister Fania has been staying in Rostov for a long time; two days ago Ernestina with her husband came to stay with the Kofmans [sister Ania and husband]. Her husband paid a visit to Patt, they were supposed to leave today in the morning. I am also informing you that I learned from Patt that all your relatives in Kiev were doing well. I only do not know whether your sister-in-law Fania has left or is still in Rostov, but this is of no great importance to you, the main thing you should know, that all of them are doing well. I don't seem to be able to write as I can when I am in a certain mood and words flow spontaneously: I am being interfered with all the time. Write to me in detail about your life, about the child, about your smallest worries, because it all interests me greatly. My table is now covered with photographs of my children and I fix my eyes on them every day. Soon "new" ones will come.

Yasha writes that he is expecting the child to be born any day now. Roza's sister has come, I'm stopping writing.

Be well and happy.

Mother.

[postscript] I finished this letter yesterday on the 29th. The Levkovs (refugees from Warsaw) came to visit, she is my first cousin, Shainov's daughter. He can play three compositions on the violin and plays the piano with such feeling that we were all very moved and papa to tears. This was an experience fitting the present general mood. Patt and Roza's sister also came. Recently we were visited by [illegible] and his wife, we spent a pleasant evening, played many fun games, remembered the times [spent?] in Kolberg, those were still the good times. Somebody comes to visit every evening but we are sad because we miss our children.

ES 18 27.I.15

I have stayed in bed for eleven days and therefore did not finish my letter. While I was in bed I received your letter in which you had written that all of you were seriously ill with influenza and I was so worried because of that. I felt terribly sorry for all of you, worried so much, thought a great deal about you. In this letter you are also writing that you are in need and ask us to send you money for a few months ahead, etc. Oh, how I was hurting for you, my child! I felt sorry that you had to suffer in vain.

By the time we received your letter papa had already sent you 300 rubles via the ministry and later 1,000 francs more. He wanted to send you 3,000 francs at once but the exchange rate was 49,50 for each hundred francs and this would have caused a great loss. Papa decided to wait a little and he will probably send you this money too. It never crossed his mind to take away even the smallest amount from you. He takes upon himself to make up for any loss due to the falling rate of exchange. The same goes for Renatochka, so go on living as before. I am keeping all the money for your and Renatochka's birthdays, it is a pity so much is lost due to the exchange rate so let the money remain with me until sending it becomes especially needed. As soon as you let me know I will send it. In addition, we are saving all the kopeck coins and we have accumulated a substantial amount for Renatochka. I was amused and pleased by the kopecks collected, still, some pin money should she wish to show herself in Zürich. In recent days I handed papa 20 single kopeck coins to get instead one 20 kopeck coin which he exchanged and then said: "What do I need them for?" I burst out laughing and put that one and the other kopecks together so now the child will be 20 kopecks richer—isn't that funny? In the summer I will sew dresses for her and Irochka. Write to me more about Renatochka. What is she saying now? It is time for her to meet other children. I am ending here. Be well and happy, wishing you all that.

Your mother.

Shura Tsaitlin was given a date to repeat his examination. In a few days the result will be known. I truly feel for him as it will turn out so badly. Yes, papa sent Yasha the full monthly amount of 300 marks for seven months without any deductions. Everything will also be sent to Sanichka.

[postscript above] Take a note of your serial numbers:

Sabina

Ser. 03180 #042

Pavlusha

Ser. 03602 #064

Renata

Ser. 03177 #092

I picked these numbers and wrote them down the corresponding name on every ticket. I wish wholeheartedly all three to win or at least yours [illegible]

Eva's postscript [fragment of another letter]. Silva and Ol.[ga] Pav.[lovna] [Yan's mother-in-law] tortured Yan—and he was probably aware of the situation with Ol. Pav. all the time—reminding him all the time that he has a wife and a child, therefore, he should abandon his scientific career and start making money. That is, to abandon science "for money". It is outrageous. Yasha, being in a well-known mood and also because he was encouraged to do this, wrote father a horrible letter about money and I can imagine how uncomfortable he will feel when he finds out that in spite of the letter he sent, he will receive the money without any mention about this. I feel sorry for him, for how badly he will feel. Yes, papa sent Yasha in full the 300 marks each month for seven months without any deductions. Sania will also be sent all the money.

ES 19

Dear Sabinochka! Rostov on/Don 4.II.15

How did you get settled all by yourself? How is your health and the child's? For God's sake, do not grudge yourself any expense on clothes, eat well and enjoy your life. When the business was very bad we only asked you to be more frugal but we did not reach a point where you should deny yourself the necessities. Remember, do not begrudge anything to yourself and the child. If necessary, papa will come to you so that you are not alone. Perhaps he will set you up in a nice and cozy little apartment. I would also like to come to see you but I have no idea how to get there, when papa returns I will come to see you. Every day now I am bathed in tears because I know so little about you and it seems to me that your mind is filled with tragedy but if I knew that you are calm I would be happy for you. You ought to feel happy to have such supportive parents. I feel so sorry that I am not with you now when you are alone.

We telegraphed you and no answer yet, nor did we receive any letters from you for quite some time. My heart is all but breaking because I have no news from you and you write so infrequently. Three weeks have passed and no letter from you. Write in detail about Renatochka. Papa gave me 30 rubles to save for Renatochka. All your and Renatochka's money is in a post office account. I will send them to you as soon as you write to me. You have a lot of money now, just don't lose it, don't deny yourself anything. Business is now somewhat better, God willing everything will be alright. Be well, happy and calm. Kisses to Renatochka.

Your mother

I will surely write tomorrow

ES 20

Dear Sabinochka! [8?].II.15

Every day I wait for your letter like manna from heaven but nothing is coming. I have already lost all my strength suffering because of you. Are you well, is Renatochka well, how is your mood? I do not know anything. I am only feeling with a mother's heart that you are suffering and feeling as badly as I do and that is already more than enough. The more I suffer the more I feel sorry for you knowing how distressing your situation is. If only your husband had enough tact to visit us and bring us greetings from our daughter, tell us about her health, explain to us all those problems that are vexing us, but instead he telephoned us calling himself Dr. Sheftel and invited papa to join him for negotiations at the Swiss pastry shop, which he calls a neutral environment and where merchants gather to make deals. He, apparently, considered the matter he wanted to discuss to be a commercial one, there is nothing holy for such people if such an upsetting problem could be discussed around people sitting at neighboring tables eyeing one with curiosity.

A letter sent from a hotel and marked "Hotel," which he didn't even bother to mark "personal," was opened in the office. Thus, a secret we concealed from everyone became known – and this must have been unpleasant for him as well – that we were paying up his debts, that he has pawned your diamonds, etc. [Concerning] your decision about a [divorce?] I know your husband well enough to realize that this was not his final decision, that he would ask for forgiveness either from you or from us, should he choose to act independently of his "dear relatives"! Oh, if you knew what kind of a family he has! Especially this Ania. It appears that many people in town know her as a piece of work. Were it not for you, I would rather forget this filth but I delve into it for your sake. In my opinion, you should be aware that your letters to him will be read by his relatives, therefore (unless he starts to discuss this issue [divorce] with you), you should not discuss this problem at all, because you do not need a divorce right now! You are now well provided for, papa will visit you soon and will furnish for you a good and comfortable apartment, so get visits from your acquaintances, have a good time, and try to think that all that happened earlier was just a dream.

I am saving money for the child, you will not be deprived of anything. Order a dress and a suit for yourself and if you do not have enough money, papa will gladly send it to you. The child is very [dear?] to us, and to father as well, and especially since her father left and abandoned the sick child we are particularly concerned for the child now. As soon as it is possible to travel, and my health permitting, I will come to be with you.

I am repeating, absolutely do not answer any letters of a certain kind, ignore them, let them get nervous, it is they who are in a hurry, it is they who need money and are eager to sell brother and son as quickly as possible, but we are not in any hurry. There is time, calm down, and in general, do not even answer letters of a different kind, should you be upset. If he asks about the child's health, answer laconically. I imagine, when the clan learns that at present, Sabina is leading a life of beauty and dignity, that she has money, ah, how sorry they will be for what has happened.

So, be smart, savvy, free, think everything over with a cool head, do not publicize anything, you can talk about everything with Miss Leibovich. One day I will tell you many interesting details but for now live a little without chains, especially the heavy chains of the Sheftel family headed by Aniechka. You should not carry this baggage all your life. I am waiting impatiently to receive your letter, I stopped eating and sleeping. Write now every day about your health and Renatochka's. Did you get the 3,000 francs that were sent to you before you asked for them in your letter? Be well, happy and calm, you have a great support in your parents. Kisses for you and Renata.

Mama

[another fragment of this letter]

This is how they succeeded [illegible] In his last letter, filled with feelings, he called papa father etc. He said he will have to return to Russia; moreover, based on a variety of weighty facts we did know, that as soon as he arrives here, "they" would grab him and start "pushing" him and working on him. The whole family was assembled in Kiev, and I immediately figured out that they would seize their prey, their "cash cow," and this indeed happened. He arrived there at the same time as they; I am not mistaken about this. I do not know everything except that he rented two rooms from his family and was waiting for patients. I think he will be drafted. I registered him [in the roster?] as a doctor because when he had first gone there, he was listed as a veterinary. A divorce, as all his relatives fervently desire, cannot even be considered before the war is over, therefore, stay perfectly calm, in my opinion, do not react to any letters from him should such be written in this spirit. As I mentioned above, let them worry themselves needlessly, they have caused me so much nervousness with their rudeness, that the glass is full. My letter was too long, but [text break]

ES 21

My dear! Rostov on/D 12.II.15

Before the postman comes I am writing a few words in order to remind you that all of us are thinking about you. Not a day or minute goes by without thinking about you. There is nothing new, well, I am living like a recluse from the world. I started going out only a few days ago, otherwise I have been sitting at home for months. The heat is unbearable and I am wearing an Astrakhan fur; willy-nilly I will have to take care of my grooming; meanwhile I mended my old suit and a green cloth dress and then I will see. Papa's business has improved a bit so that you can live better too, think some more about yourself and remember, do not ruin your face with worries, it will make you look old, on the contrary, take good care of your skin, hair, grooming, look to entertain yourself and you will see yourself revive. I would not like to even remember anything about "him", personally I would not want to know anything, but anyway, for your sake, I will try to find out whether he visits his sister and I will not try to find out anything more. However, if in spite of trying not to get involved I will find out something I will let you know, meanwhile do not think about anything, it is not worth it.

I have no letters from you, I am not occupied and I'm losing my mind. The child, the child and the child. Tell me about her. Today I received a letter from Sania in which he writes that he has not gotten any letters from us for the last 40 days, which means that letters are getting lost. Write to him that we have been sending letters frequently and that we sent money to Roza a while ago, which he has now confirmed. I'm rushing to mail the letter. Kisses to you and Renatochka.

Your mama

[postscript] Warm greetings from all of us and from [Berta?] Ilyinichna, she is living with us.

ES 22

Dear Sabinochka! Rostov on/D 13.II.15

Today I can already [illegible] letter. Milia met with your husband; they kissed each other and then had an hour-long walk. He was asking Milia about us, talking about himself and sent us greetings, asking if we received letters from you. He was in the courtyard next to us, walking toward Nikolayevskii [avenue] as Milia was leaving school, and then they [returned]. At the same time I was talking to [illegible] on Moskovskaia Street and saw Aniechka passing by. I have no letters from you; it is hurting me but I can do nothing about it. Your husband told that in Zurich you had no letters from us and that was terribly irritating, I write letters but cannot know if they will be received. I write daily, but I also don't know if you have been getting my letters. Every day I ask about you and the child but there is no answer. I will wait for two more days and then send a cable. In my previous letters I told you that your husband had not come to see us but I am afraid you have not received them.

Be well, happy, write about yourself and dear Renatochka. Kisses to you.

ES 23

Dear Sabinochka! Rostov on/D 14.II.15

I am now writing about what might be of utmost interest to you, once again before the post arrives. I went out today, got tired and therefore started writing this letter a little late. Yesterday evening we were visited by [Panin?] who had met with a relative of the Kiev Sheftels. The relative proceeded to visit the Kofmans,[100] where he spent the whole evening and next day he visited [Panin?] again about some business and sent greetings from the Kofmans. "And wasn't Pavel Naumovich there?" – "How so, is Pavlusha in Rostov?" – "They didn't they tell you about this, really?" – "No" This is strange and it makes me think that Pavlusha does not visit the Kofmans. Maybe be he had an argument with them. It is also strange that he stayed in a hotel and not with his sister. I have finally received your letter and have not found anything in it because one inside sheet was missing. I only learned that you have suffered a lot and endured a lot. Poor, poor you, how much you have suffered. El. Al. is visiting us, I am rushing

100 The lawyer Semion Evgenyevich Kofman, Ania's husband, also referred to as Semion and Senia.

to end the letter. Don't begrudge any money, take care of yourself and our dear girl. Be well and happy.

Mama

[postscript] Tomorrow I will write to Sania and I have already written to Yasha through you.

ES 24

My dear! Rostov on/D 15.II.15

Can you hear the music? It is Milia playing a concert – wonderful the way he plays. It is a pity that he has a lesson only once a week. Today was a lucky day – he was playing for four hours (Sunday), in the morning he played Mozart solo and then played the same for half an hour four hands with a young lady; and now he is having a lesson with Zelikhman[101]. I have not left home today and therefore there is nothing [illegible]. I'm waiting impatiently for a detailed letter from you. How is the child's and your health? One day you will also hear your Renatochka playing. Be careful with her now, let her be out in the sun, may God save her from catching a cold. Oh God, how hard it is when there are no letters for so long. For God's sake write to me often, I am totally sick because of suffering for you. Your husband is busy with arrangements to stay here, he opened a practice. I am very curious, do you receive letters from him? Stay calm, everything will be alright, we shall yet live in joy and happiness. We are joyful when our children are happy. I am saving money for Renatochka. I am reading cards constantly. You will certainly do well. Do not stay with Natochka near the water. Do not fire your nanny, God forbid, you will not find another one like her! Everyone is well, cordial greetings to you from relatives and acquaintances.

Kisses to you and Natochka.

Mama

ES 25

Dear Sabinochka! Rostov on/ D 16.II 15

I did not leave home today. Milia was going to his evening classes and met your husband again. For now he is working near the railway station and what he is going to do next is still unknown. He came out of the adjacent courtyard again and accompanied Milia to the streetcar. He said he regretted that Yasha was not returning to Russia, that he would easily get an engineer's job, regretted that you cannot come to Russia now, but that it is difficult with a child;

101 Perhaps a reference to Ilia(Gil') Abramovich Zelikhman (1877–1940), a violinist and teacher.

if Milia is telling the truth, he sent us greetings. It is rather strange, I can't figure it out. He does not come to visit us in person, just sends greetings. A transfer of 300 rubles through the ministry was just returned to us; the ministry does not transfer money to Switzerland, you'll get this money later. How is Silva's health? There is no letter from Yasha since his daughter was born. I would like to know how the new mother is doing, I would also like to know if there are any complications. Was the child born healthy? What is the girl's name? Don't fail to write to me about it. It is strange for me that you still have not written to me why you broke up with your husband when you were on bad terms with him. Maybe you did write, but the letter was lost. I am writing to you every day. Today I received a telegram from you informing us that you are all well, but my heart is still heavy. For God's sake write to me.

What about Renatochka? Be well and happy.

Your mama.

ES 26

Dear Sabinochka! Rostov on/D 18.II.15

There is still no letter from you. I am exhausted waiting for it. I write daily but do not know if you're getting my letters. Yesterday, finally, we got a letter from Yasha, thank God, everything is alright there. Are Sania and Roza going hungry? We sent enough money to everyone. Write to Sania and tell him not to wear himself out. My heart is pining for the children. I don't believe that Sania is doing well. Our letters are not reaching him and he writes that he has been sending us letters twice a week but we are not getting any. I can't help repeating myself. Don't deny yourself anything, eat well. I have written to you already that you should make dresses for yourself, papa has also written about this and sent you 700 francs. Now his business is doing better and it is no longer so scary. I am impatient to receive your letter. Do you write to you brothers often? I am glad that you are friends with each other. Yasha writes that Silva is well, thank God, his letter was good. Ask them to write to me more often. How is Renatochka? I ask about her every day. I hope she is healthy. Are you seeing Jung? In all, who are the people you are seeing? Make your apartment cozy and full of light and play hostess to interesting people. Go to the theatre and concerts. Why don't you mention anything about Leibovich? Tell her I would very much like to hear from her. The postman came. I am stopping. Kisses to you and Renatochka. I wish you the very best.

Mama

ES 27

Dear Sabinochka! Rostov on/D 21.II.15

There is nothing new on my horizon. What can I tell you? The mood is so awful that the mind stops working, I am writing just because you should have some news from home. When will I finally have a letter from you? I was nervous and tormented. I know nothing about you and that torments me. I am unable to write anything to Yasha and Sania until I get some news from you. I have no desire to write when I think that it will take at least a month and a half before I get an answer to my letter. I have sent you so many questions and got no answer.

Your husband would have been able to provide me with many answers and calm my tormented heart, but instead yesterday, as I was walking with Shura, he just passed us by greeting neither me nor Shura and turned [away?]. I regret that I did not stop to [to speak with] him. I wish I had confronted him with his lack of tact and showed him how proper, well-bred, cultured people would have behaved and not insensitive boors. He was probably indignant because of my behavior of not greeting him first. Never mind, I flatter myself that another opportunity may come about.

The main thing – are you and your child healthy? The 300 rubles sent to you via the ministry were returned but in a few days papa will send them to you again, you will get 500 marks through Yasha. Take care of yourself, have a good time, I hope everything will be good. I live only through you and think only about you. I am saving money for the child. Be well and happy.

Mama

Greetings to Miss Leibovich, and what about Fräulein, is she with you?

ES 28

Dear Sabina! Rostov on/D 2.III.15

I received a photograph of dear Renatochka taken with the nanny. I was so happy. Why is her face so sad on all the photographs? How is she usually, cheerful? Milchik received a telegram from you, how did you manage to remember? It is amazing. He will write to you soon. Due to the heat and [illegible]; he is getting taller, he lost a lot of weight. I'll send one of the photographs to your husband tomorrow. I send everything by registered mail. Don't worry that you have not gotten letters from him in a long time, perhaps he is very busy or perhaps he should have forwarded letters to us and we would have sent them on to you, do you understand? Perhaps I should have sent him your letters unsealed instead of putting them in envelopes. I would like to know whether he is receiving your letters, and therefore I'll take the risk and ask him briefly about it and then inform you. I'm rushing to mail the letter. I have written a lot and my hands are aching. For God's sake, write me more often about yourself and the child. It is a pity I cannot see how she is walking. Will I see her soon? It is possible that we will get a visit from uncle Adolf, I don't know for sure, but it might happen. Inform Yasha and Sania. We are very interested to learn about your work with blind patients. Keep working, you can find satisfaction in that.

Kisses to you and to dear granddaughter

Your mama

[postscript] Your dear husband has rented a room where he is receiving patients from 3–5 and he came to tell me about this 10 days ago, he is working and living in the[hospital?], but he visits his sister daily, so that the "pushing?" may be continuing. Reported by people who saw him accidentally.

ES 29

Dear Sabina! Rostov on/D 13.III.15

You shouldn't think that I caused you harm when I told Sheftel that you have enough money and I didn't say it in order to justify ourselves; you have to be here to be able to evaluate <u>everything</u>. In my conversation with him I gathered they had brainwashed him that the child is poorly cared for, that there is no money, that the child is in a poor condition. I told him point blank that the child is well cared for, that you are financially well off, that you want to take the child to some place in the summer. I said that you are completely devoted to the child and are able to sacrifice everything, even work, until the child gets stronger. Milia passed half of his examinations. I even wanted to tell you that in your letters to him you should write that the child is not lacking anything, that you have enough money to care for her, and that your parents are taking care of the child's future. You have to be very careful in your letters to him because he might be showing your letters to his relatives, slanderous people, who might want to argue in court that the mother has no means to take care of the child. It is very unlikely that he will demand to get the child, I almost don't believe it, but it doesn't hurt to be cautious. No way will we give him the child, so don't worry. So my purpose was to let him know that there is enough money, to make him regret that he mentioned divorce, that he should annoy "them" a little bit, for one, and secondly, to let him know that the child is getting the best care, that her future is secure, so why should he (unless he wants to take revenge on you) want to take the child. Regarding his request, that you should pay for his diamonds, who would have imagined that a person could humiliate himself to such an extent. Whereas he informs us, strangers according to him, that he wants to divorce our daughter, he is also asking us to pay for his diamonds. This is so ridiculous. Better yet, he avowed to me a few times that the divorce had already happened, and that only because of the war that the piece of paper is missing; at the same time he is writing to you that you should pay him back for his things, his diamonds. Where is the logic? Why doesn't he instead turn to his wonderful sister, so as not to be humiliated by "people who are strangers to him." Under such conditions, what right does he have to ask us for our support? I would have preferred to lose all those diamonds and avoid being so humiliated. Clearly, words are one thing deeds are another. "How much I would like to make money and [illegible] them to you," money which we had paid him. "But we haven't mentioned those moneys even once." "Not to me, but to my relatives." Go and prove to him that his relatives are lying. So you see, on one hand he would like to earn and throw this money at us, which he once got from us with such love, and on the other, he <u>prefers</u> to give money to Senechka [Kofman], who is certainly making demands on him, and if that is not enough, he wants you to give up 350 marks and pay for his diamonds. Where is the consistency in this. Furthermore, you yourself wrote to him about two sums you had received and only then did I tell him that you would get more. And as far as how to behave towards him is concerned, I can assure you that I will not humiliate myself and I will not humiliate you in relation to him.

I have composed for you different versions in a bunch of letters but did not mail them because in each of them willy-nilly something was mentioned about his relatives or about him and that is why I did not send them to you. But now, since you <u>yourself</u> are writing about what <u>I had wanted</u> to tell you, I took out parts of letters written at different times, and am now sending them to you. So that you can see that I myself told you that you should not humiliate yourself and avoid writing anything about yourself; that you should write infrequently, briefly, and only about the child; that nothing offensive should peep through in your letters. So how could you think that I should be trying to meet him? There was a time when he telephoned me frequently and informed me about the content of your letters and it was then evident that he was talking about it with pleasure, not even the way he did before, and I even thought that he strongly regretted what had happened. Then it turned out that a lady from whom he rented a room for his practice was telling to another one "There were rumors that he divorced his wife but he does not stop talking about his wife and a child." I've heard from other people that it was his relatives telling that he got a divorce because his wife was smart woman but an impossible spouse, and different variations thereof. Now it has been a week since he telephoned me and it is probably because I acted very cold and reserved in my telephone conversations; but I want to forget his existence but he keeps reminding me of himself. Write more often, I only your [text break?]. I am saving money for Renatochka. You received some money for her birthday, and some for you, for the 1st of June, and for a dress for you. However paying back for the diamonds should be your decision. Should you decide to pay for them, hide them in your place and one day you will be able to say that your father sent you the money to pay for the diamonds because he didn't want his daughter to scrimp on her personal expenses, and actually this the way it is; if you choose to pay 250 marks for the diamonds, then this money will have to be returned to you, so that you shouldn't suffer, and it looks as if papa paid for the diamonds, and that is ridiculous. As far as the books are concerned, it can wait till the war is over, nobody will [pay?] here. It is another matter in Switzerland.

Kisses to dear, sweet Renatochka. May God protect both of you. Mama

Your sweet husband rented a room in which he sees patients from 3–5 and he visited me about ten days ago to tell me that he works and lives in the [hospital?], that he visits his sister daily; so that ["the pushing"?] is as it should be. Lately this was reported to me daily by those who happened to see him.

ES 30

Dear Sabinochka! Rostov on/D 2nd of April

I have written you many, many letters during this time and as I was writing them I was tearing them up and a lot of them I left without mailing. I wrote because I had a need to write, to pour my heart out, to protect my child from many troubles, to tell a lot about what could bring harm to my child if I did not tell her. But it was always accompanied by this thought: "Will it be nothing but parents meddling in their daughter's life or in building her own life?" My conscience tells me: "No, it is your duty as a mother to transmit to the daughter what her husband is telling you <u>in person</u>" [probably text break].

[postscript] If you were here and knew everything the way we know, you would have said: "Oh, how happy I am." Create new work and you will forget yourself <u>for the time being</u>. We will see later.

[postscript] For now there can be no divorce and later it will depend on you. Even if you will not want to live with him, with the divorce you will torment Aniechka and the old lady.

[postscript] I kiss dear Renatochka.

ES 31

Dear Sabinochka! Rostov on/D 20.VI.15

How much I wished I could see all of you! I am missing you terribly. To alleviate all my emotional suffering I also threw myself into various social activities. It is necessary to help many poor and unfortunate people and to be somewhat useful for our beloved motherland. We have just received your telegram where you ask about our and your husband's health. What can we tell you about him? He has not sent us a word all this time and we are not on speaking terms with the Kofmans therefore there is no way to know anything. As I have written to you many times, all your letters have been forwarded to him by registered mail to the printed address; but now, I think, I will personally send him your telegram even though I consider it humiliating; but I will do this for you because I see that you are still interested in him and that he is very dear to you. But there is nothing strange about that, I am not his wife, but I would feel very aggrieved should some misfortune befall him, after all, I was devoted to him, like a mother. His attitude toward you and us, the way he insulted us, greatly numbed my feelings toward him, but should he be in an extremely difficult situation, I could even do a lot for him as a sacrifice but only on condition that he would not know about it, as I cannot bear another humiliation.

So the telegram will be forwarded to him. Therefore, I beg you, let me know what is your relationship with him like, does he still address you as "You" [the formal form]? It is <u>necessary</u> for me to know this in order to accept, for your sake, a compromise, under certain conditions, or leave my relationship as is. There were some moments when he was ready to be a little bit softer but I did not yield, I did not want him to think that I was trying to bring the two of you together. Of course, now he is far away and there are no clashes between us (and there weren't any previously either, everything went smoothly between us), i.e. we do not see each other, we do not talk to each other, but what about some happenstance? You wrote once that it depends on you whether there is a divorce. How is that possible? What does it depend on? Has he really laid down any conditions? In fact, he himself told me that divorce was unavoidable, that the war was the only obstacle. In my presence he first referred to you as "Sabina Nikolayevna" but lately he has been calling you "Sabina" and it was clear that it was a pleasure for him talk about you, and when I spoke about Renatochka and referred to you as "her mother," he was surprised and asked me why didn't I simply call you "Sabina." In my opinion, do not take any money from him, let him have enough. Briefly, I am begging you, write to me about how he is treating you, how he writes, and whether it is possible that the two of you could get back together. If there is no hope for that, we shall continue to behave toward him the same way as now – politely, correctly, coldly. Kisses to you and dear Renatochka. We are impatiently awaiting your letters.

Your mother.

Did you send his mother a photograph after all?

[postscripts from father] Hello my dear! You promised to share with me your impressions of blind people. I am also interested to know if photography plays any role in psychiatry and what role it plays. By the way, I know about experiments of photographing thoughts and in general how the brain works. In an English textbook I found the expression "fall in love" [English in the original] = to become enamored. It reminds me of the French expression "tomber malade" = to fall ill. There is [also?], although rare, *tomber amoureux* [to fall in love]. It means that "love" is equivalent to a "fall." Does "falling into sin" come from it? Your cables are not frugal. The last one contains two superfluous words, namely "Telegraphiere" [I am telegraphing] and [et?]. They are not necessary at all. But if you insist, then one word is enough: "santé" [health]. They are not necessary altogether. But if you really want it, one word "santé" should be enough. We will know what you mean.

ES 32

Dear Sabina! Rostov on/D 6.[VII?].15

I have learned that he is feeling well, and I hurry to tell you about this to calm you down. All he received was a postcard and a letter sent by you. He did not get any of the letters sent by us, and forwarded to him in [Kars?] by a registered mail and poste restante. I found this out yesterday at the post office when I wanted to send him the child's photograph by registered mail and was told that registered letters are not accepted and post restante is not allowed anymore. He must have left [Kars?] before these letters reached him and because the post office did not forward them and forwarding is not allowed; we therefore sent a written request to Kars post office with his address and asked to destroy the registered letters. I will also let him know about this. On Thursday I am leaving for Essentuki [spa] for one month, the heat is so unbearable that it is impossible to stay alive. It was 43 [centigrade] yesterday, Milia told me that. Did I write to you that Shporlinskii became a bridegroom? After the war he will marry a Christian woman, a divorcee, very rich, and will live on her money. She is a colonel's daughter and her brother is an officer. I have the impression that he is selling himself but that she is madly in love with him. This is what he is saying.

We are doing well, your husband is in good health, so this means that you should calm down. I will write more when it cools off, I have no strength to write. I write to you 2–3 times a week and I am surprised that you are not getting my letters. Take a photograph of yourself and send it to us. Write more about the child, write about everything, the way she speaks and the way she walks, and what she is doing. Regards to the children, tell Sania about Shporlinskii.

Kisses to you and Renatochka.

Mama

[postscript from Emil] Dear Sabina! Thank you for your telegram which came, by the way, one day before my birthday. As far as my examinations are concerned, mama wrote to you, those had already been over by the 1st of May and were quite successful (certificate of 4 7/12). Papa thinks that I don't need to continue studying in the 7th grade, because, as they say, I already have my certificate, but, clearly, I do not agree with him. On Thursday I will go to Essentuki with mama for about 2 weeks. Greetings to Renata and also to San'ka and Yashka.

Adio [sic], Milia

[a postscript from mother] We have just received your letter in which you write about setting up a workroom. This cost me 400 rubles of my own money; a lot of people have been coming to me daily and everybody was sewing. Fania Isayevna Gurvich helped with cutting, there were three cutters, and there were always breakfasts and dinners, a lot of work. I had to travel to Mariupol for the opening of a shelter and all of a sudden my legs got swollen, only yesterday was I able to start walking a little bit.

ES 33

Dear Sabina! Essentuki 14.VII.15

When I was getting ready to travel to Essentuki I wrote to you and to Sania, but now I do not remember if I mailed the letter to you; there was a lot in it about my work for the Mariupol children's shelter, pity if the letter was left behind at home. Some time ago I wrote to you that I had forwarded your telegram to your husband with a little postscript, that in your letters you are worried because you are not getting any letters from him, that you fear that something might have happened to him and, I must admit, it made me worried as well. In response to this, I received a few words from which I learned that while in Kars, he had received directly from you one letter and one postcard, but that he did not get any letters we had forwarded to him, either by registered mail or by post restante; but since departed, and is now on active duty, registered and poste restante letters are not allowed. We at once sent an order to the post office to return the letters to us in Rostov and from there to forward them to him without having to pay for stamps. Knowing that he is probably angry because he has not received any letters from you, on the very first day I arrived here I informed him about everything that happened and told him that he would get all those letters in eight days. I didn't write anything else, don't worry, I only informed him about this and also mentioned that it included a portrait of his daughter. I asked him to inform me about any change of address so that I would be able to send him future letters. If he writes to me, should this happen, I will let you know. He is in good health and a cheerful mood, so stay calm.

I kiss the dear child. What is she saying? I am getting treatments for my gout; I am almost a cripple. Both legs are terribly swollen, bags have appeared on the sides below on the heels and on all the lower part of the legs, I can barely move my hands, I cannot turn my neck, there is also gout in the head. I have taken a few mud treatments and I fear I won't be able to take any more, my heart got very weak. Today somebody died in the street of a heart attack. This affected me greatly. Milia is with me, he should gain weight, I should lose weight. I will stay here for a month or five weeks and then two weeks in Kislovodsk to take mineral water baths. I'm rushing to drink the water, every cup costs a lot of money. Write to Sania and Yasha and ask them to write to me, the children are my only support, they are my life, I have nothing else in my life. I'm in a rush, be well, write to Kislovodsk to post restante if you get my letter soon, otherwise write to home. Milia is now riding a horse, it gives him great pleasure. I also have to send the maid a menu for papa's dinners.

Your mama.

Greetings to madam Strashunskaya.

ES 34

Dear Sabinochka! Essentuki 22.VII.15

I am horrified reading your letter in which you write that your child was a hair's breadth away from death. I am reading and re-reading your letter, I tremble with terror; but I thank God for saving both of you for me. I am so far away from all of you and I am often bathed in tears, if I were completely healthy I would be able to distract myself by doing something but without legs and hands there is not much I can do. I am longing to work, I would like to get strong enough to offer my strength to the unfortunate and the weak and, at the same time, it would help me stop wasting my time on suffering, which is unavoidable now. We won't be able to see each other soon, so there is no other way but to be patient. My thoughts are always with all of you, I do not stop thinking and talking about all of you. This is all that keeps me alive. Do not be sad and do not suffer, God willing, everything will be alright.

You mention that your husband sent you a letter ten pages long. What did he write? Is it a good letter? It seems strange to me that you write to each other often, does this means that you have a good relationship? Does he write about the child only or about you as well? How does he address you, "Sabina" or "Sabina Nikolayevna." Since you write to me that I should see him as a person you would live with, but only as an outsider; you are wrong if you think that I should have nothing to do with him; because I will love anybody who loves you and who values you, but I will not love a person who would harm you. It so happens that a mother with a daughter and son-in-law are staying us and it makes me nervous when I see how well they are getting along. It also makes me so sick when I think about Silva. Why did we work so hard, sacrifice so much bringing up our children, and now we are not allowed to visit the home of the grandchildren. Just think, what bad things have I done to Silva? As soon as she got married I bought her a necklace and paid about 500 rubles (they reproach me that I do not love my daughter-in-law and bought nothing for her, but that they should buy for the son-in-law). When she came to stay with us I bought for her perfume, eau-de-Cologne (all very expensive), a comb, flowers, soap and furnished a room like a bonbonniere, I was attentive and caring toward her; for her birthday I sent her a chest with silverware, for the childbirth – a chest with silverware, a silver set for the child, we sewed her dresses. On her birthday Silva was abroad, I bought silver and telegraphed I always gave gifts to the child on birthdays, and more. At home in Rostov, I sent [gap in text]

On the contrary, I have written to you several times that I was impressed that he was talking about you with great satisfaction, that he took out your letters a few times and showed them to me, but I was only reading about Renatochka and not the parts addressed to you. I wrote to you that at first he referred to you as "Sabina Nikolayevna" but afterwards he called you "Sabina" all the time. So what did I upset you with? I had mentioned to you that there was one time when he almost got quite emotional, but I avoided intimacy and behaved as usual. Maybe this part appeared to you as something horrible, whereas I only wanted to show you that you unfairly reproach me for not knowing how to behave, but I just wanted to show you how carefully I behaved to avoid humiliation. I purposely described all my conversations so that you should be able to judge for yourself. There was really a clash between him and me only on the first day but thereafter everything ran smoothly and politely, so what did I write that upset you? Maybe you got such an impression because you are far away? I recall that I wrote to you that in his apartment he could not stop talking about you and the child, so that others were surprised when they heard rumors that he had divorced you. In many of my letters I informed you about all this but, for the life of me, I would never write to you anything bad.

It is only after his first letter and his meeting with me that I had ventured to say a few things because he told me at that time that the issue had already been decided, and I thought that you would suffer less if you thought poorly of him. So have it your way! You upset me terribly, terribly. All my thoughts are aimed at not uttering a sound that might affect your relationship. I think it is rare to find a mother-in-law like me. I have never done anything bad toward my son-in-law, on the contrary, have always cared for him, cooked his favorite dishes, did not confuse him, did not stir up my daughter against him, have always tried to please him, even with small gifts, to buy this or that, I never [overstated?] him. If it seemed to me that he was hard up, that he was not making any money, I comforted him, I gave him hope. Were it not for his relatives, he would have treated us better and up to the last, I have always forgiven him.

At present I treat him correctly, politely, without any reproaches and not like Ol[ga] Pav[lovna] would do, had she suffered like me. What else should I do? I am carrying out all your instructions. To get his address papa has to send somebody to Sem[ion] Evgenyevich (this is a terrible humiliation) but what can one do about it? I would like to deliver your letters, and we deliver them by registered mail. His sister is not in Rostov so everything quieted down, there are no more arguments. Semion Evgenyevich said to [Panin?] that for a long time they had no letters from your husband. Do not worry about money, we will send you as much as you need to cover your expenses. Take care of your health, eat well, get busy with activities that interest you. The current address of your husband is: Caucasus Active Army, Junior Doctor of the 3rd Special Don Cossack Battalion. Be well and happy. [postscript at the top] Write to me in detail about Renatochka, what she is saying, how she is developing, running, what she is doing. How is Renatochka's nanny? Why does she cry so often?

[postscript] Roza's family (except for mother) is visiting us often. The brother dislocated his foot and the sister is always depressed. Regards to Yasha, Sania, Roza. I will write soon. Where did Silva go with the children?

Didn't you give my letter to Yasha? Just now papa sent me your letter in which you write that I had [sent] his letter to Yasha. I can't recall now who I wrote to first, Yasha or Sania?

ES 35

Dear Sabina! Essentuki 16.VIII.15

Today I finished my treatment and felt very weak therefore I cannot write a lot, let also Yasha and Sania know that I will write when I get a little bit stronger, for now it's difficult even to sit. As a matter of fact, it seems to me that I was not very successful with my treatment, I only took eight mud poultices and 17 sulfur-alkaline baths combined with one third of a bucket of Tambukan brine, and I drank the waters and swallowed one box of [Gayadin's?] pills, that was all. Others take up to 20–25 mud poultices and 15-20 sulfur-alkaline baths.

I fear that I was not cured; it was raining yesterday and today and I am suffering from pains as I did in the winter, when I was in bed. It is a very tormenting pain in all the joints, so how did the treatment help me? I should have taken more mud treatments, but my heart would not allow it. What will be? If I should stay here for another month, I would be able to take from time to time from seven to eight mud poultices, but I am in a hurry, I have already bought a [train] ticket for the 27th, I have ten days left; during this time I will take Narzan mineral baths. The doctor says that he didn't expect I would be able to take even these treatments, and he was satisfied. I am not satisfied at all.

Accidentally I encountered the Kofmans and the unexpectedness almost caused me a heart attack. I even think that since then I've been feeling worse. Take care that you should not develop gout, it is very painful, I didn't know that it could cause such suffering and spoil the mood. I have not received letters from any of you, and in my condition it is just horrible. Ask everyone to write to me more frequently. I received a letter from Sara, Roza's sister, she misses me. I would like to help [Aron?] travel to Petrograd to study, he's a very nice fellow. One has to be a very strong person to be able to survive all the horrors of our everyday life. One scene is more horrible than the other: hundreds of refugees are wandering around in cities, homeless and hungry, exhausted both morally and physically. All of them are victims of the barbaric Germans, victims of the war. My heart is breaking for everyone and everything, at such times it is a shame to think of oneself, and the only thing I desire is to be healthy and to be able to get absorbed in work for the people who became so close and so dear to me. Yes, it is difficult to be objective at times like these, it requires a big effort to stay the course in this resort, only severe physical pains can make a person [endure?] and wish to get well and work. Kisses to you and Renatochka. Write about yourself and her in detail. Goodbye. How is Renatochka's health? What is she saying? Doctors are needed here, and it is easy to get a diploma if you came here.

ES 36

Dear Sabina! 25.VIII.15

As I finished the letter to you I received another letter from you sent to me by papa. As you can see, I was late with my letter, so much the better. "A poor peace is better than a good quarrel", I would like you to continue to behave correctly and not to give any cause for displeasure. I earnestly implore you to write letters to him in such a way that anyone could read them. You know this yourself and you certainly will not offend any of his relatives. In my opinion, it is very good that you sent him the photograph. You should have sent it to him without any words, it would have even be more beautiful not to mention anything else, as if you did not know to whom it was sent. Find the money and send him the full amount. For God's sake, take the high road, leave it to his relatives to be petty-minded, prove to him with deeds and without words that you are not a petty person. I'm rushing to take a bath, it's already late. I go home the day after tomorrow. You write little about Renatochka. Kisses to both of you.

Mama

ES 37

Dear Sabinochka! Rostov on/D 6. IX.15

Now back to what I have promised. Even though I am not in the mood to talk about this subject now other thoughts are occurring to me and I am glad that all the past experiences are behind me, but I still find it necessary to tell you everything regarding your husband. So, shortly before I left Essentuki I had received from your husband a very short little letter of an official nature in response to my letter of one-and-half months ago, referring only to registered letters and photographs which we had sent him. Apparently, he did not receive the photographs, what a pity! And now he will receive a photograph unflattering to the mother and giving the wrong impression of Renatochka. When I returned, Milia informed me that the day before Pavel Naumovich had telephoned at half past ten at night. He wanted to know whether there were any letters from Sabina, about her child's health, and where was mama? How was her health and the father's, and finally, he sent his regards. He was sent for a few days on a business trip to [Kiev?]. I expected that on his way back he would drop in and I would show him the photographs of the child or, as a last resort, promise him to take photos again and send him. A few days later the phone rang in the morning and the maid woke me up saying that the son-in-law was calling. "I am listening," I said. "Is this Eva Markovna?" "Yes, yes, it is me. Good morning!" "Doctor Sheftel is speaking." At once I understood that he had been [brainwashed?] and I continued in the same vein, I didn't want to be humiliated so I was correct and answered all his questions in a most polite and reserved manner. He asked if it had been long since we had received letters from Sabina Nikolayevna? If you and the child are well? He said that he had received one registered letter and then, suddenly, "goodbye". I do not know if he has left or is still staying in Rostov for a little longer, I am no longer interested in it. This call instantly affected me so much that I turned into an automaton and was unable to do anything the whole day. I was haunted by one question: "For what?" "Why?" God, you see all we have done for this man?! Later I took control of myself and immersed myself in work, my salvation. It is only when I am writing to you or thinking about you that I am unendingly sad. If you were here together with me, you would be suffering less, you would have understood a great deal and begin to see things differently.

The following is interesting. When I was in Essentuki, Patt came to me from Kislovodsk for a few hours. For his sake I left my room to drink some tea before supper and invited one more lady, very pretty and young (a wife of an engineer). I was very tired, I did not want to talk much, and I invited her on purpose so that he would not be bored, because he had wanted to come and see me many times, but I refused him every time. Guterman's sister also approached us, we were laughing, chatting and an hour later we went home. We didn't notice that the Kofmans were sitting across from us. The next day they were in Kislovodsk and Ania attacked Patt. "You ought to be ashamed not to have reciprocated our greetings, it is Eva Markovna who did not allow you to return our greetings." He pleaded with her that we did not see her and that Eva Markovna was incapable of behaving in such a way. "In general" she said, "why is Eva Markovna ignoring us and not returning our greetings? What have we done to her? She came here and did not let us know? She does not greet us. What do we have to do with what happened between Pavlusha and Sabina, why spoil our relationship? I wanted to approach the table and ask: what have we done to you, Eva Markovna? She used to say that she loved Pavlusha, and whatever happened between him and Sabina, even if it ended in divorce, the relationship with him would not be damaged. She even loved Semion Evgenyevich. So where is the love?" I said that I liked Semion Evgenyevich very much for his love of his wife and her relatives, that this was a rarity. I said that the relations between a son-in-law and his new family may remain good even after he divorces his wife because their characters were not compatible, etc. But is it so in this case? Even if there were a divorce, then why so inhumanely, with so much filth? When he quarreled with you, did we turn away from our son-in-law? But he instantly humiliated us by turning away from us, so why are we to blame? I wished very much that she should hurt me so that I would have the opportunity to express everything to her and to show her how much evil she had done to me; but I just kept silent. But what was there to say? She hurt me a lot, the wound is too tender to touch. She thinks that my daughter, my child, are less dear to me then she is to her own mother. I feel that I will have lots of fun, that there will be an opportunity; although a few days later I did not attend a meeting so as not to come face to face with the Kofmans. Enough about them. I received a letter from you for your husband the day he spoke to me and I forwarded it to him, and later a postcard from you and a nonregistered letter. This week I am sending you the third registered letter, in one of them there was a letter for Yasha. Tomorrow I am writing to Saniechka, I cannot write to everybody at once. Write a lot, a lot about dear Renatochka. What does she prattle? All her phrases. Who are you living with? How is your life. Kisses to you and Renatochka.

Mama

ES 38

Dear Sabina! 8.IX.15

I have a few free minutes and I would like to speak with you. This week I sent you three registered letters. I am now writing to you in order to calm you. Do not get upset about anything, take it philosophically – everything will pass. Especially your husband, he will change one thousand times. Once upon a time he sent you a rude letter and now you are reporting that he wrote you a nice letter. For example, he recently spoke to me on the telephone in such a tone that later I felt confident that he will be speaking differently, that it will depend on his mood and external influences. So, please, do not pay any attention to this, do not make yourself sick for nothing. It may be that happiness is around the corner but meantime you are making yourself sick. Get busy with something, apply your energy to some endeavor and you will forget your troubles. Regarding your medical diploma, we will soon give you an answer. It is now very easy to get a medical diploma and you do not even have to pass any examination.

I am in a hurry to write, but I am being interrupted [illegible name]. I had a visit from Noi and Aron Pochtarev, I went to see [houses?] with papa, now Noi is coming again, but I cannot walk anymore, I got very tired. Work makes me tired a lot but I am morally satisfied. Take care of yourself, stay calm, do not worry in vain. Take care of your hair, maybe you should shave your hair and get treated by a doctor, it would be pity if you lost your hair. Milia wants to write and I am giving up my space. Write a lot and often about the dear child.

Mama

[postscript from Emil] I wrote you a letter and then I tore it up myself. I will write to you next time and meanwhile I wish you all the best. Greetings to Irma-Renata. Greetings to Yashka and Sania "through the samovar".

[Your?] Milia. 8/21–IX–15

ES 39

Dear Sabina! Rostov on/D 9.X.15

Greetings to you on your forthcoming birthday, I hope my letter will reach you in time. May this day bring you new happiness, many joys in all your future life. Do not be so skeptical, I am now partially a fatalist, I believe that what has to happen will happen, and therefore, these or other sorrows in your life must have been determined by many other world events. This is my whole philosophy and right now I would not like to get into any more details, I only wanted to tell you that what will happen now is what has to happen and I am confident that life will be all good, because all the bad things are already gone. "All is well that ends well" and right now your good life will begin. God willing, everything will calm down, we will see each other, and we will organize your life anew. Gaze cheerfully into the future, show that you are an energetic woman, that [illegible] you here, you would be a great benefit to your brothers. I am working hard. I was at the station and registered many people by specialty and placed them according to their qualifications. I was responsible for setting up one family, a young woman (a masseuse) and a young man (a tie maker); later I will go to the station again and pick another group to be placed. My business is growing, many items are ready and in a few days I will be visited by a former manager [Pereselenkov?] to examine and buy lingerie for a store. Someone will come from another store to look at dresses. Ladies come to visit me and are in raptures over my house; they are amazed at my skill and my taste, I am only telling you this to bring you pleasure since you wrote that you take pleasure in your parents achieving something. I am sometimes so busy that it is difficult to find time for writing but I still manage to write a fair amount. I miss you all terribly, therefore I am glad that I immersed myself in being active but the nights are killing me – I cannot sleep and I keep thinking. There have been no letters from you and no letters from anybody else for a long time and I am suffering.

I will try to write to Yasha tomorrow. Poor boy! He was also suddenly abandoned. I don't understand what happened that Silva left him in such times, now they too are unable to see each other. Mrs. Sabsovich telephoned me that Silva was expected to arrive in Rostov and this news was like a thunder from a clear sky,

I was embarrassed that I did not know anything about it, this came up in another conversation; Silva may already be in Rostov now. Yes, anything can happen in life. Yes, who would believe that I, so generous toward people, who are either strangers or close to me and to my relatives, should have been a target of so many insults from people closest to me. How much attention have I devoted to this Silva when she lived in my home, and later, when she started getting attached to me, all of a sudden she was so indoctrinated by Olga Pavlovna against me, and I still don't know how, since I didn't try to find out from Yasha; he just told me that Olga Pavlovna turned Silva against me. So be it. I am trying to put out of my mind all that are causing me pain.

[postscript] How is your health? And how is dear Renatochka? Write more about her, I ask you for this in every letter.

ES 40

Dear Sabina! 23.X.15

There are still no letters from you, I am afraid that my intuition does not deceive me. After you wrote that you are feeling better with your ear there were no other letters from you. I wait impatiently for your letters every day and nothing is coming. I can feel that there is some misfortune somewhere.

Are Yasha and Sania alright? Ah, ho, ho, how hard it is! What can I do? I can only get hold of myself so that it won't get any worse. I'm going to be patient and keep on waiting, anyhow there is no other way. [Panin?] Isaak just came in, he was terribly depressed, almost brokenhearted. All the relatives always turn to me when they are not well, when they are in need of advice or assistance, and this is the case now. I have a new worry: [Masia?] is also not well. God knows what else can happen. Once again, patience is needed. Again I have a lot to do everywhere and I am so busy that, in spite of my desire, I may not be able to work anymore. I had a visit from Professor Gutnikov about my gout which is quite severe and makes itself felt very strongly. He again prescribed a course of treatment. I am drinking the water, [illegible], taking [selenium?] baths, he ordered mud poultices for my hands and legs. I was also feeling nervous and requested a visit from a professor for nervous diseases. I ceased sleeping at nights and I did not sleep a wink for five nights in a row. I slept a little last two nights. I hope I will get better and again I am waiting anxiously. It is a blessing that we have so many professors. Recently a professor for nervous diseases delivered a popular lecture on hysteria at the science college. I spoke to him about you. I have to stop, they are calling me. I have to tell you a lot of necessary things. I will resume tomorrow. Be well with your little one. Write more about her.

Everything, everything she saying, doing, it makes me happy to read about it. May God bless both of you and protect you for me.

Mama

[postscript] My greetings to [the children?]. I am trying to write often. Concerning providing for your livelihood do not worry – you have more than enough. You now have a sum of 30,000 rubles but you will have much more. Thank God, in this respect you are good. And so is Renatochka. I will make for you a long coat with a boa made of skunk fur. For your birthday I spent 900 rubles for fur (astrakhan) and [illegible] and bought for you very good [illegible].

ES 41

Dear Sabinochka! Rostov on/D 8.XI.15

I have already written to you a few times this week and each time I could not mail the letter. Pity, great pity! I am glad your ear is better, that you are not suffering, anyway be very careful not to catch an ear cold again. I was very worried about you because I know what a hellish pain an ear ache can cause. I am also glad the child is out of danger, thank God. But it is a pity that poor Renatochka is eating poorly. But do take care not to overdo it. She inherited her constipations from you; I also had a lot of trouble with you and still cannot forget the hard time I had with you.[102] However, one thing I find strange, the doctor determined that her constipations are caused by the food she eats; but I always fed you with my breast and afterwards with milk only, and puree and you also suffered from constipations, so what was the cause of that? It is strange! One has to find out, so as not to starve the child unnecessarily. If you are giving her less milk, it is necessary to replace her diet with something else. Take good advice from the doctor and also use your own judgment. Could you give her juice of cooked black plums to drink, this is good to make the stomach strong. Have you noticed that she has had a sick stomach for quite some time? I would like to see Renatochka very much, it would revive me if I could see her running around the room. I would like to listen to her prattle. Lucky child, what does she know now, what is happening now?

As for you, Sabinochka, instead of an astrakhan fur I bought you the very best sealskin for your fur coat. Sealskin is much more expensive than astrakhan fur. Silva's fur coat cost 1,000 rubles but your sealskin is of the highest quality and there is nothing better. For two years I wanted to make such a fur coat for me at a cost of 1,000 rubles. I bought only the skins (80 pieces) and there will

102 See the issues with constipation during Sabina's treatment by Jung at the Burghölzli.

also be enough for a muff and a hat. Each skin is thin, smooth, and even, and with a sheen. It is an amazingly beautiful thing. The ladies were very impressed. In addition, for your boa I bought a few pieces of skunk fur, also very good. You cannot imagine how glad I am that I acquired such a thing for you, you will be wearing it for many years. If you were here I would have it sewed it for you by [a Chinaman?], he has been sewing for many years. I am also saving velvet for your dress, it would be easy to make one for you. You are also well provided with lingerie. In my "factory" they make beautiful lingerie, which is appreciated not only by the ladies but also by lingerie stores. The lingerie is like the one in Vienna. If you were here, you would be dressed from head to foot, but we will do this later, when the hard times are over and we see each other again. For you and Roza we made 12 suits each. Whatever papa sees he always says "save this for Sabina." No matter whether it suits Sabina or not, but I am happy when he says this. If you were with us, money would be spent without you noticing it and nothing would be denied you, but it is much more difficult to send it to you, because papa, being a man, does not understand many things. I have just received two orders for 12 pieces each of lingerie for two girls six years old. I feel sad, when I think about it, I would like to sew things for Renatochka and Yasha's children, but I do not have them with me. What to do? We should be patient.

I forgot to answer one of your letters in which you wrote that you did not buy back the things that were pawned by your husband, because you did not receive an answer to your inquiry. I am sorry it happened that way. I wrote to you twice in detail that you should buy the things back; and from the very beginning I also told your husband about it at that time. Later I asked you the same question a number of times in my letters to you, and I was surprised that you were ignoring my questions in this regard. In conversations with papa, I always represented it as one of the losses and that you should buy the things back, and suddenly, oh horror! This is personally unpleasant for me. You should have been correct to the very end so that he would have no cause to reproach you. I am afraid this might create a new unpleasantness between the two of you. Does he know that the things were not bought back? Anyway, it doesn't matter now, it's not worth talking about it anymore.

I am working a lot every day, I host a number of ladies and a number of seamstresses, and we make visits to stores; it is an unending hustle and bustle. I now feel completely exhausted and am calling for help. In the meantime I ask for the books to be brought to me, I work on the books in the evenings and papa gets angry. I will soon give you some news. Regards to Yashen'ka and to

Roza with Sania. Today I received a letter from them. I will write to all of them. Be well and happy.

Mama

ES 42

Dear Sabinochka! 15.XII.1015

I received your letter in which you write about your surgery which struck me like thunder. Now I know the reason why such an unbearable anguish was constantly oppressing my heart and I kept telling papa that it oppressed me like a foreboding. Papa always answered me: "When does it not oppress you?" "I was oppressed all the time, either the child was ill, or Sabina was suffering with the ear, then with teeth and now a new story about her surgery." I cannot calm down, I am completely destroyed by fatigue, I work till I collapse, and I toil and work in order to drown all my sufferings.

I am anxious, it seems to me that the wound on your hand has opened. I am waiting impatiently for news about your health. Oh God, when will this hard time for all of us be over? When will you stop worrying about nannies? What a pity! How unlucky you are! It is a pity that the child has to pass from nanny to nanny; as a result she will cling to you even more, and when she grows up it will be difficult for you. How was the child's birthday? Who visited you? You were probably still sick. Write to me about everything in detail. Give thanks in my name to all your acquaintances who visited you during your illness. I am touched by this. Regards to all the children and also to madam Strashunskaya, madam Fain[illegible], and Mr. Grinfeld. Good bye, my dear! Take care of your health, don't think about anything bad.

Kisses to you and Renatochka.

Mama

[postscript from Sarra Pochtareva] Happy birthday to your little black-eyed girl. Best wishes to You, Rakhil and Sania.

Sarra Pochtareva [Isaak's mother-in-law]

[postscript from Emil] Yesterday was the birthday of your "Ziuk" [Renata] my congratulations and best wishes… The second quarter is almost over—four more days of study, and then it's finished. Are you thinking of coming to Russia?

Milia

[postscript from father] Mama asked me to write a very hot telegram for your birthday. Therefore I cabled "Felicité cent degrés" [congratulations hundred degrees]. I think that a hundred-degree letter which is a really warm enough, cannot be any warmer. The letter was delayed here till 18/12, mama wanted to write something else, I find it uncomfortable to wait any longer. Tonight you are already celebrating [a few illegible words] the New Year. Therefore Prosit Neujahr [happy new year]!

We rarely get letters from Yasha and the same is true for Sania; there were no letters from both of them for a long time. In your letter of the 7/12.15 there was no [illegible] excerpts from [family? illegible] nor Yasha's works. Apparently, they forgot to return some sheets to the envelope after the censor checked the letters; and now, even though they found them, they do not know where to send them and probably destroyed them. Next time write the return address on every sheet of paper. Perhaps they will take notice of that here, as it is done in other civilized countries.

[signature]

ES 43

Dear Sabinochka! Rostov on/D 23.XII.15

Every time we get your letter you suffer endlessly. I keep forgetting that sometimes a letter is underway for two months, like last time, and then I am overcome by impressions created by the received letters. Again, in a letter that was underway for a month you write that probably the bandage will be taken off tomorrow, that you are staying in bed a lot, the nanny is bad, and the child is pale, etc. By the way, you write that you sent two cables but we did not receive any. You did not receive our letters for a long time but we write quite often. Regarding surgery I have written already many times and I will repeat again: in my opinion, your surgery was completely unnecessary. [added in father's handwriting] On the other hand, only psychiatry is now a vast field of knowledge and very much needed in Russia. It is highly useful and very much in vogue right now.

As regards the nanny, this is a very important matter. Once again, I regret that you fired the first nanny, she loved the child and held it in her hands. It is a pity but nothing can be done, I cannot help [you with that]. I know from way back that in Switzerland it is very problematical with servants. Ask your acquaintances to recommend you a good nanny because it is very difficult without one. You cannot leave a child even with a good servant, how much more so if she is unreliable. It is a big nuisance because you are completely tied up and moreover it affects the child. How is the child? Did you take her to a doctor? What did he find? Does she take enough walks outdoors? What does she eat? How is her stomach? I wrote about this so many times but received no answer to my questions. It is difficult to write when you don't know whether your letters reach their destination. All the letters to your husband are being promptly forwarded to him, hopefully you are getting his responses. What can be done, my child, that you are sad. I would like to make it easier for you but I cannot do anything from such a distance. I am myself sad and unhappy, I miss my children and my whole soul and [text break] all but none of my [text break] will help me. I am trying to lose myself in work, even in work beyond my strength, just to stop thinking. Let us be patient and hope that [we all?] will meet in good health [a lost line?], goodbye and may everything be alright. I am waiting impatiently for a letter in which you tell me that you and the child are completely healthy. What a joyful day that would be for me! Greetings to all my dear children, I am in a rush to end my letter. A woman bather came to give me a bath. There is no time to write, the holidays are coming and I am very busy buying provisions. It is now half past 8 in the evening. Milia and his friends are in the [biograph? = movie house]. He received fourteen 5's and one 4 for art. Now he got his eye treatment and is unable to write [something is missing]. Kisses to you and my dear grand-daughter. Be well. Papa is reading.

Mama

[postscript from father] read by the censor.

ES 44

Dear Sabina! Date on stamp: December 28, 1915

Another letter from you and all its content is sad again. I have known already almost for a month that you are having problems with the nanny and it must be terribly tiring. Maybe a nanny can be referred to you by one of your acquaintances. It would be best for you, I have already written about it because it is a very bad situation – constant troubles with servants and especially with nannies. You should really take a rest after the surgery and get better but there is all this trouble, what a pity. I am waiting impatiently for pleasant news about your and the child's health. From my experience I know now that the child should not be forced to eat if she has no appetite, for if she is force-fed the stomach will not digest. Thirty years ago even papa always maintained that. It is better when the appetite comes by itself. The appetite will come when you take the child for frequent walks outdoors and when she is active a lot. Anyway, it is difficult to judge from afar, it is much clearer where you are [added by father I think so]. I would like to know what the professor will say after he examines the child. Regarding the university, I will try to find out everything today and give you an answer.

Tonight I am leaving for Ekaterinoslav for the anniversary of grandfather's death. There I will take care of the tombstone [added by father?] A long time ago, without being prompted by anybody, papa took care of that seeing that grandpa's sons do not have the time to think about such paltry matters. It is very probable that uncle Noi and Masia will accompany me, I have already asked them about it [added by father?].

Yesterday we had a visit by our relatives that lasted until two o'clock in the morning and Milia came home around four o'clock am. He had spent the evening with the Mintses. He is now getting atropine drops in his eyes and is therefore unable to read or write, he is bored with doing nothing as he is accustomed to work a lot, therefore he gets out of the house. Everything is alright with us. Where is Silva with the children? What is with Yasha? We are getting no letters from him. Is it true that Roza and Sania are in good health? I write to you two or three times a week. Kisses to you and dear Renatochka.

Mama

Dear Sabina! Cordial greetings to you and your dear little daughter.

Masses of kisses! [Masia?]

ES 45

Dear Sabinochka! 8.II.16

My head is positively empty, it is difficult to express my thoughts, as if they are blocked, and all this is due to all kinds of suffering. And I don't even know what is oppressing me first: that all the children are separated, only you are exhausted and ill, or that the child often sick. Yasha is lonely, too, he must be suffering a great deal, on the other hand Sania, though happy, must be enduring many privations. His child requires a lot of expenses and one is not permitted to send him the money. Now I worry because of Silva, the last thing was a real blow to me, to learn that the children have been in Rostov for about two months and I did not get to see them. Finally, I wrote to you that thanks to pleadings by Altshuler, Milia and Yashas's cable, I was one day able to see the little one and the next day Irochka. The first day my joy was poisoned by Olga Pavlovna. The nanny said that when Milia comes back from school at 2 o'clock he should call her. He came, telephoned, and came upon Olga Pavlovna. And now consider the height of [her] impudence: "Milia, watch that [Marianochka] does not fall out of bed, the nanny should not leave her alone, etc.". She said it despite me being there, the grandmother who had been awaiting to see the children with excitement and trepidation, who had not left the children unattended not even for one second, who did not want to lose one minute of happiness. Is this not a scandal? Who am I for this child? Aren't I the same grandmother as she? And even if the child belonged to somebody else, would I not devote to it all my attention had she been entrusted to me? I would overlook it had Silva said that to me, but she...She should have had the tact not to do this but she is a loudmouth! But I was satisfied the day after when Irunchik arrived. She did not leave my side all day long. Papa read to her, held her in his arms, danced with her, talked with her, and was all tenderness...and I... What is there to say? I was afraid to let her out of my sight even for a minute, was afraid they would not send her to us again. I was particularly gratified that she did not want to leave us at all. No matter how we insisted that she has to listen to mama, that she could be with us the next day if mama would allow this, she asked to telephone her mother but instead Mira answered the phone. [Marianochka] spoke to her, looked sad, but did not want to tell us what Mira had said to her, even though we asked. After two days of big nervousness there was a reaction: I got sick. To this day I have not heard anything about the children. Milchik just telephoned there and Silva said that Irochka had a cold, and I did not see her again. I am convinced that <u>Silva will write to Yasha that the children were sick and that is why she was not sending them</u> [perhaps text break]

ES 46

Dear Sabinochka! 24.II.16

It is long time ago since you wrote to us about the repertoire of Renatochka's vocabulary and this could have given us so much pleasure. We were delighted by her poems and papa told everybody about it with pleasure. Are you and the child well? Why did [illegible name] suddenly show up in Lausanne? Where is she living now? She probably told you many interesting things? How are all father's relatives doing? For three full months I had no letter from Yasha. I do not know what to think about this, I suffer endlessly, and worst of all, I cannot think of anything to escape this evil. I feel that something happened to Yasha, that you are hiding something, and, according to Milia and others, the only one who is calm is Silva.

27.II.16

Three days have passed and I was unable to write anything but post-scripts, prevented by my illness and other matters. During this time Silva received a telegram from Yasha in which he asked for the children to be sent to us but she expressed her displeasure to Milia because we had cabled Yasha to have him cable her and force her to send the children. Moreover, the cable contains her new address. It means that we [gave?]]. But she said: "The children were sick all the time, how could I send them?" Now she is using the children's illness as an excuse, which is such a lie. She herself admitted that the children attended a party at the [Chernikov's?] home and that they took a walk on the Sadovaia street. Needless to say, we have known for a long time that the children had arrived, as we heard accidentally from strangers. I wish they would respect her husband's parents, understand their nobility, that until now they did not complain to their son about all the offenses they had endured. It also hurts me that I do not write to him, do not complain because I feel for him; but I am still being blamed. They got to be kidding! One day the truth will be known. This minute Irochka telephoned and told she will come in two and a half hours for dinner with the Fräulein. How lovely she talks! In general, what an amazingly wonderful girl she is. She is a beauty, healthy, brimming with health, unusually wise, lively, a delight. I am rushing to order dinner for her and Fräulein. Write more about Renatochka. How I would like to see her grown up already. Kiss her for grandma. Goodbye.

Mama.

ES 47

Dear Sabina! Date on stamp: 20 March 1916

I do not know what will come out of my pen, as am completely in no mood for logical and consequential reasoning. I only know I have a lot to tell you and we will see what I am able to tell you. Today I received from you three letters all at once and was overjoyed. Had you written long letters, the pleasure would even be greater; as it is, I read them quickly and then it felt empty again. I have not written to you for a few days, because I was ill and got out of bed today. In spite of Yasha's wishes to send us the children twice a week the children did not come for ten days and finally they sent Irochka. I was very glad that prior to Yasha's request to give the children toys I had already done that. I gave the little one as present a very interesting small object (something like a sphere, all around like a swing, all in flowers, and below a music box), it cost a lot of money, I don't recall exactly but I think about 15 rubles. To Irochka I gave a gift worth 21 rubles but I got a discount. For her birthday I gave her a gold chain and a gold locket with a little ruby and diamond, with an engraved inscription "To Irochka from grandpa and grandma Shpilrein," and inside photographs of mother and father, 28.50 for the engraving. I have now sent Silva 100 rubles and said this was from Yasha. I am convinced that Olga Pavlovna will say to Silva that we did all this because we wanted to smooth out "our guilt" toward them. Every time I am surprised that there are such people in this world. When I remember that I did nothing bad to them—only good—my hair stands on end. What have I done to this fool Mira? What does she want? She behaves as if we had done something most horrible to her, nevertheless you, God, you see! I still don't feel an iota of guilt toward myself. These people are strange! How can they act friendly and then unfriendly so easily? It was awfully unpleasant for me to meet with Silva [and Mira?] in the store, [illegible] or in some other place, but they don't care. They can fling mud at you and they don't care two straws. Poor, poor Yasha! How my heart aches for him. Who are the people around him? He has no friends. The old lady and Mira do not like him because he is only a "melamed" [Yiddish, religion teacher] and makes no money. They teach Irochka, a child, to criticize grandpa and grandma, I will tell you about this in the next letter. But in fact, we never touch on such ticklish topics in the presence of Irochka and do not mention either Olga Pavlovna or Mira, the mother we only mention occasionally and always positively, "you have to obey mama" and "all that mama says is good" etc. Oh, Sabina dear, you already have your own child so you can understand how much we have suffered. If a daughter-in-law treats us, her husband's parents, in this way, who give so whole-heartedly including material support, then how can she be with someone like [illegible, somebody's initials?]. We have no letters from Yasha, there was a postcard and a letter from Sania. Are the children getting my letters? I did not receive a letter from Renatochka. We started sewing her underwear for age three to five, you will get the wardrobe when we meet. For Menikhochka we are sewing for age one to two. I am pleased with my task. Your sympathy for our relationship with Silva is a support for me and your promise to arrange for all my granddaughters and children to gather at our place brings tears of joy to my eyes. God grant that I may live to see it, my child! All these worries have severely damaged my health. I'll write soon. To Leibovich warm greetings, I like her very much. She is good.

ES 48

Dear Sabinochka! 7.IV–16

I tried to write to you a few times and each time somebody or something interfered with my being able to finish the letter. Thus, even now, I was able to scribble but a few words because uncle Pinia telephoned to say he was coming. I would like to talk with you about a lot of things but I leave this to a more convenient opportunity and I am now writing in order to give you some news about myself. I sent pastry to all of you but I fear that what all you will get is a mess because it is very friable and an inspection will cause it to crumble. This year I bought everything ready made for three reasons: 1) I did not have a good baking form, 2) I had no Jewish cook, 3) I was very weak. The pastry was not to my taste but there is nothing I could do about it. Should our parcels reach you undamaged, we would be able to send you something else but not pastry [father's remark: "the logic?"] I wanted to see you all, this would have improved my health, I wanted to see and hear little Renatochka but unfortunately we have to wait [father's remark: "What about Menikha?"] In some way you hinted that Renata had written to me and Milchik but we did not receive those letters. For a long time there were no letters from you to your husband. It is alright that you are not writing to your husband, but if you wrote to him then you should know that we have not received his letters. For the first [Passover] seder we went to Noi. For the second seder we promised to go to the Mintses but I declined because I was very tired, for the third evening we invited Patt and Shporlinskii also turned up. I read a lot, this is the only thing that pleases me. Write a lot about yourself and Renatochka. Tell me what she is prattling, this is a joy to me.

Mama

[postscript from father] Mama wants to add that "today" she will write to Sania but when "today" will happen is difficult to predict. [signature]

ES 49

My dear Sabinochka! 19th April, 1916

I have just received your letter in which you report that you passed your examination in surgery. I must tell you how happy we all were about it. I am only worried about one thing: that you are working too hard and that you do not sleep nights. If they won't accept Milia at the university and he will not take the examination, I will leave here in two weeks, but even if he passes the examination, for which there is little hope because there are no places, I will leave in three weeks and a few days. When you receive my letter, it will be only a short time before I leave and I have not yet decided where we shall spend the month of July with you. On the one hand, I would love for you to get better, and besides I would like to begin doing something in the direction well known to you. To have you travel back to Russia would need a great deal of time and papa is afraid in that if you do, you will leave the university. I talk a lot about this with him and we have many disagreements about it, but it is important that you should reach your goal and therefore you should not come back at this time. I will rest for a few more days and start packing drapery, curtains, etc. I am also facing many serious problems concerning grandfather. His wife is leaving for America, nobody wants to take him, and they burden me with all their worries. I feel tormented by all this as it is very difficult to leave him in the care of strangers. Papa is also unable to travel this year, he cannot leave the business and this is also hard on me. At least it is good that his friend and daughter will be living with us. I would like to be done with my treatment so as to be able to spend freely the month of July with you. Due to some circumstances I will be traveling via Vienna and not via Warsaw. I would like to be able to seek some advice concerning myself but I don't know who to turn to. Later that evening we were left with many flowers brought to us, we have a whole garden in the house. Masia sent me a whole basket of flowers, this was my birthday. Papa gave me a bracelet worth 400 rubles, but I want to give it back and get the money, and I told papa that I don't like keeping jewelry for a rainy day. For now, after all the losses we suffered, I don't want to accept such luxuries, this money will come in handy for me and for Sabina abroad. This was what we are discussing here, and so tomorrow I will return the bracelet. Panin gave me a silver cup and a saucer which also made me worry because it seemed to me that he only bought it because papa had pestered him. There was a lot of talk in town about our evening. We kiss you.

Your mother.

I will write to you soon, I was very [tired?]. [Receive] a lot of greetings at once? [the rest completely illegible]

ES 50

Dear Sabinochka Rostov on/Don VII.6.16

Today we received the photographs of Renatochka. She is positively a beauty and the expression of her face has something unusual. Where did she get such a serious look? She has chiseled good looks. What impressed me most is that, judging by the photograph, Renatochka is five years old, at least no less than four. She is very big and looks like a much older child. I was just leaving home to go to see Doctor Ryndziun[103] and took the photograph with me, showed it to the doctor and Matilda. They were both delighted, "Such a creation is an honor to Sabina." They were very pleased. I will show the photograph to all the relatives and acquaintances. A few days ago we had a visit from Maya Tamarkina and Nadia Bershadskaya. We spoke a lot about you and they wanted to see the portrait of your child. They will be happy for you.

You keep saying that there is a lot to write about, but all we are getting is postcards or nothing at all. I am impatiently waiting for the promised letter. It took a lot of work to arrange for Milia and Aron to travel for two weeks to the Volga river and of course we financed the trip. Milia looks so unhealthy that

103 The reference is to Ilia Galileevich Ryndziun and his wife Matilda Borisovna Raivich.

papa even insisted that he should suspend studying for two weeks, he lost a lot of weight and his eyes are sunken and he is twice as tall as we are. He is tall and stunningly thin. I am happy that he went on this trip; and now I will take care of myself and treat my gout. It seems I will go nowhere even though the heat in town is beastly. Today I received from all of you a telegram for Milia. We are very busy with Milia; we now have all the documents except the one regarding Latin. We will see if they will accept him but chances are slim. Finally I was notified that you received my parcel, I am very happy. A little bit later I will send something more. Pity that they do not allow sending any caviar. Ask Yasha and Sania to write to us more frequently. I am desperate when I get no letters. Write: how are you managing? See a doctor and ask about the state of your health. Why are you coughing? Is there no cure? Do you have enough money for everything? Write what you need. Do you have enough clothes? How is Renatochka? Do you have help? Is she trained to be clean? Tell her that Grandma misses her very much. Kissing you and wishing you all the best

Mama

ES 51

Dear Sabinochka! Rostov on/Don 9.VII.16

I am now looking at your photograph which I received today. I am sad, sad to look at you to the point of crying. Even though you look very, very attractive on the photograph, you are incredibly emaciated, and the face expresses a lot of sadness. You look like an 18 year old girl. It seems that you have cut your hair, true? It suits you. I keep looking at the photograph all the time and can't stop looking, it brings me pain and joy and I am missing you more. For God's sake, tell me, did you really lose so much weight? Are you eating well? I implore you, do not get upset and do not think that you and Renatochka are abandoned; as long as we live you will have everything, and Renatochka will be raised as if she were our own daughter, and there will be enough for her. And when we are gone, apart from your own money, there will be enough left for you. All this means money, but as for having good acquaintances and interesting intimate friends, this does not come instantly; there are opportunities for everything but nobody knows what tomorrow will bring.

There is now a global weltschmerz which has a sickening effect on everybody, but one has to get inured to it or else one cannot live. Take care of yourself, my dear, for the sake of the child, for us, and for people to whom you are very dear, and most importantly, yourself. When I received Renatochka's portrait I immediately wrote to you and expressed my delight and when I showed it to

Spielrein family 1896: Sabina, Emilia and Yan in front, Eva with Isaac middle row left, Nikolai and probably Mosya at back, others unknown.

Maternal grandfather Rabbi Mordekhai Lublinskii.

The Spielrein Mansion, 83 Pushkinskaya Street - Rostov-on-Don, where Sabina Spielrein spent her childhood and adolescence. In November 2015, the Sabina Spielrein Memorial Museum was opened in the mansion.

Sabina Spielrein (left) with her mother (center) and younger sister Emilia (right) who died in 1901, after they returned from a travel in Austria and Germany.

Eva, Sabina, Nikolai, Emil, Isaac, and Yan in 1908, when Sabina was vacationing in Rostov.

The International Psychoanalytic Congress, the Hague, Netherlands, 1920. Sabina is front row sitting, fourth from left.

Sabina Spielrein and other members of the Institut Rousseau: Godin, Claparède, Piaget, 1921. Archives Institut Jean-Jacques Rousseau (AIJJR). Sabina is second in the front row left.

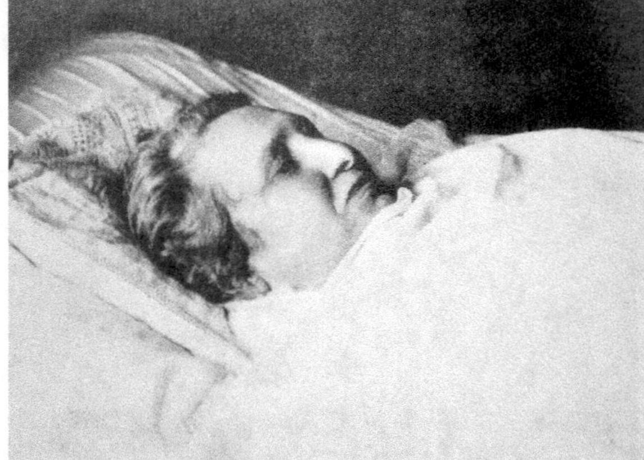

Eva Spielrein (mother) on her death bed, 1922.

Isaac Spielrein, brother of Sabina.

Nikolai and Evald, 1928.

Nikolai with a Jewish wander group.

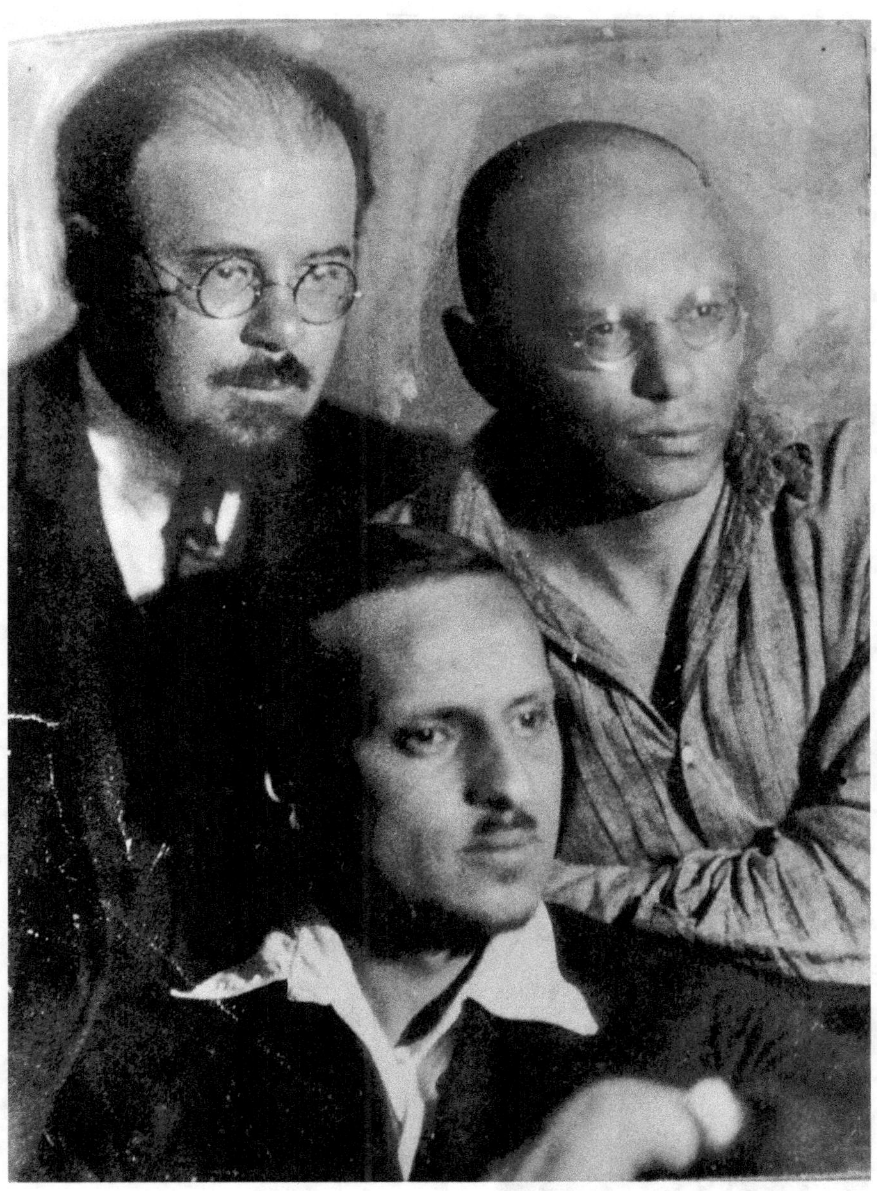

Yan, Emil and Isaac,
around 1930.

Eva Sheftel.

Sabina Spielrein's identity document, 1930s.

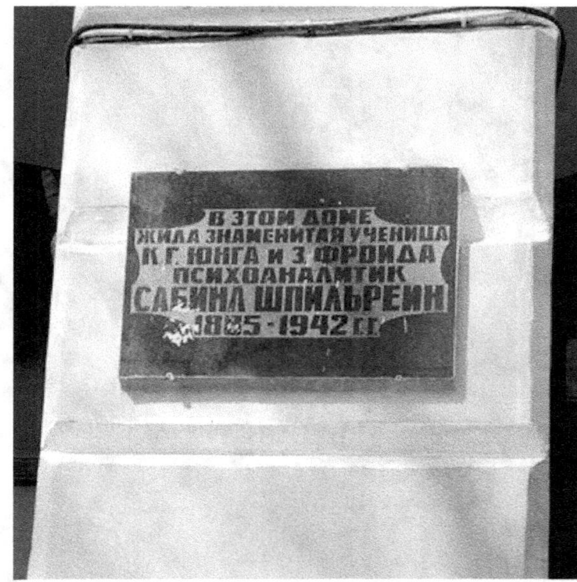

In 2002 a commemorative plaque made by the Rostov-on-Don sculptor B. N. Kondakov was installed on the building's façade. It reads:

The famous student of K. G. Jung and S. Freud, psychoanalyst Sabina Spielrein (1885-1942), lived in this house.

Memorial plaque, Sabina Spielrein, Thomasiusstraße 2, Berlin-Moabit, Germany.

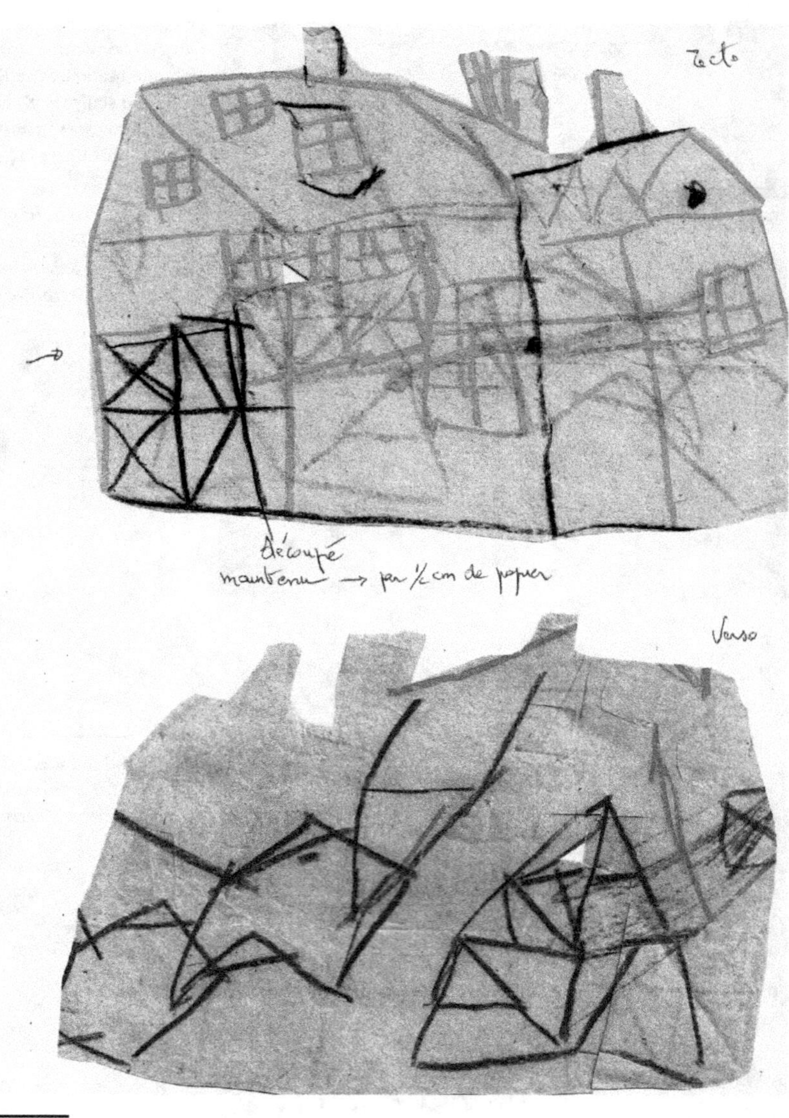

Decoupage recto-verso
inserted between some pages
of Sabina's notebook (1896?).

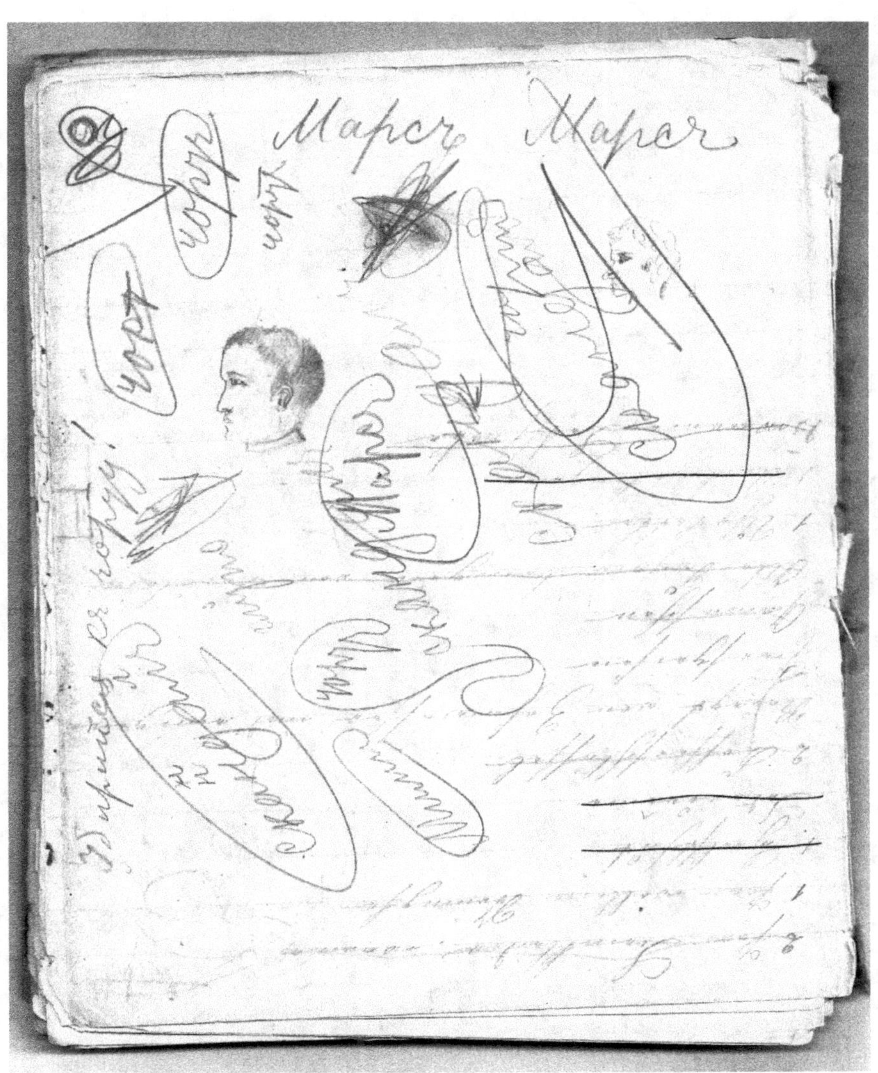

Contains the words:

May the devil take you, devil three time, Mars twice, scandal

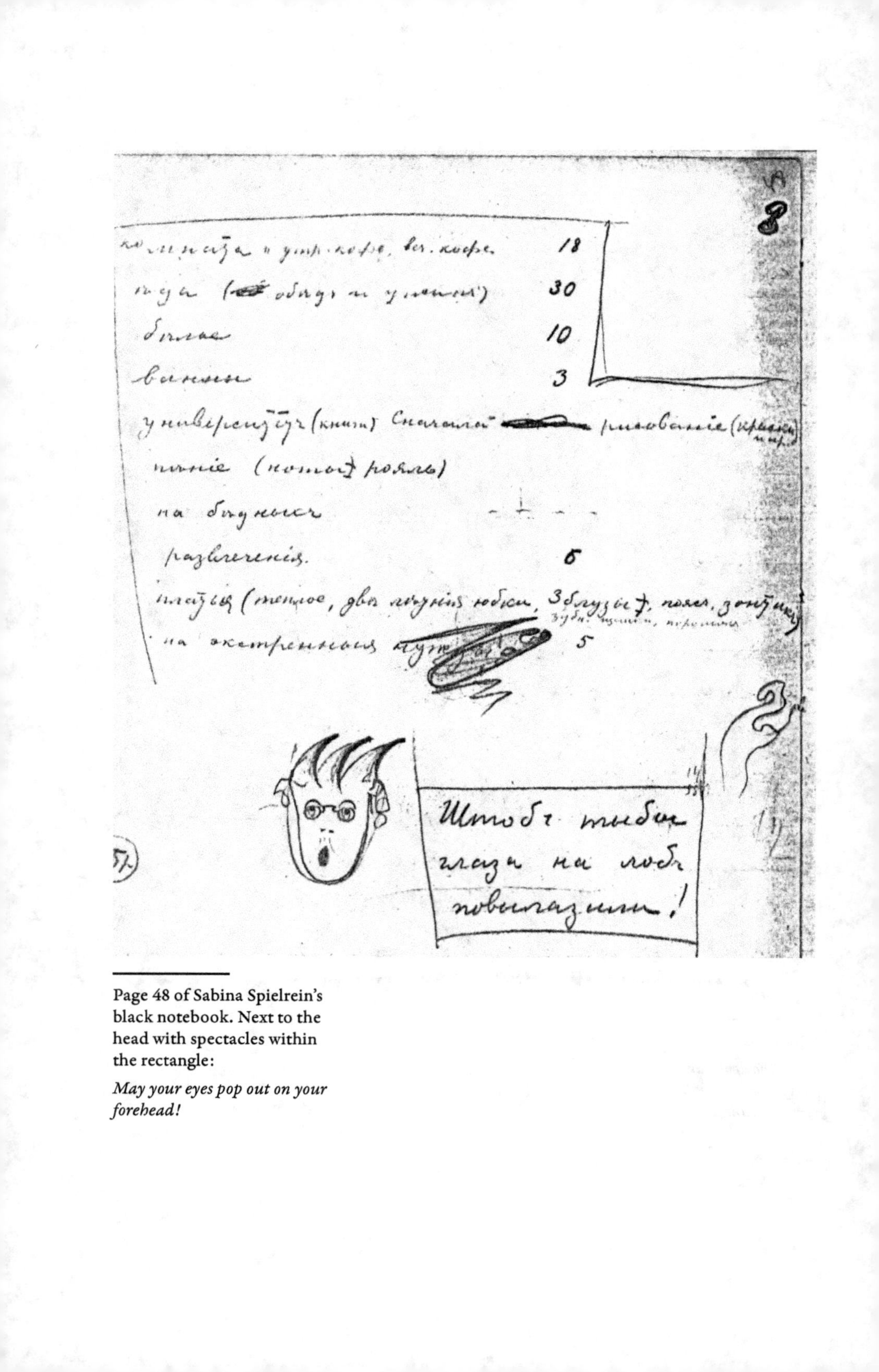

Page 48 of Sabina Spielrein's black notebook. Next to the head with spectacles within the rectangle:

May your eyes pop out on your forehead!

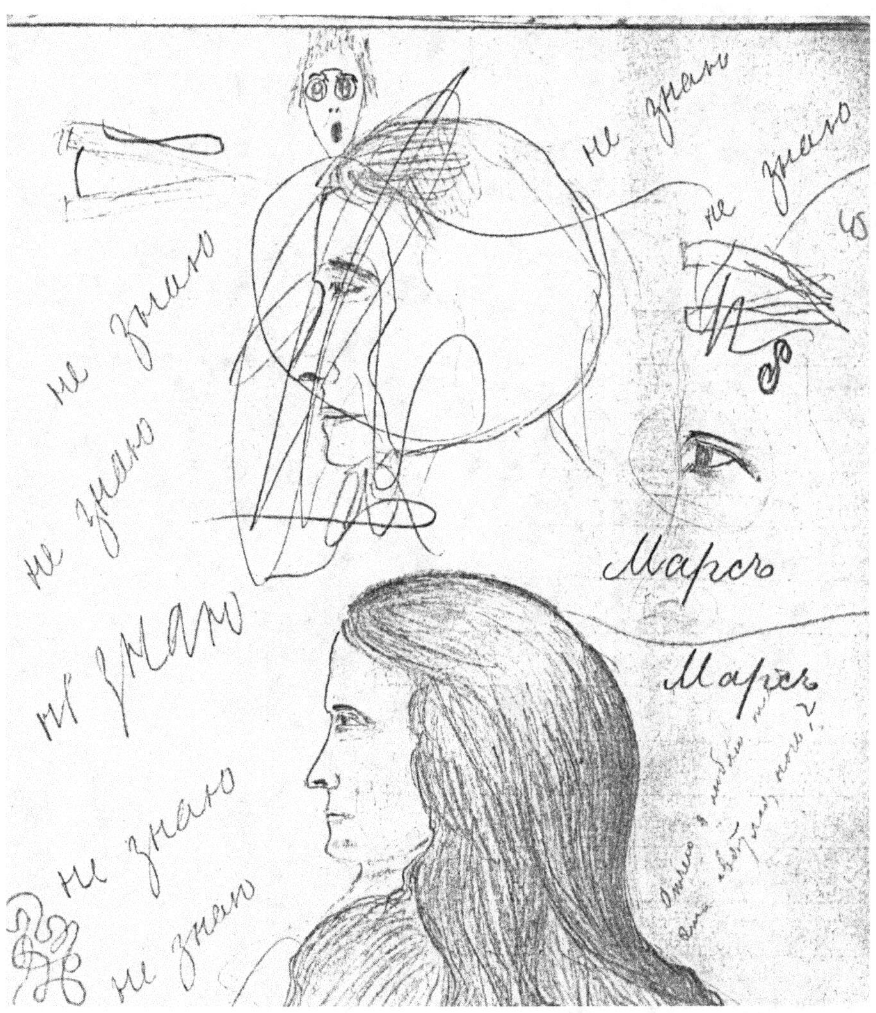

Page 49 of Sabina Spielrein's black notebook. Around and under the two heads:

I don't know (seven times)
Mars (twice)

Pages 50-51 of Sabina Spielrein's black notebook. Caricature of unknown.

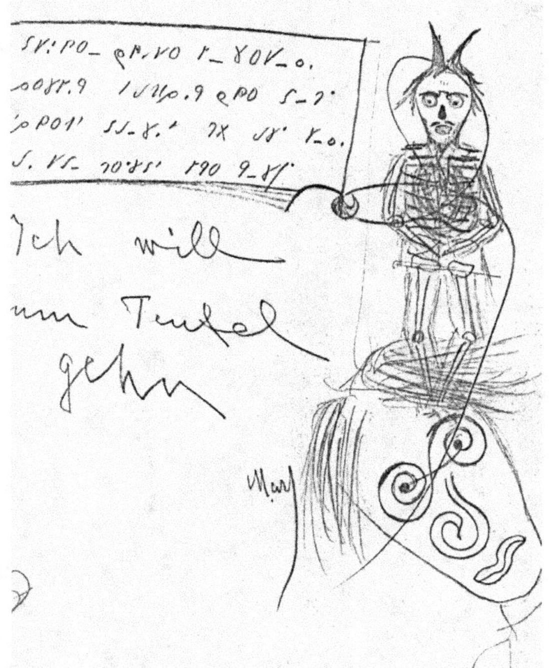

Page 52 of Sabina Spielrein's black notebook. An encoded message to the left of the little devil standing on a man's head -- a doctor?

Page 53 of Sabina Spielrein's black notebook. Caricature of unknown.

Page 54 of Sabina Spielrein's black notebook. Drawing of Meri.

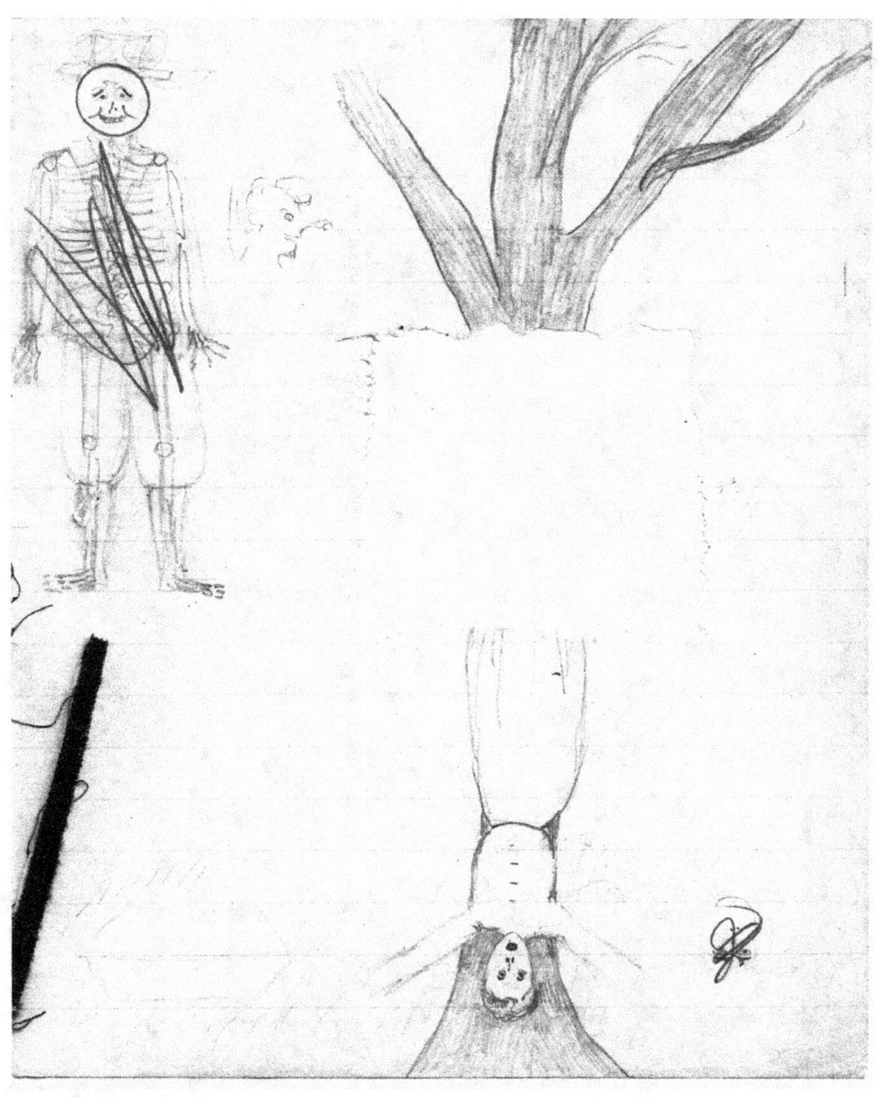

Page 55 of Sabina Spielrein's black notebook. Hospitalized Spielrein wrote in her testament how to scatter the ashes of her cremated body:

In big field (next to our home), plant an oak tree there and inscribe: "I too was once a person, and my name was Sabina Spielrein."

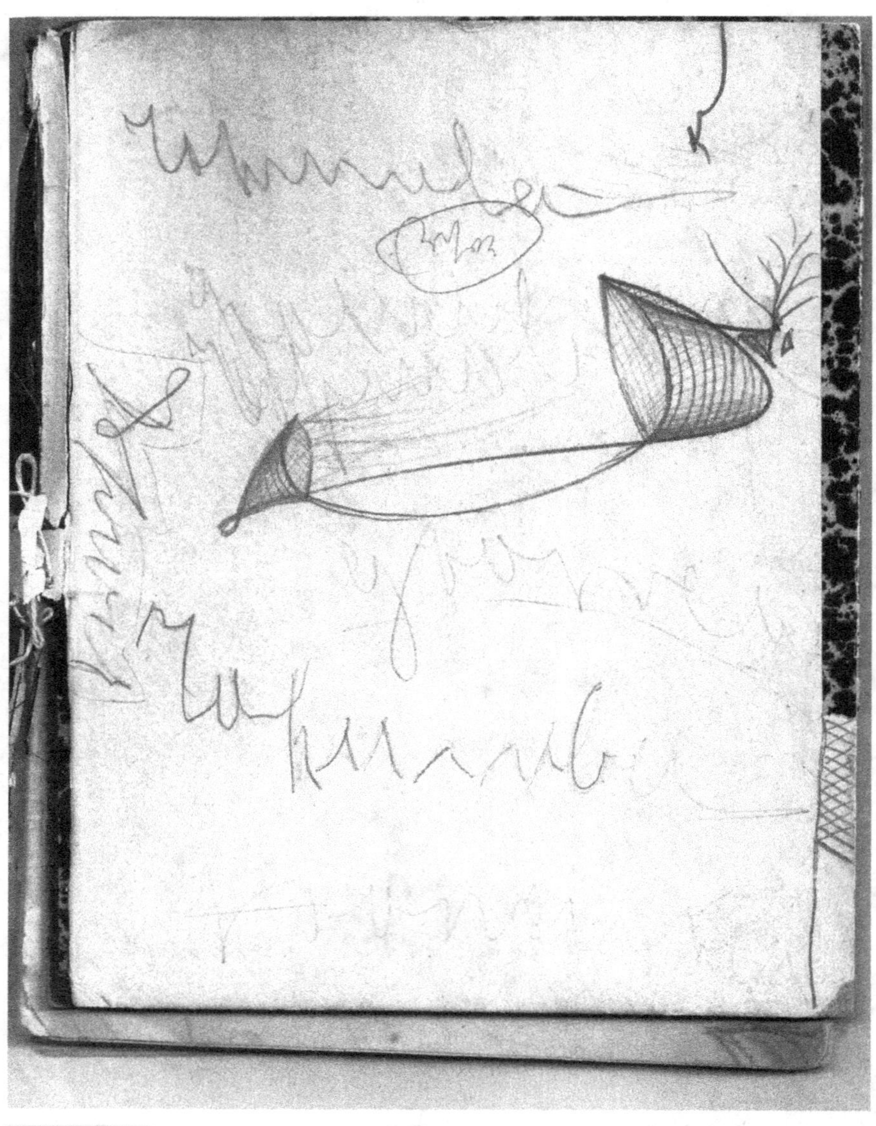

Illegible

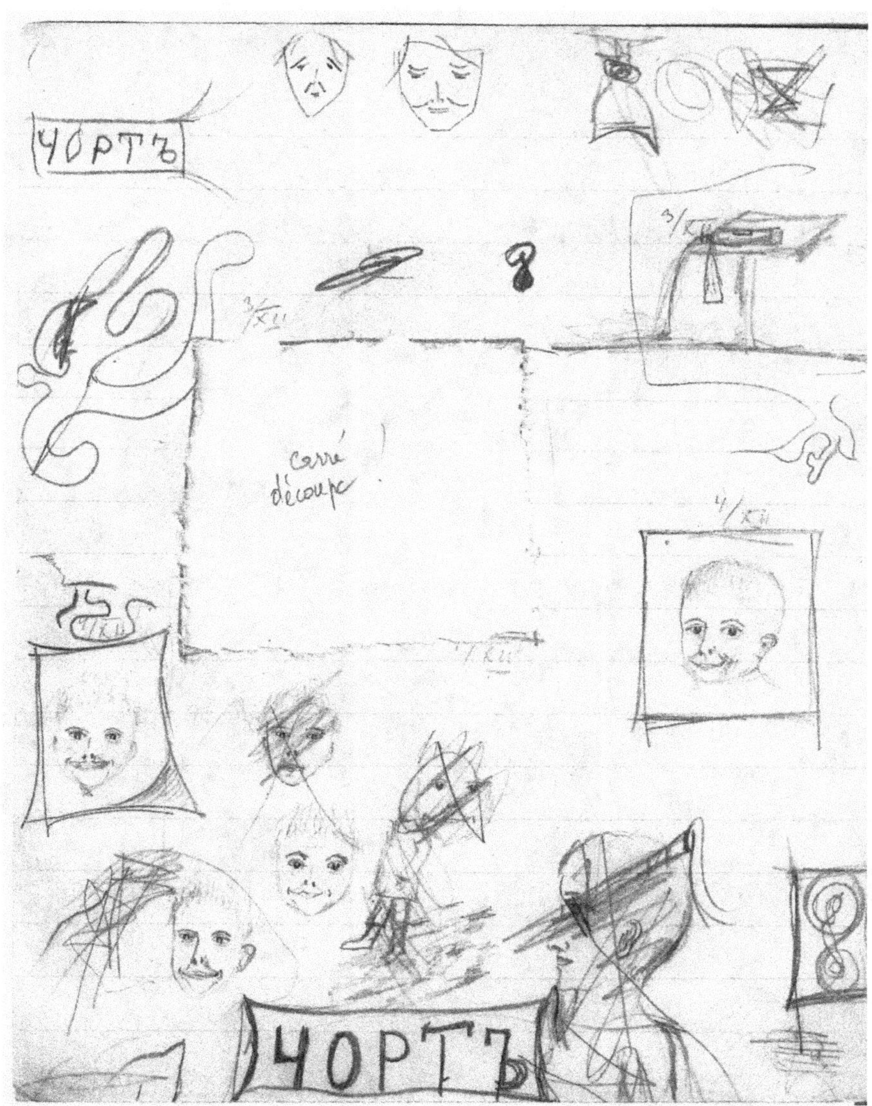

Page 56 of Sabina Spielrein's black notebook. At top and bottom: Devil; in the rectangle: Mme de Morsier's French words.

Page 57 of Sabina Spielrein's black notebook. Another illustration of Meri, "bespattered by the storm's foam."

Within the rectangle:

piglet! idiot! the devil's son! A dirty mug! If it were not that that my...won't let me say many words, I would have slapped his face and reprimanded him!

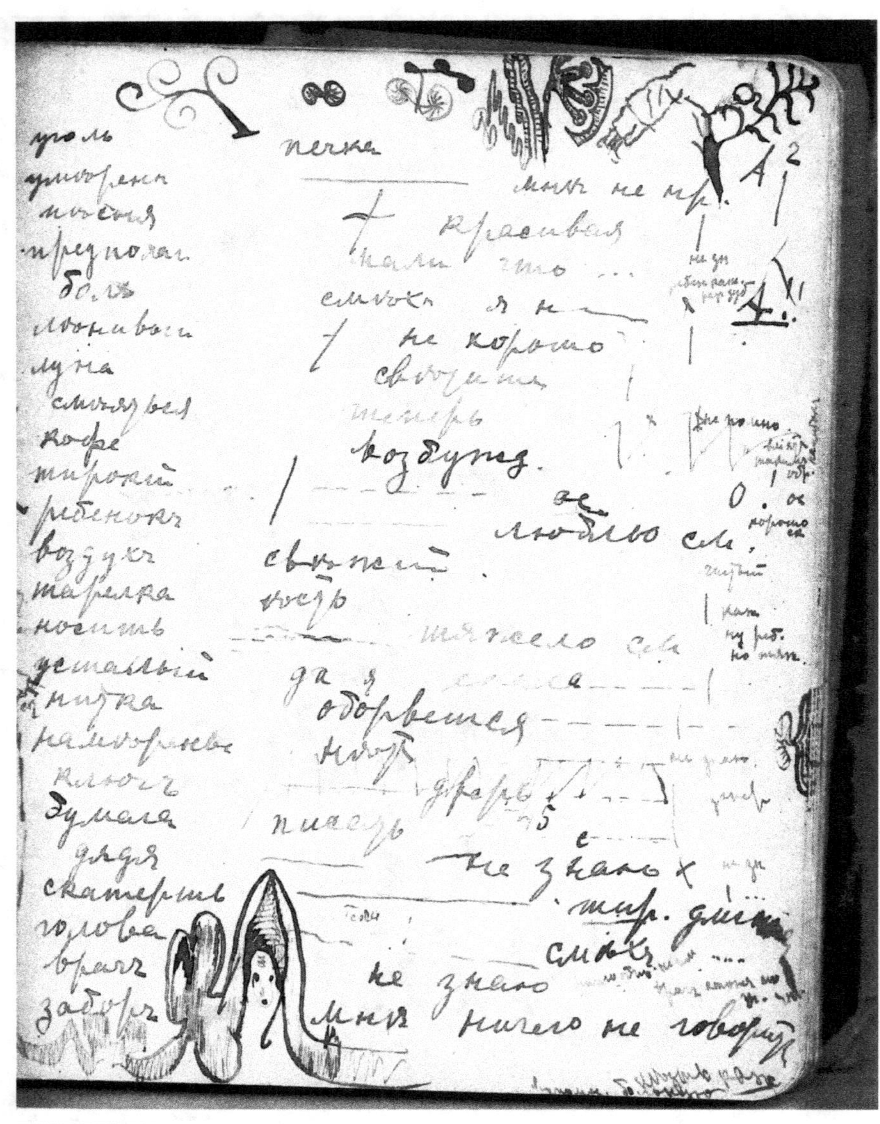

Some pairs of associations

pain laughter I don't / child I like / head doctor I don't know. The left head is male, the right female.

Sarra [Pochtareva] she oohed and aahed with delight. "Renatochka's eyes haunt you all the time," she said. "Oh what a beauty," this is everybody's opinion. This is also happiness for you. Milia has not yet seen either your photograph or Renatochka's, he is on the Volga as I wrote to you.

I went down to our little garden and was thinking about all of you there: we feel good in our garden. An apple grew on Renatochka's tree while this year Irochka's tree bore no fruit. Your cherry tree is still alive, Yasha's tree was transplanted and it is sick etc. We have a little kitchen garden. The garden is beautifully laid out. The balcony is covered in flowers, but you are not here. Strange that you are the only one who did not receive a parcel, everything takes such a long time, probably you'll get it soon. Yasha was very happy with the parcel and I am very happy. I will soon send you more parcels. If everything were easier and more available, I would be doing it more frequently. I will try to send you homemade pastries, and if they will allow it, I'll send sausages too.

I wrote to you long ago that if you have no letters from your husband, it is because it is either difficult or impossible to write; I even know that he travels frequently, but everything will be back to normal and he will write at the first opportunity. We sent him Renatochka's portrait and also telegraphed him ([did father write] to you?), and forwarded your letters to him. We took care of everything. Do you have acquaintances? Don't be alone. Loneliness always leads to sad thoughts. We hope that the sun will shine upon us and better times will come for all mankind. I got some letters from Sania but nothing from Yasha, it is sad and painful. His family is in good health and happy, tell him about it. I am taking mud treatments from Doctor Ryndziun, and I already took five mud cakes, tomorrow I will take a day off. Regards to the children, they should not forget that a mother lives only for her children and their letters are her life's only consolation. Kissing you and dear Renatochka. I wrote to her separately twice, Sarra wrote to her from Kazan.

Mama

ES 52

Dear Sabina! Rostov on/Don 6.XI.16

In your letters one feels some kind of suffering, a state of oppression. This is not surprising, nowadays most people feel like that. It is a pity that I am not with you, it could make all things easier. It is terribly hard to be far away from the children in such difficult times. It's incredibly hard on me as well, I don't go anywhere because of my rheumatism and my gout which is particularly affecting my left hand, and which I cannot move at all, I cannot dress myself etc.

I stopped all my treatments because they don't help and the doctors can't tell me anything. They say I need more mud and time will heal. What can I do? I have not been seeing anybody except those who are suffering a lot. Every day I have to listen to stories of tragedies so that I got [sucked into?] this life, and this different life became totally alien to me. It would be quite an event if I were able to breathe fresh air outdoors, or be warmed by the sun's rays. It is strange for me to think that there are such things like a theater, [a biograph?], overflowing with people. Happy people! Perhaps such joyful days will come when many people including my relatives will be alright, when my health will improve, and I will admire the beauties of life and be drawn into life's vortex. Oh, if only it were true! Just thinking about it gets me excited. Now my thoughts are occupied with one thing: that my relatives should be alright. I wish Masia should achieve his goal, that Aron should stay with us etc. Milia has not yet received his student card and he is very upset about it. His documents have not yet arrived from the ministry. I am busy arranging that he should matriculate without the documents, but everything is so difficult, and it takes such a long time. My mind is working harder than ever before. You ask me about my relations with Silva. What kind of relations can I have? She is very cold, and in general, she is only closely attached to her own family. Everything that is hers is good, everything that is not hers is devalued. She comes to visit, sits for a while, we treat her, talk about Beba [illegible name], Yasha, Sania or suchlike and the children. She will stay for an hour or so and leave. This is quite infrequent and the excuse is that she is in grief because Beba died; however, she dresses up, takes walks, has a good time etc. Silva likes money and gifts. She would be pleased if I gave her valuable gifts often. Of course, her gifts to me are seen as something valuable for my son. I would like to see her healthy and happy. But at our home she does not behave like a close relative, she is pompously playing the role of a socialite. Papa is angered by this but I take her the way she is and I say: so be it. She takes money for herself and for the children as if it is owed her, as when she was once given 300 rubles. She sends her kids to visit us and admits that they feel comfortable with us. When they have to leave they cry. So how else should we deal with Silva? I think we couldn't do any better. We never reproached her for anything, we didn't criticize anything, we do not meddle in her relationship with her husband. We shower her and the children with money and gifts, including her birthdays, so what more does she want? If she would only show us a little warmth, or at least if I saw that she loves Yasha a lot, but there is even none of that. But for this I strongly blame both Olga Pavlovna and Mira. However, outwardly it all looks decent and correct. I'll soon write to Renatochka. Yesterday they brought me her photograph, I had it shown to the family, general delight, as I was told. Her eyes [charmed?] everyone. I kiss you and your dear child.

ES 53

Dear Sabinochka! 10/23.XI–16

I just wrote a long letter to Yasha and it's a pity if he won't get it. Well, what is with you? Can't you arrange matters so that you will be spared all the fuss about the help? This is a very tedious business, especially now, in these hard times. Is it really necessary that you should be doing all this manual work for the child? To raise a child and to wash a child have nothing in common and here you are ruining your health. Perhaps you have already hired a nanny for the child. It seems to me that you should arrange to have take-out dinners from the boarding-house at home, and for the child the nanny could always cook everything on the kerosene burner. This would be good and you would not have to busy yourself with two servants but just with one. Anyway, it will be clearer once you try it. When I don't get any letters from you I suffer a great deal. It always seems to me that something has happened either to you or the child. Lately your letters have been very short and I always feel as if I want to force myself to read something into it. With whom are you corresponding in Russia? Where is Miss Leibovich? Who are you seeing in Lausanne? Do you have any intelligent acquaintances? And is Silva writing to you? Silva hasn't visited us for quite some time now. The children visit us, but not very often which I regret, because their visits infuse a fresh spirit and give us great joy, and after they leave we feel miserable again. Yasha has wonderful children and what are Sania and Roza writing about their little Menikha? Thank God, they are doing relatively well. It is only bad with you and Yasha, especially for him as he is completely alone. I am surprised that Silva was able to leave him and that neither she nor Olga Pavlovna thought to send him a parcel. Apropos parcel: pity I can't send you anything and it upsets me. Write to me more frequently about your little daughter. In general why do you write so rarely and so little about yourself? The Pochtarevs [Isaak's in-laws] are visiting us frequently. Aron is now happy and very grateful toward me, I have done a lot for him. Don't write to Roza that I have done so much for him. There is nothing new in particular that I can tell you because for the last three weeks I did not go out except twice. Today I visited Uncle Pinia and also went to see Masia to find out what is the matter with him and regretfully I found nobody home, just the children. Olia got a job as a clerk in a club [of journey men?] getting 75 rubles and after the New Year will get 100 rubles, she leased two rooms to pay their rent; for now they only have 75 rubles and later 100 rubles; perhaps everything will turn better and then everything will be alright. Uncle Noi is doing well. Adia is studying at the conservatory, Milia wants to write a few words. I kiss you and our dear and beloved granddaughter Renatochka.

Mama

[postscript]: Hooray! I am now studying mathematics, how do you like that!? Understandably, mother doesn't like it at all. What is new with you? Did you receive my letter of the 25th of October? Please write.

Your Milia

To mademoiselle Renatochka Sabinovna from grandmother Eva. Lausanne (Switzerland) To the letter of S. Shpilrein.

Dear beloved Renatochka!

Why don't you ever write to your grandmother? We often speak about you with your cousins Irochka and Marianochka. Do you write often to your cousin Menikhen'ka? Do you always obey your mama? Are you healthy? Greetings from grandfather and uncle Milia. Many kisses from your grand-mother Eva.

[Postscript from Emil] Rostov on/Don 10.XI.16. Greetings! Uncle!

ES 54

My dear! Rostov on/Don 12.I.17

Happy New Year! I have been writing less frequently lately, I was sick all the time. The hand became completely atrophied, I am completely unable to move it. Now I have some movement in it but not much and I still cannot move it freely. I suffered a lot and I am still suffering with my illness but now there is a slight improvement and the main thing is that there is hope that the new doctor will give me a lot of relief and this will also improve my mood. I am always in bed, always covered in mud, massaged twice a day, take horrible medications and baths, all this is very exhausting. My doctor is a Georgian [?]. He prescribed herbal baths (horse-tail with birch buds) and pine extract. I also have to drink herbal infusions together [with poison?], then a strong [illegible] with [massage?]. I am weak and get tired therefore I cannot write much. I started going out recently. Yesterday was papa's birthday, we were visited by the Guttermans, [Dubrov?], Noi, Panin [?], Olia, and Sara. We had a good time as a family, simply and pleasantly, the first in a long time, we are always at home. Milia and his friends played. Milia has completely abandoned music, a pity, he is very talented. Every time I get a letter from you I am happy when I read about Renatochka. I may read the same letter twenty times. She's now a big and interesting girl. May God give her happiness and health. Make a drawing of her hand and also describe her baby talk. It is very interesting, but at the same time makes one upset. Some news was delivered to us, it's very interesting and I am stopping. Write to us more frequently, goodbye and[illegible]. I kiss you and dear Renatochka.

Mama

[Postscript from father]. Greetings, [signature]. [Postscript from Emil] 14.I.17. All the best. Milia.

ES 55

Dear Sabinochka! Rostov on/Don 25th March 1917

I am writing but I am not sure you will receive my letter. It is very hard when you live so far from the children and do not even get a line from them. No news from you, except telegrams, it is so sad. If I were sure you would get my letter, I would be writing about a lot but I don't want to squander my energy for nothing. Today we were visited by Irochka. She's a beautiful girl and impresses everybody with her intelligence and her beauty, she is a tender and very lively child.

5th April

The letter was interrupted, I received telegrams from all of you and was very happy. In our current life to have a moment of happiness is also a blessing. Martselek arrived from Siberia in such a condition that it was awful to look at him. I am going to see him tomorrow and cook for him. If his mother saw him she would faint. I wish you happiness all my children and grandchildren. I kiss you all

Mama

There is a lot to write about but the uncertainty of you getting the letters interferes with writing.

[postscript from father] My Dear, Yasha wrote he hopes to get his freedom by way of an exchange for a German prisoner of war. I think that Sania is also busy arranging this for him and that he will be successful, then you and the child will be able to arrange for a permit to travel in transit through Germany. I would be so happy if this were possible for us to see each other after an almost three years long separation! Goodbye to you all. [signature] 5/4.17

ES 56

Dear Sabinochka, Rostov on/Don 18th April (May 1st) 17

I am writing about my impressions of this day. We experienced something so grandiose that it is difficult to describe it. I am too tired from so many impressions of the day and therefore will not describe the whole panorama of today's festivities. For the first time in Russia's life there was such a grandiose procession of 12,000 people celebrating this holiday. The holiday of workers and the holiday of freedom. It's no joke! A free democratic Russia! What pride this is for us now! Free Russia. How beautiful this sounds! You would be astonished to see how solemn this procession was, what order was maintained given such an enormous crowd. I was sitting on the balcony at [illegible]the pharmacy and before my eyes was a sight that can never be forgotten. Every party marched with its own banner and inscription: "Long live free Russia," "Land and Will," "In fight you will find your right," "Comrades, workers we are with you" (this was from high school students), etc. The various parties were marching singing and accompanied by music. The parties were Social-Democrats, Bundists[104], revolutionaries, etc.; there were various groups: musicians, actors, choir singers, students, school children, rag pickers, cabbies, factory employees in various departments, workers, and so on without end. It's a pity that all of you are not now in Russia where every capable person is needed, where there is much work to be done, a lot to be done for the renewal of Russia. We can talk endlessly about this topic but we will talk about it when we meet.

Tell me about yourself. For the longest time there has been one smallish letter from you. It is four months since I had a letter from Sania and Roza, I am very worried. We got a minuscule letter from Yasha. Today Milia is on call at the police station in Nakhichevan', he left at 11 in the morning and will be there until 12 o'clock next day. He serves in the police and spends a lot of energy on it, as his job is very hard. Milia is now a full-grown man and quite a brave one which you probably never expected from a "mama's boy". Today he won't get dinner and will be half-starving but what can I do? One has to make sacrifices for the motherland. I am very sad without him but I realize I have to work. So as not to repeat myself, tell the children about the content of my letter. Write more about yourself and Renatochka, she should be a very interesting young girl now. All the best to you and Natochka. Be well and happy. I kiss you

Mama

[Postscript]: For God's sake, please tell me something about Roza, Sania, Menikha, Sarra Pochtareva

ES 57

Dear Sabinochka — Rostov on/Don 31st May, 17

We answered your telegram, you should go to Stockholm and I gave you

104 Members of the Jewish leftist Bund party.

the address. After receiving your cable, I would suggest that you and the child should spend the summer in a cottage near Stockholm and then we would see, if either we could come there or if you could come to us. Two or three months would tell us a lot. We could also send you parcels there. But right now I am at a loss. Did you leave already or not yet? Did you get our telegram? I know nothing about it and I am very worried, I wait impatiently for your news, only then will I be able to write more, but now I am worried. How is yours and Renatochka's health? I am also very worried about you traveling with a child, if only you could get there safely. And so I wait for your letters and in the meantime will write to you in Stockholm. I kiss you and Renatochka

Mama

[mother's postscript]Silva and the children are getting ready to move to Moscow in the fall which will be a great loss for me.

[father's postscript] Obviously you are not able to travel to Stockholm, or else we would have been notified by you accordingly. Meanwhile, not knowing where to send the money, I made a telegraph transfer of 1,500 francs to Lausanne, adding to the 830 francs which had already been transferred there. Naturally you are now spending more than before in view of the increase in prices and that you also have to feed Sania with parcels. If anything is left over, deposit it in your savings account, in case it becomes impossible to send you money from here. Even if you had moved to Stockholm, everything could be left in Switzerland so as not to bother with moving things from place to place.

I think Milia is leading a dreadful life. He comes home late at night, more like 2 in the morning. He falls asleep late and he gets up at noon or even later. He doesn't study at all. Not even music. He has not touched the violin for months. Mother, of course, believes that the poor boy is tired, overworked, that he needs a rest, etc. but nothing you can do about it. Everybody interprets "rest" in his own way. For a long time we had no letters from you, not even telegrams. I am sending you regularly such newspapers as "Near-Azov Country" and "Russian Newsletter," but I don't know if you are getting them. At home everybody and everywhere is in an elated mood, it is only my business that has finally come to a halt. But not to worry, as long as it everything returns to normal.

[Signature]

ES 58

Dearest Sabina! Rostov on/Don 12/8.1917

For God's sake, write to us more frequently. For a long time we have not heard from you except for a little postcard. Do not get desperate, do not lose hope for a better life, think about yourself and the child so that both of you can stay healthy. Just don't lose health and the rest will come to you. I had already thought that you were coming to us and imagined what to arrange so that you would put on some weight and all of a sudden...write more about what Renatochka is saying, how does she [prattle], how does she play, what does she look like. Does she have a lively temperament? She is a big girl now and certainly very intelligent. Strange that you write nothing about her, did she put on weight? Does she have jet black hair? Is her hearing progressing? Write about everything without fail. Who are you seeing? Do you have any interesting acquaintances other than musicians? Milia has enrolled as a student in Kharkov and will be leaving us. Here he is living like a lord, has a luxurious room for which people would gladly give us more than 100 rubles a month, the very best service, but now he will be living in Kharkov in a slum, will eat poorly and pay 300 rubles in rent, so now I will have to worry about one more child. There will be no letters, it will be a time of anxiety, oh what will become of me. But what can I do? And soon he will be called up for military service and will be far away from me. I do not want to think about anything, I have suffered so much for everybody and that is the last straw. Write, write, write! This year I didn't travel to get treatments but I need them badly. I would just like to be somewhat more healthy when the children return. I have made beautiful chemises and dresses for Renatochka, for you I have made beautiful cotton lingerie. Goodbye, all the best, cheer up.

Mama

[Postscript from father]

Soeben Deine Karte erhalten. Rate dir, die Stellung [illegible word]. I have just received your postcard. Advise you, the job.

Signature

ES 59

Dear Sabinochka! 16/8.17

I just received two portraits of Renatochka. We are all struck by her beauty; moreover, in the photo with a bra, in her expression and pose, she literally looks like an eighteen-year-old coquettish young lady; she is also beautiful in the nude, but her face looks completely different. On the big photograph she looks a lot like you, but naked she looks more like her father. Amazing! The temperament shines in her eyes! She simply has the gaze of a prankster. Who taught her to hold herself like this? Some people find her more beautiful in the big photograph but I find she is beautiful in both in her own distinctive way.

We got the photographs, but no letter; that's very sad, since for a long time we had no letters from you except one that slipped through a long time ago. Endless longing and suffering! Your desperate letters were the last ones and thereafter nothing for a long time.

Yesterday we got such a desperate letter from Yasha that it was obvious that his family had pestered him so much, that finally he spilled his guts. Oh, ah, how he was suffering. Every word of his cut like a knife and my eyes were hurting from crying. We are doing what we can for his return, but the results are slow in coming, because there is so much to do; and someone else's grief is not as near as one's own. Tomorrow Milia is traveling to Kharkov on his own business and maybe from there he will continue to Petrograd on Yasha's business, depending on various circumstances.

What about your travel? Everything got quiet. For God's sake let us know. Don't stay alone, loneliness kills. Where is Leibovich? Where is Strashunskaia? Why don't you seek advice from some men how to arrange your journey. Do you have close friends? I am terribly afraid for you, you are so inexperienced and gullible. I feel that you are having a hard time and when you don't write it is worse for me. Write everything, don't hide anything. The mood is most awful; now Milia will leave us, it will become completely empty. Stand firm a little longer, my children, some day there will be an end to human suffering. All I need is to see my children healthy and happy. Let's hope, my dear ones, that we shall soon see each other. Goodbye, be as happy as is wishing you

your mother

ES 60

My dear Sabinochka! Rostov on/Don 10.X.17

It hurts me to read your letters filled with so much sadness. The main thing is that we are unable to help you. Papa is searching for a solution to this situation but so far he has only been able to send you 500 rubles and nothing certain can be said about their fate, thus we cannot send any money to Renatochka. It pains me that you are living in such awful conditions while Silva with her children is living like a queen in Kislovodsk. So far her stay there is costing us about a thousand rubles a month, may God grant you that much all your life. But in spite of this she is ranting anyway and is always displeased with something or finding something in every word; finally I lost all patience with her and I am unable to write to her. For example she is asking to be informed about what Yasha is writing: I copy the following from Yasha's letter: "I've had no letters from Silva in a long time, she mentioned something that she was very ill and it seems to me that I have no family." She answered Yasha's letter as follows, "It doesn't surprise me that it seems to Yasha that he has no family; during the last three years he managed to break the habit [of having a family]; he alone is guilty of that and he should not complain. In fact, he cannot endure anything like a man, although he knows that his situation will not last forever whereas I will have sorrow all my life. I will never see my close relatives again."

Papa sent her money for three months, and according to Yasha's request the sum was increased and we sent her the transfer document in my letter. I was in a hurry to leave and wrote in a corner of my letter: I am sending you a transfer for such and such and such an amount. Then we get her letter: "What is this account of a transfer? How can one explain it? Shouldn't I have been informed about it?" Signed Silva Shpilrein, as if we have committed a mortal offense. We always give her gifts and we surely give presents to the children. When I write to her, papa is always laughing that I am so careful that nothing should seem to her, that I explain everything, it's even disgusting. Oh, poor Yasha! How I pity you! You married a real shrew. This is our fate: we should endeavor to honor our daughter-in-law and son-in-law , look for ways to talk to them so that they are satisfied, give them money, show them attention, and then you still do not please them, because all that is best is misunderstood and misinterpreted their way. We are now more than exhausted from all this and I pray to God for us to be as far from them as possible, never have to depend on them or be forced to help them, to avoid any contact with them. Enough about that. It is necessary to ensure a good diet for Renatochka, and you also have to think about yourself. If you lose health it will not return easily. Can't you ask Jung to loan you some money with a receipt or a promissory note? Papa is taking all the measures to provide you with money. I wrote to you about Silva because of the letter that I received from her, otherwise I would not have mentioned her. I kiss you.

Mama

Postscript [upside down]: We are all doing fine. Milia is in Kharkov and he writes to you often. It is awfully nice to read about Renatochka where you write how she prattles. Always write about her. May [illegible] for happiness.

ES 61

16.X.17

There was some interference. Write more frequently and in more detail about yourself and the child. How is the health of both of you? Any detail about the child gives me joy and I imagine that she is near me. It's of no use that you sent parcels to other people when you yourself do not have enough. Apparently Sania doesn't know how difficult it is to send parcels abroad. Whatever the cost of the parcel's content, the box alone costs 3 rubles, the packing material 2–3 rubles. Mailing every parcel costs no less than 25 and sometimes up to 40 rubles. Moreover, how hard it is to get those boxes, which are difficult to send, and how exhausting all this is. I'll gladly give my last strength to my children but Sania also requested that we send parcels to a friend of his, and that's too much. Our guest now is Berta Ilyinishna [the widow of Eva's father Mordechai Lublinskii], she is traveling to her son in England. We'll have to give her a couple of hundred rubles; after grandfather's death we gave her 500 rubles and continued to give her more every holiday. Somebody else is coming to see us. Goodbye, you will suffer a bit but hopefully it will get better. I kiss you and dear Renatochka.

Mama

Postscript [upside down]: Ask for a loan from Leibovich. [another response by Eva to Silva's letters]

She was sent a money transfer but they missed mentioning who it was from, so she sent a cold letter addressing nobody and signed S. Shpilrain with an addition "it appears I ought to know why such a sum was sent to me." I always calmed papa down when he got upset and now my displeasure reached the [maximum?]. As if we exist only to give her money, to stand on our hind legs and ponder every spoken word, indeed every word a thousand times, before we write it, and then the quibbles come from God knows from where and for what. Papa, reading my letter to her, bursts out laughing and remarks, "Why are you explaining and trembling, to hell with her!"

She should have a mother in-law like me but I suffer endlessly and eat my heart out. I suffer only for Yasha's sake and I don't want to harm their relationship. I have been staying at home without going anywhere for the last three years, I am not getting any treatments and I force myself to work as never before in my entire life. My head is filled with worries for my relatives, dear people, for my children, for Masia and Pinia etc., for my motherland, for humanity entire, for myself because I am quite sick with gout and everything else, so if I didn't answer since her letter it was because she signed it as "S.[ilva] Shpilrain" with the note "I only respond to letters" etc. I don't want to tell you everything. She is living like a queen, free, doesn't write to me about the children for three weeks at a time, and when she writes it is only a few words "the children are fine." We do not deserve anything more than that. Perhaps we didn't send her enough money or didn't greet her warmly enough.

ES 62

Dear Sabinochka! Rostov on/Don 23.X.17

It is your birthday again, two days away, and how annoying and painful it is that again we are going to celebrate it without you. What can I wish you? I am thinking to say to you, may this day bring you complete mental tranquility, complete rest from all life's agitations. It is time, it's time, to shake off all this burden you have been carrying for so many years. May God grant you a new and a better life. How will Renatochka celebrate your birthday? Does she understand it? How much does she prattle? I get a lot of pleasure listening to her prattle.

About three days ago your husband turned up unexpectedly as if to ask for your address. As usual, I received him formally in the living room, rather like a stranger to me. How could it be otherwise? In the past he had struck a certain attitude toward us; out of the blue he addresses me in a letter as "madam," without any grounds or pretext on our part. We have always tried to meet him halfway. Papa never wanted to speak with him and never did, but I was courteous and would receive him, but never failed to maintain the attitude I had adopted toward him. After the "madam," I thought we would never meet again and resigned myself to this. He had sent a [business?] postcard to Milia in response to his postcard and, as expected, did not mention our name. Then all of a sudden he turned up, and you could feel that he had softened. He spoke about Yasha, Sania, and Milia with great enthusiasm, about you and Renatochka too, about all of you with such love that I was struck by this unevenness and lack of tenacity of character. He spoke about our affairs in general and told a great deal about himself etc.; all this struck me as strange, nevertheless I treated him politely, correctly, but as someone who is for me a "dear sir" and since I and papa are for him "dear sirs." Well, there you are. Our Silvochka, who despite our most perfect attitude toward her, showering her with piles of money and almost prostrating ourselves before her, has been causing grief and continues to cause grief. This is the couple God got for us. We have probably sinned greatly. May be Sania's Roza will give us consolation for those two. Poor Yashen'ka! If he only knew how much his wife dislikes him! Both we and other people are convinced of that. I would forgive her for everything if I knew that she makes him happy. But she keeps kicking him.

I am afraid that one day he will know this but certainly not from us, good Lord! And Olechka and Mira do all they can that Silva and Irochka should not like both Yasha and us, so forget it. We stay on the sidelines and other than giving money we have no relations with them.

Your husband always carries yours and Renatochka's photographs in his pocket. That means he is interested to have all this, strange! He spoke about you and Renatochka in a completely different tone compared to past times. In a word, he got emotional. He asked me to show him the big photographs of Renatochka because in his pocket he only has the small ones, but unfortunately I was unable to do it because the key to the cupboard was broken and he might interpret it the wrong way, same as Silva. She will always find an offense directed at her even in the most sincere and heartfelt words. Knowing this when I wrote to her, I always parsed every word explaining to her twenty times that no offense was meant; observing this papa laughed at me mockingly, viewing it as my humiliation. I got into a writing vein, I didn't intend to write so much about this but the painful spot, the wound, was touched and willy-nilly all the pus came out.

We are living through these times; these emotional experiences contain so much that is interesting, serious, and majestic etc. World problems are being decided and in particular problems of nations, and at the same time such paltry incidents can poison a human life. Anyway, this means that human life is a paltry affair. I asked your husband to petition his commander for a permit to send you money as his wife and thus we would be able to send you money. All the best. I kiss you and dear Renatochka.

Mama

ES 63

Dear Sabinochka! Rostov on/Don 29.X.17

There is no solution to this situation, it is so much trouble to send you money and nothing can be done about it. Papa sent you 500 rubles but it is unclear if you will get them, it is a drop in the ocean because in exchange of 500 rubles you will only get 320 francs. This is total despair. In my previous letter I wrote that I had instructed your husband as a military man to apply for a permit to send you money. Then we could send you money in his name or send the money to him. I got a letter from him which shows that he did not understand me so I wrote to him again and explained everything. We wanted to send 500 more rubles in his name so that you would have 640 francs which is not enough for you and the child [a few lines missing] How will this all end? If you had extra money that would be something else, but you don't have enough for yourself. After all, we can only send money to you. I fear for the child, should you leave her in somebody else's hands. Could you request a loan from Strashunskaya? You have so many acquaintances, ask each one for a little loan [illegible] And what about Jung? [illegible] he would not refuse you [a few illegible lines]. It is frightening to realize [illegible] that such a painful life is awaiting you and maybe even hunger. My God, there are must still be some good people in this world, take loans from everybody you can, do not be so overly scrupulous. If you do not eat enough, you might come down with acute anemia. I will wait, maybe your husband will be able to get something. We are awaiting a letter from Sevtsa. For God's sake, do everything you can so as not to go hungry, while we are trying our best to find a solution to this situation, and stay healthy. I wish you results and health. Be strong.

Mama

Ask Leibovich for money.

ES 64

Dear Sabinochka, 13/26.8.18

If I finish in time, I will send you this letter through a gentleman traveling to Switzerland. I am suffering so much for you and the child and have no words to express it. I wish you could come here, it would be a big relief for us all. If you don't have enough money, do not worry that you are spending too much; take loans from acquaintances and we'll pay them back. I am well aware that with 1,500 rubles a month to live on you have to forego a great deal. That is why I suffer so much. Here we eat pirogi, tarts, copious dinners and suppers, and you are deprived of the bare minimum, and that is why often a piece of food gets stuck in my throat. Moreover, your loneliness depresses me, too. I understand very well, without words, your mental state and worries and I am tormented thinking about it. Therefore I cannot sleep nights. In Rostov you will not be deprived of anything and that is already a big deal. Don't worry about the illnesses you mentioned, all are trifles. I never think about them: all you need is to live cleanly and not eat raw fruits. We are now having a cholera epidemic but it will be over by the time you come. There is hope that someone close to you will be in Switzerland and take you home. I can't wait for this to happen. I am so worried. After many months we finally got a letter from you through Sania. It is strange, however, that you mention sending a few words to us and something to Pavel, but there is nothing there for him, i.e., no separate letter; I read the whole contents to him except for the places where you write about Silva. The reasoning of Renatochka delighted us all and gave us great, great pleasure and, of course, papa dragged in Freud. Your husband wrote to you a few times, and also in his last letter to Yasha, but Yasha had already left; I don't know if you ever got this letter. In that letter there was also a postscript: that he was sending 35 mark to Renata and 35 mark for books. He gave me 70 mark which I added to the sum papa was sending Yasha. But Sania did not receive these monies because when Yasha ordered the letters to be forwarded to Sania, he did not mention anything about money. We have sent you a lot of money that got stuck somewhere but you will probably receive it soon. Through [Mr. Rotshtein] and others you were sent 4,000 crowns and papa is planning to send you more. We are arranging your arrival here, we want to give you peace of mind which you need so much. I am making all kinds of [plans] how I will fatten you. Tomorrow Silva and the children are going to the Crimea, and possibly Yasha will join them for a short time to see them off. So cheer up, we are thinking about you and doing all we can. Write some more about Renatochka it will give us great pleasure. I kiss you and dear Renatochka.

Mama

We are all doing well, everyone is healthy and it would be good all around if all the children were together. We just received five letters from you of which two were for Pavel and I forwarded those immediately. Mama

[Postscript from father]: We sent you money through many different persons and you will get a lot of it at once.

CERTIFICATE

Given to Rostov on/Don to citizen Eva Markovna Shpilrein, fifty five years old, to certify that she is suffering from a severe form of uric acid diathesis [gout], disseminated arteriosclerosis, cardiosclerosis with degeneration of the heart muscle and frequent attacks of angina pectoris (Arthritis urica, Atherosclerosis universalis, Cardiosclerosis c. Myodegeratione cordis et Angina pectoris), as a result of which she has to stay permanently in bed and her life is in a continually threatening state.

Certified by the signature and the attachment of the seal Rostov on/Don 16 (29 of August, 1918)

Doctor Tsaitlin

ES 65

Dear Sabinochka! Rostov on/Don 28.XI.18

I am now busy on your behalf and wrote to Petia Sheinov. So far I was unable to achieve anything for you. If madam Strashunskaya received the money, it means that her husband was in Petrograd at the right time and as a military doctor was able to send money to his family. I obtained an application from your husband and sent it to Petia in Petrograd so that he can get something done there. We are busy on your behalf all the time but we won't get a permit, rather your husband as a military doctor, but it will take a long time. Ask for a loan from Jung, Bleuler, madam Strashunskaya (according to her husband she has a lot of money). Then take some from [illegible]. Won't Jung and Bleuler trust you? Finally, pawn your diamonds but do so cautiously. Put your seal on them, or else they might replace them; they always do that. Pawn them for a whole year so they don't get lost, in case you would have no money. Realize that diamonds are now <u>ten times more expensive</u> therefore ask for more money. I think the only way you can earn money is by working at home, e.g., doing translations. Tell all to Jung and Bleuler about your situation and ask for work at home in addition to loans. Your father will gladly repay them so don't send us stupid accounts and instead write about something else. We have enough money for you, just you and the child stay healthy. Take good care of her, especially her stomach. I can't wait for your letter with news about the child's health since from your last letter I learnt that she was sick again. My poor, poor, child! How I pity you and how desperate I feel because I cannot help you.

You probably know that your husband is now living in Rostov. He is staying in Senia's apartment and Ida is living there too. He opened a practice here and is trying his luck. He has a furlough till May and then he will see, so you can write to him in Rostov if you like. As you requested I will write to you every Saturday and today is Thursday, reassure me that you found money. I kiss you and Renatochka. I am delighted to read the description of how she prattles.

Mama

[postscript] I am thinking about your wardrobe and prepared for you [a lot of lingerie], [illegible] a fur coat and money for you [illegible]. I prepared money for everybody, just come [healthy?]. My heart aches for all of you. How it hurt to read in Yasha's letter that he asked you to request more money from Silva. This will be his debt to us. To me it is both hurtful and ridiculous. As if my money, our money is not your money.

[postscript from father [upside down] All mama's advice is good but it would be better if you could think about earning some money with your own work, this is my best new year's wish for you. I am attaching a letter that was returned. How do you like this "action of military censorship," violating simple postal regulations? In general, the reason for classifying as "impecunious" is simply a crass ignorance of postal regulations. The money for you has been sent around, you will get a lot of it at once. I will gladly spend it on all of you. Just come.

[signature]

ES 66

Dear Roza and Sania! Rostov on/Don 27.IV.19

I am sending cordial greetings and best wishes to you and Menikhochka. I yearn to learn at least something about you. Are you in good health? Where do you get money to cover your living expenses? I am terrified thinking about it. May be you are broke? If you all came here I would fatten you. I have fattened Yasha so wonderfully well that the new suit does not fit him. Write to me, dear children, write about yourselves and about my little granddaughter. It is possible that we will meet soon, ah if only!... Be healthy and happy and, God willing, I'll see you soon. I kiss you all

Mama

[Postscript]: I add my cordial greeting. Milia

ES 67

Dear Sabinochka, Rostov on/Don 20.V.1919

There is another opportunity to send you a letter, lately I had many such opportunities, but are our letters reaching you? My dear child! How we suffer for all of you! When will we meet? God only knows. There is not a single moment that we forget all the suffering. How is your life? How is Saniechka with his wife? My poor children! How do you live and what do you live on? For nine months I have had no letter from you and no news! Are you alive? How is Renatochka? How is Menikhochka? I see them as if they were standing in front of me. They must be big now, are they prattling well? If I could only live long enough to see you all. How I dream of such happiness! I am forwarding this letter with a gentleman who is staying here for at least two weeks and then traveling abroad. Maybe during this time there will be other opportunities. Did you get the 10,000 francs from Odessa and 5,000 from Belgium from madame Dupont? Recently we sent a letter with a Frenchman traveling to Paris, how happy I would be to know that you received all the letters. On the one hand, I am glad that Saniechka is not here now, but I feel sorry that he is suffering because of money, and a pity we can't see each other. Poor child, how do you break for money? Where do you get the funds to live on? Turn to anyone you can for money, we will pay back everything with gratitude. I wrote you that Pavlusha visits us quite frequently and is very busy working. In the infirmary he serves as a senior physician and is tremendously busy and in his free time works in his private practice. All doctors work a lot, to exhaustion. They get 50 rubles a visit on the average. Of course we often speak with him about you and the child and he can't wait to see you both.

Papa is reading the paper and philosophizing. That's about all. The Swiss gentleman who will deliver this letter to you, is coming back soon. You can give him your letter for us. A few words about Strashunskaya: I have known for a long time that her husband has completely forgotten about his wife, and he told me in person that he never thinks about her. Other people have told me that he will marry another woman and will send his wife a divorce. I feel pity for the poor woman, it will be a big blow. Your husband has been living very frugally and, as far as I know, he only cares about his own family. His insanity is long gone, he has a good relationship with papa; clearly, he has gone through much suffering. Goodbye my dear, we are all with you, you are not alone. When you are awake at night, know that I am also awake and thinking of you. I kiss you

Mama

[postscript: Silva was just here with the children. Milia was reading in French to Ira, Yasha has wonderful children.

[postscript] Yasha's children and Silva would like to live here, what can be done? Doctors who live here are military doctors who were ill and are now recuperating.

[mother's postscript] Ma chère petite fille! Comment vas tu? Viens chez nous. Je te ferai beaucoup de cadeaux et tu choisiras tout que te plairas mieux. Je t'aime beaucoup, ma petite Renée, je veux t'avoir pour embrasser et baiser. Ta grande-maman [my darling little granddaughter! How are you? Come to visit us. I'll give you many presents and you will choose what you like best. I love you a lot my little Renée I want to see you and hug you and kiss you. Your grandmother].

[postscript] Send my letter to Saniechka. Let he and Rozochka know that we are doing fine in Rostov city. Aron is engaged in business and making money. He was here yesterday and Sarra phoned us. They say we will meet soon, if only it were true! Yasha is toiling in the kitchen like a simple laborer, boiling glycerin and selling it. Milia is on holiday and at home for the time being.

[postscript from Sarra Pochtareva] Greetings to you and your daughter.

I kiss you from Berlin.

Sarra

21.V.19 We will send money as soon as possible. If Pavlusha comes he will add a postscript if I ask him; but then I will not be able to mail my letter in time. I kiss you all my dear ones. I long to see you all healthy.

Mama

ES 68

[fragment of a letter]

I am mailing my letter to you now. Papa, Yasha and Milia went to our cottage, it was requisitioned by the military [illegible] only [illegible]. Just now Silva and the children were here. Milia read to Irina in French. Yan has wonderful [children]. [Postscript from Pochtareva] Greetings to you and your daughter. Kisses to [all three] Sarra.

[fragment from another letter]

We are doing well. Milia and his wife went to visit her parents; I'm waiting for them to come for supper. Yasha is in Ekaterinodar (he is a professor). Sania and his family are in Tiflis, they are living with Moisei; today we received a letter from them. You should not have written to Silva that Renata is sending her greetings to Pavel's [as if should be Yasha's]children. This can become fodder for gossip. Yasha's children are phenomenal, sheer delight! The younger one is not pretty but is extremely likable. Both girls amaze and delight people with their intelligence, liveliness and aptitudes. The older one is a beauty with a wonderful soul. The younger one is a little devil but quite appealing. I always tell them about Renatochka and they are awaiting her. They also tell that Sania's girl Menikhochka is wonderful; on the photograph which we received, she looks very likable, her eyes are intelligent and expressive.

ES 69

Dear Sabina, Rostov on/Don Undated

Recently, some three weeks ago, we sent you a letter and five thousand rubles with a lady traveling to Belgium and before that we sent you ten thousand rubles from Odessa. We are anxious to receive your letter confirming the receipt of all those letters and we cannot wait to have news about your life and our dear Berliners. The carrier of this letter will be returning to Russia in two months hence and you will at least be able to send us letters with her. The Belgian lady promised to send you her address, you can send your letter to her and she will deliver it to us. Also tell Sania and Roza about this. We are doing well, everybody is in good health. I told Pavlusha in a telephone conversation that a gentleman was going abroad, so he will write to you as well. By the way about him: he works a lot from morning to night, he even makes good money, he lives frugally and doesn't go anywhere and he doesn't have the time for it anyway. Naturally we always talk about both of you when we meet and we sigh, and that's how it ends. Every day, at the table ,we talk about what you live on, what you eat, where you get money, etc. Of course, this makes us worried but what can we do.

Today we learned that the Gordons[105] in Novorossiisk are going abroad. If they do, we will send money to you and Sania, we are looking for an opportunity to send you money or letters. Do not be sad, do not be depressed. We hope that all suffering will end soon and we will start a new life. How is Renatochka? Write about her in detail: what does she look like, what is she saying, how is her health? Write a detailed letter about your life, even the smallest details. Today Yasha's children visited us. They dug up the earth in the garden, wonderful children! Together with them I was planning how to arrange the garden when Renatochka and Menikhochka will come. I am in a rush to end this letter, I kiss you and dear Renatochka.

Mama

[postscript from Emil] Greetings and best wishes

ES 70

Dear Sabina, Rostov on/Don 30.VI.19

I am writing a second letter this week, I don't know if even one of them will reach you but it had to be mailed anyway. No word from you for the last eleven months. This saps what is left of my strength. How are you doing? Are you and Renatochka healthy? How are you surviving in this difficult time? What means do you live on? I feel stricken with horror at the thought that you are going hungry. Everyday we make plans how to get you and the child out of Switzerland. Papa is now trying to travel to you but it is still very difficult. We are all in good health, we suffer a lot, of course, but let us not tempt fate, thank God we are all alive. We must hope that we will meet soon so let us now be patient, perhaps the wished for sunny days will arrive soon. It would be good for all of us to get together in some spa like Kislovodsk and rest after all these hardships. For now I am very worried about all of you, it is very difficult to solve the money problem. A few days ago Pavlusha left for the Miliutino station and I think he will soon come back. Pavlusha has also written to you many times and together with us he can't wait for you to return. He is tired of being a nomad. Milia will soon end his military service. Yasha is working for the Defense Council and is getting very tired. Papa has liquidated his business because all the employees were drafted so he is languishing with nothing to do. Now he is busy with getting a permit to travel to see you. I wrote to Shura to help you with money, I think he got my letter and this calmed me somewhat. Vera is here and working in an infirmary. I wrote to you many times about

105 Probably a reference to the family of Noi Abramovich Gordon, a Rostov industrialist.

Yasha's children and there is no need to repeat it. They are charming, enough said. It's a pity that I see them so rarely but these are the circumstances. I kiss you and dear Renatochka. Till soon,

Mama

Greetings to Leibovich

[Postscript from father] I am working hard to get permission to travel abroad. Should I succeed, then perhaps we'll meet at the end of August. Just in case write to me by poste restante in Constantinople. Write there in detail about yourself, Renatochka, and Sania and family. Let Sania borrow money on my account from my firms and you ask for a loan from Shura [Kamenko?]. I sent you money a few times but I don't know the fate of these transfers. The Gordon family has gone abroad. Strashunskaya will know their whereabouts and then you will have a new source of loans. Write to Constantinople in detail about all of you. Let me know the exchange rates of various currencies, Russian rubles, marks, francs, etc. For how much can one sell Russian government securities? This letter is mailed only today, Thursday, 11/24/July 1919. Don't forget to write to Sania to send me a letter by poste restante in Constantinople, either directly there or through you. Goodbye to all of you.

[signature]

ES 71

My dear child! Rostov on/Don 28.VIII.19

I have an opportunity to write a few words. Yasha is playing and Milia is lying in bed and singing. All this is going on in what used to be the living room where I am now writing. But everything was requisitioned; eight strangers are living in our home and we are crammed into the dining room and bedroom, that's all we have. They wanted to place a general in the living room, and papa and I put him in one of the rented rooms, and now we are sorry we did because he is a very quiet and good man, and they replaced him with four other people. What can one do about it? This is not such a big evil as long as we are healthy and, meet again. Sania did not come here yet though and he has been back in Russia for the last two months. We can't send him any money, sending money [long distance?] is not allowed. Is someone thinking of sending for them? The last letter came from Tiflis. We will have to send Roza and the child to the seaside, the child is predisposed to rickets.

Silva and the children are in Kislovodsk, Yasha was there too. We have written to you that Yasha has been promoted to professor in Ekaterinodar, he just came back from there, got acquainted with colleagues and had dinner with the university rector, and on the 15th of September he will begin lecturing at the university and he will go back there. Papa is taking a rest now. Three days ago we received a letter from Pavel filled with despair, he wanted to travel and fetch you but it cannot be done. We are trying to arrange for him to be transferred to Rostov but who knows what will come of it. If you could arrange your return to Russia, we could help you get settled either in the Caucasus or in the Crimea and you and the child would have a wonderful rest. Children improve wonderfully in the Caucasus because it has a wonderful climate. For the 500 francs which you spend in Switzerland and live half-starved, here in the Caucasus [illegible] we could both live luxuriously and comfortably.

[postscript from Milia] I am rushing to go to my unit, therefore I am only adding a few words. It is in vain, dear sister, that you worry so much about my well-being, for I am completely safe, as our unit is stationed in Rostov all the time. Greetings to Renatochka.

Your Milia

[postscript from Yan] I join the preceding speaker [signature]

[postscript from mother] I was rushed to finish my letter. We pay 13 rubles for every Swiss franc and for 500 francs even more, soon instead of 13 rubles we will have to pay 15 rubles etc. Therefore, it is better to return to Russia.

ES 72 — Friday 13th November, 1919

Today I was supposed to forward this letter through a gentleman traveling to Lausanne but he did not come, what a pity! Today the Swiss consul brought us two letters from you written last year, there was also a letter to Pavel which I will forward to him today.

15th November

Tomorrow a Frenchmen, actually a Swiss, will come to tea with us and will depart on Wednesday and I hope to send you a letter with him and perhaps to send some money as well. I am very depressed because of Renatochka's illness and your condition. These problems make me cry because we cannot help either with money or with my efforts. It is difficult to send money and my health precludes me from traveling, I will not get there. These last five years have put on me an indelible stamp of aging, with its constant companions, old age ailments. I suffer endlessly for you and the child and this is all I can manage. I write relatively often, I use every opportunity, but I am not sure whether you are getting all my letters. Pavel also writes to you whenever possible; he very much wants to see you and the child and he would gladly travel to fetch you, but he cannot do this because he is serving in the military. He is not in Rostov now, he cannot write to you, but I informed him that there might be an opportunity, that he should write you a letter, and I hope you will get it soon. The other day I gave to the Swiss consul a letter from me and one from Pavel. It had been written in celebration of your birthday, was mailed and returned. I hope the child is feeling better. Papa will deposit 100,000 rubles in the bank under the name of Kamenko, and you can draw from this account each month whatever you need, just save about 250 francs for the return home in case we are unable to send you more. Meanwhile don't pay any debts, let's wait till the franc gets cheaper because now francs are causing ruination. I hope that by March the child will recover completely and you will be able to come here. It hurts me that our table is groaning with food, and you, poor thing, have to deny yourself everything. Did you get a letter from Pavlusha through Semion Evgenyevich and a sum of francs and also a sum of francs worth 2,000 rubles, I don't remember exactly. [Text break]

ES 73

Rostov on/Don 2.XII.19

Lately we have received many letters from you and I myself have written to you often. I gave my last letter to Mr. Werner who is traveling to Lausanne. I wrote to you that Papa deposited 40,000 rubles into the account of Kamenko to pay off the loan and 100,000 rubles so that you can take from as much as you need; we hope that Gordon will also give you something, in addition to the 10,000 francs which we sent you in January. I am trying to arrange all this now. So tell Noi Gordon about it, as I was told by [Janes?], that the banker's receipt [illegible] had been forwarded to him, but we did not get. Ask him to take care of this. On his recommendation, we gave this money to [Janes?], a nephew of Veisbrem[106], an absolutely honest man. We were sure you got this money but it turns out that you, poor thing, in need of that money, would have been able to get 10,000 francs for it based on the local rate of exchange. By the way, Veisbrem is now in Paris and Gordon may know that. Write to both of them. By now you should be getting a pile of letters from us, let us know. We received a postcard from Pavel and he sends you his warm greetings and a kiss. I kiss you both my dear ones, I would very much like to travel to see you but it

106 Probably the Rostov merchant Karl Vasilievich Veisbrem.

is impossible. I also wanted to travel to Tiflis but for now it is also impossible, but I am thinking about it a lot. If you were here, I would dress you from head to toe, I have got everything ready for you: velvet and fur and lingerie etc., but I am afraid I will have to sell everything, mine and yours as well. For the last six years I have made no clothes for myself, I was reduced to complete penury, but I don't regret it because it is strange to me personally to think about a wardrobe when I know, what you, poor thing, are wearing. If there is an opportunity, I will send you some francs, a little at a time. In Rostov the new rate of exchange is 40 rubles for every franc. Find out how many francs is a carat of a diamond, then perhaps I will send you a ring, you can sell it and it will be more profitable. Here a carat of a small diamond is worth 40,000 rubles and bigger ones 50,000 rubles. I have a small diamond ring of three and a half carats and was offered 165,000 for it. Of course, I won't sell it, I'll keep it for a rainy day. We are all in good health, send you our greetings, and are envious that you are living abroad. It's only a pity that the child is not in good health and that you yourself are living such a miserable life alone and without money, but all this will pass. I hope we will see each other soon. Sania is working very hard; he is organizing a psychological institute and the government is giving him money for it; he is a lecturer at the State University and working in all the social institutions. Yasha is also lecturing in [illegible] with great success. How is dear Renatochka's health? I wrote to her.

[2/15.12.19 postscript from father] Your new sister-in-law—Fanni

[Fania] Shpilrein—is still sleeping and her husband [Emil] is on active duty. Along with this we are sending you a letter through [illegible], through Sania.

ES 74

Dear Sabinochka, 15/II 20

How is your life? How is yours and Renatochka's health? I am impatiently waiting for some little news from you. Did you receive my letter through Olga Pavlovna? I also sent a letter through Ol[ga] Yakov[levna] (she is now in Moscow). I got a letter from her yesterday and she writes that somebody is going abroad and she will forward my letter to you through him. I suffer a great deal when you [a few illegible words] and I keep repeating myself, because I don't know if you are receiving my letters. Write to me immediately whether you and the dear child are in good health. Write in detail about everything. I know, my dear, that life is not easy for you, but I bend over backwards to provide for you later. I am afraid that you are going hungry, my God! How my heart aches for you and I cannot offer any help. As far as we are concerned, despite all the hardships I am grateful to fate that all my children and relatives are alive, that is the main thing. God willing we will overcome everything if only we all stay alive. Life will return to normal and in happier days we will reminisce about the hard days of the past. Papa is continually occupied with getting a business trip abroad. It is now better that you are living abroad but [morally?] it is a big quandary. Sania wrote to me that Mr. Gecker, about whom I had written to you, [a line missing?] strongly [illegible] about [illegible]. I will write to him that he should write to you [as soon as] he arrives in London. Yashen'ka is working a lot. I am helping Yasha a great deal financially, and he needs it. He earns 150,000 with perquisites per month and a half, but Silva needles him that his family is living at the expense of Olga Pavlovna. In general, he contributes to his family 70,000 in money and perquisites. In this regard she is impossible. Do not write to me about it; I don't want anyone to know about it. I bought something for you but cannot send it. If you were here I would dress you and Renatochka and help you and provide for you, but unfortunately it is now impossible to help you from afar. I implored Olga Pavlovna to help you with money and words and she promised me. But don't trust Olga Pavlovna's words, even though there is a lot of sweetness in them, but she can do a lot for you as she promised me in view of certain circumstances. Sania wrote that he had a postcard from Pavlusha from Crimea about two and a half months ago. We have had no more news from him. I know that he dreamt about traveling to see you. I am sincerely sorry for him. What happiness it would be if he could [illegible] to both of you. I kiss you and dear Renatochka and wait impatiently for your response.

Mama

[postscript on the left side, in French] My little Rennć! [sic] I hug you and kiss you. I am getting presents ready for you. Your grandmother.

[postscript] I'm terribly sorry that I can't send you the money. How do you do without money, poor thing? I'm desperate when I think about it. Let me know what you live on. What do you eat and what do you feed your child? How is Renatochka's health? Oh, I miss you! I can't bear to suffer any more when I think of you. How would you like to come to Tiflis? I would do anything to go there and to see you. Uncle Moisei would take care of you until my arrival. I am not asking for anything gratis. I did not think we would part for such a long time. We have endured a lot, a lot, we have suffered enough, but never mind, we only have to meet and all live together. I don't grumble, I just want all of you to be alive so we can all meet.

[postscript] If there is an opportunity in Moscow and you want to write to me something secret about Olga Pavlovna, write Olga Yakovlevna. Write to

Moscow and she will forward it. I kiss you and our dear child. Goodbye, may God protect you.

Mama

[postscript] Cordial greetings. Milia

[postscript] Greetings to dear Sabina and Renata. Fania

ES 75

My dear Sabinochka! Rostov on/Don 23 August 1920

Lately I sent you many letters on various occasions, but I doubt if they reached their destination, therefore I have to repeat myself. Tomorrow morning Olga Pavlovna is traveling to Moscow and from there abroad and this time I believe you will receive my letter. [In principle?] I will write what I have already written many times, and Olga Pavlovna will gradually send you all the details. I'll say the main thing: Mr. Gecker is a distant relative of ours and a very, very nice gentleman, he lives permanently in London. Before leaving Rostov he left me a check drawn on a London bank, and he did not even want to take any money from me until the rate of exchange went back to normal. For a long time there was no opportunity to send you this check and only a month and a half to two months ago I sent this check to Senia to forward it to you through Bebochka and Rozochka Lublinskiis, daughters of uncle Moisei. Now I would like to know if you received this money. Write about it to Mr. Gecker and mention that I sent money and maybe they have not yet returned home or maybe they were robbed or something else happened. Perhaps you could ask Mr. Gecker if he could offer you financial help and tell him that at the earliest opportunity I will give him all the money back with great gratitude. Here is his address: A.W. Gecker 26 Falkland Road, Kentish Town London NW. Mr. Gecker is a lawyer, a very rich man but is now busy with something else. Kamenko wrote to us that for the money you took from him we owe him 40,000 rubles because in the meantime you have taken more money from him, so we sent him 140,000 rubles and asked him in the future to give you as much as you need. This happened approximately six to seven months ago. I would like to know what was the fate of this money. You will write to Olga Pavlovna and she will forward the letter here. I cannot stop thinking about you and Renatochka. The suffering is endless, probably because there is no possibility to help you. Regarding the money, Olga Pavlovna will tell you that in order to make it possible for you to live on 500 francs a month I have to withdraw at least 150,000 rubles a month. In addition, even if I had that money, it is now forbidden to export currency from here [text break?]

[postscript] Milia asked Fania to sign "Shpilrein"

ES 76

Dear Sabinochka! [21/9.20]

Almost three weeks ago Olga Pavlovna left Rostov. I forwarded to you two letters with though her. Now Olga Yakovlevna is traveling with Nadiusha to Moscow. I gave her a letter for you, perhaps there will be an opportunity for her to mail this letter to you. We are all in good health, we and the relatives are doing well. Thank God. Don't worry about us, think only of yourself and the child.

It upsets me terribly that I cannot send you any money. How, poor child, are you doing without money? I get desperate when I think about it. Tell me what money do you live on? What are you eating and what do you feed the child? How is Renatochka's health? Oh, I miss you so much! I have no strength left to suffer when I think about you. What if you could go to Tiflis? I would do anything to travel there to see you all. Uncle Moisei would surely take care of you until I arrive and I certainly am not asking for anything [for free?]. I did not think we would be separated for such a long time. We have all been through so much, we have suffered enough, but it doesn't matter as long as we can meet again and live all together. I do not grumble, I only want one thing: that you should all live and that we should all meet again. Yasha was offered a chair in Rostov, how do you like that trick! Now the poor boy has to live economically even though he is getting a good salary. Silva has big needs and she always complains that Yasha is cavalier and does not care for the family, i.e., that he does not go to the bazaar to sell little boxes. I also suffer very much for him, poor boy. Olga Pavlovna was very angry with me that I wasn't giving Silva enough to have an opulent life at 20,000 rubles a month but now even this sum would not satisfy her, she would want a full [pantry] and at least 100,000 a month. Where can I find such money? Is Silva the only one I have to worry about? She must be kidding. Olga Pavlovna promised me to take care of you; mail your letters to her so that she would forward them to me. Your silence is oppressing me and I picture the most horrible scenes. If only I received something comforting from you. The main thing is yours, and Renatochka's health.

[postscript from father] Mama didn't leave enough space for a postscript.

Anyway, there is not much to write about. I am now rushing to work; I am serving in the provincial department for plant protection. It's your birthday soon [25/10, the old style]. If I am still alive, my thoughts will be with you and your little daughter.

Signature

[postscript] If there is an opportunity to mail a letter to Moscow and if you want to tell me a secret about Olga Pavlovna, write to Olga Yakovlevna.

A cordial greeting, Milia.

Greetings to dear Sabina and Renata, Fania, 21/9.20.

ES 77

Dear Sabinochka, Undated

We received a letter from Pavlusha and are forwarding it to you. Yesterday was his birthday; I bought pastries and went to his sisters to have tea. We spent close to an hour together. Ida seems to be a rather warm-hearted young woman. Pavlusha is suffering a great deal because he is far from his family and I feel sorry for him; he lives alone among strangers. At the same time his daughter is growing and he cannot see her. I and papa sent Renatochka a letter directly to her address; it will be interesting to see how she reacted to this letter, write to us about it. In general, in your letters, write a little bit more about Renatochka, it is our only pleasure [illegible]—from granddaughters and grandsons. Milia now has a child, he is beautiful and a very nice little boy, now six months old. You probably know that I and papa are moving to live in Moscow. We think of leaving within a month or a month and a half. Sania with family and Yasha are already there. I am very [worried?] about Sania. I will write to you separately because papa is now rushing to mail this letter. Your scientific accomplishments make us extremely happy but your finances distress us. I would like to send you a thing which you could sell and have money to live on and am waiting for an opportunity to send it. Are you in good health? Is the child healthy? Write more about yourself. Greetings from all of us and from Babitskaia. Revekka Ter-Oganesian[107].

Kisses,

Mama

[postscript from Emil]. Cordial greetings, Milia

[postscript from father] I send you my greeting. A month ago from Moscow I sent you a registered letter and a registered printed matter; did you get them? 8/7.21 A few days ago we sent a letter to Renatochka directly to Chateau d'Oex. Address your letters to us as follows: Rostovdon Postal Box No. 97 N.A. Shpilrein.

[postscript from mother]I [will make] every effort to be able to meet with you and Renatochka. Poor Pavlusha [2 illegible words] now; therefore he has a great need to have a family [illegible]. I write to you infrequently but still a fair amount, for a long time I had pain in my right hand.

107 Revekka Ter-Oganesian (see her letters).

ES 78

My dear Sabinochka, Rostov on/Don 19 August, 21

The Fräulein about whom I wrote to you has left. She was my masseuse and she was quite at home here. As I wrote to you, you can learn all about us from her. She went to work in some little town near Vienna. From her you will receive my gold watch on a bracelet, i.e. on a gold chain. You don't have to pay any duty because I didn't buy it recently and it will be considered as used. In addition, Fräulein should give you three hundred francs of her own money, she promised me that. So that you [have an idea] about the watch in case it will be necessary to sell it, I have to tell you that a long time ago I was offered a million rubles for it but didn't want to sell it. If you could do without selling it, wear it and enjoy it; I couldn't send you anything else. Exporting foreign currency is against the law, and the same applies to diamonds over a certain [carat], so those too may not be exported; [a mother?] is not allowed to carry them either, that is all. One may own only one watch, irrespective of whether I have it or my daughter has it. I have asked you many times whether you got money from a London bank through a check from Gecker, about a year and a half ago, and I still know nothing about it. It would be a great pity if this money was lost. I suffer very much because you don't have enough money and you are in need of financial help, and I cannot help you in any way now. Only when we meet will I be able to help you, but in the meantime, your young years are passing. I feel for you, I suffer with you and I cannot help. Write to Gecker in London, perhaps he is there now and will do something for you; but he was all the time in Tiflis staying with Moisei. Do write to Fräulein. I received a letter from Pavlusha for you and I attach it to the present one. He writes to us very frequently and all his letters are filled with suffering because of you and the child. He longs for you and he is sad. On the whole, he got very emotional. Did Renatochka get our letter we had sent to her address? How did she react to it? Why doesn't she answer us? It would be a pleasure to receive a separate letter written by her. Milia has a wonderful child seven months old. His name is Marochka and he is our first grandson. He is beautiful, rowdy and lively. Milia is in the Caucasus in Tiflis on a business trip, we expect him in about two to three days. Fania and the child are staying with me. Meanwhile, papa and I are moving to Moscow where papa has already landed a job. We hope to see you. This is my dream. Do not be sad, do not suffer, be a brave woman, and don't lose your presence of mind, so that you won't lose your health. You will soon have a better life. These are not just words, this is a fact. Kisses to you and Renatochka.

ES 79

My Dear Sabinochka, Moscow 23 September 21

As you can see, we are all in Moscow and Pavlusha is with us. You didn't expect that? We all have one goal, to come to you. Shall we be succeed? God only knows. Pavlusha is working to arrange it, and so does papa, but there is very little hope. I got rid of all my possessions; I am done with everything and I left for Moscow with the secret intention to travel to see you. However, in order to be able to do that I must again go to Rostov, and perhaps even to Tiflis, so as to be able, sooner or later, travel to you. Will I succeed? That is the question. And if we don't succeed, can you come to us for one month? Yasha will write to you about this. It occurred to him that you might give a few lectures here and you would have to write about it to someone, Yasha will tell you to whom, so that you will be able to leave here when you wish. I have had no letters from you for a long time and it worries me a great deal. I wrote to you often and am surprised that you have not received my letters. We are now living in terrible conditions. We are all in one room with Sania: papa, I, Sania, Yasha, and Pavlusha. Some sleep on the floor, others in beds. [We traveled?] from Rostov in separate railway cars for twelve days, it was difficult to find a room. We were in Moscow three days and unable to unpack our luggage. I am writing with Renatochka's portrait in front of me. It is night now, 10 o'clock, papa is asleep, Sania is on call today and I am expecting Pavlusha by 10:30, and if he does not come, I will lie down as we agreed and he'll spend the night on a couch at an acquaintance's place, he must be sick and tired of sleeping on the floor. I have not seen Moscow yet, I am not in the mood, my head is chock full of worries about serious problems, my thoughts are going around and around about you and Milia. By the way, Milia's child is pure joy. Everybody is delighted, including Vera [last name unclear], now in transit in Moscow on the way to Petrograd, where she was drafted as a doctor. We talked a great deal with her about you, reminisced about childhood, she admired Renatochka's photograph and found her to be a beauty. How strange that Renatochka is already a big girl. Why hasn't she answered our letter written by me and addressed to her personally? It would be so pleasant to get a little letter from her! Write to us immediately, more about yourself and personally about Renatochka. I am afraid my letter may not reach you! How is your <u>health</u>? Write immediately a letter addressed to Sania. We kiss you and dear Renatochka.

Mama

[postscript from father]. 25/9.21 Greetings. [signature]

ES 80

Dear Sabinochka! Undated

Everybody is gone, I am alone, I am very sad. I am told that I may be allowed to travel to you sooner than the others, and of course I'll do all I can to accomplish this. But anyway, I can only travel in three to four months from now, because first I have to travel to Rostov and Tiflis and back to Moscow, and then try to go to see you. It is necessary to go to Rostov and Tiflis and I'll explain why the next time. Did you get my watch and letter from Fräulein, did she give you some of her money? Let me know. We haven't received a letter from you in ages and I am so worried about you that I get exhausted. I feel that you are sick, that you are suffering, and I am powerless to help. Pavlusha is now in the library and reading some article of yours. Oh, the poor man. He is leaving Rostov with nothing about you and he wants to see you so much. If it would be possible for you and Renatochka to come temporarily for a month or two how great that would be, but you would have to [secure?] a proper document to be able to go back; you could come to Rostov or Moscow and give a few lectures in your specialty. Yasha is getting ready to write to you about it, but he doesn't find the time to do it. I wish a letter from you would come soon. Don't hide anything, tell everything. Renatochka's photograph is hanging over my table. My God, how I would like to see her. I am awaiting your letter impatiently. I kiss you and the child

Mama

[postscript] Did you get the first monies from London? Ask Gecker for money if he is in London. I am sure he will not refuse. I am afraid he is still in Tiflis. Sania and Roza [a few illegible words] he is an unusual person. But cheer up, if you only knew how much suffering there is these days, all your personal matters would seem ridiculous. The Koffmans live not far away from me—an irony of fate. Stay healthy, cheerful, your [illegible] are not idle but thinking about you. I kiss Renatochka.

Mama [omitted part of a letter, torn in places with numerous illegible words]

ES 81

My Dear Sabina! 13th October 1921

I write to you endlessly and apparently my letters are not reaching you or you would have answered or sent some news item. Therefore I have to repeat myself frequently and this gets to be boring and annoying . So now I am asking you for the hundredth time, did you receive my letter, my bracelet with a watch I had sent with the Austrian Fräulein? She could have told you about everything happening to us here. Before her, I frequently wrote and forwarded letters to you, but after the letter to Fräulein I expected to have information about you in Moscow, but in vain. We arrived here together with Pavlusha who is longing for both of you with all his heart. He also wrote to you a few times but you did not answer. Unable to wait any longer, he left without a word from you. He did not succeed to travel to you. One has to wait a few months. Papa is busy all the time to arrange something and should papa travel to you, I would have to remain in Russia for now. Yasha will explain everything to you. Sania is now here, if I could send you something with him, it would be good, but I don't know for sure. We are waiting for news from you every day. Right now papa and Yasha went together to get it. I have so many questions but all are getting lost, but since I wrote about everything a thousand times, I will now wait for your letter. The main thing is are you healthy? Is Renatochka healthy? I can't wait to know more details about you. Write a lot, a lot, and also to Pavlusha, I'll forward your letter to him. I have to leave, and I am waiting for your letter. Did you get money from London? Milia is staying in Rostov. He has a wonderful baby, Marochka. Oh, how I miss that child. He is simply a charm. I am attaching a letter to Renatochka. I kiss you.

[postscripts] Waiting for a letter. How I am suffering [together?] with you. It's a pity that Pavlusha is not near you now. He is dying to be with you. Did you sell the [fur?] I am writing to you the fourth or fifth letter from Moscow, and how painful it is to realize that you did not receive anything. Why is dear Renatochka sick so often? Is it true she has appendicitis? Poor you.

Dear Sabinochka!

Just now Yasha brought your postcard with words by Renatochka. I cried all day today because of your fate, how you are suffering, poor thing, how can I help you financially? I would have to send you 10–15 million rubles just to help you a little bit. Where can I get them? I wrote to you that Sania is so kind and will take from me one thing which will help you considerably. I am very worried about yours and Renata's health. Tell me the truth, only the truth, Yasha promises me that he will take care of you upon arrival in Berlin. He thinks you would be able to come to Moscow temporarily. He will discuss this with somebody [illegible] and [illegible] he is leaving on Thursday. Did you really get nothing from Moscow [illegible]?

ES 82

My dear Sabinochka, 27 October 1921

I am writing to you to congratulate you on your birthday but I cannot liftmy hand. It seems to me like a mockery that for some years we have all been wishing you the best, but actually each year, poor thing, you are getting worse. Every day, every hour my thoughts are about you, but what is the point of it? My thoughts and words will not make your life better. If you could find someone to help you for at least three months, then during this time I could help you by getting some money; the main thing is that I should be near you, so that you would be better off both financially and morally. Papa is doing all he can to travel to see you but it's still not a solution, because he is <u>not allowed</u> to take a lot of money with him which means that he can only help a little. The French franc costs 10,000 rubles. It means that if you receive a million you will only get 100 francs, therefore, in order to give you 500 francs a month we would have to give you five million rubles a month. If I come, I will certainly give you a full rest, but then I would have to take you out of Switzerland, because financially it means a ruin. Sixty million rubles a year is beyond our powers. I have written to you a few times that you should write to Gecker in London. If he is there, he will certainly help you and I will pay him back. He is the nicest and kindest person I have ever known. Lately he has been in Tiflis but is getting ready to go to London. In any case, write to him, he will not ignore your letter, I vouch for it. If only he is in London, he will immediately answer you and send money. I am very afraid that you will fall ill with exhaustion and suffering. I have not a minute of peace. Where are you now? How is your health? How can you, poor girl carry everything on your back? How is Renatochka? Consult another doctor, see what he can tell you. Merciful God! How everything has befallen us! I will send something for you with Sania, but he probably will only be back in Berlin in three weeks. Believe me, my dear, I think about you all the time how to help you; maybe in a few days I will be able to send you some money, as much as is allowed. I only pray to God that you and dear Renatochka should be alive and healthy. I stay awake nights thinking about you. Be strong my dear, don't lose your presence of mind, think about your health. Silva promised to handle selling your less needed things, perhaps a source of support, may be you will get a few thousand. Who knows? But I don't know what kind of things you have. You have a lot of elegant things made of silver and nickel, and also bronzes, tableware, kitchen appliances, antique things, rugs etc. [curtains?], drapes, there is plenty of it. I suggest you keep the lingerie for now. Pavlusha asked to sell his suits but I am not going to touch it. All this, i.e. your financial situation will become clear within a month. I hope that Yasha will do something for you. Meanwhile I would advise you to turn to the Professor [Bleuler], explain to him your financial situation and ask him for a job. Maybe my advice is coming too late and you have already turned to many professors and colleagues? Is it possible that none of your colleagues can understand your situation? If only I got a line from you. I am now waiting in Moscow only for you and cannot leave here without getting a letter from you. I would like to exchange a few letters with you and then travel to you. Then only will I be able to send you money. Write to me for God's sake. Did you get all my letters from Moscow? Write in detail about yourself and Renatochka, I am losing my patience waiting to hear from you. I kiss you and my dear granddaughter.

Mama

[postscripts]

Milia is in Rostov with his family taking his examinations. I wrote to you about Pavlusha. Vera [last name illegible] is visiting us daily, she is in Moscow, drafted as doctor. Babitskaia is in Rostov and working in an infirmary.

Greetings from all of us, from Olga Yakovlevna, Nadia, and [illegible]. All live in Moscow. I just talked a lot about you with Olga Yakovlevna, the letter was written yesterday. Today, again, there is not letter from you. I am losing my mind [some illegible words].

My dear Sabinochka!

I write to you endlessly but no word from you. What does it mean? Did you get my letter from Fräulein in Austria? I am now preparing a third letter for mailing. I wrote a long letter to Renatochka and will mail it tomorrow. I wrote to you frequently from Rostov. Yasha is going to Berlin and will write to you. I am waiting impatiently for your letter. Kisses for you and Renata. Greetings to all of you. I learned all the details about you from Sania. I am happy Silva now has a place where she can rest. Kisses to the children. All the best, E[va] Shp[ilrein].

[postscript form Yan]

Please forward to Sabina. I will probably travel on the 17th [?] Greetings.

[signature]

ES 83

Dear Sabinochka Moscow 17.XI.1921

Why are you silent again? In Moscow we received from you a very brief little letter and a long one. I have sent you many letters from here and hope they have been reaching you. Tell me quickly, how you are feeling? Are your lungs healthy? I recall that you used to suffer from chronic bronchitis. How are you enduring such grueling work? Are you well dressed? What kind of clothing do you have? Aren't you freezing? And what is with Renatochka? How is her health? Did you arrange surgery for her? How did Renatochka react to your taking her to live with you? Would she want to stay with your acquaintance? I believe that your situation should now improve a little bit, I did send you something, Silva will write to you and send you something from the sale of some of your less needed things. I wrote to you a long time ago that you should write to Gecker in London and have recently sent you his address, I'm sure he would help you. He is the nicest person. Tell me finally, did you get any checks from London or did somebody else get them and use them? I need to know this because we will have to pay him back. I beg you to inform me about this. I frequently get letters from Milia and Fania, they live in peace and friendship and it makes me happy. Marochka is a wonderful child, whoever comes from there speaks about him with delight. Milia is getting ready for his examinations and Fania will soon have to take hers, too. We have no letters from Pavlusha, they are probably getting lost, impossible that he shouldn't be writing to us. Milia sends letters when there is an opportunity, not by mail. I see Menikhochka and Roza very rarely; they live well, even very well. Sania is in the same room with us, which is very uncomfortable, but nothing can be done, we have to go through these tough times. I am very happy for you that you find gratification only in science, otherwise it would be totally difficult. Do you have any close acquaintances? Who do you meet with? How did poor Strashunskaia overcome her crisis? I am waiting impatiently for news from you. Write to Pavlusha separately and I will forward it to him when the occasion arises. I kiss you and Renatochka

Mama

[postscript] the letter was written a few days ago, had no time to mail it.

ES 84

My dear Sabinochka! 25/XI 21

Renatochka's birthday is coming up soon and I congratulate you on her birthday. May she grow to give joy to you and all of us. May God grant her health and happiness. On her birthday I will certainly be back in Rostov and spend the day with her father, uncle, and aunt. I am leaving very upset that there is still no letter from you. Why am I staying in Moscow? All I had was one letter and one postcard in three months. Tell me about your health. How are your lungs? Don't hide anything from me. Before starting work in Berlin, rest well with Renatochka and make sure she gets a high calories diet for about two months. You are extremely exhausted and this may lead to tuberculosis. I remember that you often complained of chronic bronchitis.

Write to Gecker in London, he is now in London, he had been in all the time in Tiflis. He is the nicest person. His address is: London NW Falkland Road

Kentish Town Gecker. Write to him frankly about everything and he will help you, and in time I will pay him back. If you knew what a wonderful person he is, you would write him without any hesitation. Write to him immediately, send him my most cordial greetings. I have no doubt that you will receive money from him, and I have just learned from Sania that he is in London. He also offered to send Sania money to Tiflis. Describe to him everything in detail, how bad your situation is, and you will get the money immediately. I am sending you Pavlusha's letter which I received. I am also sending you Fania's letter with a postscript for you. Marochka has an unusual sense of hearing, guests are delighted with him. Fabrikant cannot stop talking about him. Briefly, all my granddaughters and grandson are unusual. Write to papa addressed c/o the National Commissariat for Agriculture, Section for Plant Protection, Old Square 6. Maybe this way one will get it sooner. By the way, you should give this address to Yasha because he forwards the letters. Did you get any letters from Fräulein? Oh, how tired I am of asking the same questions. Goodbye, my dear. How hard it is for me to leave here knowing so little about you. But I have to go to get the money. If you lived in Russia, I would be able to help you financially but it's really impossible to help you in Switzerland, there are not enough riches for that, the franc is too high. I kiss you and dear Renatochka.

Mama

[postscript from Yan] Greetings, I am still unable to leave. We will see.

[signature]

ES 85

My dear Sabina! Rostov on/Don 24.XII.21

I am really tired of writing to you and not getting an answer. I do not know what is the cause of your silence, since I know that you write often to Yasha and Silva and nothing to me or Pavlusha. In every letter I have systematically asked you many questions and have received no answer till now. Previously I thought you were not getting my letters, but I know that my letters are reaching you, since Yasha and Silva are forwarding them to you. I see Pavlusha almost daily and every time my heart aches for him seeing he suffers. He is very eager to travel to you but his success is nil. If only he could spend three months with you, discuss how to organize your subsequent life together with you, see you and the child. What plans he always makes, dreaming of seeing you and Renatochka. How he will talk with her? How she will relate to him? But you both are stuck in Switzerland and do not realize how much we talk about you. I have good grounds to think that papa will soon travel to Berlin and that you will meet each other there. Papa is getting business trips abroad, the rest remains to be seen. You will learn from papa everything regarding us and Pavlusha. I am very glad that you find satisfaction in science, at least a big consolation in your loneliness. Yasha wrote us that in the last month you were getting a salary of 1250 francs a month and this made me extremely happy though it also made me think how much you must toil and tire to earn it. How is your financial situation now? How are the doctors treating you? You wrote earlier that many people envy you. Are you corresponding with Bleuler? Regarding Pavlusha, what kind of connections did you refer to thinking of helping him? Did you think about it seriously or just got carried away? Pavlusha read this phrase with trepidation.

Please write sooner and write more, your letters are so infrequent that I end up reading them 20 times and always looking for something new in them. I am now sitting alone in the room where you lived before you got married. In this room are now living Milia, Fania, and Marochka. Milia is now in Moscow, Fania went away for a few days to her family to wean Marochka from breastfeeding. It is evening now, none of the lodgers are at home, they will come either late between 1 and 2 AM or they won't come at all. I forgot to tell you that I am now living in one room with Milia and Fania, because all the other rooms are occupied by strangers. I now feel both sad and terrified, and I am up to my neck with correspondence and all kinds of matters. I wrote to papa, to Sania, I am writing to you, then to Yasha and Silva. This is what keeps me alive now. We celebrated together Renatochka's birthday, i.e., more precisely, Pavlusha and I marked it, for it is impossible to celebrate anything now. How is dear Renatochka doing? Why doesn't she write to us? It is such a joy for us when we get her little letter, written by her little hand. How is her health? How is your health? Write, for God's sake. Milia and Fania wrote to you many times and you did not answer; Marochka even sent greetings to you and Renatochka. What a charming child Milia and Fania have. There is no person who has not been charmed by him. Everyone is charmed by him, including your husband. All right, enough for today. Goodnight to you and Renatochka, I kiss you both

Mama

[illegible] with you Renatochka? Write now to this address:

Pushkainskaya 97, apartment 3, second floor.

ES 86

Dear Sabinochka! Undated

Pavlusha was rushing to work, he wrote a few words to you and left. I wrote to you yesterday and sent the letter by registered mail. When we were in Moscow and we all wrote to you together, Pavlusha wrote the Geneva address on the envelope, but the city is Lausanne, and therefore I think you did not get those Letters, an answer to which I had been waiting impatiently. Did you get a letter from Fräulein? Did you get the watch on a bracelet which I had sent through her? I have already asked you these questions twenty times. Did you receive what I had sent you with Sania? I am now leaving the house to take care of some business. I have so many things to do: busy with financial issues and matters, with your country house. They started dismantling your building, I had a very tough time with your country house, last time Pavlusha went there and I am grateful to him. I got completely exhausted because I alone have to be everywhere and I am busy day and night. Papa is getting ready to travel abroad, he received a business trip but he still has a lot of trouble with it [a few illegible words] I wrote and I have to find the letter. Milia is in Moscow, Fania and Marochka are with her family, she is no longer breastfeeding Marochka, she is returning tomorrow. Goodbye, write more frequently. I met Babitskaya who sends her greetings to you and also to [Shporlinskaya].

Mama

[postscript] I received a letter from Strashunskaya, I had written to you long ago that he married another [illegible], I will him and write a letter. [a few illegible words]

4.5 LETTERS FROM THE IN-LAW FAMILY TO SPIELREIN

SSh 1

From mother-in-law Sofia Sheftel. Undated

My dear and darling daughter Sabina

I received your letter and thank you for it. I would love to speak with you and tell you that you should not be afraid and stay calm and, with God's help, you will give birth to the child and it will turn out alright. Believe me, my dear daughter, I bore eight children and it is not at all scary to bear children. It is not such a big trouble even if it hurts a little. But the pleasure you feel later, when you see a child lying on a pillow, will make you forget that it hurt a little bit before. Therefore, I ask you, dear daughter, do not be afraid and have hope that everything will turn out well. Happy times will come, and you will see before you can say knife, that you are the mother of a happy child. It is every woman's nature to be afraid of being pregnant. Please do not be afraid and eat well, eat a lot of fruit. It is funny I should be telling you all this since you are a doctor yourself and know it better than me, but I am more experienced in the practice of giving birth and I know it better than you. And here is what I will tell you, my dear daughter. I gave birth to Fania fully dressed, I almost tossed her out, there was not enough time for the midwife to come. The maid picked Fania off the floor and afterwards I went to bed and felt completely fine as if nothing happened; but then, of course, I got sick, and this too easy childbirth became not so trouble free. I walked about a little bit in the room and then went to bed. Later an abscess developed in my abdomen and I stayed in bed for a few months. My dear late husband did not permit surgery and wanted to wait until the abscess opened by itself. After the boil burst I felt weak. For a long time poultices were applied. All the professors and doctors that came made the wrong diagnosis, and that is why my dear late husband did not allow lancing the boil. After the boil opened by itself I made a complete recovery. Then all the doctors said that I should leave my husband and have no more children because as soon as I got pregnant again I would die. I only want to tell you what these doctors and professors were saying. I went away and stayed with my parents for six months and left my husband and four children. I have to say to you, my dear daughter, that you and Pavlusha, and all my children with their husbands and wives, should live as well and as happily as I lived with my dear husband. I returned to him looking beautiful and healthy, and, of course, got pregnant again. I did think I might die but in spite of that I took hold of myself and thought to myself, I have given birth to four children and I will succeed to give birth to one more. And imagine, dear Sabina, I gave birth to Ania, I gave birth to her in one hour, and I wish you should give birth as easily to your child. I left my guests and I went to look for the midwife. I came back with her. I myself entered the house through the door and made the midwife enter through the window. I will tell you now why I did this. I was afraid to be seen walking with the midwife because they might give me the evil eye.

So you can see, dear daughter, how I died when after Fania I gave birth to Ania, Pavlusha, Katia and Ida. Well, tell me, what would the doctors say now. I ask you not to be afraid, to be cheerful and healthy, to live happily together with Pavlusha and rejoice in your life. When the happy moment arrives for you to give birth, may delivery be for you as easy and good as your loving mother wishing you wholeheartedly all the best. I kiss you warmly and ask you to keep giving me the constant pleasure of receiving letters from you.

Your loving mother

[postscript] Kisses and greetings from me to Pavlusha. Ida sends her regards, she has now gone to [Ernestina?].

Dear Sabina, I take this opportunity to add my best wishes for peace and cheerfulness of mood. I just send a hello, because my hand got tired of writing; I became my mother's letter writer and wrote everything in her name. Be well. Warm kisses.

Your loving Katia.

Greetings to Pavlusha. Today I will write to him too, perhaps, even though I sent him a postcard just yesterday.

FSh 1

From sister-in-law Fania Sheftel, undated

Dear Sabina,

I got your address from your father and I am writing to you after a long silence. My God, how surprised and happy I was when I learned that you are now a mother. My cordial congratulations, I am very happy for you. What happiness it must be to have your own dear child. I learnt about it quite accidentally; the thing is that I have been ill until now and have not yet recovered and now I am getting ready to travel to Berlin to get treatment. Knowing that you're always somewhere in Europe I asked your father for your address and how wonderfully it turned out that you are in Berlin right now. Or else we might have been in the same city and not know of the existence of each other. How are you feeling, my dear, I am so happy thinking that I will see you and, what is important, in the role of wife and mother. I will not write anything about myself now, I will tell when we meet. I think of travelling after the Christmas holidays or may be sooner. I am now living in [illegible] but will soon move to Odessa and if you are able to get up, drop me a line (and I will be very happy) to Odessa (Spiridonovskaya street, 22, to Dr. [illegible]). Warm kisses,

your Fania

4.6 LETTERS FROM YAN SHPIELREIN TO SABINA

YS 1

Hello, Sabina 7.V.10

Finally I arrived in Karlsruhe and reached a somewhat normal state; as usual, there is a lot to do and therefore I cannot tell you about it in as much detail as I would like to. I will try. So here I am. A few days later, Boris Ilyich [Silva's father] decided to help us children, because otherwise they won't be able to help themselves, and made me a kind of proposal. I accepted it, and to mark the occasion, a champagne reception was arranged by the ancestors. In my dazed state of mind

I completely forgot the existence of my own wishes, principles, etc. and let the ancestors arrange everything. As a result, my work at the factory has all gone to pot, most of the time was spent in making visits. Ten days later I came to my senses: why do we need a wedding with all the gimmicks if it is possible to arrange it quite informally. But the ancestors made an awful uproar: how can one do that, all the lady friends of the family have ordered dresses from fashionable milliners, and now for this thing to happen!...We had to agree. The wedding was arranged in the Ryss apartment; they invited various mangy and non-mangy Zhids[108], then they set up a canopy as illustrated in the drawing they placed me in the center, and then a whole gang of Jews started turning Silva around me,

Words in drawing upper: Silva Jews; middle: me; lower: direction of turning

followed thereafter by clinking glasses and accompanied by speeches of average quality. Papa made quite an impassioned speech that might have been wonderful, had he not shouted so wildly and loudly. I wanted to [illegible] Silva but was unsuccessful. Thereafter I was recognized as a married man and even kept wearing a golden ring. The in-laws arranged quite a nice evening at our place which impressed me rather pleasantly. Soon thereafter I travelled (alone) via Warsaw, Berlin, and Leipzig, Silva will arrive later. It is rather strange; all this seems to me now quite empty and drab. And indeed, all these rituals are so banal, so narrow-minded. However, it was interesting to observe all kinds of people and their behavior. I was able to observe many funny incidents but is difficult to describe it in a letter and, moreover, Karlsruhe is affecting me in such a depressing way that it kills all enthusiasm. Whereas in Russia my head was brimming with all kinds of vivid images and even "symbolic games," I presently am unable to entertain even one decent thought. But it will pass. As a result, I'm staying in Karlsruhe to complete my studies and so is Silva. Nobody knows what I will do next, even I myself don't know, there are heaps of plans and I don't know what I will choose. I have now been elected chairman of the reading room. It is an honorific duty but a lot of fuss. For now best wishes, write.

108 In Russian Zhid was the pejorative synonym of Yevrey = Jew.

[signature]

In what [illegible] did you sprain your hand? Who married Tolbitskaya and who is marrying Baryshnikova? Rabinovich would like to know. Sonia Ryss [Silva's sister] sends you her warm greetings.

YS 2

My dear ones! 13.I.13

I hasten to wish you a happy New Year and on this occasion wish you all the corresponding tzimmes[109]: to Sabina – to do a psychoanalysis on Bettmann-Holwegg[110], to Pavlusha – to be the court doctor of both von..., the chief of police and the minister, together with their wives, daughters, dogs, cats, canaries, etc. I learned from a reliable source that Sabina was ill with quinsy; the same source informed me that she is back home, but this is not enough and we do not know what happened next. I hope you will find out and let us know. It turns out that literary work in our specialty is paid very well: and so, for example, for one page 30 cm x 50 cm in an important journal we are paid 80 crowns, completely irrespective of the content, whether it be pictures, tables, or formulas – all we need is to get going. Irina caught a slight cold, yesterday the temperature was even 38.6. The doctor [illegible], and all the rest, but she is better today (*angina catarrhalis*). I had a talk with my boss about my doctoral dissertation but so far nothing is known. Now we are expecting guests to come for the first time since we arrived in Stuttgart.

[postscript by Silva]

Regards and best wishes for the New Year. How is your health, Sabina? Sania wrote that you have already recovered, how are you doing? Are you occupied? Pavel Naumovich, have you got accustomed to Germany and to your work? Yesterday we celebrated New Year and at night we took a walk in the snowy field. So long for now, all the best.

Silva.

YS 3

My dear ones! [printed] Stuttgart, 21/9 13

I didn't even suspect there was a possibility to baptize the married couple Sheftel, and even if such an unpleasant event were to happen, I would not think

109 Honey-flavored vegetable dish served at Jewish new year feast.

110 Theobald Theodor Friedrich Alfred von Bethmann-Hollweg (1856–1921) was Chancellor of the German Empire from 1909 to 1917.

of boycotting you – I am not a Zionist, after all. My (our) silence is very simple to explain. First, I write to nobody except in the most necessary cases. Second, lengthy traveling in various countries took time. Third, I intended to make copies of some lovely photographs and waited for them to be ready...but it will take a long time, so I prefer to send a letter without the photographs. We have little news to report. My patents (at least one) are ready but so far I have not received any money for it. Irina is growing up and gradually becoming wiser. Recently (in England) we had this conversation: – Mama, I would like to have a baby, I will give it food and put it to bed. –You are too small for that. –Yes, but you are not small. –Auntie Sabina will have a child and who has given it to her as a present? – Uncle Paul. [German in original]. The last words were said without any suggestion from us. And even more curious, how she cannot distinguish between "today" and "tomorrow": it is always "today" and when will "tomorrow" be? This is a profound philosophical question. Silva is doing the cooking until the first day of the month for we have no maid. She sends you her most cordial regards. Kushik would also be sending regards but she is asleep. Write about yourself, what are the most recent events? They say that mother will travel to Berlin in a month and that you are apparently settling down in Berlin. Does that mean you have decided to live among the Prussians? Wishing you all the best. Your [signature]

YS 4

My dear ones Stuttgart, 6/12 13

It is evident that the married couple Sheftel are lousy gynecologists or else we would not have had to wait so long for the "happy event" (*freudiges Ereignis*) to happen. I definitely expected to get acquainted with the new Jewish creature at end of December, mother also informed me that the child is expected at the beginning of November. I will be able to visit you probably on the 24th and, probably, stay for about five days. I expected that the whole family will gather in Berlin by that time but now I see that neither papa nor Milchik will come. At least, if Sania were able to drag himself over. Milchik should be trained very thoroughly because in many ways he has become as undisciplined as an old hag: he is nervous, he is picky with food. If he has to sit in a stuffy railway car for about half an hour he starts complaining of a headache! And when I suggested to him to travel at night in a third class car to Berlin he almost fainted: how will I be able to sleep! Briefly, he would have to live for a while wrapped in wadding. Monday and Tuesday after dinner I have work to do at the Institute and I don't know if papa will want to travel with me on Wednesday. Therefore I traveled today to see Golder. There will be more details when I see him. Already eight years ago they tried to produce galoshes but they didn't do it the right way and therefore nothing came of it. Now, upon my advice, they will test slightly modified forms. Anyway, their factory is antediluvian, more details when we meet. Regards to you all, tomorrow from 10 till 12 I'll be at the Institute.

[signature]

[Postscript from Milia] He [Yan] is a gossip monger, he created a big tattle tale that I am allegedly nervous and like a hag, he is lying, for I am neither one nor the other and as far as Berlin is concerned I simply said it would be more convenient to travel third class in the morning than at night. I implore you to write to him not to call me anymore a pregnant donkey or a pregnant horse or even a green [illegible].

[signed Emil]

YS 5

My dear ones! Stuttgart 17/4/14

I am fully aware of the character of my silence, but there's nothing I can do about it. Lately I am constantly studying and even at night I keep dreaming about elliptical integrals. My only real achievement is the improvement of my handwriting due to the necessity to write formulas slowly and clearly. We are very keenly touched by your invitation to stay with you in Berlin and we are also especially interested to see our niece, but those blessed times when we were able to travel are now over. We are not doing well with money, and if by July I have not won the lottery, the situation will become bad altogether. Time will tell, although there is not much time left (until July).

In general, living in Stuttgart has given us many delights, our entire mountain is covered with blooming fruit trees and in the evening the air is filled with such fragrance that it couldn't be better. As far as Irina's behavior is concerned, she very much likes to be guided by the experimental method. When she is confronted with the impropriety of committing forbidden acts, she explains with utmost sang-froid: I just wanted to know what mama would say if I did such a thing anyway, etc. It is also interesting that it is "mama", not "papa". There are no special events to report, everything is continuing normally.

Please, inform me about your plans and projects in the nearest future. With my best wishes

Yan

[postscript] As far as oxalic acid is concerned, I forgot, what is it about?

YS 6 (in German)

Letter from Jean Spielrein, civil prisoner in Stuttgart, to Mrs. Olga Ryss

Dear mother-in-law! 17/III/16

I am asking you, in your own interest, not to abuse the power over my children which you obtained thanks to my captivity. You have to consider that this war cannot last forever and that after the peace settlement I will regain my freedom. I was not informed by my mother of the letter you had sent to her. In your letter (missing a salutation, which is not the custom) you wrote that you will be glad should my mother visit the children. I will not engage in a discussion of your personal attitude to the visits of my mother, that is not my business. On the other hand, I would like to call your attention that the relationship of the children with my parents is *only* at the discretion of Sylvia and myself. Sylvia committed a serious breach of her duty when she had banned my parents for such a long time; she will admit it herself. But I strongly object to your having a say in this matter. I would also like to ask you, as far as possible, not to talk with Sylvia about me. Perhaps you have the best intentions in mind, but it always happens that your advice and instructions achieve the opposite get unity between us. Perhaps, for example, you might recall how at Hotel Continental you proclaimed that the absence of your late husband, i.e., the man's non-participation, was a remedy for differences of opinions in child rearing! We both have feelings and views other than different from yours about the right relationship between a man and a woman. I also see it quite unfavorably that you tell your gossip companions about your success of "punishing" my parents because it makes us all look ridiculous in the eyes of our town. But as far as that goes I should not be prescribing any rules to you. I hope you will consider my request and I remain sincerely yours. Jean Spielrein.

YS 7 (in German)

Dear Sabina! Stuttgart, 11.7.1918

I received a letter from your parents and a letter from Silva. She sends her greetings and asks about Renatchen's health and character. I also wrote that Paul had asked her about you. Our departure is becoming more and more likely. It is most desirable that you could come, too. Approach the German consulate in Bern with a detailed application: "In view of the upcoming travel of my brother Dipl. Engineer Spielrein from Stuttgart to Rostov-on-Don, and since it would be difficult for me later to travel with a small child, I take the liberty of requesting the Imperial German Consulate to allow me to travel together with my brother. I am willing to pay for the cost of a telegraphic notification." You can also apply to the representative of the Russian consul. A similar application can also be made to the representative of the General Staff of the XIIIth Army Corps in Stuttgart. It would be best if you or your proxy could apply to the German Consulate General. I will write to Sonya about this, perhaps she could help you. Everything is fine with your parents. In Rostov shoes, underwear, and clothes are very expensive (a suit is 800 rubles, an overcoat 2,000 r., a pair of stockings 50 r.). The parents have enough money. Have you received the 4,000 crowns sent by father? I estimate your assets in Rostov at 150,000–200,000 rubles but without a guarantee. All of father's money is invested in real estate and it has risen in value.

Greetings, Yan

YS 8

Dear Sabina! Berlin 26/X 21

I left for Germany on a business trip for three months, I do not know if I will get a chance to go to Switzerland because it's very expensive. In the next few days I'll be liquidating your possessions. The storage will cost about 6,000 marks = 69 francs. I think of selling part of the things and sending you the money, and leaving the rest. Having now become somewhat more familiar with your financial circumstances, I must say that I don't understand anything. Firstly, are you working for Claparède for free? Secondly, why do you work as a voluntary in Belair [hotel?] and even pay them for it? Do you really need this? We have considered a number of plans. We talked about your coming to Soviet Russia. You would be undoubtedly successful enough by giving lectures and papers on psychoanalysis, but it's uncertain whether our government will agree to your going back abroad. In any case, try to write to the Russian consulate in Berlin that you are <u>ready</u> to travel to Russia and acquaint the specialists and the general public about the contemporary status of and issues in psychoanalysis; but that you cannot live in Russia and can only go there under the absolute condition that you could return abroad where you have been living for the last 18 years. It is doubtful whether it is worth for Pavlusha to leave Russia. Even if they let him out, outside Russia he would be a completely useless person. If in all his life he has not learned how to speak Russian without a Jewish accent, then, all the more so, will he be able to learn a new language? And what will he be doing there? Therefore it would be most desirable if you could come to Russia, at least temporarily. How come your numerous professional colleagues are unable to get you a minimal income to feed yourself and the child? As you know, in Berlin people are very busy practicing psychoanalysis and other things and there is more than enough crazy people there. Based on these considerations I will now try something through the well-known Dr. Maass from Kurhaus Gubert in Schlachtensee and he could let us know if you can get work somewhere. Moreover, similar efforts will be undertaken by Sania's friend Zaidman[111]; as soon as I get some information from them I will let you know immediately. Mama is suffering terribly because she cannot help you and is planning to sell one of the houses for this purpose. She hopes she can get 200,000,000 for it i.e., 20,000 francs. In Moscow I get a salary and rations worth a total of 2 million rubles i.e., 200 rubles a month. Sania is getting the same. Father has a job and Milia is a speculator. Pretty soon a considerable alleviation of life in Russia is expected, but more about this in my next letter. Meanwhile greetings to you and Renatochka. Write to me at Sasha's address.

Your,

Yan

[Postscript] I am speaking with Rabinovich about publishing your articles in Russian journals.

YS 9

Dear Sabina! 27/1.22

We mailed your letters. There is a change in our situation as I received here the job of director of the editorial department with a salary of 10,000 marks a month (250 francs). This is completely sufficient to live decently as a family; even if we have to pay for Irina's education. I will not go to Russia again before the autumn so it will be possible for us to meet in the summer. There is reason to assume that in about 10 days Papa will arrive here (on a business trip). Do you have free time to write something about the application of psychoanalysis to child rearing? Have you worked on anything related to psychotechnics? I recently sent a parcel to Sania. Four shirts, very good ones, turned out to belong to Pavel and therefore were sent to Sania in Rostov. Pavel's cane [?] is kept with us. Here is a quotation from Irina's composition a month before arriving in Berlin, it is six pages long. Greetings

Signature

[Postscript] A list containing the names of Piaget Stern and Weber

111 Perhaps who is meant is Seidman Jankev (or Zajdman, Jakub, or Janek)(1881–1929), Polish Jew, author, lived in Berlin in the 1920's, married Martha Gertrud Freud, Freud's niece, became known as painter Tom Seidmann Freud (German Wikipedia). See also https://culturacolectiva. com/history/tom-seidmann-freud-illustrations

YS 10

Dear Sabina, Berlin 14.4.22

I mailed a letter to Mlle Feigina via the post office. This was not difficult at all since mailed letters arrive just fine now. Claparède's book was immediately sent to Lenina in Moscow to be forwarded to whom it may concern for the purpose of a new edition (and in Russia they have to decide whether this is possible). From here a warm letter about the content of the book and with gratitude for the kind sending of it was sent to Claparède. This letter was written in French and with my help was sent to Geneva.

I doubt we will go to the seaside this summer because the sea has a bad effect both on Silva and the children, but it will be possible to send them to the mountains. Now the problem of housing has been well resolved and should you come here with Renatochka, you will have a very good apartment, very close to us, so you will not have to eat out in restaurants. Regarding your official business trip to the conference, the difficulty with it has to do with the lack of specialists in psychoanalysis and therefore the name Shpilrein-Sheftel means nothing here. I did not even submit your application in this form. One would need some kind of a reference from someone with an official stationery, for example, Freud, Jung, etc. I would write as follows: having received a commission from the union of psychoanalysts, I am prepared, if you are interested, to deliver to you too a report on the congress. I have worked for years in this specialty and can present references. In general, our National Commissariat for Education is very interested in application of psychoanalysis to education and will accept any work in this field with gratitude, and if you have something new in this field, send it in. Perhaps if you could develop closer ties with Russia it might even be possible to get Faivel involved in this under some pretext. I think that your Greek woman is undoubtedly able to pay for room and board despite the fact that their government declared bankruptcy. At least take a promissory note from her and in the meantime let her pay 30 francs a month, otherwise, may she get cholera in her belly! (the latter is nowadays a salon expression). Irinochka is now a big girl studying trigonometry, she recites Schiller and Goethe and plays with dolls with great zeal. Silva cannot put on any weight and I am working like a horse and father is gallivanting in Europe. Greetings,

Yan

YS 11

Dear Sabina, Berlin 25/V.22

You now understand why I was <u>unable</u> to write to you for such a long time.

I could not bring myself to inform you of our grief, as long as you are alone without a family to share with, and to write indifferent letters would be too hard for me...But what can I do! It is awful that you were not able to ever see each other again and at the same time father had prepared everything for mama's arrival here. Milia's letter arrived at the beginning of April. We were very concerned for father's heart and made an effort to be very cautious in giving him the fatal news. It was a tremendous shock for him but the grief did not break him and the next day he went to work, continued to travel around, and do his business. Yesterday father went on business to Moscow and today in the evening he has to fly there again. His business is considered to be so important that they paid 30,000 marks for his flight. In ten days he will be in Berlin again and he may make a stopover in Rostov. Try to pull yourself together as much as possible. Now leaving Russia has become so much easier, almost as it used to be before the war. Father's business has improved somewhat financially so I think that Pavel's travel is a matter of only a few months. I will probably have to travel to Russia in September but I hope to return in four months. On the 15th of June I am traveling to a factory in Chemnitz where I will spend two months. We, that is Silva and the children, will not go to the countryside because it is too expensive, 200 marks = 4 francs a day per person. The Lichterfelde suburb is almost like the countryside, with lots of flowers and trees. Two rooms have been reserved for you and you can come immediately or any time you wish. Hold on to Milia's letter and write a few words to me. Your,

Yan

YS 12

Dear Sabina! Munich 29/V.22

I am here at a convention until Thursday, as I have already written, father reached Moscow safely and within a month will be back in Berlin. The temporary address for Sania is: Moskva Kuznietskii Most Building 5/15 Apartment 44. When do you think you will come to Germany? Write to Milchik to comfort him. He is completely unaccustomed to such a big responsibility. It's curious that only Pavel was with him and all the uncles did not find it necessary to support Milchik (morally). Currently our financial situation has become a little bit more balanced and indeed, now mother would have been able to spend a few quiet years abroad. Fate! Keep in mind that if necessary, I can always send you 200 to 300 francs which is 12,000 to 18,000 marks so that you do not have to take any more loans from anybody. What about those 1,500 francs which Henri Spilrein gave you in Paris? He now demands a reimbursement from father but since this is equivalent to the sum of 90,000 marks. I would like to find out, before I write to father, whether this is true and who is this Henri Spilrein. Kiss Renatochka,

Your [signature]

[postscript] I am awfully worried that you are now alone without a family and understandably this is very hard for you. But what can we do? Come to us as soon as possible! [signature]

YS 13

Dear Sabina! Lichterfelde 2.6.22

Upon my return I got your postcard and letter. We are all in good health. Father is in Moscow. We did not have letters yet. They will probably get here on Wednesday with the pilot. We live in a suburb almost like countryside. If you want to come now, the best would be to stay for a few days in the two rooms reserved for you and then you would be able to settle in the vicinity of Berlin, close to forests and water. Right now we don't know anything, and it is doubtful whether Silva will go anywhere until August.

Send me two notarized documents:

1) a power of attorney: I entrust to my brother Emil Shpilrein the management of all my property affairs with the right of transfer of the power at a later date.

2) the same as above, except that instead of "to brother" insert "my father, Nikolai Arkadievich Shpilrein." Send this as soon as possible so as not to delay Milchik's departure.

Signed Sabina Nikolayevna Sheftel-Shpilrein Geneva (date)

Signature

YS 14

Dear Sabina! Moscow, 30/1/23

I am back to the preceding: since you do not intend to get yourself another uncle, you should, for personal and familial considerations, return to Russia:

1) Faivel [Pavel] would be a miserable creature abroad. He may live a hundred years there and still fail to adapt to life abroad, whereas in Russia he is a person who can, with a feeling of personal dignity, sign, in notes addressed to Milchik, as "Doctor P. N. Sheftel," and even add: senior physician in such and such hospital, which he is not doing because he is so humble. Seriously, in Russia he is a person and abroad—a misunderstanding.

2) Your career in Russia could progress quite differently than in Switzerland, where, after all, you depend on Claparède's moods and rejoice at notes from a

certain Bovet[112]. Some time ago, at a reception in honor of Nansen[113], I spoke about you with Shmidt[114]. He forwarded your letter to the psychoanalysts and they were most delighted that a person with a European reputation is interested in Russian affairs. You were also remembered at a congress of psychoneurologists. Schmidt strongly advised that you should come even temporarily. In Russia you can expect the following:

a) The opportunity to practice as much as you wish due to scarcity of psychoanalysts.

b) The opportunity to apply your ideas to pre-school and school education. The Communists are very sympathetic to psychoanalysis.

c) The opportunity to participate in organizing the institute of psychoanalysis, organizing special laboratories.

d) In the not too distant future a chair of psychoanalysis and collaboration with philologists and other people.

e) Full equality and not subsisting on charity.

f) "Familial happiness" with Faivel and all your brothers together with papa, wives, and children. In Moscow you will get no peace being a popular Shpilrein. As it is, Sania is mentioned in the papers daily.

g) Financially you will have not less than in Switzerland. The Soviet Government greatly values scientific workers and without any ulterior motives. You will be getting rations, maintenance, a salary, etc.

h) Only in Russia will you be able to realize your scientific projects.

Just in case, send me the following letter:

---

112 Bovet, Pierre (1878–1965), Swiss philosopher and psychologist, joined Claparède to found Institut Jean-Jacques Rousseau.

113 Nansen, Fridtjof (1861–1930) was a Norwegian explorer, scientist, diplomat, humanitarian and Nobel Peace Prize laureate.

114 Schmidt, Otto Yulievich (1891–1956), Russian explorer, geographer and mathematician.

Esteemed Otto Yulievich!

My brother forwarded to me your advice to come to Russia. I would be glad to come to Russia for two to three months in order to create a connection between Russian and western psychoanalysts, and in many lectures acquaint Russian comrades with our work. But in order to make such a trip. I would need to receive an authorized official invitation to obtain a permit to travel to Russia and be assured of getting an apartment for the duration of my stay in Moscow. Respectfully yours,

The Government Publishing House is printing a series of Freud's works edited by Prof. Ermakov:

Introduction to psychoanalysis
The foundations of psychological theory in psycho-analysis
The technique of psycho-analysis
The interpretation of dreams
Totem and taboo
The psychoanalysis of the word and symbolism in creative writing Hypnosis
Psychoanalysis and spiritual activity of mankind
Psychoanalysis of children
The problems of incest in art
Psychoanalysis of folk art
Hypnosis and psychoanalysis
Choice of profession and psychoanalysis
Pedagogy and psycho-analysis
Psychoanalysis of religious art
Analysis of the works of Gogol, Pushkin, Griboyedov, Vrubel, Skriabin and others
Many topics have not yet been assigned to authors

[postscript] Renata can eat and study splendidly in Moscow. I [illegible] at the Scientist's Home on Kropotkin Street 16. They can place you and Renata there quite comfortably, offer you free dinners, and serve tea. Greetings

[signature]

YS 15 Moscow 8/23

Father is asleep on a bourgeois-looking bed and doesn't need anything, and should he need anything, he would buy it. Therefore he is not lolling around at all. From Berlin to Riga, there is no change of trains. From Riga to Moscow there is a sleeping car also without changing trains so you will not even think of getting tired. It snowed yesterday so there is no fear of any tropical heat, it will be hot in the end of July. Malakhovka is a God forsaken hole, but after you arrive you will get settled better. Perhaps you might even want to spend some twenty days in Crimea. We shall see later. About things: first, bring everything you need for yourself, second, for Rukhel and Fania, and then, as third in line, if it isn't too much, bring something for other Jewish girls. Sara Lublinskaya is the wife of Sen'ka Lublinskii. Upon leaving take only the money needed for travel. In any case, from Berlin to Moscow for two it costs less than 1,000 francs. Should there be any money left over, which I doubt, don't bring it with you but leave it in Geneva. Here starting in the fall you will be able to earn enough.

Greeting, Yasha

4.7 LETTTERS FROM ISAAK SHPILREIN TO SABINA

IS 1

Dear Sch[eiwe] [in German] Berlin, 17.11.18

Please let Mrs. Lüfschitz know that I will continue to forward her letters. Please tell Mrs. Straschunskaia that I received her letters of 30.X and 11.XI and forwarded them. I have also written to Mrs. Lüfschitz about your letters of 30th [illegible]. The situation with money is once again bad. I only have 500 mark and many bills to pay and no salary. I am again cut off from my parents. Perhaps you can try to write to them directly. (Rostov is already occupied by the English and, according to newspaper reports, the English are expected this week in Kiev.) Arrange for money to be sent to you and through Yankev [brother Yan] to me. Your father's letter to you of 7/9.18 states in German translation: Dear S., we had no letters from you for a long time. We have now received some meager news about you via Samovar. And mother sheds tears over her daughter. For example, she bakes pastry to feed dear S[ab]chen and Renatchen. And with Silva she will travel [illegible] to Crimea 'to recuperate' (she needs this like a hole in the head). And mother wails: "oh, those children, poor little things. I see that Menikhe is pale and Roza is skin and bones, I worry about S[ab], I [illegible] she goes hungry and is unhappy. Briefly, always anguish, sleepless nights [some illegible lines]. Miltschik worries about her, does she have any rest? But poor Miltschik is a splendid fellow: he gazes down upon us (he is a head or a head and a half to two taller than me), a man with strong muscles. I am only worried about his heart. Not because so many girls literally fall head over heels in love with him, but because he often complains of nervous heart palpitations. He even has gout phenomena at this young age. If only you, the doctor, could make some observations on him! Otherwise mama says to me: "Heal the child, don't be a doctor!" Lately mama has often been making such slips of the tongue. It makes people laugh but I worry about it. No news about S[abina's] genetic thoughts, very [illegible] Especially her theories about "downfall" and "disintegration" This is after all simple cell division! What does Freud say about this? It was he who brought out that nowadays many parents imprint all the phenomena of mental life in their children. This is most important for psychoanalysis, since *these* life periods are otherwise not accessible without psychoanalysis. And it is here that consciousness hides so as not to give away its "last stand." Now, hopefully, work will be become successful, I am anticipating that something stimulating will be discovered with psychological methods, so that many adult bodily disorders will be explained. The diagnosis, even the history of the illness, will now follow completely new paths. I remember our strolls on the beach in Kolberg when I kept asking you, "What are the practical results of psycho-analysis? What are the effects of its application to the practical development of mankind?" Yes, Freud is a great man and we are happy to share at least a part of that knowledge, that is to really "live." Is[?]. Greetings! [illegible]

IS 2

Dear Scheiwe [in German] Berlin NW 87 20.9.18

Today, with the same mail, I received your letters of 30.8 and 14.9. It is very sad that the little one is so sick, however the good thing is that she was admitted to the hospital in a satisfactory fashion. Write to me in detail about the course of the illness. I am very worried because of the news about mother although I received money in the last three weeks but no news about the parents. But an explanation might arrive any day now. You must write to me about the letter from the parents and the report of Tsaitlin. You should have somehow enough money for the time being as you will presently receive 1,000 and 1,500 marks. You probably have not received the 2,000 marks from Stau in Stuttgart. But you will get them, too, as soon as I have news from home. Personally I am doing alright. Menikha is developing as a brainy child. Yesterday she noticed the moon for the first time and called it a great ball. Today she saw from afar an electrical car and said, "Here is the 'babay'" (tramway = streetcar), and "it is so small" (she points with her finger), and they are hardly moving. She tells she should not be kissed because mama does not want it. But she herself does not kiss, "You don't know me yet, I am still a little girl." Rukh is very busy in his task because we are moving next week. As of the 1st October we will reside at NW87 Wikinger

Ufer [illegible] but in the meantime write to the old address. In a calendar I found this quote from Fichte which should be of interest to you: "Every death in nature is a birth, only in death appears the elevation of life." Can you send me a copy of your dissertation?

Best, your Izak.

IS 3

My Dear Sister Sheiva Naftulievna [in Russian] 12.I.1920

I received your letter and at the first opportunity I will forward it to Rostov. I am very happy that finally you got a job in your specialty, and I hope that you will find it gratifying. As you can see from the enclosed newspaper clipping, in my old age I am occupied with psychoanalysis, and even in with its applications to literature. I only had one letter from the parents a month or a month and a half ago. They tell me that they are very needy, that they sell their things in order to have something to eat. All of them are working but their salaries are not enough. Yankev, with wife and two children, is making about 150,000 a month, and here, of course, getting professor's rations should help. Therefore, he even left Moscow for Rostov and was there appointed a professor. Given all this, the situation in Russia regarding food and heating is improving considerably and noticeably, and one can assume that the parents will have enough things to survive this winter, and then we may be able to help them in different ways. It is evident that in general, their mood is not good because they don't give father any chances and they force him to deal with uninteresting matters. As to Milia, all the signs point to a child is about to be born, but officially I know nothing about it. I had a letter from Faivel from Feodosia some time ago about which I had written to you. Since Feodosia is now under Soviet rule it means that I will be able to forward your letters to him, should you send me any. We are doing all right. I work and I earn in your money about 300 francs a month and in Georgian money 37,000 rubles. Rukh is studying, he missed passing his tests and was left behind in the second year of his medical studies, but thanks to that he is now practicing bacteriology privately. My daughter will soon be five years old, she is already speaking Russian tolerably, studying French and can sign her name in Hebrew. She is having interesting dreams, and conversations that might interest you but that is for another time. Unfortunately, all this will be lost for future generations because the parents had no time.

And with this goodbye, with love from and with a low bow from all of us. Moreover, my best regards to my niece Renata Faivelevna and the wish that God give us all good health and lots of success in our affairs. Come to Berlin and take all your things that I left in storage with A I Grebler, Oranienburgerstrasse 65. Grebler is my friend. I left twenty places for him and of those numbers 1–8 are yours. Since storage and insurance cost 400 marks a month, it makes sense to take your things. Ask Grebler to send them to you. I have the keys to the chest and the basket and the boxes could be sent as they are. There you have lingerie, clothing, toys, tableware and books; if you need the key send a cable andI'll send it to you registered. Or perhaps you can go to Berlin and take your things?

Yours, loving and respectful brother
Itsek Naftulievich Shpilrein
Velikokniazheskya Street 34 Lublinskii apartment IS 4 (in French)
[on stationery of the International Association of Psychotechnics
President I.N. Spielrein Moscow Marx and Engels Street 1 General
Secretary J.M. Lahy Paris Avenue de l'Observatoire 22 Treasurer O.
Lipmann, Berlin Neubabelsberg II Wanseesstrasse
M. le Prof. Ed. Claparède 11 Avenue de Champel, Génève

Dear M. Claparède Moskva, 26 December, 1930

I received your card of 15th December with the list of persons invited to the international conference. The Russian translation of your *The Psychology of the Child* about which my father talked with you was not published. In fact, there was a Russian edition of that work already before the war and my father had nothing to do with it.

Receive, dear Mr. Claparède, my most cordial greetings.
[Signature]

4.8 LETTERS FROM EMIL SHPILRAIN TO SABINA AND OTHERS

EmS 1

Dear Sabina! Rostov on/D. 12.IX–15

Your letter of 3.IX-15 arrived only today. As far as agronomy is concerned, I'm not thinking much about it as I am still studying in the seventh grade, and therefore I am busy all day long. However, it interests me as it did before. As far as my classmates are concerned, none of them are interesting to me (do you understand in what sense interesting?). The 8th grade students at the Stepanov's high school are much more developed, well-read and educated than our seventh grade students. It is true that the Warsaw University is moving into our town. The Kiev conservatory and some of the high schools from the

Privislinskii region [on river Vistula] are moving in as well. This is great news as Rostov is becoming a university town and, moreover, a cultural center of the South-Russian region. Here there is nothing new. Soon (18 September) performances will start at our theatre for the winter season. As far as Kolomeytsev and Novikov are concerned, mama has no idea about their whereabouts, in any case you need not to worry because they are in prison and, thus, cannot do us any harm. With this letter I am sending you a rose-colored rose from our garden, I am not sure if it will not fall apart on its way to you. We have plenty of flowers on the terrace and a wild vine is climbing on a fine wire, and it is especially beautiful when seen from the street. Papa rented two unoccupied apartments so that all the apartments are now occupied. We received the negatives of the photographs taken by Yasha. Mama was indescribably delighted and was saying to papa: "Oh, Kolia, what do we need all our money for when we have such beautiful grandchildren?! They are part of us, our dear ones" To what papa answers: "Of course, it's a great pleasure for my six little rubles (letter mailing cost six rubles)!!!" It is an old story.

I will send you some photographs soon – mama is with me – taken while we were in Essentuki, but they are not developed yet. Alright, I am ending. Everything here is alright. The studying has resumed a short while ago. I took three examinations and got 3 fives. Write to me how you are feeling, how is Renata? Send me her photograph, it is the greatest joy for mama.

Greetings to "Ziuk" [Renata's nickname] Milchik

EmS 2

Dear Sabina. 8.XI.15

I'm now very busy, I am writing the verb alter *[Latin, other]* for tomorrow; mama is now very angry with her glasses; she has the Lublinskii saddle nose and this is why her glasses (pardon, her pince-nez) are always slipping off. Mama is saying that as long as there is no way to "fix" the glasses, so that they don't fall off, she might lose her mind! By the way, why do you like the letter Ѣ [the letter E called ЯТЬ (iat') in the old alphabet] so much! Papa says that as of the 1st of November 1915 it is now written E, take note. The first quarter is already over. My grades are eight 5's and four 4's. When you write to Yashka and Sania, please give them my regards and my best wishes for "all kinds of tsimeses" [Jewish delicacies]. Greetings to your Ziuk [Renata's nickname]. Well, I will continue writing on alter, goodbye!

Your Milia.

EmS 3

My dear niece Renata Feivelevna! Rostov on/Don 7.II–16

Why haven't you written to your relatives even once in your life, especially to your uncle?! But I am a good [illegible] and am the first to start corresponding. What language do you speak? Russian? Alright. So for starters, how are you doing? Are your ships safe, as your grandmother used to say to your uncle. Best regards to your mama and answer. Greetings.

[illegible signature](uncle)

To m-lle Renata Sheftel Lausanne

[probably a postscript from mother to Sabina]

Write about everything and in detail. For God's sake, let me know, do not [conceal?]. Is everything alright with Saniechka? Is his [Menikha?] in good health? I still do not know how it all happened. Did you get any letters for Renatochka and [Menikha]? There was not even one letter from Yasha for the last two and a half months. I don't understand, why is it only his letters that get lost. Something is not right.

EmS 4

Dear Sabina! 25/XII-21

I can say I happened to be in Moscow completely by accident and stayed in Sania's room. I'm living together with Rakhil and father (Menikha is in a sanatorium near Moscow). Before I left Rostov (five days ago) I met Pavel who gave me a letter for you; I gave it to father to be forwarded to you. Mama has just come back to Rostov and, having received the news that your financial situation has somewhat improved, she became somewhat calmer regarding her Sabinochka. I would like to believe that you will take advantage of father's trip abroad and will return with him to Moscow in two months. The main reason and benefit of this idea is to live as a whole family, either in Moscow or even in Rostov, and you will be in a much more comfortable financial situation and will be able to see all your relatives! My family is more or less in good health; the child is growing and showing, as usual, plenty of manifestations of a wunderkind, he will soon (on 18/I/22) be one year old. How is Renata, have you taken her back to live with you? Write to us at Sania's Moscow address and he will send it on to Rostov.

Goodbye, Milia

[postscript from father] Berlin, 10/2, 22 Greetings Dear Sabinochka! I have just arrived and I send you a cordial greeting. I will do my best to come to see you as soon as possible. Should this be impossible, then you and Renatochka should come to Germany for a few days. Goodbye. Yasha's address: Berlin Gross Lichterfelde Ost Lorenzstrasse 54/I. I am staying with him for now.

EmS 5

Dear Yasha! 27/3–22

On the 17th of March in the evening mama started feeling a strong headache and rheumatic pain in back and hands. The following day, unbeknownst to me, Doctor Dubrov was invited (by Dr. Ryndziun); he prescribed Aspirini, Pyramidoni 0.5 and Caffeini 0.12. The temperature was relatively low. On the 19th Pavel came, was informed about mama's indisposition, and we decided that if she does not get better to take her to stay with Pavel on Dmitrievskaya street. From the very first she was under watchful observation around the clock by a nurse, myself, Fania, and Pavel. The signs of the illness pointed to typhus, but one could not make a definitive diagnosis. Now on the 22nd , having beforehand thoroughly bundled mama up, we transferred her together with Pavel to his apartment where a separate nice big and bright room had been prepared for her. Professor Kastanayan was called immediately and said that this was most likely spotted fever (typhus exanthematicus) but without the most important sign, a clearly visible skin rash. He prescribed various heart medications like Digitalis, Camphorae, etc. Pavel didn't leave her bedside, she only took food from his hands, and it was an indescribable effort to make her eat and drink. Nurses took turns watching her day and night. The urine analysis showed 12 0/00 pro mille of albumin and an appropriate diet was prescribed. The morning temperature was in the range of 37.3–37.5 centigrade and the evening temperature 38.4–38.9 (was never any higher). On the 24th mama improved markedly (the way she felt); she was fully conscious all the time, she was satisfied that she had been moved, saying that she would have died in Ryndziun's sanatorium (a small room with poor care); she requested Pavel to accelerate her improvement so that Sania wouldn't find her lying in bed (I immediately informed Sania about mama's illness but told mama that Sania was sent on a business trip to Caucasus so that his sudden appearance would not make her nervous.) Starting on the 24th (in the evening) she stopped passing urine, in spite of the catheter, the kidneys failed and this moment, so to speak, was the fateful beginning of the end. All kinds of measures were applied to obtain urine flow. On the morning of the 25th Professor Kastanayan diagnosed brain phenomena (tremor of face and hand muscles) prescribed leeches behind the ears and subcutaneous Digalen and also a physiological enema and intravenous fluids. I instantly ran to get the leeches, found the digitalis, ordered for it a saline solution in the pharmacy statim! (immediately!). Everything was done (starting in the morning mama did not recognize me and then lost consciousness).In spite of all this, at 9 o'clock there was a stroke caused by a partial brain hemorrhage; the surgeon doctor Shostok was called immediately, he made a venesection and administered intravenous fluids. I forgot to add that all this time Dr. Tinker, assistant of professor Kastanayan, was on call; for the night on call one more surgeon from the military hospital was invited, whose services turned out to be unnecessary: at 1:25 am on the night from the 25th to the 26th of March, after the second stroke, mama died without regaining consciousness. On the 26th of March at 6 o'clock in the evening she was buried in the Jewish cemetery.

I am horrified, this unexpected calamity befell me when I was the only one of our family here and the whole responsibility became mine, but you should know, Yasha, I swear to you, I did everything that could be done; and, if, besides the 60 million spent, ten times more were needed, I would have found it, nothing would have stopped me! Clearly, not everything can be bought with money, you can buy this or that thing but not a person, not a human life. This is a colossal blow for all of us but more so for our dear papa: I am afraid even to hint to him about what happened, lest something fatal might happen to him! We, we have to do something for him, my God, he is now the only one left, he lost the "very dearest person in the whole world" to quote his words! How to prepare him?! Since you are there near him, you can better evaluate his state of mind; it is perhaps better to hide the whole truth from him; but on the other hand, he might continue bombarding with letters either his dear Evon'ka, our dear mama, who can no longer hear from him. Just the day mama died we received a postcard from papa in which he asks mama to get ready to travel to him, oh horror! Perhaps papa would like to move to Rostov, we now have rooms in our apartment; all our efforts would be aimed at making his life easier, he would not have to worry about expenses, and poor mummy was afraid all the time that she would be left penniless, afraid that she would be taking money from her children and in the end it turned out otherwise, she died and all that remains are her private possessions. In addition, I wanted personally to deliver to papa all mama's things which I took from Ryndziun and I made an inviolable list of everything until papa's arrival and his will! For God's sake take good care of papa only if there is reason to fear that telling him the truth might be dangerous; if so, hide it from him! What shall we do with Sabina! My God! Write because it is getting very hard for me without any advice or instructions. Take care of papa!

Milia

[postscript] Mama's illness remains unexplained, the professor insists that it was spotted typhus; Pavel and Dr. Tinker believe it was influenza complicated by kidney failure and uremia that caused brain hemorrhage.

[postscript, source unknown] Dear Yasha, the calamity that befell us all was great of course; but it was Milia who lived through and suffered more than anybody else, upon whom everything crashed all at once. He completely lost his head, it is scary to look at him, he can barely stand on his feet, he fainted a few times [some illegible words] For God's sake YashEn'ka [illegible] he should come [text break]

Ems 6

Dear papa! Undated

I have just received your letter of 17/ IV. As I was reading it, I was literally drowning in tears of infinite sorrow and at the same time of happiness. Yes, you are an infinitely great man, a titan! I'm proud of you and worship you! I was so firmly convinced that your attitude toward death is nothing but bravado, that you were just pretending. But you can really approach death beautifully, so beautifully – to see in it a harmony compatible with life, and finally to see life in death itself! One cannot find someone like you in tens of thousands of people! Instead of me consoling you (as I believed I would have to do), it was you who knew how to alleviate my suffering with your stoical attitude to what has happened! And how infinitely hard what happened was for me, as I have always so sincerely loved mama, I was so tormented when I saw her torments! Did she know that when she was still alive?! I think she did! I will definitely finish my university studies – I swear in the name dear to us all, so you should not worry about it! It will be probably difficult for me to travel to Berlin at this time, but on the other hand, it is impossible to abandon the entire property (I have written to you about the houses, haven't I). Meanwhile, I would like so much to see you! Perhaps, after [Genua?] I will be able to come and see you and then come back again! However, I will send [Panteleev's?] letter to Sania, let him set this affair in motion (today I received a letter from Sania: does [Menikha?] have tonsillitis?) Fania is very anxious to see you, she misses you so much. She is not at home now and that is why there is no postscript from her. I got two parcels from A.R.A; it is sad that I got both of them and not just one, but what can I do? Life is life! This morning one pound of black bread cost 250,000 rubles, and now (at 2 o'clock in the afternoon) it is already costing 320,000 rubles. So be it, you must be tired of hearing all this Russian news about food and hunger! Write to me, my dear, [postscript on the left] I kiss you many times, I am proud of you. Your Milia.

EmS 7

Dear papa! Rostov-on-Don 29/4

I visited I.D. Guterman who received me with great sympathy; when I saw on the table the postcard you sent him on 12/ IV from [illegible]. So, I.D. finds that your presence in Rostov is absolutely indispensable, but should your leaving Berlin cause a deterioration of your health, then no matter what, <u>don't do it</u>! The situation with the real estate is the following: on the basis of your power of attorney for me to have the right to manage your house (certified by I.D.), I am now able to take into possession the Griboyedov house and collect the rent in the amount of 150 thousand rubles per square meter each month; with this goal in mind, it will be necessary to [a few illegible words] and, measure the exact surface in square meters of all the apartments in the house, in order to present it officially, to the Komkhoz (Commissariat of Economy), as required by order! There is nothing I can do with the rest of the real estate, the house on Pushkinskaya is now a tenant collective of which I hope to become a member. Should you wish to sell the Griboyedov real estate, then write to me about your terms and send a power of attorney in my name. Oh, so much trouble! The long-standing watchman Petrovich died of smallpox three days ago.

Why haven't I received any letters from you until now? Waiting for them is a torture! From Moscow I received yesterday, sent by Sania, two boxes of Quaker oats [English in the original], and two boxes of sprats – this, of course, came from your parcels – thank you! Mark is devouring the Quaker with gusto! Following the introduction of collecting rent money, the Konikovs have vacated some rooms and are now living in two rooms only, although they had previously claimed they could not give up any room! [People?]! [text break]

EmS 8

Dear Silva and Yasha! Rostov on/Don 3/5–22

I received your letter of the 15th of the previous month. Everything is so difficult, almost infinitely difficult! I received your cable a long time ago but so damaged that I could not understand its content and I responded with something nonsensical. The text was as follows:

–Текст был таков: „VVLI WERDE VNRER NAECHSTENS MITTEILEN SCHONE MICH DRATHE GESUNDHEIT JASCHA"

[Gesundheit = health]

Clearly, I understood that the subject was mama's health but I could not make out the beginning! You want to know about mama's last minutes, Yasha, she was not thinking about dying at all, and nobody expected her to die the day before this disaster! Only I alone, on the second day after the onset of an innocuous illness, told Fania that I felt (!) that this illness will be fatal for mama. On the 24th of March I was at mama's bedside all day long and she felt alright, she was smiling and spoke that she wanted to see all of you soon, she expected Sania and was worried about his health, she missed Marochka whom she had not seen a whole week... (and, despite all this apparently satisfactory condition (temperature 37.3 centigrade), and looking at mama, I felt death all the time, I swear to you, I pestered Pavel with questions, is there still hope? And he would answer that there was still no danger, that the professor said the same; I left mama at 11 pm, almost on the 24th of March (she was in bed staying at Pavel's flat). The next day I came at 10 o'clock and as I approached the door I felt a real physical pain in my heart, I stood a long time before the door then I knocked and Fania Naumovma opened the door saying: mama is worse now, as since yesterday she stopped passing urine. She was catheterized as ordered by Pavel (who by the way left to go to the infirmary at 9 in the morning because he was on call); the catheterization was unsuccessful, "no urine is coming out!" I immediately ran to the Nikolayev Hospital, the Miroshnichenko Building, where professor Kastanayan was lecturing, and after he finished I took him to see mama! After examining the patient Kastanayan diagnosed brain phenomena (she had already lost consciousness), but he said it was not so bad yet and ordered to apply medicinal leeches behind the ears and cupping glasses on her back (the brain phenomena were caused by anuria), but preferably leeches. I rushed downtown and got the leeches with great difficulty and also got Digalen which could not be found in any pharmacy! The leeches were placed behind the ears and in the meantime Fania ran to Sabsovich to telephone Pavel at the hospital to send for him (R. L. did not let her in and telephoned herself!). Half an hour later Pavel came running, the situation remained the same, tremor of the facial muscles and of the right hand and unconsciousness; they also invited professor Kastanayan's assistant, doctor Tinker (seen here as a rising star) and a physiological enema, intravenous fluids, injections, and a venesection were ordered! Oh God, the Zhitomir pharmacy worked endlessly and exclusively for us, the prescriptions were marked "quickly and immediately," I ran six times in pouring rain to the hospital to see Shura Tsaitlin, then to the Bogatianovskii lane to the nurse to fetch the apparatus for physiological infusions, then to Professor Zavadskii![115]

115 Apparently, Zavadskii Igor Vladimirovich (1875–1944), Russian doctor of internal medicine.

For the night they required a surgeon to come in case of a new stroke, but in spite of everything this second stroke turned out to be fatal! After the most awful torments mama began to die very quietly, the respiration was getting fainter and fainter and at last became totally imperceptible; a mirror was placed on her mouth and it showed no moisture, this was the end! I photographed the dead mama and beforehand ordered two photographs and will order more, as soon as I have the money, and send them to you! I still cannot come to my senses after what has happened, during the day the memories become somewhat faint but at night true torments begin, all the way to hallucinations! [text break]

EmS 9

Dear papa! Rostov-on-Don5/V–22

Your letter of 17/IV was received and I answered it the day I received it, the day before yesterday. Even though you wrote that you wish to avoid all discussions about the things left behind, both personal possessions and real estate, I think that what you are doing is very wrong: 1) all that is left is undoubtedly yours only, because only you have the right to all of it, 2) you are considerably more experienced than any of us in such everyday matters. Since I am completely unaccustomed to deal with all this, it is particularly hard for me, because I feel forced to be responsible toward you! Just in case (it will soon be possible to claim inheritance) send me, if you think it's necessary, a power of attorney in your name and in the name of Yasha and Sabina, so that I could take care of it here. If you want to sell the real estate I would also need a power of attorney. By the way, why is there only a copy of the bill of sale of the Griboyedov house, where is the original? I'm only asking in order to be informed, anyway, because I'm submitting only a certified copy (in this case, a copy of a copy) to the Komkhoz [Commissariat of Economy]. Solve this problem, because this is one of the main reasons for me staying in Rostov. Furthermore, I don't mind moving with the whole family to your place, but in order to leave Rostov, I must be sure that beyond Moscow [illegible]; but to travel with the family on the off-chance, and to spend some 100 million (one ticket to Moscow costs about 12 to fifteen million), is risky.

The letter to Panteleev is being sent via Sania, but as you know, in such cases Sania has his way of "making haste", so it would be good if there is any possibility for you to intervene indirectly in some way. We are all well off financially; as you may know, I am a member of the "company" doing business with my father-in-law; this company is based on the fact that I once gave money and now we split the profits equally. I am now active again and doing quality work in a chemical laboratory. After 26/III [mother's death] and until now I was unable to pull myself together and work. I often see Lebedev and Shchelkanovtsev, greetings from them! We are sending you a test photograph of Marochka [Mark] while taking the shot he moved his hand and therefore the right side came out a little bit blurred; when we get the rest of the photographs we will send them to uncle and aunts [Mark was photographed by ZAT.] Well, goodbye, my dear!

How is your heart? Write.

Your Milia.

EmS 10

Dear Silva and Yasha with children, of course! Undated

I have already received the second letter from papa after he learned about the tragedy, on 17/4 from Berlin and on 20/IV from Eisenach addressed to mama! How awfully hard it is to read these letters, the letters of a man with colossal willpower, but at the same time very tender and loving, this combination is particularly evident now! From dad's last letter I gather that he is getting overcome by loneliness, this phenomenon is the most undesirable for us all: I implore you to do all you can to support him in his present condition. Perhaps, you will find this request of mine insulting, but that would be unfair, for you must understand what is in on my mind in the present situation?! I would love to join you in Berlin with my whole family; should father's efforts be successful, I will be able to resolve the issue in a positive way. But regarding the latter, what should be done with mother's real estate and her things?!

EmS 11

Dear Sabina! 13/V–22

We have had no letters from you for ages and were we not receiving papa's letters about your well-being, we would be downright worried. I am here attaching the photograph of your only nephew who, as they say, looks better live than in pictures; hopefully you will soon be able to see him in person and solve this problem. What about your travel to Berlin? How is Renatochka's health? I and Pavel meet almost daily and he writes to you frequently. Goodbye, kiss Renatochka!

Milia

[postscript from Emil's wife]: Rostovdon 13/V–22

Dear Sabina, how are you, any news? How is Renatochka, her health? I would very much like to see you both, and there aren't even any letters from you!

Milia and I are dreaming of traveling to see both of you. Will we be successful?... Goodbye. Write. Marin'ka kisses his aunt and his little cousin Renatochka. All the best, Fania

EmS 12

Dear papa! 14/V–22

For a whole week now I had no letters from you and because of that I walk about as if in sickening carbon monoxide fumes and bad thoughts are gnawing at my head and they cut and grind and torment me... For God's sake, write as often as possible; write about your health. You seem to deliberately avoid mentioning it in your letters and now this is for me the most important thing right now; for if I still have any presence of mind, then it is only due to the fact that in my pocket I am holding a copy of your truly heroic letter of the 17th of past month. Thinking about you gives me strength and I still want to believe that you will be completely healthy, really, and I do not want to imagine anything else. I and Fania have just visited mama's grave and planted some flowers (we will talk to the gardener about planting white stem roses); how beautiful that place is, how quiet, and it seems as if I aim becoming more honest and clean, and This Man, who brought me into this world, appears to be completely approachable as if there is an exchange of thoughts between me and Him!

From mother, we went to visit Pavel (he was in the same place today too, only a little earlier). His sister Fania N. is still ill, probably with malaria and I lost count of how long she's been ill; Pavel is of course aware that this gives no pleasure... Regarding "the house of the unfortunate" I.D. had already written in my letter that it is <u>currently</u> impossible to realize your wish [juridically?], but do not worry, at the first opportunity everything will be done the way you desire... Everything is gnawing and sucking me, it doesn't stop! If tomorrow's mail will bring nothing from you, I will send a cable to Yasha's address.

Write, I am waiting, kisses! Milia

EmS 13

Dear papa, Rostov on/Don 23/V–22

It is now about 11 pm and we are visiting with the ZAT's (Marochka was at home and asleep for quite a while). We were all sitting on the balcony, it was a moonlit night, there is a wonderful scent of acacia from the balcony and I sat for a long time in the living room improvising on the piano. As usual, the electricity was off and willy-nilly I started thinking, thinking and reminiscing about many things... darkness was conducive to this and presently a string of memories became reflected in the music. I remember how as a little chubby boy four-five years old I was sitting on your knees (dressed in a little Cherkessian suit) and saying, "Papa give me some jam!" the clock was striking the half hour (perhaps half past 7). How pleasant, to the point of hurting, it was to remember the striking of this clock! You gave me a teaspoon of sour cherry jam (I'm sure I remember it), and I licked my lips and asked for more; I received two more teaspoonfuls and then mama was saying: "It is harmful for the child to eat so many sweets!" and you stopped indulging me. Then I am being told it's time to go to bed; I asked for permission to stay a bit longer with the grownups, "with Patt"; I got permission and to my horror, a few minutes later I heard three doorbell rings and then I saw Patt's bald head appearing through the door; it could not be helped, and I went to sleep and after undressing I called mother to say "goodbye" to her before I fell asleep.

I remembered your birthday (I can't recall what year it was), sitting around were our I. Dubrov, the late Berta Vladimirovna, and our family; I approached you (do you remember your permanent tea place at the dinner table?) and gave you a drum as a present, feeling embarrassed (which caused my eyes to fill with tears), the same drum that was given to me a short while earlier by the same Berta Vladmirovna; you put me on your knees and made a gesture with your mouth as if you wanted to eat me, and you pricked me with your mustache; I was flattered and dying to tell you that I love you very much, but I felt embarrassed and then I lay in bed wide awake recalling this moment. I remembered 1905 and reminisced about all the well-known details of Sania's journey to Azov, and I began to feel heavy hearted but at the same time, for some reason, I felt very loving as a result of these reminiscences..., and all of a sudden the fingers on the keys began to play a rhapsody by Liszt (!)... then I recalled the times of the Khodosovs and the Fridmans, and in all these heavy reminiscences I felt, at the same time, much that was so close, so infinitely dear, and a great pity that all this was irreparable. I sat almost two hours at the piano and cried; I gave free expression to my feelings (thankfully, nobody saw it and nobody was suspecting what was going on inside me!), what wonderful melodies I was able to play from time to time! I can no longer reproduce those now! When I was a little boy and heard people talking about selling this or that piece of furniture from the house, I would start an awful ruckus and beg them not to do this (remember?); later when I got older, this attachment to things began to wane; now I am noticing a relapse; once again various things are enormously dear to me, connected with a variety of reminiscences!

Fanichka positively cannot stand "trash" and for me everything is insanely dear, and I won't allow anything be discarded, let alone sold. For you, of course, the love of things is an alien idea, isn't it? I positively don't know how I will be able to part with all of this once our journey becomes concrete! Today we received your postcard to Marochka but it's so short; and we wait for your letters every day, and I almost daily go to the garden to meet the postwoman. Perhaps as early as this week I'll go by myself to Moscow to find out something about taking a trip to see you; are you busy with something? Tell me, are you thinking of spending the summer in Russia in the summer? Perhaps you could come to Riga for the time being? I so want to see you, [text break]

EmS 14

Dear Sabina, 24/XII 22

From your postcard to Pavel I learned that you have not received my letter since you are surprised by my silence, apparently the letter got lost. Your husband's mood is severely depressed as he absolutely does not believe that it will be possible to see you soon. Why shouldn't you come to Russia <u>now</u>? Your scientific career here will not be lost at all, but you will see Pavel and you will be able to decide what to do in the future. Nowadays Russia is no longer a Tsarist state, there is absolutely no reason for you to be afraid of it, on the contrary, now I would not exchange living in Russia for life in Western Europe. I assure you that the intellectual life in Moscow is now in full swing, that you would instantly be able to find a use for your specialty. Moreover, you would meet and get acquainted with Fania and Marka. Oh, what a Marka this is, he is capable of saying absolutely everything! He knows by heart a whole lot of poems and songs etc. Consider my proposal! Cordial postdated greetings to Renatochka on her birthday and I wish her to grow as an <u>adult</u> in all respects. In February of this year I bought for Marka a Rönisch piano in exchange for the Blüthner grand and it makes me happy, this is my happiness! I kiss you and Renatochka. Goodbye, write.

Milia

[postscript] 14/I 23: Yasha came to see us. He is also of the opinion that it is necessary for you to come to Moscow <u>temporarily</u>. We are expecting papa on Friday. I am attaching three photographs

[postscript] Yesterday we celebrated Marka's birthday in a grandiose way! And so he is now two years old.

EmS 15

[Fragment to Yan] Undated

I wrote to papa many times about this question. I wrote that in order to sell real estate it is necessary to have a power of attorney issued to me from all the legatees; I also sent papa the order of the Komkhoz concerning revenues from real estate and the procedure for getting those. I still have not received an answer to all these questions from papa. How are you doing? How is Silva's health, the children? Be sure to write, please! For all this time I only had one letter. Goodbye

Milia

FS

Dear Nikolai Arkadievich! 6 May 1922

Not having your letter we very often thought about traveling but having received your recent letters we started thinking about it more. But Milia is quite undecided about it and is worried all the time that once we leave here and reach Moscow, we might get stuck there; and this kind of an outlook is not a happy one either for him or for me. But on the other hand, I understand that staying in Rostov will make it less possible to see you! So what should we do? We are waiting for you to dispel our doubts with something more definite than in your previous letter, dear Nikolai Arkadievich. It is painful and hard on Milia to be far from his relatives. And we want to come, but of course above all, we fear for the child. Therefore, Nikolai Arkadievich, I am turning to you for advice (in case there will be a possibility for us to get going), what household things should we take with us? And in general, what to take? I am completely inexperienced about this because I have never traveled anywhere. Milichka is now suffering from a bit of a stomach sickness, he took some castor oil and is feeling better. My Marik is developing rapidly without our influence; in the last few days he has been a little bit listless due to the heat, given his complexion. Nevertheless, he did not lose his appetite and as usual goes out for walks often, and has become quite cunning. He is beginning to chatter: whatever he hears he immediately repeats, mispronouncing words in a funny way. Overall, he is a charm! Write, dear Nikolai Arkadievich, how is your health and have your heart attacks stopped? We have heard rumors about your new important and responsible job. Don't get too tired, take a rest, dear! Wishing you all the best, we kiss you. Write,

Fania

[postscript] Greetings to Yasha and his family. How is Silva's health? Marochka sends kisses to his little cousins.

4.9 LETTERS FROM PAVEL SHEFTEL TO SABINA AND HER PARENTS

PS 1

Dear Sabina, 1917

Your letter of 8th April, addressed to your parents, was forwarded to me by them. True, due to circumstances beyond their control I received it on the 19th of July, an almost three months long delay, but thanks for that too, as it sheds some light on the complete lack of news and the silence. As I have already written in letters sent by regular and registered mail hoping they would still reach you, I am happy that you are successful in your profession and are not distressed by any attacks or rumors, for as expressed in a folk proverb, he who loves everybody, loves nobody. In other words, a more or less brilliant individual cannot please everybody and willy-nilly, as is bound to happen, shall meet friends and foes on his life's path; and the more numerous the scientific foes one has, the more it bespeaks the seriousness of that individual. There is no need to elaborate my thought any further; I think it is quite clear. Of course, it is a great pity, barring the known circumstances of personal life, that great distances make interchange of ideas difficult. However, one has to assume that despite the revolutionary frenzy that has enveloped all countries to a greater or lesser extent, [aimed at] improving the economic situation of the masses, scientific thought abroad across all disciplines, and particularly in psychiatry and psychology, has led to many interesting discoveries.

I have read Renata's letter. What a sincere, guileless, childlike and tender style: it is combined with a desire to show herself as a serious and mature person, to give, as she supposes, an account of how she spends her time, sweet and affectionate [illegible French words about Renée]. As much as would like [illegible]. However, evidently, a person is herself, a smith of her own life. I commiserate with your financial situation, it is a pity that the daughter of two doctors is living on credit. But I cannot offer any help. I am here and you have other goals and tasks. Clearly, if it were possible, I would instantly [send?], but it is difficult, very difficult. I wish you, dear Sabina, more cheerfulness, perhaps your situation will improve and you will finally be able to take Renata back and not have her raised in the manner of French counts and marquesses in [a *pension*]. I wish you health. Warm hugs to Renata. [Cordially]

Your Pavel.

[postscript] You can address your letter either to me or better yet to your parents, and they will be forwarded to me.

PS 2

Dear Sabina, 1917

On the 16th of August, according to the old calendar, I received portraits of Renata for me and her grandmother. I confess that when I opened the parcel and saw the portraits I could not believe that this was Renata, it only seemed to be some fantasy of a painter who drew a portrait of a beautiful girl. There was absolutely no similarity , nothing common, nothing between the face that I remembered since I had left Switzerland and the present portrait that would support such a comparison. To tell the truth, had I not received this portrait from you I would have never said that this was Renata. Whence this curly mass of hair, which you cannot miss, this half opened smiling mouth with a slightly pulled up upper lip, these clever little eyes reacting condescendingly to a grown-up person's fancy to photograph her; I just could not believe, and still do not believe, that this is how Renata looks. This is no longer a babbling infant wriggling in my arms but a girl perhaps with her own ego. In a word, you [the polite you] deserve complete gratitude for having cared for and raised such a beauty. May fate keep her healthy, blooming, and happy in the future. The first portrait, where she is shown as apparently making little houses in the sand, is poor, because the shadows were incorrectly applied, and only by looking attentively to make things out, one can see that Renata is dressed in a bathing suit, is squatting, and making something, but even there you can see her head with the luxurious curls.

Who knew the war would last so long, and now it is almost three years, more precisely two years and seven months, that I have not seen her. How is life in Villars? Recently, about two to three weeks ago, I received a postcard from Milia with a request to tell him if I know anything about You [the polite plural form] since they had no news for more than three months. It appears that the day they received my answer Your parents also received the portraits. Senia, i.e., Semion Evgenyevich [Kofman] informed me that he met Milia (who, he said, impressed him as an appealing young student), and that You had asked Your parents whether You should travel to Russia in a sealed car, and allegedly, having received their consent, you were going to, but since they had no news from you for a long time, they became terribly worried. Since You are in Villars, You are clearly no longer undecided and have chosen to stay in Switzerland. Tell me, please, how do You get money and how are transfers made? The rate of exchange now is terrible. How is life, your health, are You publishing in journals? You probably know from newspapers about what is happening in our country. I subscribe to *Annales de Médicine* but it's a rather dry journal, so I had asked for *Presse Médicale*. Forget it, this is no time for journals, in my situation it is difficult [to pursue?]. Perhaps I will move somewhere. Write about what is new with You, how are Your brothers, do they write anything about furniture and things left in Berlin where Sania lives? Goodbye. Before this letter reaches you on the 25th of October, I rush to greet Sabina and wish all the best.

Pavel.

PS 3

Dear Sabina, 1917.X.11

I hope my telegram was received, and you already...I do not know why, even though the experiences of my last days in Zurich have not yet died away, and also that in Your letters repeatedly slip in (slightly sarcastic) reproaches about various Rivkas or Khayas; or perhaps you perceived something intuitively. Nevertheless, I have to admit that I began to vacillate about addressing you either as "thou" or as "You." Whether it was the influence of the photograph of Renata the beautiful daughter (I received those photographs more than a month ago), or perhaps other psychological factors played a role here; and perhaps, should we meet again, the story about them might be sad an untold story of unhappiness. And I must confess that lately there was a wish to share impressions more than before, to get closer to the inner world... Yes, it means that I am now in Ekaterinodar, I serve in a public institution but I belong to a military department. The circumstances that facilitated the transfer had two causes, mainly, I got terribly bored in my village. Moreover, during the first months of the revolution I plunged head over heels into public work and since I did not have any educated coworkers, I ended up being the head of a number of many organizations in addition to my own duties, and meetings lasting from 1–2 hours, so that I became extremely exhausted. This was also especially due to the situation that I was the only physician for a district of 93,000 inhabitants and growing in numbers due to the collapse of government authority by *le peuple* [the people]. These and other kind considerations made me take measures to relocate. Thankfully, doctors who served on the front lines are now being replaced by those who serve on the home front, but having served on the front line, and since I remained in the deep home front (due to illness), I have now received a transfer to Ekaterinodar in the Kuban Province.

At first I was very glad as I hoped to have a good private practice (the salaries paid by organizations being quite low); but then this joy diminished when I found out how difficult it would be, due to the enormous influx of doctors; so the tale is told. I am now in Ekaterinodar; but it is not easy. The trips to Tiflis, the center of our district, and traveling in terribly overcrowded trains, both the ticketed and the free ones (in all classes), and due to the poor condition of the rolling stock, a heroic effort. Moreover, to an extreme degree, it is complicated by the housing problem: two rooms rented by me from intelligent and not money-hungry people, cost 125 rubles a month. I am going into all these details in order to explain why I didn't answer the letters I was receiving from you lately, and fairly regularly (the cat knows whose meat[116] he ate).

I received the photographs of Renata showing two views. The first one,

which I called a girl playing in the sand, I forwarded (in a letter) to my mother. On my way to Tiflis and back I made a stopover in Kislovodsk where [sister] Ania, who has been treated for more than three months for peritonitis, was visited by mother and also Semion Evgenyevich. Mama and Ida asked a number of times and I told them that you had sent them a number of postcards with greetings which they allegedly never answered. They declared unanimously that they have not received either letters or postcards. In general, I must say, I participated very little in conversations about my family, about you both in Switzerland, and I recall that when asked does Sabina write to me, I answered in the affirmative and thus asserted, contrary to rumors in Rostov, that there was no complete break-up between us. During my last visit in Kislovodsk they asked to convey their cordial greetings and even made a note of the address (Ida), so that they could write when they got a chance, even though Ania's health seemed to cause strong concern, I received a postcard that a few days earlier they performed a puncture and drained eight liters of fluid, probably due to peritonitis. Clearly they were in no mood to write. Right now I do not have much work to speak of and lots of free time; I visit various institutions in the hope of getting a job somewhere. I opened a private practice but the truth is that there are no patients, so all I can do is wait. The last letters I received from [Pavel crossed out and corrected] you were of 4.IX (according to the new style). So where have you settled down now, are you already in Lausanne? Anyway, send letters to the old address. By the way, about a month and a half ago I sent money to Moscow to have a set of books on pedagogy sent to you; I wonder if the store did it,

116 A reference to Krylov's fable "The cat and the cook." The moral of the fable is: don't talk much, take action.

I will make inquiries in Moscow today. And I would like to ask if it is possible to send me the journals *Münchener Medizinische Wochenschau*, *La Presse Médicale* (or another French weekly), and in addition a book published by Masson in Paris: *Les Psychonévroses* (Roussy et L'Hermitte), *Hystérie-pithiatisme* (Babinski, Froment), *Guide pratique D'expertises médico-militaires.*[117] Delving deeper into this literature and thinking that work in the city would be more interesting, I omitted asking how is Renatochka's stomach. How is she, the little darling? What is she doing? Save what she is writing. Let her have her own ideas. Maybe fate will smile upon her and I will see her, this pretty child. A real beauty! Alright, goodbye my dear ones. I wish you all the best. Write. My address: Ekaterinodar Kuban Province, Grafskaya Street 23, Doctor Sheftel.

1917.X.11 (old style) How are your brothers? Where are they and their families? How is Sania? Greetings from Leibovich (even though she put me in an awkward position regarding explanations about [illegible] and Shvartsman.

PS 4

Dear Sabina. 13/24.X.1919.

Your birthday is on the 25th of October and, of course it will not be the way it should be. On this day sad and disturbing thoughts, even more pronounced and [painful?], will invade your soul and your mood will be filled with sorrow and doubt. And indeed, separated from relatives and people close to you, worried about daily, day-to-day existence, all thoughts about and wishes for the child, living in a foreign land, isolated and lonely, on this day you have no friend to share your sorrow and worries. But nature's law is immutable and no human being can change it. However, clouds will pass, the storm will end, the loud and threatening nature will calm down, gone are the roar of thunder and flashing lightning, nature will be pacified and cheerful, and at the same time there will be a conciliatory and caressing calm. You had to overcome many hardships: the child's illness, worry about her nutrition, fear of not having a piece of bread in the literal sense of the word [illegible] could wear you down. But thank God, I hope, the child is healthy again and that you are in good health too. The main thing is that I, having experienced during this time a lot of physical privations, and even more so [incalculable?] painful sensations, such as ethnic insults as well as assaults on my personal character, I too should have health and moral

117 Roussy G., Lhermitte J. Les Psychonévroses de Guerre. Masson, Paris, 1917; Babinski J., Froment J. Hystérie-pithiatisme et troubles nerveux d'ordre réflexe en neurologie de guerre. Masson, Paris, 1917; Duco A., Blum E. Guide pratique du médecin dans les expertises médico-légales militaires. Masson, Paris, 1917 (found by Svetlana Subbotina).

satisfaction. Hopefully the rest will change over time. I hope, dear Sabina and Renata, to have some news from you. I kiss you warmly and trust fate will be good to you. Pavel.

PS 5

Dear Sabina! Simferopol, Crime 1921.VI.19

I tried to mail you a letter from Simferopol and will try to send it through your parents; hopefully it will reach you. We are now going through the 8th year of the historical shift in our national life and it is certainly also affecting us little people. Aside from the spiritual and moral sides and other forms, given the natural course of things, we do not stay put in one place, we may not count on staying in a familiar spot for many years. Having firmly settled down in Feodosia I, among others, was mobilized and assigned to be sent north (that's how we call being sent to Moscow, from where we doctors are dispersed about across the boundless expanses of Russia). But by a quirk fate, for the time being I am staying in Simferopol where I will continue to serve at the TsUKK [Central Administration of Crimea Spas] and work as chief of a reception center for evacuees. I have been in Simferopol for about three weeks and I am thinking of settling down here; in general, physicians who have a private practice have a better life here (an extra piece of bread, lard, and milk).

From you Sabina I received recently two greetings, one was a letter of 8.VII via the post office via Batum and Feodosia in April of 1921 and in the same month a second letter, marked by you 7.III of this year, addressed to your parents and forwarded to me. I am happy for you, Sabina, that you can work in a field chosen by you and that you are gradually realizing the plan we had formulated about our travel abroad in 1912. True, if science can give moral satisfaction and consolation in this vale of suffering and disenchantment, and, mainly, relieve what is peculiar to us little people, i.e., a little dose of weltschmerz, then the thirst for such an abreaction is especially pronounced now. However... not everything endures.

It is sad to hear and to know that your financial situation does only not offer a possibility of a minimum living wage but that you do not even have with you the second valuable thing in life, little Renata, who is growing up alone, on principles of a Communist weltanschauung. The main thing for me is that I cannot help financially at all. It is both offensive and hurtful. I should have foreseen that, but apparently this was fate. How are you living now, how is your and Renata's health? Where are you now and where is Renata? Goodbye, I hug you warmly,

Pavel

The address: to Doctor Kagarlitskii, Salgirnaya Street corner of Ekaterinskaya, Simferopol (for me) or Reception Center of TsUKK, No. 1 Gospitalnaya street corner of Lazaretnaya, to staff doctor Sheftel.

PS 6

Dear Sabina! 1921.IX.22

I am writing a letter in Sania's room in Moscow where we, i.e. your mother and father and I, arrived and are spending our second day here. I am making efforts to receive a business trip abroad so as to continue to Switzerland but so far without success and it looks like I will not be successful at all. I am tied up as before and even though I no longer serve directly in the army, I am still considered drafted and right now I myself do not know where I will be told to go: back to Simferopol (in Crimea) or at least whether I will be able to remain in Rostov. Of course, it is tempting to stay in Moscow, what can I say, compared to other cities of the republic Moscow lives a more conscious cultural life: libraries with foreign periodicals, hospitals, lectures, scientific societies etc. but if you do not have connections it is difficult to stay here. I myself have not had any letters from you for a long time, your parents informed me that you were getting ready for a lecture tour, but I was unable to make it out because they read the letter hastily, rushing to forward it to me to Simferopol, but in the meantime I had already left for a previously requested month long leave. Where are you working now? On what subject? Are you in contact with the scientific world in Moscow? By the way, Yasha, in spite of his talent, came up with a rather "original" idea, I mean original as far as sources [of executions?]are concerned, namely: you should come and read a few lectures in Russia for which you should be paid and—and this is the main thing—that you get a guarantee to be able to return abroad. Perhaps if you were a man, you could apply to a scientific-technical department that would enter into suitable negotiations with you; but it would not be possible for you, someone not yet adapted to the practical side of life. How is Renata? How is her health? Where is she living? What innocent simplicity and tenderness flow from her words in the letters in French—I hug you, little Renée. I would like very much to travel and see both of you and I was going to Moscow with optimistic expectations assuming that I would be able to take advantage of some acquaintances, but the influential person on whom I was counting turned out to be ill and was being treated abroad; thus the main trump card [for going abroad?][the rest illegible]. at least, they should leave me [?] in peace in Rostov. Such is life. It is true, you have the consolation of having a daughter and science. I do not have this, and all I have is to drag out this gray and monotonous work.

I feel that your letters are somewhat pessimistic and this is understandable as a reaction to current failures and efforts to arrange the intended trip abroad. I am ending my letter with a hope that fate will send both of you good health, possibilities of living comfortably, and to me the opportunity to see you. I hug you warmly and kiss you

Pavel

[postscript possibly from Yan] Try to correspond with our mission in Berlin about traveling to Russia for a period of more than a month to read lectures on psychoanalysis.

[postscript] And so now in Moscow there are mother, father, Yasha, Sania with his family, and I. I'll be leaving Moscow in a few days, but for the time being write to me in Moscow and they will forward to me.

PS 7

My dear Sabina, Moscow 1921.IX.30

As you can see, I neither succeeded to get a business trip abroad in Moscow nor was I able to settle down in Moscow; therefore I am going back to Rostov where I hope to be employed by a hospital and reopen my private practice. I will be living with my sisters: Fania, whom you probably don't know yet, and Ida. Still [hoping?] that we will all be alive and well, and by spring I hope to move back to Moscow and have a better chance of realizing [illegible] and probably some changes will take place by that time. When I was in Moscow, due to the hassle and running around, I was unable to speak with Sania about your articles. I only saw one of 1921 published in *Zeitschrift für angewandte Psychologie*.[118] What are you writing about, what are you doing? How is Renatochka? What about her appendicitis? Has a definite diagnosis been made for the child and is there hope that it is not appendicitis. What does she look like? I understand that given the strained circumstances it is not appropriate to talk about but I would very much like to see photos of both of you. It wasn't worthwhile to send you my photograph: time has put its stamp on me, or perhaps not so much the time as the war. I am going to Rostov. I hug you warmly, kiss Renata warmly for me, and [illegible] all kinds of successes. Write.

Pavel

118 The actual name of the journal founded by Freud was *Imago Zeitschrift für Anwendung der Psychoanalyse auf die Geisteswissenschaften* (journal for the application of psychoanalysis to the humanities). Actually the article "The origin of the child's words papa and mama" was the only one published in Imago in 1922.

PS 8

Dear Sabina 1921.XII.8

Even if you don't get this letter in time of our dear Renatochka's birthday (I mailed it anyway), you should know that on this day my thoughts are with you; and let fate, finally, send the child the opportunity in the nearest future to be under the cover of her father's (mine and yours) home. I do not doubt that you give her all your love, all your caring for her, and with this brighten her half-childish half-adult (due to separation), staying in [illegible]. Nonetheless, life is only harmonious when the two principles are united. But I will stop philosophizing, may God grant us a time when fate will reunite us again and the child will grow protected by our love and a rational attitude toward her.

I believe that lately you received some news about me, as I did about you, through Yasha and some letters of Silva to him, that your financial situation is unenviable and, sadly, I was able to ascertain the same from <u>your letter to a</u> certain woman named Shvarts. Perhaps with Yasha's relocation to Moscow something will get better for you, thus my plans regarding your moving to Moscow will lose their cogency and advisability. In and of itself, staying in Berlin where there is everything necessary for science and for earning a living, is more pleasant than in Russia. I don't know if you received this letter but in one of my letters, under the fresh impression of your letter to a woman called Shvarts, which was forwarded to me, I expressed the opinion that it is high time to put an end to your half-starving existence and that it would be best for you to come back to Russia. It is true, having settled in Moscow, your scientific activity would be limited due to a lack of literature, but materially, I hope, you and the child would be well fed and living amongst your family. It is true, in Moscow your scientific work would be narrowed but not obstructed. But after all, scientific work here is thriving, and even in your specialty there are ardent adherents of Freud. (In a scientific journal there was an article enthusiastically lauding Freud as a representative of a theory that in the neuroses there is an active psychological self-defense, one of the great manifestations of the law of evolution and the struggle for survival. Here in Rostov I was unable to read the whole article.) Be that as it may, you would not have to disrupt your work. Further evidence for work opportunities is the existence of various pedagogico-psychological institutes where both academic and practical psychologists are working (your brother Sania is an example thereof). But I wrote all this approximately, in case you had doubts about the chances of getting work here. But if there is a possibility to find a better life in Berlin, then there is no need to talk about Moscow. I am waiting for your letters. How is Renata, do you see her frequently, and how is her psyche? Do you see her often? How about being fed and brought up in somebody else's home? And even though there is no reason to fear that she will not develop altruistic feelings, it is not like the supply of intimate and sensitive feelings that can only be given to the child living together with her parents. Nothing special or new here, I am living in Rostov and waiting in vain for something, that is work in a hospital, which might sound overblown given the scarcity of means and materials which at present makes work quite impossible, but I am awaiting [more?]. Well, goodbye, I kiss you

Pavel

[postscript] My address: Dmitrievskaya Street 33 Apartment 3 Rostov on/Don.

PS 9

My dear ones [father and mother-in-law] 1921.XII.8

Milia will tell you more or less about how we live. Our life is rather monotonous, the least we can say. There are a few private patients and if there are any, it is only by chance, old patients are not seen; a common complaint among doctors—with the exception of three or four—is that the scarcity of patients may be due to stagnation, but this is small consolation. Serving in the department of health is not enough to make a living. The hospital staffs have been cut, briefly, the situation, God only knows, is not an enviable one; however, thank God, I have shoes, clothes, and enough food. After all, my move from Simferopol to Rostov had its positive side, I am living with my sisters and having some furniture and was able to have a better arrangement here, however, it is obvious that a life that depends on selling and being acquainted with [Senbat?] is not conducive to a particularly good mood. I lack a personal income: so what if during one month, from 24th of October when I started my private practice to the 24th of November, I made about 270,000–280,000? Considering the current high prices, you can hardly call this income; everything is forcing me to develop other plans. I am now ready for a commercial venture, but with whom and with what. Moreover, I have not given up the idea of somehow getting back to Moscow, but this will be more convenient in the spring when the freezing weather is gone, when staying in Moscow and the hustle and bustle of getting settled can take place in more favorable conditions. For some reason it seemed to me that with the help of acquaintances it would be possible to stay in Moscow but the shortness of my stay there interfered with this. It turned out that at the time I arrived there, my acquaintance Andrei Matveyevich Lezhava[119] was in Moscow but was ill, but somebody had deceived me by telling me that the ex-commissar was now living abroad. Of course, were I more intimately acquainted with him I could have asked you to go and see him with my letter in hand and get an approval for a business trip abroad, but I think that a personal meeting with him would have made him remember some facts about my relationship with the deceased Semion Evgenyevich and my sister. Therefore I suppose that this idea should now be abandoned. I had hoped that your sojourn in Moscow, and in particularly yours, mama, could help me. I think, mama, that once you get acclimated to Moscow, you will be able to help me get settled; but since you are coming here, it will be possible to solve this problem on the spot. Should you come to Rostov, mama, I ask you to stay with us. We have enough space, we now have three rooms (two were occupied by my sisters, the third one was mine), in these three rooms I and my sister Fania are living. So do not worry that you would be in our way. Ida went to Kiev so you are free to make yourself comfortable; and when you arrive in Rostov come straight to us. I told Milia about it and now I am writing to you about it. Fania, my sister, also spoke to Milia about it, she would have written to you but in her absence I am writing to you and that is why she is not adding a postscript. We hope that with Yasha's arrival the situation of Sabina and Renata will improve as well as a more orderly correspondence. In your letter to me you write that Sabina has supposedly received an invitation for a business trip from the National Commissariat for Education, but I could not figure out if it meant to go to Berlin or to Moscow. How is your life? What is father doing, what news about his business trip? It would be good if he could see Sabina. He might find some business and things might go differently. Goodbye,

Pavel

[postscript] Greetings to Sania. How is his health and Rakhil's and the child?

[postscript] Thanks for the greetings on Renata's birthday. May fate grant the child lots of health and the joy of celebrating future birthdays in the circle of intimates and relatives. My address: Dmitrievskaya 33, apartment 3, Rostov on/Don.

119 Lezhava Andrei Matveyevich (1870–1937), a soviet government agent, and in 1920–1922 vice president of the National Commissariat of Internal Commerce.

PS 10

Dear Sabina 1921.XII.30

It will soon be Renata's birthday but I don't know if my greetings will arrive in time. It seemed that with your parents moving to Moscow we will be getting more letters from you, will know more about your daily life, about your successes, about Renata; I hoped for a more frequent correspondence that would create more bonding and more intimacy. You yourself understand very well that the uncertainty of receiving letters dampens and actually kills any desire to write. However now, with new opportunities, when Yasha and his family are in Berlin, it would seem that we should be getting frequent news and we would have a clear idea of your life and you of ours. However, it is more than two months since we had a letter from you and your last letter is from the month of July. It is a great pity that nowadays letters get lost. Still your mother forwarded to me your letter sent to some woman called Shvarts. How sad and painful it was to read it. Let alone that the child, the only consolation of its mother, is, due to lack of financial means, spending her younger years separated from her mother; let alone a father whom she does not know. But it is up to you to assess the worth of your work and time spent: forced by the situation to earn some pitiful pennies, a few centimes, coupled with a deficient fitness for practical life and a passionate penchant for science. I can tell you, dear Sabina, having received your letter, I was overcome with a mixed feeling of sadness and rage. Rage, because it seemed that coming back to Russia, and having this opportunity—as Yasha and Sania were returning—to come along, you could have come too; you could have spared yourself the trouble of those brutal minutes of waiting on line to be seen by this or that committee, begging for dinners like a Russian emigrant. You would have been able to live together with your child and not have to wait till you saved enough centimes to be able to travel and see your daughter. These are the reasons for [my] discontent. On the other hand, to leave abroad with its culture, art treasures, libraries, an indispensable environment for your scientific works, to forfeit all this stuff which probably cannot be found here, to take Renata away from luxurious nature that leaves indelible traces of the love of beauty and of what ennobles the soul, to transfer her into completely different conditions of existence, into a circle of different children, and into a new country altogether—all this is not especially easy to decide and it requires a great deal of deliberation. However, a solution needs to be found. No matter how hard and troublesome it may be, one should think not only about comforts or being satiated. If you have to struggle day in and day out in the vain pursuit of a secure piece of bread for yourself and your child, you are willy-nilly faced with the decision to solve this problem by returning to Russia. All of us together would be able to settle down here somehow. It is true, my practice has not improved yet, but for now I am content. I was unable to get an official trip to where you are, so what else is left? True, some people tell me that they were sometimes lucky to go abroad on demand, and since you have been living in Switzerland for more than seven years, as a Swiss citizen you might be able to have the Swiss Republic demand that I come to Switzerland. But personally I doubt that it can be done. Perhaps, your father might be able to visit you. This would be great. I believe Yasha was able to forward to you our greetings, to tell you about our encounter and conversations. In one of your letters to someone you write about somebody with a case of appendicitis. Is that someone you? Your mother sent me your postcard to them of August 28 where you wrote that Renata was ill again. What is with her, my God. There is always something, either bronchitis or something intestinal, and now something again. How could one tell that it is now seven years since I took leave of her, so tiny, with those black eyes of hers, sitting in my arms and twirling the hair of my beard with her cute little fingers, and that now she is a big girl, with her intellect, with her soul, with her own little universe, it is hard to believe. To feel that she is our child, the rage that a father is a mere sound to her, a mere abstraction, that for her anyone else could be substituted as papa, and at the same time, [my] shyness to write, as if the letter came from a stranger. On the 17th of December Renata will be eight years old. What can I wish her? Before all else, hug her warmly, kiss her very, very warmly in my name on her cute little lips, her beautiful little head, may joy and happiness shine on her face removing all grief and worries, and may she live as a consolation for us. Be well, Sabina. I embrace you tenderly and hope that fate will smile upon us.

Your Pavel

Greetings from my sisters. I am waiting for letters from you.

[in French]My dear little Renée. Your grandmother wrote to you, I am [illegible] now with [her] and I also write a few lines to you. I would very much like to see you again but I am occupied with [illegible] in Russia and because of that I cannot [travel] to you. Write to me how you are, how is your health, what do you do, how [are] your lessons, do you see your mama often. I think you are a good and diligent girl, and [illegible] I will be able [a few illegible words], and you will tell me everything. [Kisses to mama]. I kiss you. Your papa.

Dear Sabina.

I am adding a few words to mother's letter. I have not had news from you for a long time. In his letter of 17.XI Yasha writes about a postcard written by you on 14 November. Moreover, apparently you cannot imagine the difficulties involved in traveling abroad, therefore I don't understand your question why I have not received a leave of absence. Hopefully, your father will be granted some business trips and you will soon get my 'live greeting' [?]. I am now working for the health department, I make rounds at the hospital for internal diseases, and I also take an interest in the neuroses; but here, so far, there is little thinking and less literature. In order to get some information one has to expend a great deal of energy and to get foreign literature is unthinkable. Write in detail about what you are doing, what are you occupied with, what are you writing, and in what direction is psychoanalysis currently going: in the direction of Stekel or the more complex psychoanalysis of Adler? I am being rushed, therefore I will stop here. I wish you all the best. Happy New Year. Mother will add the rest.

Pavel

PS 11

Dear Sabina [January1922?]

Had you been receiving my letters, you would have seen my complaint that we had no letters from you for a long time, but last week these complaints were pleasantly disproved. One day coming back from your mother, I thought about the letters she had received that day (it was approximately January 21) from all her children, including two letters from you, which had been forwarded to her by your father: one of approximately December 18–19 and another of 26.XII. I was pleasantly surprised and delighted: I received your letter directly from Switzerland; and there was an even greater surprise, when looking at the stamps we figured out that it had been on its way to us for only 17 days, which given the slowness of the domestic postal service seems simply incredible. But the fact is obvious. The letter is dated by you December 30 and it arrived via Moscow to Rostov on January 17 and I got it on the 21st. It seems that such a happy opportunity to correspond more often, share impressions and thoughts seems to create a mood of a certain closeness and of an intimate connection. Let us see [...] the correspondence will get better... In one of your letters to your mother was enclosed a photo of Renata. Do you believe, Sabina, when I am looking at it (your mother gave me the photo), I am overcome by a strange feeling, when I see this pensive, serious face with a noble expression, the waves of hair covering her head, you cannot determine who you are looking at. It seems that you are seeing a 15–16 years old adolescent, but the face is not as old, no. Yet this deep, deliberate gaze, this momentarily concentrated little face, the seriousness of expression and at the same time of a certain sadness—all this together somehow does not at first give the impression of an 8-year old girl; and it is only the round, low neck dress and the slender hands held on the sides, on the photo, that made me imagine a small and young Renatochka [...] as you had described her to me. Whatever it shows, regardless of the impression of age on photo, a photo remains a photo and it can never convey the liveliness of facial expressions, of the entire dynamics: for, after all, a photo is static, it fixates one moment and it is impossible to get a complete representation looking at this cute little head, the tightly pressed lips, I can hardly believe, I don't get the emotional attitude and the perception that such a big girl is the daughter of me and you. Logic says yes, it'll soon be ten years since I got married, and it is absolutely clear, the daughter is eight years old; but the feelings, the direct perception itself, somehow do not fit. Let us understand: to leave a child still in the cradle, still in her infancy, a separation for more than seven years—from January 14, 1915, when I left both of you, you and Renata, and it is the eighth year already—of course, all of this is clear and sad; because it may well be that all that happened, my separation, should not be blamed on the war, for it is we who are directly to blame, for we were the makers of our happiness, not only victims of various accidental events and *fatalité*. But why remember the past, even though it may be pleasant, as some say; yes, let us stir up the past so it will serve us as a guiding experience for the present and the future. I do not remember who said that life is in the present, but that the past spoke of a lack of hope, which should be the main incentive of our earthly existence; it is the instinct toward the new that should push us forward and pull us away from the sticky past, thus facilitate progress. Let us hope so, too. In fact, thanks to the chaotic nature of our correspondence, neither you nor I could mutually know and understand the peripeties [reversals] of our lives during these seven years, and all of this, of course, can only be clarified in a face-to-face conversation. But you seem to have had the opportunity to put down deeper roots in Switzerland, to create for yourself relatively strong material foundations. However, can you also see some resolution to the goal you had set yourself while we were betrothed and living in Russia, when during our long heart-to-heart talks lasting until early morning, we were fantasizing about the goal of your scientific career. But now, should your material situation improve, the plans I had made have lost their meaning. You know my character, don't you? While having some persistence, I confess I do not possess the hard, steely tenacity that sometimes helps a person to achieve a difficult goal extending over many years.

But sometimes I even I had passionate desires to see you and Renata that overwhelmed me and forced me to think more intensely, and look for a way out. I longed to live in the port cities Novorossiisk and Feodosia, to be by the sea and have the opportunity to travel; however, I did not have enough courage and determination to overcome the risks and difficulties of an illegal departure. And so one day, impressed by the dreary situation, when your only consolation, Renatochka, was being brought up separately, when you were forced to make a living by sewing some kind of lingerie, and this is after seven years of living in Switzerland, I have decided to propose to you to come to Russia; but I knew quite well your opinion and attitude to Russia since 1912, i.e., since nine years ago. Nevertheless, I sent your parents a letter and asked to forward it to you, expressing the opinion that now, considering your and Renatochka's half-starving existence, both of you need to come to Russia, where we would start living together. Of course, your scientific work would not the same as abroad; but the possibility of such (Sania's example), even though limited, would still exist, but most importantly, you would be well fed. There were plans for you to move to Berlin, together with Yasha; but since you wrote that the financial situation has begun to improve, it makes no sense for you to relocate anymore. And I? Well, it has been so long without me, so at least let it be going well for both of you. So that both of you should be healthy and joyfully perceive [text break]

PS 12

Dear Sabina, 1922.II.11[?]

For a long time I had no letters from you and I do not understand why! For some time it seemed as if the correspondence was going well and then it stopped again. How are you living, how is your work? How is your health? Soon on June 17th it will be ten years since a rabbi drew up the marriage contract—how many hopes, how many expectations—and how much grief, mental anguish, tears about what did not come true and what was not fulfilled. A sad and painful picture. And yet, on the path we traveled, there was a lot of joy that provided both moral satisfaction and the realization that aspirations were not only aimed at something material, but that sometimes connecting with the spiritual world smoothed over adversities. I have nothing against your reproaching me, but I recall a small gazebo in the right corner of the [semi]garden, at a time when one did not count the hours and the minutes, when the silence was more eloquent than words. You were saying then that my words were like something you read in a book; I do not know if you remember this – it happened ten years ago, as I am saying now. It was a sad and heart-breaking picture [illegible] these were vain, unnecessary, and gratuitous torments caused by morbid suspiciousness and many resentments over trifles; however, all kinds of little flames were also seen along this path, they were far away, but they enticed with a promise of comfort, warmth, and joys. We have lived through a lot of grief, doubts, hesitations, conflicts together, and separately; but when I remember how mother showed me a photograph in the stereoscope—I don't know if you have it—of our apartment [street name?], where you are in bed holding in your arms this little creature that has now developed into Renata, who writes to grandma about grandpa. When such images pass before my eyes, then I want to believe that little flames will yet shine on our path, little flames that will warm our heart and give us bodily and mental peace. Write, dear Sabina, about what you are up to. I have already written to you about the certificate. It is possible, if I had in my hands a permit of entry to Switzerland this would give me more energy and optimism to travel. Big money could buy travel to Constantinople. But without such a permit it's difficult to travel any farther. Write to me what Renata is doing, about her health. I do not do much with languages and therefore there is a lack of confidence in being able to travel any time soon; but I sometimes re-read the old medical journals which you sent me in 1917.

[postscript from Yan]: Today we received a letter from Henri

Spilrein from Paris with a request to pay back 1,500 Swiss francs which have been given to you. Did you receive 1,500 francs?

(signature)

[postscript] Father flew to Moscow. I already got a cable from him. Write to me (Signature)

PS 13

Dear father! 1922.V.4

Fate did not fulfil our dear mother's wish, after all the sorrow and suffering endured for the sake of her children and all the relatives to be together, and that you and she would have a life of your own. Fate deemed otherwise. And it seemed that there was some possibility, as this mother, grieving every minute, every free moment and was also thinking, "here, let me arrange something, specially for you, i.e. for the children"; she never said "for us" but always explicitly for others, for the children; these were her impulses, wishes and dreams: good life for all. One could hardly believe that fate would not have mercy on a mother who sacrificed herself for her children but it turned out differently. When a misfortune befalls someone the person tries to find consolation in religion; however we, even though we intellectually acknowledge the immutability of the laws of nature, rebirth and destruction, our self cannot reconcile itself with this and willy-nilly the question arises: why, who wanted this death. Lately I have been visiting her often and your letters, the letters from Sabina, were an inexhaustible source of conversations and reminiscences. And now, looking back, recalling the details of our conversations, the details of our marriage and of settling down in Berlin, reveal the whole picture of her caring attention, of kindness, and friendly compassion, taking care not to wound my pathological self-love and excessive suspiciousness at that time. And it was only lately, thanks to friendly discussions, that I deeply felt how often I had been unjust, wrong, and have sometimes offended her mercilessly; but she forgave everything for the happiness of her children was the goal of her life; because of that she tolerated taunts to her self-esteem and silently bore in her heart the wounds inflicted by close relatives. But it is not for me to offer you words of consolation, and I recall that in the Talmud there is approximately the following saying: nobody feels as acutely the loss of a mother as a husband the loss of his wife; that is, children sooner or later as they grow up, are capable of alleviating the pain of losing a mother but not a husband the death of his wife. I am saying this because I became increasingly aware of mother's character and I can only repeat that I lost not only the mother of my wife but something more, a friend to whom I was not shy to reveal my heart's pain, who listened compassionately to my complaints, who gave me approval and hope; a friend who tried to ease my situation while suffering herself; who even in the last minutes of consciousness, a few hours before her death, even though expected by all of us but which occurred sooner than expected, her intention was not to make people anxious or fearful. She was a person who sacrificed her life for other people; as she was gradually losing her consciousness, she was saying: "Milia why do you look so ill; Pavlusha go and take a rest." How much meekness and spiritual submission she showed in the days of her illness. I know, father, how difficult it is for you to read this; it breaks my heart to tears but may the luminous image of mother soar between us and inspire stoicism in our lives. As long as we are destined to live, may her love serve us as an example how to live and act for the welfare of people close to us. I kiss you

Pavel

[continuing with letter to Sabina]

For me mother's death was untimely, unnecessary and unjust, for in about two–three months she could have seen Sabina and Renata and found a little bit of satisfaction for the sleepless nights, or living in a small shabby room in a sanatorium; she is of course better off now, but we the living are terribly broken-hearted; in mother I lost a sincere and unselfish friend who brightened up many hard moments for me despite my having been so unjust. How moved she would be when someone showed her a sign of attention, but on the other hand, how much feelings of love, of selfless devotion—sometimes misunderstood by us—she was able to show to us children. I recall as if in a fog my arrival in Rostov, I do not want to dwell on it at length, but were it not for mother with her tact and humanity and sensitivity, I doubt I could now sincerely call her a mother. It was only as a friend, as a person sincerely going all out for the happiness of her children, that mother was capable of doing what she had done for me.

Recently life, and perhaps also fate, have been smiling upon me and maybe it is my destiny to be joined with both of you again. I hope my dear ones that both of you, Sabina, and you, my little dear Renée [French in the original], my child Renata, are in good health. You should know, my little Renée ,that I am living in Russia where people speak Russian, and therefore you can write to me in French [broken French in the original]. Please, Sabina, explain to Renata that she can write to me in French, and it might be interesting for you to try it too, perhaps I will derive a little bit of benefit from it. As your father and mother often tell me, I should make an effort to travel abroad, and develop in myself, so to speak, a will to travel. I do not know if I will succeed in developing in myself such [illegible] and such a strong complex of will power as in your father, but I am not giving up on the idea of traveling. I think in the spring it will be possible to make efforts in this direction. You wrote that perhaps you might succeed to arrange something for me, I do not know exactly what, but I think it would do no harm to get an entry permit; for example, they say one can get a business trip from here to Constantinople, but departures from Constantinople are being closely watched by the *Entente* [the Western Powers]; there were cases lacking such foreign permit certificates and travel was blocked. So anyway, if indeed I could get such a permit, it might be useful.

I am now working as chief doctor in a 120 bed children's hospital, there is little scientific work, not long ago I gave a short lecture on the subject of the zones described by Head[120]: this has to do with the phenomenon of hyperesthesia and algesia [= pain] as one of the differentiating signs between somatic disease and pure neurosis. But for the most part as chief doctor I have to be occupied with household matters, heating, lighting, feeding, laundry, etc. which does not interest me at all, but trying to discharge my duties conscientiously I waste a lot of time. In fact, I am an [internal medicine] therapist and pediatrician on the side but now I had <u>to get involved</u> in that specialty

120 Sir Henry Head (1861–1940), English neurologist, worked on the somatosensory system and the integrating function of the whole brain of its parts and organs of sensations, collaborating with psychiatrist W. H. R. Rivers.

as well. I think that once I organize the household, I will be able to observe children, and this will be of great value to me. Your question about which of my sisters I am living with I am answering: living here in Rostov is my sister Fania, who lived in Petersburg at the time of our wedding, and Ida who gives music lessons and sings at the opera. But now Ida moved to Kiev at her mother's request, also in Kiev is Katia who married two years ago, and Ernestina with husband and children, who are now young adults—one of whom will become an engineer and the other a lawyer; Izrail with wife and two girls and one boy, Renata's age, who is also a very intelligent boy; and of course all of them were raised in different existential conditions. As I have written already, we suffered an irreplaceable loss with the untimely death in 1917 of sister Ania and two years later the death of Semion [Senia] Evgenyevich. They liked me in their own way and when he was dying, Senia wanted to see me all the time but I did not have the opportunity. Yes, they liked me in their own way; and even if because of them there were willy-nilly some sad misunderstandings, may we be forgiven and may the earth rest lightly upon them. I have been in Rostov for over four months now; you should have received my letter from Moscow, haven't you? The practice is not doing especially well, the cold is staying on, dry freezing weather alternating with sudden rains—also kind of uneven—and all this affects the practice. We are living in the apartment of the deceased Senia, so far three people, and now even two, since Ida left, and we made an offer to your mother to come to live with us but she declined. We saw each other quite often and the topic of our conversations was dreaming how good it would be to live together, if finally the external circumstances interfering with our meeting were eliminated; we were making all kinds of plans...and cheered each other up with the hope...

A joy is awaiting you: according to letters, father is expected to travel abroad soon and you will be getting live greetings from all of us. Many Rostov citizens are now living abroad and perhaps you can learn this from Silva as well. By the way, Khosudovskaia Evgenia, who once lived in Berlin, has now settled in Berlin as a doctor. When you get a free moment write, who of the Swiss friends we knew, had you been meeting or are still meeting now. Some fifteen years ago—or maybe longer—I took a great interest in a poor but very capable young man who is now a grateful beneficiary of one of the rich Kiev Rozenberg-Brodskis, thanks to whom the man has been able to succeed in the world, he is now a professor, his last name is Lion, he should now be 35–38 years old. It would be interesting to know if he is where you are. I hope that this letter, for the writing of which I snatched a free evening in a fortunately well-heated room, will reach you and will transmit my greeting to you. I embrace you cordially, my dear ones, and expect good news from you.

Pavel

PS 14

Dear Sabina, Rostov on/Don 1922.VI.6

Father is traveling to Moscow today and I am rushing to write a few words to you. I have not had letters from you in a long time, your last postcard arrived on the 22nd of March and no word thereafter. Father told me that ten days before he left Berlin, he got some news from you, therefore I do not understand how to explain your long silence. I asked father about you and Renata. He did not have time to tell me much and even though he spent two to three days with you it was difficult to gather a lot of information about you because all of it passed so fleetingly, almost kaleidoscopically. He said that he did not find you changed. By the way, in this connection he mentioned photographs; yesterday father, Milia, Fania and Marochka were photographed but and I did not want to. Previously your deceased mother had suggested to have a photograph taken of me and sent to you but I did not want to; I always answered that I prefer to be seen live by my child and wife rather than in photographs that sometimes distort faces; for example, your deceased mother gave me a photograph of you (taken by a lady in a Lausanne park in the summer of 1920) in which your hat is pulled so much over your face that you remain unrecognizable.

[I also learned] that that you excel in sciences but are apparently not so well off financially and that you are still living in one flat and Renata in another, that Renata is a nice child, with pensive and tender character traits, that she has a well developed musicality directly responsive to the sun and bright sunny colors of the day; but that she is nonetheless rather skinny although quite healthy, that she has a lovely French accent and is in general a wonderful grandchild. But it was not mother's fate to see her, having devoted so much love, so much selfless care to you and her grandchild Renata. When we would meet, and lately it happened quite frequently, we only talked about the two of you, you and Renata; she would dream how she would talk to her, she read a lot of stuff in French and kept urging me to study languages; sometimes we spoke French and she corrected my poor pronunciation; and she always made plans to create comfort and contentment for the children and only then would take care of her personal life. During our frequent encounters in the last months, we objectively reassessed and elucidated many superfluous, unnecessary and therefore offensive moments and created an atmosphere of simple friendly chats and dreams of seeing all of us soon. But fate decided otherwise, those dreams and plans were not destined to be realized. God knows if I will be able to realize them. True, father reassures me that it will be possible and not to worry about financial matters, that my apprehensions that I will have to live at the expense of my wife are groundless, that I will be capable of participating in his publishing business (when mother was still alive he always maintained that it would be good if I could help him in his business during the day and in the evening devote myself to medicine, as long as I had no patients) and that in this way my financial situation would be more or less assured. Well, I still cannot envisage the promise that Renata would be living with us and that we could live a quiet and spiritually satisfying life in a cultural milieu. There is only one thing I can do, to be patient and can do nothing else. Anyway, I am asking you, Sabina, write to me how you are living, how are you getting on, what you are doing, how is your work. Here I am getting ready to read a lecture that recently pedagogy, having found corroboration in natural sciences, has completely changed its character, representing a new science, pedology, that requires the cooperative work of all physicians, and therefore it is necessary to establish and organize a new scientific pedological society. True, I am working in a hospital in difficult conditions which you cannot imagine so that it is impossible to speak of clinical and inpatient research; but given the present unemployment and [illegible], there are applicants for such jobs. At this time my private practice is still undeveloped. Goodbye. I am sending you, Sabina, money for a blouse (lingerie [illegible]) and, if father will take it, a dressing gown for you and Renata

[postscript in broken French]: My little daughter Renata, I send you a dress as a souvenir from your papa. I hope I and you, my little Renée, will be able to meet soon. I kiss you and [illegible] a lot from you. Your papa. On the 14th of June will be the 10th anniversary of our wedding. Remember all the good that was and try to forget the bad.

PS 15

Dear Sabina 17.01.1923

So it is 1923 now. It means we are entering a momentous year—the ninth year of our separation. "The ninth wave[121]"—as they always say—is the final,

121 *The Ninth Wave* (Russian: Девятый вал, *Dyevyatyi Val*) is an 1850 painting by the Russian Armenian marine painter Ivan Aivazovskii. It is his best-known work. The title refers to an old sailing expression referring to a wave of incredible size that comes after a succession of incrementally larger waves.

decisive outcome. You too, probably, saw the painting of the artist whose name I do not remember. The subject of it is the following: waves of a stormy sea are buffeting up and down, as if threatening to engulf the raft upon which a man is holding the steering wheel and alongside him a woman is trying to help him but apparently weakening; and here the ninth wave is approaching stealthily and mysteriously: will the fiercely raging sea carry them to the surface and give them life and freedom, or will the abyss mercilessly swallow them.

Of course, it is not necessary to interpret the person in this painting as if representing us. Our life's itinerary, even though in many ways alike, does not fit this subject: I am neither the man who is steering the wheel with a strong and brawny hand, nor are you, probably, the woman in the painting. As far as you remember and know me, your psychoanalysis will help you to criticize my analogy. Thus, I repeat, this year, without calling it fateful, must finally be settled the question: is our family (me you, Renata) finally destined to be together again or not, speaking decisively and definitively. In spite of some seemingly propitious signs, my journey to Berlin ended in failure; it seemed that as a father, I had received permission from my superiors to travel, but it failed, for in order to give me the visa, the German consul demanded an enormous bond as a precondition. Further it turned out, that the situation in Germany, both political and economic, negatively affected such a minor event as my trip. First, the dropping rate of the mark and the increasing cost of living do not offer any incentive and impetus to book-publishers like [illegible] in a direction that would favorably expedite the trip; second, the most important question, will this provide me with an independent income, which is improbable, briefly, the situation is such, that initially we would again have to live as "dependents." But, I think, we have already outgrown that state and it's time to think of becoming "independent." Such a complex, as you know yourself, especially if tied up with money matters, plays a big, big role in the lives of many people. I must tell you, Sabina, that Yasha came here for a few days; while I was still in Moscow, he claimed that the permit would be given soon, but it's been three months ,and there is still no permit. So I lost faith. I am writing this to you so that you won't have high hopes on Yasha and Sania, as you wrote in your previous letter, namely, to ask Sasha and Yasha. They are very nice guys, I am saying this without flattery, but they are too involved in their personal affairs to devote themselves to this one. Sania is pushing on with his psychotechnics, but as far as family sentiments are concerned he resembles me: at home he is hospitable, but to speak up for a relative to those in power is difficult. Rather, they are able take care of someone else, but not their own relative. Also, these are complexes, you know that yourself perfectly well. So is Sanya, So is Yasha. Of course, this is not like mother, who grieved and suffered for both of us. It was predestination. Father!? The father is in Moscow, he hasn't written anything for the third month already, some say, he is planning to come to Rostov. But there is nothing definite. We could work something out with him, but our writing relationship has soured, which is wrong. By the way, your brothers told me that they had written you about the plan, or, more exactly, that they advised you to consider the question, whether it makes sense for you to come to Moscow, to see if it is going to work for you; they also promised to find you an apartment, work, and a library. I have almost agreed, but then realized that in my case, they were wrong not to offer me assistance when I was living in Moscow; had I got a job through them, then for sure I would have found everything you and Renata needed, and on your arrival; you wouldn't have to stay with Sania, where four people are crowded in one room, where it is noisy, loud, and sometimes mismanaged. In any case, there would be no problem to find a room. Should you come to Moscow, the brothers would certainly help you. And perhaps I would be able to come to Moscow too. However, think it over, for I am aware of your understandable fears for yourself (intellectual) and for Renatusia (physical). True, financially it is now cheaper in Russia. Your 500 francs would almost be worth 4–5 billion, which is enough to live on here, without skimping anything, or food. Considerations regarding your care of Renata also have some bearing on solving this problem. I am telling you, Sabina, honestly, how much I would love finally to stop wandering from place to place and live with my own family, to work and labor for it; but the prospect of traveling to foreign lands, not knowing the language perfectly, and living off other people's money, earning nothing, is very burdensome. In this respect your mother has understood me perfectly. So, in view of all of the above, it remains an open question.

Any news? How are your spiritual and material accomplishments? Have you obtained psychoanalytic patients or are you still having trouble with it? Where are you working now, at a hospital or at home? What about Renatochka? In some ways I recognize myself in her, especially in her writing. Similar handwriting, unfinished phrases, uneven handwriting, even the spelling shows a certain similarity of character: absentmindedness, a lack of full concentration, emotionalism, but maybe it can all be improved.

[in French, with mistakes] My dear little girl Renée. Thank you for your letter. I hope you will write me many letters and tell me how you spend the time, your holidays, what presents you have received, what friends you have; that you will write to me about all you would like. Kisses, my little...

Well, goodbye my dear. Kissing you warmly. Pavel

P.S.: Fania, my sister is in Kiev. Katia, if you remember, is sending

her regards. As to your Milchik? all is well. I have delivered your letter, but I did not get your card for Marozh [?] [Mark?]

P.S.: I would like to send some money to Renata to buy some paper she doesn't have, but it is now impossible.

PS 16

Dear Sabina! 1923 [illegible] 29

I received your letter of 7th January. I also received the first real lovely child's letter from Renatochka. How difficult it is to feel that there is this really nice little girl who addresses me with the word papa, that I have in her somebody close and intimate. And I say without any hesitation or flattery, you are a woman of enormous merit for having fostered in the child such loving feelings toward a father from whom she was separated as a one-year-old child and deprived of father's care; and yes, I repeat, she needed a father to genuinely develop such ideas and feelings. And here is this guileless, sincere letter with its disarming child-like simplicity that so touched me, that made me more aware of the bitterness of separation and the impossibility of the present time. And time, the time. The travel abroad, and everywhere this accursed problem—money. As far as the travel permit is concerned, as you write, neither you nor I can get it. Yasha is not well informed about this. When I was in Moscow I was lucky to get a permission to travel abroad from the people's commissar [i.e., minister] of public health, but it was later blocked by the German consulate. As I was leaving Moscow, I got an assurance from Yasha that I will receive the permit in three weeks—and now three months have passed and there is still no permit from Berlin. First, according to your father, who is staying in Rostov before leaving for Tashkent, it is difficult to get a permit because Zaidman is busy. Second, how long will I live at the expense of other people, it's time to get used to a personally responsible life. What are the prospects of achieving this abroad. If it is not in some business, the chances are very slim. And now business abroad, and especially in Germany, as father told me, is in general not favorable for us, nothing to write home about. This is why all this is so tangled. 1) On the one hand, your basic fear, all your own, is the worry about the child and about our provincial living conditions; on the other hand, there is the legitimate and well-deserved wish to live as one family, for yours and the child's sake; further, there are problems regarding scientific work and, finally, the painful problem of financial security. How to create a situation not disruptive to development and finding satisfaction in accomplishing one's scientific projects and ideas, having a suitable cultural environment, libraries, institutions; 2) having the possibility to raise the child; 3)finally, having a life, even a private life, and transferring a part of the worries, duties, and thoughts about the child to the other half, that is to me. Of course, all this tangle of feelings, wishes, and circumstances is not easy to unravel and forces one to look for other solutions.

Another way of solving the problem might be, as I and others have written, and as father, Milchik, and Yasha have told me. Try to come to Moscow. I think this is politically more feasible than for me to travel abroad, and probably Yasha and Sania will know how to arrange it for you (you would see me, I would try to come to you); you will look around to see if you can find work (I believe in Moscow you can find a more or less suitable environment to achieve this). You will live here for about a month or two and if not possible, will decide what to do. Look, Yasha was given an official business trip, Sania went to Riga and could have gone abroad, had he wanted to. I believe that should your decision be negative, you would be able to go back. In spring they are planning a big congress of psychiatrists and neuropathologists in Petersburg, you could come. Not accustomed to the thought of staying in Russia permanently, you might be able to make it easier for yourself to discover the most important and repressed complex of your fear of our reality here. As Sania must have written to you, these days Moscow as the center of cultural life is boiling and bubbling with new quests, a striving for new goals in science, art, and literature. Youth is yearning for the light of knowledge, and Narkompros, i.e., the commissariat for education, is trying, as far as is financially possible, to meet that need; both in your profession and various pedagogical, pedological, and psychological fields new institutions are being established, so in this regard there is a lot of room. Living in Russia you can also count on a better income, if both of us can work. So this is, in general, the chain of thoughts and considerations which have occurred to me concerning our current family situation, thoughts about the present and the future. Goodbye. I wish you lots of good spirits and ongoing successes. I hug you warmly.

Your Pavel.

I will write separately to Renatochka in accordance with her wish to receive photos for her album. How is her health?

PS 17 (in German)

Dear Sabina! 10.VIII.1923

Yesterday I visited your parents and we read together the letter to your parents. In this letter that you had sent via Sania you write about many interesting things about Renatchen. Thank God, that you both are in good health. We were sorry you did not get the travel permit to return to the homeland. And, moreover, the long lasting journey home. I still don't know whether you received my letters that I had sent via the German military governor and in part via Yasha and Sania. I have already met Yasha in Rostov, he looks well but he had a long journey to Russia. I believe it would be much better if they allowed travel to Kiev via Vienna. But the main thing is that one has to have patience and trust fate, i.e., to rely on it. How are you and how is Renatchen? In your letter to Sania you mention that you will send a few lines to me, but to what address have you sent it? Otherwise for a long time, a very long time, I had no letters from you and I wanted to have news from you. With me there is nothing special. I am now living in Rostov [illegible], see patients, and, of course, what I earn would not be enough had I not been living with my brother-in-law. The practice is growing gradually, I am working in a hospital and was promised a surgery position. But for now, as long as there is a war between the Bolsheviks and the Cossacks, one cannot be sure of avoiding being drafted again.

I am very happy when I get a letter from you and I hope you will write more often, possibly the German postal service to Russia will function more efficiently than the other way around. For example, your letter via Sania arrived directly from Berlin to Rostov, but our letters could not be delivered as quickly and as regularly etc. Write what you are doing; that you are longing for the homeland is self-evident; what are you occupied with now, what is your work. What does Renatchen look like now? And why does she think of there being two sisters! Probably she has seen this at a friend's family, perhaps a Russian family in Lausanne [?] Goodbye Sabina and Renatchen and may fate protect you both. My best and warm greetings to you both,

Paul.

[postscript] Also greetings to Renatchen from me.

[postscript] The last letter to your parents came via Yan on August 22, that means it took (21?) days.

5
Letters From Spielrein's Burghölzli Friends

LETTERS FROM EUGENIA SOKOLNICKA[122]

ESo 1

Dear Sabina! Zurich, 18–VIII–1911

Why did you stop writing all of a sudden? Did you just get tired of writing or did some hurricane hit you, or has something just happened? Write, please. I am composing a scientific work. Otherwise, I'm afraid I will become a patient at the Burghölzli. First of all, I have a great deal of conflicts in analysis or, more precisely a depression (*Senkung*). I have not been attending any lectures, I sit home and the time passes, but for now I can force myself to continue writing. What will become of me. What should I do, whom can I ask for advice. And the main thing, should I continue writing, but is it any good, all I have is eight pages of the whole and it feels like it is the end, stop, I cannot go on. Please tell me, if you know anything about why dementia praecox occurs a at young age. An awfully stupid idea has occurred to me, I wrote it down and now I am ashamed that I am so inexperienced (*unerfahren*). I could discuss all of it with you. And why don't you send me your paper, the *Jahrbuch*[123] has not yet been published, and Jung gave me only the first half of your work and he is only promising. And what are you writing about now? Have you met in Zurich the bacteriology

122 Eugenia Sokolnicka (1884–1934), born in Warsaw to Maurycy Kutner and Paulina Flejszer, studied at the Burghölzli in 1911. Analyzed by Freud and Ferenczi, member of the Vienna Psychoanalytic Society; later one of the founders of the Paris Psychoanalytic Society (see French Wikipedia, Mijolla (2002).

123 *Jarhbuch für psychopathologische und psychoanalytische Forschungen*, edited by Jung, from 1909–1914.

assistant Gonzenbach[124], such a good man, kindhearted and wise, something that is rarely seen in one person. We met accidentally on Sunday and talked a great deal. You know, sometimes it is so easy to approach a person, to feel a person. At times I knew approximately from your letters how you are living now, what you are thinking about, and now it is as if a heavy curtain is covering everything that is in your mind. The semester will soon be over. And then examinations, the diploma and... I do not know what will be next. I don't even want to think about it. I am in general so afraid of the future. Yesterday I was visiting and among the guests there was a Polish woman skilled in chiromancy, and as she saw me for the first time and never heard of me and she was asked to read my palm. She found that my head line is very long, the line of heart short, and the line of happiness almost absent. How do you like that? For a long time now I have lost faith in my star. Jung says that the person who cannot see his way out of difficulty in life is a neurotic. Do you agree with that? Yes, I forgot to mention something to you. At the last Freudian meeting Dr. Nelken[125] (your sweetheart, wasn't he?) read his analysis of a beautiful case of dementia praecox. Subsequently Jung commented: "oh yes, in the paper you quite correctly cited Fräulein Spielrein's[126] words [illegible]". Perhaps I may not be quoting his words exactly, but this was their meaning (*Sinn*). I was very glad to hear this about you at that meeting. What are the good things happening to you at meetings (*Sitzungen*). I stopped reading your letter and started the book by Merezhkovsky entitled *Julian the Apostate* and read the following thought: "On her face there were traces of somebody else's happiness – that excess of life, a boundless happiness of love, when it doesn't matter to young girls whom they hug and kiss".

20/VIII

I had to stop reading your letter and only now I can continue reading it. Today I received your postcard. My dear, as you can see from the first half of my letter, I have no resistances (*Widerstände*) against you and there cannot be any. You give me so much and I can tell you a lot. But there is a snag. It seems to me all the time that you have no need to write to me, that you do not feel better

124 Wilhelm von Gonzenbach (1880–1955), from 1920 till 1950 professor of hygiene and bacteriology at ETH, Swiss Technical School in Zurich.

125 Nelken, Jan (1912). "Analytische Betrachtungen über Phantasien eines Schizophrenen" (Psycho-analytical reflections on the fantasies of a schizophrenic). *Jahrbuch*, 4:502–562.

126 Spielrein, S. (1911). Über den psychologischen Inhalt eines Falles von Schizophrenie (Dementia praecox) (On the psychological content of a case of schizophrenia). *Jahrbuch*, 3:329–400, her dissertation.

after speaking with me, that you cannot bare your soul to me, as it is called, that is, that I can give you very little or, more precisely, that you take very little from me, as if you yourself do not need this. This is what sometimes pains me and stops me from many things. I am afraid to tell you, you are surely a Freudian, but I have many, many warm feelings toward you.

What are you thinking of doing now, are you really going to stay in Munich, it's so hot there. I know a place in Oberengadin where you can find a very good boarding house for 4 fr[ancs] a day, it is wonderfully good there. If you went there I would be able to come and visit you for a week or two but, of course, before I go to Burghölzli. This would be very good. And I could show you my work. Is this possible? Think about it, and also the German gentleman could come along, for some reason I like him. Yesterday I presented a case to Bleuler, I was sitting there for an hour and a half and was terribly disgracing myself. A very interesting case, a woman with moral insanity, in my opinion not completely so, which is what I told Bleuler, he asked me why I think that, and what evidence I have for her weak but still existing morality. I said, embarrassed: "I have no evidence but I feel it" (*Beweise habe ich keine, aber ich fühle es*)." And he said that as far as feminine feeling (*weibliches Fühlen*) is concerned, this is possible, but he doesn't see it that way. Funny, he did find that I was incorrect but at the same time he showed that he was quite happy with me, that is, he looked at me, as you say, like an uncle and I got terribly red in my face. Yes, *Fühlen*, it is a funny story.

The new semester is about to begin and I am both happy and unhappy. I'm terribly exhausted, I lost so much weight because I worked a great deal, in addition to our lack of money. Please, forgive me but I am now sitting high and dry (*auf dem Trockenen*), and forgive me, I have to mail this letter to you without postage and I have already procrastinated, it was unpleasant, but after all, you are a close friend, and you will not be angry with me. In December or early January I am planning to take the examination, but to tell the truth, I haven't even read one book and now want to start reading one. It is boring but there is nothing I can do about it. During the winter I have to take a course with Dr. Roth. I don't know how that will be. Time will tell, as some wise people say. Write to me a lot, what your last work is about, and where you are planning to spend the summer and what you are doing in general.

Kisses from your Zhenia

ESo 2

Darling, dear Sabina! Zurich, 23–VIII–1911

I received your letter and wanted to answer immediately but I was unwell for a few days and even now I still feel bad. I have horrible trouble with money, I will have to return to the city soon because I don't have enough to pay my debts. But I really wanted to write about you, not about myself. But how is it possible to be so overwhelmed by a mood, God, if you only knew how hard it is for me sometimes, but one has to take hold of oneself, and that is that. But a good medicine for such a mood is a visit to the psychiatry service (Abtheilung), all that suffering that you see around makes you forget your own. No, I do not know if I will be able to stay in psychiatry, I am often afraid for myself. I am now preparing a clean copy of my work and I will soon hand it to the Professor. I cannot do my work, at times I see no point in it, and this accursed work of correcting takes up a great deal of my time. Yesterday I received your dissertation, thank you, but why didn't you write something, and could you also send me your second work, I would very much like to read it. This author, our Swiss fellow, but don't think we are not friends, is none too clever and I do not like stupid people. All the doctors are treating me very well, I have more or less good attitude only toward Klaesi[127], he is most responsive and lively. I have many acquaintances but none of them interests me. One of the reasons why Klaesi interests me is because he is a close friend of Roth, and I can gossip with him about Roth. K. told me that Russians are incapable of loving and I could only laugh at him in response to that. But this is all rubbish, this damned education, always about the same and always torture. When I come from the hospital service, I can only think about what demon is it that rules mankind. but even that is a useless subject. There is so much beauty in life, nature is so wonderful. All right then, living people don't torture each other, life is so short. As you can see, my mood has reached a dangerous level. I'm sure that either today or tomorrow I will do something stupid. Only you are a good girl, you will understand me, won't you, you are the only person to whom I can tell everything. You are such a good friend of mine, but I am sometimes such a silly girl. You, too, please, get rid of such moods. I was in such pain when I was reading your letter. Where do you want to go next, to Vienna to Freud, may be. It is interesting. Oh, you don't know how good it is when one can go and do what one wants. All right, that is all. Write, I beg you. Your letters is all I have. Kisses from your Zhenia

127 Klaesi, Jakob (1883-1980), Swiss psychiatrist, then at Burghölzli, promoted prolonged sleep treatments.

LETTERS FROM REVEKKA TER-OGANESIAN (BABITSKAYA)

Ter-O 1

Dear Sabinochka! Undated

Do you know the German proverb "he who accuses himself"[128] (*Wer klagt sich an*") Why do you always suppose that I could be offended by anything, I am somewhat offended by my fate, but it doesn't matter, it will all soon change; I'm beginning to believe, Sabinochka, that I never took any offence at you and your suspiciousness seems to me completely bizarre, or do you think that I was offended by your attitude toward me?... Do you remember how once in Zurich you suspected me of competing with you and this was absolutely baseless; I have enough of self-criticism (*Selbstkritik*) in me to think of competing with you in psychiatry. You know how highly I value you and how infinitely valuable our correspondence is for me which I hope will in time become more interesting for me and for you, but if you [illegible] should write to me because you take pity on me, I would not want it. However, let me repeat, the thought should never occur to you that I felt offended by you. Today I thought a great deal about you, about your future role as a mother, why do you write so little about what you experienced when you first felt the child's movements, for it is such happiness for a woman who loves, it contains so many beautiful, purely spiritual sensations...Don't you think how unhappy those women are who have never known such sensations? Just avoid being superstitious and don't think up any kind of fears, try to keep moving to the last minute, do some bodily work, you have difficulty breathing because you stayed in bed too long. Don't be afraid of giving birth, Sabina, here one woman recently gave birth and she is exactly the same height and build as you and she gave birth quickly and easily and this was also her first delivery. Is your mother with you? I imagine how happy she is, I'm happy for her, she has suffered enough with you, it is time for her to see you happy, you will be able to understand her even better once you become a mother yourself... Do you remember, one day you told me that you find more softness in my character, and it is really so, and I only owe this to my daughter Asyukha, if you only knew how much happiness she gives me!... Living in our out of the way place has really had a good effect on her; you remember how sickly she was, now her weight is 39 pounds, her cheeks are rosy, her figure is pure delight, I don't know whom she inherited it from, but she is strikingly

128 Perhaps a reference to "Wer sich entschuldigt, klagt sich an"—he who makes excuses himself accuses.

well-built, she dances gracefully and shows the instincts of a real woman; I'm very glad on this account, such women suffer less in life, but it is true that their psychology is less complicated; for now she impresses with her strikingly lively fantasy and facial expressions, at this moment I can hear how she is prattling in the next room and my heart is getting filled with heavenly joy. You say that "a child is half of life and the other half is given by interesting work". And a husband, according to you, what part of life does he take up? I imagine life in the form of a very complex machine with a great number of big and small screws, where each screw occupies its own place, and should only one little screw deteriorate, then the whole mechanism stops. This is why I now feel myself so jaded, so unhappy, although I can confidently say that I am happy in my family life... In two days Makich will finish his exams, he has already passed 23 examinations and most of them with excellent grades, so that I hope that he will pass his three last examinations as well and then I will get busy, I have to pass a goodly number of examinations; in the past I took supplementary examinations to get the high school diploma, then science examinations at the university and finally the state examinations. Can you imagine how much time it takes? As life goes on, I have lost a year and a half, since this work requires a whole year, if not more. But I consider this to be legitimate, more than anything else I am happy that I have to take the science examinations. It is a shame to call oneself a doctor with such kind of knowledge of science as mine, for example; the only nuisance is to take the Latin exam once more. But what will happen once I overcome all this, where will I work? Again in a province, while the best years go by and with them all the best impulses... You cannot imagine what a burden it is for me to live in a village, it is death to me. You hope that we might meet at congresses, but when will that happen, probably when my hair turn white. This is how I think when I am in a bad mood, but at other times meeting at congresses seems to me to be closer and more possible. And in the meantime I have to cram, cram, cram. Hoping I am not too tedious, write a lot about yourself and I will be happy to learn about your successes, I am grateful for the articles you sent me, I won't send you mine, now I do not like it at all: Bleuler shortened it post factum (unbeknownst to me), offered excuses, and published it in the *Neue psychiatrische Wochenschrift*.

More than two weeks later I am continuing my letter which I started on the day I received your letter, you will be the judge why I had not finished and mailed it sooner...It is now two weeks since Makich returned from Tomsk, we will soon leave this place but where is still unknown, it will depend where he will get a job, I would like it to be in the South, but even more so in the West, to be closer to the world of culture. In the meantime I registered for the graduation certificate and hope to be done with examinations no later than May. Now that Makich has passed all his examinations I am beginning to believe that one day I will be working too. Write, Sabinochka, how is your health; if you are tired of writing letters write a little but more often. How is your husband doing? Give my regards to him. I have not yet received your articles, send them, dear, and Makich will also be grateful to you. Write to the old address. I kiss you warmly.

Revekka

Ter-O 2

Dear Sabinochka! Undated

Congratulations on the birth of your daughter and I wish you and her lots of happiness. How is your health, was giving birth easy, how are you managing with the child. Write to me about everything, my dear, how strange it is for me to imagine you being a mother! I feel that we are now closer to each other, do you feel the same way? It is a pity we settled down in the Ufa Governorate and we are separated by a week long travel, if it weren't so far away I would have gone to see you no matter what. Your mother is probably staying with you, I imagine how happy grandma is, convey my warmest wishes to her. I read your articles and was amazed, I did not expect that you can write so well, with such self-confidence. The idea of "destruction as a cause of becoming" is well known to me since the Zurich days, we spoke about it many times, still, how well you developed this idea! Reading this paper I felt heavenly bliss, without any admixture of competitiveness...with no less interest I read your "Contributions to the understanding of the infantile mind" (*Beiträge zur Kenntnis der kindlichen Seele*), I recognized all three of you in that paper; why did you write so little about yourself? And this boy, Vasia, I know him too, but now you will have your own object for observations; I would very much like to know how you are raising your daughter, will you be able to manage this task so that theory will never be at variance with life? I am completely incapable of bringing up a child, everybody tells me that and I admit it myself, and yet my Asiushka is a good girl. Mention your daughter's name. Write to me often, Sabinochka, I will soon leave this place, but use my old address, your letter will be forwarded. Good bye, Sabinochka, warmest kisses, regards to your husband.

Your Revekka

I imagine your surprise receiving a postcard written by a hand that once held a knife...but times change (*tempora mutantur*).[129]

129 The complete maxim reads: the times change, and we change with them

Ter-O 3

Dear Sabinochka! Undated

Why didn't you write the name of your daughter? I keep inventing all kinds of names for her, but probably none of them will do as all my names are Russian, and you might have called her Cleopatra, Carmen, or Mignon, or perhaps given her a Jewish name? How I would like to see both of you! But, alas, it will not be possible so soon, I have to study a lot now, I'm getting ready for examinations. In three weeks I will travel to Lodz and stay there for three to four months to get ready for the supplementary examinations; in Lodz I will be 14 hours of travel away from you, but I will not be able to travel anyway to see you. Perhaps, you could consider travelling to our barbaric country, not in winter, of course, but in spring or summer, you would say that good mothers can also be found in Ural, and I even hope that one of these days you will come to see me in the summer, you will see a Russian village and get acquainted with the life of a provincial doctor. Makich is very pleased with his work and he operates left and right, he has even surpassed Sauerbruch[130]; he practices surgery only, but Makich also treats diseases of eyes and ears, practices gynecology and surgery related to midwifery. He is simply encyclopedic, something I am completely incapable of and I don't know how I would be able to work as a provincial doctor; I may have to do work in a district council after I graduate until we move into the city. Where did your husband settle down, is he happy abroad? I remember how he was against the idea of moving abroad. Write about everything, everything; write to me at the address which I am sending you; from Lodz I will send you a new address. Write, Sabinochka, write frequently, write about your daughter; for how long and how did you get settled in Berlin? Have you defended your thesis yet or is your daughter stopping you from doing that? Goodbye my dear, greetings to your husband and a kiss to your daughter.

Kisses. Your Revekka.

[postscript]Send me a photograph of your daughter and of you, if you have them, and if not, have yourself photographed. I sometimes try to remember your face and cannot see it, but sometimes I can do that; at the moment, for example, I can see you [Illegible], how the three of us are reading [illegible], in Zürich, but the most memorable is our last encounter in Rostov.

Ter-O 4

Sabina, Undated

you do not write. Oh, if you knew how much I value you, how madly I

130 Ernst Ferdinand Sauerbruch (1875–1951), a prominent German surgeon of the 20th century.

wish to see you, the impossibility of it only makes my desire stronger. I did not find it necessary to travel to accompany my brother, they are poor people, completely broke. What is with you? Were you in a sanatorium, how is your health, how is your "little gold fish" [daughter]? If I could find any work abroad, I would probably travel to see you, but there is no word from you, are you ill? For a year and a half now I've been loafing in Russia, the lack of occupation is killing me and I feel totally unimportant and worthless; and at times I lose the most valuable thing in my nature, hope, and without it, everything is so dark and dreary, you are the only one who can understand this mental hunger. I have met only two beautiful people in my life, it is my friend who is already gone and you, and you have given me so much and I am grateful to you, but what do you think, after all, it wasn't for nothing that we met each other? I know that we shall meet again in this life but meanwhile write me a long letter, write to me about problems that interest you, share everything with me! How is your husband? By the way, I don't even know where you are now, but I think my letter will reach you. Goodbye, kisses,

Ter-O 5

My dear Sabinochka! Undated

If you knew how glad, how glad I am, dear Sabinochka, that I found you, I do not want us to lose each other, I will only withdraw from you should you tell me that I am no longer of any interest to you. You and I are such different people, aren't we, but why have I always understood you so well and it turns out that I still understand you, and not only that, I share your worries... How many thoughts, how many associations were stirred up in me today by your letter. I was completely transported into the Zurich scene, I recalled our long talks on the familiar theme... I noticed this "*Sie*" [you, formal second person] in your letter and explained it exactly as you did, even before I read your comment. It appears, that he[131] is still, comparatively speaking, quite deeply lodged [in your mind], what a disappointment that you have not yet abreacted this; how unfair that you don't involve your husband in your work; of course, I do not know him well but I am somehow convinced that if you would not hold yourself so aloof from him then he, as any intelligent person and as a Jew, would soon be able to grasp psychiatry in general and Freud's theories in particular. And even Makich, who was once very much removed from all this, you would realize what an enthusiastic psychiatrist he has now become. He even surprised the professor during a recent examination. No, Sabinochka, God forbid you should isolate

131 I.e., Jung. It is unclear whether *Sie* was addressed by Jung to Sabina or by her to Jung.

yourself from you husband regarding any problem, try to have with him as many points of contact as possible, know that the first guarantee of a happy family life is mutual respect and deep understanding of each other, you as a psychiatrist, and moreover so talented, should understand this better than anybody. Don't take this as flattery; living here, amongst luck-luster people, I learnt to value you even more, besides, I am luck-luster myself, as you know, I see myself as an average person; but it seems to me that I understand more than they do, otherwise I would not be able to appreciate you as much as I do. As far as his Jewish habits and manners are concerned it seems to me that this is such a trifle, if you wished you could easily change this, considering that he loves you, I'm speaking from personal experience, after all, I have wiped out a lot of "Caucasian" traits in my husband. How I wish I could meet you and congratulate you personally regarding your "interesting situation", but as this is impossible, accept from faraway my warmest wishes; a new era will begin in your life now, you will be surprised how much your "Siegfried"[132] will bring you closer to your own father, again I say this from personal experience. Now I want to receive from you a very long, long letter the way you know how to write one. You are asking me about my "mental life" (*Seelenleben*); the only thing I cannot complain about enough is the absence of more energetic activity and the absence of at least a few interesting people. I love Makich, I infinitely believe in his honesty and decency, lately we have even been getting along much better than ever; many times a day I thank fate for my dear Asyukha, she gives me a great deal of happiness and sometimes it seems to me as if she's already quite a grown girl. But what oppresses me is my husband's attachment to Russia, where I find no place for myself; it seems to me that I am living here temporarily; but irrespective of my attitude toward Russia I must remain here. I am now cramming mathematics, physics etc. and I have to stay here to pass supplementary examinations because my husband wants that; I am at least glad that he does not insist on the Caucasus anymore. My advice to you, Sabinochka, is to avoid as far as possible mothers-in-law wearing pants and here one can see a striking analogy between the two of us...And now a little bit about psychiatry, I beg you, if you are not bored by this, please, share these issues with me, for you will give me great pleasure; I have not read your papers, I do not buy the *Jahrbuch*, we subscribe to a Russian journal called *Psychotherapie* [in the original] as it is necessary to make ourselves familiar with the Russian public and the Russian style of communicating, and I am still not comfortable with it; and therefore, when I want to understand the meaning of a word I often

132 I.e., Jung.

translate it in my mind into German. Makich will finish his exams in two weeks, send us the offprints of your papers, I will read them together with him. Well, my dear, till next time, write often and a lot, regards to your husband. Kisses.

Your Revekka.

[postscript] Why have you settled down in Berlin? And why do you think of moving back to Switzerland instead of to Vienna where I believe it would be most interesting for you to live?

Revekka.

Ter-O 6

Dear, darling Sabina! Undated

Yours and Makich's assumptions are completely wrong; I don't know where he got the idea that I have an inhibition (*Hemmung*) in relation to you. You once told me that I was competitive toward your publications and it seemed to me even then so wildly preposterous, and especially now, since I am completely far from writing any papers; it makes me laugh that you think so, for even before you started working on your paper I was sure it would be impossible to compare your work with mine. Jealousy is also out of the question, just as I cannot be jealous of Jung or any other authority. You know, Sabina, in this area I am pinning all my hopes on you and wish you success with all my heart, if you doubt that, it would hurt me a lot. I saw your paper when I visited Grebelskaya[133], she promised to give it to me once she was done reading it, she said that Jung praised it very highly, which made me very happy. You are also mistaken in what you write about Grebelskaya, I am not interested in any relationship with Jung and I do not want to publish any papers with him, and whatever relation I have to him came about only because of you – you know all this, so how can such thoughts occur to you given all this; I want to see you gay and happy in your personal life or perhaps, better yet, in your mental life. I was told that you are now in a psychiatric [illegible], write to me about how and what, I can only [illegible] with you; it would be awfully absurd if you held on to previous opinions about me. Write me a long letter, it's been long since you had written to me.

I have now started seriously to prepare for an examination in October. Where will you [a gap and illegible]. Are you already attending lectures, which ones. What are you writing about now if I may ask? I would very much like to

133 See Grebelskaya, Sch[aina] (1914). Psychologische Analyse eines Paranoiden. Jahrbuch, 4:116–140, in which she cites Schreber; also in this volume Spielrein's "Destruktion als Ursache des Werdens" and Jung's "Wandlungen und Symbole der Libido, II."

meet with you some time at the end of the semester. In August I will be in the French part of Switzerland. If you are going home for the holidays, maybe you can drop in some time. Write, Sabina about everything, you may recall, as I had told you, everything, rest assured that your interests evoke the liveliest response in me, you must feel that. You know, Sabina, the [other?] interests that brought us. closer together have lost their value for me now, they are almost completely forgotten by me; but I have never forgotten, nor will I ever forget the difficult hours I spent with you and your attitude toward me... Write more frequently, my dear. I have free time now and if you need to arrange something, let me know and I will do everything. All the very best.

Your Revekka

A LETTER FROM ESTHER APTEKMAN

EA 1

Dear Sheftel, Kherson 1/X.13

Thanks for your postcard, I was very glad that I found you again. I had already written to your father in Rostov asking where you were living but probably the address was incorrect and until now I have not received any answer. I castigated myself that I was unable to visit you prior to departure but you surely believe me how sincerely I regret that. I am glad you are in good health and, as I could tell from a few words in the postcard, that you are in a good mood too. It means that the little one is alive and making her existence noticed! It is not given to everybody to be so lucky as to permit oneself to have a child. May this little creature bring you joy and happiness.

You are asking me how I set myself up here, what my work is like? For the last three months I have been working at the Kherson Psychiatric Hospital as assistant doctor, a job similar to that of volunteer doctors at the Burghölzli. The hospital is immense: 1300 patients and you can imagine the colossal size of this clinical material which requires a great deal of time to figure out. There a few interesting patients but in the majority of cases their mental state is so abnormal that it is mostly limited to a few delusional ideas. I was terribly distressed by the inhuman frenzy which I had not seen abroad. They resembled animals ready to tear to shreds anything they could lay their hands on, others were lurking for the moment to assault and destroy anything that was in their path! It was some kind of hell in which everyone was screaming, shrieking, crying, and singing, and everything dominated by virtuoso cursing as can only be heard in our homeland Russia. You might well imagine scenes of a few nurses attending patients who were biting scratching and spitting while others, defending themselves, were relentlessly rolling in a heap all over the ward until another fantasy occurred to one of the patients. At first all this depressed me terribly, I would leave the ward all shook-up by nervous tension but thankfully the July heat passed and the patients became calmer and I got used to it. For one month I served as deputy ward chief taking care of a mixed population of mentally retarded men, women, and children and also acutely ill boys and girls up to 17 years old. The patients soon became attached to me and I approach them with an open mind. You know how sensitive they can be and I myself used sublimation but sometimes everything exploded and a terrible longing pulled me unbearably back to Zurich. Without further ado I would fantasize to excess, would get frightened by the prospect of returning, and did not have enough courage to obtain some temporary happiness instead of this prolonged and overpowering longing. I was so tempted to leave Russia, but I am convinced that I would once again become myself. And so I went back to see my patients and got all immersed in their mental suffering, as if thereby dissolve my own longing. Besides the director there are 13 doctors here; among them there are many interesting people, and all coexist collegially, without intrigues, gossip etc., which is unfortunately quite common everywhere. All of them are middle aged so that sometimes one misses a more youthful and care-free mood. All of them are quite friendly toward me, and the director banters and even flirts with me. He is an old man, 60 years old, a Pole, a very interesting man with vast knowledge in many fields, a witty and really intelligent man. It is very interesting to converse with him. Among the doctors, an especially likable one was a woman doctor, a lady somewhat older than me, with an unattractive appearance but with a very beautiful and refined soul that was reflected in her face and lent it a kind of charm. I feel well in her company and when we part I feel somewhat mentally at peace. I would like to write an article but so far nothing definite, I am searching for material. And have you written something in the meantime? What is new with Freud, did you hear more about him? Recently at all the congresses his theories have been openly and totally criticized, there is a grumbling protest against his entire theory. What is the mood of the Freudians like, how is Freud himself reacting to this? And Jung absented himself from all the congresses, he seems to have completely left this world! Write what is new in this whole field. I feel somehow sorry for Freud but he does have his strength even if the whole world is against him. Did you receive your books, I sent them to the boarding home where you have been living? Once I asked you for your papers, I would be glad to receive those. Tell me where you are living, what is new in your work. Where are you planning to spend the winter? This time I hope to hear from you soon. Goodbye, all the best, I firmly shake your hand.

Esther Aptekman[134]. Greetings to your husband. Kherson.

Kherson Psychiatric Hospital.

[postscript]. I forgot to tell you that the hospital is very well organized, with electrical lighting and steam heating. There is a lot of clothes for patients, good food and a very good and warm attitude of doctors to patients. It is a whole little town with its laws, order, customs, and demands. What is striking is the remarkable number of lower level medical personnel and, in general, the hospital system is to my liking. We live some eight [Russian] miles from the hospital and you can imagine what does this involve in terms of Russian methods and means of communication: in autumn, they say, for a couple of months, the hospital is almost cut off from the world. I will end here or perhaps something else will come to mind.

LETTER FROM S. MORGENSHTERN

SM 1

Dear Colleague! Münsterlingen 16/7 1923

You can well imagine how glad I will be when you and your daughter will come for a few weeks to Münsterlingen but I don't know if I have the right to suggest this to you. The problem is that the closest and the only hotels are on the main road, seven to ten minutes away from me, and the lake is 14 minutes from the forest. There is a lot of green all around, the air is good, but when the days are hot there is little shade and when the days are cold, the air gets chilly quickly. The food is good, but a room with meals could not be less than 12 francs a night. In addition to those two hotels, and about 3¼ hours away from me, there is a little hotel at the lake. Wouldn't Renée be a little bored in this German environment? I do not have much free time on my hands but my daughter who will arrive here in a few days will be very glad to be together with both of you. We are not afraid that Renée will be lonely, don't hesitate to come. In case you will find Münsterlingen unsuitable for you, at least make a stop here on your way to Germany for about five to six days at my place. What will depart along with you is all that was good and elevated for me in connection with my life in

134 Esther Aptekman published "Experimentelle Beiträge zur Psychologie des psycho-galvanischen Phänomens (experimental contributions to the psychology of the psychogalvanic phenomenon). Jahrbuch, 3:591-620.

Switzerland. When I came here to study, I had so many higher strivings, so many ideals, that it's hard for me to look at the end result. I have organized all my life on the principle of "by the way," but years have gone by and whatever I was striving for never arrived.

Dear colleague,

I am awaiting your answer in order to get the room ready. Sincere greetings to you and to dear Renée. From your S. Morgenshtern.[135]

A LETTER FROM R. KLEINER (SPIELREIN'S SCHOOL FRIEND)

RK 1

My dear and darling Sabina! November 7

Forgive me, my dear friend, I am addressing you by your first child's name. I do not know, i.e., I do not remember the name of your father; let me now congratulate you on your legal marriage, I wish you lots and lots of happiness and health and a long life. I have received your letter and you cannot imagine how much pleasure it gave me, my dear Sabina, as if I got a letter from [Niura?]. You write that I will realize what changes occurred in your life when I see the photograph in your letter, but, unfortunately, there was no photograph, dear, you probably forgot to put it in the envelope, therefore, I ask you if it's not difficult for you, send it to me, I will be very grateful to you, now, my dear, I want to ask you, what is the help you have given me, about which you write in your letter. In fact, the last few years have not been pleasant for me, but what could I do about it? One cannot escape one's fate. I have a lot of trouble with my sick son, he recovered but has changed dreadfully. When I was visiting him in hospital, I noticed that as he began to recover, the expression on his face became like that of an imbecile, indeed, he looked like one a little bit. On top of it, he developed some strange manners which he did not have before he got sick, so I have a lot of troubles with him. And now he will be called up on the 15th of November, he will be called up in Rostov instead of Tambov, he has already left and is now asking me to send him a certificate about his illness. And this is the question I would like you to resolve for me, if it is not difficult for you: is it better for him to serve in the army or not? You will judge me severely, but I, personally, would like him to be drafted. I think it might have a good influence on him, I ask you therefore, my dear Sabina, if it is not too difficult for you to help me resolve

135 Sophie Morgenstern (1875–1940), Polish-Jewish French psychiatrist and child psychoanalyst, trained in Burghölzli and analyzed by Sokolnicka.

this issue. Forgive me, my dear friend, that I talked so much. I'm very grateful to you for your friendship. I wish you to be healthy and happy with your dear life companion. Let me give you a kiss from afar, I remain your loving friend

R. Kleiner.[postscript] I'm sending you the address of [Nyura?]: [America?] Mr.

Berkenblit, 28 Freylinghuysen Ave Newark, NJ.

LETTERS FROM AN UNKNOWN CORRESPONDENT

UC 1

Dear Sabina! Undated

I am just now answering your letter, a bit late, it is true, but if you knew my situation, that is, to what extent I am preoccupied with my child. Do not judge me: I have not left the apartment for the whole week, except Monday, when I took a day off and delivered your lecture notebooks. I'm completely alone; I had a fight with my landlady, she is quite a mercenary woman, as all landladies are; in fact, I am chained to my room for the whole day. It will last until the first of this month. From the 1st of June I will have a wonderful apartment with full service for the child; then I will start cramming, whatever it takes, to get ready for the examination in October.

Now, you are still depressed and this is not good. Listen to me, forget all your pride and ask the promised recommendations; you know, Sabina, it is not easy for anyone to win a good place in life, you should act energetically. Perhaps, you have read Gorky's short story "Facing Life",[136] I will remind you if you forgot. Two people are facing life; the first one was saying: "I ask" and life was indifferent to him; the second one was saying: "I demand"; the short story ends with the following words: "Take, – said Life." Be more energetic! There is no need to analyze and weigh pros and cons of every step the way you do. He promised you and you have to try, in fact, he doesn't need to know that you really need it, after all, you are not corresponding with him, and he might think that you're not interested in any correspondence or any help, etc. Use skillfully and energetically means use what you possess and you will achieve the goal you are striving for. When I say "means" I do not only mean money as you sometimes misunderstood me (even though it is a big deal), but your abilities, the youthfulness of your face and all the other qualities, which are not possessed by an average [text break]

136 In: Maksim Gorky, *Collected Works in 30 volumes*, Volume 4. Foma Gordeev. Essays, Stories 1899–1900.

[the beginning is missing] it appeared to me very strange, even wild [a gap in the text], I got tired of leading an isolated life, having a hard time. One has to meet life halfway, take what is good and filled with light. I am beyond the age when one was can wait for happiness to come and choose it, now I have to take it the way it comes to me. What will come next? I cannot tell you anything about it! The future is fraught with all kinds of consequences. My uncle is 46 years old, he is 18 years older than me; he is my father's first cousin. His wife and daughter will come here soon. Probably many psychologically interesting things will happen then. What can you tell me about all this, dear Sabina? What advice can you give me? Of course, it is very difficult to offer any advice. For Christmas I traveled with him to our home. This was his first visit in our home. Everyone was terribly happy to see us and my uncle immediately charmed everybody (my mother knew him very little, brother has never seen him) with his affability and great tactfulness; but when the situation requires it, he can be a very funny and merry fellow.

I received your long registered letter: it was written in a very interesting and lively manner and I read it with great pleasure. You have apparently learned a great deal of interesting things during your stay with Freud. I found the subject "what is fear?" to be very interesting, fear comes in many shapes, for example, fear comes with all manner of inner suffering. I know this very well myself. Your second registered letter came almost together with your postcard, which arrived a day after. Do you have any news from your husband? What does he write to you? How are your parents doing? Please, send them my greetings. What is now happening in Switzerland? There is no complete peace, it seems, according to the newspapers. Does it mean that until the war ends you will not be able to come here? Of course, in the present conditions it is difficult to travel with a child. And when will this war end?!

If only it could happen soon. I thank you very much for your letter to U.; I would very much like to know what's going on with him, even if it may be an idle question. If you were told that he was killed, don't hide this from me: for some reason, it even seems to me that this was so. Given the current conditions my work is not all that satisfactory, there is a shortage of many things. My co-workers are pleasant enough. We do not have a professor, only a director of the laboratory, S. L. Frankfurt, may be you heard about him when you visited Russia. Generally speaking, during times of war, scientific work is very different from peacetime, when science was highly regarded and everybody was interested in it. It is different now.

Alright, dear Sabina, I have been writing endlessly, and now it's time to stop. My mother sends her warmest greetings. Write to me and do not be angry with me for not having written for such a long time. In the last letter I gave you my address, the Great Vladimirskaya, #14, apt. 4. It looks as if you haven't got it, because you are still writing to the Timofeyevskaya street address. all the best to you. kisses to you and your daughter. Your R.

[Another letter from the same correspondent]

[the beginning is missing] your letters. Then he told me about your life abroad, how you left Berlin, etc., briefly, almost everything that I have known from you. What I did not know is that you had been Freud's assistant in Vienna for a whole year; you probably learnt there a lot of interesting things, and generally speaking, it is probably not easy to get to him. I also didn't know that Jung and Freud went their separate ways due to differences in their opinions. That is all that I was able to discuss with your "uncle", and then we said goodbye. Thank you very much for so promptly fulfilling my request concerning U., and, of course, I would like to know what happened to him, even if it were sad news. But You are mistaken concerning my attitude toward him, assuming that I wanted the same as before. I think it is almost impossible, even if the circumstances changed after the war; of course, feelings can be more powerful than reasoning, but it seems to me that my feelings have calmed down somewhat, because I was utterly exhausted by too much worrying about him. He was a very handsome, nice, kind-hearted boy with whom I experienced the highest poetry[137] I could ever imagine: he possessed some kind of a peculiar fascination, which affected not only me but everybody who knew him. I was spellbound by feeling this most tender and moving care, given with so much affection and warmth, sometimes verging on the ridiculous. However, the difference between our intellectual development was too great and everybody who knew us could not help noticing it. Our upbringing and the direction given to us at home, our social circles, were too divergent. I never forgot that and on those grounds we had numerous conflicts. However, after a long period of knowing each other, our feelings have overcome all these obstacles; I let him have it his way and tried to understand him, he was agreeing with me and accepted my point of view and almost everything went smoothly. But when his parents learnt about it, everything fell apart. His parents became the main problem, because he was dependent on them and, you know very well this overseas law, that an impecunious man does not have the right to get married. Our Russian rules and customs are viewed abroad with complete contempt. He was a student and therefore had no right

137 An expression word echoing Spielrein's use of the word poetry in relation to her and Jung

to get married. It is true, his family was quite wealthy, but there was no way to make them yield. True, I did not intervene in this business either, because I considered offering myself to them too humiliating. Moreover, apparently, they were against me being a Russian and not of their faith. As far as my relatives were concerned, I wasn't worried too much, because I knew that one way or the other I would be able to have it my way. But the poor boy was unable to do it, he liked his relatives very much, he suffered a lot and became ill due to this conflict. And this indecisiveness and weakness of character destroyed my feelings. Therefore, I am now saying it is better the way it turned out. Especially now, in wartime, I would be utterly exhausted if I were his wife. So you can see how my story is very similar to yours. But after having suffered for five years, I got drained by this feeling so much that I became somehow inert. It's now more than a year since I have arrived here and I have no acquaintances, no energy and no desire to find any. Alright, so be it with all of them, I will live my life the way it is, even though a family, as I understand it, is a great blessing and satisfaction. But then, living with a beloved one in a hut, and if you don't love him, it is not worth it. Write to me, dear Sabina, how are you and how is your spiritual life, what are your thoughts and mood?

Your husband looks very well although he told me that [a few illegible words] sometimes he lives in difficult conditions [illegible words] [text break]

5.1 LETTER FROM MENIKHA ISAAKOVNA SPIELREIN TO DR. LOTHANE

MS 1

Dear Mr. Lothane! Moscow, 20.XII.1994

I was very glad to receive your letter which shows that in the United States there is an interest in the life and works of my late aunt Sabina Nikolayevna Spielrein. Unfortunately since 1982, when Dr. Magnus Ljunggren (Stockholm) found me in Moscow, I told and let be published practically everything I could tell about her. I believe that two of my personal reminiscences have not yet been published: (1) in 1923 I was present when Sabina was saying to my father that should she have been allowed to see Lenin, she would have certainly cured him. (2) In November of 1937, when I was booted out of the Institute and the Komsomol [youth organization], my father was in a concentration camp and my mother was exiled to Central Asia; I could not find an apartment in Moscow, Sabina's elder brother was arrested, and I decided to travel to grandfather, Sabina's and my father's father, in Rostov on Don.

At the railway station I was met by Sabina and the wife of the youngest brother of Sabina Emil. It turned out that I arrived on the morning of the night when he was arrested. When I was invited to Sabina's home she asked me if I believed what our newspapers are writing about the atrocities perpetrated by the Germans. She added she had lived in Germany for many years and cannot believe what is being printed in our newspapers since she knows the high German culture that gave the world Goethe, Heine, and Schiller and many other well-known famous people. I told her that I believe what is written in the newspapers, since two years ago I had graduated from the German translation department of the training center of foreign languages. Our teachers were émigré German communists and they told me a lot and gave me underground literature they were receiving from Germany, publications describing the crimes of the Nazis. Of course, she refused to be convinced. In her manner Sabina Nikolayevna was very amiable and polite, a kind and educated person. But at the same time she was adamant in her convictions, there was no way to change her mind.

The Nazis occupied Rostov twice. The first time Sabina was not touched. Her two daughters participated in concerts organized by the Germans: Eva played the violin and Renata the cello. This did not last long, the Germans were ejected from Rostov. But they came back. Sabina did not leave Rostov and was shot by the Germans with the other Jews on the outskirts of the city. Both her daughters died with her. I was told about it in Moscow by Eva's school friend living in Moscow.

[omitted a list of publications about Sabina Spielrein in the West and Moscow addresses and telephone numbers]

I have a question: what is the meaning of "The Sabina Spielrein Project"? At the end of November I was in Holland attending a Dutch psychoanalytic symposium. They showed us a play entitled "Victory!" about Sabina's treatment by Jung. I have the script but in Dutch. In my humble opinion, the play is a monstrosity: super modern.

I would like to inform you that living in Moscow is the younger son of Sabina's brother Emil and the younger daughter of elder brother Yan. His phone number is 164–22–15–16, hers is 431–31–81. Their names are Prof. Evald Emilievich Shpilrein and Marianna Yanovna Rodionova. They speak only Russian. There no other relatives of Sabina. I hope I have been of some help to you in some way. I wish you lots of successes in the New Year.

M. Spielrein[138]

---

138 See Grebelskaya Sch[eina] Psychologische Analyse eines Paranoiden.

PS. My phone number is 337–73–29. Perhaps it might interest you to read an article by Litvinov Aleksandr Viktorovich, "A review of Sabina Spielrein's psychoanalytical works." His home phone number is 84–0813.

6
Letters From Colleagues and Patients

SF 1

Professor Freud Wien IX, Berggasse 19

Esteemed colleague, 30.1.1923

I was very sorry about the content of your letter. We were happy that Mrs. Doctor Spielrein came to Geneva as an outpost for psychoanalysis, and we hoped that she would be able to make a living there. I was also very glad to learn that you were able to say so much that was honorable about her. Should it not be possible for her to stay there, despite the gracious assistance of her friends, I would be able to say something about the negative side [illegible], but with more difficulty about the positive side, of her future. At any rate, there are no chances in Vienna. Since the last fall the foreigners have left us, it is hardly possible for me to be fully occupied. Among the Viennese even the local analysts find it difficult to make ends meet. All the prices have risen sky high and it is almost impossible to find a modest apartment. Since Mrs. Doctor Spielrein is a Russian, she will not get an entry permit. It seems to me that the only possible city for our lady colleague is Berlin, with its unlimited resources in outpatient clinics, a mass of Russian compatriots, many Russian publishers, and currently extremely reduced living costs. All the foreigners, doctors and patients, left here to move to Berlin. No matter how insecure the future there may be, anything other than Berlin is out of the question. If psychoanalysis had funds, the problem could be quickly solved. We can expect nothing from America, its popularity there is not worth one dollar. So I am sending the most cordial greetings to you and to all the other gentlemen.

CJ 1 (postcard)

My Dear One! Lauialp 27th August 08

I have just received your friendly letter and got the impression that you are not entirely well in Rostov. I understand. I am grateful to you for your good and kind words. I am now quite calm again. The vacation has calmed my nerves considerably. Every day I take a long stroll in the mountains, mostly all by myself. That does me a great deal of good. The complexes are appreciably putting themselves in order and one can see clearly. You deserve a great bonus of friendship along with the heartfelt wish that, may your life be successful and with a minimum of inexpedient goals and the pain connected with them. Never lose hope that work done with love will lead to a good end. I can only write a short letter today because I have returned home very tired from a long hike. Please keep writing to me at the Burghölzli.

With heartfelt love

Your J.

OP 1

Oscar Pfister

Mrs. Doctor Spielrein, Geneva

Esteemed Frau Doctor! Zurich 16/III 21

Institut Rousseau is also dear to me. But from here I see no way how I could help you. Mrs. M. C. R. is a crazy chicken—brrr!!!! She only gives money to crazy people, e.g. 10,000 francs to her hotel keeper Nadel, but she says she has no money to give to a needy martyr of psychoanalysis. I do not want anything to do with this person. I myself don't know where I could beg for psychoanalysis. When I tried to provide for Professor Schneider I got nothing. Nor can I arrange either lectures or concerts. We had many concerts with heavy deficits and attendance at lectures is most uncertain. The Jungian movement, in spite of American monies in Zurich, is almost ruined and does not play a big role any more. The Jungian Society does not have meetings anymore because it has disintegrated so much. So I regret very much that I have to admit my inability to be of any help. Respectfully yours and best regards

Oscar Pfister.

WS 1

[on stationery of] *Zentralblatt für Psychoanalyse* (Medical Monthly for Psychology) Publisher Professor Dr. Sigmund Freud. Editor Dr. Wilhelm Stekel.

Dear Miss Spielrein! Vienna 12/V.1912

I should really be cross with you. You disappeared from Vienna without showing your face at my place, and on the whole, in Vienna you were not very nice toward me. Why? Jungism or phobia? I happened to read your paper recently. I like it very much. I would be glad to publish it either in the first or last issue and ask you to be prompt making corrections and sending them to me. For a change, Tausk[139] again attacked me roughly and was sharply rebuffed by everybody. The matter was [my] paper "The masks of homosexuality."

With cordial greetings, Sincerely yours,

signature and stamp Med. Dr. Wilhelm Stekel

WS 2

[on stationery of] *Zentralblatt für Psychoanalyse* (Medical Monthly for Psychology) Publisher Professor Dr. Sigmund Freud. Editor Dr. Wilhelm Stekel.

Dear Colleague, 30.5.1912

I am looking forward to receiving your manuscript and will publish your paper in the first issue of the new volume[140]. It is a great honor! I am a psychoanalyst and despite this, poetry and society have not lost their meaning for me. However, the human being does not change in his relationships by acquiring new knowledge. And now to your request: you are looking for cheap accommodations for a gentleman or a lady near the University. A poor widow with two children rents room and board and one is looked after splendidly. Ten minutes from the University. The prices are between 120 and 160 crowns per month based on mutual agreement. The room is on the ground floor, garden view. The address Frau Babette Rota, Vienna IX, Hahngasse 15, ground floor door 11. Patronage will be appreciated!

Many cordial greetings, with appreciation,

Signature and stamp

GS 1

Dear Frau Doctor, Vienna, 29.May.1912

Being overburdened with work at this time, Dr. Stekel asked me to answer your kind letter in his name. Naturally, he is agreeable to your postponing the submission of your article. He would like to let you know that despite of having practiced psychoanalysis for many years he is still good company for other people even if he does not converse about psychoanalysis. He also solemnly promises you to aggravate Freud as little as at all possible. I myself, Frau Doctor, am looking forward to your article with great anticipation. We all hope to greet

139 Tausk, Viktor (1879–1919), from Slovakia, studied medicine in Vienna funded by Freud, author of important psychoanalytic papers, who suicide became a polemic between Paul Roazen (author of the 1969 Brother Animal) and Kurt Eissler.

140 Perhaps a reference to "Destruction as a cause of becoming" published in 1912 or her paper on "Contributions to knowing the infantile mind" published in 1913.

you soon amongst us. Today is the last public session of our current activities of the Association for this year. Greetings and best wishes from Dr. Stekel and my little self,

Yours truly, Gaston Rosenstein.

EB 1 (postcard) To Miss Dr. Spielrein Wilhelmstr. 13 II

Dear Miss Doctor! Burghölzli-Zurich, 5.May.11

Your letter was forwarded to Dr. Jung to settle the matter, he is the only one who can certify that your paper is being printed and I hope that the difficulty will soon be resolved. Cordial greetings, Bleuler

EB 2 (postcard). To Miss Dr. Spielrein Wilhelmstr. 13 II

Dear Miss, Zurich, 25.X.1911

Forgive me that I have to bother you with problems in spite of your illness, but later I may not have your address. I would like to ask you kindly to send about ten copies of your dissertation. Warm wishes for your recovery and with collegial greetings,

Yours Bleuler

EB 3

Prof. Bleuler Burghölzli

Mrs. S. Spielrein-Scheftel Chez Mme. Rod 21 bis Rue St. Léger Geneva

Dear Mrs. collega! Zurich, 7.1.21

Your question perplexed me somewhat because from afar it is very difficult to make a fairly reliable diagnosis; however, based on your report, the probability that this could be dem.[entia] praecox is quite real. However, the struggle between yes and no does no longer apply to a simple obsessional neurosis. Nor does having delusions usually belong to obsessional neuroses. The fact that the patient predicted her madness is seen so frequently in schizophrenia whereas those with obsessional neurosis only have unspecific fears of this kind. Moreover, the actual thought confusion the woman felt as imminent does not belong to obsessional neuroses. Thus I do not believe that an obsession neurosis can "degenerate" into schizophrenia, however, it is certain that many schizophrenics, either in the beginning of the illness or in the course of it show obsessional symptoms. On the other hand, chronic schizophrenics that for years show no manifest obsessions usually do not have severe schizophrenic symptoms so that one came up with the apothegm that obsessional ideas are a protection against madness. And yet, at least, the catatonias that you found in the course of your patient's illness are not rare and, in any case, I would treat them as a catatonia which, for the time being, is not a bad prognosis. With cordial greetings and best wishes for New Year, yours sincerely,

Bleuler

EB 4

Prof. Bleuler Burghölzli

Dr. Spielrein-Scheftel Chez Mme Cloissac 22 rue des Sources Genève

Dear Frau Dr.! Zurich 18.IV.23

Many thanks for your beautiful report which I found really interesting and from which I learned something; however, as I always say, that thinking and time direction in dreams and in subthreshold [subconscious] thinking can be imprecise or altered, or the time direction may be totally ignored; but this is only a depth-phenomenon.156a And alongside these thought-forms and image-forms other thoughts also appear namely, those of attentive thinking while wide awake, and even in greater number. For me, subthreshold thinking is not only picture-thinking [image thinking], but that in subthreshold thinking there is a mixture of thinking in pictures and other forms as well. Thus there is no inability to initiate a certain direction, but there is no constraint to adhere to a particular direction. Occasionally one direction will be adhered to with extraordinary tenacity. For me, a "what was" is sometimes really transformed into a "what is," but only sometimes, but even then it plays a decisively more important role than in waking. These are my rejoinders which, however, do not detract from the value of your investigations but, on the contrary, make them even more important. According to your wish I am sending back your letter. With my best greetings sincerely,

Bleuler (enclosure)

EB 5

Prof. Bleuler Burghölzli

Dr. S. Spielrein-Scheftel, Chez Mme. Cloissac 22 rue des Sources

Dear Frau Dr.! Zurich 9.7.23

Many thanks for your kind sending of both your beautiful papers. As to the one about Pensèe de l'enfant I would only point out that out of an external similarity you make a partial identity. Next Monday I will leave for my vacation but perhaps immediately thereafter will be again available here for 8-10 days, in order to relieve Professor Maier. I hope that I will see you either before or during this relief action.

With collegial greetings, sincerely
Bleuler

CM 1

Doctor Cavendish Moxon[141] Box N Los Altos California, USA

Dear Doctor Spielrein, 16 December 1922

I have just read with much interest your article in Imago on "Papa and Mama" etc. Two trivial observations of my own came to mind as I read your remarks about the sound being pö rather than pa.

The Americans, instead of the British "papa", use a form which is just "pö pö".

A friend of mine when smoking his pipe has the habit of emitting a disconnected series of "pö pö pö" sounds; each [of] these is quickly emitted. I suppose most pipe smokers make the pö sound as they inhale, but in this case the infantilism was specially clear.

Please do not trouble to answer this. Indeed my wife and I may be on our way to Vienna before a reply could reach me. Perhaps we may have the pleasure of meeting you if we return via Switzerland.

Yours truly,
Cavendish Moxon

AO 1

Abraham Ott

Dear Mrs. Spielrein! Feuerthalen 11th June 1921

First of all, you might be wondering whether I am alright. Yes I am doing better than ever; had you foretold this three months ago I would have gloated over your mistake, you sly pedagogue! Forgive me that I will not tire thanking you, time and again, for the effort and the patience that you had granted to a creature as badly unhinged as myself. You can now see for yourself that it was meant to be my fortune that following my inner metamorphosis I should be able to exit my miserable life and enter an unexplored territory, this new land that I love so much, more than any other spot on earth than I have ever experienced. Have I not waxed ecstatic over all these glories to you in Geneva; and truly, I did not deceive myself, on the contrary, my expectations were surpassed. My [life in] Feuerthalen gave me exactly what I needed. But therein lay the root of my neurosis: I saw no way to escape my old [illegible: habits?] which I was

141 Moxon was an analyst in San Francisco, about whom R. Money-Kyrle published a review of Moxon's Freudian Essays on Religion and Science. *International Journal of Psycho-Analysis*, 8;133, 1927.

compelled to practice. Since I left Geneva my depressions have become just memories of some sentimental fits I could forgive any teenage girl. Every time a stroll down the awesome Rhine Falls my relativity principles are renewed and my graph returns to its usual constant level. Strange! My colleagues praise my great tranquility and wise reserve toward all things. If they only knew! But in vain, for I failed to learn my lesson. With ladies I apparently act very passive, this is what my Genevan Ursula experienced in Zurich. I visited her twice, for now I had no more time. And it would not have been wise anyway. What happens next I trustfully leave in God's hands. I was unable to do justice to matters psychoanalytic: my move to Feuerthalen, then my increased work load during the five weekly tests, have taken up all my time. Moreover, I was transferred to [teach] two classes of history and geography, subjects to which I did not apply myself as much as before, since during lessons at the gymnasium I blessedly practiced my ability to overcome sleepiness. For the last six weeks I have been busy studying the origins of the French Revolution. In addition I have put together and printed out four series of intelligence tests and subjected my poor students to them. I cannot expect too much from that because I am only able to compare my students with the test results of the last three years. Before the autumn vacation I can hardly devote myself to analyzing theoretical studies because I organized my vacation differently than I had imagined. First, we don't have a country place for two to three weeks or else I would have been in Geneva a whole week already. Eight days ago haymaking has begun everywhere. We have five weeks of vacations from 11th of July till 13th of August which I will devote to a journey through Germany and Denmark. From the 3rd till the 16th of August I will be in Jena for a vacation course so as to hear Professor Rein once again. I don't know yet if I am going to spend my autumn vacations in Geneva but it is probable. After the summer vacations I will be able to visit the Nachmansohns and Pastor Pfister and the Circle in Zurich. Meanwhile my cordial thanks to you for your friendly letter of 17.IV.21 and your friendly invitation, soon to learn something again.

In the meantime friendly greetings from your Abraham Ott.

EO 1

Dr. med. Emil Oberholzer Breitenau

Dear Miss Doctor: Schaffhausen, 27.V.1912

I received your letter today for which I thank you. I regret very much that my visit in Vienna took place during your absence. I was looking forward to chat with you. I will be in Vienna till mid-July. Would you be back by that time?

I accept with pleasure your friendly offer to be helpful to me. The boarding house Cosmopolit seems a bit too expensive. As you know, in Switzerland we psychiatrists are considered to be second-rate. In any case, upon your recommendation I will immediately contact Dr. Rank and mention you. I am sure I will find lodgings somewhere. On Friday I will be traveling so that your next letter will probably not reach me. I will look out for a yes from Freud and write to you soon about my impressions.

With cordial thanks for your future efforts on my behalf and best regards,
yours Oberholzer

EO 2

To Mrs. Doctor S. Spielrein, Geneva

Dear Colleague! 23.X.22

During our meeting on the 21st of this month you and other persons were accepted as members of the Swiss Society of Psychoanalysis. I will write to the International Psychoanalytic Publishing and the President to request that you journal and membership dues to the International [Association] remain the same as before and inform about the response in due course. In case the fee of 10 Fr. for our own dues is still too high for you, it will be my pleasure to take care of it myself; it is no special favor, as you might think, but a self-evident action for a colleague that so bravely fights for the cause and has so many meaningful things to say. The new volumes of both journals will be sent to you from Zurich.

At the last meeting I brought up your request for publications about infantile mental life. I am curious if you got something and how much of it you found unusable. I enclose two small essays which I have composed at the request of the editorial board (more will follow, fragments of individual case presentations taken apart from a whole work about childhood neuroses that became too big for the journal; therefore the lack of references in the paper about the phobia of a six year old boy; Little Hans was cited in the introduction and in the course of separating it I forgot to transfer it); and something from an earlier period and some brief observations which had occurred to me. I don't know if you will be able to use them or not. My wife would have been the one to offer something, but there I would really have to push her.

Thanks for your communications about Miss U. She attended only one-session; nobody among us would like to invite her and even less to make her a member. We need to shed a few other matters before we can enroll new questionable members. And one more request: in your beautiful essay will you allow me to replace the word "Sublimation" with "Sublimierung"? "Sublimation" is so "unfreudian", it reeks so much of chemistry and I do not know anyway why we push the preference for the unbecoming "Sublimation" rather than the elegant "Sublimierung." I wanted to tell this to you last time but I forgot.

With cordial greetings, Oberholzer.

[Added in handwriting on the left margin]. You will keep me informed about everything locally that is interesting as well as your available publications, won't you?]

EO 3

The Swiss Society for Psychoanalysis

Dear Colleague! Zurich 18.12.22

I believe that your presentation should last at least one hour. But it is all right for you to speak for as long as an hour and a half. We do not see you every day amongst us and thus this time first and foremost belongs to you. Unfortunately, I still have no news from Professor Delgado; but I will inform you as soon as I know something.

Simply, tell Bovet the following: that I have invited you to speak at the Swiss Society for Psychoanalysis and that I will advertise your lecture in the Neue Zürcher Zeitung as follows: "Frau Dr. med. S. of Geneva is lecturer at the Institut Rousseau;" you might ask him to do this in your name and should he find this objectionable, you can ask me to cancel it. I would then be able to place it as follows: "Frau Dr. med. S. of Geneva, who lectures at Institut Rousseau on educational psychoanalysis" to which he would not be able to object but which the NZZ might not add.

I take this opportunity to report a mistake: you speak again of the Zurich Psychoanalytic Society. This is incorrect and confusing. We are the Swiss Society whose members are scattered over the whole country (just recently half of the Zürichers attended) and we hold our meeting in Zurich because it suits the predominant majority, i.e., this way we are assured of maximum attendance. So just do not speak in Geneva about a Zurich society; as you know, we may soon split, as soon as circumstances will allow this, i.e., as soon there are so many in other places, that they can maintain a work community (thus like a prospective organization à la Swiss Science Society with chapters in Zurich, Basel, etc.).

With cordial greetings,

Oberholzer

You forgot that the Genevan Odier is our member, as is Morel. Thus in Geneva the members belonging to the Swiss Society are: Bovet, Morel, Odier,

Piaget, Saussure, Spielrein. However, Boven in Lausanne is not our member. Piaget does not owe us 10 Fr., as you write, but 20, i.e., 10 to the Swiss Society plus 10 to the International Association. Yours has not been received yet.[142]

EO 4

Dr. Emil Oberholzer

Specialist for Nervous and Mood

Disorders Zurich Rämi Street 2., Tel.: H.6679.

Dear Colleague! 2.VI.1923

Forgive that only today I am responding to your friendly and kind invitation, which I would have gladly accepted had circumstances permitted. But I am completely occupied with our move and am therefore burdened with expenses and other matters. The move is also the reason why I had to forego the psychiatric meeting and seeing my Geneva friends, even though it would have been tempting to meet with all of them in an intimate setting at your place and talk about all kinds of things. I was however unable to interrupt, even for a few days, a number of my analytic patients who found themselves in a critical phase, especially since the move in three weeks will once again require multiple interruptions. It was truly a pity that the conference and the move came so close to each other; the latter is now expected by 1st October, but the apartment was available a quarter of a year earlier so I will probably have to move without my wife. How did it go in Geneva and how are you doing? Please write to me and let me know when you will be in Zurich, hopefully this will not happen during my temporary absence. With cordial greetings,

Your Oberholzer

EO 5

Dear Colleague! Undated

I am returning the enclosed manuscript of your author's summary with a request to expand it so that it is at least half a printed page long. It will not affect the paper itself. In its present size, there is a big difference between yours and other authors' summaries (I was unable to gauge their content in relation to you lecture.) As to your communication about cases B. and C., I would like to say that I am happy, but I am not; for in the next few weeks —and you might not

142 In Internationale Zeitschrift f. Psychoanalyse, 1922, Spielrein is listed as member of the Geneva Group and as having "held at Institut J.J Rousseau eight lectures on "psychoanalysis and pedagogy." (8:105).

have more at your disposal, and one would hardly want to grant you more—one would hardly be able to share your conviction, on the contrary, there is a danger of a subsequent estrangement. When I analyze colleagues—and I have in mind six of yours—I do not allow them to leave before half a year is up. When will you travel? Would you be able in the meantime to do for me a French translation for a fee? Cordial greeting and best wishes to you so that perhaps at the last moment C. and B. will elevate you as their body-and soul-doctor.

Sincerely yours,

Oberholzer.

Beginning in June I will probably attend the psychiatry meeting and probably make a report. Under these circumstances a visit would not be possible. As usual, not a word from Piaget, neither in response to my question about doing a presentation for the Society in January nor to a business question about the journal. The hound of Mannheim, whom you probably know too, would have, said: "it's paltry!"

FG 1 (French)

"Vers L'Unité" Groupement de Libre Recherche Spiritualiste

Madame, Geneva 8 June 1921

I am writing to you to thank you for the very interesting talk last night at the meeting of "Vers L'Unité." You could see yourself that the listeners were numerous and attentive. I am convinced that your words will find an echo. If you are still available to work with us we would suggest establishing a psycho-analytic group within "Vers L'Unité" next fall. You would be the president of the group. Looking forward to your response and my sincere thanks for last night. I am sending you a brochure authored by me about "Vers L'Unité" and a membership card which you can sign if it interests you. Please read about our organization and see if it suits your interests. Hoping to see you in the fall, with expressions of esteem and sympathy,

Frank Grandjean, University Professor [of philosophy]

Vice-president of "Vers L'Unité"

78, Boulevard des Philosophes, Geneva

PS. Here are some messages that were handed to me after you left.

FG2

Dear Madam Flerissant 25, Geneva 16 June, 1921

Thank for having informed me about the next session, I am looking forward to hearing your lecture on phobia. Thank you also for your letter a few days ago and I am very sorry not have been able to attend your lecture held at the Group "Vers l'Unitée," nor the lecture of M. Piaget. Lately I have been extremely busy all the time due to my engagement, which you must have heard about. But as my bride had to go back to France, I now have a few free days and I will be very happy to hear from you regarding the experiences you had spoken about. In the meantime, dear madam, sincerely yours [signature partly cut off]

CO 1

Dr. Charles Odier, 6 Rue St.-Léger [Geneva] Internal medicine and nervous disorders

Dear Madame, Undated

I am very sorry that I was not free on Friday but I had a dinner, prelude to my engagement, that was decided today. It was simultaneous but less important than that of Flournoy!! The future will show if both of them happened in spite of analysis or because of it. Anyway, I am delighted insofar as my daughter is concerned. I figure I will be away nine days starting in July and in the meantime I would like to pay what I owe you. Thus I would be grateful to you if you would send me a statement of your honorarium from now till then. I thank you again for the interest you have shown me,

sincerely yours

Ch. Odier

CO 2

Dear colleague, Undated

We will be making music on Sunday evening and we are looking forward to your joining us. It will be very easy for you. You just have to come at 8 and a quarter at the entrance to the Comédie. There you will see three gentlemen and one lady. One of the gentlemen will carry a violin, another one a cello and the third will carry nothing, it will be my brother, I have informed him about your coming and you will meet him on my behalf. We will play beautiful quartets and quintets. Hoping you will decide to come, do not worry about anything, it will be quite easy, no special attire needed, should you get bored you can leave. With my best wishes, yours,

Ch. Odier.

CO 3

Dear Madame, Saturday

What's new with you? We are all back and I would like to see you. I learned about your bereavement and offer my sincere condolences. Please reserve an evening for me and come for supper, nothing formal, we will stretch out on the lawn, if you like it. I may be busy tomorrow or Wednesday, I have not decided yet, because I am awaiting your answer. Looking forward to seeing you, devotedly yours,

Odier

CO 4

Dear Madame, Undated

Would you like to come for supper tomorrow evening at half past 7? I recommended you for a case of tic in a young girl. I hope it will work.

Cordially yours, Ch. Odier

CS 1

[German, on the stationery of Dr. med. C. Schneiter Specialist for Nervous and Mood diseases]Davos Platz, Switzerland, to Frau Dr. S. Spilrein-Scheftel, Thomasiusstr. 2, Berlin

Dear Frau Collega! 29.X.14

In tranquility of working before the war, a small contribution on the psychology of dementia praecox was published in a collection of papers of the Zurich school of psychiatry which I am now offering to you. You have already gifted us repeatedly with very valuable materials from the ideational world of schizophrenics and the attached reprint offers only additional observations to those that have already been made by yourself. I have taken the liberty to cite your first article in the *Jahrbuch* in connection with various cases. I am now more aware that the connections are even more numerous and profound than the ones I have highlighted. However, the basis of my article was, as far as possible, to reconstruct a unitary structure out of the paranoiac's delusional system and therefore the various external connections were only briefly considered, which I ask you to forgive me.

With my best wishes, sincerely yours,

Dr. C. Schneiter.

NL 1

[in German] on the stationery of Dr. med. R. Nachmansohn-Leibowitz Ophthalmologist Stauffacherstr. 21

Dear Frau Doctor, Zurich 30.9.19

I assume that you are again in Lausanne but I am mailing this letter to Les

Marécottes sur/Ladran because surely your letters will be forwarded to you. The New Year is the time when we Jews are especially thinking about friends, and that fate will be favorably disposed toward them. I would be most happy to learn how you and Renatchen are doing. Do you now have news from your family? Our situation is not bad. As you can tell from the change of address, we have moved to a new apartment and I expect this change will have a good effect on my practice, seeing that my previous apartment was a bit out-of-the-way. However, due to this constant apartment hunting and finding nothing, and the move itself, I have unfortunately not been able to answer your last letter. Have you finished your article in the meantime? You asked me what and where did Havelock Ellis say anything about your article but regrettably I cannot recollect much about it. You have not sent us the most recent article of your brother, it would certainly interest us greatly. What does your brother write to you about Russia? – For the time being we are living in Switzerland but I hope to end my life either in America or in Palestine. – Did you have a good rest in the mountains and are you now satisfied with Renatchen's health condition? I hope to hear from you real soon and wish you all the best and the beautiful in the coming year.

Your R. Nachmansohn-Leibowitz.

NL 2

Dear Frau Doktor 17.VIII.20

Please forgive me that I only today I am answering your kind letter of 5.VIII and your postcard of 11.VIII. I am now very touched by your sympathy and helpfulness. Meanwhile the little one is getting better and I myself am feeling better and hope that it will continue to be trouble-free. My husband is back in Frankfurt. My two rooms are rented to a Swiss couple and I got a good maid from Germany from my mother-in-law so that everything will run smoothly. How you are doing? I am quite aghast that you are unable to pay the rent for your room. Where are you living now? And where to you want to travel on the twenty first? As far as getting a lecturer's degree in the department of philosophy, it requires submitting a habilitation[143] dissertation to the dean, and if the department agrees with it, then the candidate is invited to give a trial lecture. The habilitation thesis must be an independent scientific labor (not just the thesis itself). It is best for you is to get the advice of Bleuler. I am glad that you want to come back to Zurich soon. I am now living here as a settler, I only have

143 Habilitation in Europe still is a degree that entitles to conduct independent teaching at a university following an habilitation thesis.

a few patients from time to time. Do you have news from your family? To me the world seems so dreary that I sometimes lose all hope for a better future. But this is perhaps connected with my weakness coupled with the strain of breastfeeding and sleepless nights. Big deal, you know all this well from your own experience; ultimately this difficult time will end and be replaced by other difficulties. I hope to hear from you very soon and in the meantime send you my warmest greetings.

Your R.N.L. [Rachel Nachmansohn-Leibowitz]

EC1

Docteur Edouard Christin Privat Docent la Faculté de Médecine 2 Rue Tour de l'Ile Genève sends his thanks to Madame Dr. Spielrein and cordial congratulations on her article about the analogies between the thinking of children, people suffering from aphasia, and unconscious thinking. He sends her all his wishes for a better future and asks her to trust his good remembrance.

L. Sch. Undated

On the stationary of Hotel Westphälischer Hof Berlin NW Dear Miss and colleague!

When we parted you promised to answer me, if I write to you, and I now take this opportunity to tell your compassionate heart not to worry about my abscess: it is almost healed, withered is its noble and succulent bloom. Having duly expressed my thanks for your commiseration, I still have a bone to pick with you. I have already forgiven you that you cruelly denied me a parting kiss, an honest kiss, that nobody should resist; I can even gloss over everything else, because I have come to understand many things. Thus I understand—or, perhaps, it is a lyman's rush judgment—the mysterious depths that rise to the surface; you and the Jungian drop of blood, you! This bitter tirade shows you how seriously I take it, what a limited sense of humor I possess. Even though I just insulted you so rudely, you need not take it so tragically, and there is nothing for me to add. However, I do have something to add, for example, tragically, and yet there is nothing for me to add. However, I do have something to add, for example, that you kept all the six copies of my Lilliputian photo; I do not understand why you had to have all six; I forgave you this, too, a long time ago. But for God's sake, do not immediately turn this thing around according to your psychoanalytic habit: aha, he became turned on against me (against psychoanalysis). But here you would be committing an enormous error, as happened so often during our disputatious conversations. You would be equally mistaken if, from the fact, that in order to achieve my goal I courageously put you on to material about psychoanalysis—quasi to prove to you that psychoanalysis leaves me cold—you would deduce that "aha, he is afraid of analysis"! For God's sake, don't sniff out complexes everywhere, don't ubiquitously insinuate motives just because they immediately occurred to you, based on an assumption of types, symbols, patterns. The thing is, really, not so simple, and when the psychoanalyst condescendingly accuses the layman of naivete, it seems to me that this assumption of types is the more dangerous naivete, because psychoanalysis boastfully poses as a science. [a line missing] and I forgive psychoanalysis everything, it's "scientific" jargon, constructing concepts, such as "abreacting" etc. But there is one thing I will never forgive psychoanalysis, that you, my dear Miss, should be harmed by it and suffer. It is terrible how remembering you is so closely connected with the thought of suicide. Suicide, this horrible word! What depths of suffering it covers over! And you play with this word! It is a dangerous game. In this act, there is no logic and no awareness, as you would like to make me believe, nothing but madness, confused complexes and affects. It is madness not to use judgment when one decides cold-bloodedly and arbitrarily to cut the thread of life! You are still young and a lot of beautiful things are awaiting you in your future life; and when the youthful Sturm and Drang abates, a calmer appreciation of life will fill your soul.

Postscript. Now further details (as always in a P.S.), the most important matters, namely the misunderstandings that have intruded into our otherwise friendly and touching get-togethers. You were so afraid, as if you had to act as a mother to a child, and I behaved as I do with my wife, with whom I am used instantly to dish up all my little sorrows and discuss them with her (I hear you saying, nay, I see it in your face saying: "Aha, transference"). Hence, the misunderstandings. Indeed, I really feel like a newborn child, and, arguably, the guilty one is your psychoanalytically trained mind that is used to puzzle out the innermost shell, the core, in every harmless thing. (Only the naïve people, who take life as it is, can be happy.) However, s'excuser c'est s'accuser [he who excuses himself, accuses himself], therefore I shall not elaborate.

With cordial greeting and fond memories,
your colleague Dr. L. Schlesinger
My address: Dr. L. Sch. Libau, Russia [now Liepaja in Estonia].

7
German Diary

91. 23.VI.06 2–4 Saturday

Dementia senilis. Initial stage, course and terminal stage[144]. The initial phase of simpler symptoms. Starts with memory defect, the patients become aware of it themselves. Followed by further intellectual deterioration. Often this change causes typhus, lung diseases, often depressions, mania-like states, preoccupation. *Tram* [sic?] as in mania. Memory deficiency, then dementia senilis. Capricious, annoying behavior. Often silly deceptions, thefts, or sexual misconducts (*Johannistrieb*). Often exhibitionism, preferring a child for sexual acts. Often insomnia. (Something similar to a stroke). Course: progressive, remissions are limited and severe deterioration (cases of incompetence lasting for years). Course with mild psychoses, for example, at night time, anxious and disoriented; at day time, rage attacks (nutritional disorders of the brain). Often manic excitement or depression. Often strokes and tendency to other diseases. (What is marasmus). Marasmus without paresis, as occurs in general [?] paralysis. In strokes there is occasional paresis but not as in paralysis; only more obvious... and (urinary incontinence). In the end there is complete dementia or it can result in so-called epilepsia senilis (symptoms of cortical disorder located in "focal lesions" of the brain). The most common ultimate cause is hypostatic pneumonia. Criminality among seniles is relatively uncommon. Sometimes silly acts of revenge (e.g., arson). Complications of senile dementia, namely, alcoholism, an abuse that can also facilitate an early occurrence of the disease. Epileptic attacks can occur in so-called "late epilepsy" through which senile dementia can ultimately lead to real brain degeneration, i.e., "late paralysis," that is difficult to distinguish from the bodily symptoms of major senile dementia. Hereditary disorders. Other diseases can predispose to dementia, for example, imbecility,

144 Spielrein's numerous abbreviations were spelled out for easier reading.

dementia praecox...capable of thinking. I am totally stupid and cannot explain it any further and it is a very big hassle to see my way out of it.

92. 9.VI.6

As in any nation that is divided into different groups, each group soon gets one or another language, each one develops its "specific" expressions which in spite of all knowledge of words and grammar remain incomprehensible: the same happens in small self-enclosed "communes" and between individuals as well. It is thus conceivable that the smaller the isolated group, the more easily are the "specific expressions" naturalized in the language. You[145] are of course, familiar with the tendency to be succinct, to reduce to what is familiar, etc. In an individual there is no such counter-pressure because an individual only needs to understand himself or herself. The peculiarity of a language immensely increases the feeling of being an eccentric; these people do not expect anything more from the world for themselves, and due to the artificial coldness toward their own feelings they become similarly alienated from feelings toward other people; they react to everything with a cold smile and, because they have long since lost all faith and interest in life, they perceive all speeches as meaningless sounds in which they cannot engage, like a mother who, under the influence of some strong feelings, cannot engage in a dialogue with her beloved child: she either shows no reaction or she waits for something more to develop while showing no sign of emotion that can be observed. This rigidity is not due to an absence of emotions, but is caused by an enormous accumulation of emotions, which results in these persons' inability to distinguish discrete emotions and they can only experiences all of it as a "cover" in their head. This makes it easy to comprehend the well-known thought blocking in dementia praecox: in a brain exhausted by constant conflict, almost every word is apt to arouse a *complex* and disrupt the chain of thoughts; the interest is too feeble to be able to stick to the guiding idea so that any spontaneous incidental emotion acquires such power that it can induce thought blocking. Haven't you yourself observed that in a state of exhaustion one cannot find the right words to express one's emotions and one gets stuck: "yeah, what did I really want to say?" I can now very easily overcome this when I get into my Munich mood and thus regularly experience a thought block with every phrase and it's a very difficult to get out of it. For example, after the phrase "the interest is too feeble in order to take hold of the directing idea" I repeat a thousand times the words "in order to" until I find my way out

145 From here on Spielrein address Jung as *Sie*, You, the polite form.

of the hole. I have a few typical examples from before but I do not think they are necessary for you. Then comes the feeling of being left hanging. It seems to me, this could be caused by a loss of interest; however, I rather believe that the image is understood correctly. However, in the course of recollection there are either some images persisting in consciousness and as a result there is a more striking recollection, or, for the same reasons as in thought blocking, a sudden slowing of conscious apperception occurs and people repeat the old image and the last word. However even in normal association experiments perseverations can also occur when one does not especially direct one's attention but says the first thing that occurs to one.

Consider the following phenomenon: when one plays with one hand, the sounds are irregular and unsure, whereas when one plays the same tones, even almost inaudibly, with the other hand, then the first hand plays more clearly, regularly, and strongly. However, since abreacting is not wholly pleasant, so, for example, in order to help themselves, people choose other words to lend them the meaning of the complex (based on some similarity) and thus save themselves the trouble of bringing the entire confused complex into consciousness. Thus, other people understand these connotations and the goal of abreacting is fulfilled.

[on the upper left margin]: Construction of symbols

93. 8.VI.6

I don't need to tell you what a machine the human being is with all its emotions, but I can't help missing the schadenfreude of alerting you that people are by no means remote from children and other psychopaths. You already agree as far as mania is concerned, but dementia praecox will seem to you as something quite alien! All right, dear aunties and uncles! Do you have some atypical neologisms? Since a word is signified by an original name, you are indignant that it brings to consciousness an abundance of images and feelings that evoke in you extremely strong emotions. Therefore, you create new words, remain altogether upstanding, maintain the utmost serenity when you hear stories about the most horrifying things. The affect is inadequate throughout. However, as it is inadequate in everybody (a result of reciprocal suggestion), one considers the emotion to be adequate. When you smiled in connection with the situation of

Miss Berg[146], a situation the details of which you did not get into, your reaction was not adequate. When I called your attention to it, you said: "This

146 Jewish-Russian woman doctor Feiga Berg, interacted with Sabina when she was an inpatient at Burghölzli and later when she became a student. Berg published a vignette about her: "I will

makes one laugh." This is the typical evidence that, in this case, one would not be able to declare you insane because one would be obligated to apply it to other people as well. For now, you can laugh at me. All right! Please spare me a few more minutes. When somebody says: "This is a good pill for you!" nobody would assume that the person in question is psychotic because the analogy with the pill and substitution by a word is understood by everyone, however, a somewhat dumber person would react with some astonishment and anxiety.

When for any reason one is prevented from creating for oneself "a hand playing along" with the complex, it becomes necessary to resort to caricature in-as-much as the complex is expressed in words comprehensible only to one-self. Naturally, one deceives oneself in that one activates the mechanism necessary for instinctual gratification and gives a little free rein to the previously released energy and then promptly, as the new energy accumulates (since the effect of the cause is continuing), one seeks new sources of energy to counteract the original ones. In this way countless scandals[147] arise (from works of art to wishful dreams and wildest pranks). A special kind of scandal are the automatized scandals, or stereotypies. Stereotypies that are expressions of thinking and feeling are quite a normal phenomenon; the latter are either collective or individual stereotypies. Similarly, there are also stereotypies caused by repression. You have often observed a child who mocks a teacher for some peculiarity, and I do not need to cite any special examples thereof. You could have also observed how a person in an affective state starts performing rhythmic movements; when one succeeds once, one keeps on repeating it until finally the thing becomes automatic every time a complex strives to assert its power. In very sensitive people every little thing can become a tormenting complex and therefore they constantly have to seek refuge in processes of repression (when they cannot abreact naturally and directly). Isn't it remarkable that along with the automatisms one can also

---

cite one example of treatment by Jung of…a girl from Russia. Miss III, age 18, possessing excellent abilities, graduated with a gold medal. Before long psychical abnormalities were noticed: her speech was incoherent, she hit her mother, broke glass, etc…Was admitted in an aggressive stateof mind, in her room she barricaded the door before the doctor's visit, doused her hand with black ink to dirty the doctor's hand etc. Jung asked her to pay attention to her associations to discover the patient's complex…The complexes were mainly related to the family. The father is pronounced neurasthenic, mother a hysteric…Abreacting the complexes… and under the influence of Jung's verbal psychotherapy…the patient developed new interests…in science. Now she is studying at the university and is completely healthy" (Berg, 1909, pp. 13–14).

147 In Russian and in German, *Skandal* means a scene, a row, an outburst, i.e., dramatizing the accompanying emotions in various enactment (Lothane, 2009). In English scandal it also means a public disgrace, humiliation due to corrupt or criminal behavior.

perform other acts (i.e. one can also do good work)? Many women are able to knit and to read and nobody is amazed by this. One can even say, at least at the beginning, that a brain not exhausted by the perpetual conflict can still perform quite well; emotions proceed in wave-like manner and when they crest, the women either grumble or do something, for example, they get up; and when the wave breaks [illegible]... they again [text break].

93a. 29.8.6

I am copying the letter to Dr. Jung I finished today. I had to write the letter right away but I wanted to wait... What was present tense until now became past tense and the blues as well! Oy vey! According to my theory, if it continues this way any longer one will have to poison me as an incurable degenerate (according to your theory as well). Your penultimate letter to me brought me 20000 tons of relief, even though this is pretty dumb. For the life of me, I cannot but resort to the style of caricature. I had never the right to regard you as a liar in the usual meaning of the word and I do not assert it either. For a variety of reasons, such as integrity, vanity, or ethical concepts, you were unable to show your feelings. I know that previously you regarded me as a moral person but with time you may have changed your mind. What made me conclude that this was the case I cannot explain because of my own ambitsia.[148] However, what finally affected me was that my consciousness was not entirely clean because during all that time I was in a state of speechless despair, and when the head got completely daft due to constant studying I did nothing but engaged in creating scandals, i.e. I invented thought scandals and was flooded with the wildest anti-social pranks (when one talks about scandals one feels a little animal [crawling] on one's back on the left side). I ended up getting a small syringe filled with KCN[149] [potassium cyanide], which I brought back from the hospital, in order to entertain anyone who spoke to me. KCN was only to create an effect because the syringe was filled with water. I prefer to be silent about other plans I had. As I was traveling to the hospital, a little girl entered the streetcar looking extremely pale, gazing helplessly into the distance, carrying an enormous basket. The moment I looked at her, a tender feeling toward her awoke in me all the details of my pranks, and my depression appeared to me awful and disgusting, so that in my enthusiasm I even came to

148 In Russian ambitsia does not mean to have ambition in the sense of motivation to strive and achieve but to feel angst and anger when hurt in one's self-esteem and pride.

149 On 19 October 1910 Sabina writes in her diary: "I fell into a rage...and would poison myself in [Jung's] presence with Ken" (C 32), followed by this footnote: "probably a medicine of the period" (p. 219), thus, KCN was misread as "Ken."

the conclusion that melancholy is a moral defect. Filled with such moral sentiments I arrived at the hospital where, again, the devil gained the upper hand and wanted first and foremost to take revenge upon this moral seduction. However, you arrived sooner than the opportunity to make trouble, which made me enormously happy. However, I was not calm: first came the compulsive laughter (which still happens to me frequently and causes hellish pain). Overcome with indignation, I simply reached for schadenfreude, especially since you were just talking about pranks pulled by various patients. The fantasy reached a climax in me and I was ready to make war. However you were in the mood to speak to me with lots of kindly feelings. I do not know how it happened, but when you spoke about hysteria I was overcome, out of joy and gratitude, by tearful emotions. And when you immediately added: "Naturally, there are some moral defects in them," I attributed it to myself. In the end there was melancholy. When you spoke about the age when regression occurs you mentioned that people in uttermost misery do not forget to obtain the best morsel etc.; so do you mean that one "cannot explain this as mood determined?" Ooooooh, what priceless nonsense! Whence the cause of the misery? From the will to live, from the sensation of weakness, from anxiety about impending death. When one feels weak and helpless one wants to feel loved, protected, and cared for. When one feels death-anxiety one wants to eat as much as possible in order to live longer. Even presumed malingering can be easily explained by means of hysterical mechanisms. When you ask someone for advice, and even agree with the opinion offered, you are prone to present the dumbest contrary evidence. What for? So that all the contrary ideas will be disputed by the opponent; and here, too, the patient is anxious, she is not in the mood; she wants support and reassurance from you, she wants you to defeat her horrifying ideas with counter-associations. However, she has to depict her situation to you in most horrific thoughts and thus offer the greatest resistance to your words of consolation: and then she becomes immersed in this situation and can immediately convince herself that she cannot eat, etc. However, when left to herself (and perhaps trying to console herself a little bit, or perhaps not), she comes to the realization that she does have an appetite or that she needs to eat in order to live, and she eats. You should rather say that the label "melancholy" is not suitable for this disease picture, because here You have to do with a very clearly expressed complex. Neither is it hysteria, since the essence of hysteria, it seems to me, consists in a struggle between the transformation drive (explanation below) and repression mechanisms, which is not the case here. And yet, your lecture was wonderful (not only in the scientific, but also in the ethical, sense). Why were you able at that moment to create so much enthusiasm and emotion?

You are blessed with a wonderful potential energy and can accomplish infinitely more than you are actually doing. If you only knew how morally splendid you were at that moment (when you treated the patient so caringly and lovingly)! I looked at those present in the hospital ward (i.e. the students) and they were all filled with the same emotion and were therefore so beautiful. I was totally transformed, feeling soft and warm toward the others, and even though I went home in the throes of utmost misery, I was still calm and strong in my decision... more than that is not necessary, or else it comes from some "poetry." Since then I have not made any more scandals. (Since this page was written a week ago, I must enter a correction: a few days ago, in the gymnastics hall, I sprayed Miss Berg through a straw when she said to me something like that I should not be so impudent as to do such a thing to her), although I am again completely cold toward everybody (now perhaps not entirely so).

My work is now guided by "transformation principles." Now comes the critical point. I love you too much, therefore perhaps I imagine something that is not there (or perhaps it is there?); for example, that you despise me, that you do not want me to grovel to you, etc. Every time this creates emotional storms and self-torments. At first I thought it had to do with science, but when I happen to see you again, after so much has accumulated, everything gets so mixed up, I can find no words, I am afraid to appear stupid (or even show my face) and I become tongue-tied. And when you say something and I realize that this is not so, then perhaps half an hour later I might be able to retort (something like this never happened). When you say nothing more to me it hurts me to the point of despair. A person who allows herself to be chained by complexes is a slave and her individuality is never fully developed. For these reasons I wanted to leave Zurich for at least three years but was unable to find another suitable university! It is remarkable that now, for the second time, I am doing what I can to flee Zurich but fate brings me back time and again. You know what effect your lecture had on me, and my whimpering letter, so what do you think about it? Should I try to leave you completely alone for three years? (But it is a pity, because I so fervently yearn to hear your lecture on hysteria. To hell with it! Why should a disease complex etc. undermine the drive for science!) What is one to do? Should I not even drag myself to your lecture? Since your last lecture you have become a bright "star of virtue" to me and I wanted to become like you, that is, not exactly like you but more like all those "honest workers" above whom you stand head and shoulders thanks to an enormous intelligence and character. This sounds comical but in fact, out of respect, I...all right, enough of that, or else it will have a bad effect on you in that it could cause self-contentment.

94. 30.VIII.6

Should I see you once more, or was this the last time? Should I speak with you once more or not? Aptschebi[150]. This sounds like a romantic novel but I am not that dumb. And one can endure more than it seemed in the beginning. However, you think about this question, you must keep your word: you are first and foremost obligated, at least in connection with one of your newest physiognomies (the one that pleases you most), to send me a dream, an association, a hysterical symptom, dementia praecox or whatever else you have promised me. The rest depends on your wish: you know very well how overjoyed I am when I receive your letters. When you are up to it, write to me from time to time and without waiting for my answer. Write to me firmly: "get yourself to work" If you only knew how grateful I would be to you, which means how useful it would be for me! If you will, there are many good people in this world, and they form a crowd: they are prone to being led blindly by means of suggestive emotions. I wanted to tell you a great deal but I am too tired.

The more I associate with people the more I long for you: I have never met a person in whom intelligence (even when not like yours) is united with such moral power, character and idealism. Most of the people I know are so unhappy, like Miss Berg[151] the contact with whom turns my life into a most appalling misery. I feel anxious when I think about my current acquaintances because I instantly get into an enormous rage. It is too much and it is impossible to describe. All right: let's leave it alone. In fact, going for days on end without speaking a word can drive one crazy. I get up at 6 o'clock at the latest. After three to four hours I am exhausted by working and lapse into utmost melancholy; then again, I also get melancholy (that is despair) from contact with people so I end up preferring solitude. If I only knew what to do about it! I wanted to spend the summer working somewhere in the countryside (à la rural school) but there is no such thing even though such goal-oriented physical labor in nature, in the midst of efficient healthy people, would be very useful for me. I would like to become such an efficient (or, in your language, "useful") combination, therefore I would like you to write to me so that the better part of my personality would be inspired from time to time, so that in the moment of weakness I could think of you and become stronger. Even now I could be strong without you, but when one feels supported one is more secure, and in addition, naturally,

150 Probably Sabina's onomatopoetic word for the sound of sneezing, apchkhi in Russian, hatschi in German, a sign of an emotional reaction.

151 Here "Miss Berg" is drawn within a cage-like frame and crossed out.

I would like each time to have your work with me; could you then tell me what you have published so that I can buy it? Or, in general, when you happen to buy an interesting book?

95. 24.08.6

So this is important: do you believe, including rigorous checking, what other people tell you about me, especially one like Miss Berg: this doesn't mean that she is lying to you, but that I am lying to her. I feel this is bad on my part, and I always want to avoid this, but it happens unnoticed by me; in the midst of a most trustful conversation with her I am capable of suddenly inserting some hoax: she provokes me enormously to enact scandals. My feelings toward her are also quite remarkable: she does not meet my ideals, but it seems to be most suitable for the chain of events; perhaps I also like her because I know her fate and because the hospital has forged a bond between us. Otherwise I am in the least interested to speak with her about the hospital and especially about you, because then everything appears all too human and not as ideal as I wanted to believe. And I do believe that it will then become enormously hard for me, and I will end up always running to you so that I can regain the original clear impression. The less I want to talk with her about you the more I do, the more do truth and fiction get confusedly mixed up with each other (which concerns me more than you). As far as you are concerned, what is concocted refers only to your actions, explained as arising either from the most noble or the most abominable motives, and thus you are sometimes depicted as a wonder and sometimes as a wretch. I do not begin talking about the hospital at the outset, however when she begins [to do that], I feel imperceptibly drawn into these conversations like a moth to the fire and surely the consequences are most dire for me. And moreover this, which is actually self-evident. You must not breathe a word about my feelings toward you to anybody. You shouldn't get angry that I am speaking to you about this, which any decent person knows herself, because all this is only provisional, because in my opinion, under certain circumstances even the most ideal person can sometimes commit some meanness; should that happen to you, you would be duty-bound to inform me immediately; I have a right to ask and I ask it unconditionally: you may not say a word to anyone about my feelings toward you. Don't forget that you can only have "suppositions" but that I have given you no cause to draw any certain conclusions. But the thing remains the same even if you could know everything; I would never be able to endure your saying "oh, that's something to laugh about." Another necessary condition is that the "complexes" should leave me alone for three years at least (that is, every few months I could stand one or maximum two a day, but that is already more than enough). I have already told you this myself in a manner, that that for the sake of the harmonious development of my individuality I must be alone for three years but, obviously, it was of little use. I believe that you yourself could arrange something about this. You could write that I am proud of my family, that I like you, but despite all this, in your opinion, I must be left alone for a few years. This is "insolent" but what can one do? – Finished. I think extremely rarely (or possibly rarely), yet in circumstances of spontaneous strong emotions, I will write a few words to you. But it's dumb! This caricature of melancholy is a wretched affair! "You just work." That is the main thing. Goodbye until...? (You must decide that).

That is why I am writing now about what should happen later. The most important thing for me is that you should be as perfect as much as possible and therefore thoughts of the opposite are most frightening to me. The letter (that you sent my mother and which I read) restored my faith in you and made me wildly happy. You are a remarkably successful combination, however, unfortunately, you are too strongly influenced by the prejudices of your milieu and this could result in the good becoming eclipsed, so that the more one-sided and worse combination turn manifest. Before we proceed we have to delve into philosophy. Professor Mach[152] in Vienna, about whom you may have heard, is of the opinion that the "ego" is a combination of sensations and that the world, the body, and the like are nothing but sensations[153]. In this manner, a continuity

152 Mach, Ernst (1838–1916), Austrian physicist and philosopher, and thus psychologist, who wrote that psychology is essential for understanding the physiology of the sense organs.

153 *Empfindunge* in German means both perceptions and sensations related to feelings and emotions (Mach, 1959, with an illuminating "Introduction" by Thomas S. Szasz, citing Freud: "I read (Mach's *Analyse der Empfindunge* ...all of which [has] the same kind of aims as my work, and see what [he has] to say about dreams" (p. xviii). Mach replaced the usual word perception (*Wahrnehmung*) with the technical term sensation (*Empfindun*). However, is also connected sensations with emotions (p. 21). Freud quotes Mach in a letter to Fliess cf. June 12, 1900 (Masson, p. 417) and in his bibliography, and in the Standard Edition, 22:22 4. In English sensation, percept, and image are cognate concepts, referring either to becoming aware of stimuli from the environment or stimuli from the body, the latter either external, from the skin, or internal, as feelings of pleasure and pain. Thus "*feelings* is used more broadly to denote a response to a stimulus or a set of stimuli that is a combination of sensation, emotion, and a degree of thought; as to judge a situation by one's *feelings* rather than by the facts" (Webster, 1951). In German *Empfindun* means feeling, perception, sensation, sentiment, frame of mind. The verb *empfinde* means to sense in all these meanings. Sensations as combined ideas and emotions are also connected with the concept of *complex*, introduced by Jung, as "Organized group of ideas and memories of great affective force" (Laplanche & Pontalis, 1973). Ryle (1949) writes about "sensations, feelings, and images are things...[are] contained in the stream of consciousness (p. 199); those "connected with special organs of sense,

arises and the difference between the ego and the world disappears; one cannot ask: "who is sensing?" because the ego (i.e. the consciousness of the moment) is nothing but a clustering of sensations. (Furthermore, he points out the insignificance of the differences between conscious and unconscious in psychology). It is impossible to explain all this because it requires a lot of time; but if you are interested, I could send you his book. Its title is: *Die Analyse der Empfinungen and das Verhältnis des Physischen zum Psychischen* [analysis of sensations and the relation between the physical and the psychical]. I can quote a few sentences that I found by chance (while leafing through the book):

"Thus perceptions, presentations, volitions, and emotions, in short the whole inner and outer world, are put together, in combinations of varying evanescence and permanence, out of a small number of homogenous elements. Usually, these elements are called sensations (p. 22). That in this complex of elements, which fundamentally is only one, the boundaries of bodies and of the ego do not admit of being established in a manner definite and sufficient for all cases, has already been remarked (p. 22). In special cases, however, in which practical ends are not concerned, but where knowledge is an end in itself, the delimitation in question may prove to be insufficient, obstructive and untenable (p. 23).[154] The primary fact is not the ego, but the elements (sensations). The elements constitute the I. *I* have the sensation green, [this] signifies that the element green occurs in a given complex of other elements (sensations, memories). When *I* cease to have the sensation green, when *I* die, then the elements no longer occur in the ordinary, familiar association. That is all. Only an ideal mental-economical unity, not a real unity, has ceased to exist. The ego is not a definite, unalterable, sharply-bounded entity. None of these attributes are important; for all vary even

namely the eyes…and those which are connected with the other sensitive but non-sensory organs of the body (p. 201). "We of "describing organic sensations,… a pain as stabbing…likening it to the sort of pain…given by…instruments" (p. 203). "For here…'feel' means 'feels as if'…We might call it a 'post-perceptual' use of 'feel'" (p. 241), or as a "metaphorical expression" (p. 231). *The verb empfinde* means to sense in all these meanings. Sensations as combined ideas and emotions are also connected with the concept of *complex*, introduced by Jung, as "Organized group of ideas and memories of great affective force" (Laplanche & Pontalis, 1973). Ryle (1949) writes about "sensations, feelings, and images are things…[are] contained in the stream of consciousness (p. 199); those "connected with special organs of sense, namely the eyes…and those which are connected with the other sensitive but non-sensory organs of the body (p. 201). "We of "describing organic sensations,…a pain as stabbing…likening it to the sort of pain…given by…instruments" (p. 203). "For here…'feel' means 'feels as if'…We might call it a 'post-perceptual' use of 'feel'" (p. 241), or as a "metaphorical expression" (p. 231).

154 Here Spielrein inserts her own footnote: "fixating the complex by means of three incidental associations."

within the sphere of individual life; in fact their *alteration* is even sought after by the individual. *Continuity* alone is important. This view accords admirably with the position which Weismann has reached by biological investigations ("*Zur Frage der Untsterblichkeit der Einzelzelligen* [the question of the immortality of unicellular organisms], Vol. IV., Nos. 21, 22;[155] compare especially pages 654 and 655, where the scission of the individual into two equal parts is spoken of.) But continuity is only a means of preparing and conserving what is contained in the ego. This content, and not the ego, is the principal thing. This content, however, is not confined to the individual. With the exception of some insignificant and valueless personal memories, it remains perceived in others even after the death of the individual. The elements that make up the consciousness of a given individual are firmly connected with one another, but with those of another individual they are only feebly connected, and the connexion is only casually apparent. Contents of consciousness, however, that of universal significance, break through these limits of the individual, and, attached of course to individuals again, can enjoy a continued existence of an impersonal, superpersonal kind, independently of the personality by means of which they were developed. To contribute to this is the greatest happiness of the artist, the scientist, the inventor, the social reformer etc." (Mach, 1959, pp. 23–24)."

Even though I am not objecting to this, it does not mean that I am in complete agreement with it, but this thought, even though it might require some correction, is still very valuable. Here are two more:

"In wishing to preserve our personal memories beyond death, we are behaving like the astute Eskimo, who refused with thanks the gift of immortality without his seals and walruses (footnote 1, p. 25)." The ego must be given up. It is partly the perception of this fact, partly the fear of it, that has given rise to numerous religious, ascetic, and philosophical absurdities" (pp. 24–25) etc...

I could copy more but it is too boring. The idea of continuity in itself is not new. I had this insight when I was fifteen years old and tried to set it out clearly in my story titled "The Goal of Life;" however, what is new is concretizing this conception in all its acuity [of definition] and its demarcation; therefore, you lose sight of the whole when you don't read the evidence but only pick a few little fragments here and there. I have accidentally selected a few sentences that are suitable for my present goal; however, the work contains <u>many remarkable original thoughts</u>. <u>Thus one can simply explain the abreaction drive</u>: <u>it is a pro-</u>

155 Freud would discuss these ideas of Weismann in the 1920 *Beyond the Pleasure Principle*, pp. 45ff.

creation drive. The ego seeks to become assimilated and transformed; hence, precisely, the impossibility to suppress a complex and the remarkable relief as soon as the complex is out, therefore the relief is so much greater the more one believes oneself to be understood, the better the ego has become assimilated. Similarly, one is happy when one can observe the direct consequences and influence of one's own combination, that is, the transformation. The transformation drive is the cause of the need to communicate one's scientific views to others.

It is evident that similar attitudes or conditions are normally required for suggestion, and are also favorable for assimilation. In the first place are feelings of empathy (whether grounded in love or high esteem). That is the crux of the matter: why one wants to be loved and respected, why one seeks fame and why one works "only out of vanity." I see You as man of comfort, soft as butter, big as the moon, but also as someone who has had the patience to achieve the position you are in, even if you view the aforementioned as silly chatter. Now comes the question: did you really want to be somebody good, did you want the parts of your combination to continue developing mightily without putting a name on it, or perhaps you preferred to cover your back whilst your real combination was producing something woefully minimal? In the latter case the name C.G. Jung would mean something else and not really you.

When one is honest and dumb and praised by an ignorant crowd one is later devalued; and when one represents other people's combinations as one's own, one should be pitied for feeling blissful, the same as someone who would declare his talented adopted child as his own, or as a father using his child's fame to make himself proud. Do you think that the thoughts of a writer without fame would become extinct (especially when these are thoughts of a genius)? Quantitatively speaking, you have a rather limited reputation but qualitatively so much the better one. Should you not know this yourself, I could give you some examples. Anyway, being vain is a definite limitation. From the perspective of continuity, any personal pushing forward appears as necessary and is subjectively rather minimal. The ego, as any other combination, has its own inertia (I will not dispute what Mach's says about the ego's tendency toward variation, because everything has its transformators to whose action it is subject. However, I am unable to determine what drives the ego toward transformation and overcomes the force of inertia). What is certain, however, is that whatever is unsuitable for the present state of the ego, that every innovation—even if one wants it much and indeed recognizes its immediate advantages—is met on its path with colossal difficulties and, indeed, the latter are proportional to the persistence of what is old. In a dispute one strongly defends one's opinion and reluctantly defers to the aptitude of the opponent; it is simply a fight between the transformators and inertia. The necessary and the right will be victorious. Once the necessary finally vanquishes all else, what is the point of all manner of tricks? Is it not better simply to seek the necessary (the true), no matter on whose plate it was first clearly etched, to be published? What else is then mankind or the ego if not a clustering of infinitely inherited (let us say [cautiously]) energies? What you are now discovering has been discovered (to be quite modest about it) beforehand by thousands of others, it has been hereditarily manifest since time immemorial and it is especially pronounced in you. When similar ideas were significantly weaker in others (either in themselves or due to counter-ideas), none of them was able to assimilate your works; however, you were able to have the joy, when a few moments later, the temporary necessity (truth) restored your rights. The more necessary combinations there are to build your ego, the more valuable (if you will) a combination you become, the greater the part you create in the whole. This should add some consolation, for in view of the current state of my emotions this philosophy makes me rather melancholy. But this may mean nothing. After countless generations, the transformation instinct, if cultivated, or actually the idea of such a continuity, will become a source of pleasurable sensations. It presents a difficulty as long as it is new, as inertia (the joy of recognizing the known); but once it has become an innate instinct, it turns into the greatest bliss. For me the joy of gratifying a personal or a social drive is both conceivable and inconceivable. I wanted to say a great deal about this but I don't want to get too involved with it because so much remains. By now you were perhaps smiling at my letter, but something may have affected you even if it was just a little line, so something is better than nothing.

I am now copying an old letter I had written to you: "I hope you won't take offense that I 'dictate' to you how you should act when I tell you that in my opinion you should still pay a visit to Miss Berg. Even if you cannot help her totally you can still offer her some relief by expressing sympathy regarding her fate. I wish this for the sake of Miss Berg and for yours, because I want so much for you to be good, always get better ad infinitum (with emotion or reason alike, for after all, nobody can get out of this chaos). It is sometimes enormously important whether in a given situation someone acts with the intention of "neighborly love" or of its opposite: you do know the law of inertia in physics, here the faculty of inertia. This surely applies here as well: if you are good once, then later it will be more natural for you to be good again, whereas when you slide into comfort, you tend to maintain this state of mind and indeed it happens more easily the next time (e.g., the present generation). Why? You know that yourself. There is no need to belabor this topic.[156]

What follows will, I expect, arouse such a robust resistance that I have to say this to clear my conscience rather than saying nothing, or else the sentence is bogus. The great resistance is due to your having many associations that agree with mine and therefore you throw at me your counter associations with all your fury to be proven right. You once told Miss Berg that socialists are simply thieves ("they take the chain from one and the watch from the other"). I don't believe you meant it seriously. Perhaps, in alacrity you "went off the rails," which in general is not rare with you. Here the addiction to comfort prevented you from being fair and made you limited in everything connected with the complex. Socialism conceived in this form, that all people are equal, or should get paid proportionally to their work, or that everyone takes what is due to one (as common folk are in the habit of saying), is of course a utopia. However, socialism has a high value as an anti-capitalist movement. You say: the acquisition of wealth requires a certain level of intelligence and energy and thus the rich are the most proficient. This only applies to exceptional cases. An enterprising, intelligent person can amass his own fortune and his children may deserve it; but later we see that due to an infinity of causes, his heirs can turn into vast numbers of degenerates who own capital while capable people are reduced to poverty. We see perpetually the best people are especially incompetent in practical matters and lose all their assets. How many great men of science ended as beggars! On the other hand, the markedly egocentric people (e.g. egoists) want to have a good life for themselves only, aware of the worth of what they acquired and are holding on to it. One begins by wanting something more and gradually, as if attracted by alcohol, one becomes unwittingly inconsiderate toward the needs of other people; one feels endowed with great power and this results in a greater addiction to comfort, self-contentment, and widespread flattery, for adulation has an enormous suggestive power. (People are too stupid to realize that all this does not belong to them, that the development of their individuality is thereby inhibited. How can I express it more clearly?). They become vain. In the realm of science the real addiction to knowledge is replaced by an addiction to being admired, an addiction to power. Naturally,

156 Added Spielrein's side remark: "This letter belongs to the time when the brother of Miss Berg was ill, a concrete case." Another side remark: "I also held forth in favor of abstinence. I was able to convert one person probably at least until he gets together with his cronies, which will happen tomorrow.

all this develops step by step, gradually and steadfastly, unbeknownst to the individual, while gaining an ever-increasing power over his descendants. (I do not mean to claim that vanity is created by riches alone. It always develops when one pays too much attention to one's own person.) Just imagine: your parents were unable to support you when you were a student; but I believe that after all they reached the right decision, but how much time and energy you had to expend at first! To begin with, you had to remain stuck for a long time in some office and cursed your fate until you could earn the money you needed. Would that be fair? Furthermore, had you desired to marry a girl who was not wealthy, how would you be able to exist given your enormous needs? Again, would that be fair? You would have been able to become "something," given your gigantic character and vital energy. However, many capable people, not as strong as you, might have easily fallen into despair, or those who, for the time being, were not drawn to pursue knowledge, so that they lost confidence in their own powers and did not think it necessary to fight for an opportunity to study. It could also happen that a young man with a talent for science might be the biggest fool in business and forego a decent income. Even despite my limited life experience I have personally known such cases; and you can also learn about them from literature and history. Moreover, there are countless examples to the contrary, that is, all kind of globetrotters who "enjoy" life. I find it comical that I have to instruct you how unfairly wealth is distributed as if you don't know this better than me. Here I have considered extremes, and between the extremes there are naturally intermediate degrees, not as pronounced but still unfair; at every step you meet people with bigger needs caused by lack of money who are forced to vegetate for long periods, or often something even more awful, while others utilize their capital surplus in the service of further enhancing their vanity. It seems foolish of me to want to give you more examples because civilized society is teeming with such cases; it takes prejudice not to see that capital is not at all distributed according to the worth or the needs of people; and further, that the real worth of people remains hidden from view causing enormous damage. "You can discuss this with Forel.[157]" You believe that if people work less they will drink more; this might be true in present-day conditions, but why should only the poor work more? And, moreover, have to do work that does not offer them any gratification? Why should people less gifted, or those with lesser needs, not be forced to work, instead, of those with less money? Or do you think perhaps that the rich are the most intelligent people? But this is pure nonsense. Take Miss

157 Forel, August Henri (1848–1931), former director of Burghölzli.

Rähmi who is conspicuously superior in her intelligence to most fellow students I know. Or another girl, working as a saleswoman in a store, who would rank as the third or a fourth in class (or the second, barring the Russians). Should you want to judge according to your experiences with your patients, you would have to do the greatest violence to ordinary circumstances: you find nervousness more often among the rich than among the poor whose mental powers are still preserved; the [rich] people, with their lesser tenacity and less self-control, are more prone to being antisocial. Poor people, if you will, are more sociable, they can better submit to circumstances; therefore here (in the hospital) the poor are almost the only ones who are truly demented; I believe that poor people are almost never admitted to the hospital voluntarily while this is more often the case with rich people. The rich person should become somewhat freer in his actions, forgo his reputation (usually quite high) to a certain degree, but when one is poor and "crazy" the situation is so much the more serious. Moreover, please do not forget that rich people who brood over the world have more opportunities to get an education, and this is why the rich compared to the uneducated with some intelligence, seem to be more intelligent. You can analyze this yourself.

What an esthetic benefit did I get when you were the last one to enter and to leave Professor Schumann's lecture! This was true awe, an awe of what the man has achieved. The main thing is who the person is, not what the person has or shows. Wealth distribution should be in keeping with a person's individuality, that is, everyone should have as much as is necessary for the harmonious development of all his powers. Whereas there exists a social compulsion that certain unpleasant kinds of work should be performed, these should be imposed on the least capable people. Theoretically, this goes at a good paces, but practically, for the time being, one could quite easily be helped by some substitute thought trends [underlined with dots!!!][158]. And yet it does not mean that one must lapse into comfort so that the bad is converted into an abstraction or embellished while the good is treated with mildness. I believe that the way toward individualism, as I understand this word, must pass through socialism (I believe less that socialism will actually take place, if only for a few days); but there must exist an extreme, and socialism is the extreme that combats the contemporary capital hegemony. When one starts out with equality etc., one realizes immediately that people are not equal and can never be equal; this sets off endless storms until, as it seems to me, one unavoidably gets to individualism (assuming that people, or whatever you call them, do not die out in the meantime). Philosophy,

158 Unclear, perhaps a pun on Strich (trend) and gestreichelt (dotted).

science, art—all propagate individualistic concepts. Education is becoming increasingly individualistic, one now studies psychology and pedagogy with greater zeal. Then again, one fervently wishes that highly placed individualists who own lots of capital will meet individualism halfway; that they will first learn to be just toward themselves, that is, to become conscientiously aware of what is necessary for them and stay within these limits; and give the rest to talented individuals and to innovative schools; anyway, there is a plenty of applications. It has always been my most ardent wish that you should belong to such noble innovators and not let yourself be carried away by the egoism and suggestions of the milieu. Perhaps you feel it would be an injustice toward your wife, should you deny her the luxuries to which she has been accustomed? I can only repeat: the main thing is what one is, not what one has or shows. If you are fond of your wife, then the most important thing for you is that she should really be a good person and that you can influence her accordingly. Your wife is so enormously fond of you that your overabundant joy could serve as compensation for the loss of some comfort. Moreover, she has a good heart, so it seems to me, that influencing her in this way should be easy, or, at least, not difficult. And you (conscious of your good deeds) can easily ignore neighborhood gossip because the future does not belong to these people and the more they shout, the more they will realize they are wrong and feel they are dying out.

When one deals with complexes one has to proceed with caution: I understand "necessary" not only to mean that without it one must die right away but also what is necessary for the spiritual (including esthetic) development. (Everyone should have as much as he needs for the optimal development of his powers, or at least for the most important ones.) "Necessary" is a relative concept and determining its scope should be left to conscientiousness. I think, as long as one is not acting under compulsion, one has to take it himself; everything should be left to one's conscientiousness, and one had better take less than more.

~~You should not get mad or lapse into negativism for, first and foremost, I am not reproaching you for anything. I don't know what you possess and what you give, nor do I presume to judge what is necessary for you. Since every "good" there is a "better," I would like to bring about is much as possible a far-reaching "better." I am concerned only with the good parts of your nature.~~ [crossed out by her].

I am only calling your attention to phenomena about which you may have reflected less, and I touch provisionally upon the good sides of your nature, so as to get you going; the rest (that is everything) I leave to your individuality.

The right to do this was given to me by my devotion that went so far that I have devoted two weeks to this letter to you.

Finished on 31.8.1906 9:30 in the morning Seefeld Street 69 III

Zurich

The motto for this letter is: if you would like to read this letter, you have to observe two conditions:

(1) you should only read it at times when you are not silly but are up for it;

(2) Once you already started, you should be very mindful to read everything to the end. I wanted to say too much therefore the ideas are in such a jumble, mostly so fleetingly intimated, that some of them might appear contradictory. Therefore a greater measure of attention is required of you. Should it appear to you as presented in a rambling manner, which it obviously is, you must still be patient enough to read it to the end.

8
Essay On Transformation (Letter To Jung)[159]

Undated[160]

Two speakers. Of these two speakers, one who is able to achieve the whole rationality of his pursuit, is the one who surrenders to passion, that pumps enough blood and heat into his brain so as to force his high spirituality to reveal itself. The other speaker attempts here and there to achieve the same: with the help of passion, he brings forth his pursuit in a manner sonorous, fervent, and fascinating but usually with a poor result. Before long his speaking becomes obscure and confused, he exaggerates, he makes omissions creating mistrust in the rationality of his pursuit; moreover, he himself senses this mistrust and this explains the sudden outbursts in the most glacial and disagreeable tones which make the listener doubt the authenticity of his whole passionateness. In him every time passion overruns the mind; perhaps because in him the passion is stronger than in the first one. However, he is at the peak of his power when he is able to resist the overpowering storm of his sensations and to scorn it. In this way his mind emerges fully out of its hiding, a logical, mocking and playful mind and an awe-inspiring one at that.

[*Transformation theory and what it is related to*]

If we take as the starting point a case of a young woman unhappy in love: marrying a man who did not protect her from falling ill with dem[entia] prae-c[ox]. In the course of her illness the complex is expressed as "mobilized." This case raises a number of questions. Above all, from the perspective of preservation of the species, it is in fact completely inconceivable why one cannot love any person who is healthy, why the new marriage was insufficient to erase the complex, why the endless torments regarding a person who perhaps elicits a mocking

---

159 A new translation of the German original, first published in French by Jeanne Moll (1983) and in English (Covington & Wharton, 2015)

160 By internal evidence the date is 1908: "tomorrow the studies resume" (p. 458 below).

smirk in her environment, who is perhaps both a physical and mental cripple? You say: "it is a perverse instinct." From the perspective that all this for the sake of preservation of the species, yes; however, from another perspective it is normal. Let us suspend basic causes and goals and ask ourselves what really is this dreadful thing love? The more highly evolved a living being, the more meaningful is this word for it. A dog would hardly distinguish love from sexual attraction but a human being can experience real deep love only a limited number of times, in most cases it will be a fleeting fascination. Two years ago you yourself asked me a question you regarded as crucial to decide whether I love you, namely: "do you share many similarities with me?" You received a "furious no." Well now, with a beloved one shares many similarities. People who markedly resemble each other, like animals, are thus less selective (careful here!) and have almost no love grievances; an uneducated young woman can more easily find a beloved and should you wish to quote authorities, remember *Wilhelm Meister*: there you encounter a maiden who remains a virgin for so long because she stands above her milieu. Goethe says that, too. The more differentiated a person, the more disastrous the situation (do not mix things up: I mean the degree of love of which the individual in question is capable of, and not a passing attraction). We also have to consider the fundamental difference between man and woman that is still the rule. The man wants to clasp, the woman wants to be clasped. For now it cannot be the other way around, seeing that men are unremarkably differentiated. And what are the consequences? The woman is much more selective because it is more difficult for her to find a personality corresponding to her <u>ideal</u>; for this reason, the woman who really loves is as a rule monogamous; obversely, the man is not as selective and is more or less polygamous. As a remedy against unfaithfulness Forel recommends that the woman should share more of her husband's interests, be more his friend, more indispensable. Forel is the man who dedicated his book to his wife "with love and esteem."[161] He constantly expresses the highest love for his wife. The same thought is conveyed by Ibsen, for example in his "Nora".[162] A commoner once told me: the man is polygamous until he finds a woman whom he can truly love; then he becomes monogamous (again, barring small passing

161 The book is Forel's popular 1906 (first edition 1904) *The sexual question. A scientific, psychological, hygienic and sociological study for the educated* where he dedicates his book to "my wife Emma née Steinhel in love and respect" and writes: "The sexual love in woman differs from that in a man in that [its] outstanding characteristic is the dominant role in the brain, is more that of a life goal than in a man. Without love a woman ceases to be a right normal woman" (p. 127).

162 In the play *A Doll's House* whose heroine Nora is a married woman seeking self-actualization in a male-dominated society, a most controversial issue at that time.

attractions). Do you want examples from history? [Czar] Ivan the Terrible (1533–1584) was a kind and benevolent ruler during the years when the love for his wife illuminated all his actions; he became "terrible" after his wife had died, when his unsatiated love needed nourishment. We might return to him later as an example. This is how men feel. Is there a contradiction? We see time and again that for a man what is most decisive is a beautiful feminine form! Don't get excited! What does it mean, a beautiful form? After all, there is no such thing as absolute beauty; the ideal of beauty arose from seeing female forms among women with whom one had relations, that is, women whose qualities were found to be most suitable. You know too well that beauty, as a value, need not be connected with the purpose of procreation. The latter is usually seen in degenerates,[163] and aren't the ideas of degenerates—even when connected with other matters—yet eternally alive? When a generation of women, in keeping with their fine sentiments and thereby conditioned lifestyles, finally develops new and more refined forms, then the sexual automatism will adapt itself directly to those forms. Innovators are actually rare, especially when an instinct is involved. Thus it is still the rule that a certain form is the cause of a sexual excitation, a form that perhaps only simulates a particular similarity, or if it contains a rather slight similarity, but more than just a similarity between two people. Finally, there are also similarities between animals and people, which for some individuals are sufficient to initiate sexual intercourse; such people are even less selective because the animal in them can correspond to an even smaller component of their personality. Indeed, when in need,[164] one might conclude, based on small similarities, that one could even be understood by a cow and confide to it one's highest emotions. A woman colleague of mine, while still a child (at an age when animals and humans are close to each other), had a tender affection for a dog; she would confide to it all the thoughts that weighed on her and this usually happened in a forest, accompanied by shedding bitter tears; she was sure that the dog understood her. And in a certain way the dog did! In need one could also confide everything to a tree and you would clearly sense how the tree understands you and finally how it expresses its empathy in the soft whisper of its leaves! "And I always

163 Spielrein quotes Max Nordau's 1895 bestseller *Degeneration* where he defined "degenerates are not always criminals, prostitutes, anarchists, and pronounced lunatics; they are often authors and artists" (p. viii), the latter seen as 'higher degenerates' (*dégénérés supérieurs*) (p. 18), among whom were listed Wagner, Tolstoy, Ibsen, and Nietzsche.

164 In English the word need, in addition to want, also mean privation and hardship. In German the word *Not* has the additional meanings of emergency, urgency, effort, trouble, grief, distress, and danger.

heard them whisper, as if they called to me, come to me, mate, here you will find your rest,"[165] etc. ad infinitum. Thus one can love nature as a living being to whom one confides one's inner world, in that one finds similarities, for example, between a storm in nature and what one constructs in one's own soul; and this similarity actually exists because our inner world is a part of, or if you prefer, an echo of the world entire. Therefore, everybody loves nature, and especially that in which one has mostly lived, which also forms the greater and more powerful part of the personality. Turning to Nietzsche again to help us: "We must rest from ourselves occasionally by contemplating and looking down upon ourselves, and by laughing or weeping over ourselves from an artistic remoteness: we must discover the hero, and likewise the fool, that is hidden in our passion for knowledge; we must now and then be joyful in our folly, that we may continue to be joyful in our wisdom!"[166]

The note I wrote in the hospital chart about the value of reacting is based on the premise that we see our own pain arise in the soul of the other, that is we treat it objectively, and thus the other's pain is alleviated. Every complex extends beyond personality boundaries, every complex is searching to find what is similar to it or co-participating with it, creating its mirror image, and when you show the complex its mirror image, laughter arises, although there is nothing laughable at all in ego-consciousness. Freud's idea that laughter develops as a result of comparing two energy quantities such that the energy surplus is abreacted through laughter.[167] The question "why?" would go too far. But the fact remains that joint work (not to be confused with work called joint work which is no joint work at all) is much easier, because a shared pain is half the pain. Shared pain means when the same complex thinks itself welcomed both in one's own soul and in the mirror, i.e., in a transformed state (expressed in the form of a scandal[168]). Each participant thinks: now I am the boss!, they act together, and "from the saved energy quantity, which previously went into resistance (Freud), laughter arises."

165 Imprecisely quoted from Schubert's song "*Der Lindenbaum*" (in the cycle *Die Winterreise*): "Und seine Zweige rauschten,/Als riefen sie mir zu:/Komm her zu mir, Geselle,/ Hier find'st du deine Ruh' !"(And its branches rustled/as if they were calling to me:/Come here to me, lad,/here you will find your rest).

166 *The Joyful Science*, II p. 146. https://archive.org/stream/completenietaschl0nietuoft/complete- nietaschl0nietuoft_djvu.txt, p. 146.

167 See Freud 1905, pp. 148–149.

168 Here the word scandal suggests a shared, interpersonal enactment.

Art is nothing but a complex gone independent or "gone wild to lead a life of pleasure" (your expression), or one that "wants to become transformed," my expression. When an artist creates, it is not in the slightest the drive (*Trieb*)[169] to communicate something to people that takes effect. The complex simply has to get out! For a long time the artist can admire his work as external to himself but eventually feels the urge (*Drang*)[170] to view his work as understood by others. (Here no laughter ensues because "the beautiful" does not have to overcome any resistance?) The same takes place in science, a thought worked out after many trials and tribulations, whatever it may be, needs to be understood by others. It seems to me that very few researchers care primarily about fame. The love of fame as a striving to get everybody's attention to oneself can only prevail in people unable to feel their own personality as powerful, the "normal" ones. Those in whom thoughts have developed in a process of prolonged ordeals view their thoughts as more important than fame; for them fame is at most a means to an end, a wish to be understood better and to remain alive. Or I must make a correction: fame does not matter to scientific workers, it only serves science as a means of directing general attention to itself. Those in whom thoughts have developed in the course of prolonged suffering and really became a part of their own personality, can fame at the most be better understood as a means to an end, needed to sustain their thoughts as eternally living thoughts. A person who agrees with me can sense Galileo's words "and yet it moves"[171] and sensing them throughout his or her life.

I am now resuming our apparent contra[dictions?] about the sexual [crossed out by her] sphere namely, since associations about death are associations about sexuality.

When we consider folklore poetry—and we must consider it because it always contains truths—we see that sexual power is often viewed as diabolical power, as a destructive power, and the sexual act as a sin! How did this happen? How does it happen that every person always puts up so much resistance against his or her sexual sensations? Why are these covered up and perceived as unseemly,

169 Freud began using *Trieb*, meaning an internal energy, force, impulse, and motive Freud began using in the 1905 *Three Essays on the Theory of Sexuality* is In the *Standard Edition Trieb* translated as instinct. There Freud also mentioned the hybrid scopophilic drive and the drive to cruelty. Freud also made the distinction between internal drives and external stimuli. Spielrein used drive and instinct interchangeably and this is adhered to here.

170 *Drang* can mean need, impulse, desire, passionate longing, and craving.

171 *Eppur sie muove*, allegedly spoken by Galileo Galilei (1564–1642) after being forced by the Church and the Inquisition to recant his claim that the earth turns around the sun.

why may these be expressed only in sublimated or symbolic forms? Why must every young woman (and perhaps every young man as well) go through a period when she experiences the deepest shyness toward everything sexual (when she also has no inkling that there are some pains there)? In this way an antagonism between sexuality and the rest of the personality is established, an antagonism most intensely felt at the moment of emergence of sexual sensations, clearly a source of multiple psychological disorders during puberty. Until this "demonic drive" in part suppresses the former personality and is in part is suppressed by it. What is the origin of the primal sensations of this antagonism (primal sensations are always the strongest, because sensations act like logarithms derived from stimuli). What is the origin of the unwillingness to accept these primal sensations? What is the origin of this alienation? Not even for a moment should you fail to consider that current sexual sensations are not the genuine but the suppressed ones. When I once asked a healthy and passionate young woman: "how can one tell when one is in love? One can also want to hug and kiss one's mother?" She explained: "when you kiss your lover, you want him to die from your kisses and you yourself to perish in him" (she also used another quite peculiar expression) etc.; there are expressions ad infinitum. Extreme instincts always arise as murderous instincts. Starting with the little brother who calls the cat: "Hey, kitty! My little heart! I love you! I am going to torture you to death!" Continuing with this well-known fact that people in love readily tease and torture <u>each other</u>, <u>all the</u> way up or down from martyrs to sex-murderers.

Everywhere you see people busy destroying or dying. In young people you see an indefinite urge to sacrifice their life for something elevated, something "lofty." The soul wants to yield to this slyly contrived demand. However, it can also happen that it is some relatively modest wish, for example, a wish for an eight-hour [work?] day. But when such a wish is both entertained and demanded by a great mass of people, it results in such a heightening of the sensation that the entire personality becomes this monster sensation. This sensation can only be gratified when it alone persists, when the entire remaining and microscopically small personality is destroyed. And in this way young men, totally transformed by their wish, sally forth with burning torches, assume glorious postures, make pathetic speeches about death. Their wish should live forever in this new enchanting form—everything else should perish!

Essentially, every complex has the need to reshape the entire personality in the service of its role; and when a complex becomes expressed to a degree greater than allowed by the milieu, then the emotion is labeled as exaggerated and its owner is called a simulator, an actor depending on the whim. Yet every human being is an actor, or "actor is a relative concept". The degree of being an actor is determined by the power of the complex. At its culmination point the complex can, as was shown above, eventually lead the whole individual to sacrifice for the sake of himself, but then this is just a kind of "sacrificing." The death of an individual constitutes the essence of one complex only—the sexual complex. Every individual as such must disappear. Actually in an ameba the whole "personality" also disappears; in a human being, or in other animals, only an extract (I cannot find a more fitting expression); however, the instinct is always death, annihilation of the personality, as when two individuals merge into one. In this way one can also explain the numerous representations of the drive (*Trieb*) as a destructive diabolical power, etc. In this way one can also explain the resistance that every person exhibits toward the sexual drive. I spoke earlier about the "essence" of the sexual drive; this does not mean that two individuals who are sexually attracted to each other continually wish to disappear as an entity or something like that. The sexual emotion[172] is always subdued by other emotions; even during the sexual act it restrained, or else you would get either sex-murderers or martyrs. I might also say that in the sexual act the man basically wants to lead to annihilation, the woman wants to be led to annihilation. You can also see that there are many male martyrs. You can also see how one's own martyrdom is significantly connected with cruelty toward other people, as was, for instance, Ivan the Terrible, who was a martyr, too: he repented after his every act and was also very devout. To tell the truth, I don't really know! Perhaps I am here trying to conceptualize martyrdom as the female nature, to comprehend it as a contrast emotion! In very passionate artists, as was [Richard] Wagner, the culmination of love is to be sought in death. His heroes must die, thus dies Siegfried and Brünnhilde. In this way the idea that love prevails is expressed as follows:

The race of gods is vanished like a breath,
And masterless I leave the world behind:
The brightest treasure of my wisdom's hoard
I therefore give to you. Not goods, nor gold,
Nor royal pomp, nor palaces, nor halls,
Nor costly shows of wealth's magnificence;
Nor yet the empty kindness of false leagues,

172 Significantly, Spielrein writes Sexualgefühl, sexual feeling. A suggested differentiation: one becomes aware of a feeling, one enacts it as an emotion.

Nor canting custom's merciless decrees:
Care not for these, let Love reign paramount
In sorrow and in joy.[173]

The complex achieves its greatest enhancement when it is placed above death. I would have used this explanation here as well had I not known, about the nature of the sexual act, and had I not cited the aforementioned numerous examples at every step and stride showing the "willingness to die," the destruction drive. In *The Flying Dutchman* we also see the culmination point of love placed in or above death: "I remain faithful to you until death."[174] These are my recent impressions, besides, you know these things well enough yourself, situations where he kills both her and himself, or the other way around; so you too can analyze! I have to finish here quickly because tomorrow the studies resume.

So to sum up. The sexual drive, a drive for the renewal of the whole personality, a partial case of the transformation drive, is held-by every single complex, sexual attraction, attraction between similar individuals (individuals of the same kind, a partial case, when the individuals are less differentiated). Similar [individuals], i.e., in the sense of "qui se ressemblent, s'assemblent" [birds of a feather flock together] or the expression "les contrastes se touchent" [contrasts attract each other][175]. A person who is put off by smoking can understand a smoker, but a person who knows nothing about smoking cannot. What an individual really is, nobody knows. An individual consists of sensations[176] and counter-sensations occurring in various ratios. Overly identical relations between individual complexes would be bothersome for the suppressed part of the psyche, that is why very similar people do not fare well together. Sexual attraction is elicited by either positive or negative sensations but not by similar sensations. One might explain "the negative" by assuming that the suppressed sensation is the more active one. No! This is simply unnecessary! The man clasps, the woman wants to be clasped, and therefore it is quite amazing that you, for example, only wanted to say "my baby" whereas your wife, at most, wanted to say "our" baby, if not "my husband's baby." You loved yourself in the baby and your wife loved herself

173 Wagner, Richard (1901). *The Twilight of the Gods* Volume Two Done into English verse by Reginald Rankin. London: Longman's, Green, and Co.

174 "Here my hand to the man of the sea:—Unto death I will faithful be" (Senta, Second Act).

175 A variation on maxim 71 of Labruyère, les extremes se touchent, "extremes meet together." http://www.gutenberg.org/files/46633/46633-h/46633-h.htm
the idea that extremes closely resemble each other.

176 See footnote 148

in you. It is worth noting the phenomenon that when one no longer loves one's beloved, one nevertheless loves the beloved's former image; one loves one's own ideals in the other; a small separation makes love stronger because one always prefers remembering what was right, what was ideal; but ideals are nothing but what—as a result of endless circumstances—remains markedly ingrained in the psyche. Similar ideals, similar sensations, similar experiences attract each other. It can soon happen that various ideals can occupy the foreground of the psyche and thus alter one's sexual preference. However, the more ideals can be found in the beloved, the more enduring the love. There are circumstances that make people approachable to each other. I believe that is what Turgeniev meant: "when a woman feels sorry about something, you can know what the consequences will be."[177] You feel compassion, that means you imagine yourself in a similar situation. It means that in the moment you imagine you are having the same complex in the foreground, and similar complexes trigger sexual sensations. When two individuals are of the same gender, slight erotic expressions of love arise, when they are of different genders—the attraction goes farther. This explains the sexual attachment between patient and doctor who are in a psychic rapport with each other. There the sexual feeling is not the primary one or else one could choose everybody to be one's doctor. One comes to a doctor with the need to get freed from a complex, the doctor is trusted because one is aware of his interest and sympathy, or the lack of it; likewise, his interest is to understand the complex and its owner. Hence the sexual feeling. It is entirely unnecessary that one should react with a sexual complex, however, every compassion between man and woman arouses sexual sensations. Two people looking at each other's beautiful gray eyes can heighten compassion because these eyes are saying a lot to each other, that is, they are connected through some powerful complex of sensations or perhaps are expressing some form of feeling. The sexual feeling awakened by similar complexes disappears as soon as other complexes move

177 Spielrein's paraphrase of a scene in Turgeniev's 1862 novel *Fathers and Sons*: "Bazarov was standing with his back to her. "Let me tell you then that I love you like a fool, like a madman… There, you've got that out of me."…it was passion beating within him, a powerful heavy passion not unlike fury and perhaps akin to it…Madame Odintsov began to feel both frightened and sorry for him. "Evgeny Vassilich," she murmured, and her voice rang with unconscious tenderness. He quickly turned round, threw a devouring look at her—and seizing both her hands, he suddenly pressed her to him. She did not free herself at once from his embrace, "You misunderstood me," she whispered in hurried alarm" (p. 91). Odintsova did not marry him, she visited him as he lay semi-delirious on his deathbed. http://intersci.ss.uci.edu/wiki/eBooks/Russia/BOOKS/Turgenev/Fathers% 20and%20Sons%20 Turgenev.pdf

to the foreground of the psyche (to occupy the foreground means "to be more powerful") and are no longer mutually experienced.

Transformation of the sexual complex

The sexual feeling causes a series of images which we combine into a sexual complex, i.e., the sexual complex in its narrower meaning. However, since each strong complex, as soon as it is experienced together with the other gender, activates that sexual complex, it becomes a part of the sexual complex. In this way the most important part of the psyche can become the sexual complex, the sexual complex is not a determinable quantity. In the broader sense, the entire sexual complex—the sum total of the feelings toward the beloved, including all that was experienced with him—must, in the case of unhappy love, be transformed as a whole. The person to whom this is communicated gains a great value. When such a transformation takes place between man and woman, the reciprocal feelings create a new sexual attraction. Transformation can also occur in works of art; then one is not attached to any particular personality and protected from new affairs. In this way, a sexual complex in the extended sense can become a powerful driving motive especially in art but it does not have to be. When, as usual, the ideals want to attach themselves to sexual transformation, when the enchanting form for a man is often a woman, i.e. experienced by him as resonating with the ideal in the woman, then—seeing that it is only an effect of transformation or of the self-preservation drive of each and every complex— it is not obligatory that the complex should get attached to a sexual act. However, it is not that the sexual feeling becomes the driving motive of art etc. but that the transformation drive possessed by each and every complex, and that each part of the personality, wants to have its own resonance. Thus sexual complex has a transformation instinct, and the sexual act is but a special form of this transformation which achieves a fresh and corresponding connection for these complexes. Based on its nature, the sexual feeling does not need an urge (*Drang*) for transformation but nevertheless this urge exists; however, the transformation urge needs the sexual feeling, the latter is a necessary part of the former; how else can such combinations go on existing? Otherwise, the combinations would indeed have to die out eventually. As stated above, complexes requiring transformation don't have to be attached to sexual complexes; thus a painter who lived through a storm can immortalize a sea storm in a painting without the arousal of a sexual complex at all; so it was not the sexual feeling that compelled the individual to paint: it was simply "a complex gone wild that wanted to come out to enjoy life to the full." Thus the aroused sexual complex was also transformed. For example, people like Marx, who devoted his life to social problems, contended that one can derive all sensations and feelings from politico-economic conditions and that therefore all emotional expressions, i.e., including those of science and art, would be changed in a new social order. Isn't this an enormous exaggeration? Anyway, we do not know what is the cause of sensations and perhaps we may never know! At the most, we can discuss the foundations of feeling; but it seems clear to me that the foundation of feeling is the alpha and omega of the transformation drive that could possibly be gratified by the sexual act.

It is indeed good that I have a principle not to act when I first get upset. I am now indeed very tired yet, it seems to me, calm. Last night's conversation feels like a heavy dream that continues to oppress me. Yes! Now I feel I have to react! Should I enact my *ambitsia*[178]? Play the role of the righteous and the offended? That would mean lying to myself and to you. Yes! I wish that my whole being should agree with me that I am right! I find it appalling that you spoke to me in this manner. Nevertheless, you have to understand that my "unconscious" does not want what your "unconscious" does not want. But the thing is, that I can be frank (I must) and you cannot. Well, I have been constantly reproached for misusing my outspokenness but how could I do otherwise? This complicated situation makes me enact the unnatural role of a man and you that of a woman. Far be it from me to attribute any kind of absolute meaning to all this; I understand quite well that you had to put up a resistance but I also recognize that these resistances irritate me. I am also quite aware that if everything depended on me, I would have put up a frantic resistance. This word provoked a storm and I wrote many stupid things and therefore rewrote everything. Now I came back from the violin lesson and this produced a soft and serene mood. Oh, you! If you knew how fond I am of you, without the slightest thought about a child. Is not the wish to have a child above all a wish to possess you in some small way? Is it not above all a wish to give you a special gift? Oh, if only I had a friendly relationship with you! However, you seek to suppress all the stronger feelings you might have toward me. As a result you are nothing but diplomacy and lies. Another result is that your semi-unconscious makes all kinds of detours, so you handed me a paper by Dr. Binswanger[179] in which everything is as transparent as glass. Should I explain all this to you? What for? Firstly, most of it is probably known to you, and secondly, you would undoubtedly feel obliged to deny

178 In Russian the word means pride which can make one feel hurt and angry.

179 Binswanger, Ludwig (1881–1966), Swiss psychiatrist, whose grandfather was German-Jewish, director of the famed Bellevue Sanatorium in Kreuzlingen, founder of existential psychoanalysis, and a trusted friend of Freud.

everything. Previously you were able to discuss abstract matters with me, you showed me various things either in the laboratory or in your suite—some-thing like illustrations, or some old book. Now everything that does not have a closer connection to the sexual complex you call "holding a lecture," which you find irritating; but this is because the complex is so strong that you are no longer fully master of it. I do not know: is one always so stupid about oneself or that you just won't admit it to me; it would, however, be rather striking if with all your psychoanalytical abilities, you failed to notice what case histories you have reserved for me! Let us return to yesterday's conversation. After a long pause, rather striking given your language facility, you brought up the story of S.W.[180] It is clear, that this comparison presupposes a similar situation, how else would you have brought up this ancient saga? Mark well, however, mentioning the girl you didn't mean yourself, you had me in mind (unless you wanted to speak of the cunning of your unconscious). However, as you say, it is the unconscious of the girl (not yours) that was more remarkably cunning, and it is even more remarkable that you highly respected the girl and thought and that she was intended for you. However, with time the girl plainly started to cheat; you became disappointed and broke up with her. Isn't this proof how cunning your unconscious is? Blessed are those who believe! Yet I do not belong to the blessed and I think differently. You felt that the "little goblin" was beginning to be dangerous for you and you called for help. Compare the words "to have a child" and "to put on a hat," associations[181] that came rushing in; and it took quite a long time till you passed through fire and indeed were finally able to catch on that "for so many years I had known a similar woman that appeared to me like a goddess but in the end she was merely an impostor."

I do not feel at ease when I speak to you like this. But what can I do? I myself cannot allow that you defend yourself against me in this way, that you put me down. It would be incomparably more horrible if I had to die in order to leave you alone. What should I do? I completely agree with you never again to speak about the unconscious. I will soon take a trip to Locarno and hope that the new impressions and the long period during which I will not be seeing you will make the whole situation more reasonable. I am, however, totally stupid and am writing mechanically. It also occurs to me that when I staged a little scene of justified rage at the university, Miss Floroff thought that I looked as

180 Jung's cousin Helly Preiswerk and whom Jung held mediumistic séances

181 Perhaps a reference to association experiments conducted at the Burghölzli with the participation of Jung and Spielrein.

if I was gazing at "children dripping with blood." This is a quote from "Boris Godunov," the well-known ballad by Pushkin. One usually quotes this phrase when one was really furious. Yet, why did this phrase occur to me? Yes, it also brought to mind : "Pitiful he whose conscience is unclean !" quoted from the same monologue. You may well know that Boris Godunov was a Russian czar. His reign only lasted six years, and yet, in spite of all the unrest of that time, it was beneficial for Russia. He was certainly no ordinary personality. And yet he did not come from czarist stock. And in order to ascend the throne, he had to have the successor (a nine year old child) murdered. The successor was the son of Ivan the Terrible, and you can imagine what he would have become. According to Pushkin's drama, Boris Godunov was a very good person. His hunger for power reflected a real talent. And so he says in his monologue:

> Six years
> Already have I reigned in peace; but joy
> Dwells not within my soul...
> I thought
> To satisfy my people in contentment,
> In glory, gain their love by generous gifts,
> But I have put away that empty hope;
> The power that lives is hateful to the mob,—
> Only the dead they love[182]

followed by the aforementioned bloody children and unclean conscience. Briefly: he died shortly afterwards during a popular uprising, probably by his own hand (P.S. your speeches about death were very timely.) Thereafter his two children were murdered. Evidently, an unclean conscience is also raging inside me. Yet it is just a feeling, I am not afraid that fate will pay me back with the same coin as to the czar. Now, my crime would be that I want to steal you from your wife; and then somebody will steal my husband from me, but for now, I don't give a damn! But then it does not occur to me at all to grab you from your wife! "It is of no use to scare the foxes," that is for sure; "if you want to protect your geese, you have to watch them well,"[183] the devil is singing to me right now,

182 The quotes as in the original http://www3.nmtl.gov.tw/Russia/Ebook/Pushkin/Boris%20Godunov -a %20drama%20in%20 verse.pdf

183 The last stanza of the folk song "The Thief" starting with "Fox you have stolen my goose."

so there! I find this whole story too boring. My serene mood has not remained so serene. The devil won't let me speak.

2. III

I'm so tired of endlessly ruminating! Should I write this, or should I not, because I didn't like to reread this letter? And yet I had to! Because I cannot, when you speak this way to me: either we decide that such topics should not be discussed again, and when they are discussed, I must react according to your remarks referring to this matter. Naturally, I could not alter my wishes after one conversation because this required quite a long and conscious reflection. The wish never sounded like this: "I want a child from you," because above all it meant: "I agree to renounce you forever". And it seems to me that only at those moments when I felt greatly offended by you and was overwhelmed by the wish to have a child from you. Anyway, I can't help it and therefore I put up an adequate resistance against the complex. As a rule I got frightened by the thought that our relationship will no longer be as beautiful as happens in an altruistic friendship. Yet there are times when the fact that I will never have a child from you seems terrible. When that hour comes, I will definitely have to leave you...well, then, I really don't know anything... But this will go on for a long time, and one never knows what fate will bring and I do not think it's impossible that I will win someone else's love, since you had made another decision about me. I am talking to you like a devil because now the devil is the suppressed one. It would be a big mistake on your part to think that I equate my high decision with my happiness. I never thought that a son was meant to be mine, I know only too well that he will have a life of his own and belong to me as little as I belong to my parents. I will then become aware of how lonely I am. But one does not think just about oneself; the dark powers of fate work as they see fit without being the least bit concerned with the overall will of the individual [text break]

Look, I do not love you now, I mean, in the ideal sense, and this state is more horrible than death. But it is all the same to me...Preservation of the species is indeed much more important than preservation of the individual. Then why don't you want to kill me off, if you like me and know that I am a degenerate? But yet, it is not the same to me, and once I can explain it, I will be free! I understand quite well that you are older than me and possess all the other qualities that deserve respect, and yet, it cannot be denied that in some circumstances even a child can have rational thoughts and vice versa. And therefore I am taking the risk. To prove that everything serves the preservation of the species you gave me an example that could just as well be evidence against you. A woman has two children, why then weren't they both equal for her? Why is there love in the first place and not just raw sexual attraction? Why are the mentally higher species more selective? How can the sexual emotion be displaced to something else, or, better yet, is this more expedient from the standpoint that everything should serve the preservation of the species? Please, don't get too impatient right away! I don't want you to make a wrong transformation. This is an essential difference between your view and my view of it, and should we not agree on this, then I won't be able to prove to you why it seems to me that a given phenomenon can have some other manifestation, some other cause, and this distresses me. So this is how I think. The ultimate goal and similar problems. Nonsense. What strikes me as the highest tangible entity is inertia and the transformation drive. Preservation of the species is only a part of this instinct, and this is very important because it explains so much. But wait! Should you give some consideration to art, you will see: plastic art begins by presenting its own ideals. In other words: a warrior does not necessarily portray any girl but the warrior's ideal woman etc. I am looking at the drawings of my little brother; I can send them to you for analysis; one simply creates one's own person and its immediate environment: the more evolved the individual, the bigger his own person and the greater the part of the environment that belongs to it. A phrase from Leonardo da Vinci is engraved in my mind: (approximately) that every hand involuntarily imitates its own corporeal forms. When I was still in the gymnasium it struck me that we girls only drew feminine forms whereas the boys preferred men (we had separate gymnasium). One could explain this via the environment. In poetry we also see diverse objects represented and one can say again, that is the way a person expresses herself. I cannot easily prove this in German literature because I am not familiar with German writers, on the other hand, we have Gorky whose character "The Traveling Companion" (or whatever else you want to call him) has many similar traveling companions[184]. Dostoevsky, the hysterical epileptic, portrays only hysterical epileptics, and Andreyev[185], in "Madness and Fear," only deals with madness and fear. Gogol, steeped in the humor of Little Russia, created corresponding personalities, and yet, why go so far?

Recently, I encountered an excellent case. A girl my age, a complete stranger, approached me with an overwhelming desire to speak with me. She wanted to

184 Maksim Gorky's "My Fellow Traveler" ("Мой спутник," 1894), about the narrator's long walk from Odessa to Crimea with a destitute Georgian prince. The latter, an aggressive free loader, mocks the man working and feeding him. Perhaps. Sabina is hinting at her relationship with Jung.
185 Leonid Nikolayevich Andreyev (1871–1919) was an author of plays, novels, and short stories.

ask me a series of questions which I readily promised to answer (I knew that the complexes of [her] people were so different from mine that she could not ask me any dangerous questions). The questions turned out to be as follows: has it ever happened to you that you were telling a story that was only understandable to you etc. I don't know anymore which of us said what; I explained to her step by step how one tells one's own story in a circuitous way, how one eventually adopts a method of questioning and in this way tells all, how the complex grasps all possible means in order to become transformed. For you this means, just as here, that a part of the ego, i.e., the complex, wants to be assimilated and transformed, even in contradiction to all the rest of the contents of consciousness. Thus, the girl digressed from talking about Jews and after some time she quickly reverted to preceding themes and said: "you are a thinking person."

And now the last art form, music, here too, there is nothing but "self-expression" or, more precisely, an expression of the rhythm of a particular complex. Apropos, a little digression. Naturally, I thought a great deal about dem[entia] praec[ox] and there one encounters peculiar stereotyped acts (repetitive standing up, even though between two acts of standing up the person can function quite well). I cannot assert anything but I have a modest hypothesis (compare curves caused by muscle contraction, tetanus caused by a too rapid succession of stimuli). I imagine that a feeling is not a single impact but a wave-like succession of stimuli; in everyday psychic life—like in a calm lake when a boat passes by—you have a rhythmic series of waves corresponding to a stronger feeling. In countless cases I had the opportunity of observing how an affect causes one to behave rhythmically, for example, appearing and leaving, rubbing one's hands, dancing, or moaning rhythmically. Thus we can quite easily explain it the other way around: why is it so easy to walk and work rhythmically. If you don't think that the interval between two wave crests as too short, you can very easily undertake another task in the interim. For example, it happened that something stupid I did irritated me enormously; nevertheless I was somewhat able to listen to the lecture on physics except that every time the story distinctly emerged in my consciousness. I ground my teeth and said to myself "go to hell!" In dem[entia] praec[ox] the complex can remain unconscious and for it to become conscious a certain degree of illumination is necessary; just think of symbols! A symbol is nothing but a side association that possesses the feeling of the main association but to a lesser degree. In fact you can see: things that are emotionally-toned are symbolized, and especially sexual ones. Perhaps you will say: "the sexual ones because these become repressed?" This, however, would not be an explanation. What does it mean: they become "repressed?" And why do they get "repressed?"

Are they positively or negatively emotionally-toned? Here a key point comes into play again. In and of itself every complex is positively toned, however, when we consider the psyche as a whole, the stronger complexes are mostly negatively toned. Why? Simply, because the other complexes possess inertia and do not want to be destroyed by the stronger ones. In this way, the whole psyche turns inimical toward the stronger complex. Do you mean that amnesia takes place as a result of the strength of counter-images? (repression). I am less convinced of this: if so, then simply, the counter-image should become conscious for not everything is unconscious (a physical law: for every movement there is a [counter] force = resistance). When a mother's child dies, "repression" should have the effect of "the child is still alive" and not total amnesia. This is seen more clearly in sexual matters, to wit: when amnesia is caused by a counter-image, the entire chain of associations disappears because the resistance is proportional to an increase or decrease in energy (or else it would be impossible that a complex, composed of different nuances, could disappear); we see that this is not the case, but that symbols endures.

Now, to resume, you can see that in sexual selection not only are individuals of the same kind chosen but also those who correspond to an ideal, that is, those who are capable of assimilating and transforming a corresponding combination. Then this: individuals whose instincts or ideals are not adapted to nature perish and only those survive whose ideals contain features necessary for the preservation of the species. He who is incapable of adapting is called a cripple. The more evolved social life, the more means there are to transform the personality differently, to a certain degree, and there the sexual motive can recede. This does not mean that sexual energy for having affairs can serve music, or something like that, but that there is a shared energy quantum whereby, naturally, the more is spent for the raw sexual transformation, the less there is for the other kind, and vice versa. You see this particularly clearly in women who are mainly destined for renewal by sexual procreation. Thanks to the preponderance of this form of transformation the more a woman is selective and ever more original, the more difficult it is for her to find a man. The less a woman can count on a spiritual transformation—seeing that by nature (at least for the time being) she is destined for sexual transformation and is thus otherwise not sufficiently independent—the more we can see the well-known phenomenon that a woman seeks a man who can clasp her. Among the primitive races, it is perhaps expressed in this way: the man can hold her emotions and instincts. You yourself know that one always discovers similarities in the beloved and the other way around. However, since the sexual attraction is induced by psychical attraction, it is clear that certain psychical sensations are closely connected with corresponding sexual ones, especially when we are dealing with two different genders.

The expression "libido" (i.e., "sexual feeling" in its narrower sense), when applied to art and science is, strictly speaking, wrong, for there is no specific sexual feeling that is the foundation of all feeling, but only an inertia faculty and a transformation drive (*Trieb*); it can possibly tend toward a sexual aspect and then it can be called "libido." I would not stick to using this word so strictly because wrong words are such a frequent cause of wrong concepts. I want to produce an extreme case for you because you are so passionate about your new theories that you cannot recognize the possibility of a sexual transformation at all. In the case of Mama you are unable to consider the simple fact: Mama does not have the slightest sexual affinities toward her former beloved but she cannot tolerate that the valuable parts of his psyche persist in her as a caricatured image. This is how it also happens between me and Professor Bleuler, toward whom I have not the slightest sexual affinity; and this is how it happens to me with every female colleague even if she has the slightest value for me. It is a thousand times better that people don't understand one at all than if they misunderstand one; the latter is terrible. I hope I have not written in vain until past one o'clock in the morning. Should you want to throw this letter away, I prefer that you return it to me; I will ponder the thoughts broached here later. You have to understand me correctly. When you treat hysteria you must to consider two different matters:

N1 To provide a transformation (mostly, or always) for the psychosexual component of the ego (be it by means of art or a simple reaction—whichever you prefer); in this way the component is always weakened, à la a playing a phonograph disk, and moreover, the feeling guides the corresponding innervations and the psyche is not exhausted in resistances.

N2 Perhaps it would more often appear necessary to inhibit the excitation of the psychosexual component as much as possible by shifting the feeling to another part of the ego combination. It is dangerous to pay too much attention to the complex, to enrich it with new images; only an artist can live this way, and also for him, there are definite limits that exceed his powers, which means that the remainder of his psyche acts as an enemy toward the complex. In my case, the family has now arranged that I am snatched from my studies and remain stuck in the complex. The misery is once again immeasurable. Will I be able to get out of it unscathed once more?

Afterword

Sabina Spielrein and Carl Jung: Rumors vs. Reputation

During her life Sabina Spielrein had a reputation as a practicing psychoanalyst, who presented papers at international psychoanalytical congresses in The Hague and Berlin,[186] authored numerous works[187], and was cited by Freud and Dalbiez.[188] However, posthumously, she also acquired a notoriety as Jung's mistress: for instance, the book by Jungian analyst Coline Covington[189] opens as follows: she is "perhaps best known for her love affair with Carl Jung." The Oxford Universal Dictionary defines "love-affair an amour" and "amour a love-affair, love-making." Thus one might wonder why was Spielrein singled out? Why is not Jung, too, known for his love affair with her, thus as an adulterer and guilty of professional misconduct to boot? I will examine the creation and course of this myth.

In 1906 Jung sent Freud a copy of his *Diagnostic Association Studies* initiating their historic friendship and correspondence. Responding to Freud's thanks Jung declared: "it seems to me that though the genesis of hysteria predominantly, it is not exclusively sexual. I take the same view of your sexual theory." By 1906 Jung would have read Freud's *Studies on Hysteria*, *Three Essays on the Theory of Sexuality* and the *Dora Case*. Freud responded: "I venture to hope that in the course of years you will come much closer to me than you now think possible." By 1913, Jung's replacing Freud's sexual libido with his own transformed theory of libido he called "genetic," as well as his brazen personal attack on Freud, would lead to their historic breakup. For now, Jung replied: "at the risk of boring you, I must abreact my most recent experience. I am currently treating a Russian girl student, ill for 6 years. First trauma between the 3rd and 4th year."[190] This is triple

186 Hague 1920, Berlin 1922.

187 Spielrein, 1987, also partially cited in Grinstein (1958).

188 Freud 1911, Dalbiez 1941.

189 Covington, 2nd edition 2015, p. 1.

190 Freud Jung Letters, p. 4–5, p. 539, p. 7.

deception: the student is Jewish-Russian, she is *his* student at the Zurich medical school, he is not treating her anymore, and no fees are being paid either to Jung or to the hospital. Unpaid therapy is no less an ethical problem than mixing therapy with a sexual relationship.[191] The anonymity of the patient is surprising yet understandable. Jung could have also sent Freud his 1905 report about Spielrein addressed to Freud (copied in Lothane 1996) in which he claimed that Sabina had the misfortune of falling in love with him. These omissions suggest Jung feared revealing his own falling in love with her and it suggests a consciousness of his feelings of guilt. Jung dissembled again in 1907: (1) presenting Spielrein at a conference in Amsterdam as "a case of psychotic hysteria" and publishing it in 1908,[192] thus blatantly falsifying Bleuler's formal assessment: "Miss Sabina Spielrein is not psychotic (*geisteskrank*). She came here for treatment of nervousness with hysterical symptoms" (see p. 27 in "Introduction"). In his 1907 *Psychologie der Dementia Praecox* Jung included

> Case 1. A young lady cannot bear to see the dust beaten out of her mantle. This peculiar reaction is based on the fact that she is somewhat masochistic. As a child her father frequently chastised her by spanking her *a posteriori* which eventually caused sexual excitement. For this reason, to whatever even remotely resembles this form of chastisement, she is forced to react with marked rage, which rapidly changes into sexual excitement and masturbation. On saying to her once on a quite indifferent occasion, "You must obey," she went into a condition of sexual excitement (p. 45).

There is nothing schizophrenic in this vignette but her rages, more than her infantile neurosis, were the important factor when she was an inpatient and thereafter, which Jung did not consider.

The Jungian psychoanalyst Carotenuto[193] went Jung one better claiming that Spielrein had "a psychotic transference" to Jung, was "schizophrenic," a case of "psychotic love," and that in Spielrein's 'poetry' "we must surmise a metaphorical significance known only to Jung and Sabina [on the] analogy that [in Proust's] Swann and Odette used the metaphor "*faire cattleya*" to express the

191 This conclusion was endorsed by Martin Stingelin, German Studies Professor at Dortmund University, review of Lothane 1999, "Explosion im Psycho-Labor," *Frankfurter Allgemeine Zeitung*,
192 (Jung, 1961, p. 20).
193 Carotenuto (1992/1994): pages 157, 158, 161, 219, respectively.

physical act of possession." But why must we? John Kerr (1993) equivocated: calling their relationship a "liaison"— "an illicit sexual intercourse—he also found "it at least plausible that the two stopped short of intercourse" but ended concluding: "Clearly, in their own minds, they had sinned."[194] And for good reason: as a married man with children his affair would amount to committing adultery, and if it involved a patient, serious professional misconduct[195], reacting to Freud's analysis of a dream that was also included in *The Psychology of Dementia Praecox*, Jung thanked Freud for his analysis of it and confesses: "I know the dreamer intimately: he is myself...My wife is rich...I was turned down when I first proposed...I am happy with my wife in every way...there has been no sexual failure, more likely a social one...hiding an illegitimate sexual wish that had better not see the light of day" (*FJL*, pp. 14–15). Conceivably, the 31 year old Jung may have felt sexually deprived while his wife was busy with pregnancies and childbirths: Agathe in 1904, Gret in 1906. and Franz in 1908, thus Sabina represented a constant temptation. The social issue was money: if the wife became aware of his infidelity, she would have sued for divorce and he would have lost her riches. Freud commented neither on Jung's marital matters nor his illegitimate sexual wish but differentiated love writ large from sexual love: "essentially, one might say, the cure if effected by love (*eine Heilung durch Liebe*). And actually transference provides the most cogent, the only unassailable proof that neuroses are determined by the individual's love life."[196] Certainly by healing though love Freud never meant satisfying a patient's real sexual demands. Equally clearly, Jung was not referring to love life in his postcard to Spielrein[197] but to love as benevolent care and concern.

In 1907 there was a bizarre reference to Spielrein Jung sent Freud on July 6: "An hysterical patient told me about a poem by Lermontov...about a prisoner whose sole companion is a bird in a cage...He opens the cage and lets the bird fly out...in her dream she is condensed with me. She admits that actually her greatest wish is to have a child with me. For that purpose I would naturally have to let "the bird out" first (In Swiss-German we say: "Has the birdie whistled?"). A pretty little chain, isn't it? Do you know Kaulbach's pornographic picture: 'Who Buys Love-gods?'"[198] It turns out that pornography is on the mind of the letter writer: in the German the vulgar verb for sexual intercourse is *vögeln,* from

194 Kerr, 1993, p. 224.

195 See Lothane, "Afterword" in Carotenuto, 2003, and Lothane, 2007.

196 *Freud Jung Letters*, pp. 12–13.

197 See Jung's letter CJ1.

198 *FJL*, pp. 72–73.

Vogel, a bird; but the eight line poem, *Ptichka* (a little bird), was composed by Aleksandr Pushkin in 1823 about an exiled man who "set[s] at liberty a little bird on the bright holiday of spring...the gift of freedom."[199] On October 28 Jung confesses to Freud: "My veneration for you has something of the character of a "religious" crush...[with an] undeniable erotic undertone. This abominable feeling comes from the fact that as a boy I was the victim of a sexual assault by a man I once worshipped. Even in Vienna the remarks of the ladies ("enfin seuls" [finally alone with each other," etc.) sickened me."[200] Perhaps Jung's sexual banter in the July 6 letter was a projection of Jung's own sexual wish on Spielrein and reassuring himself he was not a homosexual.

It is still mystifying why three years later, on March 7 1909, a freaked out Jung again reports to Freud that Spielrein had unleashed "a vile scandal solely because [he] denied [himself] the pleasure of giving her a child."[201] But the "scandal" was no more than a quarrel, not a public disgrace. After Spielrein unmasked him to Freud, on June 4 1909, Jung invented a new story: "I finally broke with her. She was, of course, systematically planning my seduction which I considered inopportune. Now she is seeking revenge. Lately she has been spreading a *rumor* that I shall soon get a divorce from my wife and marry a certain girl which has thrown not a few of my colleagues into a flutter."[202] Jung was dissembling again: at most, Sabina would have talked to close friends but she never spread rumors nor planned revenge against Jung, on the contrary, she repeatedly wrote about her compassion for and tenderness to him.[203]

On June 11 1909 Saina wrote: "Four years and half ago was my doctor, then he became my friend and finally my poet, i.e., my beloved. Eventually he came to me and things went as they usually do with poetry. He preached polygamy" (C p. 95).

Jung's "breaking up" pushed Sabina over the edge on June 12 1909: "he could stand it no longer and wanted "poetry"...But when he asked me what would happen next (because of the "consequences")...I said that first love has no desires, that I had nothing in mind and did not want to go beyond a kiss, which I also could do without if need be. And he now claims he was too kind to me, that I want sexual involvement with him because of that, something he, of course, never wanted etc...My ideal personality was completely destroyed...I

199 Cited in *FJL*, p. 72, note 2.
200 Cited in Lothane, 1997.
201 *FJL*, p. 207.
202 *FLJ*, 228–229; emphasis added.
203 See Spielrein's German unpublished letter to Freud, p. 159).

stood there with a knife in my left hand, I resisted. I have no idea what happened then...Suddenly he went very pale, he clapped his hand to his left temple:" You struck me!"...My left arm and forearm were covered with blood. "That's not my blood, that's his: I murdered him!" (C, pp. 96–97).

Jung's panic turned out to be paranoia. On June 21 1909 Sabina "turned up at my home and had a *very decent* talk with me during which it transpired that the rumor buzzing about me does not emanate from her at all...I am largely to blame for the high flying hopes of my *former* patient [first italics Jung's, second italics added]...Caught in my delusion that I was a victim of the sexual wiles of my patient, I wrote to her mother that I was not a gratifier of her daughter's sexual desires but merely her doctor and that she should free me from her."[204]

In letters to Freud Spielrein's quoted the following from Jung's letter to her mother:

> I moved from being her doctor to being her friend when I ceased to push my own feelings into the background. I could drop my role as a doctor the more easily because I did not feel professionally obligated, for I never charged a fee...You understand, of course, that a man and a girl cannot possibly continue indefinitely to have friendly dealings without the likelihood that something more may enter the friendship. For what would restrain the two from drawing the consequences of their love? A doctor and his *patient* can talk about the most intimate things...and the patient may expect her doctor to give her all the love and concerns she requires. But the doctor knows his limits and will never cross them, for he is *paid* for his trouble...My fee is 10 francs per consultation (C p. 94; Jung's italics).

The "scandal" shows the various faces of anger and aggression in their relationship. Freud coolly concluded: "Such experiences, though painful, are necessary and hard to avoid...But no lasting harm is done. They help us to develop the thick skin and we need to dominate "countertransference,"... they teach us to displace our own affects to best advantage. They are a "*blessing in disguise*" [English in the original].[205]

204 FJL, p. 236.

205 On page 235 Freud added: "In view of the kind of matter we work with, it will never be possible to avoid little laboratory explosions."

It was Carotenuto who converted a personal quarrel into a sensational sex scandal, thereafter copied ad nauseam in journals, books, plays, and feature films[206] in which either Jung or Spielrein were depicted as seducer or seduced, victor or victim. For Deirdre Bair[207] Spielrein was a seductive temptress. Many commentators condemned Jung as a Spielrein's abuser. At first I myself agreed that the two had a sexual relationship[208] but fair about Jung's caring attitude toward Spielrein.[209] I rebutted the sexual myth in 1999.[210] The allegations about sex precluded seeing tender love as poetry with erotic coloration. Spielrein might have also read in the 1905 book by August Forel,[211] the former director of the Burghölzli, about the "poetry of love raptures" stimulated by music, painting, and literature; or, perhaps, read Anton Chekhov's short story "Ariadna"[212] in which physical love is poeticized. A former friend wrote to Spielrein about a young

---

206 FLJ, p.231. Bettelheim, B. (1983). Scandal in the Family. *New York Review of Books*, June 30, 1983, reprinted in Carotenuto 1982, as "Comments by Bruno Bettelheim," pp. xv–xxxix; Kerr, 1993; Cremerius, J. Foreword to Carotenuto, 1986; Höfer, R. Sabina Spielrein (1885—1941). In: WahnsinnsFrauen: Zweiter Band. Herausgegeben von Sibylle Duda und Luise F. Pusch. Frankfurt/Main: Suhrkamp, 1996, pp. 156–166; Stephan, I. (1992); „Täuschobjekt zwischen Jung und Freud. SABINA SPIELREIN (1885–1941). In: Die Gründerinnen der Psychoanalyse: eine Entmythologisierung Sigmund Freuds in zwölf Frauenportraits. Stuttgart: Kreuz-Verlag, pp. 83–87; Krutzenbichler, H. S. & H. Essers. Muß denn Liebe Sünde sein? Über das Begehren des Analytikers. Freiburg/Br.: Kore, 1991; Richebächer, S. (2000). „Bist mit dem Teufel du und du willst Dich vor der Flamme scheuen?" Sabina Spielrein und C. G. Jung: ein verdrängtes Skandalon der frühen Psychoanalyse. In: Specher, T., Hrsg., Das Unbewusste in Zürich Literatur und Tiefenpsychologie um 1900. Zürich: NZZ Verlag. However, Sabine Richebächer (2005) is the only author of a thoroughly researched and authoritative biography and a major source for John Launer's 2015 book (reviewed by Lothane, 2015). Appignanesi and Forrester (1992) equivocated: "However the question of the sexual consummation is answered, Jung and Spielrein had been acting for some years as if they were engaged in an illicit affair" (p. 211). Recently Harris (2015) reaffirmed this myth in a paper dealing with Spielrein's contributions to the study of language and their connections with language investigations by Piaget, Luria and Vygotsky. In her 2017 book Sabina Spielrein The Woman and the Myth cites my Spielrein papers and yet equivocates about Sabina's "affair" with Jung. Sex was exploited in plays and films. In the1988 Snoo Wilson's play Sabina Jung reassures Sabina he has enough condoms and the 2002 Christopher Hampton's play The Talking Cure shows a defloration scene of Spielrein by Jung with red blood stains on the sheets and a foreplay scene with spanking. The latter became the screenplay based for David Cronenberg's 2011 egregious kitsch A Dangerous Method, paraphrasing Kerr's 1993 title (see Lothane, 2012).

207 Her 2003 Jung biography was reviewed by Lothane in 2005.

208 Lothane, 1987.

209 Lothane, 1996, p. 216.

210 See also my "Discussion" on love in Covington & Wharton, 2015, pp. 147–153 and my "Afterword" in Carotenuto 2003

211 Pages 307 and 535.

212 Chekhov, 1895.

man she loved: "He was a very handsome, nice, kind-hearted boy with whom I experienced the highest poetry."[213] But what did Spielrein mean by poetry?

Spielrein's answer came from her aforecited 1909 letter to her mother which I had the good luck of finding in Geneva. In response to mother's admonition to remain at the level of friendship alone, Sabina wrote: "we have remained at the level of poetry that is not dangerous and we shall remain at that level for a long time."[214] I believe Sabina told the truth but whether one believes her or not, nobody can now categorically claim that they consummated coitus. But even if, *per impossibile*, they did, it would have been between teacher and student and *not* between patient and doctor, thus a case different both ethically and legally, as I claimed in 2016, exonerating both Spielrein and Jung.[215]

The aforementioned stabbing episode brings us full circle back to the crisis that led to her hospitalization. It was not so much the memory of spankings by her father as the problems she had with him over many years culminating in the violent scene in Zurich. In Carl Jung she encountered a doctor, a mentor, and a benevolent father figure who was empathetic to and patient with her many so-called "scandals" enacted with the nurses. Jung did not mention anger as a dynamic factor in his hospital notes, in the 1905 report or in letters to Freud for another reason he shared with Freud for decades Freud theorized about libido, aggression surfaced only after his 1917 essay on "Mourning and Melancholia" where he discussed "sadism, hate," and "hostility"[216]. The stabbing episode was Sabina's dramatized hostile reaction to Jung's threatening a breakup and to his habitual "diplomacy and lies"[217] and perhaps transference rage at father. She got over her rage at Jung in short order but it may have played a role in the relationship with her husband. Her continuing longing for Jung was another factor, as implied by the remarks about Jung in the letters from her mother and some of her women friends during the Zurich years.[218]

213 Letter from UC.
214 Letter from UC.
215 Spielrein's third letter, her underlining, also cited in Lothane, 1999, p. 1197.
216 For a further discussion of these matters see my book review Lothane, 2015.
217 Standard Edition, volume 14, p.251.
218 See page 435 above.

Conclusion

In the German diary, Sabina described her "friendship" with Jung as "the tragedy of our situation" (C p. 15). And the tragedy was a part of her life. And tragedy was also the fate of her family. The word fate is a recurrent motif in the family correspondence. She had "made a conscious decision that psychology will be my profession. Can I be sure I am not making a mistake?" (C p. 73). She also considered another career: "in a few years I would also have enough musical training" (C p. 81). But what else could she have chosen, since there was no medical training at the Burgholzli? Financially her career as psychoanalyst was a big disappointment. And so was her marriage: the "brilliant" (C p. 19) and charismatic Jung who overshadowed the decent Sheftel. Thus a question she left unanswered: how did she emotionally handle not being with a man all these years?

The war and the Russian revolution were a tragedy for all of them. Stalin murdered her scientific and patriotic brothers, the husband died of heart illness, the father of grief. Hitler murdered Sabina and her two beautiful daughters. Sabina used to daydream and worry about her future (see pages 20, 103, 156–157). Let Sabina have the last word, her testament, written in German and enclosed in the hospital chart:

> When I die, I only permit my head to be dissected, only if it does not look too ugly. A young person may not be present at the autopsy. Only the most proficient students may observe it. I bequeath my skull to the gymnasium, it should be placed in a glass box and adorned with immortal flowers. Write the following on the box (in Russian): "And when put it in the grave let young life play and uncaring nature shine in eternal magnificence." I give my brain to you, place it in a beautiful vessel similarly adorned, and write the same words upon it. The body should be cremated but nobody should be present. The ashes should be divided into three parts. Put one part in an urn and send it home, scatter the other one in the soil, in the middle of a big, big field (next

> to our home), plant an oak tree there and inscribe: "I too was once a person and my name was Sabina Spielrein ["] What to do with the third part a brother will tell you.

Trees are still growing on the mass graves of Rostov Jews in the Zmiyevskaia Ravine.

Henry Zvi Lothane, New York, February 2023

References

Bair, D. (2003). *Jung a biography*. Boston: Little, Brown, & Co.

Bleuler, E. (1912). Autistic thinking. In Rapaport, 1951, pp. 399 437.

Brinkmann, E. & Bose, G. (1986). *Sabina Spielrein Marginalien*. Berlin: Brinkmann & Bose.

Carotenuto, A. (1982, 1984[1980]). *A secret symmetry Sabina Spielrein between Jung and Freud*. New York: Pantheon Books.

Carotenuto, A. (editor) (1986). *Sabina Spielrein Tagebuch einer heimlichen Symmetrie Sabina Spielrein zwischen Jung und Freud Vorwort Johannes Cremerius*. Freiburg i. Br.: Kore Verlag Traute Hensch.

Carotenuto, A. (2003). *Sabina Spielrein Tagebuch und Briefe*. Hrsg. (edited by) von Traute Hensch. Veränderte (altered by) um den Nachwort (afterword) von Zvi Lothane und den Epilog von Chista von Petersdorf ergänzte Neuauflage (enlarged new edition). Giessen: Psychosozial-Verlag.

Chekhov, A. (1895). Ariadna. http://livros01.livrosgratis.com.br/ln000380.pdf

Claparède, E. (1903). *L'association des idées*. Paris: Octave Doin.

Covington, C., & Wharton, B. (2015). *Sabina Spielrein Forgotten pioneer of psychoanalysis*. Second edition. London: Routledge, second edition.

Dalbiez, R. (1941[1936]). *Psychoanalytical method and the doctrine of Freud. Volume 1 Exposition*. London: Longman's, Green and Co.

Erdelyi, M., Lippmann, O., Spielrein, I., Stern, W. (1933). *Prinzipienfragen der Psychotechnik. Abhandlungen über Begriff und Ziele der Psychotechnik und der praktischen Psychologie* (principal issues of psychotechnics.Essays on the concept and goals of p. and of practical psychology). Berlin: Barth.

Etkind, A. (1977[1993]). *Eros of the impossible: The history of psychoanalysis in Russia*. Boulder, CO: Westview Press.

Federn, P. (1913). Sabina Spielrein: *Die Destruktion als Ursache des Werdens. Internationale Zeitschrift für ärztliche Psychoanalyse*, 1:89–93.

Feldman, S. (1964). The attraction of "the other woman." *Journal of the Hillside Hospital*, 13:3–17.

Forel, A. (1906). *Die sexuelle Frage. Eine naturwissenchaftliche, psychologische hygienische und soziologische Studie*. 4. Und 5. Auflage. Munich: Reinhardt.

Freud, S. (1915). Observations on transference love. *Standard Edition*, 12:159–171.

Freud. S. (1920). Beyond the pleasure principle. *Standard Edition*, 18:7–64.

Freud, S. (1923). The ego and the id. *Standard Edition*, 19:12–66.

Grinstein, A. (1958). *The index of psychoanalytic writings*, IV. New York: International Universities Press.

Freud Jung Letters, The (1974). Princeton, NJ: Princeton University Press, p. 20.

Harris, A. (2015). "Language is there to bewilder itself and others": theoretical and clinical contributions of Sabina Spielrein. *Journal of the American Psychoanalytic Association*, 63(4):727–767.

Hoffer, A. (2001). Jung's analysis of Sabina Spielrein and his use of Freud's free association method. *Journal of Analytical Psychology*, 46(1):117–128.

Jodl, F. (1896). *Lehrbuch der Psychologie*. Stuttgart: Cotta Nachfolger.

Guttman, S. (1984). *The concordance to the Standard Edition of the Complete Psychological Works of Sigmund Freud.* New York: International Universities Press.

Jung, C.G. (1961[1908]). The Freudian theory of hysteria. In *Collected Works of C.G. Jung*, Volume 4. Princeton: Princeton University Press.

Jung, C.G. (1909). *The psychology of dementia praecox.* Authorized translation of with an introduction by Frederick Peterson and A.A. Brill. New York: The Journal of Nervous and Mental Disease Publishing Company.

Kerr, J. (1993). *A most dangerous method. The story of Jung, Freud, and Sabina Spielrein.* New York: Knopf.

Laplanche, J. & Pontalis, J.–B. (1973). The language of psychoanalysis. New York : Norton & Company.

Launer, J. (2015). *Sex vs. survival: The life and ideas of Sabina Spielrein*. New York: Overlook Duckworth.

Litvinov, A. V. (1994). K istorii psikhoanaliza v Rossii. Avtoreferat, unpublished dissertation.

Ljunggren, M. (1989). The psychoanalytic breakthrough in Russia on the eve of the First World War. In: Rancour-Laferriere, D.(ed.). Russian literature and psychoanalysis. Amsterdam: John Benjamin Publishing Company, pp. 173–191.

Ljunggren, M. (2001). Sabina and Isaak Spielrein. *Slavica Lundensis*, 21:79–95.

Lothane, Z. (1987). Love, seduction, and trauma. *Psychoanalytic Review,* 74(1):83–105. Lothane, Z. (1996). In defense of Sabina Spielrein. *International Forum of Psychoanalysis*, 5:203–217.

Lothane, Z. (1997). The schism between Freud and Jung over Schreber: its implications for method and doctrine. *International Forum of Psychoanalysis,* 6:103–115.

Lothane, Z. (1999). Tender love and transference: unpublished letters of C.G. Jung and Sabina Spielrein. *International journal of psychoanalysis*, 80(6):1189–1204.

Lothane, Z. (2000). Tenero amore e transfert: lettere inedited tra C. G. Jung e Sabina Spielrein. *Studi Junghiani*, 6(2):97–121.

Lothane, Z. (2001). Zärtlichkeit und Übertragung—Unveröffentlichte Briefe von C. G. Jung und Sabina Spielrein. In A. Karger, O. Knellessen, G. Lettau & C. Weismüller (Hg.), *Sexuelle Übergriffe in Psychoanalyse und Psychotherapie* (pp. 35–70). Göttingen: Vandenhoeck & Ruprecht.

Lothane, Z. (2001). Niezhnaia liubov i transfer: neopublikovannyie pis'ma K. G. Iunga i Sabiny Shpilrein. *Vestnik psikhanaliza* (Spets. Vypusk Nr. 1), S. 87–106.

Lothane, Z (2003a). Tender love and transference: unpublished letters of C. G. Jung and Sabina Spielrein (with an addendum/discussion). In: Covington, C. & Wharton, B., eds. *Sabina Spielrein Forgotten Pioneer of Psychoanalysis.* Hove and New York: Brunner-Routledge, pp. 191–225. Second edition 2015.

Lothane, Z. (2003b). Nachwort. In: Carotenuto 2003, pp. 249–278.

Lothane, Z. (2004). Czuła milosc i przeniesienie: nie opublikowane listy C.G. Junga i Sabiny Spielrein. In: Błocian, I. & Saciuk, R. (eds.), *Gabinet Luster Psychoanalityczne krytyki poznania.* Toruń: Adam Marszałek.

Lothane, Z. (2005). Review of Deirdre Bair's *Jung A biography. Journal American Psychoanalytic Association*, 53:317–324.

Lothane, Z. (2006).Verführung/Entführung, mit/ohne Psychoanalyse. Oder: was suchen jüdische Mädchen bei germanischen Helden und vice versa? *psychozial,* 29(106, III):97–124.

Lothane, Z. (2007).The snares of seduction in life and in therapy, or what do young Jewish girls (Spielrein) seek in their Aryan heroes (Jung), and vice versa? *International Forum of Psychoanalysis*, 16 (No. 1):12–27, 16:81–94.

Lothane, Z. (2009). Dramatology in life, disorder, and psychoanalytic therapy: A further contribution to interpersonal psychoanalysis. *International Forum of Psychoanalysis*,18(3): 135–148.

Lothane, Z. (2012). Sabina Spielrein between Carl Gustav Jung and Sigmund Freud: the naked truth vs. salacious scandals. *Off the Couch, an zine of Psychoanalysis and Culture*, volume 2 No. 1, pp. 8–15.

Lothane, H.Z. (2014). Emotional reality: A further contribution to dramatology. *International Forum of Psychoanalysis*, 24(4). 191–203.

Lothane, H.Z. (2015). Review of John Launer's *Sex vs. Survival The life and ideas of Sabina Spielrein. Journal of the American Psychoanalytic Association*, 63:1057–1068.

Lothane, H.Z.(2016). Sabina Spielrein's Siegfried and other myths: facts vs. fictions. *International Forum of Psychoanalysis*, 25:40–49.

Lothane, H.Z. (2018). Free association as the foundation of the psychoanalytic method and psychoanalysis as a historical science. *Psychoanalytic Inquiry*, 38:416–434.

Lothane, H. Z. (2019). Wilhelm Reich revisited: The role of ideology in character analysis of the individual versus the character analysis of the masses and the Holocaust. *International Forum of Psychoanalysis*, 28(2):104–114.

Lothane, H.Z. (2020). Chapter 1. Lessons learned. In: Brenner I. (ed.). *The Hand-book of Psychoanalytic Studies Holocaust Studies*. London: Routledge, pp. 3–17.

Mach, E. (1959[1906]). *The analysis of perceptions and the relation of the physical to the psychical.* Fifth edition. New York: Dover Publishing Inc., with an "Introduction to Dover Edition" by Thomas S. Szasz, M.D

Metchnikoff, É. (1903). *The nature of man Studies in optimistic philosophy*. New York: G.P. Putnam's Sons.

Metchnikoff, É. (1908). *The prolongation of life Optimistic studies*. New York: G.P. Putnam's Sons.

Mijolla, A. de (2002). *Dictionnaire international de la psychanalyse*. Paris: Calmann-Lévy.

Minder, B. (1994). Sabina Spielrein, Jungs Patientin am Burghölzli. *Luzifer-Amor*,14:55–127. Burghölzli hospital records of Sabina Spielrein. *Journal of Analytical Psychology*, 46(1):15–42.

Moll, J. (1983). Extraits inédits d'un journal: de l'amour, de la mort, et de la transformation. *Le Bloc-notes de la psychanalyse*, 3:149–170.

Misiak, H. & Sexton, F.S. (1966). *History of psychology An overview*. New York: Grune & Stratton.

Nietzsche, F. https://www.gutenberg.org/files/1998/1998-h/1998-h.htm

Nitzschke, B. (2001). "Poesie" und Prosa. Eine Nachgetrachtung zum Beitrag von Zvi Lothane über Sabina Spielrein und C.G. Jung. In Karger, A., et al., *Sexuelle Übergriffe in Psychoanalyse und Psychotherapie. Psychoanalytische Blätter*, 18:71–81.

Nordau, M. (1898[1895]). *Degeneration.* http://www.gutenberg.org/files/51161/51161-h/51161-h.htm

Nunberg, H. & Federn, P. (1974). *Minutes of the Vienna Psychoanalytic Society*. Volume III:1910–1911. New York: International Universities Press.

Ovcharenko, V.I. (1994). *Psikhoanaliticheskii glossarii*. Prilozhenie (addendum). Dokumenty i materialy. Minsk: Vysheishaia Shkola.

Ovcharenko, V. I. (1996). Istoria rossiiskogo psikhoanaliza i problem ee periodizatsii. *Arkhetip*, 3–4:145–150.

Ovcharenko, V. I. (n.d.). Vekhi v zhizni Sabiny Shpilrain (milestones in the life of S.S.).

Ovcharenko, V.I. (2000). *Rossiiskiie psikhoanalitiki* (Russian psychonalysts). Moscow: Federal Publishing House.

Oxford English Dictionary, The (1933). Oxford: at Clarendon Press. Oxford Universal Dictionary (1955). Oxford: at Clarendon Press.

Poliakov, L. (1974). *The Aryan myth A history of racist and nationalist ideas in Europe.* New York: New American Library.

Rapaport, D. (1951). *Organization and pathology of thought.* New York: Columbia University Press.

Reich, W. (1932). Der masochistische Charakter Eine sexualökonomische Widerlegung des Todestriebes und des Widerholugnszwanges. *Internationale Zeitschrift für ärztliche Psychoanalyse*, 18:303–351.

Reik, T. (1948). *Listening with the third ear.* New York: Farrar, Straus and Company.

Reich, W. (1945[1936]). *The sexual evolution.* New York: Farrar, Straus and Giroux.

Richebächer, S. (2008[2005]). *Sabina Spielrein Eine fast grausame Liebe zur Wissenschaft.* Munich: btb-verlag.

Russell, B. (1984). *Human knowledge its scope and limits.* New York: Simon & Schuster.

Ryle, G. (1949). *The concept of min.* New York: Barnes & Noble Books.

Shpilrein, Isak Nikolaievich (1924). *Raboty Laboratorii Promyshlennoi Psikhotekhniki NKT Narodnyi Komissariat Truda SSSR.* Pod obshchei redaktsiei I. N. Shpilreina. I. Meto-dy prikladnoi psikhologii v poslevoiennyi period. II. Laboratoria Promyshlennoi Psikhotekhniki pri Narodnom Komisariate Truda (god raboty) (proceedings of the laborartory for industrial psychotechnics, at National Komissariat of Labor, general editor I.N.S.I. Methods of psychology in the postwar period. II. The laboratory of industrial psychotechnics at NKT (a year's work). Moskva: Izdatel'stvo Voprosy Truda. Citing his 7 papers 1922–1928.

Shpilrein, Itshe Maier (1926). *Idish A konspekt fun a kurs in dem 2-tn Moskwer Meluchishn Uniwersitet* (Yiddish a synopsis of a course at the 2nd Moscow State University). Moskwe: Varlag „Shul un Bukh."

Silberer, H. (1912). On symbol formation. In Rapaport, 1951, pp. 208–233.

Spielrein, S. (1911). Über den psychologischen Ihalt eines Falles von Schizoprhenie (Dementia praecox) (on the psychological content of a case of s.). *Jahrbuch für psychonalytische und psychopathologische Forschungen*, 3:329–400.

Spielrein, S. (1912a). Die Destruktion als Ursache des Werdens (destruction as cause of becoming). *Jahrbuch*, 3:465–503.

Spielrein, S. (1912b). Beiträge zur Kenntnis der kindlichen Seele (contributions to knowing the child's soul). In : Spielrein 1987, pp. 144–166.

Spielrein, S. (1921). Russische Literatur, in: *Bericht über die Fortschritte der Psychoanalyse in den Jahren 1914–1919* (report on progress in psychoanalysis), pp. 356–365; reprinted in Spielrein, 1987, pp. 356–365.

Spielrein, S. (1922). Die Entstehung der kindlichen Worte Papa und Mama (the origin of the infantile words mama and papa). In Spielrein, 1987, pp. 238–262.

Spielrein, S. (1923). Quelques analogies entre la pensée d'enfant, celle de l'aphasique et la pensée subconsciente (some analogies between infantile thinking and that of aphasic patients and unconscious thinking). *Archives de Psychologie*, 18:305–322.

Spielrein, S. (1986). *Tagebuch einer heimlichen Symmetrie. Sabina Spielrein zwischen Jung und Freud*. Herausgegeben von A. Carotenuto. Vorwort Johannes Cremerius. Freiburg i. Br.: Kore Verlag Traute Hensch.

Spielrein, S. (1987). *Sämtliche Schriften*. Freiburg i. Br: Kore Verlag Traute Hensch. Swales, P. (1992). What Jung didn't say. *Harvest*, 38:30–43.

Tchaikovsky (Chaikovskii, P.[iotr] I.[lyich]). *Dnevniki* (diaries). Moskva: "Nash Dom—L'Age d'Homme" Ekaterinburg: "U Faktoriya."

Wackenhut, I. & Willke, A. (1994). *Sabina Spielrein Missbrauchüberlebende und Psychoanalytikerin Eine Studie ihres Lebens und Werkes unter besonderer Berücksichtigung ihrer Tagebücher un ihres Briefwechsels*. Inaugural-Dissertation, Medizinische Hochschule (abuse survivor and psychoanalyst). A study of her life and work with special consideration of her diaries and correspondence.)

Webb, J. (1980). *The occult establishment*. La Salle, IL: Open Court.

Webster (1951). Webster's dictionary of synonyms. Springfield, MA: G. & C. Merriam CO.

Varendonck, J. (1921). *The psychology of day-dream* . New York: Macmillan.

Weizmann, C. (1949). *Trial and error: The autobiography of Chaim Weizmann*. New York: Harper & Row Publishers.

Wyman, H. Rittenberg, S. (1992). The analyzing instrument in the teaching and conduct of the analytic process by Otto Isakower, M.D. Journal of Clinical Psychoanalysis, 1(2):33–48

www.ingramcontent.com/pod-product-compliance
Lightning Source LLC
Chambersburg PA
CBHW050309120526
44592CB00014B/1840
* 9 7 8 1 9 4 2 2 5 4 2 0 1 *